History Alive!

The United States Through Industrialism

Student Edition

TCi

Teachers' Curriculum Institute

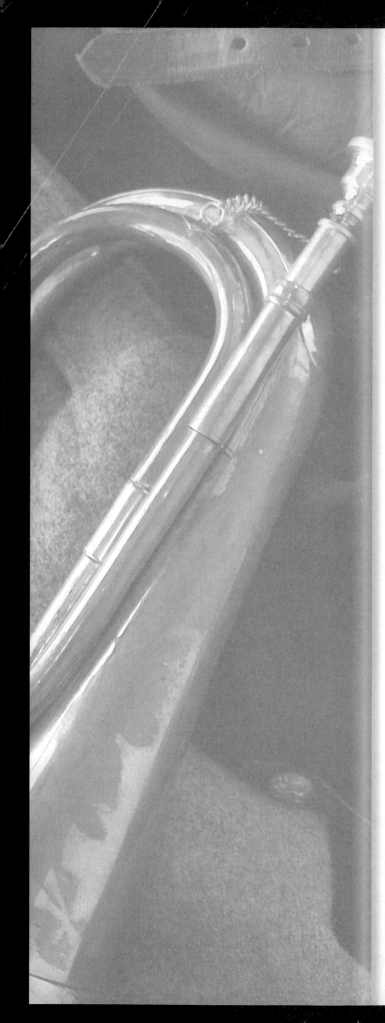

Managing Editor: Laura Alavosus
Developmental Editor: John Bergez
Production Editor: Beverly Cory
Editorial Assistant: Anna Embree
Art Director: Tim Stephenson
Production Manager: Lynn Sanchez
Graphic Designers: Jeff Kelly, Christy Uyeno
Photo Editors: Lindsay Kefauver, Margee Robinson
Operations Manager: Ellen Mapstone

This book is published by Teachers' Curriculum Institute.

TCi®   Teachers' Curriculum Institute
PO Box 50996
Palo Alto, CA 94303

ISBN 1-58371-401-4

6 7 8 9 10 -WC- 09 08 07

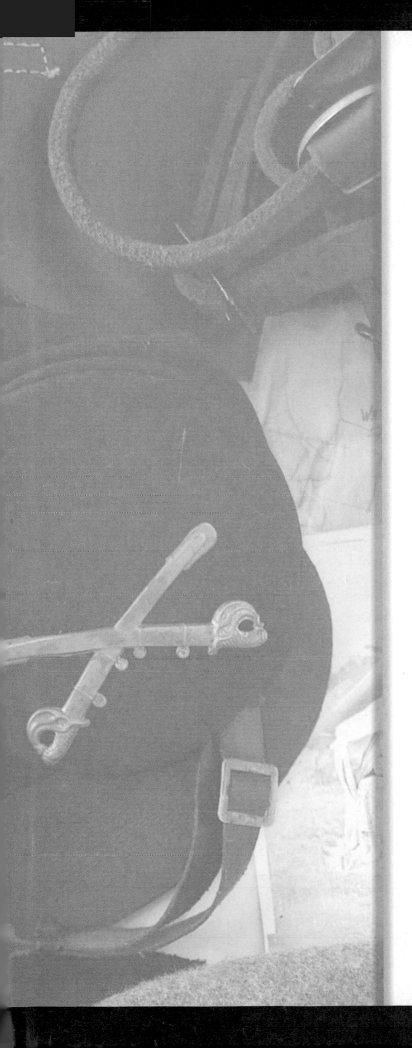

Diane Hart is a writer and consultant specializing in history and social studies. She is the author of several social studies textbooks as well as resources for teachers, including *Authentic Assessment: A Handbook for Educators*. She has written texts for special needs and limited English students that are used not only in schools, but also in prisons, adult literacy, and citizenship classes. Recently she has been developing materials for video, multimedia, and the Internet.

A former teacher and Woodrow Wilson Fellow, with a master's degree in history from Stanford University, Diane remains deeply involved in social studies education. She is an active participant in the National and California Councils for the Social Studies.

In both her professional and volunteer activities, Diane has served as a bridge between social studies teachers and students on the one hand, and textbook publishers and media developers on the other. Her goal is always to help the latter better meet the needs and goals of the former.

Acknowledgments

Program Directors

Bert Bower

Jim Lobdell

Author

Diane Hart

Contributing Writers

Laura Alavosus

John Bergez

Jill Fox

Christine Freeman

Andrew Goldblatt

Tedd Levy

Curriculum Developers

Joyce Bartky

Vern Cleary

Terry Coburn

Steve Seely

Kelly Shafsky

Reading Specialist

Kate Kinsella, Ed.D.

Reading and TESOL Specialist

Department of Secondary Education,

College of Education

San Francisco State University

San Francisco, California

Teacher Consultants

Melissa Aubuchon

City of Ladue School District,

St. Louis, Missouri

Connie Davidson

San Leandro Unified School

District, San Leandro, California

Nicolle Hutchinson

Broward County Public Schools, Miramar,

Florida

Julie Peters

Woodstock Community Union School

District #200, Woodstock, Illinois

Debra Schneider

Tracy Unified School District, Tracy,

California

Scholars

Dr. Eric Avila

César E. Chávez Center for Chicana and

Chicano Studies

University of California,

Los Angeles

Maureen Booth

Constitutional Law Consultant

Maynard, Massachusetts

Dr. Eun Mi Cho

Department of Special Education

California State University, Sacramento

Dr. William Deverell

Department of History

University of Southern California

Dr. Dan Dupre

Department of History

University of North Carolina, Charlotte

Dr. Ben Keppel

Department of History

University of Oklahoma

Dr. Stanley J. Underdal

Scholar of Native American Studies,

Ethnicity, and Race

in U.S. History and History

of the West

San Jose State University

San Jose, California

Dr. Dan Wickburg

School of Arts and Humanities

University of Texas, Dallas

Readability Consultant

Jeanne Barry

Jeanne Barry and Associates, Inc.,

Incline Village, Nevada

Geography Specialist

David Knipfer

Mapping Specialists

Madison, Wisconsin

Internet Consultant

Chuck Taft

University School of Milwaukee

Milwaukee, Wisconsin

Diverse Needs Consultants

Erin Fry

Glendora, California

Colleen Guccione

Naperville, Illinois

Welcome to *History Alive! The United States Through Industrialism*

History Alive! The United States Through Industrialism was developed by middle school teachers at Teachers' Curriculum Institute (TCI). We, Bert Bower and Jim Lobdell, are two former high school teachers who started TCI. Our goal is to help students like you succeed in learning about history in a way that is fun and exciting. With the help of teachers from around the nation, we've created the TCI Approach to learning. This chapter explains how the TCI Approach will make U.S. history come alive for you.

The TCI Approach has three main parts. First, during class you'll be involved in a lot of exciting activities. For example, by playing a game of Capture the Flag, you'll learn how the Continental Army defeated the British in the Revolutionary War. You'll participate as a delegate to the Constitutional Convention to understand the important debates that influenced the design of our Constitution. You'll explore the experience of immigrants at the turn of the 20th century by creating and sharing immigrant scrapbooks. Every lesson is built around an activity like these.

Second, during and after these activities, you get to read this book. You'll discover that your reading connects closely to the activities that you experience. We've worked hard to make the book interesting and easy to follow.

Third, during each lesson you'll write about your learning in your Interactive Student Notebook. You'll end up with your very own personal account of U.S. history.

With the TCI Approach, you'll not only learn more about history than ever before, but you'll have fun doing it. Let's take a closer look at how this approach will help you learn U.S. history.

Two teachers, Bert Bower (above) and Jim Lobdell (below), started TCI. They work with teachers and students like you to develop new ways to learn history.

Theory-Based, Active Instruction

History Alive! The United States Through Industrialism is probably unlike any other history program you have ever encountered. Perhaps you have been in history classes where you listen to the teacher and then read a textbook and answer chapter questions. Does this approach make you excited about learning history? Most students would say no, and educational researchers would tend to agree. Researchers have discovered new ways of reaching all students in the diverse classroom. This program relies on three of their theories.

Researchers have found that students learn best when they are given the opportunity to use their multiple intelligences, work cooperatively with their peers, and build on what they know.

Students learn best through multiple intelligences. Howard Gardner, an educational researcher, discovered that people use their brains in very different ways to learn the same fact or concept. From this discovery, he created a theory called multiple intelligences. There are at least seven intelligences. You can think of them as different ways of being smart—with words, with pictures, with numbers, with people, with your body, with music and rhythms, and with who you are. Everyone has multiple intelligences. Using one or more of these ways of being smart can make learning easier.

Cooperative interaction increases learning gains. Through research, Elizabeth Cohen discovered that students learn more when they interact by working with others in groups. Interactive learning includes working with your classmates in many kinds of activities. You'll work in groups, do role plays, and create simulations. This kind of learning requires you and your classmates to share your ideas and work together well.

All students can learn via the spiral curriculum. Researcher Jerome Bruner believed that learning isn't just up to students. Teachers need to make learning happen for all students. Bruner believed, as the TCI Approach does, that all students can learn through a process of step-by-step discovery. This process is known as a spiral curriculum.

These three theories are the foundation of the TCI Approach. Putting them into practice in *History Alive! The United States Through Industrialism* gives you what you need to succeed.

History Alive! The United States Through Industrialism has been carefully developed to provide the information and learning you need to succeed on state tests.

Standards-Based Content

A lot of people care about what you are learning in history. These people include your parents, your school administrators, your teachers, and even your state and national elected officials. In fact, if you're like students in most states, you take tests at the end of the year to measure your progress.

Most end-of-year tests are based on standards. Standards are the key pieces of information about history that elected officials think are important for you to remember. When you read most standards, you might scratch your head and think, "These seem really hard to understand, and they're probably even harder to learn and remember." There's no need to worry about that with *History Alive! The United States Through Industrialism*. Every lesson is based on standards. So every day, while you're having fun learning U.S. history, you are also learning key standards.

You'll be recording everything you learn in your Interactive Student Notebook. When it's time to prepare for tests, your notebook will make it easy to review all the standards you've learned.

In fact, students across the nation using the TCI Approach are getting better scores than ever on standardized tests. A big reason for this success is that the TCI Approach is based on interactive learning. That means you won't just read about history. You'll be actively involved in experiencing it and recording what you learn. Now let's look at what you'll do during each part of a lesson with the TCI Approach.

Preview Assignments

With the TCI Approach, learning starts even before you begin studying. Most of the lessons in *History Alive! The United States Through Industrialism* begin with a Preview assignment. Previews are short assignments that you complete in your Interactive Student Notebook. They allow you to make a personal connection to what you will study.

After you complete a Preview assignment, your teacher will hold a brief class discussion. Several students will share their answers. Your teacher will then reveal how the assignment "previews" what is to come in the lesson.

Here are some examples of the kinds of Preview assignments you will complete:

Preview assignments like the ones shown here help introduce you to new topics.

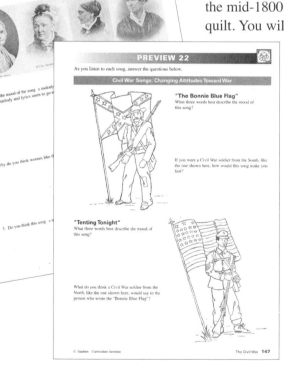

- Before learning about daily life in colonial America in Chapter 4, you will look at a set of statements about the colonies in a fictitious British tabloid newspaper. You'll become a British reporter and travel to colonial America to evaluate the accuracy of these claims.
- Before learning about the Bill of Rights in Chapter 10, you will reflect on the powers given to parents in a "Parents' Constitution." You will determine if the powers should be restricted to protect the rights of children.
- Before learning about the lives of African Americans in the mid-1800s in Chapter 20, you will analyze a story quilt. You will use the quilt to find clues about the varied experiences of African Americans during this time period.
- Before learning about the Civil War in Chapter 22, you will listen to two period songs. You will describe the mood and lyrics of each song as if you were a Confederate or a Union soldier.

Preview assignments like these will spark your interest and get you ready to tackle new concepts. Next come the exciting activities that make up the heart of each lesson. As you're about to see, these activities draw on many ways of being smart—our multiple intelligences.

Multiple Intelligence Teaching Strategies

The teaching strategies in the TCI Approach are based on hands-on learning. Every lesson in *History Alive! The United States Through Industrialism* is built around a fun and exciting activity. We mentioned some examples earlier. Here are some other things you and your classmates will do to experience U.S. history:

- For Chapter 3, you'll prepare a booth for a colonial fair to see the similarities and differences between the New England, Middle, and Southern colonies.
- For Chapter 16, you'll become groups of people traveling to the West in the 1800s, bringing to life the challenges and successes of your move westward.
- For Chapter 25, you'll pretend to be workers in a garment factory, experiencing life on the assembly line.

Using your multiple intelligences helps you learn and remember what you study.

Activities like these will challenge you to use your multiple intelligences. Think about times when learning new things has been easier for you. Were you looking at pictures about the new ideas? Were you writing about them? Does acting out an event help you to better understand what happened? Studying history is a lot easier and more fun when you learn new ideas in ways that best suit your learning styles. Here's a list of seven different intelligences:

- Linguistic (word smart)
- Logical-mathematical (number/reasoning smart)
- Spatial (picture smart)
- Body-kinesthetic (body smart)
- Musical (music smart)
- Interpersonal (people smart)
- Intrapersonal (self smart)

While you're engaged in fun and exciting activities, you'll also be reading this book to learn more about U.S. history. The next page explains why this book is so easy to read.

Considerate Text

The TCI Approach is all about being successful and having fun while you learn. You're about to discover that *History Alive! The United States Through Industrialism* is interesting to read and easy to understand. That's because this book is "reader friendly," which is another of saying that it makes readers want to read it. Some people call this *considerate text.* The writers of this book considered your needs as a reader and made sure you would have fun reading.

Here are some of the ways this book is considerate of all levels of readers:

- Each chapter is organized around key concepts. The summary section reminds you of the big ideas in the chapter.
- Each chapter begins with a graphic organizer—a picture that represents the main ideas of the chapter. The graphic organizer also appears in the Reading Notes in your Interactive Student Notebook. It will help you remember key ideas long after you've read the chapter.
- Short chapters make it easier for you to understand and remember what each one is about.
- Each section has a clear focus and a subtitle that provides an outline for your reading. Research shows that presenting new information in easy-to-manage chunks makes it easier to understand.
- Important new words are in bold teal-colored type. These words are defined in the margins and in the Glossary at the back of the book.
- Photos and illustrations provide additional infor mation about the topic on the page. A great way to check your understanding is to ask yourself, "How does this picture show what I just read?"

Most importantly, *History Alive! The United States Through Industrialism* is as exciting to read as a good story. The next section explains a special way of taking notes that will help you remember what you read.

You'll use *History Alive! The United States Through Industrialism* during classroom activities. You'll be turning to it over and over again to find the information you need to know.

Graphically Organized Reading Notes

Note taking is very important in the TCI Approach. As you read this book, you'll complete Reading Notes in your Interactive Student Notebook. You'll answer important questions, find main ideas, and connect new ideas to what you already know.

Your Reading Notes will leave you with a picture in your mind of each chapter's key ideas. The graphic organizers at the start of each chapter will be a visual reminder of what you read. In your Reading Notes, you'll use those same graphic organizers to help you record key ideas. For example, in Chapter 6, you'll use a visual metaphor of a rope tying the American colonies to Britain. You'll take notes on the rope's unraveling strands to record the weakening ties that led to the Declaration of Independence. For Chapter 15, you will take notes on map of the United States. You will trace and annotate new boundaries to follow the country's expansion across the continent. For Chapter 18, you'll take notes on signs carried by people demonstrating for change. The signs represent the different reform movements of the mid-19th century.

Completing your Reading Notes will help you study in two ways. First, it will encourage you to think carefully about what you read. Second, recording key ideas will help you remember them for a long time.

There's one more part of the TCI Approach that will help you remember the important ideas you are learning. Read the next page to find out.

You'll record key ideas on the Reading Notes pages in your Interactive Student Notebook. This will help you remember what you learned long after the lesson is over.

Processing Assignments

At the end of each lesson, you'll complete a Processing assignment in your Interactive Student Notebook. Here you'll show that you understand the key concepts of the lesson.

These pages encourage you to relate ideas to one another. You'll make connections between the past and present. You'll show your understanding of concepts by creating illustrations, diagrams, flowcharts, poetry, and cartoons. As one student said, "It's really cool to have a place in our notebooks where we can record our own ideas. It makes learning history a lot more fun."

Here are some examples of the kinds of Processing assignments you'll complete:

- In Chapter 5, you will learn about the tensions between the colonies and Britain from 1763 to 1775. In the Processing assignment, you'll write a dialogue between the two sides.
- In Chapter 14, you will assess the presidency of Andrew Jackson. In the Processing assignment, you'll design a hero's commemorative plaque to highlight his positive contributions and a Wanted poster to show his negative impact.
- In Chapter 28, you will analyze early 20th-century political cartoons to learn about U.S. expansionism. In the Processing assignment, you'll create your own political cartoon to show your support or opposition to U.S. involvement in World War I.

Students across the country report that their Processing assignments have helped them understand and remember what they have learned. As a result, they are earning higher test scores.

In Processing assignments, you'll show that you understand the new ideas of the lesson.

Multiple Intelligence Assessments

Do you dread taking chapter and unit tests? If so, maybe you feel that most tests don't let you show what you've learned. The tests for *History Alive! The United States Through Industrialism* are different. They let you show how well you understand each lesson's key ideas.

These tests also allow you to use your multiple intelligences. Each test has some of the usual multiple-choice questions. These will help prepare you for taking more formal tests. But other parts of the assessments will challenge you to use more than just your "word smart" intelligence. They'll give you a chance to shine if you are good in other areas, such as reading maps, using charts and graphs, drawing, understanding music, or analyzing historical paintings. You may also be asked to show how well you read. You'll be invited to express your ideas and your understanding of historical events in writing, too.

The secret to doing well on tests is preparation. You have the perfect tool for this purpose: your Interactive Student Notebook. Right there on those pages are your notes about all the key ideas in each chapter. Students who study their Reading Notes and Processing assignments before a test usually earn good test scores.

Success on tests is important, but the most important thing of all is learning. We've designed our tests not just to assess your understanding but to help you remember key ideas. That's because the lessons you learn from U.S. history can help you make sense of your world and guide your future decisions. We hope that what you learn in *History Alive! The United States Through Industrialism* will remain with you for years to come.

Your teacher may give you test pages to complete at the end of a lesson. These tests include questions with multiple-choice answers as well as questions that let you draw or write your answers.

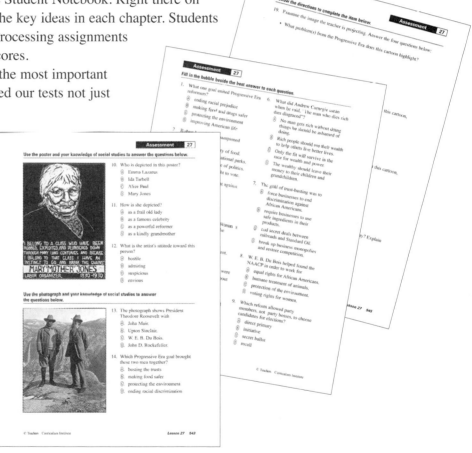

Contents

Chapter 1
The Native Americans 1
Meet the Native Americans who lived in
different regions of North America. Discover
how the different environments affected these
original settlers.

Chapter 2
**European Exploration
and Settlement** .17
Read about the European countries that
competed for control of the New World and
its riches. Learn what devastating effects their
arrival had on the native population.

The Granger Collection, New York

Chapter 3
The English Colonies in America 35
Travel with the first English settlers who came
to start a new life in America. Consider the
advantages and disadvantages of life in the
New England, Middle, and Southern Colonies.

Chapter 4
Life in the Colonies 49
Experience the joys and hardships of daily life
for the American colonists, their servants, and
slaves. Learn about their work, their pleasures,
their food, their religion, and their schooling.

Chapter 5
Toward Independence 63
Discover what happened as tensions grew
between the colonists and their government in
far-off England. Meet the people who would
rather risk their lives than give up their rights.

The Granger Collection, New York

The Granger Collection, New York

The Granger Collection, New York

Chapter 6
The Declaration of Independence 79
Examine the events that led the colonists to declare independence. Witness the brave men who created a document that changed the world.

Chapter 7
The American Revolution 87
Relive the challenges faced by poorly trained and ill-equipped solders, locked in a war against the most powerful nation in the world. Learn how the colonies won the revolution and their independence from Great Britain.

Chapter 8
Creating the Constitution 103
Share the frustrations of the delegates to the Constitutional Convention as they struggled to organize a new government. Recognize the compromises they made for the sake of presenting a united plan.

Chapter 9
The Constitution:
A More Perfect Union 119
Why has the Constitution endured for more than 200 years of extreme social change? Examine this remarkable document that describes the organization and powers of the national government and its unique system of checks and balances.

Chapter 10
The Bill of Rights 133
Explore the power of the first ten amendments to the Constitution. Learn how they are used by the Supreme Court to protect the basic freedoms we enjoy in our daily lives.

The Granger Collection, New York

The Granger Collection, New York

Chapter 11
**Political Developments in
the Early Republic** 145

Compare the two rivals in the election of
1800—Hamilton and Jefferson. Note how their
opposing views gave rise to the country's first
political parties and led to a new way of
electing the president.

Chapter 12
Foreign Affairs in the Young Nation . . .161

Follow the foreign policy debates as the young
America faces threats from powerful European
nations. Learn which presidents were willing to
risk war and which preferred to keep their
country at peace.

Chapter 13
A Growing Sense of Nationhood 175

Learn how the United States developed a
national identity in the first half of the 19th
century. Take a look at the politics, art, music,
and literature that helped define what it meant
to be an American.

Chapter 14
**Andrew Jackson and the Growth
of American Democracy** 185

Evaluate Andrew Jackson, one of the nation's
most colorful presidents, through the eyes of
his contemporaries. Understand why some
thought he was a villain and others considered
him a hero.

Chapter 15
Manifest Destiny and
the Growing Nation **197**
Trace the expansion of America across the
continent. Discover why many Americans
believed it was both their right and their duty
to spread their way of life into the West.

Chapter 16
Life in the West **211**
Join the explorers, the trappers, the
missionaries, and other pioneers on their
difficult journey to settle the rugged West.
Discover the unique contributions each
group made to American culture.

Chapter 17
Mexicano Contributions to
the Southwest **229**
Recognize the many Mexicano innovations
adopted by Anglos. Appreciate their
contributions that enabled settlers to prosper
in the hot, dry climate of the Southwest.

Chapter 18
An Era of Reform **241**
Find out about the efforts of American
reformers in such causes as ending slavery,
promoting women's rights, and improving
education. Judge the progress women have
made toward full equality.

Chapter 19
The Worlds of North and South **253**
Step back in time to experience life in a
northern city and on a southern plantation.
Explore the differences that would ultimately
shatter the unity of the country.

The Granger Collection, New York

The Granger Collection, New York

Chapter 20
African Americans at Mid-Century **269**

Share the misery and admire the courage
of black Americans living as slaves. Learn
about their struggle to escape racism and
discrimination.

Chapter 21
A Dividing Nation **285**

Discover the deep divisions over slavery
that would threaten to tear the country apart.
Join the search for compromises on the issues
that divided the nation.

Chapter 22
The Civil War **303**

Visit battlegrounds to relive the Civil War.
Face the terrors and hardships of those who
suffered through America's bloodiest war.

Chapter 23
The Reconstruction Era **323**

Track the progress of African Americans
toward full citizenship following the
Civil War. Feel the disappointment and
bitterness of former slaves who lost their
newly gained rights.

Chapter 24
Tensions in the West **337**

Follow the groups that swept across the West
after the Civil War. Observe their clashes with
the Native Americans and consider their impact
on the West's native peoples.

The Granger Collection, New York

The Granger Collection, New York

Chapter 25
The Rise of Industry 353

Learn how the rise of big business changed American life. Explore the innovations that transformed society, and witness the benefits and the abuses of industrialization.

Chapter 26
The Great Wave of Immigration 371

Step off a steamship or cross the border with some of the many immigrants from Europe, Asia, and Mexico. Learn about their hopes, their struggles, and their disappointments.

Chapter 27
The Progressive Era 385

Investigate the problems in America and discover how social leaders proposed to deal with them. Understand that while the "Progressives" fought for many different causes, all sought a better American society.

Chapter 28
America Becomes a World Power 399

Revisit America as the 20th century begins, and learn how expansionists moved to extend the nation's power across the Western Hemisphere and around the world.

Chapter 29
Linking Past to Present 417

Consider the tremendous changes in social and economic conditions in the United States since 1914. Recognize the role that dedicated individuals have played and will always play in shaping the world around them.

Resources 425

What materials were used to make these houses?

What materials were used to make these people's clothes?

What are these people trading?

xx

The Native Americans

1.1 Introduction

As a cold winter wind howls outside, the children huddle under thick fur blankets. They listen to their grandmother's soothing voice. "In the beginning there was the Great Spirit," Grandmother begins, "who ruled over a world of sky and water." Then the Great Spirit, says Grandmother, created land, plants, and animals. Finally, from living wood, the Great Spirit carved people for the new world.

These Abenaki children of New England are learning how their people began. Most groups have beliefs about where they came from. You may have heard stories about how your own relatives first arrived in America. But do you know where your ancestors were living 10,000 years ago?

Only if you are Native American did you have relatives in America that long ago. Europeans and other groups did not start arriving until a little more than 500 years ago. For thousands of years, these First People had the American continents to themselves. In this chapter, you will learn about these resourceful people and the creative ways they developed to live in tune with the natural world.

Even today, scientists are trying to find out more about the first Americans. These early people left few written records to tell us what their lives were like, so researchers study other items they left behind. What has survived? Not much. A few animal and human bones, some stone and metal tools, bits of pottery. Like detectives, scientists sift through these clues, trying to imagine how these people lived and how their lives changed over time. When scientists find a new object, they try to figure out whether it supports their current ideas or suggests new ones.

In your lifetime, scientists will probably learn much more about the first Americans and may revise many of their conclusions. This chapter tells these people's stories as we know them today.

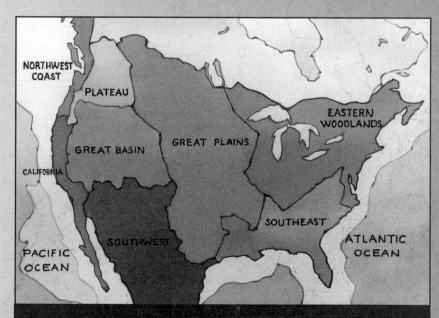

Graphic Organizer: Map of Cultural Regions
You will use this map to learn about the adaptations made by Native Americans living in eight cultural regions.

1.2 Migration Routes of the First Americans

migrate To move from one place and establish a home in a new place. A move of a large number of people is called a *migration,* and the people who move are called *migrants.* Some animals also migrate, usually with the seasons.

The first Americans probably **migrated** on foot from Siberia, in Asia, to present-day Alaska. Today, Alaska and Asia are separated by a strip of ocean called the Bering Strait. But there was a time when a land bridge connected them.

Across a Land Bridge   About 30,000 years ago, the most recent Ice Age began. As temperatures fell, much of the earth was covered by glaciers, sheets of ice up to a mile thick. With water locked up in the glaciers, the level of the oceans dropped 200 feet. This exposed a wide bridge of land between Asia and North America that scientists call Beringia.

In the summer, Beringia's grasslands attracted large Asian mammals, such as mammoths, long-haired cousins of the elephant. Over thousands of years, the animals slowly spread eastward. Generations of Siberian hunter families followed. Armed with only stone-tipped spears, they killed these huge, powerful animals for food. Eventually, perhaps between 10,000 and 20,000 years ago, some of them reached America. Other migrants may have traveled along the coast of Beringia by boat to catch fish, seals, and other marine mammals.

Scientists believe that the first Americans migrated from Siberia to Alaska across a land bridge called Beringia. These people were following mammoths and other prey that moved east in search of grazing land.

Migrating East and South   Once in America, hunters followed the animals south, where spring brought fresh grasses. Then, about 10,000 years ago, the earth warmed up again. As the glaciers melted and the oceans rose, the land bridge disappeared. Mammoths and other traditional prey began to die off, perhaps from disease, overhunting, or the change in the climate.

Native Americans now had to find new sources of food and new materials for clothing and shelter. So they became hunter-gatherers, catching smaller animals, fishing more, and collecting edible plants and seeds. Over thousands of years, they spread across the two American continents, from the Pacific to the Atlantic, and from Alaska all the way to the tip of South America.

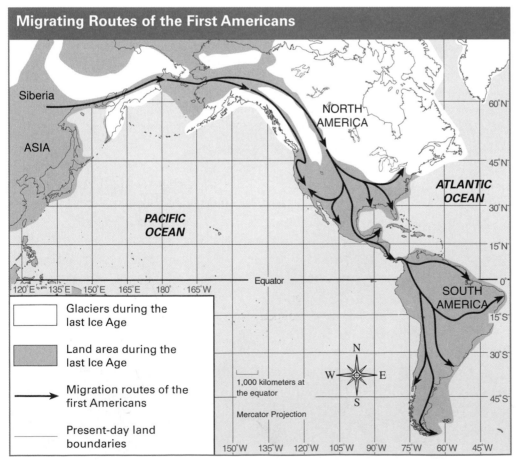

Migrating Routes of the First Americans

Siberia

ASIA

NORTH AMERICA

PACIFIC OCEAN

ATLANTIC OCEAN

Equator

SOUTH AMERICA

120°E 135°E 150°E 165°E 180° 165°W

60°N
45°N
30°N
15°N
0°
15°S
30°S
45°S

Glaciers during the last Ice Age

Land area during the last Ice Age

Migration routes of the first Americans

Present-day land boundaries

1,000 kilometers at the equator

N W E S

Mercator Projection

150°W 135°W 120°W 105°W 90°W 75°W 60°W 45°W

1.3 Native Americans Adapt to the Environment

Native Americans lived in a variety of places, from snowy forests to dry deserts and vast grasslands. Each of these kinds of places is an **environment**. An environment includes everything that surrounds us—land, water, animals, and plants. Each environment also has a climate, or long-term weather pattern. Groups of Native Americans survived by adapting, or changing, their style of living to suit each environment, its climate, and its **natural resources**.

The tents in this Inuit camp in Northern Alaska were made from seal and caribou skins. The Inuit used the inflated seal skins, hanging from the poles, as floats.

Using Natural Resources   Native Americans learned to use the natural resources in their environments for food, clothing, and shelter. In the frigid regions of the far north, early Americans survived by hunting caribou in the summer and sea mammals in the winter. They fashioned warm, hooded clothing from animal skins. To avoid being blinded by the glare of the sun shining on snow, they made goggles out of bone with slits to see through.

The people of the north lived most of the year in houses made from driftwood and animal skins. In winter, hunters built temporary shelters called *iglus* out of blocks of snow.

In warmer climates, early Americans gathered wild plants. Then, about 7,000 years ago, they learned to raise crops such as squash, chili peppers, beans, and corn. Growing their own food enabled them to settle in one place instead of following animals or searching for edible plants in the wild. These early farmers built the first villages and towns in America.

Native American Cultural Regions   Over generations, groups of Native Americans developed their own **cultures,** or ways of life. Many became part of larger groupings that were loosely organized under common leaders.

Groups living in the same type of environment often adapted in similar ways. Forest dwellers often lived in houses covered with tree bark, while many desert peoples made shelters out of branches covered with brush.

Using such artifacts (items made by people), historians have grouped Native American peoples into **cultural regions**. A cultural region is made up of people who share a similar language and way of life.

By the 1400s, between one and two million Native Americans lived in ten major cultural regions north of Mexico. Later in this chapter, you will take a close-up look at eight of these regions. They include the Northwest Coast, California, the Great Basin, the Plateau, the Southwest, the Great Plains, the Eastern Woodlands, and the Southeast.

environment all of the physical surroundings in a place, including land, water, animals, plants, and climate

natural resources useful materials found in nature, including water, vegetation, animals, and minerals

culture a people's way of life, including beliefs, customs, food, dwellings, and clothing

cultural region an area in which a group of people share a similar culture and language

Native American Cultural Regions

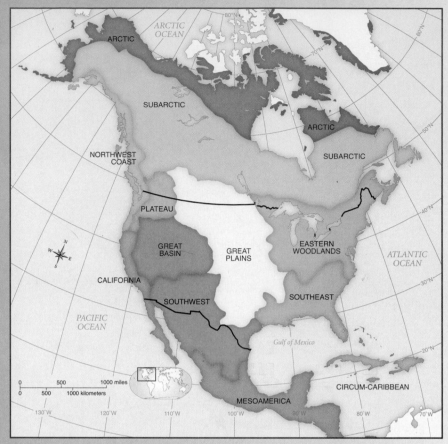

Native American Clothing

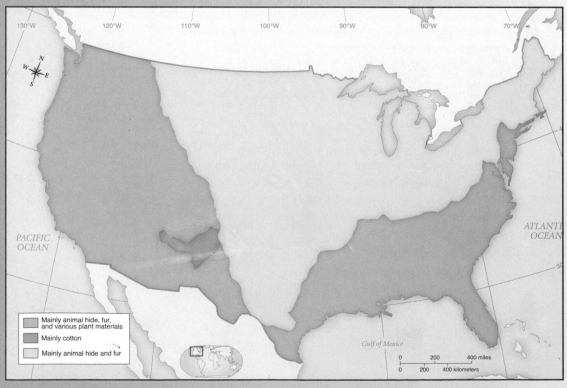

Mainly animal hide, fur, and various plant materials

Mainly cotton

Mainly animal hide and fur

Native American Housing

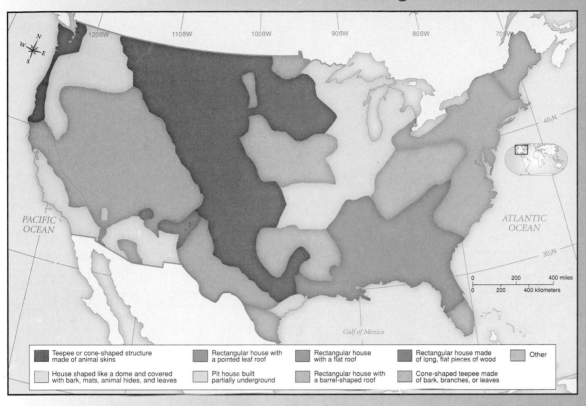

■ Teepee or cone-shaped structure made of animal skins	■ Rectangular house with a pointed leaf roof	■ Rectangular house with a flat roof	■ Rectangular house made of long, flat pieces of wood	■ Other
■ House shaped like a dome and covered with bark, mats, animal hides, and leaves	■ Pit house built partially underground	■ Rectangular house with a barrel-shaped roof	■ Cone-shaped teepee made of bark, branches, or leaves	

Native American Food

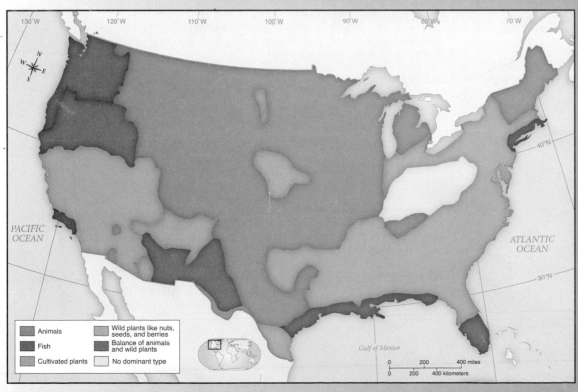

■ Animals	■ Wild plants like nuts, seeds, and berries
■ Fish	■ Balance of animals and wild plants
■ Cultivated plants	☐ No dominant type

1.4 First Americans' View of Their Environment

Wherever they lived, Native Americans had a strong connection to their surroundings. They viewed themselves as a part of the community of plants, animals, and other natural objects. As a Sioux said, "From Wakan Tanka, the Great Spirit, there came a great unifying life force that flowed in and through all things—the flowers of the plains, blowing winds, rocks, trees, birds, animals—and was the same force that had been breathed into the first man."

Nature's Spirits   Native Americans generally believed that each part of nature had its own spirit. Each person had to maintain a balance with these spirits.

These beliefs were expressed in various customs. Southwest farmers, for example, made corn a part of every ceremony. Hunters gave thanks to the animals they killed.

Using the Land   Unlike Europeans, Native Americans did not believe that land could be owned as private property. But each group was deeply connected to its homeland—the area where its people lived most of the year. If necessary, Native Americans would fight to protect their right to this land.

Native Americans believed humans, animals, plants, and even inanimate objects had their own spirits. Because of this belief, Native Americans felt related to all parts of nature.

Native Americans adapted the land to suit their needs. Woodlands people set fires to clear heavy forest growth, so deer could browse and berries could grow. Southwest farmers built ditches to carry water to dry fields.

These practices had seldom harmed the environment. As one Native American historian explains, "We dug our clams here, caught our salmon over there, got…seagull eggs on another island…. By the time we came back here, this place had replenished itself."

Native Americans tried not to waste anything taken from nature. A California woman recalled, "When we…kill meat, we eat it all up. When we dig roots we make little holes…. We shake down acorns and pine nuts. We don't chop down the trees."

1.5 Native Americans of the Northwest Coast

The Northwest Coast cultural region extends from southern Oregon into Canada. Winters along the ocean are cold but not icy, and summers are cool. To the east, thick forests of fir, spruce, and cedar cover rugged mountains. The mountains trap Pacific storms, so there is heavy rainfall much of the year.

Abundant Food Northwest people found food plentiful, particularly from the sea. They built their villages along the narrow beaches and bays of the coastline, and on nearby islands. They gathered clams, other shellfish, and seaweed from shallow waters. They ventured onto the sea in canoes to hunt seals, sea lions, and whales, as well as halibut and other fish. The forests provided deer, moose, bear, elk, beaver, and mountain goat.

For each kind of creature, hunters developed special weapons. To catch seals, for example, they made long wooden harpoons, or spears. The harpoon had a barbed tip made of bone that held firmly in the seal's hide once it was struck. At the other end, hunters fastened a long rope so that they would not lose either the weapon or their prey.

In early summer, masses of salmon swam from the ocean up the rivers to lay their eggs. Men built wooden fences across the rivers to block the fish, making them easier to net. Women dried salmon meat so that it could be eaten all year long.

Builders and Carvers The forests of the Northwest provided materials for houses and many useful objects. Using wedges and stone-headed sledgehammers, men cut long, thin boards from logs or living trees. They joined these planks to build large, sturdy houses. To keep out the rain, they made roof shingles out of large sheets of cedar bark.

Women cut strips from the soft inner bark and used them to make baskets, mats, rope, and blankets. They even wove the strips of bark into waterproof capes.

With abundant food nearby, the Northwest people had time to practice crafts. Women made decorative shell buttons and sewed them onto their clothing with ivory needles. Men used tools such as wooden wedges, bone drills, stone chisels, and stone knives to carve detailed animal masks and wooden bowls.

Native Americans of the Northwest relied on the thick forests, abundant seafood, and plentiful game to meet their needs.

The California cultural region contains many different environments. Along the coast, huge redwood trees cover coastal mountains. In the inland areas, oaks and berries grow on rolling hills.

1.6 Native Americans of California

The California cultural region stretches from southern Oregon through Baja California. Ocean storms bring winter rains to this region. But summers are hot and dry, particularly inland.

The California region includes not only the coast, but also the coastal foothills, an inland valley, deserts, and the western side of the Sierra Nevada mountain range. Over 100 small groups made their homes in these diverse environments, more than in any other cultural region.

Many Sources of Food

Groups living along the coast of Northern California depended on salmon for much of their food. Farther south, coastal people relied more on shellfish. Away from the coast, groups hunted deer with bows and arrows. They set snares to trap rabbits and used nets to capture ducks. California people also gathered roots, berries, and pine nuts.

Most people in the region relied on acorns from oak trees as a basic food. In the fall, women harvested the acorns, shelled them, and pounded the nuts into meal. Water was rinsed through the meal to remove its bitterness. Women cooked the meal by mixing it with water in tightly woven baskets and then dropping hot cooking stones into the mixture.

Clothing, Houses, and Baskets
As they worked, the women wore simple aprons or skirts made from grasses or other plants, or sometimes from leather strips. In colder months, they wrapped themselves in animal hides.

Because the climate was mild, California people built simple homes. In forested areas, men used tools made from the antlers of deer and elk to strip large slabs of bark from redwood trees. They draped these into a cone shape to form a house. In marshy areas, people wove thick mats of reeds to drape over a cone-shaped framework of poles.

California people wove plant materials into many useful items. They made cooking baskets, storage baskets, sifters, and fish traps. Women used fine weaving and elegant patterns to make beautiful baskets, decorating their work with clamshells and bird feathers.

1.7 Native Americans of the Great Basin

To the east of California lies the Great Basin, a low area between the Sierra Nevada and the Rocky Mountains. The mountains on either side of this region block the rain, making this land mostly desert.

The plants that grow in this area are those that need little water, such as low grasses, sagebrush, and craggy piñon trees. Only small animals, such as rabbits and lizards, live in this harsh region.

With limited food and water, only a few families could live in a place at one time. For this reason, people of the Great Basin traveled in small groups and spent much of their time looking for food.

Extreme Heat and Cold Wherever people camped, they made temporary shelters of willow poles shaped into a cone and covered with brush or reeds. Almost all year, they carried water in baskets coated with sap from pine trees.

When winter came, temperatures dropped below freezing. To keep warm, people made robes out of rabbit hides. First they twisted long strips of hide so that only the fur showed. Then they wove these strips on a willow loom. Each adult robe required about 100 rabbit skins.

Life was difficult for Native Americans who lived in the Great Basin. Because of extreme temperatures and sparse rainfall, few plants and animals survive there.

Searching for Food In this arid (dry) environment, people followed food sources from season to season. In spring, they camped by valley lakes and streams swollen with melted snow. Men attracted migrating ducks with floating decoys made from reeds. When birds landed, the men chased them into nets. Meanwhile, women gathered duck eggs and the tender shoots of cattail plants.

When the streams dried up in summer, Great Basin people enjoyed snakes and grasshoppers as treats. But mostly they ate plants, almost 100 kinds. Women used sharp sticks to dig up roots. To knock seeds loose from plants, they wove flat baskets called *seed beaters*. From the mountain slopes they gathered ripe berries.

In autumn, bands harvested pine nuts and hunted fat jackrabbits. As winter arrived, the Great Basin people bundled into their rabbit robes in the warmer hills. In huts and caves, they lived off food they had dried earlier, waiting for the ducks to return in spring.

1.8 Native Americans of the Plateau

North of the Great Basin lies the Plateau cultural region. This region is bounded by the Cascade Range to the west, the Rockies to the east, and the Fraser River, in present-day Canada, to the north.

The mountains in this area have dense forests. The flatter, central part is drier and covered with grass and sagebrush. Winters are long and cold, while summers remain gentle.

The Plateau people hunted and gathered with the seasons. The cool, wet climate made it fairly easy to find enough to eat. So, too, did the Plateau's two mighty river systems, the Columbia and the Fraser.

Sturdy Houses and Clothing   Plateau people built their villages along major rivers. The rivers provided drinking water, fish, and driftwood to use for houses and firewood.

Food was so plentiful that some groups were able to live in their villages year-round. To stay cool in summer and warm in winter, they built their homes partly underground. They dug a pit, lined it with a frame of logs, and covered everything with saplings, reeds, and mud.

Plateau people used their weaving skills to create many kinds of baskets, as well as elaborate hats. As the cold months approached, they spent more time making clothes. In the fall, men hunted antelope and deer. Then women scraped and softened the hides for dresses, leggings, and shirts. They decorated their work with designs of seeds and shells.

Camas and Salmon   Although hunting usually provided plenty of meat in the fall, most of the time Plateau people relied on fish and plants for food. In spring, they gathered sprouts of wild onions and carrots from the low grasslands. Their particular favorite was camas, a starchy root related to lilies. Women uprooted it with willow digging sticks for eating raw, for roasting, and for grinding into flour.

The food most important to Plateau people was salmon. When the salmon migrated upstream, men stood on wooden platforms built over the water. From there, they could spear or net fish easily.

The Plateau cultural region features flatlands, rolling hills, and steep gorges. Large rivers provide water.

1.9 Native Americans of the Southwest

The Southwest cultural region includes present-day Arizona, New Mexico, southern Utah and Colorado, and portions of Texas, Oklahoma, and California. This region has many environments—canyons, mountains, deserts, and flat-topped mesas. It even has two major rivers, the Colorado and the Rio Grande. But rain seldom falls anywhere.

The heat and lack of water made living in the Southwest a challenge. Yet some Native Americans learned to love this arid land. "The whole Southwest was a House Made of Dawn," goes an old Indian song. "There were many colors on the hills and on the plain, and there was a dark wilderness on the mountains beyond."

Survival in the Southwest was a challenge. The area contains mountains, flat-topped mesas, canyons, and deserts. Sparse rainfall prevents the growth of many trees and plants.

Mesa People Different groups found different ways of surviving in the Southwest. Some lived as nomadic (wandering) desert hunters. Along the Colorado River, small groups hunted, gathered, and farmed. Others planted fields of corn, beans, and squash on the tops of high, flat areas called *mesas*.

The mesa people lacked trees for building homes. Instead, they made homes from the earth itself. Using bricks of *adobe* (sun-baked clay), they built thick-walled houses that protected them from summer heat and winter cold. Their villages looked like apartment houses that reached up to four stories high and had hundreds of rooms. A single village, called a *pueblo*, might house 1,000 people.

To protect their bodies from the sun, mesa people wore clothes made of cotton that they grew, spun, and wove into cloth. Using plants and minerals, they dyed fabrics with bright colors.

Corn Culture Despite living in a desert, the early mesa people learned to grow corn, beans, and squash. Corn was by far their most important crop.

To make the most of infrequent rain, farmers planted near naturally flooded areas like the mouths of large streambeds or the bases of mesas, where rain runoff flowed. Men dug irrigation ditches from the streams to the fields, and built small dams to hold summer rain.

Girls spent many hours a day grinding corn kernels into cornmeal. The women cooked the cornmeal into bread in clay ovens. In clay pots, they cooked stews of corn, rabbit meat, and chili peppers.

The Great Plains region is mostly tree-less grassland with cold winters and hot summers. Buffalo and other animals grazed freely over a vast territory.

1.10 Native Americans of the Great Plains

The Great Plains cultural region is a vast area of treeless grasslands. The Great Plains stretch for 2,000 miles from the Rockies to the Mississippi Valley, and from Canada to the Gulf of Mexico. The eastern part of this region has more water and softer soil than the western part. In the drier west, short, dense grasses provided perfect grazing for millions of buffalo.

Buffalo Hunters   On the Eastern Plains, various groups took up farming, going on buffalo-hunting trips only a few months each year. On the Western Plains, Native Americans followed buffalo herds much of the year.

In the spring and early summer, small groups lay in ambush where buffalo came to drink. The hunters gripped hardwood bows reinforced with strips of buffalo tendon. Taking aim, each man let loose a wooden arrow tipped with a sharp stone and arrayed with feathers to help it fly straight.

In the fall, huge buffalo herds gathered, and Plains people traveled in larger bands. The men sometimes made a trap for the buffalo by heaping stones into two short walls to form a V-shaped passage. The walls forced the buffalo closer together as they approached a cliff. Behind the herd, people set a grass fire or made loud noises to panic the buffalo. The animals stampeded between the walls and over the cliff edge. Below, waiting hunters finished them off with spears or bows and arrows.

Using the Buffalo   Buffalo provided the main food for Plains people. Women and children cut up the buffalo with bone knives. Extra meat was dried and kept for winter.

Plains people used every part of the buffalo. Buffalo hides were turned into shields, waterproof containers, warm robes, and bedding. For clothing and bags, women softened the hides with bone scrapers and rubbed in buffalo brains and fat.

Buffalo hair and sinew were twined into bowstrings and ropes. Horns and hooves became spoons and bowls, or were boiled down to make glue. Dried buffalo dung provided fuel for fires.

Buffalo provided materials for housing as well. Using tendons as thread, women sewed 8 to 20 buffalo skins together. The skins were then fastened around a tall cone of poles to make a *tipi,* a Plains word for "dwelling."

Plains people became even more successful when Spanish explorers introduced horses to the region. With horses, hunters could bring down more buffalo and move faster and more comfortably to new hunting grounds.

1.11 Native Americans of the Eastern Woodlands

The Eastern Woodlands cultural region reaches from the Mississippi River eastward to the Atlantic Ocean, and from Canada to North Carolina. Here, winter snows and summer rains produce endless forests, lakes, and streams.

Two language groups emerged in this region. In most of the territory, people spoke Algonquian languages. In New York and around the southern Great Lakes lived the Iroquois-speaking groups described in this section.

Plentiful Woods   The forests provided most of what Iroquois people needed to live. For food, hunters prowled through the forests to track deer. Men also hunted bears, trapped beavers, caught birds in nets, and speared fish. Women gathered fresh greens, nuts, and berries. They made syrup by boiling down sap from maple trees.

Instead of walking through the thick forests, Iroquois often paddled log and bark canoes along lakes and rivers. Because waterways also provided fish and drinking water, the Iroquois built their villages nearby.

Each village had dozens of sturdy log-frame houses covered with elm bark. Such longhouses were usually about 20 feet wide and over 100 feet long. Several related families lived in sections of the longhouse.

Women Farmers   To clear a space for farming, Iroquois men burned away trees and underbrush. Women did the rest. After hoeing the soil, they planted corn, sometimes several varieties. Around the cornstalks, they let beans twine. Squash stayed near the ground, keeping down weeds and holding moisture in the soil.

When the planting was done, women tanned deerskin to make skirts, capes, and moccasins (soft shoes). They ground corn with wooden sticks in hollowed-out tree trunks or between two stones. In the fall, they stored the harvest, often in large bark bins in the longhouses. Iroquois crops included sunflowers, tobacco, and many vegetables that are still planted in American gardens today.

Dense forests are home to deer, beavers, and other wildlife, and provided food, clothing, and shelter for the Native Americans of the Eastern Woodlands.

1.12 Native Americans of the Southeast

The Southeast cultural region stretches from the southern part of the Ohio Valley to the Gulf of Mexico, and from Texas to the Atlantic Ocean. This region's fertile coastal plains, river valleys, mountains, and swamps all have long, warm, humid summers and mild winters. In this green countryside, the people of the Southeast found growing crops fairly easy.

Towns Built Around Mounds

Some Southeastern peoples built towns dominated by large earthen mounds. The first mounds were burial sites. Centuries later, people made mounds several stories high as platforms for temples.

Building these mounds took months, even years, because people had to move the dirt one basketful at a time. Workers building mounds had no time to help grow or find food. But Southeastern groups had developed a type of corn that grew so fast, they could harvest two crops a year. Farmers raised enough food to feed the people building the mounds.

A single Southeastern town might have had 2 to 12 mounds arrayed around a central town plaza. Around these mounds, people clustered their houses. They built their homes from strips of young trees woven into a rectangular frame and plastered with clay. Roofs were pointed and made of leaves.

The Southeast cultural region includes river valleys, mountains, coastal plains, and swamps. The mild climate allowed Native Americans of the Southeast to grow corn, beans, squash, and other crops.

A Fertile Region Beyond their homes, fields lay in all directions. With the region's long growing season, Southeastern people relied on corn, beans, squash, pumpkins, and sunflowers for most of their food.

Women worked the fields with hoes made of stone, shell, or animal shoulder blades fastened to wooden handles. Men sometimes hunted, using blowguns for squirrels, rabbits, and turkeys, and bows and arrows for large animals like deer. They even brought home alligators and turtles.

To complete their varied diet, women gathered edible plants like sweet potatoes, wild rice, and persimmons. Because they wore simple, short deerskin skirts, they didn't spend much time making clothing. Instead, they used stones, shells, feathers, pearls, bones, and clay to fashion rings, earrings, arm rings, and hairpins.

1.13 Chapter Summary

In this chapter, you read about the first people to settle in North America. You used a map to study the adaptations made by Native Americans living in eight cultural regions.

The ancestors of Native Americans migrated to America from Asia across a land bridge during the last Ice Age. As their descendants traveled east and south, they had to adapt to the challenges of living in many different environments.

Wherever they settled, Native Americans had a special relationship with the world around them. They believed they were part of nature, and they treated the environment with respect.

Native Americans were a diverse group who spoke many languages. People living in different cultural regions developed distinctive ways of life that were suited to their environment's climate and natural resources. Scientists study these ways of life by examining the artifacts America's first people left behind.

Depending on where they lived, Native Americans ate different food, built different kinds of houses, and clothed themselves in different ways. They also practiced many kinds of crafts, making such things as jewelry, fine baskets, and animal masks. Native Americans built the first towns and villages in North America, and they were the continent's first farmers.

For thousands of years, these First People had the Americas to themselves. That would change when Europeans learned of the existence of the American continents. In the next chapter, you will read about the first explorers and settlers to arrive in America from European countries.

This drawing by John White, one of the first English colonists in North America, shows the village life of the Secotan people who lived in North Carolina.

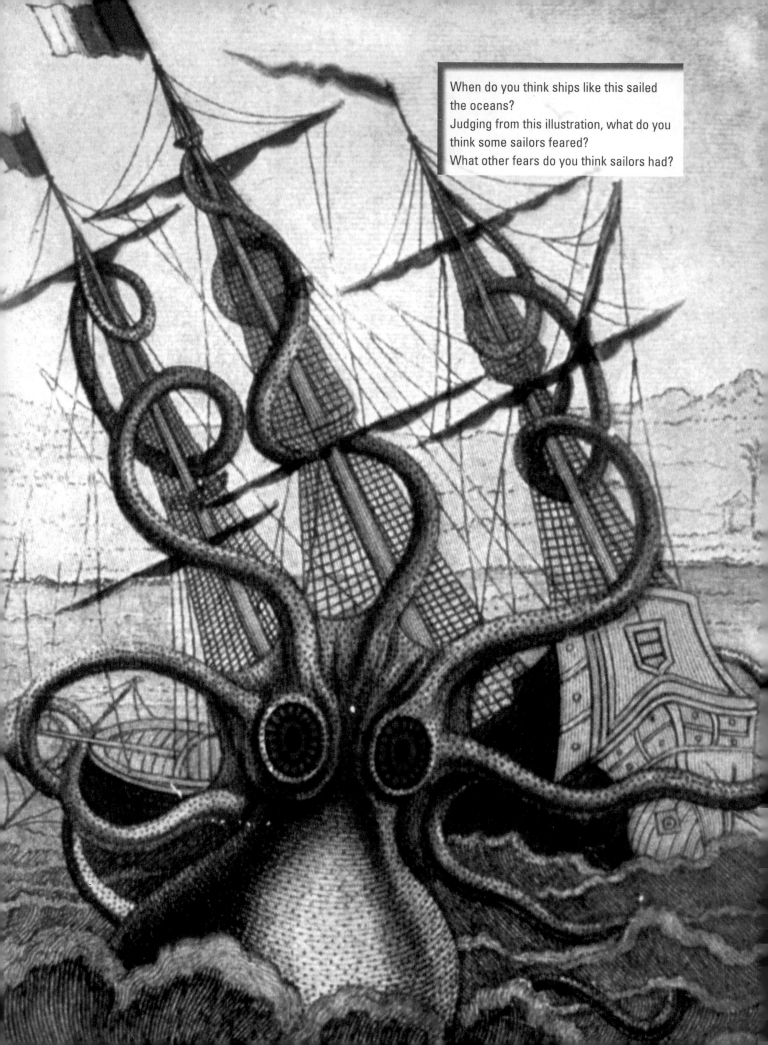

When do you think ships like this sailed the oceans?
Judging from this illustration, what do you think some sailors feared?
What other fears do you think sailors had?

European Exploration and Settlement

2.1 Introduction

Half a world away from where Native Americans made their homes, Europeans had no knowledge of these peoples or the land where they lived. When Europeans looked west, they saw only a vast ocean.

Europeans were far more interested in the lands that lay to the east. In the late 1200s, a young man named Marco Polo traveled through Asia with his father, a merchant and trader from Venice, Italy. Marco Polo spent 17 years in China. When he returned to Venice, people flocked to hear his stories of "the Indies," as India and East Asia were then known. He was called "the man of a million tales."

Eventually, a writer helped Marco Polo put his adventures into a book. The book described the wonders Polo had seen in China. It told of rich silks and rare spices, gold and jewels, and luxurious palaces.

When Marco Polo's book was published, only a few people in Europe could read. Those who did read it were fascinated by its description of riches to the east. Merchants and traders were eager to find the fastest way to get there. The land route that Polo had traveled was long and dangerous. His tales inspired explorers to find a route by sea.

Some **explorers** would seek a route to China by going around the southern tip of Africa. But a few brave souls looked to the west for another route. This took courage, because no one knew how far west sailors would have to sail to reach Asia or what monsters and terrors might await them far from Europe's shore.

In this chapter, you will learn how Christopher Columbus defied these dangers and sailed west to find a route to China. As you will see, his unexpected discovery of America led to competition among European nations to explore and profit from the land they called the **New World**.

Graphic Organizer: Illustration
You will use this illustration to learn about European exploration and settlement of the Americas.

2.2 Spain Starts an Empire

Marco Polo's book continued to be read over the next two centuries. This was a time of great change in Europe. The rediscovered writings of ancient Greeks and Romans inspired a new interest in learning and art. This period of lively new thinking has become known as the Renaissance, a word that means "rebirth."

During this time, the invention of the printing press made books, including Marco Polo's, more available. As Europeans learned about the world beyond Europe, they became eager to explore these far-off lands.

Columbus's Discoveries   One of the people who was inspired by Marco Polo's writings was an Italian seaman named Christopher Columbus. After studying maps of the world, Columbus became convinced that the shortest route to the Indies lay to the west, across the Atlantic Ocean.

Columbus looked for someone who could pay for the ships and men he needed to test his idea. Eventually, he was able to convince King Ferdinand and Queen Isabella of Spain to sponsor a voyage.

In August 1492, Columbus sailed west with three small ships. After more than a month at sea, his sailors raised the cry of "Land!" The land turned out to be a small island in what we now call the Caribbean Sea.

Columbus was thrilled. In a later

On October 12, 1492, Columbus stepped on land and claimed for Spain an island he named San Salvador. The people he encountered were peaceful, their only weapons being small wooden spears.

letter, he wrote, "I write this to tell you how in thirty-three days I sailed to the Indies with the fleet that the illustrious King and Queen...gave me, where I discovered a great many islands, inhabited by numberless people." Mistakenly believing that he had reached the Indies, Columbus called these people Indians.

In reality, the islanders were Native Americans who spoke a language called Taino. The Taino lived in a peaceful fishing community. Never had they seen people like the ones who had suddenly appeared on their shores. Yet they were friendly and welcoming. Columbus wrote, "They are so unsuspicious and so generous with what they possess, that no one who had not seen it would believe it."

Columbus promptly claimed the island for Spain and named it San Salvador, which means "Holy Savior." From there he sailed on to other islands. Convinced that China lay nearby, Columbus sailed back to Spain for more ships and men.

Columbus made four trips to the Caribbean, finding more islands, as well as the continent of South America. Each time he discovered a new place, he claimed it for Spain. Columbus died still believing he had found Asia, but later explorers quickly realized that he had actually stumbled on a "New World" unknown to Europe—the continents of North and South America.

The Columbian Exchange   The voyages of Columbus triggered a great transfer of people, plants, animals, and diseases back and forth across the Atlantic Ocean. This transfer, which still continues today, is called the Columbian Exchange. The Columbian Exchange brought valuable new crops such as corn and potatoes to Europe. These foods greatly improved the diet of the average European. Many Europeans also found new opportunities by crossing the Atlantic to settle in the Americas.

For Native Americans, however, the exchange began badly. The Europeans who came to America brought with them germs that caused smallpox and other diseases deadly to Native Americans. Historians estimate that in some areas, 90 percent of the native population was wiped out by European diseases.

Slavery Comes to America   This high death rate contributed to the introduction of African slaves to the Americas. Some of the Spanish settlers in the Caribbean had started gold mines. Others raised sugar, a crop of great value in Europe. At first the settlers forced Indians to work for them.

At first, Spanish settlers relied on the forced labor of Native Americans to work their sugar plantations. When disease wiped out this labor force, the Spanish turned to African slaves to perform the backbreaking task of harvesting and refining sugar cane.

The Granger Collection, New York

But as native people began dying in great numbers from European diseases, the settlers looked for a new work force. Before long, enslaved Africans were replacing Indians.

Slavery had existed around the world since ancient times. Often people who lost wars were enslaved, or treated as the property of their conquerors. By the late 1400s, European explorers in West Africa were trading guns and other goods for slaves captured by Africans.

In the 1500s, European slave traders began shipping slaves to the Caribbean for sale. Over the next three centuries, millions of Africans would be carried across the Atlantic in crowded, disease-infested ships. The terrible voyage lasted anywhere from weeks to months. Many died before it was over.

When the Africans arrived in the Americas, they were sold to their new masters at auctions. Many perished from disease and overwork. Those who survived faced a lifetime of forced labor as slaves.

Cortés, shown here with his translator, is trying to convince a group of Native Americans to help him conquer the Aztecs. With the help of Aztec enemies and smallpox, Cortés captured the Aztec capital of Tenochtitlán.

slavery The treatment of people as property for the purpose of forcing them to do labor. People who are denied freedom in this way are called *slaves* and are said to be *enslaved.*

conquistadors Spanish soldier-explorers, especially those who conquered the native peoples of Mexico and Peru

Cortés Conquers Mexico After Columbus's voyages, Spain began sending soldiers called **conquistadors** across the Atlantic. Their mission was to conquer a vast empire for Spain. Along the way, the conquistadors hoped to get rich.

In 1519, Hernán Cortés arrived in Mexico with horses and 500 soldiers. There he heard about the powerful Aztecs who ruled much of Mexico. When Cortés and his men reached the Aztec capital of Tenochtitlán, they could not believe their eyes. A beautiful city seemed to rise out of a sparkling lake. One Spaniard wrote, "Some of our soldiers asked whether the things that we saw were not a dream."

The Aztecs were not sure what to make of the strangers. They had never seen men dressed in metal armor and riding horses. Some mistook Cortés for the great Aztec god Quetzalcoatl and welcomed him as a hero. They would soon change their minds.

With the help of Indians who hated their Aztec rulers, and smallpox—which killed large numbers of Aztec warriors—Cortés conquered Tenochtitlán. The Spaniards pulled the city down and used its stones to build Mexico City, the capital of a new Spanish empire called New Spain.

Pizarro Conquers Peru   Smallpox also helped another Spanish conquistador, Francisco Pizarro, conquer an empire in South America. In 1532, Pizarro led an attack on the powerful Inca empire in present-day Peru. Luckily for Pizarro, smallpox reached Peru many months before him, killing thousands of Incas and leaving their empire badly divided.

Pizarro captured the Inca ruler, Atahualpa, but promised to release him in exchange for gold. To save their ruler, the Incas filled three rooms with gold and silver treasures. Pizarro killed Atahualpa anyway and took over the leaderless Inca empire. From there, Spanish conquistadors conquered most of South America.

Exploration of the Americas

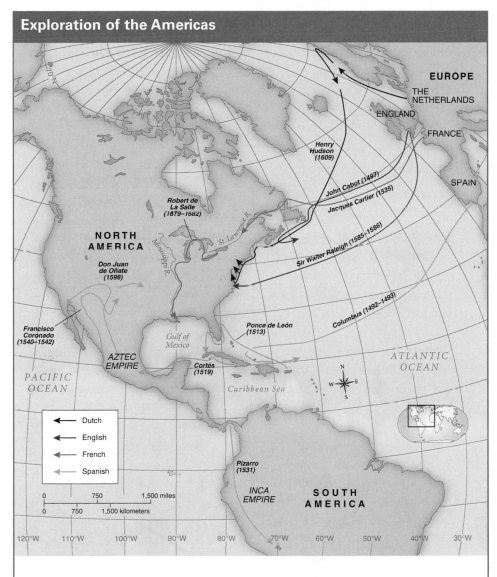

- Identify at least four details about this map.
- What do the different arrows represent?
- Which sections of the Western Hemisphere were explored by the Spanish?
  By the French? By the English? By the Dutch?
- Which country explored the most territory in the Western Hemisphere?
- Why do you think this country explored the most territory?

2.3 The Spanish Borderlands

In both Mexico and Peru, conquistadors found gold and silver riches beyond their wildest dreams. Hoping for still more, they pushed north into lands that are now part of the United States. Because these lands were located on the far edges of Spain's North American empire, they were known as the Spanish borderlands.

Florida   One of the first Spanish expeditions into North America was led by a man named Juan Ponce de León. He had sailed with Columbus to the Caribbean and made his fortune by discovering gold on the island of Puerto Rico. Despite his wealth, Ponce de León couldn't stop thinking about Indian rumors of a "fountain of youth" that made old people young again. Restless for more adventure, he set off to find the truth about these tales of everlasting youth.

Ponce de León landed on a sunny peninsula of North America in April 1513. Because he had sighted this lush new land on Easter Sunday, he called it La Florida, meaning "flowery." (The name is short for "flowery Easter.") Eight years later, he returned to Florida with 200 men to establish a Spanish settlement, or **colony**. Native Americans in the area used poisoned arrows to drive off the invaders. Instead of finding a fountain of youth, Ponce de León died from a poisoned arrow in his stomach.

Although Coronado never found the Seven Cities of Cíbola, his explorations opened a new area for Spanish settlement.

The "Seven Cities of Cíbola"   Another legend sparked new Spanish expeditions into North America. An old European tale told of the "Seven Cities of Cíbola." These cities were said to be so fabulously rich that the

The Granger Collection, New York

streets and houses were decorated with gold and jewels. When the Spanish heard Indians tell similar tales, they became convinced that the Seven Cities of Cíbola were somewhere in North America.

Spanish explorers first looked for the seven cities in Florida and in present-day Texas. They found plenty of adventure, but no golden cities. Then a Spanish priest named Marcos de Niza claimed to have seen a shimmering golden city in what is now New Mexico. He raced back to Mexico City with the news.

The Coronado Expedition In 1540, a famed conquistador named Francisco Vásquez de Coronado set out from Mexico City with a large expedition and de Niza as his guide. Their goal was to find the legendary golden cities.

After traveling north more than 7,000 miles, the expedition found a Native American *pueblo* (a village of apartment-like buildings made of stone and adobe rising four and five stories high). To de Niza, this might have looked like a golden city. But to Coronado, it was a "little, crowded village…all crumpled up together." The enraged expedition leader sent the priest home.

St. Augustine was originally a presidio, or fort, built by the Spanish to protect their claim to Florida. It is the oldest permanent European settlement in the United States.

The Coronado expedition continued north onto the Great Plains before giving up the search for golden cities. Disappointed, Coronado reported to Spain, "Everything is the opposite of [what] was related, except the name of the cities and the large stone houses…. The Seven Cities are seven little villages."

Settling the Borderlands As conquistadors explored new territories, they claimed the areas for Spain. By 1600, the Spanish borderlands extended west from Florida across present-day Texas, New Mexico, Arizona, and California.

At first, Spain did little to encourage settlement in these far-flung areas. But when rival European nations also began to show an interest in the land, small bands of soldiers were sent to these regions to protect the claims. The soldiers lived in walled forts called *presidios*.

In 1565, for example, a Spanish naval officer named Pedro Menéndez de Avilés was sent to Florida to protect the area from French explorers. Menéndez successfully drove the French out of their Florida base and built a fort on the peninsula's Atlantic coast. Menéndez named the fort Saint Augustine. Over the years, Spanish soldiers based at St. Augustine successfully defended the fort, and Spanish claims to Florida, from both French and English rivals. Today, St. Augustine is the oldest permanent settlement founded by Europeans in the United States.

Catholic **missionaries** accompanied the soldiers to the borderlands. Missionaries are priests who try to persuade people to convert to their religion. The priests built settlements called *missions* where they taught local Indians new skills and the Christian faith. Each mission grew its own food and produced most of what the missionaries needed to survive far from towns and trading centers.

Hardy bands of settlers also moved into the borderlands. There they established towns and farms. Juan de Oñate, who had made a fortune mining silver in Mexico, led the settlement of New Mexico. In 1598, Oñate brought 400 settlers and 7,000 animals from Mexico to New Mexico. The long overland journey took a year and a half to complete.

At first, the Pueblo Indians of New Mexico welcomed the newcomers. Unfortunately, the Spanish repaid the Indians' kindness with cruelty. Indians were made to work for the settlers as slaves. Catholic priests ordered the whipping of Pueblo religious leaders who continued to practice their traditional rituals. Such treatment led the Pueblo people to rise up in revolt and drive the Spanish out. Twelve years would pass before Spanish settlers returned to New Mexico.

During the 1600s and 1700s, settlement of the Spanish borderlands proceeded slowly. But in time, the language, religion, and culture of Spain spread across much of the American Southwest.

Impact on Native Americans The arrival of Spanish settlers had a great impact on the native peoples of the borderlands. The Pueblo people, for example, learned from the Spanish how to use new tools, grow new foods, and raise sheep for wool. In turn, the Indians introduced the Spanish to new techniques for growing crops in the desert soil.

From Florida to California, some Native Americans converted to the Catholic faith. The converts often lived and worked in and around the missions, growing crops and helping to maintain the churches and other buildings. However, even converts often continued to practice their traditional religious rituals as well.

Unfortunately, wherever the Spanish settled, they brought with them diseases to which native peoples had no resistance. Smallpox, measles, and influenza often wiped out entire villages. Before Coronado's expedition, there had been more than 100 Indian pueblos in New Mexico. By 1700, only 18 remained.

Missions were established to convert Native Americans to Christianity and increase Spanish control over the land. Missions included a church and the farmland on which missionaries produced almost all of what they needed to survive.

missionaries people who travel to a territory or community in order to make converts to their religion

2.4 New France

As Spanish colonies sent ships loaded with gold and silver home to Spain, all of Europe watched with envy. Every year, Spain seemed to become more wealthy and more powerful. Other nations wanted their share of riches from the New World. But none was strong enough to challenge Spain's American empire. Instead, they would have to seek their fortunes in areas not yet claimed by Spain.

Claiming New France   In 1534, France sent Jacques Cartier to explore the Atlantic coastline of North America. His goal was to find a Northwest Passage, an all-water route through the North American continent to the Pacific Ocean. Such a passage would provide a shortcut for ships sailing west to Asia.

Cartier failed to find such a passage. But he did claim for France the land we know today as Canada. He later named this land New France. Cartier also discovered something almost as valuable as Spanish gold— beaver fur. Beaver hats were a hot fashion item in Europe, and French hatmakers were willing to pay high prices for beaver pelts.

Settling New France   The first settlement in New France was founded by Samuel de Champlain. In 1608, Champlain sailed up the St. Lawrence River and built a trading post he called Quebec. For the next 150 years, Quebec would be a base for French explorers, soldiers, missionaries, traders, and fur **trappers**.

From Quebec, fur trappers pushed west in search of beaver. They called themselves *coureurs de bois,* which means "wood rangers" in French. Catholic missionaries followed the trappers, seeking converts among the native peoples.

Like the Spanish borderlands, New France failed to attract large numbers of settlers. The harsh climate of New France discouraged French farmers from crossing the Atlantic. So did the colony's policy of granting the best land along the St. Lawrence River to French nobles who then planned to rent it out to farmers. The few settlers who did come soon got tired of renting and left their farms to search for furs.

The image below shows two *coureurs de bois,* which means "wood rangers" in French. These fur trappers, who roamed New France in search of beaver pelts, learned trapping skills from the Native Americans.

Native American Business Partners

Because the French were more interested in furs than farming, they did not try to conquer the Indians and put them to work as the Spanish had done. Instead, the French made Native Americans their business partners.

After founding Quebec, Champlain made friends with the nearby Indians, especially the Huron. Fur trappers lived in Huron villages, learned the Huron language, and married Huron women. From the Huron they learned how to survive for months in the wilderness. Unfortunately, the friendship between the French and Huron exposed the Huron to European diseases, which swept through their villages and killed many of them.

Champlain even joined the Huron in an attack on their enemies the Iroquois. He later wrote:

The French made friends with the Native Americans in New France, and often assisted them in battles with their enemies. Here, Samuel de Champlain, in the center, helps the Huron Indians defeat the Iroquois.

> *I marched some 20 paces ahead of the rest, until I was about 30 paces from the enemy…. When I saw them making a move to fire at us, I rested my musket against my cheek and aimed directly at one of their three chiefs. With the same shot, two fell to the ground, and one of their men was wounded…. When our side saw this shot…they began to raise such loud cries that one could not have heard it thunder. Meanwhile, the arrows flew on both sides.*

The astonished Iroquois, who had never seen or heard gunfire before, fled in terror. From that day on, the Iroquois would be the bitter enemies of the French.

Claiming Louisiana

The search for furs led the French far inland from Quebec. In 1673, two explorers, Father Marquette and Louis Joliet, explored the great Mississippi River. They hoped that this waterway would be the long-sought Northwest Passage. But they discovered that, instead of flowing west to the Pacific Ocean, the river flowed south toward the Gulf of Mexico. Disappointed, they returned to New France.

Nine years later, Robert de La Salle explored the entire length of the Mississippi River. On April 9, 1682, he planted a French flag at the mouth of the river and claimed everything west of the Mississippi River for France. La Salle named this vast area Louisiana for the French monarch, King Louis XIV.

2.5 Jamestown: The First English Colony

Columbus's voyages inspired John Cabot, an Italian living in England, to seek his own western route to Asia. In 1497, Cabot, who had moved to England from Venice, sailed west across the Atlantic. He landed in Newfoundland, an island off the coast of Canada. A fellow Venetian living in London wrote of Cabot's brief landing:

He coasted for three hundred leagues and landed; saw no human beings, but he has brought here to the king certain snares which had been set to catch game, and a needle for making nets; he also found some felled trees, by which he judged there were inhabitants, and he returned to his ship in alarm…. The discoverer…planted on this newly-found land a large cross, with one flag of England and another of St. Mark [the patron saint of Venice] on account of his being a Venetian.

John Cabot, an Italian exploring for England, sailed to Newfoundland and Nova Scotia, off the coast of present-day Canada. He believed he had reached Asia, and claimed the land for England. Two years later, he was lost at sea when he set out on an expedition to find Japan.

Like Columbus, Cabot mistakenly believed that he had landed in Asia. Later, however, England would claim all of North America because of the flag planted by Cabot in 1497.

The Lost Colony of Roanoke

Nearly a century later, an English noble named Sir Walter Raleigh tried to start a colony on Roanoke Island off the coast of present-day North Carolina. Indians on the island welcomed the settlers and gave them traps for catching fish. The newcomers, however, were more interested in looking for gold than fishing. When their supplies ran low, they returned to England.

In 1587, Raleigh sent a second group of colonists to Roanoke. Unfortunately, they arrived too late in the season to plant crops. Their leader, John White, sailed back to England for more supplies. While White was in England, however, fighting broke out between England and Spain. As a result, his return to Roanoke was delayed for three years.

When White finally reached the island, the colonists had disappeared. Carved on a doorpost was the word CROATOAN. To this day, both the meaning of this word and what happened to the lost colony of Roanoke remain a mystery.

The Granger Collection, New York

The first colonists at Jamestown settled in an area they believed would be easy to defend against Native Americans and the Spanish. However, the land was marshy and infested with malaria-carrying mosquitoes.

Settling Jamestown Twenty years went by before a permanent English colony was established in America. In 1607, a group of merchants formed the London Company to start a money-making colony in Virginia. The company crammed 144 settlers into three tiny ships and sent them across the Atlantic. The settlers were to ship back valuable goods such as furs and timber.

When they reached Virginia, the colonists settled on a swampy peninsula they believed could be easily defended against Native Americans or Spanish ships. They called their new home Jamestown after King James I. What the settlers didn't know was that the spot they chose to settle would soon be swarming with disease-carrying mosquitoes. It was also surrounded by a large and powerful Native American group.

To make matters worse, the Jamestown settlers were a mix of gentlemen and craftsmen. None of them knew much about farming. Nor were they willing to work very hard at it. They thought they were in Virginia to look for gold, not to provide for themselves.

As the food the settlers had brought with them disappeared, they began to trade with the Indians, bartering glass beads and iron hatchets for corn and meat. But barter wasn't easy. Many Indians decided they would sooner kill the English—or just let them starve—than trade. Hunger and disease soon took their toll. Every few days, another body was carried off to the graveyard.

In 1608, a natural leader named Captain John Smith took control of Jamestown. "If any would not work," announced Smith, "neither should he eat." The men were hungry, so they worked.

While scouting for food, Smith was captured by the Indians and brought to a smoky longhouse. Seated at one end, he saw Powhatan, the Indians' powerful chief. The Indians greeted Smith with a loud shout and a great feast. But when the meal ended, the mood changed. Smith was about to be clubbed to death when a young girl leapt out of the shadows. "She took my head in her arms and laid her own upon mine to save me from death," Smith later wrote.

Smith's savior was Pocahontas, Chief Powhatan's favorite daughter. From that moment on, she would think of Smith as her brother. Pocahontas helped Smith save Jamestown by bringing food and keeping peace with her people. "She, next under God," Smith wrote, "was...the instrument to preserve this colony from death, famine, and utter confusion."

The Starving Time Jamestown's troubles, however, were far from over. In the fall of 1609, after being injured in a gunpowder explosion, Smith returned to England. The following winter was the worst ever—so bad that it came to be known as the "Starving Time."

Without Smith and Pocahontas to act as go-betweens, the Indians refused to trade with the settlers. The English ate dogs, rats, and even human corpses to survive. By spring, only 60 of the 500 people Smith had left in the fall remained alive.

When supply ships arrived the following spring, the survivors were ordered to abandon their failed colony. Then three more English ships arrived with food, 150 new colonists, and 100 soldiers. Jamestown was saved again.

Jamestown Survives Even with more settlers, the people of Jamestown lived in constant danger of Indian attacks. To end that threat, the English kidnapped Pocahontas and held her hostage. For a year, Pocahontas remained a prisoner—but a willing and curious one. During that time she learned English, adopted the Christian faith, and made new friends.

Among those new friends was a widower named John Rolfe. Rolfe had already helped the colony survive by finding a crop that could be raised in Virginia and sold for good prices in England—tobacco. The happy settlers went tobacco mad, planting the crop everywhere, even in Jamestown's streets.

Now Rolfe helped again by making a proposal of marriage to Pocahontas. Both the governor of Jamestown and Chief Powhatan gave their consent to this unusual match. Maybe they hoped that the marriage would help end the conflict between their peoples.

The union of Pocahontas and John Rolfe did bring peace to Jamestown. In 1616, Rolfe wrote, "Our people yearly plant and reap quietly, and travel in the woods...as freely and securely from danger...as in England."

Pocahontas, the daughter of a powerful Indian leader, brought food to the Jamestown settlers and helped them survive. Pocahontas later married John Rolfe and visited England with him. This portrait of her in European dress is the only authentic painting of her.

Peter Minuit is shown offering Native Americans knives, beads, blankets, and trinkets worth about $24 in exchange for Manhattan Island.

2.6 New Netherland: The Short-Lived Dutch Settlement

While John Smith was struggling to save the colony of Jamestown, an English sailor named Henry Hudson was exploring the coastline farther north for the Netherlands. Henry Hudson's voyage was sponsored by Dutch merchants who hoped to find the Northwest Passage. (The people of the Netherlands are called the Dutch.)

In 1609, Hudson discovered a deep river full of fish, and thought it might just take him all the way across the continent. It didn't, of course, but he claimed the land along its banks for the Netherlands. The river was later named the Hudson in his honor, and the territory he claimed became known as New Netherland.

In 1621, Dutch merchants formed the Dutch West India Company to start a colony in America. The first Dutch colonists settled along the upper Hudson where they built Fort Orange, near present-day Albany, New York. The new colonists quickly found that there were good profits to be made in the fur trade. They established trading posts along the Hudson River. The largest was on Manhattan Island at the river's mouth.

Relations with Native Americans   In 1626, the Dutch West India Company sent Peter Minuit to New Netherland as the colony's governor. Wanting peaceful relations with the Indians, the company told Minuit that any native peoples on Manhattan Island "must not be expelled with violence or threats but be persuaded with kind words…or should be given something."

Following orders, Minuit offered the island's Indians iron pots, beads, and blankets worth about $24 in exchange for their land. The Native Americans didn't believe that anyone could own land. Laughing at the foolishness of the white men, they made the trade.

Dutch traders also made deals with members of the powerful Iroquois Confederacy, an alliance of five Indian groups who lived across the northern portion of New Netherland. The French had long supplied the Huron, the Iroquois' great rivals, with guns in exchange for furs. It made sense for the Iroquois to become partners with the Dutch, who supplied them with the weapons they needed to stand up to the Huron.

This partnership also made sense for the Dutch. The French were their main rivals in the fur trade. For most of the 1600s, the Iroquois kept the French from moving into the fur-rich Ohio Valley.

New Amsterdam   As the fur trade expanded, the Dutch settlement on Manhattan swelled to over 1,000 people. In 1647, the Dutch West India Company hired Peter Stuyvesant as the colony's new governor. When he arrived at Manhattan, Stuyvesant declared that the settlement would be called New Amsterdam, after the capital city of the Netherlands.

Stuyvesant had lost his right leg in battle, and he stomped around on a wooden leg that was decorated with silver nails. People called him "Old Silvernails" or "Peg Leg Pete." Although he was a strong leader, "Old Silvernails" was generally disliked. When Dutchmen who had been elected as city councilors disagreed with him, he called them "ignorant subjects" and threatened to ship them back to the Netherlands in pieces if they gave him trouble.

Despite his reputation as a grouch, Stuyvesant governed New Amsterdam for 17 years. During this time, he captured a nearby Swedish colony and invited its settlers to live in New Amsterdam. By 1660, the colony had nearly 8,000 people, including Europeans from many nations as well as enslaved Africans. New Amsterdam also provided refuge for Jews who were seeking freedom to follow their religion in peace.

Peter Stuyvesant, the Dutch governor of New Amsterdam, surrendered the settlement to the British without a shot being fired. Outnumbered and outgunned, Stuyvesant bowed to the pleas of his people to avoid bloodshed and destruction.

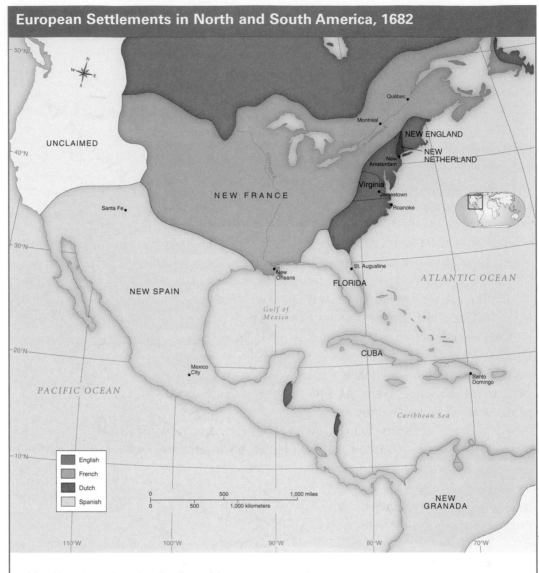

European Settlements in North and South America, 1682

- Identify at least four details about this map.
- What do the different colors on the map represent?
- Which country settled the largest area? Which country settled the smallest area?
- What connections do you see between this map and the map "Exploring the Americas"?
- Which European country first settled the area in which you live?

New Netherland Becomes New York Stuyvesant's biggest problem was that the English wanted to drive the Dutch out of North America. England's king, Charles II, refused to recognize Dutch claims to New Netherland. In 1664, Charles gave his brother, James, the Duke of York, ownership of all Dutch lands in America—if he could conquer them.

James promptly organized a small invasion fleet to take the colony. When the English arrived, they sent Stuyvesant a letter demanding his surrender. Stuyvesant tore up the note and refused to consider giving up until New Amsterdam's chief gunner reported that the city's supply of gunpowder was damp and useless. Without firing a shot, the English took over New Netherland and renamed the colony New York.

2.7 Chapter Summary

In this chapter, you read about the first European settlements in the "New World." You used an illustration to learn about the European exploration and settlement of the Americas.

Europeans called the Americas the "New World" because their discovery came as a surprise to them. Explorers like Christopher Columbus were actually looking for a westward route to Asia when they stumbled onto these continents.

European nations competed to claim these new lands and the riches they might contain. Spain claimed vast territories, including Mexico and the southwestern portion of the future United States. In their search for gold and other treasures, Spanish conquistadors conquered the Aztecs of Mexico and the Incas of Peru. The Spanish also brought enslaved Africans to the Americas to plant and harvest crops. In the American Southwest, Spanish missionaries worked to convert Native Americans to Christianity.

The French, meanwhile, staked a claim to much of present-day Canada, as well as Louisiana, the territory west of the Mississippi River. Most French settlers were more interested in trapping and trading furs than in farming or establishing large settlements.

The English based their claim to North America on John Cabot's voyage in 1497. After several attempts, the English established their first permanent colony at Jamestown in Virginia.

The Dutch established their own foothold in North America by founding the colony of New Amsterdam. The English, however, drove the Dutch out and renamed the colony New York.

For Native Americans, the arrival of Europeans brought many changes. The newcomers brought new technology and ideas to the native people. But they also brought deadly diseases that killed great numbers of the first Americans.

The exploration and settlement of the Americas brought amazing changes both to Europe and to the New World.

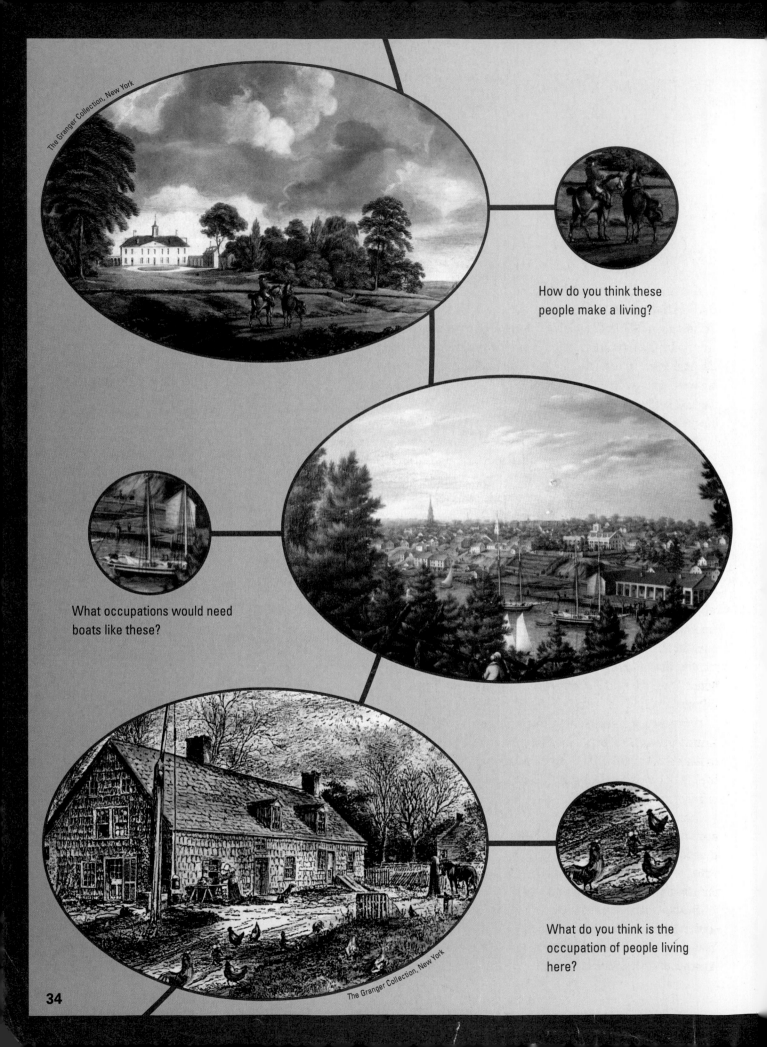

How do you think these people make a living?

What occupations would need boats like these?

What do you think is the occupation of people living here?

3

The English Colonies in America

3.1 Introduction

In the mid-1700s, a German schoolteacher named Gottlieb Mittelberger boarded a ship bound for the colony of Pennsylvania, in far-off America. Mittelberger had borrowed the cost of his passage by signing on as an **indentured servant**. When he arrived in the colonies, he would have to settle his debt by working for several years for the master who bought his services.

As Mittelberger discovered, the voyage across the Atlantic was horrible. Most passengers suffered greatly from illness and hunger. "The people are packed densely," Mittelberger wrote, "like herrings so to say, in the large sea vessels. One person receives a place of scarcely 2 feet width and 6 feet length.... There is on board these ships terrible misery, stench, fumes, horror, vomiting, many kinds of seasickness, fever, dysentery, headache, heat, constipation, boils, scurvy, cancer, mouth-rot, and the like, all of which come from old and sharply salted food and meat, also from very bad and foul water."

When the nightmarish voyage ended, Mittelberger had to stay on board the ship until his service was bought. Depending on their age and strength, most indentured servants were obliged to work for their masters for three to six years. But, as Mittelberger noted, "young people, from 10 to 15 years, must serve till they are 21 years old."

Why were people willing to go through such hardships to come to the colonies? Many colonists came to America for the chance to own land and start a new life. Others were seeking freedom to practice their religion.

There were some who did not have a choice. A number of convicts (people in jail) were forced to go to America to work off their debts as indentured servants. And millions of Africans were kidnapped from their homelands and brought to the colonies as slaves.

In this chapter, you'll read about the people who settled the English colonies, and why they came. You'll also read in detail about 8 of the 13 colonies. As you do, try to find out what made each one unique.

Graphic Organizer: Spoke Diagram
You will use a spoke diagram to record important features of 8 of the original 13 colonies.

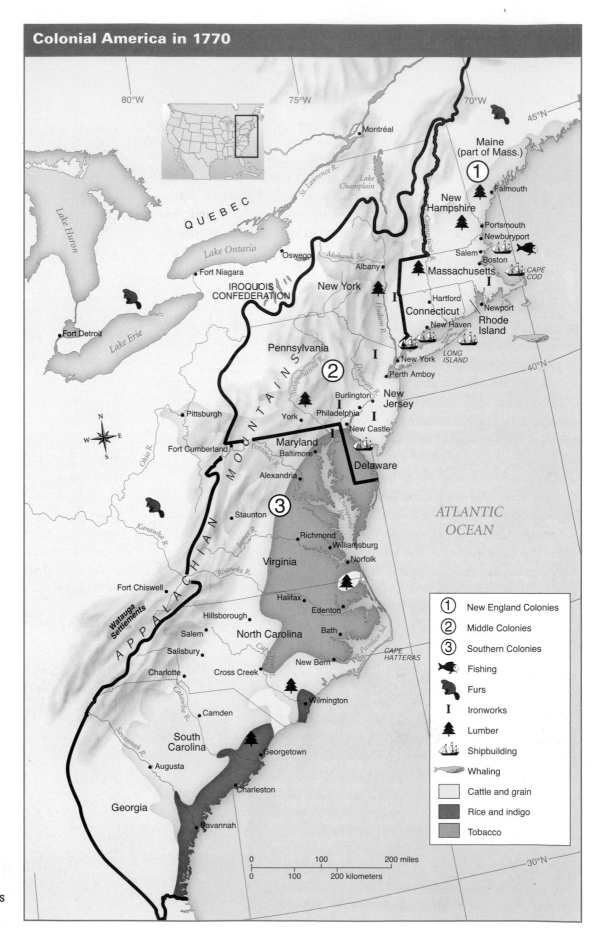

Colonial America in 1770

80°W 75°W 70°W

45°N

Montréal

Maine (part of Mass.)
① Falmouth

New Hampshire
Portsmouth
Newburyport
Salem
Boston
CAPE COD

QUEBEC

St. Lawrence R.

Lake Champlain

Lake Huron

Lake Ontario
Oswego
Fort Niagara

Mohawk R.
Albany

IROQUOIS
CONFEDERATION

New York

Massachusetts

Hartford
Connecticut
New Haven
Rhode Island
Newport

Hudson R.

Fort Detroit

Lake Erie

Pennsylvania
②

LONG ISLAND
New York

40°N

Perth Amboy

Susquehanna R.

Pittsburgh
York

Burlington
Philadelphia
New Jersey
Delaware R.

New Castle
Maryland

Fort Cumberland
Potomac R.
Baltimore

Ohio R.

Delaware

Alexandria

Staunton
③

Chesapeake Bay

ATLANTIC OCEAN

Kanawha R.

James R.

Richmond
Williamsburg
Norfolk

Virginia

Roanoke R.

Fort Chiswell

APPALACHIAN MOUNTAINS

Watauga Settlements

Halifax
Edenton
Bath

Hillsborough

Salem
North Carolina

Pamlico Sd.

CAPE HATTERAS

Salisbury

Cape Fear R.

New Bern

Charlotte
Cross Creek

Catawba R.

Wilmington

Camden

South Carolina
Georgetown

Savannah R.

Augusta

Georgia

Charleston

Savannah

N
W E
S

0   100   200 miles
0   100   200 kilometers

30°N

Legend
① New England Colonies
② Middle Colonies
③ Southern Colonies
🐟 Fishing
🦫 Furs
I Ironworks
🌲 Lumber
⛵ Shipbuilding
🐋 Whaling
◻ Cattle and grain
◼ Rice and indigo
▩ Tobacco

By 1770, the 13 American colonies had developed distinctive ways of life that would affect the development of America for years to come.

3.2 The New England, Middle, and Southern Colonial Regions

English settlers established colonies in North America for many reasons. Some colonies were set up by groups of businessmen who hoped to profit from resources found in the "New World." Several colonies were settled by people looking for a place to practice their religion freely. One colony was established as a refuge for debtors (people who owe money). The debtors would otherwise have been tossed into prison. The English government supported all these efforts in part because it was competing for land in the New World with such nations as France and Spain.

By 1733, there were 13 British colonies strung along the Atlantic coastline. They can be grouped into three distinct regions: the New England, Middle, and Southern Colonies. These regions had different climates and resources that encouraged settlers to develop different ways of life.

The New England Colonies The New England region included the colonies of Massachusetts, Rhode Island, Connecticut, and New Hampshire. As you will read in the next section, the first settlers of these colonies came to America seeking religious freedom.

In New England, farming was difficult because of the long, cold winters and the region's rocky, hilly wilderness. But the forests and the sea provided useful resources and ways to make a living. New Englanders built their economy on small farms, lumbering, fishing, shipbuilding, and trade.

The Middle Colonies The four Middle Colonies were New York, Pennsylvania, New Jersey, and Delaware. The landscape of this region ranged from the rich soil of coastal New Jersey and Delaware to the valleys and wooded mountains of New York and Pennsylvania. Farmers in the Middle Colonies raised a-wide variety of crops and livestock. Lumbering, shipbuilding, and other occupations added to the variety of opportunities in these colonies.

By the 1700s, Philadelphia, in the Middle Colony of Pennsylania, had become a bustling trading center and one of the most important cities in the English colonies. It was the first city in America to establish a public school or a newspaper. It was also the first to use a grid or checkerboard pattern to set up its streets.

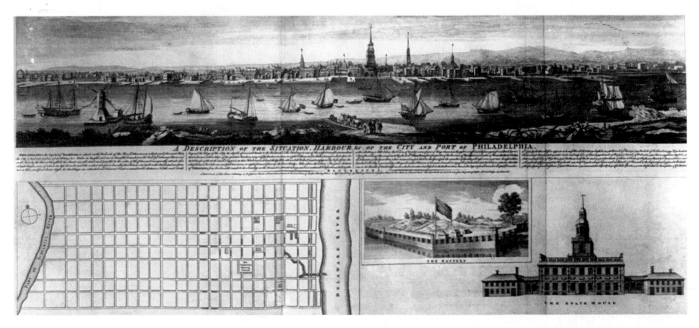

A DESCRIPTION of the SITUATION, HARBOUR &c. of the CITY and PORT of PHILADELPHIA.

cash crops crops, such as tobacco, sugar, and cotton, raised in large quantities in order to be sold for profit

assembly an elected group of lawmakers

democratic Ruled by the people. In a democracy, citizens elect representatives to make and carry out laws.

The people who settled the Middle Colonies represented many cultures and religions. One important group, the Quakers, started the colony of Pennsylvania. Like the early settlers of New England, the Quakers were looking for freedom to practice their religion. Others seeking religious freedom soon followed. Settlements of French, Dutch, Germans, Swedes, Danes, Finns, Scots, Irish, and English spread throughout the Middle Colonies.

The Southern Colonies   The five Southern Colonies were Maryland, Virginia, North Carolina, South Carolina, and Georgia. This region featured broad rivers and vast wetlands that gradually merged with the sea. Here, the soil and the hot, wet climate were ideal for growing tobacco, rice, and other **cash crops**.

Wealthy colonists took advantage of these conditions by establishing large farms called *plantations*. Plantation owners relied on indentured servants and enslaved Africans to sow and harvest their fields. After being harvested, the crops could be brought by river to the coast and loaded on ships for transport to other colonies and to Europe.

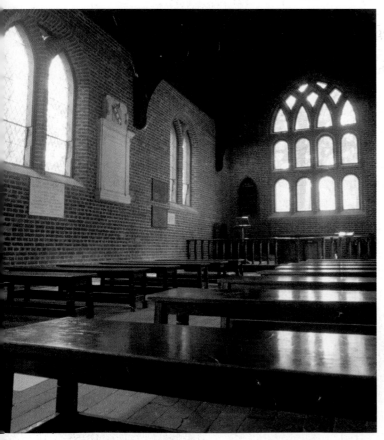

In New England, the church was at the center of both religious and political life. This church's pews could be removed to make room for tables used in town meetings.

Government in the Colonies   All the colonies were settled with the permission of the king of England. For each colony, the king issued a charter, a formal document that outlined the colony's geographic boundaries and specified how it would be governed.

Because the colonies were so far away from England, however, they needed to be able to make their own laws and keep peace and order.

The colonies developed different forms of government, depending on the purpose of the settlement. Most of the colonies were self-governing. Colonists elected members of their community to a general **assembly**, which made their laws.

Many colonies also had a governor appointed by the king. As the king's representative, the governor could overrule the elected assembly. Some colonies also had councils, groups of men who represented the English businessmen involved in starting the colony.

In Massachusetts, religious-minded colonists established a theocracy, a government whose leaders ruled in the name of God. In time, however, a system of town meetings evolved in which colonists voted for representatives to govern them.

In many ways, the colonies were more **democratic** than England. Still, not all colonists had a voice in the government. Usually, only free, white, land-owning men were allowed to vote. In some colonies, voters also had to belong to the preferred church. Other colonists—including women, servants, slaves, and skilled tradesmen who were not landowners—had no voting rights.

3.3 Massachusetts: New England Colony

In the early 1600s, religion was very important in England. The king ruled the official Church of England, also called the Anglican Church. However, not everyone agreed with the Church's ideas and practices.

One group, called **Puritans** by their opponents, wanted to "purify" the Church by making services simpler and doing away with ranks of authority. Some of the Puritans, called Separatists, wanted to separate from the English church and form their own congregations. When Separatists were put in jail for not going to Anglican services, some of them moved to Holland, where they could practice their religion freely.

But Holland wasn't home, and the Separatists wanted their children to grow up in an English culture. In 1620, about 50 Separatists set sail for America aboard the *Mayflower*. The Separatists had become Pilgrims, people who travel for religious reasons. The Pilgrims hoped to build their idea of a perfect society in America. During their voyage, they signed an agreement called the Mayflower Compact that described the way they would govern themselves in the new world.

After a long, uncomfortable journey across the Atlantic, the Pilgrims landed at Plymouth, near Cape Cod. Luckily for them, the local Indians welcomed them. Without the help of these Native Americans, the Pilgrims might not have survived their first winter. The Indians taught them how to plant crops, trap animals, and catch fish. In 1621, the Pilgrims invited the Indians to share their first harvest in a three-day feast of thanksgiving. Americans still celebrate this holiday.

Ten years later, a large group of Puritans decided to follow the Pilgrims to America. The king was relieved to see them go and sent them off with a charter for the colony of Massachusetts Bay. The charter said that the Massachusetts colonists would govern themselves. The Puritans were pleased with the charter, because they wanted to build a community governed by the rules of the Bible. They hoped to set an example for the rest of the world. Their governor, John Winthrop, said, "We must consider that we shall be as a city upon a hill. The eyes of all people are upon us."

Puritans People who wanted to "purify" the English Church. Puritans wanted to simplify the Church's ceremonies and its ranks of authority.

Massachusetts
New England Colony

Founders
Pilgrims led by William Bradford (1620); Puritans led by John Winthrop (1630)

Settlers
Puritans seeking escape from religious persecution

Climate
Harsh winters and warm summers

Geography
Sandy coast with good ports, rich pastures, forests

Economy/Occupations
Crop and livestock farming, lumber, shops, shipping

Religion
Puritan

Government
Self-governing with strong religious influence

John Winthrop was a founder and later the governor of Massachusetts. Here, we see him giving a blessing to soldiers in the colony.

slave trade the business of capturing, transporting, and selling people as slaves

Rhode Island
New England Colony

Founders
Roger Williams
and Anne Hutchinson

Settlers
People seeking religious freedom

Climate
Hot, humid summers and
cold, snowy winters

Geography
Coastal lowlands;
flat, rocky woodlands

Economy/Occupations
Farming (large cattle and dairy farms,
small independent farms), lumber,
shipbuilding, fishing, whaling, trade

Religion
Various faiths

Government
Self-governing

3.4 Rhode Island: New England Colony

The Puritans of Massachusetts gained religious freedom, but it was a liberty they kept to themselves. They set up a government that required everyone in the colony to worship in the same way.

When a young minister named Roger Williams began preaching different ideas, the Puritans put him on trial. Williams believed that all people should be able to worship in any way they chose. "Forced worship," he declared, "stinks in God's nostrils."

The Puritans ordered Williams sent back to England. Instead, on a cold winter day in 1636, he left his wife and children and fled south. After trudging through snow for days, he met a group of Indians near Narragansett Bay. The Indians cared for him until spring. When his family and a few followers joined him, Williams bought land from the Indians for a settlement. He called it Providence, a word meaning "the guidance and care of God."

Roger Williams welcomed people with different religious beliefs. Two years after he and his followers settled Providence, a colonist named Anne Hutchinson was also forced to leave Massachusetts for preaching against the Puritans. She and her family followed Williams and established a settlement called Portsmouth. In 1647, these and other settlements became the colony of Rhode Island.

The ideal of freedom in Rhode Island did not extend to enslaved Africans. Sea merchants soon discovered the riches that could be made in the **slave trade**. As a result, Rhode Island became one of the largest slave-trading centers in the world. Slave trading helped make the fortunes of some of the wealthiest families in New England. At the same time, the isolated coves along the Rhode Island coast provided perfect hiding places for pirates and their stolen goods.

Puritans in other colonies were disgusted by these activities. Reverend Cotton Mather of Boston called Rhode Island "the sewer of New England." To these Puritans, Rhode Island represented people and ideas that they rejected from their own communities. Using a word that implied "criminals," they invented their own name for the colony: "Rogues' Island."

This woodcut shows Roger Williams building a crude cabin after he fled Massachusetts in the bitter cold of winter.

3.5 Connecticut: New England Colony

Even in Massachusetts, not all Puritans shared exactly the same ideas. Thomas Hooker was a Puritan clergyman who lived in New Towne, a fast-growing community next to Boston. Hooker didn't always agree with the laws and leadership in Massachusetts. When he heard about a fertile valley along a river to the west, he convinced his family and about 100 other people to move there with him.

It took Hooker and his followers two weeks to travel to the Connecticut Valley with all their animals and belongings. There they established a settlement on the site of an old Dutch fort where an earlier group of English colonists had settled. They called their new community Hartford. In 1639, Hartford joined with two other settlements to form the colony of Connecticut.

Hooker believed that government should be based on the "free consent of the people, to whom belongs the choice of public magistrates [officials], by God's own allowance." He helped draw up the first written plan of government for any of the colonies. This document was called the Fundamental Orders. The Fundamental Orders guaranteed the right to vote to all men who were members of the Puritan church.

Meanwhile, other Puritans formed a separate colony nearby called New Haven. The Puritans of New Haven agreed to live by the "Word of God." Their laws were more strict than those in Hooker's Connecticut colony.

Neither of these colonies, however, was legally authorized by the king. Then, in 1662, King Charles II granted a charter for a new Connecticut Colony that included New Haven. This charter gave the colonists of Connecticut more rights than those enjoyed by any other colonists except in Rhode Island. Legend says that when King James II sent Governor Andros to Hartford 15 years later to take back the colonists' charter, someone stole it and hid it in the trunk of a huge white oak tree. The "Charter Oak" became a symbol of Connecticut's freedom.

Connecticut
New England Colony

Founders
Thomas Hooker

Settlers
Puritans seeking a new settlement

Climate
Cold winters, mild summers

Geography
Forested hills, seacoast

Economy/Occupations
Farming (crops and livestock), shipbuilding, fishing, whaling

Religion
Puritan

Government
Written constitution (the Fundamental Orders), self-governing

Thomas Hooker and about 100 others established the community of Hartford in the fertile Connecticut Valley. It later became a part of the colony of Connecticut.

New York
Middle Colony

Founders
Dutch West India Company (1624);
James, Duke of York (1664)

Settlers
Dutch and English seeking new lives

Climate
Cold, snowy winters and
hot, humid summers

Geography
Wetlands along the coast and Hudson River,
forested mountains to the north

Economy/Occupations
Fur trapping, lumber, shipping,
slave trade, merchants and tradesmen,
farming, iron mining

Religion
Various faiths

Government
British-appointed governor and
council alternating with elected assembly

3.6 New York: Middle Colony

In Chapter 2, you read about how the English took control of the settlement of New Netherland in 1664. The English renamed the colony New York in honor of its new proprietor (owner), James, the Duke of York. The duke gave huge chunks of his colony to two friends, Sir George Carteret and Lord John Berkeley. These men then established the colony of New Jersey to the south of New York.

The duke also awarded large estates along the Hudson River to wealthy Englishmen. The new landowners charged high rents to farmers working their land. This practice created a great difference in wealth between the landowners and their poor tenants. It also discouraged people from settling in New York.

The duke of York expected his colony to be a money-making business. As its owner, he appointed the people who ran the colony. He also issued his own laws and decided what New Yorkers should pay in taxes.

New York's rich landlords approved of the duke's approach to governing his colony. But farmers, fishermen, and tradespeople did not. They demanded the right to elect an assembly to make laws for New York. The duke refused, saying that elected assemblies had a habit of "disturbing the peace of the government."

After years of protest, the duke finally allowed New Yorkers to elect an assembly in 1683. This first assembly passed 15 laws. The most important was a charter listing a number of rights that most colonists thought they should have as English citizens. Among them were the right to elect their own lawmakers, the right to trial by jury, and the right to worship as they pleased.

When the duke saw what the assembly had done, he abolished it. New Yorkers did not get a new assembly until, under the leadership of Jacob Leisler, they rebelled in 1689. Leisler was elected commander in chief of a democratic council that governed until 1691. That year, New York was finally granted the right to elect an assembly with the power to pass laws and set taxes for the colony.

Ships navigate the harbor of New Amsterdam in the 1660s. The city was later renamed New York and became one of the busiest and most important ports in the world.

3.7 Pennsylvania: Middle Colony

This picture shows William Penn making a treaty with Indians about 1770. Penn insisted that the Delaware Indians be treated fairly and paid for their land.

When William Penn asked King Charles II to let him establish a colony in America, the king had two very good reasons for granting his request. First, he could repay a large debt that he owed to Penn's father, Admiral Penn. Second, he could get rid of William. The younger Penn had been a thorn in the king's side for a long time.

William Penn was a member of the Society of Friends, or Quakers. The Quakers believed in a simple lifestyle and in treating all people as equal. They refused to bow before the king, fight in wars, or pay taxes to the Church of England.

In 1668, the king threw Penn in jail, hoping to stop him from preaching the Quakers' ideas. To the king's dismay, Penn continued preaching after his release.

With the Quakers unwelcome in England, Penn wanted to establish a colony in America where they would be safe. In 1681, the king granted Penn a huge area of land between the Puritan colonies of New England and the Anglican colonies of the South. In honor of Penn's father, the colony was called Pennsylvania.

Penn advertised his colony all over Europe. In his Great Law of 1682, he promised that people of all faiths would be treated equally.

Penn's appeal attracted settlers from several countries. An early colonist in Pennsylvania marveled at the prosperity and peace in the colony. He wrote, "Poor people (both Men and Women) of all kinds, can here get three times the Wages for their Labour they can in England or Wales…. Here are no Beggars to be seen…. Jealousie among Men is here very rare…. nor are old Maids to be met with; for all commonly Marry before they are Twenty Years of Age."

Penn named his capital city Philadelphia (Greek for "City of Brotherly Love"). From there, he wrote great documents of government that made Pennsylvania the first democracy in America.

Pennsylvania
Middle Colony

Founders
William Penn

Settlers
English Quakers and other Europeans seeking freedom and equality

Climate
Cold winters and hot, humid summers

Geography
Rolling hills, trees, and fertile soil

Economy/Occupations
Farming (crops and dairy), merchants and tradesmen, lumber, shipbuilding

Religion
Various faiths

Government
Self-governing

The English Colonies in America **43**

Sir Cecilius Calvert, or Second Lord Baltimore, the founder of Maryland. Calvert established laws to protect Catholics from persecution in the colony.

3.8 Maryland: Southern Colony

The founding of Maryland was a family enterprise. Sir George Calvert, named Lord Baltimore by King James I, was an English gentleman who became a Roman Catholic. In England, with its official Anglican Church, Catholics were treated harshly. Calvert wanted to start a colony "founded on religious freedom where there would not only be a good life, but also a prosperous one for those bold enough to take the risk." As a businessman, he also hoped the colony would make his own family more prosperous (wealthy).

Unfortunately, Calvert died while he was still bargaining with the king. The new king, King Charles I, granted a charter for the colony to Calvert's son Cecil, the new Lord Baltimore. The charter gave the Calverts complete control of the colony, which was called Maryland.

Armed with these powers, Cecil named his brother Leonard to be governor. In order to make money from the colony, Cecil needed to attract both Protestant and Catholic settlers. He told Leonard to be "very careful to preserve unity and peace…and treat the Protestants with as much mildness and favor as justice will permit."

Leonard's expedition arrived in Maryland in 1634. There, he and his followers built St. Mary's City on a high, dry bluff they purchased from Native Americans. The following year, Leonard agreed to let Maryland elect an assembly.

As more and more settlers arrived, Leonard could see that Catholics would always be outnumbered in the colony. To protect their rights, in 1649 he helped pass America's first law guaranteeing religious liberty, the Act Concerning Religion. This law, however, applied only to Christians. Atheists (people who deny the existence of God) and Jews were not included.

Despite the Calverts' efforts, Protestants and Catholics remained suspicious of one another and waged a tug-of-war in Maryland for more than a century. During this time, the colony's founding family lost and regained power several times. Still, George Calvert's dream was fulfilled. Catholics in Maryland worshipped freely and took part in the colony's government alongside Protestants.

Maryland
Southern Colony

Founders
Cecil Calvert (Lord Baltimore)

Settlers
Catholics and Protestants seeking religious and political freedom

Climate
Cold, rainy winters and hot, humid summers

Geography
Low, fertile land surrounding the Chesapeake Bay

Economy/Occupations
Farming, (crops, beef, dairy), lumber, shipping, fishing, iron mining

Religion
Various faiths, particularly Catholic

Government
Self-governing

3.9 Virginia: Southern Colony

In Chapter 2, you read about Jamestown, Virginia, the first successful English settlement in America. After a shaky start, Virginia began to grow and prosper. By 1700, the descendants of those early settlers were wealthy landowners and the most important people in Virginia.

The economy of Virginia was based on tobacco. Tobacco planters needed vast areas of land to be successful. They also needed a large number of workers to grow their crop.

At first, planters tried putting Indians to work. But Indians in this area were not used to farming. Worse, many of them died of diseases they caught from the colonists. The others faded into the forests and disappeared.

Next, tobacco planters tried bringing poor people from England to work their land. In exchange for free passage to Virginia, the workers agreed to become indentured servants for a period of five to seven years. Many men, women, and children came to Virginia as indentured servants. After completing their service, they were given their freedom along with a small plot of land, some clothing, tools, and seeds.

The first Africans brought to Virginia were also treated as indentured servants. At first they had the same rights and freedoms as white servants. Once their service ended, they could buy land and servants of their own.

Gradually, however, planters turned to slaves to solve their labor problem. Slaves brought from Africa cost twice as much as servants, but they did not leave after a few years.

For the planters, enslaving Africans had other advantages as well. Most Africans were hard workers who were used to farming. And because of their dark skin, it was hard for them to escape from their owners and blend into the rest of the population.

In 1661, the Virginia House of Burgesses passed a law making African workers slaves for life. By 1700, Virginia had more than 16,000 enslaved Africans—more than one fourth of the colony's population. For Virginia, slavery had become a way of life.

The first African slaves were brought to Jamestown, Virginia, in 1619, the year before the Pilgrims landed at Plymouth Rock.

Virginia
Southern Colony

Founders
Sir Walter Raleigh and the Virginia Company

Settlers
English landowners, skilled laborers (shoemakers, bricklayers, tailors, etc.), people seeking profits

Climate
Mild winters and hot, humid summers

Geography
Coastal lowlands; wooded mountains

Economy/Occupations
Farming (plantations and small independent farms)

Religion
Church of England

Government
Self-governing

The Granger Collection, New York

Georgia
Southern Colony

Founders
George II and
James Edward Oglethorpe

Settlers
Debtors from English prisons, Europeans
seeking religious freedom and cheap land

Climate
Short, mild winters and
long, hot, humid summers

Geography
Wetlands and red-clay plains;
forested mountains

Economy/Occupations
Farming (plantations and independent
farms), trade, skilled labor

Religion
Various faiths

Government
Self-governing

3.10 Georgia: Southern Colony

Georgia, the 13th and last colony, was founded by a group of Englishmen whose business plan was based on a grand and noble idea. They wanted to help poor people in England stay out of debtor's prison. In England at this time, people who couldn't pay their bills went to jail. James Oglethorpe inspired wealthy Englishmen to give money to help establish a colony where the poor could build better lives instead of going to jail.

King George II and his government liked this plan because the Georgia colony would help keep the Spanish from moving north out of Florida. Georgia would stand between Spanish Florida and the rest of the British colonies to the north.

The Englishmen's plan depended upon getting the cooperation of settlers. But there weren't many poor debtors who wanted to start new lives in the wilderness of North America. Some thought prison would be a safer place.

Instead of an army of poor people, the colonists who went with Oglethorpe to Georgia in 1732 were adventurers much like the settlers in the other colonies. In addition, many Protestants, Catholics, and Jews came to Georgia in search of religious freedom.

As many had feared, life was not easy in Georgia. The Spaniards in Florida wanted to control Georgia, and they continually attacked the new settlements. The Georgians fought them off without any help from the other British colonies. To make matters worse, Oglethorpe had specific ideas about how the colonists should live. He established laws against drinking alcohol and owning slaves. He thought the settlers should live on small farms and learn to farm their land themselves.

The settlers weren't about to go along. They wanted to farm large plantations and own slaves like the wealthy planters in neighboring colonies. They disliked some of Oglethorpe's other rules as well.

Trying to mold Georgia into his idea of a perfect society, Oglethorpe lost all his money. For its settlers, however, Georgia became as successful as the other Southern Colonies.

The Granger Collection, New York

James Oglethorpe, the founder of Georgia, is pictured here in Scottish dress.

3.11 Chapter Summary

In this chapter, you read about the settlement of the 13 English colonies in the future United States. You used a spoke diagram to record important features of eight of these colonies.

Settlers had many reasons to come to America in the 1600s and 1700s. Two important reasons were freedom of religion and the chance to start a new life. However, even though colonists treasured freedom for themselves, enslaved Africans were taken to America by force.

The New England, Middle, and Southern Colonies all had distinctive geographies and natural resources. As a result, different ways of life developed in each of these regions. Colonies also varied in their form of government. All, however, were democratic to some degree.

In the New England Colonies, religion and geography were key influences. Although Puritans sometimes disagreed with one another, they hoped to establish model communities based on their religious faith. New England's forests and coastline made lumbering, shipbuilding, and trade very important to the region's economy.

The Middle Colonies were geographically, culturally, and religiously diverse. Catholics, Quakers, Anglicans, and members of other Protestant faiths all found homes in this region.

In the Southern Colonies, climate and geography encouraged the planting of cash crops and the development of large plantations. In time, slave labor would become a major part of the economy of this region.

What was daily life like for the settlers, servants, and slaves who came to America? You'll find out in the next chapter.

Handbills like this one lured colonists from Europe to the American colonies.

NOVA BRITANNIA.
OFFERING MOST
Excellent fruites by Planting in
VIRGINIA.
Exciting all such as be well affected
to further the same.

LONDON
Printed for SAMVEL MACHAM, and are to befold at
his Shop in Pauls Church-yard, at the
Signe of the Bul-head.
1 6 0 9.

What do these men have in their cart and where might they be going?

What different classes of people do you see?

Life in the Colonies

4.1 Introduction

In 1723, a tired teenager stepped off a boat onto Philadelphia's Market Street wharf. He was an odd-looking sight. Not having luggage, he had stuffed his pockets with extra clothes. The young man followed a group of "clean dressed people" into a Quaker meeting house, where he soon fell asleep.

The sleeping teenager with the lumpy clothes was Benjamin Franklin. Recently, he had run away from his brother James's print shop in Boston. When he was 12, Franklin had signed a contract to work for his brother for nine years. But after enduring James's nasty temper for five years, Franklin packed his pockets and left.

In Philadelphia, Franklin quickly found work as a printer's assistant. Within a few years, he had saved enough money to open his own print shop. His first success was a newspaper called the *Pennsylvania Gazette.*

In 1732, readers of the *Gazette* saw an advertisement for *Poor Richard's Almanac.* An *almanac* is a book, published annually, that contains information about weather predictions, the times of sunrises and sunsets, planting advice for farmers, and other useful subjects. According to the advertisement, *Poor Richard's Almanac* was written by "Richard Saunders" and printed by "B. Franklin." Nobody knew then that the author and printer were actually the same person.

In addition to the usual information contained in almanacs, Franklin mixed in some proverbs, or wise sayings. Several of them are still remembered today. Here are three of the best-known:

"A penny saved is a penny earned."

"Early to bed, early to rise, makes a man healthy, wealthy, and wise."

"Fish and visitors smell in three days."

Poor Richard's Almanac sold so well that Franklin was able to retire at age 42. A man of many talents, he spent the rest of his long life as a scientist, inventor, political leader, diplomat, and national postmaster.

Franklin's rise from penniless runaway to wealthy printer was one of many colonial success stories. In this chapter, you will learn what life was like for people throughout the colonies in the early 1700s.

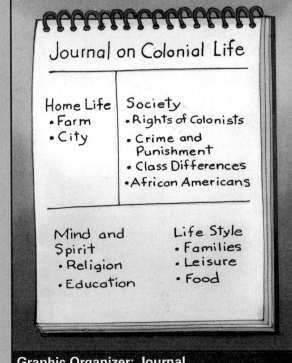

Graphic Organizer: Journal
You will use a journal to organize information about various aspects of colonial life.

Although most farmers lived in one-room farmhouses, they held out hope that they would achieve wealth like that pictured above.

economy the way a society organizes the manufacture and exchange of things of value, such as money, food, products, and services

4.2 Life on a Farm

The colonists developed an **economy** based on farming, commerce (buying and selling goods), and handcrafts. Nine out of ten people lived on small family farms. Most farm families either raised or made nearly everything they needed. One farmer wrote with pride about a typical year: "Nothing to wear, eat, or drink was purchased, as my farm provided all."

The first and hardest task facing farm families was to clear the land of trees. The colonists had only simple, basic tools. They cut down trees with axes and saws. Then they used the same tools to cut square timbers and flat planks for building houses, barns, and fences.

Imagine living on a colonial farm. Your home is a single large room with a chimney at one end. In this room, your family cooks, eats, and sleeps. Your parents sleep in a large bed built into one corner. Your younger brothers and sisters sleep in a smaller "trundle" bed, a bed that can slide under the big bed during the day. At bedtime, you climb a ladder next to the chimney to sleep in an attic or a loft. As your family grows, you help to build another room on the other side of the chimney.

The fireplace is the only source of heat for warmth and cooking. So, keeping a supply of firewood is important. The fire is kept burning all the time because, without matches, it is very difficult to light a new one.

Cooking is one of the most dangerous jobs on your farm. Food is cooked in heavy iron pots hung over an open fire. While lifting or stirring these pots, your mother might burn her hands, scorch her clothes, or strain her back.

Life on your farm starts before sunrise. Everyone wakes up early to share the work. Chores include cutting wood, feeding animals, clearing land, tending crops, building fences, making furniture and tools, gathering eggs, spinning thread, weaving cloth, sewing clothes, making candles and soap, cooking, cleaning, and caring for babies.

How does this compare with life in your home today?

4.3 Life in Cities

In 1750, one colonist out of 20 lived in a city. Compared to the quiet farm life, cities were exciting places.

The heart of the city was the waterfront. There, ships brought news from England as well as eagerly awaited items such as paint, carpets, furniture, and books.

Just beyond the docks, a marketplace bustled with fishermen selling their catch and farmers selling fresh eggs, milk, and cheese. Close by were taverns, where food and drink were served. People gathered there to exchange gossip and news from other colonies.

The nearby streets were lined with shops. Sparks flew from the blacksmith's block as he hammered iron into tools. Shoemakers, clockmakers, silversmiths, tailors, and other craftspeople turned out goods based on the latest designs from England. There were barbers to cut colonists' hair and wigmakers to make it look long again.

Cities were noisy, smelly places. Church bells rang out daily. Carts clattered loudly over streets paved with round cobblestones. The air was filled with the stench of rotting garbage and open sewers, but the colonists were used to it. Animals ran loose in the street. During hot weather, clouds of flies and mosquitoes swarmed about.

City homes were close together on winding streets. Most were built of wood with thatched roofs, like the houses the colonists had left behind in Europe. Their windows were small, because glass was costly.

For lighting, colonists used torches made of pine that burned brightly when they were wedged between hearthstones in the fireplace. Colonists also burned grease in metal containers called "betty lamps" and made candles scented with bayberries.

With torches and candles lighting homes, fire was a constant danger. Colonists kept fire buckets hanging by their front doors. When a fire broke out, the whole town helped to put it out. Grabbing their buckets, colonists formed a double line from the fire to a river, pond, or well. They passed the buckets full of water from hand to hand up one line to the fire. Then the empty buckets went hand over hand back down the opposite line to be filled again.

Colonial cities were very small by today's standards. Boston and Philadelphia, the two largest, had fewer than 20,000 people in 1700.

The Granger Collection, New York

4.4 Rights of Colonists

Colonists in America saw themselves as English citizens. They expected the same **rights** that citizens enjoyed in England. The most important of these was the right to have a voice in their government.

The Magna Carta   The English people had won the right to participate in their government only after a long struggle. A key victory in this struggle came in 1215, when King John agreed to sign the Magna Carta, or "Great Charter." This agreement established the idea that the power of the monarch (ruler) was limited. Not even the king was above the law.

The next major victory was the founding of **Parliament** in 1265. Parliament was made up of representatives from across England. Over time, it became a lawmaking body with the power to approve laws and taxes proposed by the king or queen.

In 1685, James, the Duke of York, became King James II. As you read in Chapter 3, King James did not want to share power with an elected assembly in New York. Nor did he want to share power with an elected Parliament in England. When he tried to rule without Parliament, James was forced off his throne. This event, which took place without bloodshed, is known as the Glorious Revolution.

The English Bill of Rights

In 1689, Parliament offered the crown to Prince William of Orange and his wife, Mary. In exchange, they had to agree to an act, or law, known as the English Bill of Rights. This act said that the power to make laws and impose taxes belonged to the people's elected representatives in Parliament and to no one else. It also included a bill, or list, of rights that belonged to the people.

Colonists established assemblies to promote citizen rights. The English tradition of self-government thrived in all 13 colonies. Here we see a depiction of the first colonial assembly of Virginia in 1619.

Among these were the right to **petition** the king and the right to trial by jury.

English colonists saw the Glorious Revolution as a victory not only for Parliament, but for their colonial assemblies as well. They wanted to choose the people who made their laws and set their taxes. After all, this was a cherished right of all English citizens.

4.5 Crime and Punishment

Each colonial assembly passed its own laws defining crimes and punishments. However, most crimes were treated similarly in all the colonies.

Certain very serious crimes could be punished by death. These included murder, treason (acts of disloyalty toward the government), and piracy (robbery at sea). Puritans in New England added other crimes to this list based on their understanding of God's law in the Bible. In New England, colonists could be put to death for "denying the true God" or for striking or cursing their parents.

Crimes such as theft, forgery, and highway robbery carried harsh punishments in every colony. For these crimes, people might be jailed, whipped, or branded with hot irons.

Lesser crimes, such as drunkenness and breaking the Sabbath (working or traveling on Sunday), were punished with fines, short jail terms, or public humiliation. A colonist caught breaking the Sabbath, for example, might be locked in the town stocks. Stocks were a heavy wooden frame with holes for a person's neck, wrists, and ankles. Lawbreakers were locked for hours in this device in a public place where others might make fun of them.

No group had firmer ideas about right and wrong than New England's Puritans. The Puritans required everyone to attend church on Sundays. They also forbade anyone to work or play on that day. The Puritans wrote their Sunday laws in books with blue paper bindings. For this reason, these rules came to be known as *blue laws*. Some blue laws persist to this day. In Massachusetts, for example, it is still illegal to sell liquor on Sundays.

The Puritans were constantly on the watch for signs of Satan (an evil angel who rebelled against God). Satan was thought to work through witches. In 1691, fear of witchcraft exploded in Salem, Massachusetts, when several young girls were seen acting strangely in church. When they were questioned, the girls accused their neighbors of being witches and putting spells on them. Twenty accused witches were put to death in the Salem Witch Trials before calm was restored and the townspeople realized that the girls' accusations were not true.

Courts, like the one pictured above, were important to social life in the colonies. This painting depicts a woman being tried for witchcraft in Salem, Massachusetts, in 1692.

class A part of society defined by such qualities as wealth, occupation, and inherited titles or honors. A society may have an upper class, a middle class, and a lower class.

4.6 Class Differences

Like many people today, those living in colonial times were eager to "move up in the world." In England, "moving up" was difficult. A person's **class,** or place in society, was determined largely by family, inherited titles (such as "duke" or "baron"), and wealth.

In colonial America, however, titles and family background meant little. Most colonists started out poor. Those with ambition could use their brains and talents to climb the social ladder. A poor boy, for example, might turn into an upper-class gentleman by becoming a successful planter, merchant, or lawyer. A poor girl could move up by marrying a man of a higher social class. In America, what set the classes apart was not family background, but money.

"Clothing makes the man!" This old saying aptly describes colonial society. In the colonies, people's clothes showed their social position. Only the gentry, or wealthy class, wore gold or silver, colored lace, buttons, boots, and wigs. Some colonies forbade ordinary citizens from wearing such "excess apparel" (clothing) and even fined those who disobeyed.

The middle class was made up of farmers and artisans (skilled craftspeople). These were people who owned their own land or businesses. Many had enough property to qualify to vote. During the week, people of the middle class wore plain but brightly colored clothes. On Sundays, they wore dark, somber clothing.

The lower class was mostly made up of farmhands and other workers. Members of this class depended on others for their wages. With little or no property of their own, they were not allowed to vote. Some were able to save enough money to buy land or start a business and rise to the middle class. Others remained wage earners their entire lives.

At the bottom of colonial society were indentured servants and slaves. Indentured servants made up a third of New England's settlers, and almost half of those who settled the Middle Colonies. Some eventually saved enough money to buy land and rise to the middle class. Others became wage earners. But even the poorest white laborers were better off than most African Americans.

Class divisions are apparent in this painting. The wealthy sit high on a wagon, surrounded by stacks of trunks carrying their many possessions. The children of the farmhands and servants bid the travelers farewell.

4.7 Life for African Americans

You read in Chapter 3 how slavery first came to Virginia. From there, it spread both north and south. By the early 1700s, enslaved Africans were living in every colony. Even Benjamin Franklin owned slaves for a time. But like most people in the New England and Middle Colonies, Franklin found that hiring workers when he needed them cost less than owning slaves.

In the Southern Colonies, however, slavery expanded rapidly. From Virginia to Georgia, slaves helped raise tobacco, rice, indigo, and other cash crops.

The Atlantic Slave Trade Most of the slaves who were brought to the colonies came from West Africa. Year after year, slave ships filled with cloth, guns, and rum sailed from the colonies to the coast of West Africa. There, these goods were traded for Africans. The ships then returned to the Americas carrying their human cargoes.

For the Africans packed onto slave ships, the ocean crossing—known as the Middle Passage—was a nightmare. Olaudah Equiano was just ten years old when he was put onto a slave ship. He never forgot "the closeness of the place…which was so crowded that each had scarcely room to turn himself." Nor did he forget "the shrieks of the women, and groans of the dying." The terrified boy refused to eat, hoping "for the last friend, Death, to relieve me."

Although Equiano survived the voyage, many Africans died of sickness or despair. Even so, the Atlantic slave trade was very profitable. Many colonial merchants built fortunes trading in human beings.

Work Without Hope The slaves' masters in America demanded hard work. Most enslaved Africans were put to work in the fields raising crops. Others worked as nurses, carpenters, blacksmiths, drivers, servants, gardeners, and midwives (people who assist women giving birth). Unlike other colonists, slaves had little hope of making a better life. Their position was fixed at the bottom of colonial society.

Some slaves rebelled by refusing to work or running away. But most adapted to their unhappy condition as best they could. Slowly and painfully, they began to create a new African American way of life.

The first slaves were brought to the United States in 1619 to help produce tobacco in the Virginia colony. Above, we see slaves tending tobacco while their owner relaxes, feet up, smoking his pipe.

4.8 Religion

Religion was an important part of colonial life. Most colonists tried to lead good lives based on their faith. Children grew up reading the Bible from cover to cover several times over.

Puritan Church Services   In New England, the sound of a drum or horn called Puritans to worship on Sunday morning. "Captains of the Watch" made sure everyone was a "Sabbath-keeper." Sometimes, houses were searched to ensure that everyone was at church.

Church services were held in the town meetinghouse. This was the most important building in the community and was used for all public meetings. Inside were rows of wooden benches called *pews,* and a pulpit (a platform where the preacher stood). A "Seating Committee" carefully assigned seats, with the best ones going to older, wealthy people.

Services could last as long as five hours. At midday, villagers would go to "noon-houses" near the church to warm themselves by a fire, eat, and socialize. Then they returned to church for the long afternoon sermon.

Colonial society had a strong religious flavor. Above, we see colonial citizens gathered around a church on Sunday.

The First Great Awakening

Beginning in the 1730s, a religious movement known as the **First Great Awakening** swept through the colonies. This movement was spurred by a feeling that people had lost their religious faith. "The forms of religion were kept up," a Puritan observed, but the "power of Godliness" was missing.

To revive people's religious spirit, preachers traveled from town to town holding outdoor "revival" meetings. There they delivered fiery sermons to huge crowds. Their words touched the hearts and souls of many colonists. Benjamin Franklin wrote about the change he observed in Philadelphia: "It seemed as if all the world were growing religious, so that one could not walk through the town in an evening without hearing psalms [Bible songs] sung in different families of every street."

The Great Awakening had a powerful effect on the colonies. It helped spread the idea that all people are equal in the eyes of God. Ordinary people could understand God's will if they had an open heart and a desire to know God's truth. By encouraging ideas of liberty, equality, and resistance to authority, the Great Awakening helped pave the way for the American Revolution.

4.9 Education

Except in New England, most children in the colonies received little formal education. Neither the Middle nor the Southern Colonies had public schools.

In the Southern Colonies, most families were spread out along rivers. A few neighbors might get together to hire a teacher for their children. Often, wealthy planters hired tutors to educate younger children at home. Older children were sent to schools in distant cities, or even England, to complete their education.

In the Middle Colonies, religious differences among Quakers, Catholics, Jews, Baptists, and other religious groups slowed the growth of public education. Each religious group or family had to decide for itself how to educate its children. Some groups built church schools. Others were content to have parents teach their children at home.

The Granger Collection, New York

Children gather with their teacher in a colonial school. These children were among a minority of children who received formal education. Most children did not go to school beyond the elementary level.

Only in New England were towns required to provide public schools. The Puritans' support for education was inspired by their faith. They wanted their children to be able to read God's word in the Bible.

To encourage education, Massachusetts passed a law in 1647 that required every town with 50 families or more to hire an instructor to teach their children to read and write. Towns with more than 100 families were required to build a school. Similar laws were passed in other New England colonies.

Parents were asked to contribute whatever they could to the village school. This might mean money, vegetables, firewood, or anything else the school needed. Often, land was set aside as "school-meadows" or "school-fields." This land was then rented out to raise money for teachers' salaries.

Schools were one-room buildings with a chimney and fireplace in the center. There were no maps, or boards to write on. Pencils and paper were scarce. Students shouted out spelling words and wrote sums in ink on pieces of bark. There was usually one book, the *New England Primer*, which was used to teach the alphabet, syllables, and prayers.

Most colonists believed that boys needed more education than girls. "Female education, in the best families," wrote Abigail Adams, "went no further than writing and arithmetic; in some few and rare instances, music, and dancing."

Family life was at the center of colonial society. Here, a family is gathered around a fire on a cold, wintry evening. A mother and grandmother work while the father relaxes and the children play.

4.10 Colonial Families

The concept of family has changed many times throughout history. Today, most people think of a family as being made up of parents and their children. In colonial times, however, families might include grandparents, aunts and uncles, cousins, and stepchildren.

Marriage   Colonial men and women generally married in their early to mid-20s. Those who arrived in America as indentured servants were not allowed to marry until they had gained their freedom.

Men outnumbered women throughout the colonies. As a result, almost every woman was assured of receiving a marriage proposal. "Maid servants of good honest stock [family]," wrote a colonist, could "choose their husbands out of the better sort of people." For a young woman, though, life as a wife and mother often proved to be even harder than life as an indentured servant.

Large Families   Colonial families were generally large. Most families had between seven and ten children. (Benjamin Franklin had 17 brothers and sisters!) Farm families, in particular, needed all the hands they could get to help with the chores.

Religious and cultural backgrounds influenced colonists' ideas about raising children. But almost everywhere in the colonies, children were expected to be productive members of the family.

Married women gave birth many times, but nearly half of all children died before they reached adulthood. Childhood deaths were especially high in the Middle and Southern Colonies, where the deadly disease of malaria raged. Adults often died young as well. After the death of a wife or husband, men and women usually remarried quickly. Thus, households often swelled with stepchildren as well as adopted orphans (children whose parents had died).

Whether colonists lived in cities, in villages, or on isolated farms, their lives focused on their families. Family members took care of one another because there was no one else to do so. Young families often welcomed elderly grandparents, aunts, uncles, and cousins into their homes when they could no longer care for themselves. It didn't matter if there was barely enough room for everyone. No one would turn away a needy relative.

4.11 Leisure

While most colonists worked hard, they enjoyed their periods of leisure (time away from work). They also took advantage of gatherings, such as town meetings and Sunday services, to talk with neighbors and make friends.

Bees and Frolics   When possible, colonists combined work and play by organizing "bees" and "frolics." New settlers might hold a "chopping bee" in which all the neighbors helped clear the trees off their land. Other frolics included corn-husking bees for men and quilting bees for women. Sharing the work made it faster and a lot more fun.

The Germans introduced house and barn raisings to the colonies. At these events, neighbors joined together to build the frame of a house or barn in one day. The men assembled the four walls flat on the ground and then raised them into place. Meanwhile, the women prepared a huge feast. At the end of the day, everyone danced on the barn's new floor.

Here, we see Dutch settlers in a spirited game of bowls in New Amsterdam. Below, colonists enjoy a form of billiards called "trock."

Toys and Sports   Colonial children had a few simple toys, such as dolls, marbles, and tops. They played games of tag, blindman's bluff, and stoolball, which was related to the English game of cricket (a game like baseball). Children in New England also enjoyed "coasting" downhill on sleds. Adults must have thought coasting was dangerous, because several communities forbade it.

Adults enjoyed several sports. Almost every village had a bowling green. Here men rolled egg-shaped balls down a lane of grass toward a white ball called a "jack." Colonists also played a game similar to backgammon called "tick-tack" and a form of billiards (pool) called "trock."

In the Southern Colonies, fox hunting with horses and hounds was a popular sport. Card playing was another favorite pastime, one that New England Puritans disapproved of strongly. Horse racing, cockfighting, and bull baiting were also popular.

Fairs were held throughout the colonies. At these events, colonists competed in contests of skill and artistry. There were footraces, wrestling matches, dance contests, and wild scrambles to see who could win a prize by catching a greased pig or climbing a greased pole.

Life in the Colonies   **59**

The Granger Collection, New York

Food preparation occupied a great deal of time in the colonies. Here, we see one woman rolling corn meal while another cooks on the stove. The woman in the doorway is using a butter churn.

4.12 Food

The first colonists in North America traded with Indians for their food. The Indians taught them how to grow and cook corn, which became a major part of the colonists' diet. Colonial children knew that morning and evening meals would probably consist of something made from corn.

Most colonists ate ground cornmeal cooked into a mush or a cake every day. Women pounded corn for hours in wooden bowls called *mortars*. It is said that fishermen lost in a fog would know they were close to land when they heard the pounding sound.

Meat was a favorite food for many colonists. Colonists hunted wild deer, rabbits, and birds. They also raised pigs, cattle, and chickens. Their biggest problem with meat was how to keep it from going bad. Without refrigerators, meat had to be salted, smoked, or pickled to keep it from rotting. Colonists often used pepper and other spices to disguise the bad taste of old meat.

Fruit was another major food. Apple trees grew well in the New England and Middle Colonies. "Apple pie is used through the whole year," wrote a visitor to Delaware in 1758. "And when fresh apples are no longer to be had, dried ones are used. It is the evening meal of children." In spring and summer, children picked wild huckleberries, blackberries, blueberries, grapes, and strawberries. In the Southern Colonies, colonists had more peaches than they could eat.

Many colonists thought vegetables were unhealthy, particularly if eaten raw. Still, they learned to be thankful for native pumpkins, squash, beans, peas, and sweet potatoes. They also planted root vegetables, such as parsnips, turnips, carrots, and onions. In the English tradition, they cooked these vegetables into mushy stews seasoned with meat and herbs from their gardens.

Great iron pots of stew simmered 24 hours a day in colonial fireplaces. Keeping food hot reduced the chances that it would spoil. Each day, bowls of stew were served at the main meal, which was eaten between noon and three o'clock. For breakfast and dinner, colonists ate mostly some form of corn mush sweetened with milk, fruit, honey, molasses, or maple syrup.

4.13 Chapter Summary

In this chapter, you read about life in the American colonies during the early 1700s. You used a journal to organize information about various aspects of colonial life.

The colonists developed an economy based on farming, commerce, and crafts. Farm families produced most of what they needed for themselves. In the villages and cities, many trades and crafts developed.

American colonists expected to enjoy all the rights of English citizens, especially the right to have a voice in their own government. Crimes and punishments were defined by colonial assemblies. Often, punishments were harsh.

Class differences in the colonies were based mostly on wealth. Most people in lower classes could hope to move up through hard work. Enslaved African Americans had almost no such hope. After being brought to America in chains, they faced a life of forced obedience and toil.

Religion was very important to the colonists. The First Great Awakening revived religious feeling and helped spread the idea that all people are equal.

Except in New England, most colonial children received little education. Instead, they were expected to contribute to the work of the farm or home. Most colonial families were large. Often they included many relatives besides the parents and their children.

Much of colonial life was hard work, even preparing food. But colonists found ways to mix work with play. They also enjoyed sports and games.

For most of the 1700s, the colonists were content to be ruled by English laws. In the next chapter, however, you'll learn how tensions grew between the colonists and the government in far-off England.

This panorama of Philadelphia in 1702 reveals a number of aspects of colonial life. Church steeples, government buildings, colonial homes, ships, and citizens on unpaved colonial roads are all evident in the painting.

PHILADELPHIA IN THE OLDEN TIME.

The Granger Collection, New York

What is happening here? Who is the man on horseback?

Why might this man be happy? Is he a Loyalist or a Patriot?

What might these Loyalists be thinking?

Toward Independence

5.1 Introduction

An almost full moon cast a pale light over Boston on April 18, 1775. But the night was anything but quiet. Mounted on Brown Beauty, one of the fastest horses in Massachusetts, Paul Revere woke up the countryside with alarming news. British troops stationed in Boston were on the move! They had orders to march to the nearby town of Concord and seize weapons that the colonists had stored there.

This was news that local Patriots had been waiting for. **Patriots** (also called Whigs) were Americans who believed that the colonies had the right to govern themselves. On hearing Revere's warning, Patriots around Concord grabbed their muskets and prepared to meet the British troops.

The same news filled Loyalists (also called Tories) with dread. **Loyalists** were Americans who felt a deep loyalty to Great Britain. They saw themselves as faithful subjects of the king. They were horrified by the idea of taking up arms against British troops. How did colonists become so divided in their feelings about the British? As you read in the last chapter, most Americans were content with British rule in the early 1700s. In this chapter, you will learn what happened to change the relationship between Britain and the colonies.

The story begins in the 1750s, when Britain and the colonies fought a war against the French and their Indian **allies**. The French and Indian War left Britain with huge debts and a vast new empire to protect. To solve its problems, the British government passed new laws that tightened its control of the colonies. Some of these laws also placed new taxes on the colonists.

Americans were stunned. They had always had the right to make their own laws and taxes. Suddenly, Britain was changing the rules. It wasn't right, the colonists protested. It wasn't fair!

You probably know just how they felt. In this chapter, you will see how these feelings led the colonists to the brink of war.

Graphic Organizer: Metaphor
You will use a metaphor to compare the tensions between Britain and the colonies to the strained relationship between a principal and students.

Before 1763, the colonies enjoyed life free from British control.

5.2 Before 1763

By 1750, the American colonies were bursting with growth. In just a century, the population of the colonies had grown from 50,000 to more than a million people. What brought about this rapid growth? Cheap land? Religious tolerance? Economic opportunity? All of these were important in attracting people to the colonies. But there was another reason.

For more than a century, the British government had mostly left the colonies alone to solve their own problems. During this time, Americans had learned to govern themselves. Each colony elected its own assembly. Like the British Parliament, the assemblies had the power to pass laws and create taxes. Each assembly also decided how the colony's tax money should be spent. Americans had more freedom to run their own affairs than ordinary people in any country in Europe.

Conflict in the Ohio Valley   As the colonies grew, settlers began to dream of moving across the Appalachian Mountains and into the Ohio Valley—the region between the Ohio and Mississippi Rivers. Both Britain and France claimed this area. In 1754, the French made good on their claim by building a fort where the city of Pittsburgh stands today. They called it Fort Duquesne.

News of the fort alarmed the governor of Virginia. He ordered a small force of Virginia **militia** to drive the French out of the Ohio Valley. Militias are small armies of citizens who are trained to fight in an emergency. To head the militia, the governor chose a 22-year-old volunteer named George Washington.

Today, Americans remember George Washington as a great Patriot, a military hero, and the first president of the United States. In 1754, however, he was just an ambitious young man with no land or money. Washington believed that his best chance of getting ahead was to become an officer in the British army. There was only one problem with his plan. Most British officers believed that colonists made lousy soldiers.

The expedition into the Ohio Valley gave Washington a chance to prove them wrong. Near Fort Duquesne, he came across a French scouting party that was camped in the woods. Washington ordered his men to open fire. It was an easy victory. "I heard the bullets whistle," he wrote afterward. "And, believe me, there is something charming in the sound."

militia   a small army made up of ordinary citizens who are available to fight in an emergency

The French and Indian War   Washington's whistling bullets were the first shots in a conflict known as the French and Indian War. This war was part of a long struggle between France and Britain for territory and power. Because many Native Americans fought with France in this latest conflict, the colonists called it the French and Indian War.

In 1755, Britain sent 1,400 British soldiers to Virginia to finish the job that Washington had begun. They were led by a bumbling general named Edward Braddock. The soldiers' job was to clear the French out of the Ohio Valley. Washington joined the army as a volunteer, hoping to make a good impression on General Braddock.

The British army's march into the Ohio Valley was a disaster. The troops' bright red uniforms made them perfect targets for French sharpshooters and their Indian allies. Two-thirds of the soldiers were killed.

Washington himself narrowly escaped death. "I had four Bullets through my Coat and two horses shot under me," he wrote in his journal. Showing great courage, Washington led the survivors back to Virginia. There, he was greeted as a hero.

The French and Indian War raged for seven long years. The turning point came in 1759, when British troops captured Canada. In 1763, Britain and France signed a peace treaty ending the war. In this treaty, France ceded, or gave, Canada to Great Britain.

Americans were thrilled with this victory. Great Britain now controlled a vastly expanded American empire. Never before had the colonists felt so proud of being British. And never before had the future of the colonies looked so bright.

Here, we see George Washington tipping his hat to the British flag at Fort Duquesne. The British captured the badly damaged fort in 1758. It was rebuilt and called Fort Pitt. The city of Pittsburg was later built here.

The Granger Collection, New York

5.3 Early British Actions

Changes that were taking place in Britain soon clouded the colonists' bright future. A new king, George III, had been crowned in 1760. He was not a bright man. One historian wrote that "he was very stupid, really stupid." He was also proud and stubborn. Worse yet, he was determined to be a "take-charge" kind of ruler, especially in the colonies.

Unfortunately, the people George III chose to help him were not much brighter than he was. And they knew very little about conditions in America. Before long, they were taking actions that enraged the colonists.

The Proclamation of 1763   The British government faced a number of problems after the French and Indian War. One was how to keep colonists and Native Americans from killing each other as settlers pushed westward. No problem, said George III. Simply draw a line down the crest of the Appalachian Mountains. Tell settlers to stay east of that line and Indians to stay west of it.

This was what the king ordered in his Proclamation of 1763. To Americans, the king's order suggested **tyranny,** or the unjust use of government power. They argued that the lands east of the Appalachians were already mostly settled. The only place that farmers could find new land was west of the mountains. Besides, the Proclamation was too late. Settlers were already crossing the mountains.

The British government ignored these arguments. To keep peace on the frontier, it decided to expand the British army in America to 7,500 men.

tyranny The unjust use of government power. A ruler who uses power in this way is called a *tyrant.*

North America in 1763

CANADA

Bay

Missouri R.

St. Lawrence R.

ORIGINAL 13 COLONIES

LOUISIANA

Colorado R.

Ohio R.

ATLANTIC OCEAN

Rio Grande

Mississippi R.

NEW SPAIN

GULF OF MEXICO

WEST INDIES

PACIFIC OCEAN

N
W E
S

0   500 miles
0   500 km
Parallel scale at 45°N 90°W
Conic Projection

Claimed by Spain

Claimed by Britain

Claimed by France

Claimed by Russia, Spain, and Britain

13 Colonies

Proclamation Line of 1763

The Proclamation of 1763 prohibited settlers from moving west of the Appalachian Mountains. King George hoped this would prevent conflict between the colonists and Native Americans.

The Stamp Act angered the colonists, who felt that taxation without representation was unfair. Protests, such as the one shown here, forced Parliament to repeal the act.

The Stamp Act   The British government had other problems besides keeping colonists and Native Americans from killing each other. One was how to pay off the large debt left over from the French and Indian War.

The solution seemed obvious to Prime Minister George Grenville, the leader of the British government. People in Britain were already paying taxes on everything from windows to salt. In contrast, Americans were probably the most lightly taxed people in the British Empire. It was time, said Grenville, for the colonists to pay their fair share of the cost of protecting them.

In 1765, Grenville proposed a new act, or law, called the Stamp Act. This law required colonists to buy a stamp for every piece of paper they used. Newspapers had to be printed on stamped paper. Wills, licenses, and even playing cards had to have stamps.

Once again, the colonists sensed tyranny. One newspaper, *The Pennsylvania Journal,* said that as soon as "this shocking Act was known, it filled all British America from one End to the other, with Astonishment and Grief."

It wasn't just the idea of higher taxes that upset the colonists. They were willing to pay taxes passed by their own assemblies, where their representatives could vote on them. But the colonists had no representatives in Parliament. For this reason, they argued, Parliament had no right to tax them. They saw the Stamp Act as a violation of their rights as British subjects. "No taxation without representation!" they cried.

Some colonists protested the Stamp Act by sending messages to Parliament. Loyalists simply refused to buy stamps. Patriots, however, took more violent action. Mobs calling themselves "Sons of Liberty" attacked tax collectors' homes. Protesters in Connecticut even started to bury one tax collector alive. Only when he heard dirt being shoveled onto his coffin did the terrified tax collector agree to resign from his post.

After months of protest, Parliament **repealed,** or canceled, the Stamp Act. Americans greeted the news with great celebration. Church bells rang, bands played, and everyone hoped the troubles with Britain were over.

According to the Stamp Act, colonists had to buy stamps like this and place them on all paper products, such as newspapers, wills, and playing cards.

repeal to take back, or to cancel, a law

The Quartering Act   As anger over the Stamp Act began to fade, Americans noticed another law passed by Parliament in 1765. Called the Quartering Act, this law ordered colonial assemblies to provide British troops with quarters, or housing. The colonists were also told to furnish the soldiers with "candles, firing, bedding, cooking utensils, salt, vinegar, and...beer or cider."

Of course, providing for the soldiers cost money. New Jersey protested that the new law was "as much an Act for laying taxes" on the colonists as the Stamp Act. New Yorkers asked why they should pay to keep troops in their colony. After all, they said, the soldiers just took up space and did nothing.

In 1767, the New York assembly decided not to vote any funds for "salt, vinegar and liquor." The British government reacted by refusing to let the assembly meet until it agreed to obey the Quartering Act. Once again, tempers began to rise on both sides of the Atlantic.

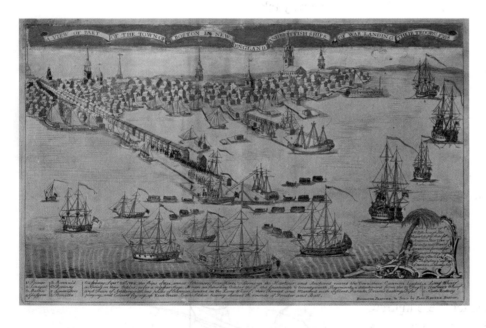

In 1768, the British government sent soldiers to Boston to enforce the Townshend Acts. This Paul Revere engraving shows the troops landing.

5.4 The Townshend Acts

The next British leader to face the challenge of taxing the colonies was Charles Townshend. He was also known as "Champagne Charlie" because of his habit of making speeches in Parliament after drinking champagne. Townshend believed that the colonists' bad behavior made it even more important to keep an army in America. Once he was asked in Parliament if he would dare to make the colonists pay for that army. Stamping his foot, Townshend shouted, "I will, I will."

And he did. In 1767, Townshend persuaded Parliament to pass the Townshend Acts. The new laws placed a duty, or tax, on certain goods the colonies imported from Britain. These goods included such popular items as glass, paint, paper, and tea.

Having kept his promise, Townshend caught the flu and died. But his new laws increased the unhappiness of the colonists.

A Boycott of British Goods   To many colonists, the Townshend duties were simply taxes in disguise. Once again, they were determined not to pay taxes that their assemblies had not voted on.

A Boston Patriot named Samuel Adams led the opposition to the Townshend Acts. Adams was not much to look at, and he was a failure at business. But he was gifted at stirring up protests through his speeches and writing. The governor of Massachusetts once complained, "Every dip of his pen stung like a horned snake."

Adams wrote a letter protesting the Townshend Acts that was sent to every colony. The letter argued that the new duties violated the colonists' rights as British citizens. To protect those rights, the colonies decided to **boycott** British goods. This was a peaceful form of protest that even Loyalists could support. One by one, all of the colonies agreed to support the boycott.

Women were very important in making the boycott work, since they did most of the shopping. The *Virginia Gazette* wrote that one woman could "do more for the good of her country than five hundred noisy sons of liberty, with all their mobs and riots." Women found many ways to avoid buying British imports. They sewed dresses out of homespun cloth, brewed tea from pine needles, and bought only American-made goods.

Repeal of the Townshend Acts   Meanwhile, a new leader named Lord North became head of the British government. Described as a "great, heavy, booby-looking man," Lord North embarrassed his supporters by taking naps in Parliament. But he was good with numbers, and he could see that the Townshend duties were a big money-loser. The duties didn't begin to make up for all the money British merchants were losing because of the boycott.

Early in 1770, North persuaded Parliament to repeal all of the Townshend duties, except for one—the tax on tea. Some members of Parliament argued that keeping the duty on tea was asking for more trouble. But stubborn King George wasn't ready to give up on the idea of taxing Americans.

"I am clear that there must always be one tax to keep up the right," the king said. "And, as such, I approve the tea duty."

5.5 The Boston Massacre

On the same day that Parliament repealed most of the Townshend duties, a brawl broke out between soldiers and colonists in Boston. When the dust cleared, five Bostonians were dead and ten were injured.

Patriots called this incident the "Boston Massacre." A massacre is the killing of defenseless people. What really happened was a small riot.

Trouble had been brewing in Boston for months before the riot. To the British, Boston Patriots were the worst troublemakers in the colonies. In 1768, the government had sent four regiments of troops to keep order in Boston.

Bostonians resented the British soldiers. They made fun of their red uniforms by calling them "lobsterbacks." Sam Adams even taught his dog to nip at soldiers' heels.

Despite such insults, the troops were forbidden to fire on citizens. Knowing this only made Bostonians bolder in their attacks. General Thomas Gage, the commander of the British army in America, wrote that "the people were as Lawless…after the Troops arrived, as they were before."

boycott To refuse to buy one or more goods from a certain source. An organized refusal by many people is also called a boycott.

Paul Revere's famous engraving of the Boston Massacre stirred up deep colonial resentment.

Mob Violence Breaks Out   On March 5, 1770, a noisy mob began throwing rocks and ice balls at troops guarding the Boston Customs House. "Come on you Rascals, you bloody-backs," they shouted. "Fire if you dare." Some Patriot leaders tried to persuade the crowd to go home. So did Captain Thomas Preston, the commander of the soldiers. But their pleas had no effect.

As the mob pressed forward, someone knocked a soldier to the ground. The troops panicked and opened fire. Two bullets struck Crispus Attucks, a large black man at the front of the crowd. He was the first to die, but not the last. The enraged crowd went home only after receiving a promise that the troops would be tried for murder.

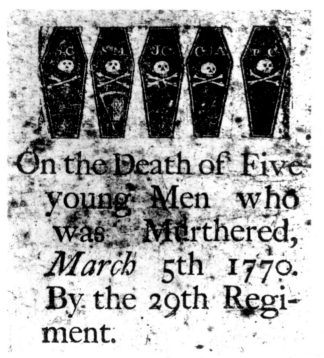

Paul Revere's engraving of five coffins showing the victims of the Boston Massacre appeared on flyers to remind colonists of British brutality.

On the Death of Five young Men who was Murthered, March 5th 1770. By the 29th Regiment.

Massacre or Self-Defense?   Sam Adams saw this event as a perfect opportunity to whip up anti-British feeling. He called the riot a "horrid massacre" and had Paul Revere, a local silversmith, engrave a picture of it. Revere's engraving shows soldiers firing at peaceful, unarmed citizens.

Prints of Revere's engraving were distributed throughout the colonies. Patriots saw the Boston Massacre as proof that the British should pull out all of their troops from the colonies. Loyalists saw the tragedy as proof that troops were needed more than ever, if only to control Patriot hotheads.

One hero came out of this sad event. He was a Boston lawyer named John Adams. Like his cousin Sam, John Adams was a Patriot. But he also believed that every person had the right to a fair trial, even the hated redcoats (British soldiers). Adams agreed to defend the soldiers, even though he knew that his action would cost him friends and clients.

At the murder trial, Adams argued that the troops had acted in self-defense. The jury found six of the soldiers not guilty. Two of them were found guilty only of manslaughter, or causing death without meaning to.

Throughout his long life, John Adams remained proud of his defense of the British soldiers. He said that upholding the law in this case was "one of the best pieces of service I ever rendered to my country."

5.6 The Boston Tea Party

Despite the hopes of Patriots like Sam Adams, the Boston Massacre did not spark new protests against British rule. Instead, the repeal of the Townshend duties led to a period of calm. True, there was still a small duty on tea. But the tax didn't seem to bother Loyalists very much. And Patriots could always drink Dutch tea that had been smuggled into the colonies without paying duties.

Things did not stay peaceful, however. In 1773, a new law called the Tea Act prompted more protests. One of them was the incident that became known as the Boston Tea Party.

The Tea Act The Tea Act was Lord North's attempt to rescue the British East India Company. This large trading company controlled all the trade between Britain and Asia. For years it had been a moneymaker for Britain. But the American boycott of British tea hurt the company badly. By 1773, it was in danger of going broke unless it could sell off the 17 million pounds of tea that was sitting in its London warehouses.

The Tea Act lowered the cost of tea that was sold by the British East Indian Company in the colonies. As a result, even taxed British tea became cheaper than smuggled Dutch tea. The Tea Act also gave the British East India Company a monopoly, or complete control, over tea sales in the colonies. From now on, the only merchants who could sell the bargain-priced tea were those chosen by the company.

Lord North may have thought he could trick Americans into buying taxed tea by making it so cheap, but colonists weren't fooled. They saw the Tea Act as still another attempt to tax them without their consent.

In addition, many merchants were alarmed by the East India Company's monopoly over the tea trade. They wondered what the British government might try to control next. Would there be a monopoly on cloth? On sugar? Nervous merchants wondered what would happen to their businesses if other goods were also restricted. The thought of more monopolies made them shudder.

Tea Ships Arrive When the British East India Company's tea ships sailed into American ports, angry protesters kept them from unloading their cargoes. More than one ship turned back for England, still filled with tea. In Boston, however, the governor ordered the British navy to block the exit from Boston Harbor. He insisted that the three tea ships would not leave until all their tea was unloaded.

On December 16, 1773, the Sons of Liberty decided to unload the tea, but not in the way the governor had in mind. That night, about 50 men dressed as Mohawk Indians boarded the three ships. One of them, George Hewes, described what happened:

To protest the tax on tea, Patriots disguised as Native Americans threw 342 chests of tea overboard from three British ships. Colonists later called this the Boston Tea Party.

> *We then were ordered by our commander to open the hatches and take out all the chests of tea and throw them overboard...and we immediately proceeded to execute his orders, first cutting and splitting the chests with our tomahawks.... In about three hours from the time we went on board, we had thus broken and thrown overboard every tea chest to be found on the ship.... We were surrounded by British armed ships, but no attempt was made to resist us.*

About 90,000 pounds of tea was dumped into the sea that night. Nothing else on the ships was touched.

News of the Boston Tea Party excited Patriots throughout the colonies. "This is the most magnificent moment of all," wrote John Adams in his journal the next day. "This Destruction of the Tea is so bold, so daring, so firm…it must have…important Consequences." He was right.

The British considered those who protested the Tea Act to be lawless troublemakers. In this cartoon, the tax collector, who has been tarred and feathered, is being forced to drink tea.

5.7 The Intolerable Acts

Lord North was stunned by news of the Boston Tea Party. As he saw it, he had tried to help the colonists by sending them cheap tea. And what did they do? They threw it in the sea! This time they had gone too far!

King George agreed. To him, the issue was no longer about taxes. It was about Britain's control over the colonies. "We must master them totally," he declared, "or leave them to themselves." And the king wasn't about to leave the colonies to themselves.

Britain's anger led Parliament to pass a new series of laws in 1774. These laws were so harsh that many colonists called them "intolerable," or unacceptable. Throughout the colonies, they became known as the Intolerable Acts.

Parliament Punishes Massachusetts   The Intolerable Acts were designed to punish Massachusetts for the Boston Tea Party. The first law closed Boston Harbor to all shipping until the ruined tea was paid for. The second law placed the government of Massachusetts firmly under British control. Colonists in Massachusetts could not even hold a town meeting without the governor's permission. The third law said that British soldiers who were accused of murder would be tried in England, not in the colonies. Finally, more troops were sent to Boston to enforce the new laws.

A few British leaders worried that the Intolerable Acts might push the colonies into rebellion. But George III was sure they would force the colonists to give in to British authority.

The Colonies Begin to Unite   In fact, the Intolerable Acts did not force the colonists to give in. Boston Patriots declared they would "abandon their city to flames" before paying a penny for the lost tea. Merchants in other cities showed their support by closing their shops. Many colonies sent food and money to Boston so that its citizens would not starve.

In Virginia, lawmakers drafted a resolution in support of Massachusetts. The Virginians said that everyone's rights were at stake. "An attack made on one of our sister colonies," they declared, "is an attack made on all British America."

The Virginians also called for a congress, or meeting, of delegates from all the colonies. The purpose of the congress would be to find a peaceful solution to the conflicts with Great Britain.

Not all Americans agreed with this plan. In every colony, there were Loyalists who thought that Bostonians had gone too far and should pay for the tea. If they were forced to choose, they would side with the king against Sam Adams and his Sons of Liberty. To them, it was the misguided Patriots who were causing all the trouble.

The First Continental Congress   In September 1774, some 50 leaders from 12 colonies met in Philadelphia. The meeting brought together delegates from most of the British colonies on the North American continent. For this reason, it was called the First Continental Congress.

The delegates were used to thinking of themselves as citizens of their own colonies. Patrick Henry, a leader from Virginia, urged them to come together as one people. "I am not a Virginian," he declared, "but an American." But only strong Patriots like Sam and John Adams were ready to think of themselves this way. Many delegates were strong Loyalists who still thought of themselves as British. Still others, like George Washington, were somewhere in between. Only one thing united the delegates—their love of liberty and hatred of tyranny.

In spite of their differences, the delegates agreed to send a respectful message to King George. The message urged the king to consider their complaints and to recognize their rights.

The delegates also called for a new boycott of British goods until Parliament repealed the Intolerable Acts. Finally, they agreed to meet again the following May if the boycott didn't work.

The Colonies Form Militias   In towns and cities throughout the colonies, Patriots appointed committees to enforce the boycott. In case the boycott didn't work, they also began organizing local militias. In New England, the volunteers called themselves Minutemen because they could be ready to fight in just 60 seconds.

Across the colonies, militias marched and drilled. In New Hampshire, unknown persons stole 100 barrels of gunpowder and 16 cannons from a British fort. Similar thefts occurred in other colonies. Rather than forcing the colonies to give in, the Intolerable Acts had brought the two sides to the brink of war.

Colonies began forming militias after the Intolerable Acts to enforce a boycott of British goods. Shown here is a statue of a member of the New England militia known as the Minutemen.

5.8 Lexington and Concord

King George had made many mistakes in his decisions about the colonies. The Continental Congress listed all these mistakes in its message to the king. Now he made another one.

Rather than consider the colonists' complaints, King George refused even to answer their message. "The New England governments are in a state of rebellion," he said. "Blows must decide whether they are to be subject to this country or independent." In Boston, General Gage, the king's commander of British troops in America, got ready to deliver those blows.

This hand-colored engraving by Amos Doolittle shows the British firing upon the Minutemen who are gathered at Lexington. This was the first battle in what would be a seven-year war.

The First Blow at Lexington   In April 1775, a spy told General Gage that the colonists were hiding a large supply of gunpowder and weapons in the nearby village of Concord. Gage decided to strike at once.

The general ordered 700 of his best troops to march to Concord and seize the weapons. To keep the colonists from moving the weapons, the attack had to be a surprise. And so Gage had his troops march the 20 miles to Concord at night.

The colonists had their own spies. When Gage's troops slipped out of Boston on April 18, 1775, Patriots were watching their every move. Soon

Paul Revere and William Dawes were galloping through the countryside, warning colonists that the British were coming.

At Lexington, a village on the road to Concord, a small band of Minutemen gathered nervously in the chilly night air. "Stand your ground," ordered Captain John Parker. "Don't fire unless fired upon! But if they mean to have a war, let it begin here."

Suddenly, British troops appeared in the early morning mist. A shot rang out—from where, no one knew for certain. Without orders, the soldiers rushed forward, shooting wildly.

When the firing stopped, eight colonists lay dead or dying. Another ten were limping to safety with painful wounds. The British gave three cheers for victory and marched on to Concord.

The Second Blow at Concord
By breakfast time, the British were in Concord, looking for gunpowder and weapons. But colonists had moved the gunpowder and hidden the weapons. In frustration, the soldiers piled up a few wooden tools, tents, and gun carriages and set them on fire.

On a ridge outside the city, militiamen from the surrounding countryside watched the smoke rise. "Are you going to let them burn the town down?" shouted one man.

At the North Bridge in Concord, the Minutemen fired upon British troops who had occupied the town. Surprised by the fury of the colonial attack, the British fled in panic. The Amos Doolittle engraving above shows the bridge at the time of the battle. The photo below shows the bridge today.

"No!" replied Captain Isaac Davis. "I haven't a man that's afraid to go."

Captain Davis marched his volunteers down the hill. As they approached Concord's North Bridge, British troops opened fire. Davis fell dead, a bullet through his heart.

The British expected the Americans to break and run. To their surprise, the Minutemen stood their ground and fired back. Two minutes later, it was the redcoats who were running away in panic.

The retreat back to Boston was a nightmare for the British. More than 4,000 armed and angry Minutemen lined their route, shooting at every red-coat they saw. By the end of the day, 74 British soldiers were dead, and another 200 were wounded or missing. The colonists counted their own losses as 49 dead and 41 wounded.

A British officer described what it was like to face the colonists' fury that day. "Whoever looks upon them as an irregular mob," the officer said, "will find himself much mistaken."

Indeed, since the French and Indian War, the British had been mistaken about Americans again and again. Their biggest mistake, however, was in thinking that ordinary people—farmers, merchants, workers, and house-wives—would not fight for rights that they held dear. At Lexington and Concord, Americans proved they were not only willing to fight for their rights. They were even willing to die for them.

5.9 Chapter Summary

In this chapter, you read about tensions between the colonies and Britain between 1763 and 1775. You used the metaphor of a principal and students to describe that relationship. American colonists had grown used to governing themselves, and they felt strongly about their right to do so.

The French and Indian War left Britain with huge debts and a much larger empire to govern. Parliament tried to deal with these challenges by imposing new taxes and passing new laws. These actions divided many of the colonists into opposing camps. Loyalists urged obedience to Britain, but Patriots resisted "taxation without representation" through protests, boycotts, and riots.

In 1774, delegates at the First Continental Congress sent a formal complaint to the king. Meanwhile, Patriots began forming militias to defend themselves against British troops.

King George III was determined to teach the colonists a lesson. But at Lexington and Concord, Patriots showed they would rather fight than give up their rights. In the next chapter, you will see how these clashes triggered an all-out war and the birth of a new nation.

Sons of Liberty raise a Liberty Pole in 1776. Liberty Poles were used to promote patriotism.

The Granger Collection, New York

Thomas Jefferson

Benjamin Franklin

John Adams

What role did each of these three men play in drafting the Declaration of Independence?

6

The Declaration of Independence

6.1 Introduction

As you read in Chapter 5, the bloodshed at Lexington and Concord marked a turning point for the colonies. The day after the clashes, horseback riders galloped through the colonies with news of Britain's "barbarous murders" of innocent militiamen. Most Americans were deeply shocked by the news. More urgently than ever before, they debated what the colonies should do about the trouble with Great Britain.

The choices were clear enough. The colonies could declare their independence—a course that would surely lead to war. Or they could continue with protests and petitions. This choice would keep the colonies at peace, but at what cost to the colonists' freedom?

No one was more outspoken in his support for independence than Patrick Henry of Virginia. After the passage of the Intolerable Acts, Henry delivered to the Virginia House of Burgesses one of the most famous speeches in American history.

"There is no room for hope," Henry began. "If we wish to be free… we must fight! Our chains are forged. Their clanking can be heard on the plains of Boston. The war is inevitable—and let it come!"

Then Henry spoke to those who treasured peace above freedom:

Gentlemen may cry, peace, peace—but there is no peace. The war is actually begun. The next gale that sweeps from the north will bring to our ears the clash of resounding arms!… What is it that gentlemen wish?… Is life so dear, or peace so sweet, as to be purchased at the price of chains and slavery? Forbid it, Almighty God! I know not what course others may take; but as for me, give me liberty, or give me death!

Despite the passionate words of Patriots like Patrick Henry, most colonists remained reluctant (hesitant) rebels. As you will read in this chapter, only after war had already started did the colonies decide to declare their independence.

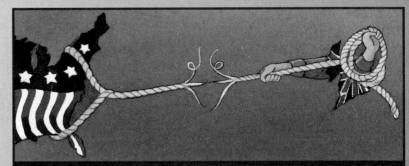

Graphic Organizer: Visual Metaphor
You will use this visual metaphor of an unraveling rope to understand the historical events that led the colonists to declare independence.

The Granger Collection, New York

6.2 The War Begins

On May 10, 1775, the Second Continental Congress met in Philadelphia. By then, New England militia had massed around Boston. The first question facing Congress was who should command this "New England Army." The obvious answer was a New Englander.

George Washington and the Continental Army John Adams of Massachusetts had another idea. He proposed that Congress create a "continental army" made up of troops from all the colonies. To lead this army, Adams nominated "a gentleman whose skill as an officer, whose…great talents and universal character would…unite…the colonies better than any other person alive." That man was George Washington of Virginia.

The delegates agreed. They unanimously elected Washington to be commander-in-chief of the new Continental Army.

The Battle of Bunker Hill Meanwhile, militiamen near Boston made plans to fortify two hills that overlooked the city—Bunker Hill and Breed's Hill. On the night of June 16, Israel Putnam led a few hundred men up Breed's Hill. In four hours of furious digging, they erected a crude fort on the top of the hill.

The fort worried British general William Howe, who had just arrived from England with fresh troops. Howe ordered an immediate attack. Under a hot June sun, some 2,000 redcoated troops formed two long lines at the base of Breed's Hill. At Howe's order, they marched up the slope.

As the lines moved ever closer, Putnam ordered his men, "Don't fire until you see the whites of their eyes." Only when the British were almost on top of them did the militiamen pull their triggers. The red lines broke and fell back in confusion.

The British regrouped and attacked again. Once more the Americans stopped their advance. On their third attack, the redcoats finally took the hill—but only because the Americans had used up all their gunpowder and pulled back.

This clash, which was misnamed the Battle of Bunker Hill, was short but very bloody. More than 1,000 British troops were killed or wounded, and nearly half that many Americans. British and Americans alike knew that this was no small skirmish on a village green. A war had begun.

Orderly rows of British soldiers marched up Breed's Hill and eventually defeated American forces when the rebels ran out of gunpowder. The fierce fighting proved the British would not easily defeat the colonists.

6.3 The Siege of Boston

A week later, George Washington took command of his new army. He found "a mixed multitude of people…under very little discipline, order, or government." Washington worked hard to impose order. One man wrote, "Everyone is made to know his place and keep in it…. It is surprising how much work has been done."

Ticonderoga   A month later, a dismayed Washington learned that the army had only 36 barrels of gunpowder—enough for each soldier to fire just nine shots. To deceive the British, Washington started a rumor in Boston that he had 1,800 barrels of gunpowder—more than he knew what to do with! Luckily, the British swallowed this tall tale. Meanwhile, Washington sent desperate letters to the colonies begging for gunpowder.

Washington got his powder. But he still did not dare attack the British forces in Boston. To do that he needed artillery—heavy guns, such as cannons—to bombard their defenses. In desperation, Washington sent a Boston bookseller named Henry Knox to Fort Ticonderoga to round up some big guns.

Ticonderoga was an old British fort located at the southern end of Lake Champlain in New York. A few months earlier, militiamen led by Ethan Allen and Benjamin Arnold had seized the fort. The Americans had little use for the run-down fort, but its guns would prove priceless.

As winter set in, Knox loaded 59 cannons onto huge sleds and dragged them 300 miles to Boston. Knox's 42 sleds also carried 2,300 pounds of lead for future bullets. Boston was about to be put under siege.

George Washington turned an undisciplined army, composed of troops from all the colonies, into an effective fighting force.

The British Abandon Boston

On March 4, 1776, the British soldiers in Boston awoke to a frightening sight. The night before, the ridges of nearby Dorchester Heights had been bare. Now they bristled with cannons, all aimed on the city.

Rather than risk another bloodbath, General Howe abandoned the city. Within days, more than a hundred ships left Boston Harbor for Canada. The ships carried 9,000 British troops as well as 1,100 Loyalists who preferred to leave their homes behind rather than live with rebels.

Some Americans hoped the war was over. Washington, however, knew that it was only beginning.

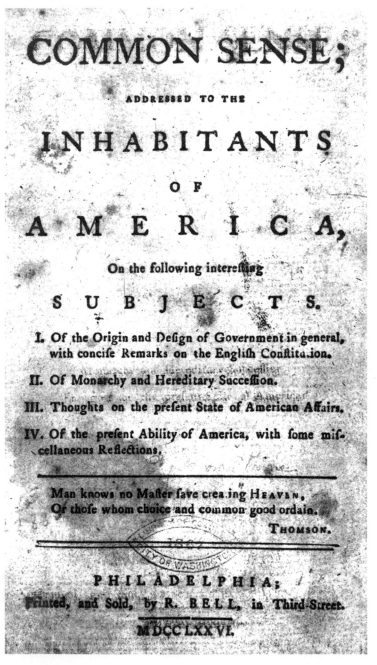

6.4 Toward Independence

Nearly a year passed between the skirmishes at Lexington and Concord and the British retreat from Boston. During that time, there was little talk of independence. Most colonists still considered themselves loyal British subjects. Their quarrel was not with Great Britain itself, but with its policies toward the colonies.

The Olive Branch Petition Many Americans pinned their hopes for peace on King George. In July 1775, Congress sent a petition to George III asking him to end the quarrel. John Adams called the petition an "olive branch," because olive tree branches are an ancient symbol of peace.

By the time the petition reached London, however, the king had declared the colonies to be in "open and avowed rebellion." He ordered his ministers "to bring the **traitors** to justice."

Being called a traitor was enough to change the mind of one of Washington's generals. The general confessed that he had long "looked with some degree of horror on the scheme of separation." Now he agreed with Patrick Henry that "we must be independent or slaves."

Common Sense Many colonists, however, still looked with "horror" at the idea of independence. Then, early in 1776, a Patriot named Thomas Paine published a fiery pamphlet entitled *Common Sense*. Paine scoffed at the idea that Americans owed any loyalty to King George. "Of more worth is one honest man to society," he wrote, "than all the crowned ruffians who ever lived."

Paine also attacked the argument that the colonies' ties to Britain had benefited Americans. Just the opposite was true, he said. American trade had suffered under British control. Americans had also been hurt by being dragged into Britain's European wars.

Paine ended with a vision of an independent America as a homeland of liberty. "Ye that love mankind!" he urged. "Ye that dare oppose not only the tyranny, but the tyrant, stand forth!… The sun never shined on a cause of greater worth."

Within a few months, more than 120,000 copies of *Common Sense* were printed. Paine's arguments helped persuade thousands of colonists that independence was not only sensible, but the key to a brighter future.

Thomas Paine's pamphlet *Common Sense* persuaded many colonists to support independence.

6.5 Thomas Jefferson Drafts a Declaration

A few weeks after the British left Boston, the Continental Congress appointed a committee to write a declaration, or formal statement, of independence. The task of drafting the declaration went to the committee's youngest member, 33-year-old Thomas Jefferson of Virginia. A shy man, Jefferson said little in Congress. But he spoke brilliantly with his pen.

Jefferson's job was to explain to the world why the colonies were choosing to separate from Britain. "When in the course of human events," he began, if one people finds it necessary to break its ties with another, "a decent respect to the opinions of mankind" requires that they explain their actions.

Natural Rights Jefferson's explanation was simple, but revolutionary. Loyalists had argued that colonists had a duty to obey the king, whose authority came from God. Jefferson reasoned quite differently. All people are born equal in God's sight, he began, and all are entitled to the same basic rights. In Jefferson's eloquent words:

We hold these truths to be self-evident, that all men are created equal, that they are endowed by their Creator with certain unalienable rights, that among these are life, liberty, and the pursuit of happiness.

After Thomas Jefferson wrote the first draft of the Declaration of Independence, Benjamin Franklin and John Adams suggested changes.

Governments are formed, Jefferson said, "to secure these rights." Their power to rule comes from "the consent of the governed." If a government fails to protect people's rights, "it is the right of the people to alter or abolish it." The people can then create a new government that will protect "their safety and happiness."

The King's Crimes King George, Jefferson continued, had shown no concern for the rights of colonists. Instead, the king's policies had been aimed at establishing "an absolute tyranny over these states [the colonies]."

As proof, Jefferson included a long list of the king's abuses. In all these actions, Jefferson claimed, George III had shown that he was "unfit to be the ruler of a free people."

The time had come, Jefferson concluded, for the colonies' ties to Britain to be broken. "These United Colonies are," he declared, "and of right ought to be, free and independent states."

6.6 The Final Break

On July 1, 1776, the Second Continental Congress met in Philadelphia's State House to debate independence. By noon, the temperature outside had soared into the nineties, and a thunderstorm was gathering. Inside the State House, emotions were equally hot and stormy. By the end of the day, the issue was still undecided.

The next day was cooler and calmer. On July 2, all but one of the 13 colonies voted for independence. New York cast no vote.

No delegate was more excited about the colonies' decision than John Adams. He wrote to his wife Abigail, "The second of July…will be celebrated by succeeding generations…with pomp and parade, with shows, games, sports, guns, bells, bonfires and illuminations, from one end of the continent to the other, from this time forward forevermore."

Debate over Slavery   Adams was wrong about the date that would be celebrated as America's birthday, but only because Congress decided to revise Jefferson's declaration. Most of the delegates liked what they read, except for a passage on slavery. Jefferson had charged King George with violating the "sacred rights of life and liberty…of a distant people [by] carrying them into slavery."

Almost no one liked this passage. Southerners feared that it might lead to demands to free the slaves. Northerners worried that New England merchants, who profited from the slave trade, might be offended. Even delegates who opposed slavery felt that it was unfair to blame the king for enslaving Africans. The passage was struck out.

Independence Day   On July 4, the delegates approved a final version of the Declaration of Independence. One by one, they stepped forward to sign it. In doing so, they pledged to support independence with "our lives, our fortunes, and our sacred honor."

This was a serious pledge. Every signer knew that he was committing an act of treason against Great Britain. If the new "United States of America" failed to win its freedom, each of them could end up swinging from a hangman's rope. Knowing this, Benjamin Franklin told the delegates, "We must all hang together. Or most assuredly we shall all hang separately."

Slavery was not mentioned in the Declaration of Independence because the slave trade was important to the economy of many of the colonies. In the triangular trade shown on this map, rum and iron were shipped from New England to West Africa. In West Africa, these products were exchanged for slaves. Then the slaves were taken to the West Indies (Caribbean), where they were traded for molasses and sugar. Finally, the molasses and sugar were brought back to New England.

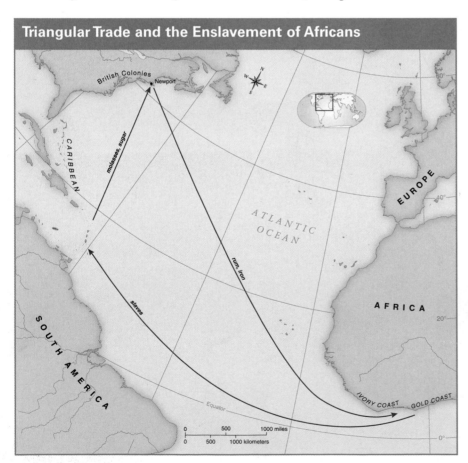

Triangular Trade and the Enslavement of Africans

6.7 Chapter Summary

In this chapter, you read how the American colonies took the dramatic step of declaring their independence. You used a visual metaphor to describe the key historic events that led up to the Declaration of Independence. Soon after the skirmishes at Lexington and Concord, the struggle with Great Britain turned into all-out war. The Second Continental Congress elected George Washington as the head of the Continental Army. After the bloody Battle of Bunker Hill, American troops threatened the city of Boston with heavy guns. The British decided to abandon the city.

The failure of the Olive Branch Petition, and Thomas Paine's eloquent pamphlet, *Common Sense,* moved the colonies closer to a declaration of independence. Thomas Jefferson, a delegate to the Second Continental Congress, was selected to write a draft of the declaration.

On July 4, 1776, the delegates took their lives in their hands by signing the Declaration of Independence. For the first time in history, a government was being established on the basis of the natural rights of people and the duty of government to honor those rights.

But independence could not be won with words alone. As you will read in the next chapter, the colonies now faced the challenge of winning a war against the most powerful nation in the world.

This poster shows the delegates leaving Independence Hall to announce the signing of the Declaration of Independence.

What differences can you
see between the soldiers in
these two armies?

The American Revolution

7.1 Introduction

When the **Revolutionary War** began in 1775, 15-year-old Joseph Martin was too young to join the Continental Army. But when recruiters returned to his Connecticut village a year later, he was ready to go.

The recruiters were looking for volunteers to go to New York, where the British were rumored to have landed 15,000 troops. "I did not care if there were fifteen times fifteen thousand," Martin said later. "I never gave a thought about numbers. The Americans were invincible [unbeatable] in my opinion."

Just two days after the Declaration of Independence was signed, Martin traded his plow for a musket (an early type of rifle). A week later he arrived in New York City, where he hoped to "sniff a little gunpowder." As he recalled, "I was now what I had long wished to be, a soldier. I had obtained my heart's desire; it was now my business to prove myself equal to my new profession."

If Martin had known what lay ahead, he might not have been so pleased about his new profession. The army in New York was ill trained, ill equipped, and just plain ill. "Almost the whole regiment are sick," reported a Massachusetts officer of his unit.

The British army, in contrast, was well trained, well equipped, and well supported by the Royal Navy. Rather than the 15,000 troops Martin had heard about, the British had assembled a force of 25,000 men in New York. More than 400 British ships bobbed in New York Harbor. This was the biggest army and the largest fleet the British had ever sent overseas.

In the face of such overwhelming force, the Americans should have been easily defeated. But they were not. In this chapter, you will read how soldiers like Joseph Martin stood up to mighty Britain to win a revolution and a new nation.

Graphic Organizer: Metaphor
You will use this metaphor of a game of Capture the Flag to understand the factors that helped decide the outcome of the Revolutionary War.

7.2 American Strengths and Weaknesses

The Patriots began their revolution in a weak position. They had a hastily organized, untrained army and a tiny navy. Their weaknesses were far more obvious than their strengths.

At first, the Continental soldier was poorly trained and poorly equipped. He suffered a lack of gunpowder, rifles, food, and clothing. Some men had only spears or axes for weapons.

American Weaknesses   The Continental Army was always short of men. General Washington never had more than 20,000 troops at one time and place. Many soldiers enlisted for six months or a year. Just when they were learning how to fight, they would pick up their muskets and go home to tend to their farms and families.

Few Americans were trained for battle. Some could shoot well enough from behind a tree. But when facing a mass of well-disciplined redcoats, they were likely to turn and run.

The army was plagued by shortages. Guns and gunpowder were so scarce that Benjamin Franklin suggested arming the troops with bows and arrows. Food shortages forced soldiers to beg for hand-outs. Uniforms were scarce as well. In winter, one could track shoeless soldiers by their bloody footprints in the snow.

Such shortages outraged Washington. But when he complained to the Continental Congress, nothing changed. Congress, the new nation's only government, lacked the power to raise money for supplies by taxing the states (the former colonies).

In desperation, Congress printed paper money to pay for the war. But the value of this money dropped so low that merchants demanded to be paid in gold instead. And like everything else, gold was scarce.

American Strengths   Still, the Americans had strengths. One was the patriotism of people like Joseph Martin, who willingly gave their lives to defend their liberty and their homes. Without them, the war would have been quickly lost.

The Americans also received help from overseas. Motivated by their old hatred of the English, the French secretly aided the rebels. During the first two years of the war, 90 percent of the Americans' gunpowder came from Europe, mostly from France.

The Americans' other great strength was their commander. George Washington was more than an experienced military leader. He was also a man who inspired courage and confidence. In the dark days to come, it was Washington who would keep the ragtag Continental army together.

7.3 British Strengths and Weaknesses

Britain, in contrast to the American colonies, entered the war with many advantages. But looks can be deceiving, and the British encountered many problems as well.

British Strengths With a professional army of 50,000 troops, British forces greatly outnumbered the Continental Army. In addition, George III hired 30,000 **mercenaries**. These hired soldiers were known as Hessians because they came from a part of Germany called Hesse-Cassel. The British were also able to recruit many Loyalists, African Americans, and Native Americans into their forces.

British and Hessian troops were well trained in European military tactics. They excelled in large battles fought by a mass of troops on open ground. They also had far more experience than Americans at firing artillery.

The British forces were also well supplied. Compared to the pitifully equipped Continental Army, they seldom lacked for food, uniforms, weapons, or ammunition.

British Weaknesses Even so, the war presented Britain with huge problems. One was the distance between Britain and America. Sending troops and supplies across the Atlantic was slow and costly. News of battles arrived in England long after they had occurred, making planning difficult.

A second problem was that King George and his ministers were never able to convince the British people that defeating the rebels was vital to Britain's future. There were no Joseph Martins in England volunteering to fight the Americans. The longer the war dragged on, the less happy British taxpayers were about paying its heavy costs.

A third problem was poor leadership. Lord George Germain, the man chosen to run the war, had no real sense of how to defeat the rebels. How could he? He had never set foot in America. Nor did it occur to him to go see for himself what his army was up against. If he had, Germain might have realized that this was not a war that could be won by conquering a city or two. To end the revolution, his forces would have to crush the Patriots' will to fight, state by state. Instead, Germain kept changing plans and generals, hoping that some combination of the two would bring him an easy victory.

> **mercenaries** professional soldiers who fight for anyone who will pay them

The British soldier was a trained professional. He was well equipped with ammunition, a good musket, adequate food, and uniforms.

The Granger Collection, New York

7.4 Britain Almost Wins the War

After abandoning Boston in the spring of 1776, Germain came up with his first plan for winning the war. British forces, led by General William Howe, were ordered to capture New York City. From that base, British troops would then move north to destroy the rebellion at its heart—Massachusetts.

To block the British invasion, Washington hurried with his army from Boston to New York. It was there that he heard good news: Congress had finally declared the colonies to be "free and independent states."

Washington had the Declaration of Independence read aloud to his troops. The time had come, he said, to "show our enemies, and the whole world, that free men, contending for their own land, are superior to any mercenaries on Earth." Most of his men agreed that independence was a prize worth fighting for.

African Americans faced a difficult decision during the Revolution. Would the Americans or the British give them freedom at the end of the war? At the Battle of Cowpens in South Carolina, pictured above, the Continental Army, which included African Americans, soundly defeated the British.

African Americans and the War

For African Americans, however, the Declaration of Independence raised both hopes and questions. Did Jefferson's words, "all men are created equal," apply to them? Would independence bring an end to slavery? Should they join the Revolution?

Even before independence was declared, a number of African Americans had joined the Patriot cause. Black militiamen fought at Lexington, Concord, and Bunker Hill. Early in the war, however, blacks were banned from the Continental Army. Washington did not want the army to become a haven for runaway slaves.

In contrast, the British promised freedom to all slaves who took up arms for the king. As a result, thousands of runaways became Loyalists and fought for Britain.

A shortage of volunteers soon forced Washington to change his mind. By 1779, about 15 percent of the soldiers in the Continental Army were African Americans. Large numbers of black sailors also served in the Continental Navy.

As black Americans joined the war effort, whites began to question their own beliefs. How could they accept slavery if they truly believed that all people are created equal, with the same rights to life, liberty, and happiness? By the time the war ended, Vermont, Connecticut, Massachusetts, New Hampshire, Rhode Island, and Pennsylvania had all taken steps to end slavery.

While chasing the retreating Continental Army, British soldiers looted the homes of Americans, both Patriots and Loyalists. Such actions turned many former supporters into enemies.

Defeat in New York   On August 27, 1776, the American and British armies met in Brooklyn, New York, for what promised to be a decisive battle. The Americans began their defense of the city "in high spirits." But the inexperienced Americans were no match for the British, with their greater numbers and superior training. In two days of fighting, the British lost only 377 men, while the Americans lost 1,407.

Satisfied that the war was nearly won, Howe ordered a halt to the British attack. Washington, he assumed, would do what any self-respecting European general would do in a hopeless situation. He would surrender honorably. And so Howe waited.

Washington had no intention of giving up. But for his army to survive, he would have to retreat. Even though Washington knew this, he could not bring himself to utter the shameful word "retreat."

An officer named Thomas Mifflin rescued him from his pride. "What is your strength?" Mifflin asked. "Nine thousand," Washington replied. "Not enough," said Mifflin bluntly, "We must retreat."

Fading Hopes   The battle for New York City was the first of many defeats for the Americans. In the weeks that followed, British forces chased the Americans out of New York, through New Jersey, and finally across the Delaware River into Pennsylvania.

For Joseph Martin and his comrades, this was a trying time. There was little food to eat, and the soldiers grew weak from hunger. As the weather turned cold, muddy roads and icy streams added to their misery. With their terms of enlistment nearly up, many soldiers headed for home. Along the way they spread the word that anyone who volunteered to risk his life in the Continental Army had to be crazy.

By the time Washington reached Pennsylvania, he had only a few thousand men. Many of his remaining troops, he reported, were "entirely naked and most so thinly clad [clothed] as to be unfit for service." More troops had to be found, and found quickly, he wrote his brother. Otherwise, "I think the game will be pretty well up."

7.5 A Pep Talk and Surprise Victories

By the end of 1776, the British also thought the war was just about won. General Howe offered to pardon all rebels who signed a statement promising to "remain in peaceful obedience" to the king. Thousands took him up on his offer.

The Crisis Washington knew that he had to do something, and quickly. Gathering his last troops together, he read to them from Thomas Paine's new pamphlet, *The Crisis*:

> *These are the times that try men's souls. The summer soldier and the sunshine patriot will, in this crisis, shrink from the service of their country; but he that stands it NOW, deserves the love and thanks of man and woman.*

Next, Washington outlined a daring plan to attack Hessian troops who were camped for the winter in Trenton, New Jersey. Heartened by Paine's words, his men did not "shrink from the service of their country."

With morale low and his soldiers threatening to return home, George Washington planned a daring attack on the Hessians at Trenton. Crossing the ice-choked Delaware River, he surprised the enemy, overwhelming them completely.

Victory in Trenton Late on December 25, 1776, Washington's army crossed the ice-choked Delaware River in small boats. On the New Jersey shore, Washington gave his men the password for the long night march ahead: "Victory or Death."

As the Americans made their way toward Trenton, a driving snow chilled them to the bone. Ice and rocks cut through their worn-out shoes. One officer reported to Washington that the troops' guns were too wet to fire. "Use the bayonets," the general replied. "The town must be taken."

When the Americans reached Trenton, they found the Hessians happily sleeping off their Christmas feasts. Caught completely by surprise, the mercenaries surrendered. Washington took 868 prisoners without losing a single man. A week later, the Americans captured another 300 British troops at Princeton, New Jersey. These defeats told Howe that it would take more than capturing New York City and issuing pardons to win the war.

News of Washington's victories electrified Patriots. "A few days ago they had given up their cause for lost," wrote an unhappy Loyalist. "Their late successes have turned the scale and they are all liberty mad again." The game was not yet up.

7.6 The Tide Begins to Turn

When the Revolution began, both sides adopted the same military strategy, or overall plan for winning the war. That strategy was to defeat the enemy in one big battle.

After barely escaping from New York, Washington revised his strategy. In the future, he wrote Congress, he would avoid large battles that might put his army at risk. Instead, the war would be "defensive." Rather than defeating the British, Washington hoped to tire them out.

A New British Strategy   Germain revised the British strategy as well. His new plan was to divide the rebels by taking control of New York's Hudson River Valley. Control of this waterway would allow the British to cut New England off from the rest of the states. Without men and supplies from New England, the Continental Army would surely collapse.

To carry out this plan, General John Burgoyne left Canada in June 1777, with about 8,000 British soldiers and Indian warriors. He planned to move this army south to Albany, New York. There he would meet up with General Howe, who was supposed to march his army north from New York City.

Problems with Burgoyne's Plan   There were two big problems with Burgoyne's plan. The first was that what looked like an easy invasion route on a map was anything but easy. The route Burgoyne chose from Canada to Albany took his army through more than 20 miles of tangled wilderness. His army had to build bridges, chop down countless trees, and lay out miles of log roads through swamps as it crept toward Albany.

To make matters worse, Burgoyne didn't travel light. His army was slowed by more than 600 wagons, 30 of them filled with his personal baggage. Even in the wilderness, "Gentleman Johnny" Burgoyne sipped champagne with his supper.

The second problem with Burgoyne's plan was that General Howe had his own ideas about how to win the war. Instead of marching to Albany, Howe headed for Philadelphia, the rebels' capital. There he hoped to lure Washington into another major battle. Howe hoped it would be the last one.

> **strategy** An overall plan (for example, for winning a war). Specific ways of carrying out a strategy are called *tactics*.

The wife, children, and slave of General Philip Schulyer burned the family wheat fields, so as to leave nothing useful for British forces advancing toward Saratoga.

The Granger Collection, New York

The American Revolution **93**

Washington, however, refused to risk his army in another big battle. He would not fight for Philadelphia. Instead, he played hide-and-seek with Howe, attacking here and there and then disappearing into the countryside.

A Turning Point   By the time the slow-moving Burgoyne finally reached Saratoga Springs on the Hudson River, the area was swarming with militia. Although the rebels outnumbered his army, Burgoyne ordered an attack. Again and again the rebels beat back Burgoyne's troops. On October 17, 1777, Gentleman Johnny accepted defeat.

Burgoyne's surrender marked a turning point in the war. Before the victory at Saratoga, the American cause had looked hopeless to most of the world. Now the Americans had shown they could stand up to a British army and win.

Not long after this victory, France came into the war as an **ally** of the United States. The French government sent money, weapons, troops, and warships to the Americans. Spain also entered the war against Britain. The American cause no longer looked quite so hopeless.

The Granger Collection, New York

George Washington is shown with the Marquis de Lafayette at Valley Forge. Lafayette, a Frenchman who aided the Americans, described the American soldiers there as "in want of everything; they had neither coats, nor hats, nor shirts nor shoes; their feet and their legs froze until they grew black."

Winter at Valley Forge

Saratoga was a stunning victory, but the war was far from over. While General Washington's army roamed the countryside, Howe's forces still occupied Philadelphia.

Late in 1777, Congress declared a day of thanksgiving. By this time, Washington and his army were on their way to Valley Forge, Pennsylvania, to make camp for the winter. Joseph Martin described the army's "celebration":

We had nothing to eat for two or three days previous.... But we must now have what Congress said, a sumptuous [lavish] Thanksgiving.... It gave each and every man a gill [a few ounces] of rice and a tablespoon of vinegar! The army was now not only starved but naked. The greatest part were not only shirtless and barefoot, but destitute of [without] all other clothing, especially blankets.

Washington's troops were hungry because many farmers preferred to sell food to the British. The British paid them in gold, while Congress paid them in paper money. As for uniforms and blankets, merchants had raised the prices for these items sky-high. This desire for profits at the army's expense outraged Washington. "No punishment," he fumed, "is too great for the man who can build his greatness upon his country's ruin."

To distract his men from their misery, Washington put Baron Friedrich von Steuben, a volunteer from Prussia, in charge of training. The Prussian's method, wrote Martin, was "continual drill." It worked wonders. "The army grows stronger every day," wrote one officer. "There is a spirit of discipline among the troops that is better than numbers."

Another foreign volunteer, the Marquis de Lafayette, also helped raise the troops' spirits. Although he was one of the richest men in France, Lafayette chose to share the hardships of Valley Forge. He even used his own money to buy the men warm clothing. "The patient fortitude [courage] of the officers and soldiers," Lafayette wrote, "was a continual miracle."

When at last spring arrived, Washington received news that the British were about to abandon Philadelphia. The time had come to put his newly trained army to the test.

The Battle of Monmouth   By this time, Sir Henry Clinton had replaced General Howe as commander of the British forces in America. In Clinton's view, taking over Philadelphia had gained the British nothing. He ordered his army to retreat to New York City, where the Royal Navy could keep it supplied by sea.

Now it was Washington's turn to chase an army across New Jersey. On June 28, 1778, he caught up with the retreating British near Monmouth, New Jersey. In the battle that followed, Washington was everywhere, constantly rallying his men to stand and fight. "Cheering them by his voice and example," wrote Lafayette, "never had I beheld [seen] so superb a man."

Late that night, the British slipped across the Hudson River to safety in New York City. Washington camped with his army nearby. It was pleasing, he wrote, "that after two years maneuvering…both armies are brought back to the very point they set out from." Neither army knew it yet, but the war in the North was over.

At the Battle of Monmouth in New Jersey, George Washington led his troops in an attack on retreating British forces. Although the Americans won, the British were able to slip away during the night and sail safely to New York.

7.7 The War Goes South

After failing to conquer any state in the North, the British changed strategies yet again. Their new plan was to move the war to the South. There, they believed, thousands of Loyalists were just waiting to join the king's cause.

Clinton began his "southern campaign" with a successful attack on Savannah, Georgia. From Georgia, he moved on to take control of North and South Carolina. At that point, Clinton returned to New York City, leaving Lord Charles Cornwallis to run the war in the South.

This engraving shows Francis Marion crossing the Pee Dee River in South Carolina. Marion, known as the Swamp Fox because of his tactic of ambushing the British from the marshes of the South, never led a force of more than 70 men.

Saving the South Cornwallis soon learned that he did not really control the Carolinas after all. Guerrillas—soldiers who are not part of a regular army—kept the American cause alive. One of them was Francis Marion, who was also known as the "Swamp Fox." Marion's band of rebels harassed the British with hit-and-run raids. Then they faded into the swamps and forests like foxes.

Late in 1780, Washington sent General Nathaniel Greene to slow the British advance through the South. Greene's army was too small to meet Cornwallis in a major battle. Instead, Greene led Cornwallis's troops on an exhausting chase through the southern backcountry. He wrote of his strategy, "We fight, get beat, rise, and fight again."

Greene's strategy worked wonderfully. In April 1781, Cornwallis wrote that he was "quite tired of marching about the country." He moved his army to Yorktown, a sleepy tobacco port on Chesapeake Bay in Virginia, for a good rest.

guerrillas soldiers who operate on their own and are not part of a regular army

A Trap at Yorktown By the time Cornwallis was settling into Yorktown, France had sent nearly 5,000 troops to join Washington's army in New York. In August, Washington learned that another 3,000 troops were scheduled to arrive soon in 29 French warships.

Washington used this information to set a trap for Cornwallis. Secretly, he moved his army south to Virginia. When they arrived, they joined the French and surrounded Yorktown on land with more than 16,000 troops.

Meanwhile, the French warships showed up just in time to seal off the entrance to Chesapeake Bay. Their appearance was a crucial help to the Americans. Now Cornwallis was cut off from the British navy and any hope of rescue by sea.

The trap was sprung on October 6, 1781. Joseph Martin watched as a flag was raised to signal American and French gunners to open fire on Yorktown. "I confess I felt a secret pride swell in my heart," he wrote, "when I saw the 'star-spangled banner' waving majestically." The shelling went on for days, until "most of the guns in the enemy's works were silenced."

Cornwallis Surrenders With Yorktown exploding around him, at first Cornwallis clung to the hope that the British navy would come to his rescue. When no ships arrived, he finally agreed to surrender.

On October 19, 1781, American and French troops formed two long lines that stretched for more than a mile along the road to Yorktown—the French on one side, the Americans on the other. The two lines could not have looked more different. The French were dressed in elegant uniforms that gleamed with gold and silver braid in the afternoon sun. The Americans' uniforms—and not everyone even had uniforms—were patched and faded. Behind the lines stood civilians who had traveled for miles to witness this glorious event.

After hours of waiting, the crowd watched as 8,000 British troops left Yorktown to lay down their arms. The defeated troops moved "with slow and solemn step." They were accompanied by a slow tune known as "The World Turned Upside Down." This same sad tune had been played at Saratoga after the British surrender.

Cornwallis did not take part in this ceremony, saying that he was ill. In reality, the British commander could not bear to surrender publicly to an army that he looked down on as "a contemptible and undisciplined rabble [mob]." While Cornwallis sulked in his tent, his men surrendered their arms. Many of them wept bitter tears.

To the watching Americans, there was nothing sad about that day. "It was a noble sight to us," wrote Martin, "and the more so, as it seemed to promise a speedy conclusion to the contest."

This painting by John Trumbull shows the British surrender at Yorktown on October 19, 1781. At the center is General Benjamin Lincoln leading the British. On the right is General Washington in front of the American flag. On the left are French, Polish, and Prussian soldiers.

80°W   75°W   70°W

45°N

Maine
(part of Mass.)

New
Hampshire

*Battle of Saratoga,
October 1777*

New York   Massachusetts

Connecticut   Rhode
Island

*Battle of Fort Washington,
November 1776*   40°N

*Battle of Princeton,
January 1777*   *Battle of Long Island, August 1776*

Pennsylvania   *Battle of Trenton, December 1776*
*Valley Forge,
Winter 1777–78*   New Jersey

Maryland
Delaware

N
W   E
S

Virginia   *Battle of Yorktown,
October 1781*

Proclamation Line of 1763   35°N

North Carolina

American military victory
British military victory
American winter camp
- - - Proclamation line
New England Colonies
Middle Colonies
Southern Colonies

*Battle of Cowpens,
January 1781*

South
Carolina

Battle of Charleston, May 1780

0   100   200 miles
0   100   200 kilometers

Georgia

Battle of Savannah, December 1778

30°N

80°W   75°W

1. Identify at least four interesting details on this map.

2. What do the blue, white, and red sections of the map represent?

3. In which region(s)—New England Colonies, Middle Colonies, or Southern Colonies—did the key battles of the American Revolution take place?

4. How does this map show why the British were not able to defeat the Americans in the American Revolution?

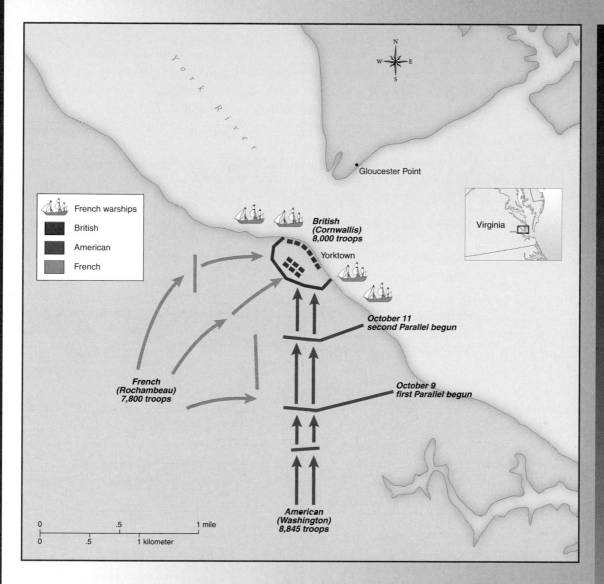

French warships

British

American

French

Y o r k   R i v e r

Gloucester Point

N
W — E
S

**British
(Cornwallis)
8,000 troops**

Yorktown

Virginia

**October 11
second Parallel begun**

**October 9
first Parallel begun**

**French
(Rochambeau)
7,800 troops**

**American
(Washington)
8,845 troops**

0   .5   1 mile
0   .5   1 kilometer

1. Identify at least four interesting details on this map.

2. Which three countries were involved in this battle?

3. According to the map, what did American and French forces do to defeat the British at the Battle of Yorktown?

4. How do you think Americans responded to the outcome of the Battle of Yorktown? The British? The French? Explain.

7.8 The War Ends

The conclusion of the war was not quite as speedy as Martin had hoped. When Lord North, the British prime minister, heard about Cornwallis's defeat, he paced up and down the room repeating, "Oh God! It is all over!" The British public agreed. Yorktown took the heart out of whatever support was left for the war. Still, months dragged by before King George was finally forced to accept defeat.

For most Americans, the end of the war was a time for joy and celebration. They had gained the freedom to govern themselves and create their own future. But liberty came at a high price. At least 6,200 Americans had been killed in combat. An estimated 10,000 died in camp of diseases, and another 8,500 as British prisoners. As a proportion of the total population, more Americans died fighting the Revolutionary War than in any other conflict except the Civil War, in which Americans fought one another.

The Treaty of Paris   Early in 1783, representatives of the United States and Britain signed a peace **treaty** (agreement) in Paris. The Treaty of Paris had three important parts. First, Great Britain agreed to recognize the United States as an independent nation. Second, Britain gave up its claims to all lands between the Atlantic Coast and the Mississippi River, from Canada south to Florida. Third, the United States agreed to return all rights and property taken from Loyalists during the war.

Many Loyalists did not trust the treaty's promise of fair treatment—and for good reason. During the war, Loyalists had been badly treated by Patriots. More than 80,000 black and white Loyalists left the United States to settle in British Canada.

The ideals of the American Revolution helped inspire calls for "Liberty, Equality, and Fraternity" in France. In addition, France's support for the American war deepened its national debt and caused suffering among its people. In 1789 France's monarchy was overthrown. This image shows a violent clash between French commoners and King Louis XVI's troops.

The Influence of the American Revolution   The Revolutionary War had a major impact in other parts of the world. In the 1800s, it would help inspire revolts against European rule in South America. In Europe, it thrilled liberals who dreamed of creating their own democracies. The American example was especially influential in France, which soon had its own revolution. As one Frenchman wrote, "They [Americans] are the hope of the human race; they may well become its model."

7.9 Chapter Summary

In this chapter, you read how the American colonies won their independence from Great Britain. You used a visual metaphor to record factors that helped to decide the outcome of the Revolutionary War.

At the start of the war, the Americans seemed sure to lose the fight with Britain. The poorly trained and poorly equipped American forces were no match for Britain's professional army and huge navy. But patriotic feeling, help from overseas, and a magnificent commander helped to overcome British strengths. In addition, fighting a war in far-off America posed major problems for the British.

Still, the British enjoyed a string of victories in the early part of the war. After the loss of New York, only Washington's leadership kept the Americans going. Then, beginning with the victory at Saratoga, the tide began to turn. When France and Spain joined in the conflict, the Americans had the help they needed to outlast the British.

The war's climax came when the Americans, with the help of the French, trapped Cornwallis's army at Yorktown. After Cornwallis surrendered, it was only a matter of time until Britain gave up the fight.

The conflict ended officially with the signing of the Treaty of Paris. In this agreement, Britain recognized the United States as an independent country.

At great cost in lives and property, Americans had won their freedom. They had also set an example that inspired people in other countries to dream of winning their own liberty. Now they faced the task of organizing a government for their new nation.

The Revolutionary War officially ended with the signing of the Treaty of Paris in 1783. British troops agreed to leave American soil "with all convenient speed."

Why would the delegates want George Washington to lead the Constitutional Convention?

Why would Benjamin Franklin be a good delegate to the Constitutional Convention?

What might these men be thinking?

Creating the Constitution

8.1 Introduction

When the Revolutionary War ended, no one was happier than a small, bookish Virginia Patriot named James Madison. And no one was more worried about the future of the United States. While serving in Congress during the war, Madison had tried and failed to get the states to work easily together. He doubted that things would improve now that the war was over.

After declaring independence in 1776, Congress had tried to unite the states under one national government. This proved to be a difficult task. Most members of Congress were nervous about creating a strong central government. They feared that such a government would trample the very rights they were fighting to preserve.

Their solution was a plan of government known as the **Articles of Confederation**. The Articles created "a firm league of friendship" in which "each state retains its sovereignty, freedom, and independence." This "league of friendship" was a loose union in which the 13 states cooperated for common purposes. It was run by Congress, in which each state had one vote.

On paper, the Articles of Confederation gave Congress several important powers. It could make war and peace, raise an army and a navy, print money, and set up a postal system.

In reality, however, these powers were limited by the inability of Congress to impose taxes. Instead, Congress had to ask the states for funds to do anything. All too often, the states ignored Congress's "humble requests." The result, said Madison, was that the Articles were no more effective at binding the states into a nation than "a rope of sand."

In this chapter, you will read about the new nation's shaky start under the Articles of Confederation. You will also learn how Madison and other leaders came together in Philadelphia's Independence Hall in 1787 in the hope of forming "a more perfect union."

Graphic Organizer: Illustration
You will annotate this drawing of the Assembly Room at Independence Hall to organize information about the Constitutional Convention.

territory A region designated by Congress and organized under a governor. A territory may apply to become a state when it has a large enough population.

8.2 Early Quarrels and Accomplishments

Even before the Revolutionary War ended, the states began quarreling among themselves. Many of their quarrels were about taxes on goods that crossed state borders. New York, for example, taxed firewood from Connecticut and cabbages from New Jersey. The states also quarreled over boundaries. The inability of Congress to end such disagreements was one of the key weaknesses of the Articles of Confederation.

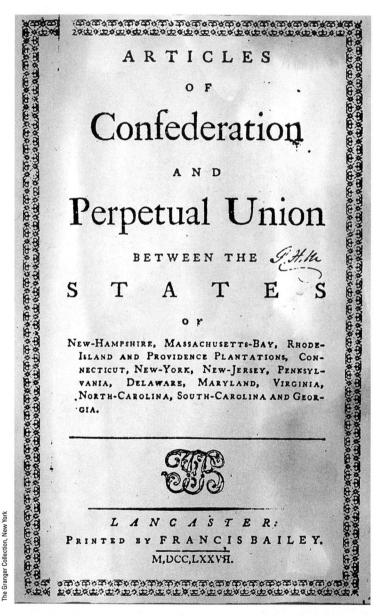

ARTICLES

OF

Confederation

AND

Perpetual Union

BETWEEN THE *G.H.W*

S T A T E S

OF

NEW-HAMPSHIRE, MASSACHUSETTS-BAY, RHODE-ISLAND AND PROVIDENCE PLANTATIONS, CONNECTICUT, NEW-YORK, NEW-JERSEY, PENNSYLVANIA, DELAWARE, MARYLAND, VIRGINIA, NORTH-CAROLINA, SOUTH-CAROLINA AND GEORGIA.

L A N C A S T E R :
PRINTED BY FRANCIS BAILEY.
M,DCC,LXXVII.

This is the title page from the Articles of Confederation, the first constitution of the United States. Under the Articles, the states held the most power. The national government could not collect taxes or settle disputes between states.

Developing Western Lands Congress did get the states to agree on one important issue: how to develop the western lands acquired by the United States in the Treaty of Paris.

At that time, there was no orderly way of dividing up and selling these lands. Settlers walked into the wilderness and claimed the land they liked. Disputes over who owned what land clogged the courts.

To end this confusion, Congress passed the Land Ordinance of 1785. Under this law, western lands were divided into six-mile squares called *townships*. Each township was then divided into 36 sections of 640 acres each. One section of each square was set aside to support the township's public schools. The other sections were to be sold to settlers.

Surveyors proceeded to lay out townships in the Ohio Valley, then known as the Northwest Territory. By 1787, the government was ready to sell sections to settlers. This raised the question of how these areas should be governed. Were they to be colonies of the United States or new states?

The Northwest Ordinance Congress answered this question in the Northwest Ordinance of 1787. This law divided the Northwest Territory into smaller territories, each governed by a territorial governor. As soon as a territory had 5,000 free adult males, it could elect its own legislature, or lawmaking body. When the population reached 60,000, a territory could apply to Congress to become a state.

The Northwest Ordinance included a list of rights that gave settlers the same privileges as other citizens, except for one. Slavery was banned in the Northwest Territory.

This system of settlement served the nation well. Over time, the United States would continue to establish territories as it spread to the Pacific Ocean and beyond.

8.3 Shays's Rebellion and the Need for Change

Under the Articles of Confederation, the new nation also had serious money problems. The paper money printed by Congress during the war was worthless. Congress had the power to make coins that would not lose their value. But it lacked gold or silver to mint into coins.

The states reacted to the money shortage by printing their own paper currency (money). Before long, bills of different sizes and colors were floating from state to state. No one knew what any of these currencies were worth, but most agreed that they were not worth much.

The Granger Collection, New York

arsenal a place where weapons and ammunition are stored

Massachusetts Farmers Rebel

The money shortage was particularly hard on farmers who could not earn enough to pay their debts and taxes. In Massachusetts, judges ordered farmers to sell their land and livestock to pay off their debts. Led by Daniel Shays, a hero of Bunker Hill, Massachusetts farmers rebelled.

First, Shays and his followers closed down courthouses to keep judges from taking their farms. Then they marched on the national **arsenal** at Springfield to seize the weapons stored there. Having disbanded the Continental Army, Congress was unable to stop them.

Massachusetts ended Shays's Rebellion by sending militia troops to Springfield to restore order. To many Americans, however, the uprising was a disturbing sign that the nation they had fought so hard to create was falling apart. "No respect is paid to the federal [national] authority," Madison wrote to a friend. "It is not possible that a government can last long under these circumstances."

A Call for a Convention

Shays's Rebellion shocked Congress into calling for a convention to consider "the situation of the United States." Each state was invited to send delegates to Philadelphia in May 1787, "for the sole and express purpose of revising the Articles of Confederation."

Madison was ready. For the past year he had devoted himself to the study of governments, both ancient and modern. The lesson of the past was always the same. A nation that was made up of many groups needed a strong central government, or it was soon torn apart by quarrels. The question was, would Americans heed this lesson?

Daniel Shays, shown at the top right, and his followers closed down courthouses to prevent judges from seizing their land when they could not pay their debts. Many American leaders saw the rebellion as a sign that the government under the Articles of Confederation was not working.

8.4 Opening the Constitutional Convention

Philadelphia was already hot and sticky when delegates began drifting into the city. On May 25, the Constitutional Convention met for the first time in the east room of the Pennsylvania State House (later known as Independence Hall). The Declaration of Independence had been debated in this very room just 11 years earlier. The delegates would meet in the east room all summer on days so steamy that, as one visitor wrote, "the slightest movement is painful."

The delegates' first action was to elect George Washington president of the convention. No man was more admired and respected than the former commander in chief of the Continental Army. When the war ended, Washington could have used his power and popularity to make himself a king. Instead, he went home to Virginia to resume his life as an ordinary citizen. But despite his reluctance to return to public life, Washington would play a key role by presiding over the convention and lending it his prestige.

The Delegates   Fifty-five delegates from 12 states attended the convention. Rhode Island, which prided itself as "the home of the otherwise minded" and feared a strong national government, boycotted the meeting.

Some leaders of the revolution were missing. John Adams and Thomas Jefferson were representing the United States in Great Britain and France. Others who did not attend included Sam Adams, John Hancock, and Patrick Henry. They feared a strong national government would endanger the rights of states.

The delegates to the Constitutional Convention met on May 25, 1787, in the same hall where the Declaration of Independence was signed. Today, the building is called Independence Hall.

As a group, the delegates were, in the words of a modern historian, "the well-bred, the well-fed, the well-read, and the well-wed." Their average age was 42. At 81, Benjamin Franklin of Pennsylvania was the oldest. He arrived at the convention each day in a sedan chair carried by four good-natured prisoners from a nearby jail.

Most of the delegates brought extensive political experience to the meeting. More than two thirds were lawyers. More than one in three owned slaves. Thomas Jefferson was so impressed by the ability and experience of these men that he called the convention "an assembly of demi-gods."

The Father of the Constitution   The best prepared of these "godlike" figures was James Madison of Virginia. One delegate wrote of Madison, "In the management of every great question he evidently took the lead in the Convention." Indeed, Madison's influence was so great that later he would be called the "Father of the Constitution."

Madison addressed the convention more than 200 times. When he was not speaking, he took notes. Sitting near the front of the room so that he could hear everything that was said, Madison wrote down nearly every word. When collected together, his notes covered more than 600 printed pages. From this remarkable record, we know what went on inside the convention day by day.

Benjamin Franklin, the oldest delegate to the Constitutional Convention, had doubts about the final Constitution. However, he said, "The older I grow, the more apt I am to doubt my own judgment and pay more respect to the judgment of others."

The Rule of Secrecy   At the time, however, no one outside the convention knew what was happening. After choosing a president, the delegates voted on rules for the convention. The most important was the rule of secrecy. The delegates wanted to feel free to speak their minds without causing alarm or opposition among the general public. They agreed to keep secret whatever was said in the meeting room until their work was done.

One day Washington was handed some notes that had been dropped in the hall outside the east room. Washington pocketed the paper until the end of debate the next day. Then, in his sternest voice, he lectured the delegates on the importance of secrecy. "I know not whose paper it is," Washington said as he flung the notes on his desk. "But here it is, let him who owns it take it." The notes were never claimed. Instead, they lay on Washington's desk for days.

Like Washington, the delegates took the rule of secrecy very seriously. During that long summer, not a single word about the convention debates appeared in any newspaper.

Shared Beliefs and Clashing Views   Once the convention was organized, the delegates got down to business. As a group, the delegates had much in common. But they also had very different views on many of the issues facing the new nation.

To be sure, all the delegates were committed to the ideals of the Declaration of Independence. The basic purpose of government, they believed, was to protect the rights to "life, liberty, and the pursuit of

Enlightenment the "Age of Reason" in 17th and 18th century Europe. Enlightenment thinkers emphasized using rational thought to discover truths about nature and society.

republic a country governed by elected representatives

constitution a written plan that provides the basic framework of a government

happiness." And they agreed, in the words of the Declaration, that the "just powers" of governments came from "the consent of the governed."

In part, these beliefs reflected the liberal ideas of **Enlightenment** thinkers like England's John Locke. Human institutions, these thinkers had argued, should be based on "laws of nature." Among these laws were the rights to liberty and equality. The best way to protect these rights, the delegates agreed, was through some form of **republic**.

From New England's town meetings to lawmaking bodies like the Virginia House of Burgesses, Americans had a long tradition of participating in their own government. After the Revolution, all the states had adopted **constitutions** that embraced republican ideals. Despite many differences in details, every state had some form of representative government. States had also expanded the right to vote and to hold office. These state constitutions helped to shape the delegates' thinking.

Despite delegates' broad agreement on a government "of the people," many questions were left unanswered. For example, who exactly should have a say in a truly "representative" government? Even in liberal Pennsylvania, only free, white males could vote. Some states allowed only wealthier citizens to vote or hold office. Women could not vote in any state except New Jersey. (And New Jersey women would lose the right to vote in 1807.)

Perhaps the most troubling question of all was how powerful the national government should be. Many delegates wanted to keep government close to the people by preserving the rights of the states. They feared that a strong national government would threaten individual liberty. Others, including James Madison, argued just the opposite. Look at what has happened under the Articles of Confederation, they said. If the central government is too weak, it cannot do its job of protecting liberty and property.

As they met behind closed doors, the delegates wrestled with these and other issues. Tempers often flared. Several times it seemed that the convention might collapse in failure. But as you will see, in the end the delegates found ways to save the convention—and the nation.

Delegates with opposing views were Pennsylvania's James Wilson (left) and New Jersey's William Paterson (right). Wilson, one of the most vocal delegates at the convention, argued for a strong national government. Paterson tried to protect the rights of the states. Many delegates of small states shared his fear of being "swallowed up" by the larger states.

The Granger Collection, New York

The Granger Collection, New York

8.5 Issue: How Should States Be Represented in the New Government?

When the convention began, most delegates believed that their task was to revise the Articles of Confederation. To their surprise, the Virginia delegation presented them with a completely new plan of government. After a lengthy debate, the delegates made a bold move. They agreed to throw out the Articles of Confederation and write a new constitution.

While the delegates—later known as the *framers*—agreed to design a new framework of government, they were divided on a key issue. Where should the government's power to rule come from? The states? Or the people? Under the Articles of Confederation, the answer was the states. Madison's answer in the Virginia Plan was that the government's power should come directly from the people.

The Virginia Plan The Virginia Plan called for a strong national government with three branches or parts. A legislative branch, or congress, would make laws. An executive branch would carry out ("execute") the laws. A judicial branch, or system of courts, would apply and interpret the laws.

Under the Virginia Plan, Congress was to be made up of two houses, the House of Representatives and the Senate. The number of lawmakers that a state could send to Congress depended on its population. States with a large number of people would have more representatives than smaller states.

Delegates from Virginia, Pennsylvania, and other large states liked the Virginia Plan. Having the new government represent people, not states, would give them more representatives and more power in both houses of Congress.

The New Jersey Plan Not surprisingly, delegates from the small states disliked the Virginia Plan. Just as the convention was about to vote on it, William Paterson of New Jersey introduced a rival proposal.

Like the Virginia Plan, the New Jersey Plan called for a government with three branches. However, the legislative branch would have just one house, not two. And each state would have an equal vote in Congress, no matter how big or small. This plan, Paterson argued, would keep the small states from being "swallowed up" by their more populous neighbors.

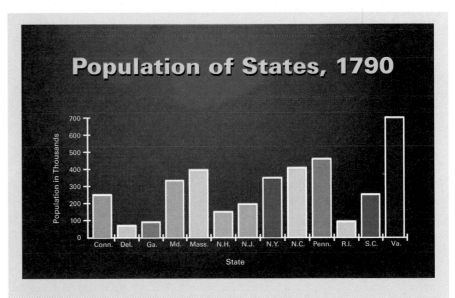

A major issue that confronted the Constitutional Convention was how to determine representation in the new government. Should each state have the same number of representatives, or should representation be based on population? Looking at this chart, which states would want equal representation for each state?

Roger Sherman, a signer of the Declaration of Independence, helped construct the Great Compromise that called for a Congress of two houses. Each state had equal representation in one house and representation based on population in the other house.

8.6 Resolution: The Great Compromise

The New Jersey Plan was warmly received by delegates from small states. The majority of delegates, however, saw Paterson's plan as little improvement over the Articles of Confederation and rejected it. But they could not agree on what should replace it.

Tempers Rise   The debate over who Congress should represent continued into July, with tempers rising day by day.

To most delegates from large states, representation based on population seemed both logical and fair. "Can we forget for whom we are forming a Government?" asked James Wilson of Pennsylvania. "Is it for men, or for the imaginary beings called States?"

To Wilson, the answer was obvious. But his logic could not overcome the fears of small-state delegates. One hot Saturday afternoon, Gunning Bedford of Delaware tore into the delegates from large states. "They insist," he said, "they will never hurt or injure the lesser states." His reply was, "I do not, gentlemen, trust you!" If the large states continued trying to "crush the smaller states," Bedford warned, "the small ones will find some foreign ally of more honor and good faith who will take them by the hand and do them justice."

Rufus King of Massachusetts was shocked at this reference to foreign powers. He shot back that he was "grieved, that such a thought had entered into the heart." Still, every delegate knew that Britain, France, and Spain were just waiting for the United States to fall apart so that they could pick up the pieces.

compromise an agreement in which both sides in a dispute agree to give up something they want in order to achieve a settlement

A Compromise Is Reached   Finally, a **compromise** was proposed based on a plan put forward earlier by Roger Sherman of Connecticut.

The compromise plan kept a two-house Congress. The first house, the House of Representatives, would represent the people. In this house, the number of representatives from each state would be based on the state's population. The second house, the Senate, would represent the states. Each state would have two senators, to be elected by their state legislatures.

The vote was very close, but the compromise plan was approved. This plan saved the convention and became known as the Great Compromise.

8.7 Issue: How Should Slaves Be Counted?

The Great Compromise kept the framers working together. But having agreed to base representation in one house of Congress on state population, they faced a new and difficult question. As Gouverneur Morris of Pennsylvania put it, "Upon what principle shall the slaves be computed in the representation?"

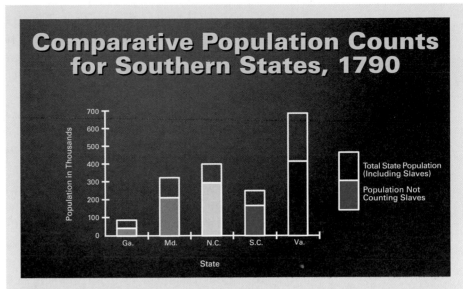

Comparative Population Counts for Southern States, 1790

How would representatives from the states shown in this chart want slaves to be counted? Would they want slaves to be counted as population for determining representation in Congress, or would they want slaves to be counted as property that could be taxed?

People or Property?   By the time of the convention, nine tenths of the slaves lived in the South. Like everyone else, southerners wanted as many representatives in the House as possible. They argued that slaves should be counted the same as any other people in determining representation.

Delegates from the North challenged this idea. Were slaves to be considered people with a right to be represented in Congress? Or were they property?

"Blacks are property and are used to the southward as horses and cattle to the northward," argued Elbridge Gerry of Massachusetts. Most northern delegates agreed. Slaves should be counted only as property that could be taxed like any other property. If slaves were to be counted as people in determining representation in Congress, said Morris, "then make them citizens and let them vote."

New Thinking on Slavery   This argument signaled a growing division over slavery among white Americans. As you read in Chapter 7, the Declaration of Independence and the Revolutionary War forced many whites to reexamine their views on slavery. Some became active in trying to end what they now saw as a great evil. Benjamin Franklin, for example, became president of an antislavery society in 1787. In the North, this new thinking led one state after another to pass laws ending slavery.

Although many southerners were uneasy about slavery, they were not yet ready to abolish it. The South's economy was still too dependent on the labor of enslaved African Americans. But some southern states did pass laws making it easier for owners to free their slaves.

The question facing the framers was how far they could take this new thinking in a nation that was becoming half-slave and half-free.

8.8 Resolution: The Three-Fifths Compromise

After a bitter debate, Madison proposed a compromise. Count each slave as three fifths of a person, he suggested, when determining a state's population. The delegates approved this idea, known as the *three-fifths compromise*.

The three-fifths compromise made a mockery of the statement in the Declaration of Independence that "all men are created equal." Still, the delegates adopted the compromise because it seemed the only way to keep the convention moving forward.

The Slave Trade A dispute over trade raised another question about slavery. To help business in the North, northern delegates favored giving Congress broad power to control trade between the states and other countries. This proposal made southern delegates nervous. They worried that Congress might try to tax southern export crops such as rice and tobacco. Southerners also worried that Congress would use its power over trade to outlaw the slave trade—the importing of slaves from Africa.

Southerners had reason to be fearful. By 1787, several states had outlawed the slave trade within their boundaries. And a majority of the convention's delegates favored ending the slave trade completely.

South Carolina and Georgia, however, objected that their economies would collapse without a constant supply of fresh slaves. Neither state would agree to any constitution that threatened the slave trade.

Again, the delegates settled on a compromise. Congress would have the power to control trade, but with two limitations. First, Congress could not place any tax on exports going to other countries. Second, Congress could not interfere with the slave trade for 20 years, or until 1808.

To satisfy southerners, the delegates also agreed to a provision known as the "fugitive slave clause." This clause said that escaped slaves had to be returned to their owners, even if they were caught in a free state.

Without such compromises, the states might never have come together in a single union. Still, the compromises only postponed the day when Americans would have to resolve the terrible contradiction between slavery and the ideals of liberty and equality. Meanwhile, generations of African Americans would spend their lives in bondage.

Northern and southern delegates agreed to a compromise regarding the slave trade. Congress could control trade but could not tax exports or interfere with the slave trade for 20 years.

Miss Fillis and child, and Bill, Sold at publick Sale in May 12th Christiansburg. montgomery County.

8.9 Issue: How Should the Chief Executive Be Elected?

Another major question facing the delegates concerned who would head the new government's executive branch. Early in the convention, Charles Pinckney urged the creation of a "vigorous executive." James Wilson followed with a proposal that a single person serve as the chief executive.

A sudden silence fell over the convention. A single executive? Just the words brought to mind unhappy memories of King George III.

Wilson broke the silence by explaining that good government depends on clear, timely, and responsible leadership. Such leadership, he said, is most likely to be found in a single person.

Many delegates felt that ordinary citizens, such as those pictured above, were not suited to elect the president. Roger Sherman stated, "The people should have as little to do as may be about the government. They want information, and are constantly liable to be misled."

One Executive or Three? Edmund Randolph of Virginia disliked this proposal. He preferred a three-member executive drawn from different parts of the country. Three people, he argued, could lead the country better than one.

Benjamin Franklin opposed a single executive for different reasons. "The first man put at the helm will be a good one," said Franklin, thinking of George Washington. "Nobody knows what sort may come afterwards." The next chief executive, he warned, might be overly ambitious or too "fond of war."

In spite of these objections, the framers agreed to a single executive, to be called the *president*. To keep this leader from becoming too kinglike, they limited the president's term to four years. A vice president was also to be elected to fill that term if the president died in office.

Choosing the Chief Executive Equally troubling was the issue of how to choose the chief executive. Some delegates wanted Congress to appoint the president. Gouverneur Morris objected. The president "must not be made a flunky of the Congress," he argued. "It must not be able to say to him: 'You owe your appointment to us.'"

Several delegates thought that the people should elect the president. Madison, however, argued that voters would naturally vote for someone from their own state. As a result, this method would not be fair to candidates from small states.

Still others suggested that the president be elected by a specially chosen group of "electors" from each state. Such a group, they felt, would be able look beyond state interests to make a wise choice for the entire country.

8.10 Resolution: The Electoral College

After some 60 votes on the issue of how to elect the president, the framers reached another compromise. Neither Congress nor the people, they decided, should choose the president and vice president. Instead, a special body called the **Electoral College** would elect the government's leaders.

The Electoral College System   The Electoral College is made up of electors who cast votes to elect the president and vice president every four years. Each state has as many electors in the Electoral College as the number of senators and representatives it sends to Congress.

The delegates left the method of choosing electors up to each state. Before 1820, state legislatures chose electors in most states. Today, the people choose their state's electors when they vote in presidential elections. The electors then cast their ballots for president and vice president on a date chosen by Congress.

Originally, the electors voted for two candidates without saying which one they preferred for president or vice president. The candidate receiving the most votes became president. The runner-up became vice president. As you will read in Chapter 11, this system caused great confusion in the election of 1800 and was later changed.

Political Parties and Elections   The Electoral College system looks very odd to most Americans today. In our age of instant communication, it is hard to appreciate the framers' concern that voters would not know enough about candidates outside their own state to choose a president wisely.

The delegates could not have predicted how quickly communications would improve in the United States. Nor could they foresee the rise of national political parties. Within a few years of the convention, political parties were nominating candidates for president and educating voters in every state about those candidates.

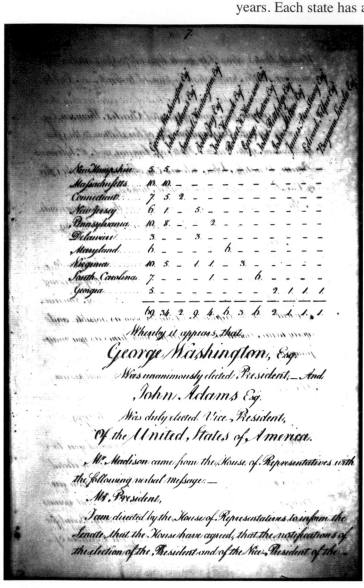

This is a copy of the Electoral College vote for the election of 1789. At that time, which states had the most electoral votes?

The Electoral College system still affects presidential elections today. In most states, the candidate who gets the most votes—even if less than a majority—gets all of that state's electoral votes. As a result, a candidate can win a majority in the Electoral College without necessarily winning a majority of the votes cast across the country. In fact, in the election of 2000, George W. Bush won the presidency over Al Gore, even though more voters nationally chose Gore.

8.11 The Convention Ends

By the end of summer, the hard work of designing the Constitution was finished. But the new plan still had to be accepted by the states.

ratify To formally approve a plan or an agreement. The process of approval is called *ratification*.

Approving the Constitution The first question was how many states would have to **ratify,** or approve, the Constitution before it could go into effect. Should ratification require approval by all 13 states? By a majority of 7 states? The framers compromised on 9 states.

The second question was who should ratify the Constitution—the people, or state legislatures? Ratification by state legislatures would be faster and easier. Madison, however, argued strongly that the people were "the fountain of all power" and should decide. The majority of delegates agreed. The Constitution would be ratified at special conventions by delegates elected by the people in each state.

Signing the Constitution
On September 17, 1787, the delegates declared the Constitution complete. As this last meeting began, Franklin shared his final thoughts, which would be printed in more than 50 newspapers.

"I confess that I do not entirely approve of this Constitution," he began. But no convention could produce a perfect plan. "It therefore astonishes me," he continued, "to find this system approaching so near to perfect… and I think it will astonish our enemies." Franklin added that he approved the final plan "because I expect no better, and because I am not sure that it is not the best." He urged "every member of the convention" to "put his name to this instrument."

Not everyone was won over by Franklin's words. Fourteen delegates left the convention before it ended, and three other doubters—Edmund Randolph and George Mason of Virginia, and Elbridge Gerry of Massachusetts—did not sign the Constitution either. Mason felt it gave too much power to the national government. Gerry refused to sign because he believed the new plan did not protect the rights of the people.

When the signing was over, Franklin confessed that he had often looked at the sun carved on the back of George Washington's chair and wondered whether it was about to rise or set. "But now," he said, "I have the happiness to know that it is a rising and not a setting sun." A new day was dawning for the United States.

Only 38 of the original 55 delegates signed the Constitution on September 17, 1787. Fourteen delegates had returned home before the conclusion of the convention, and three others also refused to sign.

8.12 The Constitution Goes to the Nation

Newspapers in every state printed the Constitution as soon as they could get it. What readers found was a plan that would create a "federal" system of government, in which a strong national government shared power with the states. Before long, the entire country was debating the same issues that had kept the convention in session for four long months.

The Federalists   Supporters of the Constitution called themselves Federalists. The Federalists argued that the Constitution would create a national government that was strong enough to unite the quarreling states into a single republic.

James Madison, Alexander Hamilton, and John Jay led the Federalist campaign for ratification. In a series of newspaper articles, they recalled the weaknesses of the government under the Articles of Confederation. They showed how the Constitution would remedy those weaknesses by creating a stronger, more effective Union of the states.

The Federalist leaders also addressed the fears of many Americans that a strong government would threaten their freedom or take away their rights. The powers given to the government, they pointed out, were strictly limited. In addition, those powers were divided among three branches so that no one branch could become too powerful. The influential articles written by Madison, Hamilton, and Jay were later collected and published as *The Federalist Papers*.

The Constitution had to be approved by 9 states. This political cartoon shows 11 states, pictured as columns, supporting the Constitution, while 2 states are hesitating.

The Anti-Federalists   Opponents of the Constitution were known as Anti-Federalists. They found much to dislike about the new plan. Congress, they feared, would ruin the country with taxes. The president had power enough to rule like a king. And the judicial branch would swallow up state courts.

The Anti-Federalists also complained about what was missing from the plan. Their main complaint was that the plan listed the powers of the government but not the rights of the people. Most of all, the Anti-Federalists feared change. The idea of giving up any state power to form a stronger Union made them uneasy.

After listening to the arguments, Madison wrote that the question facing the nation was "whether the Union shall or shall not be continued. There is, in my opinion, no middle ground to be taken."

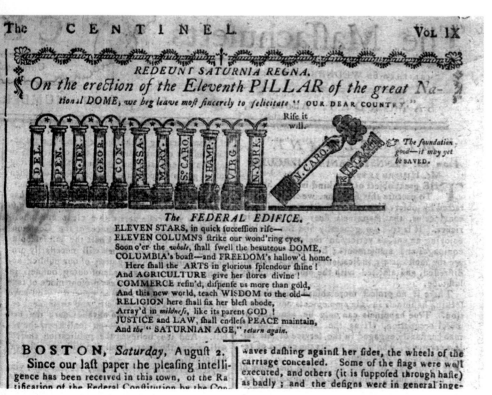

8.13 Chapter Summary

In this chapter, you read about the Constitutional Convention, the historic meeting that replaced the Articles of Confederation with a new plan of government for the United States. You used an annotated drawing of the Assembly Room at Independence Hall to organize information about the convention.

Both the Articles of Confederation and the Constitution that replaced it were attempts to realize the ideals of the American Revolution and the Declaration of Independence. Americans wanted a government that would protect their rights to "life, liberty, and the pursuit of happiness." The challenge was to create a government that was strong enough to guarantee these rights, yet not so strong that it could take them away.

The Articles of Confederation, which were America's first attempt at self-government, created a loose union of states under a weak central government. This government saw the new nation through the Revolutionary War. It also established a procedure for settling western territories. But, as Shays's Rebellion showed, it was too weak in peacetime to keep order or protect its own property.

Delegates to the Constitutional Convention quickly agreed to create a new constitution. For four long months, they argued in secret over a number of issues that often threatened to destroy the meeting. In the end, the framework they created included a series of compromises.

One of these agreements, the Great Compromise, established how the states were to be represented in the legislative branch of government. The three-fifths compromise settled how slaves were to be counted in determining a state's population. A third set of compromises created a single chief executive, to be chosen by the Electoral College.

The labors of the framers were only the beginning. Their new Constitution had to be ratified by the people through special state conventions. Federalists, who supported the Constitution, were opposed by Anti-Federalists, who feared the power of the proposed national government. Now it was up to the people to decide.

During the convention, Benjamin Franklin wondered if the sun painted on the back of George Washington's chair was rising or setting. At the conclusion of the convention, Franklin optimistically concluded it was a rising sun.

What are these buildings?

The Constitution: A More Perfect Union

9.1 Introduction

When the delegates left Independence Hall in September 1787, they each carried a copy of the Constitution. Their task now was to convince their states to approve the document that they had worked so hard to write.

As you read in the last chapter, writing the Constitution involved many compromises. Most of all, the framers, or writers, wanted a central government that would be strong and lasting, but not so strong that it endangered people's freedoms. In this chapter, you will see how the Constitution meets these goals.

The delegates wanted ordinary citizens to understand and support the Constitution. For this reason, they organized its contents very clearly. After a short introduction, they divided the Constitution into parts called *articles*. Then they split each article into numbered sections that present topics in a careful order.

This structure can help you find information in the Constitution. For instance, the first section in the article on the president describes how the president is chosen. The second section lists the president's powers. The third section lists presidential duties, and the fourth explains how the president can be removed from office. If you wanted to find out whether the president can sign treaties, where would you look?

One of the marvels of the Constitution is the way it combines a strong framework for the government with flexibility. In general, the delegates allowed Congress, the president, and the courts to add details to the basic framework. They also included procedures for changing the Constitution.

This combination of strength and flexibility makes the Constitution a "living document." Like a plant or an animal, the Constitution keeps its basic nature, yet it also changes with the times. The "living" quality of the Constitution helps to explain why it has survived for so long.

The delegates did their work well. More than 200 years after the Constitution was created for a new nation, a vastly different United States is still governed by this ingenious document.

Graphic Organizer: Illustration
You will use an image of the original parchment Constitution to record information about the organization and powers of the federal government.

The Pennſylvania Packet, *and Daily Advertiſer.*

[Price Four-Pence.] WEDNESDAY, SEPTEMBER 19, 1787. [No. 2690.]

WE, the People of the United States, in order to form a more perfect Union, eſtabliſh Juſtice, inſure domeſtic Tranquility, provide for the common Defence, promote the General Welfare, and ſecure the Bleſſings of Liberty to Ourſelves and our Poſterity, do ordain and eſtabliſh this Conſtitution for the United States of America.

ARTICLE I.

Sect. 1. ALL legiſlative powers herein granted ſhall be veſted in a Congreſs of the United States, which ſhall conſiſt of a Senate and Houſe of Repreſentatives.

Sect. 2. The Houſe of Repreſentatives ſhall be compoſed of members choſen every ſecond year by the people of the ſeveral ſtates, and the electors in each ſtate ſhall have the qualifications requiſite for electors of the moſt numerous branch of the ſtate legiſlature.

No perſon ſhall be a repreſentative who ſhall not have attained to the age of twenty-five years, and been ſeven years a citizen of the United States, and who ſhall not, when elected, be an inhabitant of that ſtate in which he ſhall be choſen.

Repreſentatives and direct taxes ſhall be apportioned among the ſeveral ſtates which may be included within this Union, according to their reſpective numbers, which ſhall be determined by adding to the whole number of free perſons, including thoſe bound to ſervice for a term of years, and excluding Indians not taxed, three-fifths of all other perſons. The actual enumeration ſhall be made within three years after the firſt meeting of the Congreſs of the United States, and within every ſubſequent term of ten years, in ſuch manner as they ſhall by law direct. The number of repreſentatives ſhall not exceed one for every thirty thouſand, but each ſtate ſhall have at leaſt one repreſentative; and until ſuch enumeration ſhall be made, the ſtate of New-Hampſhire ſhall be entitled to chuſe three, Maſſachuſetts eight, Rhode-Iſland and Providence Plantations one, Connecticut five, New-York ſix, New-Jerſey four, Pennſylvania eight, Delaware one, Maryland ſix, Virginia ten, North-Carolina five, South-Carolina five, and Georgia three.

When vacancies happen in the repreſentation from any ſtate, the Executive authority thereof ſhall iſſue writs of election to fill ſuch vacancies.

The Houſe of Repreſentatives ſhall chuſe their Speaker and other officers; and ſhall have the ſole power of impeachment.

Sect. 3. The Senate of the United States ſhall be compoſed of two ſenators from each ſtate, choſen by the legiſlature thereof, for ſix years; and each ſenator ſhall have one vote.

Immediately after they ſhall be aſſembled in conſequence of the firſt election, they ſhall be divided as equally as may be into three claſſes. The ſeats of the ſenators of the firſt claſs ſhall be vacated at the expiration of the ſecond year, of the ſecond claſs at the expiration of the fourth year, and of the third claſs at the expiration of the ſixth year, ſo that one-third may be choſen every ſecond year; and if vacancies happen by reſignation, or otherwiſe, during the receſs of the Legiſlature of any ſtate, the Executive thereof may make temporary appointments until the next meeting of the Legiſlature, which ſhall then fill ſuch vacancies.

No perſon ſhall be a ſenator who ſhall not have attained to the age of thirty years, and been nine years a citizen of the United States, and who ſhall not, when elected, be an inhabitant of that ſtate for which he ſhall be choſen.

The Vice-Preſident of the United States ſhall be Preſident of the ſenate, but ſhall have no vote, unleſs they be equally divided.

The Senate ſhall chuſe their other officers, and alſo a Preſident pro tempore, in the abſence of the Vice-Preſident, or when he ſhall exerciſe the office of Preſident of the United States.

The delegates to the Constitutional Convention met in secret at Independence Hall in Philadelphia in 1787. Ordinary citizens got their first look at the Constitution in newspapers like the *Pennsylvania Packet,* pictured above.

popular sovereignty the idea that the authority of government comes from the people

9.2 The Preamble Tells the Goals of Government

The delegates who crafted the Constitution chose each word carefully. Some of their best-known words come in the introduction, called the *Preamble.* The Preamble explains the reasons for the new government.

The Constitution begins with the memorable phrase "We the People." With these words, the delegates announced that the Constitution based its authority on the people themselves. The power to form the government did not come from the states or from the existing government. It did not come from a sovereign (ruler) appointed by God. Instead, the power came from ordinary Americans. This concept is known as **popular sovereignty**.

The Preamble then lists the goals of the new government. First, the delegates wanted to "form a more perfect Union." This meant building a country that could take advantage of the strengths the states gained from working together.

The Constitution also aims to "establish Justice." Americans wanted to be ruled by laws, not by the might of soldiers or the decisions of kings. The same laws would apply to all people.

The delegates hoped that the new government would "insure domestic Tranquility." By "tranquility," they meant peace and order. If the new system worked well, people would not fight the government or each other.

The new government would "provide for the common defense." In other words, the national government would be responsible for protecting Americans from foreign invaders. This would allow for stronger protection than if each state had its own army and navy.

The delegates wanted the new government to "promote the general Welfare." This means that it could support an economy and society in which people could prosper.

Finally, the delegates hoped to "secure the Blessings of Liberty to ourselves and our Posterity." By "posterity," the delegates meant the generations that would come after them. They wanted Americans to enjoy freedom then and in the future. We are their future, their posterity.

The delegates knew that these goals required a national government, but many people were suspicious of a strong central government. For this reason, the delegates tried to create a balanced framework that people could trust.

9.3 The Legislative Branch Makes Laws

For the framers of the Constitution, the first step in building a trusted government was to create a fair way to make laws. Article I of the Constitution gives the power to make laws to the **legislative branch** of government.

The Structure of Congress The Constitution creates a **bicameral** (two part) national legislature, called Congress. The two parts, or "houses," of Congress are the House of Representatives and the Senate.

Members of the Senate serve six-year terms so that they can enjoy some independence from the day-to-day opinions of voters. In contrast, members of the House serve two-year terms. As a result, they have to face the voters much more often. In this way, the framers tried to balance the independence and thoughtfulness of the Senate with the House's responsiveness to the changing wishes of the voters.

The framers also designed Congress to balance the rights of large and small states. Thus, while every state gets two senators, representation in the House is based on population. States with more people have more House representatives. To determine the number of representatives for each state, the Constitution calls for a census (a count of the population) every ten years. In time, the number of representatives in the House was set at 435.

The framers considered the Senate to be the "upper house" of the legislature. Its members are supposed to be wiser and more experienced than members of the "lower house." Senators must be at least 30 years old, while House members must be 25. Senators must have been citizens for nine years, House members for just seven years.

Originally, the Constitution allowed state legislatures to choose the two senators to represent their state. Today, however, senators are elected by popular vote (direct vote by the people).

legislative branch The law-making part of government, called the *legislature*. To *legislate* is to make a law.

bicameral Having two law-making parts. *Bicameral* comes from Latin words meaning "two rooms."

Senators and members of Congress listen to a speech given by the president in the chambers of the House of Representatives. The president must get congressional approval for his ideas before they can become law.

bill a proposed law

veto To reject a proposed law or a bill. Only the president can veto bills.

How Congress Passes Laws   The primary job of Congress is to make laws. Any member of the House or Senate can submit a proposal for a new law, called a **bill**. However, only the House can propose new taxes. If a majority in one house votes in favor of the bill, it is sent to the other house for debate. If both houses approve the bill, it goes to the president. The bill becomes a law if the president signs it.

The president can **veto** (reject) any proposed law. Congress can override the president's veto, which means passing the bill over the president's objections. But to do so requires a two-thirds majority in both houses.

The Powers of Congress   Article I spells out other powers of Congress. For example, only Congress can decide how to spend the money raised through taxes. Other congressional powers include the power to raise an army and navy, to declare war, to pay government debts, and to grant citizenship.

In addition, Congress may "make all laws which shall be necessary and proper" to carry out its other powers. This power, known as the "elastic clause," gives Congress the flexibility needed to do its job. Over the years, the elastic clause has been stretched to allow Congress to do many things that were never listed among its powers in the Constitution.

How a Bill Becomes Law

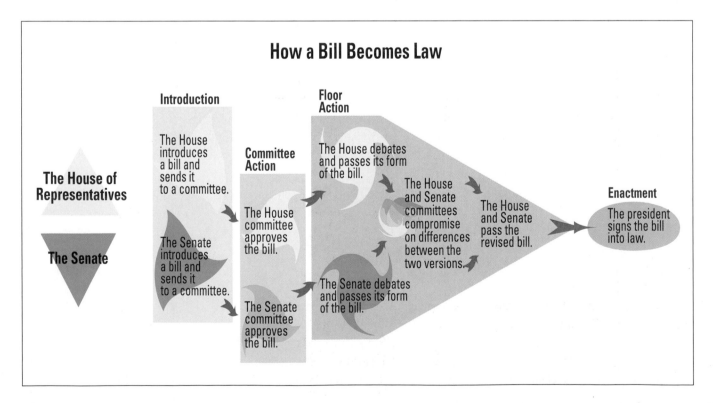

The House of Representatives

The Senate

Introduction

The House introduces a bill and sends it to a committee.

The Senate introduces a bill and sends it to a committee.

Committee Action

The House committee approves the bill.

The Senate committee approves the bill.

Floor Action

The House debates and passes its form of the bill.

The Senate debates and passes its form of the bill.

The House and Senate committees compromise on differences between the two versions.

The House and Senate pass the revised bill.

Enactment

The president signs the bill into law.

9.4 The Executive Branch Carries Out the Laws

A government needs people to carry out, or execute, the laws passed by the legislature. For instance, when Congress approves a tax, someone must collect the money. When Congress appropriates, or sets aside, money for low-cost housing, someone must build and manage the housing.

Article II of the Constitution describes the branch of government that fills this role, the **executive branch**. The head of the executive branch is the president. The president is often called the Chief Executive.

Electing the President As you read in Chapter 8, delegates at the Constitutional Congress were not prepared to let the people elect the president directly. Instead, they decided that the president would be selected by a group of "electors." Each state would have the same number of electors as it had representatives and senators. To win the presidency, a candidate needs a majority of the "electoral vote."

The president serves a four-year term. Under the Twenty-second Amendment, a president may be reelected only once. A new president makes a solemn promise called the *oath of office*. The Constitution gives the exact words of the oath. Notice that the president promises to "defend the Constitution." These words reinforce the importance of the Constitution as the basic law of the land.

A president must be a natural-born American citizen and at least 35 years old. The Constitution always refers to the president as "he." The delegates to the Constitutional Convention probably assumed that only men would ever vote or hold office. But nothing in the Constitution prevents a woman from being elected president.

Presidents are at the center of the American political stage. Here we see President Bush meeting with his cabinet and other close advisors.

executive branch the part of government that "executes" (carries out) the laws

impeach to formally accuse an official of a crime related to official duties

judicial branch the part of government, consisting of the Supreme Court and lower federal courts, that interprets the laws

The Powers of the President   The president does more than carry out laws passed by Congress. The president is commander in chief of the nation's military forces. He or she can, with the consent of the Senate, make treaties, or formal agreements, with other nations. The president nominates, or recommends, ambassadors (official representatives to other countries) and Supreme Court justices (judges). Finally, the president can grant pardons to people convicted of violating federal (national) laws.

The framers expected that the executive branch would need organizations called "departments" to carry out its duties. For example, the State Department handles relations with other nations. The Justice Department is involved in law enforcement as well as in court actions. The heads of executive departments are members of the president's cabinet, a formal group of advisors.

Today, the executive branch has over a dozen departments. Each department contains smaller, specialized agencies. For instance, the Department of Health and Human Services contains the Food and Drug Administration. This agency works to ensure that foods and medicines meet safety standards that have been set by Congress.

Removing the President   The Constitution gives Congress the power to remove a president or other officials from office if they commit certain crimes related to their duties. The House of Representatives can vote to impeach the president. To *impeach* means to formally accuse the president of the crimes specified in the Constitution. These include "Bribery, or other high Crimes and Misdemeanors." If the House votes to **impeach,** the Senate puts the president on trial, with the senators serving as the jury. If found guilty, the president is removed from office.

9.5 The Judicial Branch Interprets the Law

The framers intended the Constitution to be the "supreme Law of the Land." That means no other laws or actions by the government or by any state can conflict with the Constitution. Protecting the Constitution is one of the principal responsibilities of the third branch of government, the **judicial branch**. The judicial branch consists of the system of federal courts and judges.

Article III of the Constitution gives the basic framework of the judicial branch. It establishes the country's highest court, the Supreme Court. It also gives Congress the power to create "inferior" (lower) courts to meet the nation's needs.

In addition to protecting the Constitution, federal courts have the power to resolve disputes that involve national laws, the federal government, or the states. People accused of breaking national laws can be tried in federal courts.

The Federal Court System   Congress has authorized two main sets of inferior federal courts. These lower courts are called *district courts* and *appellate courts*.

Most cases involving federal laws are first heard in district court. The United States is divided into large geographic districts. Each district covers several states. Citizens can "appeal" decisions given in district court, which means asking a higher court to review the case. Courts that review cases are called *courts of appeal* or *appellate courts*. An appellate court only considers whether the original trial was fair and legal. A decision by an appellate court can be appealed to the Supreme Court.

The Powers of the Supreme Court   The Supreme Court is the last stop in the judicial system. Its decisions are final, and they are binding on all lower courts. The Constitution does not specify the size of the Supreme Court. Congress has set it at nine members, who are called *justices*. The Constitution says that all federal judges, including Supreme Court justices, serve for "good behavior." Once they are appointed, the justices usually serve on the Court for life.

A dispute goes directly to the Supreme Court only if it involves a state or an ambassador from another country. Any other case comes to the Supreme Court after a trial and an appeal in lower courts. Participants in either national or state courts may eventually appeal cases to the Supreme Court.

Every year, lawyers ask the Supreme Court to review thousands of cases, but they agree to consider only about a hundred. The Supreme Court usually reviews a case only if the justices think that the decision made by a lower court might conflict with the Constitution or a federal law. After hearing state-

The nine members of the U. S. Supreme Court hold very important positions in American government. Their legal opinions on such issues as gun control, the death penalty, abortion rights, and prayer in schools are enforced in every state.

ments from both sides, the justices debate among themselves and vote. Supreme Court decisions are announced and explained in writing. These decisions then guide later decisions in lower courts.

Early in its history, the Supreme Court defined the power of "judicial review." This is the power to decide whether laws and actions by the legislative and executive branches conflict with the Constitution. Courts all over the country rely on the Supreme Court for guidance about what is constitutional. Judicial review gives the Supreme Court great power in its role of protecting the "supreme Law of the Land."

9.6 Checks and Balances Between the Branches

The framers of the Constitution were very concerned about achieving a balance between a strong national government and protection for American freedoms. Dividing the federal government into three branches was one way they hoped to limit the government's power. But what would keep one branch from dominating the others? As one delegate to the Constitutional Convention pointed out, "From the nature of man, we may be sure that those who have power in their hands...will always, when they can...increase it."

Because of this concern, the framers developed a system that would enable each branch of the government to limit the power of the other branches. This system is called **checks and balances**.

Checking the Power of Other Branches   "Checks" allow one branch to block the actions of another branch. For instance, Congress has the power to pass laws. But the president can check this power by vetoing a bill before it becomes law. In turn, Congress can check the president's power by overriding the veto by a two-thirds vote in both houses.

Similarly, the judicial branch can check the actions of the other two branches. Through its power of judicial review, the Supreme Court can declare that a law, a treaty, or an executive action is unconstitutional.

This diagram illustrates the concept of checks and balances, one of the most significant features of the Constitution. Checks and balances prevent one branch of government from gaining too much power.

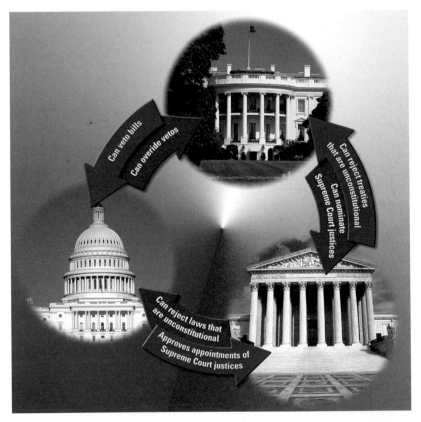

Can veto bills

Can override vetos

Can reject treaties that are unconstitutional

Can nominate Supreme Court justices

Can reject laws that are unconstitutional

Approves appointments of Supreme Court justices

Balancing the Power of Other Branches   "Balances" allow each branch of the government to have some role in the actions and power of the other branches. For instance, judges, ambassadors, and cabinet members are appointed only if the president nominates them and the Senate approves the nomination. Similarly, the president has the power to sign treaties, but they take effect only if the Senate approves them.

The powers of the judicial branch are also balanced against the powers of the other branches. Even though the Supreme Court can declare laws unconstitutional, it is the president who chooses federal judges—and the Senate must approve these appointments. In addition, Congress can impeach federal judges. In these ways, the legislative and executive branches have some role in the actions of the judicial branch.

These checks and balances keep any one branch of the federal government from being too strong. This balance of powers is one of the most important features of the American system of government.

9.7 The Amendment Process Changes the Constitution

amendment a change to the Constitution

The framers knew that the Constitution would need to be changed over time. As Thomas Jefferson said, the Constitution "belongs to the living and not to the dead." At the same time, they wanted the Constitution to provide a lasting and stable framework for the government. To maintain that stability, the framers made changing the Constitution possible, but difficult.

Changing the Constitution

Article V describes how changes, called **amendments,** can be made to the Constitution. Proposing an amendment requires a vote of two thirds of both houses of Congress, or a national convention called by Congress at the request of two thirds of the legislatures of all the states. Thus, either Congress or the states can start the process of amending the Constitution.

Proposing an amendment is only the first step. Before an amendment can become part of the Constitution, it must be approved by the legislatures (or by special conventions) in three quarters of the states. Once an amendment is approved, it becomes part of the supreme law of the land.

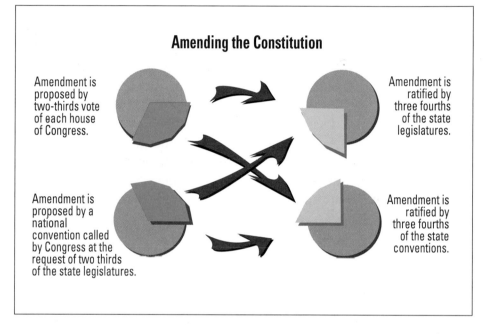

Amending the Constitution

Amendment is proposed by two-thirds vote of each house of Congress.

Amendment is proposed by a national convention called by Congress at the request of two thirds of the state legislatures.

Amendment is ratified by three fourths of the state legislatures.

Amendment is ratified by three fourths of the state conventions.

This chart shows the different ways that amendments to the Constitution can be proposed and approved. Amendments are proposed in Congress on a regular basis. The vast majority of the proposals fail.

Amendments So Far

Over the years, people have suggested more than 10,000 amendments to the Constitution. Only 27 of these have been approved.

The first ten amendments were added almost immediately after the Constitution was ratified (approved by the states). These amendments were demanded by many Americans in exchange for their support for the Constitution. Called the Bill of Rights, these ten amendments primarily guarantee specific rights to citizens. The Bill of Rights is so important in American history that the next chapter is devoted to it.

The other 17 amendments became part of the Constitution one at a time. Some of them changed the way certain public officials are elected. Others guaranteed the rights of certain groups of Americans. For instance, the Thirteenth Amendment made slavery illegal. The Nineteenth Amendment guaranteed women the right to vote. And the Twenty-sixth Amendment gave the right to vote to all citizens over the age of 18. Ideas for other amendments are proposed from time to time, but chances are that very few of them will become part of the Constitution.

The Constitution divides power between the federal and state governments. The idea behind the separation of powers is to create a unified nation while also protecting local control.

interstate commerce trade and other business dealings that cross state lines

9.8 The Federal System Connects the Nation and the States

The framers of the Constitution wanted a strong national government, but they also wanted the states to keep significant powers. They accomplished both goals by creating a federal system of government in which power is shared between the national and state governments.

Powers Belonging to the National Government Some powers are given solely to the national government. In general, these are powers best exercised by one central authority, such as declaring war and making treaties. The Constitution also says that only the national government can print and coin money. The framers had learned from bitter experience that having separate state currencies made no sense.

Similarly, Article I gives Congress the power "to regulate Commerce with foreign Nations, and among the several States, and with the Indian tribes." Known as the "commerce clause," this provision gives the national government the power to regulate **interstate commerce**. For example, a state cannot try to protect its own businesses and industries by taxing goods imported from other states. Under the Articles of Confederation, many states had done just that. As a result, interstate trade threatened to grind to a halt. In effect, the commerce clause made the entire United States a common market, or "free-trade zone."

There were several advantages to having the states share a common market. First, goods and resources could flow more easily across the country. This is important because different regions do different things well. For example, New Englanders might be very good at making cloth, but their region is not good for cotton growing. Southerners, meanwhile, might have lots of cotton but few factories for turning it into cloth. Making interstate trade easier for cloth makers and cotton growers helps both businesses thrive.

Second, the common market made it easier to create large businesses that crossed state lines. This was very important to companies like those that built the nation's railroads in the 19th century.

Third, the common market helped to create a single national economy. Under the Articles of Confederation, it was almost as if the country had 13 small economies. These could never have grown so diverse or powerful as the United States economy did.

Notice that the commerce clause also gives the national government the right to regulate trade with Indian tribes. In effect, the Constitution treats native tribes as foreign governments. Relations with these "nations within a nation" are the responsibility of Congress, not the states.

In the decades that followed, the national government made hundreds of treaties with different tribes, as if they were separate countries. But the promises made in those treaties were seldom kept. You will learn more about the fate of Native Americans in later chapters.

Powers Belonging to the States The Constitution does not spell out specific powers of the states. Instead, it says that the states retain any powers that are not given to the national government. For instance, the Constitution does not say anything about schools, marriage, establishing local governments, owning property, licensing doctors and lawyers, or most crimes. The states make the laws that guide these areas of American life.

The Constitution does, however, outline the responsibilities of states to each other. Article IV says that each state must give "full Faith and Credit" to the laws and court decisions of other states. This means accepting other states' laws and decisions as legal. For example, a

Under the Constitution, states make their own laws in most areas of everyday life, such as marriage. But states must honor marriages and other legal arrangements made in other states.

marriage or divorce legalized in one state is legal in every state. Similarly, states cannot negate contracts that people have made in other states. Like the commerce clause, the "full faith and credit" provision brings stability to business dealings.

States are also required to help each other track down fleeing criminals. Criminals cannot escape justice by fleeing to another state.

Finally, the Constitution does not allow one state to discriminate unreasonably against a citizen of another state. A state may not, for example, refuse to let a child who was born in another state attend its public schools.

Shared Powers   Federal and state governments also share some powers. For example, both can raise taxes, build roads, and borrow money.

If you think **federalism,** or the sharing of power, sounds complicated, you're right. Consider presidential elections. Congress sets the date for national elections, but the states register voters and run the elections. States count the ballots, but the national government organizes the Electoral College vote, which determines who will be president.

Federalism is also complicated because the Constitution provides only a general framework for the sharing of powers. Of course, there was no way for the framers to spell out rules for every possible situation. The federal system continues to evolve through new laws, court decisions, and constitutional amendments. No doubt it will continue to evolve long into the future.

federalism the constitutional system that shares power between the national and state governments

The Law of the Land   Americans may disagree about how to interpret the Constitution, but they may not ignore it. Article VI states that the Constitution and the laws flowing from it are the "supreme Law of the Land." This means that a state's constitution, laws, and judicial decisions must agree with the Constitution. They must also not conflict with any other federal laws or treaties. In addition, everyone who holds a state or federal office must promise to support the Constitution.

Political parties are not mentioned in the Constitution, but they have become a central part of the American political system.

9.9 Popular Participation in Government

The framers of the Constitution designed a government based on the will of the people. They expected people to take part in their own government and to hold leaders responsible for their actions.

If government is to reflect the popular will, then it makes sense for decisions to be based on what most people want. The Constitution therefore establishes the principle of majority rule. Laws are passed in Congress by majority vote, and elections are decided by a majority of voters.

It is through elections that most people have a say in what the government does. Leaders must listen to the voters, or they will not be elected (or reelected). Elections serve the vital function of expressing the will of the people.

But who exactly are "the people"? The framers did not specify who would have the right to vote. Over the years, states established various requirements for voting. It took many years of struggle to establish the principle that all citizens should have the right to vote. Women, for example, were not guaranteed this right until the Nineteenth Amendment was ratified in 1920.

Popular participation in government has evolved in other ways that are not part of the Constitution. For example, the Constitution makes no mention of political **parties.** Today, parties select most candidates for political office. Becoming active in party affairs is another way that voters can help choose their leaders and influence the positions they take on issues. You will learn about the first political parties in Chapter 11.

People also take part in government indirectly through **interest groups.** There are interest groups for almost any issue people might care about. Some interest groups represent businesses, industries, and workers. Some represent groups of people, such as churchgoers, women, or minorities. Some are organized around issues, such as the environment or health care.

Interest groups influence government in several ways. They rally public opinion, work to elect candidates who promise to listen to them, and try to persuade lawmakers and government officials to take actions they favor.

If the framers were alive today, they might be surprised to see the changes in the system they created. Yet the remarkable thing is how successful they were in building the basic framework of American democracy. As one historian has said, the Constitution "would become the rule of life for a country larger than any of the founders imagined, and would last longer than most of them dared hope."

9.10 Chapter Summary

In this chapter, you used an old parchment document to organize information as you studied how the Constitution defines the organization and powers of the federal government.

The Constitution created in 1787 is both strong and flexible. As the first words of the Preamble tell us, its authority comes directly from the people, not the states. Power is divided among three branches of government. The legislative branch makes the laws, the executive branch carries out the laws, and the judicial branch makes sure that the actions of the other two branches agree with the Constitution and federal laws. A system of checks and balances keeps any branch from gaining too much power. The Constitution also ensures that power is shared between the states and the national government in a system known as *federalism*.

For all its strength, the Constitution has been flexible enough to adapt to changing times. The framers purposely made the process of amending the Constitution difficult. Still, 27 amendments have been added since it was written. The first 10 amendments, called the Bill of Rights, guarantee the most cherished rights of American citizens. You will read about these amendments in the next chapter.

Americans have good reason to celebrate the Constitution. It has worked effectively for more than 200 years, ensuring that the American system of government remains strong today.

BILL OF RIGHTS

What is this bell?

What does it symbolize?

132

The Bill of Rights

10.1 Introduction

To James Madison, the creation of the Constitution seemed nothing less than "a miracle." By 1788, however, it seemed that it would take another miracle to get it adopted.

The adoption of the Constitution depended upon ratification, or approval, by 9 of the 13 states. Ratification started off smoothly, with Delaware, Pennsylvania, New Jersey, Georgia, and Connecticut all saying yes. Then came Massachusetts, where opposition ran strong.

When the Massachusetts ratification convention met early in 1788, defeat seemed certain. Opponents objected that the Constitution did not list the rights of the people. Many delegates said that they would not vote in favor of ratification unless such a list were added at once.

In desperation, the Constitution's supporters, the Federalists, looked to John Hancock, the state's governor. Hancock had stayed away from the convention, pleading a painful attack of gout. In fact, he was waiting to make an appearance until he could be sure to be on the winning side.

The Federalists tried to take advantage of Hancock's vanity. Virginia, they hinted, might not ratify the Constitution. If it did not, then George Washington, a Virginian, could not run for president. And if Washington didn't run, who was the best choice for the honor? Why, none other than the great governor of Massachusetts!

Hancock swallowed the bait. The governor was carried into the convention, his feet swathed in bandages. In a dramatic speech, he urged the delegates to approve the Constitution as it was. At the same time, he promised that the first task of the new Congress would be to amend the Constitution by adding a **bill of rights**.

The vote was close, but Massachusetts chose to ratify. The Federalists' strategy, "Ratify now, amend later," also worked well in other states. By the end of 1788, the Constitution was the law of the land.

In this chapter, you will learn how Federalists made good on their promise to add a list of rights to the Constitution. You will also learn how these rights work to protect Americans from abuses of government power.

Graphic Organizer: Visual Metaphor
You will use this visual metaphor of a protective shield to learn about the rights protected by the Bill of Rights.

10.2 Creating the Bill of Rights

For all his hopes, John Hancock never got to be president. By a narrow vote, Virginia did ratify the Constitution. In the first presidential election, held in 1789, George Washington became the nation's first president. John Adams of Massachusetts was chosen to be vice president.

When the first Congress met that year, no one seemed in much of a hurry to amend the Constitution. Representative James Madison, however, did not forget the promises made during the ratification debate. Originally, he had opposed adding a bill of rights to the Constitution. Such a listing seemed unnecessary to him. Thomas Jefferson helped change his mind. In a letter to Madison, Jefferson argued that "a bill of rights is what the people are entitled to against every government on Earth…and what no just government should refuse."

While Congress debated other issues, Madison sifted through nearly 100 proposed amendments. He chose those that seemed least controversial (likely to cause conflict) and presented them to Congress on June 8, 1789.

Critics jumped on Madison's proposals as meaningless "milk and water" cures for imaginary problems. The debate that followed was, in Madison's words, "extremely difficult." As months dragged on with no agreement, he wrote to a friend that the Bill of Rights had become a "nauseous project." Still, he persevered until Congress finally approved 12 amendments.

A young James Madison is pictured here. Often called "the Father of the Constitution," Madison also crafted the Bill of Rights that was debated and approved in 1791.

Ratification by the States   Under the Constitution, three quarters of the states must ratify an amendment before it can become law. The states rejected the first two amendments, which dealt with the size of congressional districts and congressional pay raises. Both amendments were considered unnecessary. By 1791, the required number of states (nine) had approved the other 10 amendments. Together, these 10 amendments form the Bill of Rights.

When Madison first proposed the Bill of Rights, some people saw his amendments as useless "paper barriers" against abuses of government power. For more than 200 years, however, his "paper barriers" have proven far stronger than even Madison might have hoped.

10.3 First Amendment Rights

Madison combined five basic freedoms into the First Amendment. These are freedom of religion, of speech, of the press, and of assembly, and the right to petition the government. Many people consider these basic freedoms to be the most important part of the Bill of Rights.

These First Amendment rights would have been meaningless, however, without some way to protect them. When a person believes that the government has violated these rights, he or she may challenge the government's action in court. The same is true of all other rights protected in the Constitution.

If the case reaches the Supreme Court, the nine Supreme Court justices decide how the Constitution applies to the situation. After hearing both sides, the justices vote on their decision. One of the justices from the majority side then writes a majority opinion. This document explains how the Court interpreted the Constitution to reach its decision. Any justices who disagree with the majority decision may write minority opinions explaining their reasoning.

As you read about First Amendment rights, you will see how the Supreme Court has applied these rights to real-life situations.

The Right to Worship Freely   The First Amendment has two guarantees of religious freedom. The first says, "Congress shall make no law respecting an establishment of religion." This means that Congress cannot make any faith the official religion of the United States. Nor can it make laws that favor any religion over another. In Thomas Jefferson's words, the amendment builds "a wall of separation between church and state."

How high should that wall be? The founders of the American republic disagreed about this question. For example, lawmakers in Virginia proposed using state taxes to help pay for teachers of religion. George Washington was among those who supported the idea as long as no particular church was favored. Opponents of the proposal, like James Madison, argued that government and religion should be completely separate.

In a 1971 case known as *Lemon v. Kurtzman,* the Supreme Court sided with Madison's view. This case challenged a Pennsylvania law that used public tax money to pay for books and teachers' salaries at private religious schools. The Court ruled that the law was unconstitutional because it allowed too close a connection between government and religion.

The beliefs of minority religious groups, like the Hare Khrishnas in this image, are protected by the Bill of Rights.

The second religious guarantee in the First Amendment says "Congress shall make no law … prohibiting the free exercise" of religion. This means that people can believe whatever they want about religion, without fear of punishment. However, they can't necessarily do whatever they want in the name of religious freedom. For instance, the Supreme Court has ruled that parents are not free to deny their children medical treatment or vaccinations because of their religious beliefs.

The Right to Free Speech and Press   The First Amendment protects freedom of speech and freedom of the press. The Supreme Court often treats these rights together as the right of free expression.

Freedom of the press is important because of the vital roles that the press plays in a democratic society. Newspapers, magazines, and other media such as books and television act as watchdogs on the government. They also allow for the free flow of ideas that citizens need to stay informed and to make up their own minds about important issues. Without a free press, democratic self-government would be impossible.

Americans had learned in colonial days that a free press was their best protection against abuse of government power. In 1735, John Peter Zenger was arrested for printing reports that the governor of New York had taken bribes. The prosecutors said that it was illegal to damage the governor's good name, even if Zenger had published the truth. Zenger's lawyer argued that no one should be jailed for "exposing and opposing arbitrary power by speaking and writing the truth." The jury agreed, and Zenger was freed.

Freedom of speech and the press are two of the most cherished rights held by Americans. Rallies, such as the one you see here, have been an important part of the American tradition since colonial times.

Freedom of the press also brings responsibilities, such as taking care not to spread false accusations or publish information that would be helpful to an enemy in wartime. In a similar way, freedom of speech brings responsibilities as well. Although the First Amendment protects the right to speak freely in public places, like streets and parks, that right is not unlimited. The Supreme Court has allowed limits on some kinds of speech, such as speech that endangers public safety. As one justice said, "The most stringent [strongest] protection of free speech would not protect a man in falsely shouting, 'Fire!' in a theater and causing a panic."

On October 16, 1995, hundreds of thousands of black men marched and assembled at a rally on the steps of the United States capitol. The demonstration was called the "Million Man March," and it illustrates the importance of the First Amendment.

The Supreme Court has ruled that "speech" means more than just words. Free expression includes "symbolic speech," or actions people take to express their opinions.

Protection of symbolic speech was an issue in the case of *Texas v. Johnson.* This case involved a man who had been convicted in Texas of burning an American flag as a form of protest. When he appealed his case to the Supreme Court, the justices overturned his conviction. No form of expression can be banned, the Court ruled, just because "society finds the idea itself offensive or disagreeable."

The Right to Assemble and Petition   The final two rights protected in the First Amendment are the right to peaceably assemble (meet together with others) and to petition (appeal to) the government.

The right to assembly means that citizens can use public property for meetings and demonstrations. Parades, protest marches, and political rallies are all forms of peaceful assembly protected by the First Amendment.

While the First Amendment protects peaceful meetings, it does not give people the right to close streets or buildings, or to protest violently. Police can arrest a speaker who urges listeners to riot or to break the law.

What if an assembly is peaceful, but the people watching it are not? This question came up in the case of *Gregory v. Chicago.* The case began when comedian Dick Gregory led a protest march to the home of Chicago's mayor. Residents in the neighborhood began throwing eggs and shouting insults at the marchers. Fearful of a riot, the police asked the marchers to leave. When the marchers refused, the police arrested them.

The marchers challenged their arrests in court, claiming that their protest was protected under the First Amendment's right of assembly. The Supreme Court agreed that the marchers had assembled peacefully. If anyone should have been arrested, it was the mayor's neighbors.

10.4 Citizen Protections

The next three amendments protect citizens from different kinds of government abuse. All three reflect the unhappy experience of American colonists under British rule.

Second Amendment: The Right to Bear Arms   During colonial times, Britain had used a standing (permanent) army to keep the colonists in line. After winning their independence, Americans remained suspicious of standing armies. They preferred to rely on volunteer state militias to protect their new nation. The Second Amendment states that "A well-regulated militia, being necessary to the security of a free state, the right of the people to keep and bear arms, shall not be infringed [limited]."

The meaning of this amendment has been much debated. Some argue that it protects the right of people to own guns *only* if they are part of an organized militia. (An example is today's National Guard.) Others believe that the Second Amendment protects the right of individuals to own weapons for their own self-defense.

Third Amendment: Quartering Troops in Homes   Before the Revolution, Britain had forced colonists to open their homes to British soldiers. The Third Amendment gave Americans the right to refuse such requests. "No soldier," it says, "shall…be quartered [housed] in any house, without the consent of the owner."

Today, soldiers are not quartered in homes. The Third Amendment remains important, however, as a warning to the government to respect the privacy of people's homes. As Justice Joseph Story said, "A man's house shall be his own castle, privileged against all civil and military intrusion."

In colonial America, guns were an important part of everyday life. They were used for hunting and for protection in a time when the police were often very distant. Also, militias protected colonists against outside invasion and Indian attacks.

The Granger Collection, New York

Fourth Amendment: Searches and Seizures The Fourth Amendment protects people and their belongings from "unreasonable searches and seizures." (A *seizure* is the act of forcibly taking control of a person or property.) Before arresting a person or searching someone's home, the police must show a judge that there is good reason for allowing the action. The judge then issues a **warrant** that says exactly who will be arrested or what will be searched.

The purpose of protections such as this one, wrote Justice Louis Brandeis, is to guarantee "the right to be left alone—the most comprehensive of rights and the right most valued by civilized men."

The police must follow careful guidelines in searches and seizures of private property.

10.5 Legal Rights and Protections

The next four amendments lay out the rights and protections that apply to people who are accused of crimes or are involved in other legal disputes.

Fifth Amendment: Legal Rights The Fifth Amendment is the longest amendment in the Bill of Rights. It lists five important rights of citizens involved with the justice system.

First, this amendment gives people who are accused of serious crimes the right to a grand jury hearing. A *grand jury* is a group of citizens who hear the government's evidence and decide whether it justifies a trial. If so, the grand jury issues an indictment, or formal charge. If not, the accused person is released.

Second, the amendment protects citizens from "double jeopardy." (*Jeopardy* means risk.) This means that a person who is tried for a crime and found not guilty cannot be tried again for that same crime.

Third, the amendment prohibits **self-incrimination**. This means that the police cannot force people to say things that might be used against them in a trial.

Today, police are required to remind people of their right to remain silent before they start to question them. They must also warn people that anything they do say can be used against them at a trial. This reminder is known as the "Miranda warning," after the case in which the Supreme Court defined this requirement.

The protection against self-incrimination also applies to **defendants** testifying in court. They may refuse to answer questions that might damage their case. This refusal is called "taking the Fifth."

warrant an order from a judge that authorizes police or other officials to take a certain action, such as searching someone's property

self-incrimination the act of giving testimony that can be used against oneself

defendants people who are required to defend themselves in a legal action; an example is an accused person who is put on trial for a crime

Next, the amendment says that a person cannot be "deprived of life, liberty, or property, without due process of law." The term *due process* means that the government must follow clear rules and act reasonably as it carries out the law. For example, the Supreme Court has ruled that every person should be presumed innocent until proven guilty. In addition, the government must prove its case against a defendant "beyond a reasonable doubt."

Finally, the Fifth Amendment says that the government cannot take someone's private property for public use "without just compensation." This means that the government must pay a fair price when it takes over a person's property for purposes such as building roads or parks.

Sixth Amendment: Criminal Trial Rights   The Sixth Amendment lists a number of rights that are designed to provide accused persons with fair trials. It begins with the right to "a speedy and public trial, by an impartial jury."

The right to a speedy trial means that people cannot be kept in jail for long periods before being judged at a trial. Speedy trials also ensure that witnesses testify while their memories of events are still fresh.

"Public" means that trials may not be held in secret. Citizens have a right to attend trials to make sure that justice is being done.

An accused person also has the right to be judged by a jury of people who live in his or her area. The jury must be "impartial," which means that jurors are not prejudiced (influenced) against the defendant. Courts have also said that prosecutors cannot exclude potential jurors just because of their race or gender.

Before a trial, the prosecutor must tell the accused person not only the charge, but the time and place of the supposed crime. This information is essential to the accused person in preparing his or her defense.

A defendant also has the right to hear and question all witnesses who testify at the trial. In addition, the defendant can ask the court to order reluctant (unwilling) witnesses to testify against their wishes.

Lastly, a defendant has the right to an attorney to assist in his or her defense. The Supreme Court has called this the most important of all the rights of accused persons. Without legal help, an innocent person may all too easily be convicted of a crime. In the past, only people with money to hire lawyers enjoyed this important right. Today, people accused of crimes are provided with a lawyer if they cannot afford to pay for one.

Seventh Amendment: Civil Trial Rights   Not all trials involve criminal actions. Some trials decide civil cases, or disputes between people or businesses. Civil cases typically involve money,

Lieutenant Colonel Oliver North testified before Congress in 1987. He took the Fifth Amendment to avoid giving evidence regarding his involvement in a government arms deal.

property, or family matters, such as divorce. The Seventh Amendment says that in all but the most minor cases, people involved in a civil case have a right to a jury trial.

The Seventh Amendment also says that "no fact tried by a jury shall be otherwise reexamined." This means that after a jury decides the facts of a case, no judge can overrule the jury's decision.

Eighth Amendment: Bail and Punishments The Eighth Amendment protects an accused person's rights both before and after trial. Before a trial, it forbids a judge from demanding "excessive" bail. *Bail* is money or property given to the court to hold until an accused person shows up at trial. If a defendant cannot pay bail, he or she stays in jail until trial. The Eighth Amendment prevents judges from using unreasonably high bail to keep someone in jail before his or her day in court.

After trial, if the person is found guilty, the Eighth Amendment forbids "excessive fines" and "cruel and unusual punishments." It does not say what such punishments are. In 1791, physical punishments like whipping and branding were common. Today, they are considered cruel. As Justice Thurgood Marshall has written, "A penalty that was permissible at one time in our nation's history is not necessarily permissible today."

The Supreme Court has interpreted this amendment to mean that punishments must be "proportionate" to the crime. Judges cannot, for example, impose long prison terms on people convicted of minor crimes. The Court has also ruled that the amendment prohibits inhumane prison conditions, such as depriving prisoners of food.

Today, Americans continue to debate whether the death penalty should be banned under the Eighth Amendment. Opponents of the death penalty have argued that executing anyone is a cruel and unusual punishment, no matter how horrible their crime. The Supreme Court has disagreed. In a 1976 case known as *Gregg v. Georgia,* the Court ruled that "the punishment of death for the crime of murder does not under all circumstances, violate the Eighth Amendment."

A lawyer tries to convince the jury to decide in his client's favor during a trial. The right to a jury trial is one of a number of citizen protections found in the Sixth Amendment.

Your Legal Rights and Protections

Before being charged with a crime, you are protected from • a search of your property without a search warrant. • arrest by the police without a warrant or good reason.	After an arrest, you have the right to • remain silent when questioned. • talk to a lawyer. • have a grand jury hearing to weigh the evidence against you.	Once indicted, you have the right to • know the charges against you. • reasonable bail. • a speedy trial. • a jury trial.
At your trial, you have the right to • question witnesses against you. • call witnesses in your defense. • refuse to answer questions that could harm you. • be defended by a lawyer.	If found innocent, you are protected from • double jeopardy.	If found guilty, you are protected from • excessive fines. • cruel or unusual punishments.

10.6 Other Rights and Powers

The last two amendments were included to help keep a proper balance of rights and power among the federal government, the people, and the states.

Amendment Nine: Rights Retained by the People One argument raised against putting a bill of rights in the Constitution was that no list could be complete. If some rights were listed and others were not, did this mean that people had only the listed rights?

The Ninth Amendment says that even though "certain rights" are listed in the Constitution, other rights not listed there are also "retained [kept] by the people." An example of this is the right to privacy.

Amendment Ten: Powers Reserved to the States The Tenth Amendment was included to protect the states from excessive federal power. It says that powers not given to the national government by the Constitution are "reserved to the states…or to the people."

This amendment was tested in *McCulloch v. Maryland*. The case began in 1816 when Congress chartered a national bank. Many states protested that the Tenth Amendment prohibited Congress from creating a bank because this power is not listed in the Constitution. In 1818, Maryland expressed its disapproval by levying a tax on the national bank.

James McCulloch, an officer of the Baltimore branch of the bank, refused to pay the tax. If the tax were set high enough, he protested, the state could drive the bank out of business. The effect would be the same as letting Maryland veto an act of Congress.

Maryland took McCulloch to court for failing to pay the tax. The state argued that not only was the bank unconstitutional, but under the Tenth Amendment, Maryland had the power to tax it.

The Supreme Court sided with McCulloch. It ruled that the Tenth Amendment did not forbid the chartering of a federal bank. The "necessary and proper clause" of the Constitution gave Congress the power to do so. The Court also ruled that when state and national power conflict, national power is supreme. Since Congress's power to create a bank was superior to Maryland's power to tax, the tax was unconstitutional.

This cartoon illustrates how passionate Americans are about their rights, even those that don't exist.

Calvin and Hobbes

by Bill Watterson

CALVIN AND HOBBES © 1990 Watterson. Reprinted with permission of UNIVERSAL PRESS SYNDICATE. All rights reserved.

10.7 Chapter Summary

In this chapter, you read about the Bill of Rights, the first 10 amendments to the Constitution. You used a visual metaphor to organize information about the amendments.

The promise of a bill of rights was key to getting the Constitution ratified by the states. As a member of the first Congress, James Madison proposed the amendments that guarantee the rights of citizens of the United States.

The First Amendment spells out five basic freedoms enjoyed by all Americans, from freedom of speech to the right to petition the government. The Second, Third, and Fourth Amendments specify protections for ordinary citizens against the abuse of government power.

The Fifth through Eighth Amendments are intended to guarantee fair treatment for people who are involved in legal actions.

The Ninth and Tenth Amendments concern the relationships among the federal government, the states, and the people.

As with other parts of the Constitution, the Supreme Court has interpreted the provisions of the Bill of Rights over time and applied them to new situations. But the spirit of these amendments remains much the same as when James Madison drafted them more than 200 years ago. His "unnecessary" addition to the Constitution has become the foundation of the rights and liberties Americans have learned to cherish.

The Bill of Rights contains many of the rights that we think of as American freedoms.

The Bill of Rights

Amendment I
...pecting an establishment of religion, or prohibiting the free exerci... ...t of the people peaceably to assemble, and to petition the Govern...

Amendment II
...essary to the security of a free State, the right of the people to kee...

Amendment III
...be quartered in any house, without the consent of the Owner, n...

Amendment IV
...re in their persons, houses, papers, and effects, against unreasona... ...but upon probable cause, supported by Oath or affirmation, a... ...s to be seized.

Amendment V
...for a capital, or otherwise infamous crime, unless on a present... ...naval forces, or in the Militia, when in actual service in time of... ...ce to be twice put in jeopardy of life or limb; nor shall be con... ...ed of life, liberty, or property, without due process of law; nor...

Amendment VI
...used shall enjoy the right to a speedy and public trial, by an im... ...mmitted, which district shall have been previously ascertained... ...be confronted with the witnesses against him; to have compulso... ...Counsel for his defence.

Amendment VII
...lue in controversy shall exceed twenty dollars, the right of tri... ...e-examined in any Court of the United States, than according to...

Amendment VIII
...r excessive fines imposed, nor cruel and unusual punishments a...

Amendment IX
...f certain rights, shall not be construed to deny or disparage oth...

Amendment X
...ed States by the Consti...

Thomas Jefferson was the first secretary of state. What were his responsibilities?

Alexander Hamilton was the first secretary of the treasury. What were his responsibilities?

Political Developments in the Early Republic

11.1 Introduction

The picture to the left shows four leaders in the first government formed under the Constitution. On the far right stands George Washington, who had been lured out of retirement to serve as the nation's first president. Seldom has a leader seemed more reluctant (hesitant) to take power. "My movements to the chair of government," he wrote on leaving home, "will be accompanied by feelings not unlike those of a culprit [criminal] who is going to the place of his execution."

Henry Knox sits opposite Washington. During the Revolutionary War, this Boston bookseller became a general and Washington's close friend and advisor. When Washington became president in 1789, he made Knox his secretary of war.

Take a close look at the two men facing out in the middle of the picture. Alexander Hamilton, who stands beside the president, served as Washington's secretary of the treasury. Thomas Jefferson, who stands behind Knox, served as secretary of state. It was his job to manage relations between the United States and other countries.

Washington chose Hamilton and Jefferson for these positions because of all they had in common. Both were strong patriots. Both had served their country during the Revolutionary War—Hamilton in the Continental Army and Jefferson in the Continental Congress. Both had brilliant minds.

For all they had in common, the two men were opposites in many ways. Hamilton dressed with great care. Jefferson was sloppy with clothes. Hamilton moved with precision. Jefferson slouched. Hamilton was a doer who moved briskly from task to task. Jefferson was a thinker who took time to explore ideas.

The expression "opposites attract" may be true in love, but not in politics. As you will discover in this chapter, Hamilton and Jefferson soon became political rivals. Their rivalry eventually gave rise to the nation's first political parties and a new way of electing the nation's president.

Graphic Organizer: Character Collage
You will make a character collage for these two men to understand the political differences between the Federalist and the Democratic-Republican Parties.

11.2 Launching the New Government

On April 30, 1789, George Washington took the oath of office as the first president of the United States. After his **inauguration,** Washington addressed both houses of Congress. He asked Congress to work with him to put into place "the wise measures on which the success of this government must depend." At times his hands shook so much that he had trouble reading his speech.

The Title Debate   Washington had reason to be nervous. The first Congress was deeply divided. Some members were eager to build a strong national government. Others were just as eager to limit the power of the new government. These differences showed up immediately in a debate over what title to use when addressing the president.

Vice President John Adams pointed out that European heads of government had titles like "Your Excellency" that showed respect for their office. The president, he argued, should have a similar title. Supporters of a strong national government agreed.

Others argued that such titles smelled of royalty and had no place in a democracy. A few members of Congress joked that the rather plump Adams should be given the title "His Rotundity" (His Roundness). The debate finally ended when Washington let it be known that he preferred the simple title "Mr. President."

Setting Up the Executive Branch   Next, Congress turned to the task of creating executive departments. As Washington had feared, arguments broke out at once over what those departments should be and what powers they should have.

Congress eventually approved three departments. A Department of State was set up to handle relations with other countries. A Department of War was established to defend the nation. A Treasury Department was set up to oversee the nation's finances. Congress also created an attorney general to serve as the president's legal advisor, and a postmaster general to head the postal system.

Washington chose men he trusted—such as Jefferson, Hamilton, and Knox—to fill these positions. He often met with them to ask for their ideas and advice. As you learned in Chapter 9, the heads of the executive departments became known as the president's *cabinet.*

Martha Washington, shown on the left, held tea parties on Friday evenings at the presidential mansion in New York City. At these parties, people could discuss important issues with President Washington, shown near the center.

11.3 Washington as President

The most critical problem facing the new government was money. The national treasury was empty. Congress had the power to raise funds through taxes. But its members argued endlessly about what to tax and by how much. In 1791, Congress finally agreed to place an excise tax on whiskey and other "luxury" goods, such as carriages. An *excise tax* is a tax on the production or sale of a product.

The Granger Collection, New York

The Whiskey Rebellion

Settlers living west of the Appalachian Mountains howled in protest. Western farmers found it too costly to haul their grain across the mountains to sell in eastern cities. Instead, they distilled their bulky wheat into whiskey, which could be shipped more cheaply. Many farmers complained that the tax made their whisky too expensive, and refused to pay it.

To end these protests, Congress lowered the excise tax in 1793. Most farmers began to pay up, but not the tax rebels of western Pennsylvania. These "Whiskey Boys" tarred and feathered tax collectors who tried to enforce the law.

Hamilton and Washington saw the Whiskey Rebellion as a threat to the authority of the national government. At Hamilton's urging, Washington led 13,000 state militia troops across the mountains to crush the rebels. Faced with overwhelming force, the rebellion melted away.

Jefferson thought that the idea of sending an army to catch a few tax rebels was foolish. Even worse, he believed, Hamilton was prepared to violate people's liberties by using armed force to put down opposition to government policies.

The Whiskey Rebellion was a serious challenge to the new nation's ability to enforce its laws. When several hundred Whiskey Boys refused to pay a federal whiskey tax, President Washington personally led 13,000 state militia troops to put down the rebellion.

The French Revolution   Meanwhile, the nation was caught up in a debate over events in France. In 1789, the French people rebelled against their king. The leaders of the French Revolution dreamed of building a nation based on "Liberty, Equality, and Fraternity," or brotherhood. Three years later, France became a republic and declared "a war of all peoples against all kings."

Many Americans were thrilled by the French Revolution. This was especially true of Jefferson and his followers, who began calling themselves Democratic-Republicans, or simply Republicans. The Republicans saw the French Revolution as part of a great crusade for democracy.

In time, news from France caused supporters of the revolution to think again. Cheered on by angry mobs, France's revolutionary government began lopping off the heads of wealthy nobles. Some 20,000 men, women, and children were killed.

Hamilton and his followers, who called themselves Federalists, were appalled by the bloodshed. Many Federalists were themselves well-off. After hearing about the fate of wealthy families in France, they began to finger their own necks, wondering whether such terrors could happen in the United States. "Behold France," warned one Federalist, "an open hell…in which we see…perhaps our own future."

When the French Revolution turned violent, and an endless stream of nobles was beheaded on the guillotine, many Americans withdrew their support for the revolution.

Washington's Farewell Address   The growing division between Republicans and Federalists so disturbed Washington that he agreed to run for a second term as president in 1792. He was the only person, Hamilton and Jefferson told him, who could keep the nation from pulling apart.

Near the end of his second term, Washington announced that he would not run again. Before leaving office, the president prepared a farewell address, or message. In it he reminded Americans of all that bound them together as a people. "With slight shades of difference," he said, "you have the same religion, manners, habits, and political principles. You have in a common cause fought and triumphed together."

Next, Washington warned of two threats to the nation's future. You will read about one of those threats— problems with other countries—in the next chapter. The other threat was "the spirit of party." It was natural for people to hold different opinions, Washington said. But he warned against the dangers of passionate loyalty to parties. If fighting between parties was not controlled, it could tear the young nation apart.

Despite his worries for the future, Washington had much to be proud of as he left office. The new government was up and running. The nation was growing so fast that it had added three new states—Kentucky, Tennessee, and Vermont. Most of all, Washington had steered his government safely through quarrelsome times. He left the nation united and at peace.

11.4 Alexander Hamilton and the Federalist Party

Washington's warnings did not stop the rise of political parties in the young nation. The Federalist Party appeared first during the debates over the ratification of the Constitution. Its most influential leader was Washington's energetic treasury secretary, Alexander Hamilton.

Personal Background   Hamilton was born in the West Indies and raised on the Caribbean island of St. Croix. When Hamilton was 13, a devastating hurricane struck the island. Hamilton wrote a vivid description of the storm that impressed all who read it. A few St. Croix leaders arranged to send the talented teenager to New York, where he could get the education he deserved. Once in America, Hamilton never looked back.

Hamilton grew up to be a small, slim, handsome man. His blue eyes were said to turn black when he was angry. But most of the time they sparkled with intelligence and energy. With no money or family connections to help him rise in the world, he made his way on ability, ambition, and charm.

George Washington spotted Hamilton's talents early in the Revolutionary War. Washington made the young man his aide-de-camp, or personal assistant. Near the end of the war, Hamilton improved his fortunes by marrying Elizabeth Schuyler. His new wife came from one of New York's richest and most powerful families. With her family's political backing, Hamilton was elected to represent New York in Congress after the war. Later, he served as a delegate from New York to the Constitutional Convention.

View of Human Nature   Hamilton's view of human nature was shaped by his wartime experiences. All too often, he had seen people put their own interests and personal profit above patriotism and the needs of the country. "Every man ought to be supposed a knave [scoundrel]," he concluded, "and to have no other end [goal] in all his actions, but private interests."

Most Federalists shared Hamilton's view that people were basically selfish and out for themselves. For this reason, they distrusted any system of government that gave too much power to the "the mob," or the common people. Such a system, said Hamilton, could only lead to "error, confusion, and instability."

This portrait of Alexander Hamilton was painted by John Trumbull, a famous American artist. Hamilton rose from poverty to become a leader of the Federalist Party. His brilliant career was cut short when he was killed in a duel with Vice President Aaron Burr, whom he had accused of being a traitor.

Best Form of Government   Federalists believed that the country should be ruled by "the best people"—educated, wealthy, public-spirited men like themselves. Such people had the time, education, and background to run the country wisely. They could also be trusted to make decisions for the general good, not just for themselves. "Those who own the country," said Federalist John Jay bluntly, "ought to govern it."

Federalists favored a strong national government. They hoped to use the new government's powers under the Constitution to unite the quarreling states and keep order among the people. In their view, the rights of states were not nearly as important as national power and unity.

Hamilton agreed. Having grown up in the Caribbean, Hamilton had no deep loyalty to any state. His country was not New York, but the United States of America. And he hoped to see his adopted country become a great and powerful nation.

Ideal Economy   Hamilton's dream of national greatness depended on the United States developing a strong economy. In 1790, the nation's economy was still based mainly on agriculture. Hamilton wanted to expand the economy and increase the nation's wealth by using the power of the federal government to promote business, manufacturing, and trade.

Before this could happen, the new nation needed to begin paying off the huge debts that Congress and the states had piled up during the Revolutionary War. In 1790, Hamilton presented Congress with a plan to pay off all war debts as quickly as possible. If the debts were not promptly paid, he warned, the government would lose respect both at home and abroad.

Hamilton's plan for repaying the debts was opposed by many Americans, especially in the South. Most southern states had already paid their war debts. They saw little reason to help states in the North pay off what they still owed.

To save his plan, Hamilton linked it to another issue—the location of the nation's permanent capital. Both northerners and southerners wanted the capital to be located in their section of the country. Hamilton promised to support a location in the South if southerners would support his debt plan. The

Alexander Hamilton believed that to become strong, the United States needed to develop businesses such as this foundry (factory for melting and shaping metal) in Connecticut.

debt plan was passed, and the nation's new capital—called the District of Columbia—was located in the South on the Potomac River between Maryland and Virginia.

Next, Hamilton asked Congress to establish a national bank. Such a bank, Hamilton said, would help the government by collecting taxes and keeping those funds safe. It would print paper money backed by the government, giving the nation a stable currency. Most important, the bank would make loans to businesspeople to build new factories and ships. As business and trade expanded, Hamilton argued, all Americans would be better off.

Once again, Hamilton's proposal ran into a storm of opposition. Where in the Constitution, his opponents asked, was Congress given the power to establish a bank? In their view, Congress could exercise only those powers specifically listed in the Constitution.

Hamilton established the first national bank, pictured here in 1933. The bank collected taxes, printed money, and made loans to businesses.

Hamilton, in contrast, supported a loose construction (broad interpretation) of the Constitution. He pointed out that the "elastic clause" allowed Congress to "make all laws which shall be necessary and proper" for carrying out its listed powers. Since collecting taxes was one of those powers, Congress could set up a bank to help the government with tax collection.

After much debate, Hamilton was able get his bank approved by Congress. Once established, the Bank of the United States helped the nation's economy grow and prosper.

Relations with Britain and France   When the French Revolution began, Hamilton hoped that it would lead to the "establishment of free and good government." But as he watched it lead instead to chaos and bloodshed, his enthusiasm for the revolution cooled.

When war broke out between France and England in 1793, most Federalists sided with Britain. Some were merchants and shippers whose business depended on trade with America's former enemy. Others simply felt more comfortable supporting orderly Britain against revolutionary France.

Hamilton leaned toward Britain for yet another reason. Great Britain was all that he hoped the United States would become one day: a powerful and respected nation that could defend itself against any enemy.

Thomas Jefferson was one of America's greatest patriots. His strongest support came from the middle class: farmers, laborers, artisans, and shopkeepers.

11.5 Thomas Jefferson and the Republican Party

Hamilton's success in getting his plans through Congress alarmed Thomas Jefferson and his fellow Republicans. In Jefferson's view, almost everything Hamilton did to put the United States on the path to greatness was instead a step down the road to ruin. The two men held very different views on almost everything.

Personal Background Jefferson was born in Virginia to an old and respected family. One of ten children, he was gifted with many talents. As a boy, he learned to ride, hunt, sing, dance, and play the violin. Later, he carried a violin with him in all his travels.

Jefferson was also a gifted student. When he entered college at age 16, he already knew Greek and Latin. He seemed to know something about almost everything. He once wrote that "not a sprig of grass [is] uninteresting to me." This boundless curiosity would remain with him all his life.

Jefferson grew up to be a tall, lanky man with reddish brown hair. Abigail Adams, the wife of John Adams, wrote that his appearance was "not unworthy of a God." With land inherited from his father, Jefferson set himself up as a Virginia tobacco planter. Like other planters, he used slaves to work his land.

Once he was established as a planter, Jefferson entered Virginia politics. As a politician, he lacked the ability to make stirring speeches. Instead, Jefferson spoke eloquently with his pen. His words in the Declaration of Independence and other writings are still read and admired today.

View of Human Nature Jefferson's view of human nature was much more hopeful than Hamilton's. He assumed that informed citizens could make good decisions for themselves and their country. "I have so much confidence in the good sense of men," Jefferson wrote when revolution broke out in France, "that I am never afraid of the issue [outcome] where reason is left free to exert her force."

Jefferson had great faith in the goodness and wisdom of people who worked the soil—farmers and planters like himself. "State a problem to a ploughman [farmer] and a professor," he said, and "the former will decide it often better than the latter."

Best Form of Government   Republicans favored democracy over any other form of government. They had no patience with the Federalists' view that only the "best people" should rule. To Republicans, this view came dangerously close to monarchy, or rule by a king.

Republicans believed that the best government was the one that governed the least. A small government with limited powers was most likely to leave the people alone to enjoy the blessings of liberty. To keep the national government small, they insisted on a strict construction, or interpretation, of the Constitution. The Constitution, they insisted, meant exactly what it said, no more and no less. Any addition to the powers listed there, such as the creation of a national bank, was unconstitutional and dangerous.

Along with a weak national government, Republicans favored strong state governments. State governments, they argued, were closer to the people, and the people could control them more easily. Strong state governments could also keep the national government from growing too powerful.

Ideal Economy   Like most Americans in the 1790s, Jefferson was a country man. He believed that the nation's future lay not with Federalist bankers and merchants, but with plain, Republican farm folk. "Those who labor in the earth," he wrote, "are the chosen people of God, if ever He had a chosen people."

Republicans favored an economy based on agriculture. They opposed any measures, such as the national bank, designed to encourage the growth of business and manufacturing. In their view, the national bank was not only unconstitutional, but anti-farmer. While the bank was happy to loan money to businesspeople to build factories and ships, it did not make loans to farmers to buy land.

Relations with Britain and France   Another issue that sparked heated arguments between Republicans and Federalists was the French Revolution. Most Americans favored the revolution until it turned violent and led to war. As you have read, most Federalists then turned against the new French republic and sided with Great Britain. For this change of heart, a Republican newspaper branded the Federalists "British bootlickers."

Despite the violence of the revolution, most Republicans continued to support France. While regretting the bloodshed, they argued that a few thousand noble heads was a small price to pay for freedom. For their

Agriculture, according to Jefferson, was the most important part of the economy. He believed farming was the best occupation because it kept people out of corrupt cities.

The Granger Collection, New York

Edmond Genet, who called himself Citizen Genet, was the French representative to the United States. During his stay, he attempted to convince Americans to join the French in their war with Britain. After Genet insulted President Washington, he was ordered to leave the country.

loyalty to France, Republicans were scorned in a Federalist newspaper as "frog-eating, man-eating, blood-drinking cannibals."

In 1793, the French government sent Edmond Genet to the United States as its new official representative. Genet preferred to be called "Citizen," using the title adopted by French revolutionaries to emphasize the equality of all people. His mission was to convince Americans that they should join France in its war against Great Britain.

Citizen Genet was welcomed by Republicans as a conquering hero. As he traveled about the country preaching against kings and nobles, he was cheered by large crowds. In Philadelphia, the nation's temporary capital, a great banquet was held in his honor. Throughout the city, people drank toasts to Citizen Genet and to France.

The cheering crowds quickly went to Genet's head. When he formally presented himself to President Washington, he expected another warm and enthusiastic reception. Washington, however, did not want to be drawn into war with Britain. His response to Genet was cool and dignified.

Genet began making speeches attacking the president. "I live in the midst of continual parties," he crowed. "Old man Washington is jealous of my success, and of the enthusiasm with which the whole town flocks to my house." These attacks on Washington brought thousands of Genet's supporters into the streets of Philadelphia. "Day after day," recalled Vice President Adams, the protesters "threatened to drag Washington out of his house, and effect [bring about] a revolution in the government, or compel it to declare war in favor of the French revolution."

This was too much, even for Jefferson. Washington's cabinet agreed that Genet had to go. Calling him "hotheaded...disrespectful, and even indecent toward the President," Secretary of State Jefferson asked the French government to recall its troublesome representative.

154 Chapter 11

11.6 The Presidency of John Adams

When the framers of the Constitution created the Electoral College, they imagined that the electors would simply choose the two best leaders for president and vice president. That was how the nation's first two presidential elections worked. By the third election in 1796, however, it was clear that political parties had become part of the election process.

The Republicans backed Thomas Jefferson for president that year. His support came mainly from farmers in the South and the West. The Federalists supported John Adams, who appealed to lawyers, merchants, shipowners, and businesspeople in the North. When the electoral votes were counted, John Adams was elected president by just three votes. Jefferson came in second, making him vice president. The nation's new top two leaders were political enemies from opposing parties.

The Alien and Sedition Acts   At first, President Adams tried to work closely with Jefferson. "Party violence," he found, made such efforts "useless." Meanwhile, Federalists in Congress passed four controversial laws known as the Alien and Sedition Acts. They argued that these laws were needed to protect the country from troublemakers like Citizen Genet. In fact, the real purpose of the Alien and Sedition Acts was to make life difficult for the Federalists' rivals, the Republicans.

Three of the laws, the Alien Acts, were aimed at **aliens** (noncitizens). The first lengthened the time it took for an immigrant to become a citizen with the right to vote—from 5 to 14 years. Since most immigrants voted Republican, Jefferson saw this law as an attack on his party. The other two Alien Acts allowed the president to either jail or deport (expel) aliens who were suspected of stirring up trouble. Although these laws were never enforced, they did frighten a number of French spies and rabble-rousers into leaving the country.

The Sedition Act made **sedition**—encouraging rebellion against the government—a crime. Its definition of *sedition* included "printing, writing, or speaking in a scandalous or malicious [hateful] way against the government… Congress…or the President." Hamilton approved of this law, believing that it would punish only those who published vicious lies intended to destroy the government.

aliens people who have come from other countries and are not yet citizens

sedition the crime of encouraging rebellion against the government

John Adams, a Federalist, was elected the second president of the United States by the slim margin of 71 votes to 68 votes in the Electoral College. Thomas Jefferson, a Democratic-Republican, became the vice president.

The Granger Collection, New York

In this cartoon, the devil and the British lion encourage a Federalist editor, represented by the hedgehog, to cross out important phrases from America's great documents. Liberty weeps at Benjamin Franklin's tomb.

Instead, the Sedition Act was used to punish Republican newspaper editors who delighted in insulting Adams. One, for example, called him "old, querulous [whiny], bald, blind, crippled, toothless Adams." Twenty-five people were arrested under the new law. Ten of them were convicted of printing seditious opinions.

The Virginia and Kentucky Resolutions Republicans viewed the Sedition Act as an attack on the rights of free speech and free press. Since the federal government was enforcing the act, they looked to the states to protect these precious freedoms.

Jefferson and Madison drew up a set of resolutions, or statements, opposing the Alien and Sedition Acts and sent them to state legislatures for approval. They argued that Congress had gone beyond the Constitution in passing these acts. States, therefore, had a duty to **nullify** the laws—that is, to declare them to be without legal force.

Only two states, Virginia and Kentucky, adopted the resolutions. The arguments put forward in the Virginia and Kentucky Resolutions were based on the **states' rights** theory of the Constitution. This theory holds that the states created the Constitution. In doing so, they gave up certain rights. Rights not specifically given to the federal government remained with the states. Of these, one of the most important is the right to judge whether the federal government is using its powers properly.

When no other states approved the Virginia and Kentucky Resolutions, the protest died. The states' rights theory, however, was not forgotten. It would be raised and tested again in the years ahead.

The New National Capital

In the fall of 1800, the federal government moved to the city of Washington in the District of Columbia. Most of the government's buildings were still under construction. President Adams' wife, Abigail, described the new "President's House" as a "castle" in which "not one room or chamber is finished." She used the large East Room for hanging laundry, as it was not fit for anything else.

After years of wandering from city to city, the national government finally had a permanent home.

The Granger Collection, New York

11.7 The Election of 1800

The move to Washington, D.C., came in the middle of the 1800 presidential election. Once again, Republican leaders backed Jefferson for president. Hoping to avoid the strange outcome of the last election, they chose a New York politician named Aaron Burr to run as his vice president.

The Federalists chose John Adams to run for reelection as president. Charles Pinckney of South Carolina was selected to run for vice president. Some Federalists would have preferred Hamilton as their presidential candidate, including Hamilton himself. But Hamilton was not eligible to run, because the Constitution requires the president to be an American-born citizen.

The Campaign The candidates outlined their campaign issues early. Jefferson supported the Constitution and states' rights. He promised to run a "frugal and simple" government. Adams ran on his record of peace and prosperity.

The campaign, however, was run more on insults than on issues. Republican newspapers attacked Adams as a tyrant. They even accused him of wanting to turn the nation into a monarchy so that his children could follow him on the presidential throne.

Charles Pinckney, above, and Aaron Burr, below, were vice presidential candidates in the election of 1800.

Federalist newspapers called Jefferson a "howling atheist" (someone who denies the existence of God). Jefferson, they charged, would "destroy religion, introduce immorality, and loosen the bonds of all society." Frightened by these charges, some elderly Federalists buried their Bibles to keep them safe from the "godless" Republicans.

The Divided Federalists Meanwhile, Hamilton and his followers refused to support Adams because of disagreements over the president's foreign policy. You will read more about this split in the next chapter. "We shall never find ourselves in the straight line of Federalism while Mr. Adams is President," moaned Oliver Wolcott, one of Hamilton's close allies.

As the campaign heated up, Hamilton worked feverishly behind the scenes to convince the men chosen for the Electoral College to cast their presidential ballots for Pinckney over Adams. Pinckney seemed more likely than Adams to value Hamilton's advice and his firm Federalist principles. With Pinckney as president, Hamilton believed that he would be able to personally guide the United States into the new century.

Political Developments in the Early Republic **157**

11.8 A Deadlock and a New Amendment

When the Electoral College voted early in 1801, it was clear that Adams had lost the election. But to whom? Under the Constitution, each elector cast two votes, with the idea that the candidate finishing second would be vice president. All of the Republican electors voted for Jefferson and Burr. The result was a tie between them.

Here, Republican women help Thomas Jefferson win the election in New Jersey in 1800. Women were allowed to vote in New Jersey until 1808.

Breaking the Tie   In the case of a tie, the Constitution sends the election to the House of Representatives. There, each state has one vote. Burr should have told his supporters in the House to elect Jefferson president, as his party wanted. Instead, he remained silent, hoping the election might go his way. When the House voted, the vote was another tie.

After 6 days and 35 ballots, it was Federalist Alexander Hamilton who broke the deadlock. He asked his supporters in the House to vote for Jefferson. Of the two Republicans, he said, "Jefferson is to be preferred. He is by far not so dangerous a man." The tie was broken, and Jefferson was elected president.

In 1804, the Twelfth Amendment was added to the Constitution to prevent such ties. The amendment calls for the Electoral College to cast separate ballots for president and vice president. If no presidential candidate receives a majority of electoral votes, the House of Representatives chooses a president from the top three candidates. If no candidate for vice president receives a majority, the Senate chooses the vice president.

A Peaceful Revolution   The election of 1800 was a victory for Jefferson and his Republican Party. But it was also a victory for the new system of government established by the Constitution. In other countries, power changed hands by means of a war or revolution. In the United States, power had passed from one group to another without a single shot being fired.

No one was more pleased by this outcome than the nation's third president. "The Revolution of 1800," Jefferson wrote with pride, was not brought about "by the sword." Americans had learned that it was better to fight for power with parties and ballots than with armies and bullets.

11.9 Chapter Summary

In this chapter, you read about the beginnings of political parties in the United States. You used character collages of Alexander Hamilton and Thomas Jefferson to learn about the political differences of the Federalist and Democratic-Republican Parties during the 1790s.

Both Alexander Hamilton and Thomas Jefferson served in President Washington's cabinet. Their responses to the Whiskey Rebellion and the French Revolution revealed the sharp differences between these talented men, and between their supporters.

Hamilton and the Federalists believed in a strong national government run by wealthy and well-educated men. Hamilton also favored using the national government's power to support business, manufacturing, and trade. Alarmed by the violence of the French Revolution, he and other Federalists favored Great Britain in its war with France.

In contrast, Jefferson and the Republicans looked to the mass of informed citizens to safeguard democracy. They championed the rights of states and the interests of farmers and planters. Republicans saw the French Revolution as a step toward democracy, and they attacked the Federalists' support for Great Britain.

During the presidency of John Adams, Federalists used the Alien and Sedition Acts to attack the Republicans. In response, Republicans urged states to nullify these laws.

The emergence of political parties revealed a need to change the Constitution. The election of 1800 resulted in a tie between the Republican candidates for president and vice president. To prevent such a tie from happening again, the Twelfth Amendment calls for electors to cast separate ballots for president and vice president.

While the young nation worked to strengthen its political institutions, it also faced threats from other countries. In the next chapter, you will read about how the United States responded to these threats.

The Granger Collection, New York

Thomas Jefferson, left, and Alexander Hamilton, right, led the first political parties of the new nation. Sharp differences existed between these two parties.

What does each of these
symbols stand for?

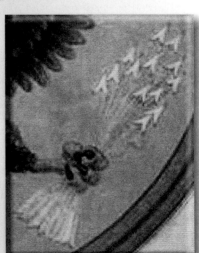

Foreign Affairs in the Young Nation

12.1 Introduction

Did you know that you are carrying a history lesson in your pocket or purse? You'll find it on any $1 bill. Take out a dollar and see for yourself!

Look first at the portrait of George Washington. Americans still honor this leader as "First in war, first in peace, and first in the hearts of his countrymen." But few remember that Washington defined our nation's first **foreign policy**. During his presidency, Washington set principles that would guide the United States in its future dealings with other nations.

Turn the dollar bill over. You will see two circles showing the Great Seal of the United States. For thousands of years, governments have used seals like this one to mark their approval of important documents. Our nation's founders thought that a national seal was so important that they began work on it the same day that they declared independence—July 4, 1776. In 1782, Congress approved the design we see today on our money.

The elements on the Great Seal represent the founders' hopes and dreams for the United States. For example, the unfinished pyramid on one side of the seal signifies strength and endurance. The bald eagle on the other side is a symbol of national power. In one talon, it grasps the arrows of war. In the other, it holds an olive branch of peace.

The arrows and olive branch are perfect symbols of two foreign policy choices. The United States could be actively involved in world affairs, risking war. Or it could avoid involvement in other nations' conflicts in the hope of staying at peace. Arrows or olive branch? Which choice would you have made for the new nation? In this chapter, you will read about four dilemmas faced by early presidents of the United States. Their decisions influenced the future of U.S. foreign policy.

Isolationism   Involvement

Graphic Organizer: Spectrum
You will use a spectrum to chart the range of U.S. foreign policy from isolationism to involvement.

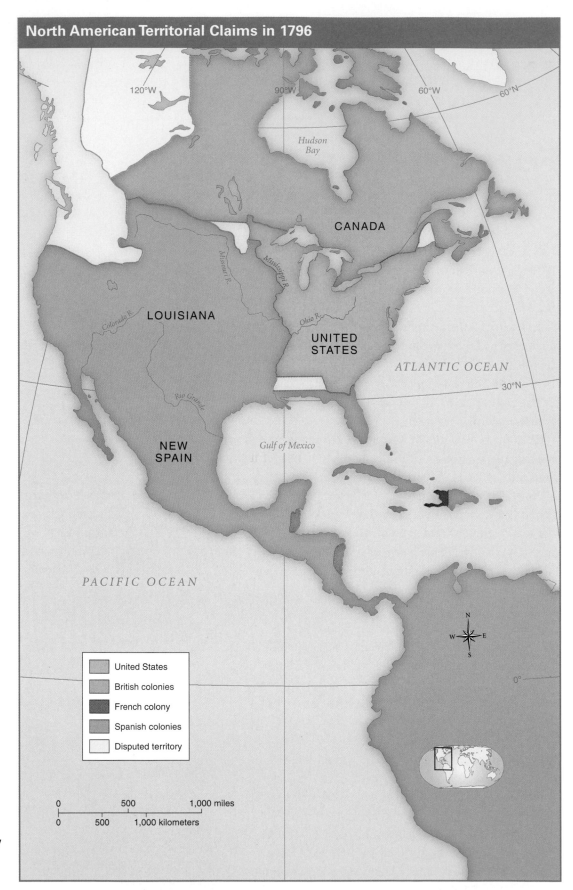

North American Territorial Claims in 1796

120°W
90°W
60°W
60°N

Hudson Bay

CANADA

Missouri R.

Mississippi R.

LOUISIANA

Colorado R.

Ohio R.

UNITED STATES

ATLANTIC OCEAN

30°N

Rio Grande

Gulf of Mexico

NEW SPAIN

PACIFIC OCEAN

N
W E
S

0°

	United States
	British colonies
	French colony
	Spanish colonies
	Disputed territory

| 0 | | 500 | | 1,000 miles |
| 0 | 500 | | 1,000 kilometers | |

In 1796, the United States was surrounded by colonies that belonged to European countries. What problems might this have caused for the newly independent United States?

12.2 President Washington Creates a Foreign Policy

neutrality a policy of not choosing sides in a war or dispute between other countries

isolationism a policy of avoiding political or military agreements with other countries; first established by George Washington

When George Washington took office as the nation's first president in 1789, America was looking weak. The army that Washington had commanded during the Revolutionary War had gone home. It had not been replaced for two reasons. First, an army would cost money that the government did not have. Second, Americans had learned that a standing army could be used to take away their liberty. State militia troops, they believed, could handle any threats the country might face.

And there were threats. The new nation was surrounded by unfriendly powers. To the north, Britain still controlled Canada. The British also refused to abandon their forts in the Ohio Valley, even though this region now belonged to the United States. To the south and west, Spain controlled Florida and Louisiana.

Events in Europe also threatened the new nation. As you read in Chapter 11, in 1789, the French people rose up against their king and declared France a republic. Most Americans were thrilled by the French Revolution. However, when France went to war with Britain in 1793, President Washington faced a difficult decision. During its own revolution, the United States had signed a treaty of alliance with France. (*Alliances* are agreements made with other nations to aid and support each other.) In that treaty, the United States had promised to aid France in time of war. Many Americans were eager to honor that pledge, even if it meant going to war with Britain.

Washington knew that the United States was not prepared for war. Instead, he announced a policy of **neutrality**. Under this policy, the United States would do nothing to aid either France or Britain in their war against each other.

Before leaving office, Washington summed up his foreign policy in his famous farewell address. The United States, he said, could gain nothing by becoming involved in other nations' affairs. "It is our true policy," he declared, "to steer clear of permanent alliances with any portion of the foreign world." Washington's policy of avoiding alliances with other countries became known as **isolationism**. For the next century, isolationism would be the foundation of American foreign policy.

George Washington was considered a hero even in his own time. Here we see Lady Liberty crowning a bust of Washington. The inscription on the bust reads "First in War, First in Peace, First in the Hearts of His Countrymen."

12.3 Dilemma 1: What Should President Adams Do to Protect American Ships?

Isolationism sounded good in theory. But it was often hard to stay out of other countries' conflicts. No one knew this better than John Adams, the nation's second president. Adams tried to follow Washington's policy of neutrality. With France, however, staying neutral proved difficult.

The Jay Treaty   French leaders hoped that Britain's refusal to leave the Ohio Valley would lead to war between England and the United States. Those hopes were dashed when Washington sent Chief Justice John Jay to London to settle things with the British. In the Jay Treaty, the British finally agreed to pull their troops from the Ohio Valley. French officials viewed the Jay Treaty as a betrayal by the United States. In July 1796, the French navy began attacking American merchant ships bound for Britain. Over the next year, French warships seized 316 American ships.

The XYZ Affair   President Adams sent three envoys, or representatives, to France to end the attacks. French Foreign Minister Talleyrand refused to receive the Americans. Instead, they were met by secret agents, later identified only as X, Y, and Z. The agents said that no peace talks would be held unless Talleyrand received a large sum of money as a tribute. (A *tribute* is a payment of money as the price of protection.) "No! No! Not a sixpence!" responded the shocked envoys.

The XYZ Affair outraged Americans. At the president's urging, Congress voted to recruit an army of 10,000 men. It also voted to build 12 new ships for the nation's tiny navy. The slogan "Millions for defense, but not one cent for tribute!" was heard everywhere as Americans prepared for war.

Meanwhile, Congress authorized American warships and privately owned ships, called *privateers,* to launch a "half-war" on the seas. During this undeclared war, American ships captured more than 80 armed French vessels.

As war fever mounted, John Adams—never a lovable leader—found himself unexpectedly popular. His Federalist Party also gained support in all parts of the country. The question facing Adams was whether doing the popular thing by unleashing the arrows of war on France was also the best thing for the country.

In this cartoon, American envoys meet with a French diplomat, depicted as a multiheaded monster holding a dagger. The cartoonist shared the very negative view of French diplomacy held by most Americans in the 1790s.

12.4 What Happened: Adams Pursues Peace

Adams knew that no matter how good war might be for the Federalist Party, it would not be good for the country. In February 1799, the president announced that he was sending a peace mission to France. Federalist leaders were furious. They pleaded with the president to change his mind, but Adams would not budge.

By the time the peace mission reached France, Napoleon Bonaparte had taken over the French government. The Americans found that Napoleon was eager to make peace with both Britain and the United States. He had already ordered an end to the seizure of American ships and the release of captured American sailors.

More importantly, Napoleon agreed to end France's 1778 alliance with the United States. While the alliance with France had been essential to the United States during the Revolutionary War, it had brought nothing but trouble since then. In exchange, the Americans agreed not to ask France to pay for all the ships it had seized. This meant that the U.S. government would have to pay American ship owners for their lost property. To Adams, this seemed a small price to pay for peace.

Choosing the olive branch cost Adams political popularity. His pursuit of peace caused strong disagreements within the Federalist Party. These disagreements cost Adams and the Federalists votes when he ran for reelection in 1800. As you read in Chapter 11, Jefferson defeated Adams, and the Federalist Party lost much of its support. Over the next few years, Adams would watch his Federalist Party slowly fade away.

Still, Adams had no regrets. He wrote:

I will defend my missions to France, as long as I have an eye to direct my hand, or a finger to hold my pen.... I desire no other inscription over my gravestone than: "Here lies John Adams, who took upon himself the responsibility of the peace with France in the year 1800."

Adams left the nation at peace and with no permanent alliances that might drag it into war. He had a right to feel proud.

The Granger Collection, New York

President Adams believed the United States needed a strong navy. Congress approved the construction of 12 warships, including the *Philadelphia*, which is shown under construction in the image above.

Foreign Affairs in the Young Nation   **165**

12.5 Dilemma 2: How Should President Jefferson Deal with Pirates?

Peace with France did not last long. By 1803, France and Britain were again at war. As the conflict heated up, both nations began seizing American ships that were trading with their enemy. President Thomas Jefferson, who took office in 1801, complained bitterly that "England has become a den of pirates and France has become a den of thieves." Still, like Washington and Adams before him, Jefferson tried to follow a policy of neutrality.

Impressment Remaining neutral when ships were being seized was hard enough. It became even harder when Britain began impressing, or kidnapping, American sailors to serve in the British navy. The British claimed that the men they impressed were British deserters. This may have been true in some cases, as some sailors may well have fled the terrible conditions on British ships. Yet thousands of unlucky Americans were also impressed and forced to toil on Britain's "floating hells."

American anger over impressment peaked in 1807 after a British warship, the *Leopard,* stopped an American warship, the *Chesapeake,* to search for deserters. When the *Chesapeake*'s captain refused to allow a search, the *Leopard* opened fire. Twenty-one American sailors were killed or wounded. This attack triggered another case of war fever, this time against Britain.

In the late 1700s and early 1800s, the Mediterranean Sea was filled with pirates who attacked American merchant ships. The United States paid tribute to leaders of the Barbary Coast states to prevent these attacks.

Piracy American ships faced a different threat from the Barbary States of North Africa: piracy, or robbery at sea. For years, pirates from Morocco, Algiers, Tunis, and Tripoli had preyed on merchant ships entering the Mediterranean Sea. The pirates seized the ships and held their crews for ransom.

Presidents Washington and Adams both paid tribute to Barbary State rulers in exchange for the safety of American ships. While Americans were shouting "millions for defense, but not one cent for tribute" during the XYZ Affair, the United States was quietly sending money to the Barbary States.

By the time Jefferson became president, the United States had paid the Barbary States almost $2 million. The ruler of Tripoli, however, demanded still more tribute. To show that he was serious, he declared war on the United States. Jefferson hated war. But he also hated paying tribute. The question was, which was worse?

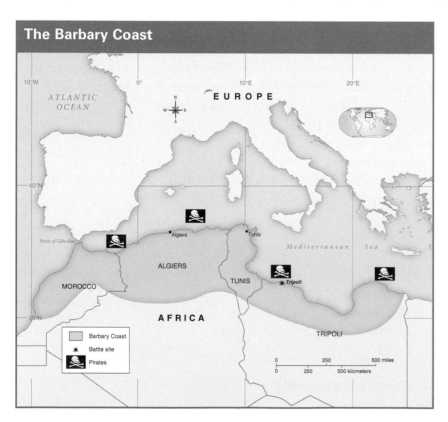

The Barbary Coast

12.6 What Happened: Jefferson Solves Half the Problem

As much as Jefferson hated war, he hated paying tribute more. In 1802, he sent a small fleet of warships to the Mediterranean to protect American shipping. The war plodded along until 1804, when American ships began bombarding Tripoli with their cannons. One of the ships, the *Philadelphia,* ran aground on a hidden reef in the harbor. The captain and crew were captured and held for ransom.

Rather than let pirates have the *Philadelphia,* a young naval officer named Stephen Decatur led a raiding party into

the heavily guarded Tripoli harbor and set the ship afire. A year later, Tripoli signed a peace treaty with the United States. Tripoli agreed to stop demanding tribute payments. In return, the United States paid a $60,000 ransom for the crew of the *Philadelphia.* This was a bargain compared to the $3 million first demanded.

Pirates from other Barbary States continued to plunder ships in the Mediterranean. In 1815, American and European naval forces finally destroyed the pirate bases.

Meanwhile, Jefferson tried desperately to convince both France and Britain to leave American ships alone. All of his efforts failed. Between 1803 and 1807, Britain seized at least a thousand American ships. France captured about half that many.

When diplomacy failed, Jefferson proposed an **embargo**—a complete halt in trade with other nations. Under the Embargo Act of 1807, no foreign ships could enter U.S. ports, and no American ships could leave, except to trade at other U.S. ports. Jefferson hoped that stopping trade would prove so painful to France and Britain that they would agree to leave American ships alone.

The embargo, however, proved far more painful to Americans than to anyone in Europe. Some 55,000 seamen lost their jobs while their ships rotted at deserted docks. In New England, newspapers cursed Jefferson's "Dambargo." They also pointed out that *embargo* spelled backward reads "O-grab-me," which made sense to all who were feeling its pinch.

Congress repealed the unpopular Embargo Act in 1809. American ships returned to the seas, and French and British warships continued to attack them.

President Jefferson ordered an embargo—a halt of trade with foreign countries—to force Britain and France to leave American ships alone. This political cartoon pictures the embargo (Ograbme) as a snapping turtle hurting U.S. merchants more than Britain or France.

embargo a government order that stops merchant ships from leaving or entering a country's ports

12.7 Dilemma 3: What Should President Madison Do to Protect Sailors and Settlers?

President James Madison, who took office in 1809, tried a new approach to protecting Americans at sea. He offered France and Britain a deal: If you agree to stop attacking American ships, the United States will stop trading with your enemy.

Napoleon promptly agreed to Madison's deal. At the same time, he gave his navy secret orders to continue seizing American ships headed for British ports. Madison, who desperately wanted to believe Napoleon's false promise, cut off all trade with Britain.

Meanwhile, the British continued seizing ships and impressing American sailors. Madison saw only one way to force Britain to respect American rights. He began to think about abandoning Washington's policy of isolationism and going to war with Britain.

New Englanders and Federalists generally opposed going to war. Merchants in New England knew that war would mean a **blockade** of their ports by the British navy. They preferred to take their chances with the troubles at sea.

Many people in the South and to the west, however, favored war. Like all Americans, they resented Britain's policy of impressing American sailors. They also accused the British of stirring up trouble among Native Americans in the states and territories to the northwest.

Trouble with the Indians was growing as settlers moved into the Ohio

This lithograph shows William Harrison, on the far left, encouraging his troops during the battle of Tippecanoe Creek. After the battle, Harrison's men discovered that the Indians were armed with British guns, which added to Americans' anger at the British.

The Granger Collection, New York

and Mississippi Valleys, pushing Indians off their lands. Two Shawnee Indians—a chief named Tecumseh and his brother, the Prophet—tried to fight back by uniting Native Americans up and down the Mississippi River into one great Indian nation. On November 7, 1811, Tecumseh and his warriors fought with a militia force led by Indiana governor William Henry Harrison in the Battle of Tippecanoe Creek. After the battle, Harrison's men found British guns on the battlefield.

Americans were outraged. Several young congressmen from the South and West, including Henry Clay of Kentucky and John C. Calhoun of South Carolina, were so eager for war with Britain that they were nicknamed "War Hawks." They argued that the way to make the northwestern frontier safe for settlers was to drive the British out of Canada. Once that was done, Canada could be added to the United States.

Losses at sea, national pride, and a desire to make the frontier safe for settlement all contributed to the reasons for war. Still, Madison hesitated. Was the nation strong enough to launch the arrows of war? Or should he hold tightly to the olive branch of peace?

12.8 What Happened: Madison Launches the War of 1812

Madison chose to abandon isolationism. At his request, Congress declared war on Britain on July 17, 1812. This was a very bold step for a nation with an army of 7,000 poorly trained men and a navy of only 16 ships.

Battles on Land and Sea   War Hawks were overjoyed when war was declared. They thought that conquering Canada was "a mere matter of marching." They were wrong. In 1812, 1813, and again in 1814 American forces crossed into Canada, but each time they were turned back.

The British, too, found the going much rougher than they expected. On September 10, 1813, an American naval force under Oliver Hazard Perry defeated and captured a British fleet of six ships on Lake Erie. Perry's victory enabled William Henry Harrison to push into upper Canada, where he defeated the British in a major battle. Chief Tecumseh, who was fighting on the side of the British, was killed in the fighting. But in December, the British drove the Americans back across the border.

By 1814, Napoleon had been defeated in Europe, and Britain was able to send 15,000 troops to Canada. American hopes of conquering Canada were at an end.

Meanwhile, in August 1814, another British army invaded Washington, D.C. The British burned several public buildings, including the Capitol and the White House. President Madison had to flee for his life.

Next the British attacked the port city of Baltimore. On September 13, an American lawyer named Francis Scott Key watched as the British bombarded Fort McHenry, which guarded the city's harbor. The bombardment went on all night. When dawn broke, Key was thrilled to see that the American flag still waved over the fort. He captured his feelings in a poem that was later put to music as "The Star-Spangled Banner."

The Shawnee leader Tecumseh, pictured above, united Native Americans in an attempt to halt the advance of white settlers onto Indian lands.

The United States gained control of Lake Erie during the War of 1812 as a result of the victory of naval forces under the leadership of Oliver Hazard Perry in 1813.

The Battle of New Orleans

Two days before the unsuccessful attack on Baltimore, a British fleet had surrendered to American forces after the Battle of Lake Champlain in New York. In Britain, news of this defeat would greatly weaken the desire to continue the war. But the news took time to travel, and in the meantime British commanders in America launched another invasion. This time their target was New Orleans.

The city was defended by General Andrew Jackson and a ragtag army of 7,000 militia, free African Americans, Indians, and pirates. On January 8, 1815, more than 7,500 British troops marched confidently into battle. Jackson's troops met them with deadly fire, turning the field of battle into a "sea of blood." Some 2,000 British soldiers were killed or wounded, compared with only about 20 Americans.

The Battle of New Orleans was the greatest American victory of the war. It was also totally unnecessary. Two weeks earlier, American and British diplomats meeting at Ghent, in Belgium, had signed a peace treaty ending the war. The news did not reach New Orleans until after the battle was fought.

Results of the War   Although both sides claimed victory, neither Britain nor the United States really won the War of 1812. And the Treaty of Ghent settled none of the issues that had led to the fighting. Instead, the problems of impressment and ship seizures faded away as peace settled over Europe. Still, the war had important effects.

First, Indian resistance in the Northwest weakened after Tecumseh's death. Over time, most of the Native Americans who fought with Tecumseh would be driven out of the Ohio Valley.

Second, national pride in the United States surged. Many Americans considered the War of 1812 "the second war of independence." By standing up to the British, they felt, the United States had truly become a sovereign nation.

Third, the war had political effects. The Federalists were badly damaged by their opposition to the war, and their party never recovered. Two of the war's heroes—William Henry Harrison and Andrew Jackson—would later be elected president.

12.9 Dilemma 4: What Should President Monroe Do to Support the New Latin American Nations?

James Monroe became president in 1817. After the excitement of the War of 1812, he was happy to return the nation to its policy of isolationism. Americans began to turn their attention away from Europe to events happening in their own backyard. From Mexico to the tip of South America, colonial peoples were rising up in revolt against Spain.

Latin America's Revolutions   In Mexico, the revolt against Spanish rule was inspired by a priest named Miguel Hidalgo. On September 16, 1810, Hidalgo spoke to a crowd of poor Indians in the town of Dolores. "My children," Hidalgo cried, "when will you recover lands stolen from your ancestors three hundred years ago by the hated Spaniards? Down with bad government! Death to the Spaniards!" Hidalgo's speech, remembered today as the "Cry of Dolores," inspired a revolution that lasted ten years. In 1821, Mexico finally won its independence from Spain.

Two other leaders liberated South America. In 1810, a Venezuelan named Simón Bolívar launched a revolution in the north with the cry: "Spaniards! You will receive death at our hands! Americans! You will receive life!" José de San Martín, a revolutionary from Argentina, led the struggle for independence in the south. By the end of 1825, the last Spanish troops had been driven out of South America.

The New Latin American Nations
Many Americans were excited by what Congressman Clay described as the "glorious spectacle of eighteen millions of people struggling to burst their chains and be free." The British also supported the revolutions, for their own reasons. Spain had not allowed other nations to trade with its colonies. Once freed from Spanish rule, the new Latin American nations were able to open their doors to foreign trade.

Other European leaders were not so pleased. Some even began to talk of helping Spain recover its lost colonies. In 1823, Britain asked the United States to join it in sending a message to these leaders, telling them to leave Latin America alone.

President James Monroe asked former presidents Thomas Jefferson and James Madison for advice. Should the United States do something to support the new Latin American nations? If so, what?

A Catholic priest, Miguel Hidalgo (lower center), inspired an independence movement in Mexico. In his upraised hand, Hidalgo holds the flames of revolution that spread throughout Latin America in the early 1800s.

Foreign Affairs in the Young Nation   **171**

secretary of state The head of the State Department, who oversees matters relating to foreign countries. The secretary of state is an important member of the president's cabinet.

doctrine a statement of official government policy, especially in foreign affairs

With the Monroe Doctrine by his side, Uncle Sam puts out his hands in warning to foreign powers to keep their "hands off" the Americas. Even though the Monroe Doctrine is over 180 years old, it still guides American presidents as they make foreign policy decisions.

12.10 What Happened: The U.S. Issues the Monroe Doctrine

Both Thomas Jefferson and James Madison liked the idea of joining with Britain to send a warning to the nations of Europe. Jefferson wrote to Monroe, "Our first and fundamental maxim [principle] should be, never entangle ourselves in the broils [fights] of Europe. Our second, never to suffer Europe to meddle with…America, North and South."

President Monroe's **secretary of state,** John Quincy Adams, agreed with Jefferson's principles. But he insisted that "it would be more candid [honest], as well as more dignified," for the United States to speak boldly for itself. Though never a bold man himself, Monroe agreed.

In 1823, President Monroe made a speech to Congress announcing a policy that became known as the Monroe **Doctrine**. Monroe stated that the nations of North and South America were "not to be considered as subjects for future colonization by any European powers." The United States, he said, would view efforts by Europeans to take over "any portion of this hemisphere as dangerous to our peace and safety."

Europeans denounced Monroe's message as arrogant. "By what right," asked a French newspaper, did the United States presume to tell other nations what they could do in "the two Americas"?

Americans, however, cheered Monroe's message. It made them proud to see the United States stand up for the freedom-loving people of Latin America. If Europeans "attempt to control the destinies of South America," boasted a Boston newspaper, "they will find…an eagle in their way."

In the years ahead, the Monroe Doctrine joined isolationism as a basic principle of U.S. foreign policy. The doctrine asserted that the United States would not accept European interference in American affairs. It also contained another, hidden message. By its very boldness, the Monroe Doctrine told the world that the United States was no longer a weak collection of quarreling states. It had become a strong and confident nation, a nation to be respected by the world.

12.11 Chapter Summary

In this chapter, you learned about the birth of foreign policy in the United States. You used a spectrum to chart the range of U.S. foreign policy from isolationism to involvement.

Our first president, George Washington, knew that the young United States was not prepared for war. He established a policy of isolationism that stated America would avoid alliances with other countries. Each president following Washington faced new dilemmas that required decisions about what was best for America.

During the presidency of John Adams, the dilemma involved French attacks on American ships. Adams followed Washington's policy of isolationism and kept America at peace.

President Thomas Jefferson also faced threats at sea. When peace talks failed, he declared an embargo on American ports. It, too, was unsuccessful. President James Madison then tried offering a trade deal to both France and Britain. But the attacks at sea continued. Madison finally abandoned isolationism and declared war on Britain in 1812. The War of 1812 resulted in a peace treaty with Britain.

President Monroe's dilemma was whether or not to support the new Latin American states. Monroe issued a policy called the Monroe Doctrine. In it, he warned the nations of Europe to leave the Americas alone. The Monroe Doctrine established the United States as a strong and confident nation, willing to stand up for its own freedom and that of others. In the next chapter, you will learn how the United States developed a stronger national identity in the first half of the 19th century.

The American eagle holds the olive branch of peace in one talon and the arrows of war in the other. Both are necessary to protect the "liberty" (at the top) that Americans hold so dear.

How is the flag above different from the one we use today?
How old do you you think it might be?
Can you guess why this flag is so famous?

13

A Growing Sense of Nationhood

13.1 Introduction

From a distance on that rainy night of September 13, 1814, you might have mistaken the bombardment for thunder, because sometimes the fuses burned too fast and the bombs burst in air. But Maryland lawyer Francis Scott Key knew better. He huddled in a boat in Baltimore harbor and watched as British warships fired on Fort McHenry.

Fort McHenry had a flag so big "that the British would have no trouble seeing it from a distance," boasted the fort's commander. It was 30 feet high and 42 feet long. Key knew that if the flag came down, it meant that both the fort and Baltimore had been lost. But when the sun came up, the flag was still there, and the British were retreating.

Key celebrated by writing a poem called "The Defence of Fort McHenry." Six days later it was published in the *Baltimore Patriot*. Before long, Key's poem had been reprinted across the country. In October 1814 it was set to music and sung as "The Star-Spangled Banner." This song stirred the pride of Americans for generations. In 1931 it was proclaimed the national anthem.

Inspirational moments like these during the War of 1812 helped give Americans a feeling of national identity. But what did being American mean? How was it different from being European? Alexis de Tocqueville, a French nobleman who toured the United States in 1831 and 1832, had an answer. "I do not know a country where the love of money holds a larger place in the heart of man," he wrote in his book *Democracy in America*. The pursuit of wealth was an important element of the emerging American identity. But there were other elements as well. And not all Americans wanted to be alike. In this chapter you will learn how a growing sense of nationhood developed during the early 19th century in spite of significant regional differences.

Graphic Organizer: Illustration
You will use an illustration of the American flag to organize information about Americans' growing sense of national identity.

13.2 Developing a Nation in a Land of Differences

The United States of the early 1800s was a very young country. Older adults could still remember when they were British subjects—and proud of it. (George Washington had once yearned to be a British officer.) Even after the Revolution, America seemed less a single nation than a collection of states.

A surge of patriotism following the War of 1812 helped forge a new national identity. The opposition of many Federalists to the war—a stance which their opponents denounced as disloyal—all but killed off the Federalist party. Leaders like James Monroe hoped that partisan strife (bitter fighting between political parties) was a thing of the past. Most Americans looked with pride on a rapidly growing country whose brightest days, they believed, lay ahead.

The American Landscape in the Early 1800s   Americans' image of their country in 1800 was very different from what it is today. Two out of every three Americans still lived within 50 miles of the Atlantic coast. Fewer than one in ten lived west of the Appalachians. These round-topped, forested mountains stretched like a bumpy spine from Maine through Georgia. They made travel between east and west very difficult.

Beyond the mountains the land flattened out, but was covered by dense woods. More and more settlers crossed the Appalachians in the early 1800s, felling trees and starting farms and mills. For Americans of the day, this land between the eastern mountains and the Mississippi River was "the West." Across the Mississippi lay a vast, unexplored wilderness.

Everywhere, travel was difficult and slow. Nothing moved faster than a horse could run —not people, not goods, not messages. News could take weeks to travel from one city to another, as the post office labored to deliver letters and newspapers over rutted, muddy roads.

In part because of the geographical differences, distinct regional lifestyles developed. This led to stereotypes, or exaggerated and sometimes scornful images of different groups. The "Yankees" of the Northeast, with its growing cities and bustling trade, were seen as enterprising, thrifty, and (in the eyes of southerners) quick to chase a dollar. The rich plantation owners of the South were seen as gracious, cultured, and (in the eyes of Yankees) lazy. The frontiersmen

America in 1820

CANADA

Oregon Country

ROCKY MOUNTAINS

Missouri R.

Mississippi R.

Michigan Territory

Unorganized Territory

Vt.   Me.
N.H.
N.Y.   Mass.
R.I.
Pa.   Conn.
N.J.
Ohio   Md.   Del.

Ill.   Ind.   Ohio R.
Ky.   Va.
APPALACHIAN MTS.
Tenn.   N.C.

Arkansas Territory
S.C.
Miss.   Ala.   Ga.
La.

ATLANTIC OCEAN

MEXICO

Fla. Terr.

N W E S

PACIFIC OCEAN

Gulf of Mexico

0   250   500 miles
0   250   500 kilometers

who sought their fortunes in the West were deemed rugged, hardy, and (in the eyes of easterners) crude. Many of America's leaders knew they would have to overcome geographical obstacles in order to truly unite the country. Among other ideas, they favored an ambitious program of building roads and canals to make transportation easier and faster.

Along with the White House, the rebuilt Capitol building, shown here in an 1824 painting, became a powerful symbol of national unity.

Symbols and Values   Uniting America required more than roads and waterways. It required citizens to *feel* American. One way to accomplish that was to build on Americans' pride in their government. After the British burned Washington, D.C., during the War of 1812, Congress hired architects to rebuild the White House and the Capitol in a style that would rival the grand, stately buildings of Europe. Congress complained about the cost, but not about the result. These magnificent buildings are revered to this day as national symbols.

Another national symbol was born during this period—Uncle Sam. Legend has it that the name came from Sam Wilson, a New York butcher. "Uncle Sam," it was said, had provided the army with meat during the War of 1812. More likely the name was made up to match the initials *U.S.,* for United States. After the war, Uncle Sam became a popular nickname for the federal government. (The cartoon figure of Uncle Sam came later.)

A national identity required more than symbols. There had to be shared values as well. White American men saw themselves as devoted to individualism and equality. Their commitment to these values may not have extended to slaves, Native Americans, or women. Still, they were united in the belief that they were different—and better—than Europeans.

Alexis de Tocqueville sensed this feeling just four days into his visit. "The Americans carry national pride to an altogether excessive length," he noted with irritation. By the end of his trip, however, he had come to admire this distinctly American spirit. That spirit was reflected in every aspect of life, from politics to art, music, and literature.

James Monroe was the last president to have fought in the Revolutionary War and the last to dress in the fashions of the 18th century. When he ran for reelection, no one opposed him. He won the Electoral College vote, 231 to 1.

capitalism an economic system based on the private ownership of farms and businesses

13.3 Politics: The Era of Good Feelings

After being elected president in 1816, James Monroe went on a "goodwill tour." Huge crowds greeted him so warmly that a newspaper proclaimed an Era of Good Feelings. Monroe's eight years as president are still known by this name today. To many Americans at the time, it seemed that a new period of national unity had dawned.

Economic Nationalism   The swelling of nationalist spirit was reflected in proposals that the federal government take a more active role in building the national economy. One of the leading supporters of such measures in Congress was Henry Clay of Kentucky.

Clay was a tall, slender man and an eloquent speaker, full of charm and intelligence. Driven by ambition, Clay longed to be president. He campaigned for the office five times, but never succeeded. A man of principle, Clay once stated proudly, "I would rather be right than be president."

Clay believed that America's future lay in **capitalism,** an economic system in which individuals and companies produce and distribute goods for profit. But he also believed that the national government had a role to play in encouraging economic growth. His "American System" called for high tariffs to protect industry, as well as federal spending on transportation projects like roads and canals.

A third part of Clay's plan was a new national bank to standardize currency and provide credit. Congress adopted this idea in 1816 when it created the second Bank of the United States. (The first national bank had been allowed to lapse in 1811.) The bank was a private business, but the federal government owned one fifth of it and deposited government funds there.

Another early champion of economic nationalism was South Carolina's John C. Calhoun. At six feet two inches, Calhoun was extremely tall for his time. He looked even taller because his thick black hair stood up as if he had seen a ghost. In Congress, Calhoun supported the national bank, a permanent road system, and a protective tariff. Yet in other ways he resisted federal power. By the 1830s, he would become the leading spokesman for states' rights, largely to protect slavery in the South. His career illustrates the tensions between nationalism and the pull of regional differences.

A third proponent of nationalism was Daniel Webster of Massachusetts. Nicknamed "Black Dan" for his dark hair and eyebrows, Webster served several terms in both the House and Senate. Unlike Clay, who was a War Hawk, Webster bitterly opposed the War of 1812. After the war, however, he voiced strong support for Clay's American System. "Let us act under a settled conviction, and an habitual feeling, that these 24 states are one country," he urged in 1825. Later, Webster would strongly debate Calhoun's claim that states had the right to defy the federal government.

Judicial Nationalism   Both nationalism and commerce had a friend in the Supreme Court's Chief Justice, John Marshall. Appointed by John Adams in 1801, Marshall wrote some of the most important court decisions in American history.

Marshall's decisions had two major impacts. First, they strengthened the role of the Court itself, as well as federal power over the states. Second, his rulings encouraged the growth of capitalism. Several specific cases show how. In *McCulloch v. Maryland* (1819), the Court confirmed Congress's power to create a national bank that was free from state interference. This strengthened the federal government's position. In another case, Marshall's Court ruled that business contracts were inviolable—they could not be broken, even by state legislatures. This ruling gave contracts a fundamental place in constitutional law. And in *Gibbons v. Ogden* (1824), the Court further reduced state powers. This case struck down a monopoly that New York State had granted to a steamboat company operating between New York and New Jersey. Only Congress, the Court said, had the authority to regulate interstate commerce. Besides strengthening the power of the federal government, this decision promoted business growth by limiting the ability of states to regulate transportation.

The End of the Era of Good Feelings   In 1824, four candidates (including Clay) competed to succeed Monroe as president. As you will learn in the next chapter, none of the candidates won a majority in the Electoral College. As a result, the election ended up in the House of Representatives. The House elected John Quincy Adams, the son of John Adams.

The House's action enraged the candidate who had received the most votes on election day, war hero and Indian fighter Andrew Jackson of Tennessee. Jackson vowed to renew the fight in the next election. The voters who rallied around him in 1828 would become the heart of a new political party, the Democrats. The Era of Good Feelings was over. "Partisan strife" was here to stay.

Americans were on the move in the 1800s, many of them bound for the frontier. Henry Clay envisioned a government-built sytem of roads and canals, linking the nation's far-flung regions.

13.4 Early American Art

Americans had brought European art traditions with them to the colonies, but by the 1800s they were developing styles all their own. Not all artists were professionals. Ordinary people produced many kinds of **folk art.** Men carved weathervanes and hunting decoys. Women sewed spare bits of cloth into quilts. Untrained artists created signs, murals, and images of national symbols like the flag. Such folk art was simple, direct, and often very colorful.

Most professional artists made a living doing portraits. The best-known portrait artist was Gilbert Stuart. The picture of George Washington on a dollar bill is adapted from a Stuart painting. When the British attacked Washington, D.C., during the War of 1812, President Madison's wife, Dolly, saved Stuart's painting of Washington from the burning White House.

Strangely enough, it was an Englishman whose work led to a uniquely American brand of fine art. When Thomas Cole arrived from England in 1818, he fell in love with America's immense and varied landscape. His most famous works feature both storm clouds and sunny skies over broad stretches of unspoiled land. The glowing light made a striking contrast to the stormy darkness. Fellow artists followed Cole's example and started what became known as the Hudson River School of painting. These painters focused on nature rather than people, often choosing to paint broad, scenic vistas. The gorgeous light in their paintings had an almost religious quality, as if God were smiling on America.

Other artists portrayed more particular aspects of nature. John James Audubon painted 435 finely detailed portraits of birds. In some respects, Audubon was more a naturalist than an artist. He made accurate, realistic studies of the species he observed in the fields and woods. No one in America would print his four-volume book, so he found a publisher in England. *The Birds of America* made him America's first internationally famous artist.

Philadelphia's George Catlin turned his eye on the natives of the American West. He saw that Native Americans' traditional ways were disappearing. For years Catlin crisscrossed the West, drawing the native people. He captured in rich colors their villages, their hunts, and their rituals.

By choosing as their subject the wondrous features of their new country, Americans gave their art a distinct identity. At times they may have presented dangerous landscapes in deceptively warm tones. Still, the vividness and optimism of their work accurately reflected the national outlook.

In *The Subsiding of the Waters of the Deluge* (1829), painter Thomas Cole bathed his scene in a soft, glowing light. Like other painters of the Hudson River School, Cole favored grand vistas that celebrated America's natural beauty.

13.5 Early American Music

Until the 19th century, music in America was performed and heard mostly in church. There were popular songs, too, but they were usually old tunes with new lyrics. The music for "The Star-Spangled Banner," for instance, came from an English drinking song.

With growing prosperity came an outburst of musical activity. In the North, orchestras played classical music from Europe. They also provided the music for the *cotillion,* in which groups of four couples danced together with elegantly coordinated movements. Dancers swirled through ballrooms, performing lively minuets, gavottes, mazurkas, and waltzes. Sometimes female dancers lifted their floor-length petticoats to show off their footwork. Displaying their ankles was considered quite daring.

In the South, slaves combined the hymns of white churchgoers with African musical styles to create **spirituals.** They also entertained themselves, and sometimes their masters, with rowdy folk songs accompanied by violin, drum, and banjo (an African American invention). In the South and West, square dances became common. These were less formal versions of the popular cotillion. As the fiddles played, a "caller" told dancers which steps to perform.

As demand for popular songs grew, composers answered with a stream of patriotic anthems. The best known is "America," written in 1832 by Samuel Francis Smith. It begins "My country, 'tis of Thee" and is sung to the tune of England's "God Save the King."

White composers from the South, inspired by the music of black slaves, created a type of music known as *minstrel songs.* The songs honored black music by mimicking it. But at the same

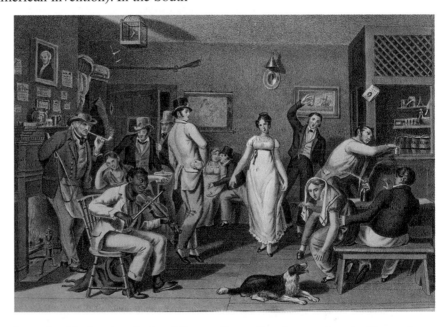

Some Americans relaxed with rowdy folk songs and fiddle tunes, while others listened to classical orchestras and performed formal dances. From North to South, music was a popular form of entertainment.

time, the performers mocked African Americans by blackening their white faces, wearing shabby clothes, and singing in exaggerated African American dialects. In 1828 Thomas Dartmouth Rice caused a national sensation with his song "Jump Jim Crow":

> *Weel about and turn about and do jis so*
> *Ev'ry time I weel about I jump Jim Crow.*

The racist phrase "Jim Crow," which came from Rice's black minstrel show character, had a long life. Many years later, laws that discriminated against African Americans would be known as "Jim Crow laws."

Minstrel shows became the most popular form of entertainment in America. They inspired composer Stephen Foster to write such famous songs as "Old Folks at Home," "Camptown Races," and "Oh! Susanna." Foster earned nationwide fame, proof that a truly American musical tradition had arrived.

13.6 Early American Literature

In 1820, a British writer sneered, "Who reads an American book, or goes to an American play, or looks at an American picture or statue?" In the eyes of Europeans, the United States was a culturally backward nation. Yet America was finding its cultural voice, especially in literature.

Like the painters of the Hudson River School, writers began to use uniquely American subjects and settings. One of the first to achieve literary fame was Washington Irving. He drew on German folklore for his colorful tales of "Rip Van Winkle" and "The Legend of Sleepy Hollow," but set them in the wilds of upstate New York. Irving's enchanted stories were an immediate hit.

The nation's first novelist was James Fenimore Cooper. In books such as *The Pioneers* and *The Last of the Mohicans,* Cooper wrote about the adventures of rugged frontiersmen venturing into the wilderness. His descriptions of frontier life and Native Americans attracted worldwide interest. In France, 18 publishers competed to publish *The Pioneers.*

Davy Crockett was a real-life frontiersman who spun tall tales about his life as a hunter, scout, soldier, and explorer. His election to Congress from Tennessee horrified Alexis de Tocqueville. The Frenchman described Crockett as a man "who has no education, can read with difficulty, has no property, no fixed residence, but passes his life hunting, selling his game to live, and dwelling continuously in the woods." But that very image captivated Americans, who saw Crockett as the fictional frontier hero come to life. Crockett's autobiography, which was full of his plain backwoods speech and rough humor, helped give popular literature a new, distinctly American accent.

New England's Henry Wadsworth Longfellow was one of the first serious American poets. He wrote America's first epic poem, *The Song of Hiawatha,* based on stories of Native Americans. Other poems, like his famous "Paul Revere's Ride," touched on patriotic themes. In "The Building of the Ship," Longfellow celebrated America's growing importance to the world:

> ...Sail on, O Ship of State!
> Sail on, O Union, strong and great!
> Humanity with all its fears,
> With all the hopes of future years,
> Is hanging breathless on thy fate!

In both subject matter and style, writers like these helped nurture the growing sense of national identity. In particular, they encouraged the myth of rugged individualism that for many people—at home and abroad—best characterized America.

Vol. 2.]   "GO AHEAD!!"   [No. 3.
THE CROCKETT ALMANAC 1841.

Tussel with a Bear. See page 9.

Containing Adventures, Exploits, Sprees & Scrapes in the West, & Life and Manners in the Backwoods.

Nashville, Tennessee. Published by Ben Harding.

In a typical humorous boast, frontiersman Davy Crockett described himself as "half-horse, half-alligator." Crockett became a national celebrity, and books bearing his name were best-sellers in the 1830s.

13.7 Chapter Summary

In this chapter, you read about the growing sense of nationhood in the United States after the War of 1812. You used an illustration of the American flag to organize information about the art, music, politics, and literature that helped define the American identity.

People in the United States during this time were extremely proud of their country. Despite regional differences, it seemed that Americans were building a nation unlike any seen before. Rulers served the people, rather than the other way around. Men who started with nothing became wealthy merchants or powerful statesmen. That was what it meant to be *American*. It was what made you different from a European.

But was it really true?

Yes, answered Frenchman Alexis de Tocqueville—but it was not the whole truth. African slaves and Native Americans, he wrote, "both occupy an equally inferior position in the country that they inhabit; both experience the effects of tyranny." Still, de Tocqueville was impressed with the spirit of equality and national pride among white men of different classes.

The growing sense of national identity was reflected both in politics and culture. Congress and the Supreme Court took action to strengthen the national economy and the power of the federal government. Distinctly American themes and styles developed in art, music, and literature.

Yet, beneath the surface, inequalities in wealth and regional differences—especially over slavery—threatened national unity. How much longer could America remain united? Not long, concluded de Tocqueville. "Slavery, in the midst of the democratic freedom and enlightenment of our age, is not an institution that can endure…. One must expect great misfortunes." Later on you will learn just how tragically right he was.

As a spirit of national pride swept the nation, painter George Caleb Bingham captured democracy at work on the frontier. *The Verdict of the People* (1855) shows a rough and lively crowd of voters, eager to hear the results of a local election.

What do you think
these voters are
talking about?

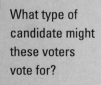

What type of
candidate might
these voters
vote for?

What type of
candidate might
these voters
vote for?

184

14

Andrew Jackson and the Growth of American Democracy

14.1 Introduction

The presidential campaign of 1828 was one of the dirtiest in American history. The election pitted John Quincy Adams, the nation's sixth president, against Andrew Jackson, the popular hero of the Battle of New Orleans.

During the campaign, both sides hurled reckless accusations at each other, a practice called *mudslinging*. Adams was called a "Sabbath-breaker" for traveling on Sunday. He was falsely accused of being an alcoholic. He was accused of using "public money" to purchase "gambling furniture" for the White House. In reality, he had used his own money to purchase a billiard table. Strangely, his opponents missed the one truth that might have shocked most Americans of the day. The very formal and proper Adams had a habit of swimming naked in the Potomac River.

The president's supporters lashed back. They called Jackson a crude and ignorant man who was not fit to be president. They also raked up old scandals about his wife, Rachel. She was accused of marrying Jackson while she was still knowingly wed to her first husband (not true). One newspaper even charged Jackson's mother with immoral behavior (not true). Jackson was called "Old Hickory" by his troops because he was as tough as "the hardest wood in creation." But when he read these lies, he broke down and cried.

When the votes were counted, Jackson was clearly the people's choice. But he was not the choice of the rich and **well-born** people who were used to running the country—the planters, merchants, bankers, and lawyers. "Nobody knows what he will do," wrote Senator Daniel Webster gloomily. "My fear is stronger than my hope."

Jackson proved to be a controversial president. In this chapter, you will discover how he was viewed by several groups of Americans, including not only the rich and well-born, but also the common people, Native Americans, and supporters of states' rights.

Graphic Organizer: Character Portraits
You will draw facial expressions on the figures to record various groups' reactions to Andrew Jackson's presidency.

185

People of every color, age, and class mobbed the White House to see Andrew Jackson take his oath of office. One observer claimed that the scene was like the invasion of barbarians into Rome.

14.2 The Inauguration of Andrew Jackson

On March 4, 1829, more than 10,000 people from every state crowded into Washington, D.C., to witness the inauguration of their hero. The visitors overwhelmed local hotels, sleeping five to a bed and drinking the city dry of whiskey. "I have never seen such a crowd here before," observed Senator Webster. "Persons have come 500 miles to see General Jackson, and they really seem to think the country has been rescued from some…disaster."

Many of the people flocking into the capital were first-time voters. Until the 1820s, the right to vote had been limited to the rich and well-born. Only white men with property, it was said, had the education and experience to vote wisely.

The new states forming west of the Appalachians challenged this argument. Along the frontier, all men—rich or poor, educated or not—shared the same opportunities and dangers. They believed they should also share the same rights, including the right to vote.

With the western states leading the way, voting laws were changed to give the "common man" the right to vote. This expansion of democracy did not yet include African Americans, Native Americans, or women. Still, over one million Americans voted in 1828, more than three times as many as voted in 1824.

Many of these new voters did believe that they had rescued the country from disaster. In their view, the national government had been taken over by corrupt "monied interests"—that is, the rich. Jackson had promised to throw these rascals out and return the government to "the people." His election reflected a shift in power to the West and to the farmers, shopkeepers, and small business owners who supported him.

After Jackson was sworn in as president, a huge crowd followed him to the White House. As the crowd surged in, the celebration turned into a near riot. "Ladies fainted, men were seen with bloody noses, and such a scene of confusion took place as is impossible to describe," wrote an eyewitness, Margaret Bayard Smith. Jackson was nearly "pressed to death" before escaping out a back door. "But it was the people's day, and the people's president," Smith concluded. "And the people would rule."

14.3 From the Frontier to the White House

self-made achieving wealth or influence through one's own effort rather than being born to a privileged family

The "people's president" was the first "**self-made** man" to occupy the White House. Jackson was born in 1767, on the South Carolina frontier. His father died before he was born, leaving Jackson, his mother, and two brothers in poverty. Young Andrew loved sports more than schoolwork. He also had a hot temper. He would pick a fight at the drop of a hat, a friend recalled, and "he'd drop the hat himself."

The American Revolution ended Jackson's childhood. When he was just 13, Jackson joined the local militia and was captured by the British. One day, a British officer ordered Jackson to polish his boots. "Sir," he replied boldly, "I am a prisoner of war and demand to be treated as such." The outraged officer lashed out with his sword, slicing the boy's head and hand. Jackson carried the scars to his grave.

The Frontier Lawyer   After the war, Jackson decided to become a lawyer. He went to work in a law office in Salisbury, North Carolina. He quickly became known as "the most roaring, rollicking, game-cocking, horse-racing, card-playing, mischievous fellow" in town. The wonder is that he learned any law at all.

In 1788, Jackson headed west to Nashville, Tennessee, to practice law. At that time, Nashville was a tiny clump of rough cabins and tents beside the Cumberland River. But the town grew quickly, and Jackson's practice grew with it. He soon earned enough money to buy land and slaves and set himself up as a gentleman planter.

Despite his success, Jackson never outgrew his hot temper. A slave trader named Charles Dickinson found this out when he called Jackson "a worthless scoundrel" and insulted his wife, Rachel. Enraged, Jackson

Andrew Jackson was born in this cabin in a small, rural South Carolina town. He received little formal education, but in his teens he studied law to become a lawyer.

Andrew Jackson and the Growth of American Democracy   **187**

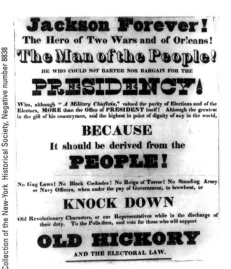

Jackson is shown here at the Battle of New Orleans, where he became a national hero after defeating the British.

challenged Dickinson to a duel (fight) with pistols, even though the slave trader was said to be the best shot in Tennessee. At that time, duels were accepted as a way of settling disputes between gentlemen.

Dickinson shot first, hitting Jackson in the chest. Jackson stiffened, raised his pistol, and fired a single shot. Dickinson fell dead to the ground.

"My God," a friend exclaimed on spotting Jackson's wound. "He missed your heart only by an inch." In fact, Dickinson's bullet was lodged so close to Jackson's heart that doctors were not able to remove it. "I would have hit him," replied Jackson, "if he'd shot me through the brain!"

The People's Choice Jackson entered politics in Tennessee, serving in both the House and Senate. But he did not become widely known until the Battle of New Orleans during the War of 1812. His glorious defense of the city made "Old Hickory" a national hero.

In 1824, the hero of New Orleans ran for president against three other candidates—Henry Clay, William Crawford, and John Quincy Adams. Jackson won the most popular votes, and the most electoral votes as well. But he did not have enough electoral votes for a majority. When no candidate has an electoral majority, the House of Representatives chooses a president from the three leading candidates.

Clay, who had come in fourth, urged his supporters in the House to back Adams. That support gave Adams enough votes to become president. Adams then chose Clay to be his secretary of state.

It made sense for Adams to bring Clay into his cabinet, because the two men shared many of the same goals. Jackson's supporters, however, accused Adams and Clay of making a "corrupt bargain" to rob their hero of his rightful election. And they promised revenge in 1828.

Jackson's supporters used the time between elections to build a new political organization that came to be called the Democratic Party, the name it still wears today. This new party, they promised, would represent ordinary farmers, workers, and the poor, not the rich and well-born who had taken control of the Republican Party.

Jackson's supporters worked feverishly to reach the nation's new voters. Besides hurling insults at Adams, they organized huge parades, picnics, and rallies. At these events, supporters sang "The Hunters of Kentucky"—the nation's first campaign song—and cheered for Old Hickory. They wore Jackson badges, carried hickory sticks, and chanted catchy campaign slogans like "Adams can write, but Jackson can fight."

The result was a great victory for Jackson. But it was also a victory for the idea that the common people should control their government. This idea became known as Jacksonian Democracy.

This campaign poster shows the theme of Jackson's presidential campaign. His supporters claimed that if Jackson were elected, government would finally be in the hands of ordinary people, not just the rich and well-born.

14.4 Jackson's Approach to Governing

Jackson approached governing much as he had approached leading an army. He listened to others, but then he did exactly what he thought was right.

The Kitchen Cabinet   Unlike earlier presidents, Jackson did not rely on his cabinet for advice. He made most of his decisions with the help of trusted friends and political supporters. These advisors were said to meet with him in the White House kitchen. For this reason, they were known as the "kitchen cabinet."

The rich and well-born looked at the "kitchen cabinet" with deep suspicion. In their eyes, the men around the president were not the proper sort to be running the country. One congressman accused Amos Kendall, Jackson's closest advisor, of being "the President's…lying machine!" Jackson ignored such charges and continued to turn for advice to men he trusted.

The Spoils System   Jackson's critics were even more upset by his decision to replace many Republican officeholders with loyal Democrats. Most of these **civil servants** viewed their posts as lifetime jobs. Jackson disagreed. Rotating people in office was more democratic than lifetime service, he said, because it gave more people a chance to serve their government. After a few years in office, civil servants should "go back to making a living as other people do."

Jackson's opponents called the practice of rewarding political supporters with jobs the **spoils system**. This term came from the saying that "to the victor belong the spoils [prizes] of war." They also exaggerated the number of Republicans removed from office. Only about 10 percent of all civil servants were replaced, and many who were dismissed from their jobs deserved to be. One was an official who had stolen $10,000 from the Treasury. When he begged Jackson to let him stay in office, the president replied, "Sir, I would turn out my own father under the same circumstances."

But Jackson could put patriotism above party loyalty. One dismissed postmaster started to undress to show the president his wounds from the Revolutionary War. Jackson snapped, "Put your coat on at once, sir!" The next day, the postmaster got his job back.

civil servants employees of the government

spoils system the practice of rewarding political supporters with government jobs

In this cartoon, titled "Office Hunters for the Year 1834," Andrew Jackson is a puppet master. He is pulling strings attached to people who want to be appointed to public offices. What is the cartoonist's opinion of Jackson?

The Granger Collection, New York

Andrew Jackson and the Growth of American Democracy   **189**

14.5 The Nullification Crisis

Jackson's approach to governing was tested by an issue that threatened to break up the United States. In 1828, Congress passed a law raising **tariffs,** or taxes, on imported goods such as cloth and glass. The idea was to encourage the growth of manufacturing. Higher tariffs meant higher prices for imported factory goods. American manufacturers could then out- sell their foreign competitors.

Northern states, humming with new factories, favored the new tariff law. But southerners opposed tariffs for several reasons. Tariffs raised the prices they paid for factory goods. High tariffs also discouraged trade among nations, and planters in the South worried that tariffs would hurt cotton sales to other countries. In addition, many southerners believed that a law favoring one region—in this case, the North—was unconstitutional.

Based on this belief, John C. Calhoun, Jackson's vice president, called on southern states to declare the tariff "null and void," or illegal and not to be honored.

Jackson understood southerners' concerns. In 1832, he signed a new law that lowered tariffs—but not enough to satisfy the most extreme supporters of states' rights in South Carolina. Led by Calhoun, they boldly proclaimed South Carolina's right to nullify, or reject, both the 1828 and 1832 tariff laws. Such an action was called *nullification*.

The constitutional issue of nullifi- cation had been raised by the Virginia and Kentucky Resolutions 30 years before. But now South Carolinians took the idea of states' rights even farther. They threatened to **secede** if the national government tried to enforce the tariff laws.

Jackson was outraged. "If one drop of blood be shed there in defi- ance of the laws of the United States," he raged, "I will hang the first man of them I can get my hands

In this cartoon, John C. Calhoun is the figure at the top of the staircase. Calhoun, who believed that states have the right to nullify, or reject, federal laws, is reach- ing toward a crown. The crown is a symbol of his desire for power. Andrew Jackson is pulling on the coattails of a Calhoun supporter. He wants to prevent Calhoun from trampling on the Constitution and destroying the Union.

on from the first tree I can find." He called on Congress to pass the Force Bill, which allowed him to use the federal army to collect tariffs if needed. At the same time, Congress passed a compromise bill that lowered tariffs still further.

Faced with such firm opposition, South Carolina backed down and the nullification crisis ended. However, the tensions between the North and the South would increase in the years ahead.

14.6 Jackson Battles the Bank of the United States

Jackson saw himself as the champion of the people, and never more so than in his war with the Bank of the United States. As you learned in Chapter 13, the Bank was partly owned by the federal government, and it had a monopoly on federal deposits. Jackson thought that the Bank benefited rich Eastern investors at the expense of farmers and workers as well as smaller state banks. He felt that the powerful Bank stood in the way of opportunity for hopeful capitalists in the West and other regions. He also distrusted the Bank's president, Nicholas Biddle, who was everything Jackson was not—wealthy, well-born, highly educated, and widely traveled.

The Bank's charter was due to come up for renewal in 1836, and Jackson might have waited until then to "slay the monster," as he called it. But Henry Clay, who planned to run for president against Jackson in 1832, decided to force the issue. Clay pushed a bill through Congress that renewed the Bank's charter four years early. He thought that if Jackson signed the bill, the president would lose votes from farmers who shared his dislike of banks. But if Jackson vetoed the bill, he would lose votes from businesspeople who depended on the Bank for loans. What Clay had forgotten was that there were many more poor farmers to cast votes than there were rich bankers and businesspeople.

Jackson vetoed the recharter bill. Even though the Supreme Court had ruled that the Bank was constitutional, Jackson called the Bank an unconstitutional monopoly that existed mainly to make the rich richer. The voters seemed to agree. Jackson was reelected by a large majority.

Rather than wait for the Bank to die when its charter ran out, Jackson decided to starve it to death. In 1833, he ordered the secretary of the treasury to remove all federal deposits from the Bank and put the money in state banks. Jackson's enemies called these banks "pet banks" because they were run by the president's supporters.

Delegations of business owners begged Jackson not to kill the Bank. Jackson refused. Slaying the Bank, he believed, was a victory for economic democracy.

GENERAL JACKSON SLAYING THE MANY HEADED MONSTER.

Andrew Jackson, on the left, is attacking the many-headed Bank of the United States with a veto stick. Nicholas Biddle is in the center wearing a top hat. The many heads represent the 24 state directors of the Bank. Vice President Van Buren is choking Massachusetts and Delaware.

Andrew Jackson and the Growth of American Democracy **191**

14.7 Jackson's Indian Policy

Sequoyah, pictured above, was a Cherokee Indian who developed an 86-letter alphabet for the Cherokee language. The alphabet contained both Roman letters and symbols that Sequoyah created. Even though these Native Americans developed what many whites considered an advanced civilization, wealthy planters and poor settlers were determined to force them out and seize their lands.

As a frontier settler and famous Indian fighter—Native Americans called him "Sharp Knife"—Jackson had little sympathy for Indians. During his presidency, it became national policy to remove Native Americans from the East by force.

White settlers had come into conflict with Native Americans ever since colonial days. After independence, the new national government tried to settle these conflicts through treaties. Typically, the treaties drew boundaries between areas claimed for settlers and areas that the government promised to let the Indians have forever. In exchange for giving up their old lands, Indians were promised food, supplies, and money.

Despite the treaties, Native Americans continued to be pushed off their land. By the time Jackson became president, only 125,000 Indians still lived east of the Mississippi River. Warfare and disease had greatly reduced the number of Indians in the East. Others had sold their lands for pennies an acre and moved across the Mississippi. Jackson was determined to remove the remaining Indians to a new Indian Territory in the West.

Most of the eastern Indians lived in the South. They belonged to five groups, called *tribes* by whites: the Creek, Cherokee, Chickasaw, Choctaw, and Seminole. Hoping to remain in their homelands, these Indians had adopted many white ways. Most had given up hunting to become farmers. Many had learned to read and write. The Cherokee even had their own written language, a newspaper, and a constitution modeled on the U.S. Constitution. Whites called these Indians the "Five Civilized Tribes."

While the Five Civilized Tribes may have hoped to live in peace with their neighbors, whites did not share this goal. As the cotton kingdom spread westward, wealthy planters and poor settlers alike looked greedily at Indian homelands. The Indians, they decided, had to go.

The Indian Removal Act   In 1830, urged on by President Jackson, Congress passed the Indian Removal Act. This law allowed the president to make treaties in which Native Americans in the East traded their lands for new territory on the Great Plains. The law did not say that the Indians should be removed by force, and in 1831 the Supreme Court ruled that Indians had a right to their lands. An angry Jackson disagreed. Groups that refused to move west voluntarily were met with military force, usually with tragic results.

This was true of the Sac and Fox of Illinois. Led by a chief named Black Hawk, the Sac and Fox fought removal for two years. Black Hawk's War ended in 1832 with the slaughter of most of his warriors. As he was taken off in chains, the chief told his captors:

The Granger Collection, New York

Black Hawk is an Indian. He has done nothing for which an Indian ought to be ashamed. He has fought for his countrymen, the squaws [women] and papooses [young children], against white men who came, year after year, to cheat them of and take away their land. You know the cause of our making war. It is known to all white men. They ought to be ashamed of it.

The Trail of Tears   Many whites *were* ashamed. Washington was flooded with protests over the treatment of Indians. Still the work of removal continued. In 1836 thousands of Creeks who refused to leave Alabama were rounded up and marched west in handcuffs. Two years later, under President Martin Van Buren, more than 17,000 Cherokee were dragged from their homes in Georgia and herded west by federal troops. Four thousand died during their long walk to Indian Territory. Those who survived remembered that terrible journey as their "Trail of Tears." A soldier who took part in the Cherokee removal called it "the cruelest work I ever knew."

Led by a young chief named Osceola, the Seminoles of Florida resisted removal for ten years. Their long struggle was the most costly Indian war ever fought in the United States. A number of Seminoles were finally sent to Indian Territory. But others found refuge (safety) in the Florida swamps. Their descendants still live in the state today.

When Jackson left office, he was proud of having "solved" the Indian problem for good. But as you will learn in the next two chapters, Jackson had simply moved the conflict between Indians and whites across the mighty Mississippi.

This artist painted an unrealistic picture of the Trail of Tears. Most of the Cherokees had no horses or warm blankets. They were dragged from their homes and allowed to take only the clothes they had on. Many died as they walked barefoot for hundreds of miles.

Geography Challenge

The Indian Removals

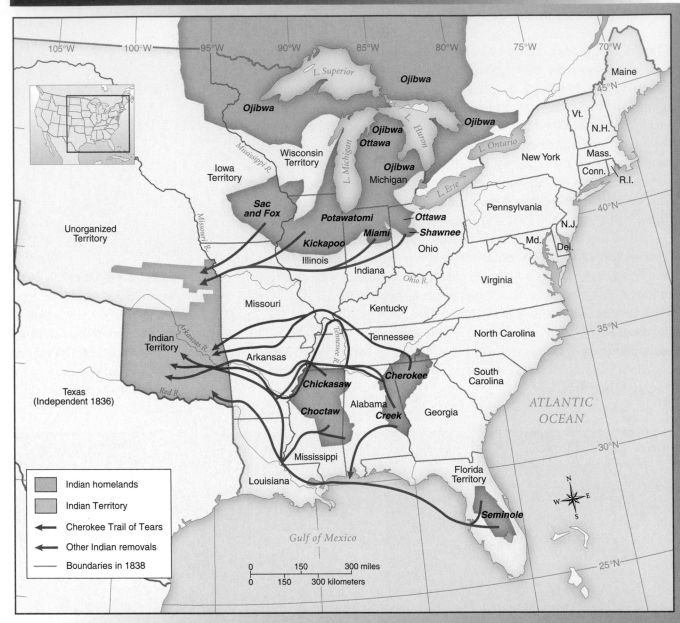

1. From which states were Indians removed?

2. To what future state were they moved?

3. How does the size of Indian Territory compare to the size of their homelands?

4. How far were Indians forced to travel to reach Indian Territory?

5. Which Native American tribe was involved in the Trail of Tears?

6. How many other tribes were forced into Indian Territory?

7. In what direction were Indians pushed? Why were they pushed in this direction?

14.8 Chapter Summary

In this chapter, you read about the presidency of Andrew Jackson. You used character portraits to evaluate Jackson's presidency from the perspective of different groups.

First-time voters, many of them farmers and frontiersmen, flocked to the polls to help elect Andrew Jackson in 1828. Jackson's supporters celebrated his election as a victory for the "common man" over the rich, well-born, and powerful. Jackson, after all, was a self-made man who rose from poverty to become president of the United States.

As president, Jackson fought a number of battles for "the people"—and rewarded his friends and supporters at the same time. For advice, he relied on his "kitchen cabinet," rather than the official cabinet. He replaced a number of Republican civil servants with Democrats. And he waged war on the powerful Bank of the United States.

A controversy over higher tariffs led to the nullification crisis, in which South Carolinians threatened to separate from the United States. Although Jackson forced them to back down, the crisis was an early sign of developing tensions between northern and southern states.

Jackson's Indian policy was simple: move the eastern Indians across the Mississippi to make room for whites. The Indian Removal Act caused great suffering for thousands of Native Americans. Furthermore, Jackson had only moved the conflict between whites and Indians to the West, not solved it. For, as you will read in the next chapter, the West was just where many white Americans were looking for new opportunities and the chance to expand their way of life across the continent.

Andrew Jackson was America's first frontier president. He came to office with great popular support. His supporters viewed him as a president of the people. His enemies saw him as a president hoping to become a king.

How do these people feel about settlers moving west?

Why is this man going west?

15

Manifest Destiny and the Growing Nation

15.1 Introduction

A century and a half ago, the words *"Manifest Destiny"* inspired vast hopes and dreams among Americans. They led to a war with Mexico. And they changed the map of the United States.

The phrase *manifest destiny* means "obvious fate." It was coined in 1845 by John O'Sullivan, a New York newspaperman. O'Sullivan wrote that it was America's "manifest destiny to overspread and to possess the whole of the continent." Looking at the land beyond the Rocky Mountains, he argued that "the God of nature and nations has marked it for our own."

The fact that Great Britain claimed part of this land—a huge territory known as Oregon—made no difference to O'Sullivan. After all, the United States had stood up to Britain in the War of 1812 and survived.

Nor was O'Sullivan impressed by Mexico's claims to much of the West. Like many Americans, he believed that America had a duty to extend the blessings of democracy to new lands and peoples. It was God's plan, he wrote, for Americans to expand their "great experiment with liberty."

When Americans began their "great experiment" in 1776, the idea that the United States might one day spread across the continent seemed an impossible dream. By 1848, however, the dream was a reality. In this chapter, you will learn how the United States tripled its size in a little more than a single lifetime.

As America grew, it became far more diverse. Its new territories were home to many native peoples, as well as settlers from France, Spain, Mexico, and other countries. America's growth would have a major impact on the people who were already living in the West.

Manifest Destiny took many forms. America grew through treaties, through settlement, and through war. As you read this chapter, think about the way each new territory was acquired. Was O'Sullivan right that this expansion was a matter of destiny? Or was it a matter of diplomacy and sometimes dishonorable dealings? Could Americans have made different decisions along the way?

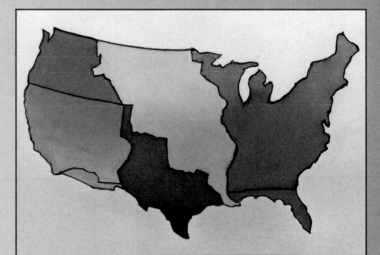

Graphic Organizer: Map of Territorial Acquisitions
You will use this map of America's acquisitions to study how and why the United States expanded across the continent.

15.2 The Louisiana Purchase

America's first opportunity for expansion during the early nineteenth century involved the vast territory to the west of the Mississippi River, then known as Louisiana. The United States wanted the port city of New Orleans, near the mouth of the Mississippi River. By 1800, thousands of farmers were settling the land to the west of the Appalachian Mountains. To get their crops to market, they floated them down the Mississippi to New Orleans. There they loaded the crops onto ships bound for Europe or for cities on the East Coast.

The farmers depended on being able to move their crops freely along this route. "The Mississippi," wrote James Madison, "is to them everything. It is the Hudson, the Delaware, the Potomac, and all the navigable rivers of the Atlantic States formed into one stream."

Louisiana   Across the Mississippi lay the unexplored territory of Louisiana. This immense region stretched from Canada south to Texas. From the Mississippi, it reached west all the way to the Rocky Mountains. First claimed by France, Louisiana was given to Spain after the French and Indian War. In 1800, the French ruler Napoleon Bonaparte convinced Spain to return Louisiana to France.

Napoleon had plans for Louisiana. He hoped to settle the territory with thousands of French farmers. These farmers would raise food for slaves who toiled on France's sugar plantations in the Caribbean.

Napoleon's plans alarmed frontier farmers. New Orleans was part of Louisiana. If Napoleon closed the port to American goods, farmers would have no way to get their crops to market.

"A Noble Bargain"   President Thomas Jefferson understood the concerns of American farmers. So, in 1803, he sent James Monroe to France with an offer to buy New Orleans for $7.5 million. By the time Monroe

American diplomats (standing) work out the final details of the Louisiana Purchase with Tallyrand, the French foreign minister.

THE LOUISIANA PURCHASE.
MESSRS. MONROE AND LIVINGSTONE COMPLETING NEGOTIATIONS WITH TALLYRAND, APRIL 30, 1803

reached France, Napoleon had changed his plans. A few years earlier, a slave named Toussaint L'Ouverture had led a slave revolt in the French Caribbean colony known today as Haiti. The former slaves defeated the French troops who tried to take back the colony. As a result, Napoleon no longer needed Louisiana.

In addition, France and Britain were on the brink of war. Napoleon knew that he might lose Louisiana to the British. Rather than lose Louisiana, it made sense to sell it to the United States.

Napoleon's offer to sell all of Louisiana stunned James Monroe. Instead of a city, suddenly the United States had the opportunity to buy an area as big as itself!

It didn't take long for Monroe to agree. On April 30, 1803, he signed a treaty giving Louisiana to the United States in exchange for $15 million. Said the French foreign minister, "You have made a noble bargain for yourselves, and I suppose you will make the most of it."

The Purchase Debate   To most Americans, the Louisiana Purchase looked like the greatest land deal in history. The new territory would double the country's size at a bargain price of just 2 to 3 cents an acre!

The Granger Collection, New York

In this painting, the American flag is raised in New Orleans as the French flag is taken down. The ceremony marked the official transfer of the Louisiana Territory in 1803.

Still, not everyone approved. Some people worried that such a large country would be impossible to govern. Politicians in the East fretted that they would lose power. Sooner or later, they warned, Louisiana would be carved into enough new states to outvote the eastern states in Congress.

Others fussed about the $15 million price tag. "We are to give money of which we have too little," wrote a Boston critic, "for land of which we already have too much."

Opponents also accused Jefferson of "tearing the Constitution to tatters." They said that the Constitution made no provision for purchasing foreign territory.

Jefferson was troubled by the argument that the purchase was unconstitutional. Still, he believed that it was better to stretch the Constitution than to lose a historic opportunity.

Late in 1803, the Senate voted to ratify the Louisiana Purchase treaty. Frontier farmers cheered the news. "You have secured to us the free navigation of the Mississippi," a grateful westerner wrote Jefferson. "You have procured an immense and fertile country: and all these great blessings are obtained without war and bloodshed."

Manifest Destiny and the Growing Nation   **199**

15.3 Florida

15.3 Florida

diplomacy The art of conducting negotiations with other countries. People who engage in diplomacy are called *diplomats*.

Having acquired Louisiana through **diplomacy,** President Jefferson turned next to Florida. Spain had colonized this sunny peninsula in the late 1500s. By the 1800s, Florida had a diverse population of Seminole Indians, Spanish colonists, English traders, and runaway slaves. In 1804, Jefferson sent two diplomats to Spain to buy Florida. Spain's answer was "no deal."

Many white Americans in the Southeast wanted the United States to take over Florida. Slave owners in Georgia were angry because slaves sometimes ran away to Florida. (Some of the runaways were accepted and welcomed by the Seminole Indians.) In addition, white landowners in Georgia were upset by Seminole raids on their lands.

Over the next few years, Spain's control of Florida weakened. The Spanish government could do nothing to stop the raids on farms in Georgia by Seminoles and ex-slaves.

BILLY BOWLEGS. CHOCOTE TUSTENUGGEE. ABRAM. JOHN JUMPER. PARATCHEE EMARTHLA. SARPARKEE YOHOLA.
BILLY BOWLEGS AND CHIEFS OF THE SEMINOLE INDIANS.

Escaped slaves were accepted into Seminole Indian communities, and often intermarried. Here we see Chief Abraham, a Seminole leader of both African and Seminole heritage.

Andrew Jackson Invades Florida   In 1818, President James Monroe sent Andrew Jackson—the hero of the Battle of New Orleans—to Georgia with orders to end the raids. Jackson was told that he could chase raiding Seminoles into Florida. But he did not have authority to invade the Spanish colony.

Despite his orders, Jackson marched into Florida with a force of 1,700 troops. Over the next few weeks, he captured nearly every military post in the colony. He arrested, tried, and executed two British subjects for stirring up Indian attacks. He also replaced the Spanish governor with an American. Later Jackson said that he was sorry that he didn't execute the governor as well. Spain demanded that Jackson be called back to Washington and punished for his illegal invasion.

"Govern or Get Out"   Fearing war, Monroe asked his cabinet for advice. All but one of his cabinet members advised him to remove Jackson and apologize to Spain. The exception was Secretary of State John Quincy Adams. Rather than apologize, Adams convinced Monroe to send a blunt message to Spain. The message was, either govern Florida properly or get out.

Equally fearful of war, Spain decided to get out. In 1819, the Spanish government agreed to yield Florida to the United States. In exchange, the United States agreed to pay off $5 million in settlers' claims against Spain. The United States also agreed to honor Spain's longtime claim to Texas.

Not all Americans were happy about leaving Spain in charge of Texas. One newspaper declared that Texas was "worth ten Floridas." Even so, the Senate ratified the Florida treaty two days after it was signed.

15.4 Texas

There was a reason many Americans felt that Texas was so valuable. Much of this region was well suited for growing cotton, the South's most valuable cash crop, and many southerners hoped that one day it would become part of the United States.

Americans Come to Texas   The Texas tale begins with Moses Austin, a banker and businessman who dreamed of starting an American colony in Spanish Texas. In 1821, Spanish officials granted Austin a huge tract of land. When Moses died suddenly that year, his son Stephen took over his father's dream.

Stephen arrived in Texas just as Mexico declared its independence from Spain. Now Texas was a part of Mexico. Mexican officials agreed to let Austin start his colony—under certain conditions. Austin had to choose only moral and hardworking settlers. The settlers had to promise to become Mexican citizens and to join the Catholic Church.

Austin agreed to the Mexican terms. By 1827, he had attracted 297 families—soon known as the "Old Three Hundred"— to Texas.

Rising Tensions   The success of Austin's colony started a rush of settlers to Texas. By 1830, there were about 25,000 Americans in Texas, compared to 4,000 Tejanos, or Texans of Mexican descent. Soon tensions between the two groups began to rise.

The Americans had several complaints. They were used to governing themselves, and they resented taking orders from Mexican officials. They were unhappy that all official documents had to be in Spanish, a language most of them were unwilling to learn. In addition, many were slaveholders who were upset when Mexico outlawed slavery in 1829.

The Tejanos had their own complaints. They were unhappy that many American settlers had come to Texas illegally. Worse, most of these new immigrants showed little respect for Mexican culture and had no intention of becoming citizens.

The Mexican government responded by closing Texas to further American immigration. The government sent troops to Texas to assert its authority and enforce the immigration laws.

The Texans Rebel   Americans in Texas resented these actions. Hotheads, led by a young lawyer named William Travis, began calling for revolution. Cooler heads, led by Stephen Austin, asked the Mexican government to reopen Texas to immigration and to make it a separate Mexican state. That way, Texans could run their own affairs.

Stephen Austin made his father's dream a reality when he founded a colony in Texas in 1822. In this painting, we see a young and charismatic Austin talking with a group of Anglo American settlers about the rules Mexico required them to live by.

Manifest Destiny and the Growing Nation   **201**

In 1833, Austin traveled to Mexico and presented the Texans' demands to the new head of the Mexican government, General Antonio López de Santa Anna. The general was a power-hungry dictator who once boasted, "If I were God, I would wish to be more." Rather than bargain with Austin, Santa Anna tossed him in jail for promoting rebellion.

Soon after Austin was released in 1835, Texans rose up in revolt. Determined to crush the rebels, Santa Anna marched north with approximately 6,000 troops.

The Alamo   In late February 1836, a large part of Santa Anna's army reached San Antonio, Texas. The town was defended by about 180 Texan volunteers, including eight Tejanos. The Texans had taken over an old mission known as the Alamo. Among them was Davy Crockett, the famous frontiersman and former congressman from Tennessee. Sharing command with William Travis was James Bowie, a well-known Texas "freedom fighter."

The Alamo's defenders watched as General Santa Anna raised a black flag that meant "Expect no mercy." The general demanded that the Texans surrender. Travis answered with a cannon shot.

Slowly, Santa Anna's troops began surrounding the Alamo. The Texans were outnumbered by at least ten to one, but only one man fled.

Fewer than 200 Texans fought 4,000 Mexican troops at the Alamo. When the battle was over, they were all dead—including James Bowie and the fabled frontiersman Davy Crocket.

Meanwhile, Travis sent messengers to other towns in Texas, pleading for reinforcements and vowing not to abandon the Alamo. "Victory or death!" he proclaimed. But reinforcements never came.

For 12 days, the Mexicans pounded the Alamo with cannonballs. Then, at the first light of dawn on March 6, Santa Anna gave the order to storm the fort. Desperately, the Texans tried to stave off the attackers with a hailstorm of rifle fire.

For 90 minutes the battle raged. Then it was all over. By day's end, every one of the Alamo's defenders was dead. By Santa Anna's order, those who had survived the battle were executed on the spot.

Santa Anna described the fight for the Alamo as "but a small affair." But his decision to kill every man at the Alamo filled Texans with rage. It was a rage that cried out for revenge.

Texas Wins Its Independence Sam Houston, the commander of the Texas revolutionary army, understood Texans' rage. But as Santa Anna pushed on, Houston's only hope was to retreat eastward. By luring Santa Anna deeper into Texas, he hoped to make it harder for the general to supply his army and keep it battle-ready.

Houston's strategy wasn't popular, but it worked brilliantly. In April, Santa Anna caught up with Houston near the San Jacinto River. Expecting the Texans to attack at dawn, the general kept his troops awake all night. When no attack came, the weary Mexicans relaxed. Santa Anna went to his tent to take a nap.

Late that afternoon, Houston's troops staged a surprise attack. Yelling "Remember the Alamo!" the Texans overran the Mexican camp. Santa Anna fled, but he was captured the next day. In exchange for his freedom, he ordered all his remaining troops out of Texas. Texans had won their independence. Still, Mexico did not fully accept the loss of Texas.

To Annex Texas or Not? Now an independent country, Texas became known as the Lone Star Republic because of the single star on its flag. But most Texans were Americans who wanted Texas to become part of the United States.

Despite their wishes, Texas remained independent for ten years. People in the United States were divided over whether to **annex** Texas. Southerners were eager to add another slave state. Northerners who opposed slavery wanted to keep Texas out.

Others feared that annexation would lead to war with Mexico. The 1844 presidential campaign was influenced by the question of whether to expand U.S. territory. One of the candidates, Henry Clay, warned, "Annexation and war with Mexico are identical." His opponent, James K. Polk, however, was a strong believer in Manifest Destiny. He was eager to acquire Texas. After Polk was elected, Congress voted to annex Texas. In 1845, Texas was admitted as the 28th state.

The flag of the Lone Star Republic. Sam Houston was elected the first president of the independent country of Texas in 1836. In 1845, Texas was admitted to the United States. Today, Texas is known as the Lone Star State. This is the only known official Lone Star flag of the Republic of Texas of the period 1836-1846.

annex To add a territory to a country. Such an addition is called an *annexation*.

In the 1800s, wagon trains like the one depicted in this William Henry Jackson painting transported thousands of American families from established eastern settlements to the rugged West. This wagon train is winding its way across Nebraska toward Oregon Country.

15.5 Oregon Country

Far to the northwest of Texas lay Oregon Country. This enormous, tree-covered wilderness stretched from the Rocky Mountains to the Pacific Ocean. To the north, Oregon was bounded by Russian Alaska. To the south, it was bordered by Spanish California and New Mexico.

In 1819, Oregon was claimed by four nations—Russia, Spain, Great Britain, and the United States. Spain was the first to drop out of the scramble. As part of the treaty to purchase Florida, Spain gave up its claim to Oregon. A few years later, Russia also dropped out. By 1825, Russia agreed to limit its claim to the territory that lay north of the 54°40′ parallel of latitude. Today that line marks the southern border of Alaska.

That left Britain and the United States. For the time being, the two nations agreed to a peaceful "joint occupation" of Oregon.

Discovering Oregon America's claim to Oregon was based on the Lewis and Clark expedition. Between 1804 and 1806, Meriwether Lewis and William Clark had led a small band of explorers to the Oregon coast. You will read more about their epic adventure in the next chapter.

Lewis thought that many more Americans would follow the path blazed by the expedition. "In the course of 10 or 12 years," he predicted in 1806, "a tour across the continent by this route will be undertaken with as little concern as a voyage across the Atlantic."

That was wishful thinking. The route that Lewis and Clark had followed was far too rugged for ordinary travelers. There had to be a better way.

In 1824, a young fur trapper named Jedediah Smith found that better way. Smith discovered a passage through the Rocky Mountains called

South Pass. Unlike the high, steep passes used by Lewis and Clark, South Pass was low and flat enough for wagons to use in crossing the Rockies. Now the way was open for settlers to seek their fortunes in Oregon.

Oregon Fever   The first American settlers to travel through South Pass to Oregon were missionaries. These earnest preachers made few **converts** among Oregon's Indians. However, their glowing reports of Oregon's fertile soil and towering forests soon attracted more settlers.

These early settlers wrote letters home describing Oregon as a "pioneer's paradise." The weather was always sunny, they claimed. Disease was unknown. Trees grew as thick as hairs on a dog's back. And farms were free for the taking. One joker even claimed that "pigs are running about under the great acorn trees, round and fat, and already cooked, with knives and forks sticking in them so you can cut off a slice whenever you are hungry."

These reports inspired other settlers who were looking for a fresh start. In 1843, about 1,000 pioneers packed their belongings into covered wagons and headed for Oregon. A year later, nearly twice as many people made the long journey across the plains and mountains. "The Oregon Fever has broke out," stated a Boston newspaper, "and is now raging."

All of Oregon or Half?   Along with Texas, "Oregon fever" also played a role in the 1844 presidential campaign. Polk won the election with stirring slogans such as "All of Oregon or none!" and "Fifty-four forty or fight!" Polk promised that he would not rest until the United States had annexed all of Oregon Country.

Settlers who braved the 2,000 mile trek from Independence, Missouri, to Oregon Country were rewarded by fertile land in the Willamette Valley.

But Polk didn't want Oregon enough to risk starting a war with Britain. Instead, he agreed to a compromise treaty that divided Oregon roughly in half at the 49th parallel. That line now marks the western border between the United States and Canada.

The Senate debate over the Oregon treaty was fierce. Senators from the South and the East strongly favored the treaty. They saw no reason to go to war over "worse than useless territory on the coast of the Pacific." Senators from the West opposed the treaty. They wanted to hold out for all of Oregon. On June 18, 1846, the Senate ratified the compromise treaty by a vote of 41 to 14.

Polk got neither "fifty-four forty" nor a fight. What he got was even better: a diplomatic settlement that both the United States and Great Britain could accept without spilling a drop of blood.

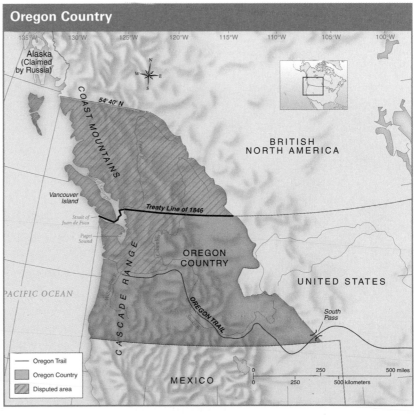

Oregon Country

- Oregon Trail
- Oregon Country
- Disputed area

Alaska (Claimed by Russia)

COAST MOUNTAINS

54° 40' N

Vancouver Island

Strait of Juan de Fuca

Puget Sound

PACIFIC OCEAN

Treaty Line of 1846

BRITISH NORTH AMERICA

CASCADE RANGE

OREGON COUNTRY

OREGON TRAIL

UNITED STATES

South Pass

MEXICO

0 250 500 miles
0 250 500 kilometers

Volunteers from Exeter, New Hampshire, line up as they leave New England to fight in the war against Mexico.

15.6 War with Mexico

You might think that Texas and Oregon were quite enough new territory for any president. But not for Polk. This humorless, hardworking president had one great goal. He wanted to expand the United States as far as he could.

Polk's gaze fell next on the huge areas known as California and New Mexico. He was determined to have them both—by purchase if possible, by force if necessary.

These areas were first colonized by Spain, but they became Mexican territories when Mexico won its independence in 1821. Both were thinly settled, and the Mexican government had long neglected them. That was reason enough for Polk to hope that they might be for sale. He sent a representative to Mexico to try to buy the territories. But Mexican officials refused even to see him.

War Breaks Out in Texas When Congress voted to annex Texas, relations between the United States and Mexico turned sour. To Mexico, the annexation of Texas was an act of war. To make matters worse, Texas and Mexico could not agree on a border. Texas claimed the Rio Grande as its border on the south and the west. Mexico wanted the border to be the Nueces River, about 150 miles northeast of the Rio Grande.

On April 25, 1846, Mexican soldiers fired on American troops who were patrolling along the Rio Grande. Sixteen Americans were killed or wounded. This was just the excuse for war that Polk had been waiting for. Mexico, he charged, "has invaded our territory and shed American blood on American soil." Two days after Polk's speech, Congress declared war on Mexico.

To Mexico, the truth was just the opposite. Mexican president Mariano Paredes declared that a greedy people "have thrown themselves on our territory.... The time has come to fight."

The Fall of New Mexico and California A few months later, General Stephen Kearny led the Army of the West out of Kansas. His orders were to occupy New Mexico and then continue west to California.

Mexican opposition melted away in front of Kearny's army. The Americans took control of New Mexico without firing a shot. "General Kearny," a pleased Polk wrote in his diary, "has thus far performed his duties well."

Meanwhile, a group of Americans led by the explorer John C. Frémont launched a rebellion against Mexican rule in California. The Americans arrested and jailed General Mariano Guadalupe Vallejo, the Mexican commander of Northern California. Then they raised a crude flag showing a grizzly bear sketched in blackberry juice. California, they declared, was now the Bear Flag Republic.

When Kearny reached California, he joined forces with the rebels. Within weeks, all of California was under American control.

The United States Invades Mexico The conquest of Mexico itself was far more difficult. American troops under Zachary Taylor battled their way south from Texas. Taylor was a no-nonsense general who was known fondly as "Old Rough and Ready" because of his backwoods clothes. After 6,000 troops took the Mexican city of Monterrey, an old enemy stopped them. General Santa Anna had marched north to meet Taylor with an army of 20,000 Mexican troops.

In February 1847, the two forces met near a ranch called Buena Vista. After two days of hard fighting, Santa Anna reported that "both armies have been cut to pieces." Rather than lose his remaining forces, Santa Anna retreated south. The war in northern Mexico was over.

A month later, American forces led by General Winfield Scott landed at Veracruz in southern Mexico. Scott was a stickler for discipline and loved fancy uniforms. These traits earned him the nickname "Old Fuss and Feathers." For the next six months, his troops fought their way to Mexico City, the capital of Mexico.

Outside the capital, the Americans met fierce resistance at the castle of Chapultepec. About 1,000 Mexican soldiers and 100 young military cadets

In this painting by Hal Stone, we see the American cavalry overwhelming the enemy in the Battle of Resaca de la Palma, Texas, in May 1846.

fought bravely to defend the fortress. Six of the cadets chose to die fighting rather than surrender. To this day, the boys who died that day are honored in Mexico as *Los Niños Héroes*—the heroic children.

Despite such determined resistance, Scott's army captured Mexico City in September 1847. Watching from a distance, a Mexican officer muttered darkly, "God is a Yankee."

Mexican Cession

As this map shows, Manifest Destiny was accomplished by the 1850s. The country stretched from the Atlantic to the Pacific, and the present outline of the United States was complete.

The Treaty of Guadalupe Hidalgo   Early in 1848, Mexico and the United States signed the Treaty of Guadalupe Hidalgo. Mexico agreed to give up Texas and a vast region known as the Mexican Cession. (A *cession* is something that is given up.) This area included the present-day states of California, Nevada, Utah, Arizona, and New Mexico, as well as parts of Colorado and Wyoming.

By this agreement, Mexico gave up half of all its territory. In return, the United States agreed to pay Mexico $15 million. It also promised to protect the 80,000 to 100,000 Mexicans living in Texas and in the Mexican Cession. (As you will learn in Chapter 17, most of these promises were not kept.)

In Washington, a few senators spoke up to oppose the treaty. Some of them argued that the United States had no right to any Mexican territory other than Texas. They believed that the Mexican War had been unjust and that the treaty was even more so. New Mexico and California together, they said, were "not worth a dollar" and should be returned to Mexico.

Other senators opposed the treaty because they wanted even more land. They wanted the Mexican Cession to include a large part of northern Mexico as well. To most senators, however, the Mexican Cession was a Manifest Destiny dream come true. The Senate ratified the treaty by a vote of 38 to 14.

"From Sea to Shining Sea"   A few years later, the United States acquired still more land from Mexico. In 1853, James Gadsden arranged the purchase of a strip of land just south of the Mexican Cession for $10 million. Railroad builders wanted this land because it was relatively flat and could serve as a good railroad route. With the acquisition of this land, known as the Gadsden Purchase, the nation stretched "from sea to shining sea."

Most Americans were pleased with the new outlines of their country. Still, not everyone rejoiced in this expansion. Until the Mexican War, many people had believed that the United States was too good a nation to bully or invade its weaker neighbors. Now they knew that such behavior was the dark side of Manifest Destiny.

15.7 Chapter Summary

In this chapter, you read about how Americans extended their nation to the west and the south. You used a map of America's acquisitions to study how and why the United States expanded into these territories.

In the 1800s, many Americans believed that they had both the right and the duty (an idea called *Manifest Destiny*) to spread their way of life across the continent.

America's first great expansion was the Louisiana Purchase. Next, Florida was added to the United States through a treaty with Spain. A treaty with Great Britain added Oregon Country.

Americans in Texas rebelled against the Mexican government there and created the Lone Star Republic. Ten years later, the United States annexed Texas.

In 1846, the United States went to war with Mexico and acquired California and New Mexico as part of the Mexican Cession. Later, the Gadsden Purchase completed the outline of the contiguous United States.

America's expansion across the continent was now complete. Yet much of the West was only thinly settled. In the next chapter, you will learn about the people who moved into this vast area.

As the 19th century progressed, more and more settlers were lured to the West by hopes of free land and an independent and prosperous life.

Emigrants Crossing the Plains by Albert Bierstadt, 1867. Oil on canvas. Catalog Number 72.19. National Cowboy & Western Heritage Museum, Oklahoma City, OK.

Why are these
people moving
west?

16

Life in the West

16.1 Introduction

The vast region that stretches from the Mississippi River to the Pacific Ocean is one of the most extraordinary landscapes on earth. Today, tourists come from all over to see its towering mountains, deep canyons, painted deserts, and fertile plains.

To American settlers from across the Mississippi, this great expanse of grasslands, mountains, and deserts was the West. For all its beauty, the West was a challenging environment. Look at the names settlers gave to its features. Where else can you find a confusion of mountains called the Crazies, a scorching desert named Death Valley, a blood-red canyon called Flaming Gorge, or a raging river known as the River of No Return?

Despite its daunting challenges, the West was never empty. Perhaps as many as 3 million Native Americans lived there before Europeans arrived. These first westerners were far more diverse in language and culture than the Europeans who claimed their land.

For most Americans in the early 1800s, however, the West was mostly a blank map. By 1850, it had become the land of opportunity. The West boasted wide open spaces and great natural wealth in timber, gold, silver, and other resources. It became a magnet for immigrants and for easterners looking for a new start in life. And as Americans began their westward trek, they created new markets for eastern merchants. In time the West changed the nation's economy and politics. It also created a folklore of "rugged individualism" that has become a lasting part of American culture.

Newspaperman Horace Greeley captured the growing enthusiasm for "going west" when he wrote, "If you have no family or friends to aid you, and no prospect [opportunity] opened to you…turn your face to the great West, and there build up a home and fortune." In this chapter, you will learn about eight groups of people who turned their faces to the West in the first half of the 1800s. You will find out why they came, what hardships they faced, and what legacy they left.

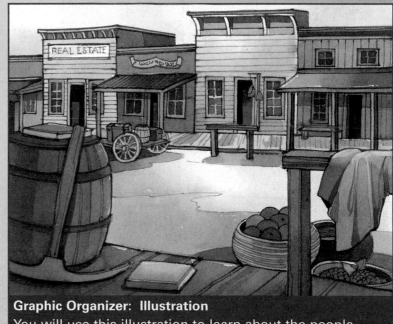

Graphic Organizer: Illustration
You will use this illustration to learn about the people who settled the West.

16.2 The Explorers

In the early 1800s, a number of expeditions set out from the United States to explore the West. The most famous was the Lewis and Clark expedition, a pet project of President Thomas Jefferson.

The public purpose of the expedition was to make friendly contact with Indian groups that might be interested in trade. Its secret purpose was to find the "Northwest Passage," a water route across North America that explorers had been seeking ever since Columbus bumped into America. With the purchase of Louisiana from France in 1803, the expedition gained a third purpose—finding out just what the United States had bought.

Up the Missouri River   In May 1804, the 45-member expedition left St. Louis, Missouri, in three boats. The group was led by Jefferson's private secretary, Meriwether Lewis, and his friend William Clark. Its members included soldiers, frontiersmen, and Clark's slave York.

It was hard going from the first day. Rowing upstream against the Missouri River's strong current left the explorers' hands blistered and their muscles sore. Hungry mosquitoes feasted on sunburned faces.

By summer, the explorers had reached Indian country. Most groups welcomed the strangers, and York fascinated the Indians. They had never seen a black man before. Again and again, wrote Clark in his journal, York allowed his skin to be rubbed with a wet finger to prove "that he was not a painted white man."

The explorers made camp for the winter near a Mandan village in what is now North Dakota. There, a French fur trapper joined them along with his 16-year-old wife, a Shoshone woman named Sacagawea, and their infant son. As a girl, Sacagawea had been kidnapped from her people by another group. Lewis and Clark hoped she would translate for them when they reached Shoshone country.

This painting shows members of the Lewis and Clark expedition at Three Forks, Montana. The woman is Sacagawea. To her right are Meriwether Lewis, William Clark, and Clark's slave, York.

To the Pacific and Back   In the spring of 1805, the explorers set out once more. As they moved up the Missouri, their progress was slowed by rapids and waterfalls. When they hauled their boats by land around these obstacles, the thorns of the prickly-pear cactus pierced their feet. Meanwhile, grizzly bears raided their camps, and game became scarce.

By late summer, the explorers could see the Rocky Mountains looming ahead. To cross the mountains before the first snows of winter closed the high passes, they would have to find horses—and soon.

Fortunately, the expedition had reached the land of Sacagawea's childhood. One day a group of Indians approached. To Sacagawea's great joy, they proved to be Shoshone. Learning that her brother was now a Shoshone chief, Sacagawea persuaded him to provide the explorers with the horses they desperately needed.

The explorers made it over the Rockies, but they were more dead than alive. The Nez Percé, an Indian people living in the Pacific Northwest, saved them from starvation. A grateful Lewis wrote in his journal that the Nez Percé "are the most hospitable, honest and sincere [people] that we have met with on our voyage."

As winter closed in, the explorers reached their final destination, the Pacific Ocean. Clark marked the event by carving on a tree, "William Clark December 3rd 1805 By Land from the U. States."

The Explorers' Legacy   After a wet and hungry winter in Oregon, the explorers headed homeward. In September 1806, two years and four months after setting out, they returned to St. Louis. Lewis proudly wrote to Jefferson, "In obedience to our orders, we have penetrated the continent of North America to the Pacific Ocean."

Lewis and Clark had good reason to be proud. They had not found the Northwest Passage, for it did not exist. But they had traveled some 8,000 miles. They had mapped a route to the Pacific. They had established good relations with western Indians. Most of all, they had brought back priceless information about the West and its peoples.

Other explorers added to this legacy and helped prepare the way for the settlement of the West. In 1806, the same year Lewis and Clark returned to St. Louis, 26-year-old army lieutenant Zebulon Pike set out to explore the southern part of the new Louisiana Territory. Pike and his party traveled up the valley of the Arkansas River into present-day Colorado. There Pike saw the mountain that today is called Pikes Peak.

Pike went on to explore Spanish territory along the Rio Grande and the Red River. His reports of the wealth of Spanish towns in the Southwest brought many American traders to the region. But Pike was not impressed with the landscape. He called the West a "Great American Desert."

Another famed explorer, John C. Frémont, helped to correct this image. Nicknamed "the Pathfinder," Frémont mapped much of the territory between the Mississippi Valley and the Pacific Ocean in the 1840s. His glowing descriptions of a "land of plenty" inspired many families to try their luck in the West.

Zebulon Pike's published reports of his expedition spurred American interest in the Southwest. Part of his path would become the Santa Fe Trail, used by thousands of pioneers.

Geography Challenge
Lewis and Clark Expedition

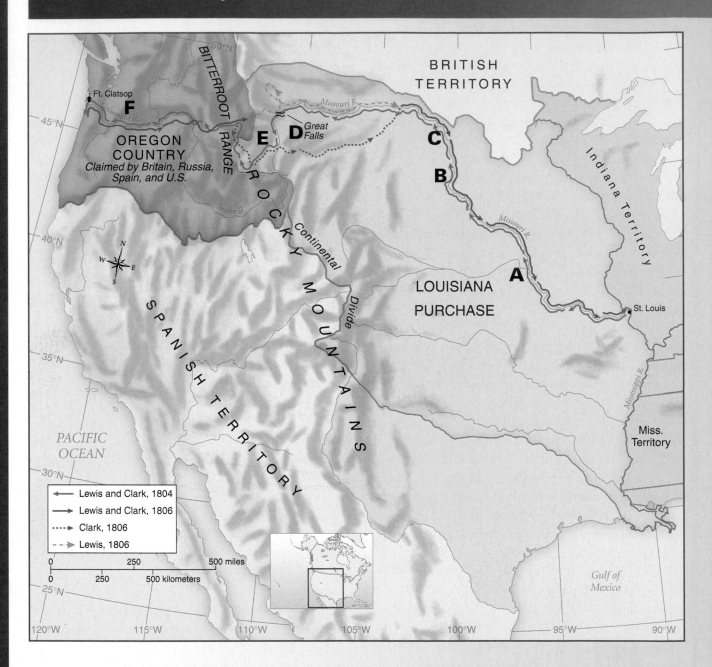

1. What details do you see on this map?

2. What specific geographic features did Lewis and Clark encounter?

3. What challenges might these features have created for them?

4. What other challenges might Lewis and Clark have faced on their expedition?

Image A: August 3, 1804. Excerpts from William Clark's journal: "chiefs," "long speech," "wishes of our government," "trading," and "a canister of (gun) powder."

Image B: November 3, 1804. Excerpts from William Clark's journal: "plenty of timber," "building," "our camp," and "we received a visit from Kagohami."

Image C: March 9, 1805. Excerpts from William Clark's journal: "grand chief of the Minnetarees," "surprised," "examined him closely," and "wash off paint."

Image D: August 6, 1805. Excerpts from Meriwether Lewis's journal: "rapid current," "baggage wet," "several articles lost," and "thrown out of one of the canoes."

Image E: August 17, 1805. Excerpts from William Clark's journal: "companions in childhood," "embraced with the most tender affection," "conference," and "interpret."

Image F: November 3, 1805. Excerpts from Joseph Whitehouse's journal: "fog so thick…we cannot see," "met several Indians in a canoe," "they signed to us," and "two hundred miles…to the ocean."

16.3 The Californios

mission A place established by missionaries for their work. A typical California mission included such things as a church, a residence, workshops, and large areas of land for raising crops.

rancho A grant of land made by the Mexican government. Most ranchos were used for raising cattle and crops.

If Lewis and Clark had turned south from Oregon after reaching the Pacific, they would have found Spain's best-kept secret, a sun-drenched land called California.

The California Missions   In 1769, a Spanish missionary named Junipero Serra led soldiers and priests north from Mexico to California. Serra's goal was to convert the California Indians to Christianity. To do this, he began a chain of **missions** that eventually stretched from San Diego to just north of San Francisco. Each mission controlled a huge area of land, as well as the Indians who worked it.

Although the missionaries meant well, the missions were deadly to native Californians. Indians were sometimes treated harshly, and thousands died of diseases brought to California by the newcomers.

Settlers followed the missionaries to California. "We were the pioneers of the Pacific coast," wrote Guadalupe Vallejo, "building pueblos [towns] and missions while George Washington was carrying on the war of the Revolution." To reward soldiers and attract settlers, the Spanish began the practice of making large grants of land.

When Mexico won its independence in 1821, California came under Mexican rule. In 1833, the Mexican government closed the missions. Half of the mission land was supposed to go to Indians. Mexico, however, established its own system of land grants in the Southwest and gave most of California's mission lands to soldiers and settlers. The typical Spanish-speaking Californian, or *Californio*, was granted a **rancho** of 50,000 acres or more.

Life on the Ranchos   Life on the ranchos combined hard work and the occasional *fiesta*, or social gathering. Most families lived in simple adobe houses with dirt floors. The Californios produced almost everything they needed at home. Indian servants did much of the work.

The ranchos were so huge that neighbors lived at least a day's journey apart. As a result, strangers were always welcome for the news they brought of the outside world. During weddings and fiestas, Californios celebrated with singing, dancing, and brilliant displays of horsemanship.

In the 1830s, cattle ranching became California's most important industry. Cattle provided hides and tallow (beef fat) to trade for imported goods brought by ship. An American sailor named Richard Henry Dana described the goods his trading ship carried to California:

The prosperity and pride of the Californios is evident in this painting, *Hacendado y Su Mayordomo*, meaning "The Landowner and His Foreman."

We had...teas, coffee, sugars, spices, raisins, molasses, hard-ware, crockery-ware, tin-ware, cutlery, clothing of all kinds, boots and shoes...shawls, scarfs, necklaces, jewelry...furniture...and in fact everything than can be imagined, from Chinese fire-works to English cart-wheels.

Because California was so far from the capital in Mexico City, the territory was neglected by the Mexican government. Soldiers were not paid, and they took what they needed to survive from the people they were supposed to protect. Officials sent to govern California were often unskilled and sometimes dishonest.

The Californios' Legacy

In 1846, the United States captured California as part of the war with Mexico. Before long, Californios were a minority in California.

Still, the Californios left a lasting mark. California is full of Spanish place names such as San Diego, Los Angeles, and San Francisco. The Californios also introduced many of California's famous crops, such as grapes, olives, and citrus fruits. Most of all, they opened California to the world. As you will see, the world soon rushed in.

16.4 The Mountain Men

The Lewis and Clark expedition stirred new interest in an old industry, the fur trade. Inspired by the explorers' reports of finding beaver in the Rockies, a Spanish trader named Manuel Lisa followed their route west. In 1807, Lisa led 42 trappers up the Missouri River. The next year, he took 350 trappers into the Rockies. For the next 30 years, trappers crisscrossed the West in search of valuable furs.

The Trapper's Life

The trappers, who were also called *mountain men,* lived hard and usually died young. During the spring and fall, they set their traps in icy streams. In July, they traveled to trading posts to swap furs for supplies or gathered for an annual "rendezvous," or get-together. Here is how writer Washington Irving described one rendezvous:

This, then, is the trapper's holiday.... [The men] engaged in contests of skill at running, jumping, wrestling, shooting with the rifle, and running horses.... They drank together, they sang, they laughed, they whooped; they tried to outbrag and outlie each other in stories of their adventures and achievements. Here were the free trappers in all their glory.

Mountain men, like this one pictured in a Frederick Remington painting, were rugged individualists. They often wore shirts and trousers made from animal hides and had hair that hung to their shoulders.

The Granger Collection, New York

In their search for furs, mountain men established new routes to Oregon and California.

The rendezvous may have been fun, but the trappers' lives were filled with hazards. Trappers were attacked by fur thieves, Indians, wolves, and bears. Mountain man Hugh Glass was mauled by a mother bear that threw chunks of his flesh to her hungry cubs before friends rescued him.

Accidents were common, too. A single misplaced step on a mountain, or a misjudged river rapid, often meant sudden death. Disease also took a heavy toll. When one man asked for news about a party of trappers, he learned that "some had died by lingering diseases, and others by the fatal [rifle] ball or arrow." Out of 116 men, he wrote, "there were not more than sixteen alive."

Freedom and Adventure   Trappers braved this dangerous way of life because of its freedom and adventure. A good example is Jim Beckwourth, a slave who fled Virginia to become a fur trapper. While hunting beaver in the Rockies, Beckwourth was captured by Crow Indians. According to Beckwourth, an old woman identified him as her long-lost son, and he was adopted into the tribe. "What could I do?" he wrote later. "Even if I should deny my Crow origin, they would not believe me."

Beckwourth lived with the Crow for six years and became a chief. By the time he left the tribe in the 1830s, the fur trade was in decline. Like other mountain men, however, Beckwourth continued his adventurous life as an explorer, army scout, and trader. In 1850, he discovered the lowest pass across the Sierra Nevada mountain range, known today as Beckwourth Pass.

The Mountain Men's Legacy   In their search for furs, the mountain men explored most of the West. The routes they pioneered across mountains and deserts became the Oregon and California Trails. Their trading posts turned into supply stations for settlers moving west along those trails.

A surprising number of mountain men left another kind of legacy as well—personal journals. Their stories still have the power to make us laugh and cry—and to wonder how they lived long enough to tell their tales.

16.5 The Missionaries

Ever since Lewis and Clark appeared among them, the Nez Percé had been friendly toward Americans. In 1831, three Nez Percé traveled to St. Louis to learn more about the white man's ways. There, the Nez Percé asked if someone would come west to teach their people the secrets of the "Black Book," or Bible.

Several missionaries answered that call. The best known were Marcus and Narcissa Whitman and Henry and Eliza Spalding. In 1836, the two couples traveled west from St. Louis along the **Oregon Trail**.

It was a difficult journey. Narcissa described the Rockies as "the most terrible mountains for steepness." Still, the missionaries arrived safely in Oregon, proving that women could endure the journey west.

A Difficult Start On reaching Oregon, the group split up. The Spaldings went to work with the Nez Percé. The Whitmans worked among a neighboring group, the Cayuse. Neither couple knew very much about the people they hoped to convert. The result was a difficult start.

After three years the Spaldings finally made their first converts. In 1839, Henry baptized two Nez Percé chiefs. A year later, one of the chiefs had his infant son baptized as well. The child would grow up to be the leader best known as Chief Joseph. You will meet him again later in this book.

The Whitmans were less successful. The Cayuse were far more interested in the whites' weapons and tools than in their religion. The couple also offended the Cayuse. They refused to pay for the land they took for their mission or to offer visitors gifts, as was the Indians' custom. Not a single Cayuse converted to the new faith.

A Pioneer's Paradise Marcus Whitman was far more successful at converting Americans to the belief that Oregon was a pioneer's paradise. "It does not concern me so much what is to become of any particular set of Indians," he wrote. "Our greatest work is…to aid the white settlement of this country and help to found its religious institutions."

In 1842, Marcus traveled east on horseback. Along the way, he urged Americans to settle in Oregon. On his return, he guided a large group of settlers along the Oregon Trail. More settlers soon followed. "The poor Indians are amazed at the overwhelming number of Americans coming into the country," observed Narcissa. "They seem not to know what to make of it."

Oregon Trail an overland route that stretched about 2,000 miles from Independence, Missouri, to the Columbia River in Oregon

In 1836, Marcus and Narcissa Whitman married and set out for Oregon to establish a mission. Here they are seen offering prayers for a safe journey.

In 1847, measles came west with settlers and swept through the Whitman mission. Marcus treated the sick as best he could. The Cayuse noticed that whites usually recovered, while their own people were dying. Rumors spread that Whitman was giving deadly pills to Indians. Angry warriors attacked the mission, killing both Marcus and Narcissa.

The Missionaries' Legacy   Like the Spanish priests in California, American preachers in Oregon hoped that their legacy would be large numbers of Christian Indians. In fact, relatively few Indians became Christians. Many, however, died of the diseases that came west with the missionaries. The missionaries' true legacy was to open the West to settlement. In California, Oregon, and other territories, settlers followed in the footsteps of western missionaries.

The Whitmans were killed by angry Cayuse warriors who blamed them for a deadly outbreak of measles.

16.6 The Pioneer Women

Women pioneers shared in the danger and the work of settling the West. Most of these women were wives and mothers, but some were single women seeking **homesteads**, husbands, or other new opportunities. Pioneer women not only helped to shape the future of the West, but also earned new status for themselves and for women throughout the United States.

On the Trail   Between 1840 and 1869, about 350,000 people traveled west in covered wagons. Most westward-bound pioneers gathered each spring near Independence, Missouri. There they formed columns of wagons called *wagon trains*.

The journey west lasted four to six months and covered about 2,000 miles. Wagon space was so limited that women were forced to leave most of the comforts of home behind. The few treasures they managed to fit in often had to be tossed out when the way became steep. The Oregon Trail was littered with furniture, china, books, and other cherished objects.

Women were expected to do the work they had done back home, but while traveling 15 to 20 miles a day. They cooked, washed clothes, and took care of the children. Meals on wheels were simple. "About the only change we have from bread and bacon," wrote Helen Carpenter, "is to bacon and bread."

The daily drudgery wore many women down. Lavinia Porter recalled, "I would make a brave effort to be cheerful and patient until the camp work was done. Then starting out ahead of the team and my men folks, when I thought I had gone beyond hearing distance, I would throw myself down on the unfriendly desert and give way like a child to sob and tears."

Trail Hazards   The death toll on the trail was high. Disease was the worst killer. Accidents were also common. People drowned crossing rivers.

homestead a plot of land where pioneers could build a home, farm, or ranch

Children fell from wagons and were crushed under the wheels. Indian attacks were rare, but the prospect added to the sense of danger.

By the end of the journey, each woman had a story to tell. Some had seen buffalo stampedes and prairie fires on the Great Plains. Some had almost frozen to death in the mountains or died of thirst in the deserts. But most survived to build new lives in the West.

One group of pioneer women faced a unique set of dangers—African Americans who had escaped from slave states or who were brought west by their owners. Even though slavery was outlawed in most of the West, fugitive slaves were often tracked down by bounty hunters. But for some African American women, the move west brought freedom. For example, when Biddy Mason's owner tried to take her from California (a free state) to Texas, Biddy sued for her freedom and won. She moved to Los Angeles, where she became a well-known pioneer and community leader.

The Pioneer Women's Legacy   The journey west changed pioneer women. The hardships of the trail brought out strengths and abilities they did not know they possessed. "I felt a secret joy," declared one Oregon pioneer, "in being able to have the power that sets things going."

And women did set things going. Wherever they settled, schools, churches, libraries, literary societies, and charitable groups soon blossomed. A good example is Annie Bidwell. When Annie married John Bidwell, she moved to his ranch in what is now the town of Chico, California. There she taught sewing to local Native American women and

Pioneers who wished to go west met in Independence, Missouri, in the spring. There they formed wagon trains before setting out on the trail.

The Granger Collection, New York

Although pioneer women had to travel 15 to 20 miles a day, they were still expected to take care of household chores when the wagon train stopped for the night.

helped their children learn to read and write English. Annie convinced John to give up drinking—he closed the tavern that had been part of his home—and encouraged the building of Chico's first church.

Annie was active in other causes as well, including the movement to give women a right that had long been denied them in the East—the right to vote. Wyoming Territory led the way by granting women the right to vote in 1869. By 1900, a full 20 years before women across the nation would win the right to vote, women were voting in four western states. The freedom and sense of equality enjoyed by women in the West helped pave the way for more equal treatment of women throughout the United States. This was perhaps the greatest legacy of the women pioneers.

16.7 The Mormons

In 1846, a wagon train of pioneers headed west in search of a new home. Looking down on the shining surface of Great Salt Lake in what is now Utah, their leader, Brigham Young, declared, "This is the place!"

It was not a promising spot. One pioneer described the valley as a "broad and barren plain...blistering in the rays of the midsummer sun." A woman wrote, "Weak and weary as I am, I would rather go a thousand miles further than remain." But that was one of the valley's attractions. No one else wanted the place that Brigham Young claimed for his followers, the Mormons.

A Persecuted Group   The **Mormons** were members of the Church of Jesus Christ of Latter-Day Saints. This new church was founded in New York by Joseph Smith in 1830. Smith taught that he had received a sacred book, *The Book of Mormon*, from an angel. He believed that it was his task to create a community of believers who would serve God faithfully.

Smith's followers lived in close communities, working hard and sharing their goods. Yet wherever they settled—first New York, then Ohio, Missouri, and Illinois—they were persecuted by their neighbors.

Many people were offended by the Mormons' teachings, especially their acceptance of polygamy—the practice of having more than one wife. Others resented the Mormons' rapidly growing power and wealth. In 1844, resentment turned to violence when a mob in Illinois killed Joseph Smith.

After Smith's murder, Brigham Young took over as leader of the Mormons. Young decided to move his community to Utah. There, the Mormons might be left alone to follow their faith in peace.

West to Utah Young turned out to be a practical as well as pious leader. "Prayer is good," he said, "but when baked potatoes and pudding are needed, prayer will not supply their place."

Young carefully planned every detail of the trek to Utah. The pioneers he led west stopped along the way to build shelters and plant crops for those who would follow.

Even with all this planning, the journey was difficult. "We soon thought it unusual," wrote one Mormon, "to leave a campground without burying one or more persons."

When he arrived at Great Salt Lake, Young laid out his first settlement, Salt Lake City. By the time he died in 1877, Utah had 125,000 Mormons living in 500 settlements.

To survive in this dry country, Mormons had to learn new ways to farm. They built dams, canals, and irrigation ditches to carry precious water from mountain streams to their farms in the valley. With this water, they made the desert bloom.

The Mormons' Legacy The Mormons were the first Americans to settle the Great Basin. They pioneered the farming methods adopted by later settlers of this dry region. They also helped settlers make their way west. Salt Lake City quickly became an important stop for travelers in need of food and supplies.

To the Mormons, however, their greatest legacy was the faith they planted so firmly in the Utah desert. From its center in Salt Lake City, the Mormon church has grown into a worldwide religion with more than 7 million members.

When Mormons were unable to purchase wagons or oxen for the journey to Utah, they pulled their belongings in handcarts. What cultural features will these settlers bring to the cities of the West?

16.8 The Forty-Niners

In 1848, carpenter James Marshall was building a sawmill on the American River in northern California. Suddenly, he spotted something shining in the water. "I reached my hand down and picked it up," he wrote later. "It made my heart thump, for I felt certain it was gold."

When word of Marshall's discovery leaked out, people across California dropped everything to race to the goldfields. "All were off to the mines," wrote a minister, "some on horses, some on carts, and some on crutches."

The World Rushes In   By 1849, tens of thousands of gold seekers from around the world had joined the California gold rush. About two thirds of these **forty-niners** were Americans. The rest came from Mexico, South America, Europe, Australia, and even China.

The forty-niners' first challenge was simply getting to California. From China and Australia, they had to brave the rough crossing of the Pacific Ocean. From the East, many traveled by ship to Panama in Central America, crossed through dangerous jungles to the Pacific side, and boarded ships north to San Francisco. Others made the difficult journey overland.

Most forty-niners were young, and almost all were men. When Luzena Wilson arrived in Sacramento with her family, a miner offered her $5 for her biscuits just to have "bread made by a woman." When she hesitated, he doubled his offer. "Women were scarce in those days," she wrote. "I lived six months in Sacramento and saw only two."

The search for gold was difficult. Miners spent long days searching through the mud and stones of freezing streams for this precious metal.

Life in the Mining Camps   Wherever gold was spotted, mining camps with names like Mad Mule Gulch and You Bet popped up overnight. At Coyote Diggings, Luzena found "a row of canvas tents." A few months later, "there were two thousand men…and the streets were lined with drinking saloons and gambling tables." Merchants made fortunes selling eggs for $6 a dozen and flour for $400 a barrel.

With no police to keep order, the camps were rough places. Miners frequently fought over the boundaries of their claims, and they took it on themselves to punish crimes. "In the short space of twenty-four hours," wrote Louise Clappe, "we have had murders, fearful accidents, bloody deaths, a mob, whippings, a hanging, an attempt at suicide, and a fatal duel."

Digging for gold was hard and tedious work. The miners spent long days digging up mud, dirt, and stones while standing knee-deep in icy streams. All too soon, the easy-to-find gold was gone. "The day of quick fortune-making is over," wrote a miner in 1851. "There are thousands of men now in California who would gladly go home if they had the money."

Miners shoveled gravel into a narrow box called a *sluice*. The water running through washed away the lighter particles, and the gold remained.

The Forty-Niners' Legacy   By 1852, the gold rush was over. While it lasted, about 250,000 people flooded into California. For California's Indians, the legacy of this invasion was dreadful. Between 1848 and 1870, warfare and disease reduced their number from about 150,000 to just 30,000. In addition, many Californios lost their land to the newcomers.

The forty-niners also left a prosperous legacy. By 1850, California had enough people to become the first state in the far west. These new Californians helped to transform the Golden State into a diverse land of economic opportunity.

16.9 The Chinese

Gam Saan—"Gold Mountain"—was what people in China called California in 1848. To poor and hungry Chinese peasants, Gam Saan sounded like paradise. There, they were told, "You will have great pay, large houses, and food and clothing of the finest description.… Money is in great plenty."

By 1852, more than 20,000 Chinese had ventured across the Pacific to California. That year, one of every ten Californians was Chinese.

An Uncertain Welcome   At first the Chinese were welcome. Lai Chun-Chuen, an early immigrant, observed that they "were received like guests" and "greeted with favor." In 1852, the governor of California praised Chinese immigrants as "one of the most worthy classes of our newly adopted citizens."

As gold mining became more difficult, however, attitudes toward immigrants began to change. A miner from Chile complained, "The Yankee regarded every man but…an American as an interloper [intruder] who had no right to come to California and pick up the gold." The Chinese, too, came under attack.

American miners called on the government to drive foreigners out of the goldfields. In 1852, the state legislature passed a law requiring foreign miners to pay a monthly fee for a license to mine. As the tax collectors arrived in the camps, most of the foreigners left. One traveler saw them "scattered along the roads in every direction," like refugees fleeing an invading army.

The Chinese Stay   The Chinese, however, paid the tax and stayed on. When the miners' tax failed to drive off the Chinese, Americans tried to bully them into leaving. Whites hacked off the long *queues,* or braids, worn by Chinese men. They burned the shacks of Chinese miners. Beatings followed burnings.

Discouraged Chinese immigrants left the mines to open restaurants, laundries, and stores in California's growing cities. "The best eating houses

in San Francisco," one miner wrote, were those opened by the Chinese. So many Chinese settled in San Francisco that local newspapers called their neighborhood Chinatown. Today, Chinatown remains the oldest and largest Chinese community in the United States.

Other Chinese put their farming skills to work in California's fertile Central Valley. They drained swamps and dug irrigation ditches to water arid fields. In time, they would help transform California into America's fruit basket and salad bowl.

Thousands of Chinese left their homeland and flocked to the California goldfields. Most failed to strike it rich. However, many settled in California's Central Valley, where their knowledge of farming helped the area develop.

The Legacy of the Chinese Immigrants   Most of the Chinese who came to California in search of gold hoped to return to China as rich men. A few did just that. Most, however, stayed on in America. Despite continued prejudice against them, their hard work, energy, and skills greatly benefited California and other western states. "In mining, farming, in factories and in the labor generally of California," observed a writer in 1876, "the employment of the Chinese has been found most desirable."

The Chinese not only helped to build the West, but they also made it a more interesting place to live. Wherever they settled, Chinese immigrants brought with them the arts, tastes, scents, and sounds of one of the world's oldest and richest cultures.

16.10 Chapter Summary

In the 1800s, the West became a magnet for people seeking adventure and opportunity. In this chapter, you learned about the people who settled the West. You used an illustration of a western town as you studied eight groups of settlers and their contributions to the West.

The Lewis and Clark expedition went west to find the Northwest Passage and to establish friendly relations with the native peoples. By mapping and collecting information about the West, the expedition helped prepare the way for future settlement.

In California, Spanish-speaking settlers followed in the footsteps of missionaries. The Californios' way of life centered on the rancho and the raising of cattle.

Valuable beaver furs—and a life of freedom and adventure—attracted fur trappers to the West. Many of these hardy "mountain men" stayed on as scouts, guides, and traders.

Missionaries traveled to Oregon and other western territories in hopes of converting Indians to Christianity. Although they made few converts, the missionaries attracted other settlers to the West.

Many women pioneers sought new opportunities in the West. Besides working to establish homes and farms, women brought education and culture to new settlements.

Mormon pioneers traveled to Utah in search of religious freedom. The Mormons built cities and towns, and they introduced new methods of farming to the dry plains.

Gold seekers from all over the world rushed to California in 1849. Few became rich, but many stayed to help build the economy of the new state.

The gold rush attracted thousands of Chinese immigrants to California. Although they often had to fight prejudice, most of them remained in the United States, working as laborers and starting new businesses and farms.

Many settlers who moved west built small towns. Some became huge cities. This painting shows an already sprawling Los Angeles, California, in the early 1800s. What physical and cultural features can you observe?

Why does this man need a burro?

What do these packs contain?

How is this man helping the other man?

Mexicano Contributions to the Southwest

17.1 Introduction

The Texas war of independence and the war with Mexico in the 1840s had a lasting effect on the people of the Southwest. Spanish-speaking people had made their homes in the region since the days of the conquistadors in the 1500s. By 1848, from 80,000 to 100,000 *Mexicanos*, or Mexican citizens, lived in the territories given up by Mexico in the Treaty of Guadalupe Hidalgo. Most of these people remained in the Southwest and became citizens of the United States.

The treaty with Mexico promised Mexican Americans full citizenship rights, the right to keep their property, and the right to use their language. These promises were not kept. Armed with the belief that they were a superior people, white settlers pushed Mexicanos off their land. Whites also made it illegal for Mexicano children to speak Spanish in schools. They found ways to keep Mexicanos from exercising their right to vote.

Mexicanos protested each of these assaults on their rights. But the government did little to protect them. Before long, Mexican Americans found themselves, in the words of one historian, "foreigners in their native land."

The problems of prejudice, poverty, and the lack of political power persisted well into the 20th century. Despite much progress, many of these problems remain today.

Yet Mexican Americans also had a deep influence on their new country. Even though most white settlers had little respect for Mexican Americans, they freely borrowed much that was useful from the Mexican **heritage**. Spanish words and Mexican foods, laws, technology, and architecture all became a lasting part of the culture of the Southwest. In this chapter, you will learn about these and other contributions that Mexicanos made to American life.

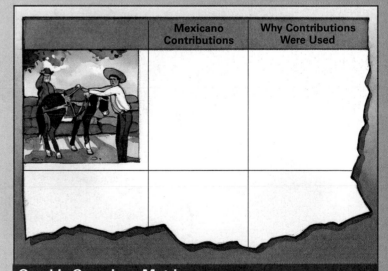

	Mexicano Contributions	Why Contributions Were Used

Graphic Organizer: Matrix
You will use this matrix to learn about Mexicano contributions to the Southwest.

tradition a belief, custom, or way of doing something that has existed for a long time

17.2 Mexicano Mining Contributions

Mining in the West developed in three waves—gold, silver, and copper. Each wave depended on the contribution of Mexican miners. Mexicanos came to the Southwest with a rich mining **tradition**. They knew where to look for precious metals and how to get them out of the ground.

Gold Mining   The Americans who rushed to California in 1849 had many skills. But they knew nothing about mining. Mexicanos introduced them to the *batea,* or gold pan. Miners scooped up mud from streambeds with the batea. Then they swished it around to wash away the lightweight sand. The heavier flakes of gold sank to the bottom of the pan.

Mexicanos also brought the riffle box to the goldfields. The bottom of this long box was crossed with pieces of wood called *riffles.* As mud washed through the box, the heavy gold sank and was trapped behind the riffles. The riffle box was used extensively by both American and Chinese miners.

Before long, miners discovered that the gold they were picking up in streams came from veins of quartz rock in the Sierra Nevada. Quartz mining was a mystery to Americans, but it was familiar to Mexicanos. Mexicanos taught other miners how to dig the quartz out of mountains. They also showed miners how to use a simple *arrastra,* or grinding mill, to crush the rock so they could easily remove the gold.

Shown below is an arrastra, or grinding mill. A horse moved a round stone to crush gold-bearing rocks from which miners could remove the precious metal.

Silver and Copper Mining   A Mexican miner sparked the West's first big silver strike. In 1859, a prospector named Henry Comstock was looking for gold in Nevada. Much to his annoyance, his gold was mixed with a lot of worthless "blue stuff." One day, a Mexicano miner looked at the blue stuff and started shouting, *"Mucha plata! Mucha plata!"* ("Much silver!") In its first 20 years, the Comstock lode yielded over $300 million in silver and gold.

Mexicanos discovered copper in the Southwest in the early 1800s. When Americans began to mine copper in Arizona, they turned to Mexican miners for help. By 1940, Arizona mines had produced $3 billion worth of copper—copper that carried electricity and telephone calls to millions of homes across America.

17.3 Cattle Ranching

Cattle ranching in the West was built upon traditions brought north from Mexico. Spanish colonists imported the first cattle to the Americas. The animals **adapted** well to the dry conditions of Mexico and the American Southwest. In time, millions of Spanish cattle ran wild in Texas and California.

Spanish cattle were thin, wiry creatures with long, wide-spreading horns. They moved quickly and were dangerous. *Californios* (Mexicanos in California) often found themselves dodging behind trees or diving into ditches to escape the charge of an angry longhorn.

With cattle so abundant, Californios and *Tejanos* (Mexicanos in Texas) found ranching to be a good business. So did the Americans who learned the cattle business from Mexican *rancheros,* or ranchers.

The Rancho   Western cattle ranching was nothing like dairy farming in the East. Dairy farms in the East were small family businesses that produced mostly milk, butter, and cheese. Compared to these farms, western ranchos were huge. In the arid Southwest, large grants of land were needed to provide enough food and water for cattle herds. Instead of dairy products, the main products of ranchos were meat, hides, and tallow.

Ranch life followed traditions that had been developed in Spain and perfected in Mexico. Rancheros spent most of their day on horseback, overseeing their land and herds. Caring for the cattle was the work of hired *vaqueros,* or cowboys.

The Roundup   Among the vaqueros' most important jobs were the *rodeo,* or roundup, and branding (using a hot iron to burn a mark into the hide of cattle). Branding was essential because herds belonging to different owners mixed together on unfenced grasslands. To avoid conflicts, every owner had to mark his cattle with a distinctive brand.

During the rodeo, vaqueros drove unbranded calves to a roundup area. There, the calves were branded with the brand their mothers bore.

As Americans took up ranching, they adopted the rancheros' practice of branding cattle. Along with cowboys and the roundup, cattle brands are still part of ranch life in the West.

During the rodeo, or roundup, vaqueros drove unmarked cattle to special roundup areas. There the animals were branded with a rancho's distinctive identification mark. Such a practice was necessary because cattle belonging to different owners grazed together on the same open range.

adapt to change in order to survive in a new or different environment or situation

17.4 The Cowboy

Hollywood movies make it seem that nothing is more American than the western cowboy. Cowboys, however, learned their job from the Mexican vaquero. Across the Southwest, vaqueros were admired for their skill at riding, roping, and handling cattle. American cowboys adopted the vaqueros' clothes and gear, and much of their language.

Cowboy Clothes and Gear   From head to toe, cowboys dressed in clothing borrowed from the vaqueros. For example, the cowboys' "ten-gallon hats," which shaded their eyes and sometimes served as a water pail or a pillow, came from the vaqueros' wide-brimmed *sombreros*. The leather chaps that protected the cowboys' legs from cacti and sagebrush were modeled on the vaqueros' *chaparreras*. The high-heeled, pointed-toe boots that slipped so easily into the cowboys' stirrups were based on the vaqueros' *botas*. Even the *poncho* that protected cowboys from cold and rain was borrowed from the vaqueros.

Mexicanos also invented the western (or cowboy) saddle, with its useful horn. The saddles brought to America from Europe did not have horns. When a vaquero on a European saddle roped a steer, he had to tie his rope to the horse's tail to keep it anchored. This method was hard on both the horse and the rider. By adding a horn to the saddle, vaqueros made their job easier—and their horses' job as well.

Cowboys borrowed another essential piece of gear from the vaqueros— *la riata* (the lariat). Vaqueros were masters of the art of throwing a 60-foot rope long distances with amazing accuracy. This skill was especially useful for roping calves during a roundup. In a remarkable display of roping skill, a vaquero named José Romero once roped a full-grown eagle right out of the sky!

From his hat to his boots, the American cowboy copied the dress of the Mexican vaquero. Each item of the vaquero's clothing helped him with his work. His sombrero shaded him from the sun. His neckerchief, when worn over his mouth, protected him from dust. His high-heeled, pointed boots kept him secure in the stirrups of his saddle.

Cowboy Lingo
American cowboys borrowed or adapted many ranching words from the vaqueros as well. The terms *bronco, stampede, corral, lasso, burro, buckaroo,* and *vamoose* all come from Spanish-Mexican words. So do *mesa, canyon, mesquite, chaparral,* and other terms used to describe the southwestern landscape. The cowboy slang word for jail, *hoosegow,* came from the Spanish *juzgado.* And of course, the terms *ranch* and *rancher* came from *rancho* and *ranchero.*

17.5 Sheep Raising

In New Mexico, the most important industry was sheep raising. From the founding of the province up to the Mexican Cession, sheep fed, clothed, and supported Spanish and Mexican settlers.

The Spanish brought a long tradition of sheep raising to the Americas. Two kinds of sheep were raised in Spain—the beautiful *merinos* with their fine wool, and the ugly *churros* with their coarse wool. The Spanish brought the scrawny churro to New Mexico, and for good reason. This tough little sheep knew how to survive in a dry environment like that of the Southwest.

The Spanish Sheep-Raising System   When Americans came to New Mexico, they did not think of sheep raising as a business. In the East, a farmer might raise a few sheep as a sideline, but not large herds. Once they saw the Spanish sheep-raising system in New Mexico, however, some Americans changed their minds.

Under the Spanish system, sheep raising was a big, well-organized business. The Spanish governor of New Mexico, for example, once owned 2 million sheep and employed 2,700 workers.

At the top of this business stood the *patron,* or owner of the herds. Below him were several layers of managers. These supervisors and range bosses spent their days on horseback, checking range conditions and the health of the sheep.

Sheep raising was the most important industry in New Mexico when the area belonged to Mexico. An owner of a sheep ranch might have over a million sheep.

The lowest-level worker was the *pastor,* or herder. Each pastor was responsible for 1,500 to 2,000 sheep. A pastor stayed with his flock night and day, slowly guiding it from place to place so that the sheep could graze as they moved. During spring lambing season, the pastor assisted with difficult births, cared for orphaned lambs, and helped the newborns survive. One pastor described this busy time as a "month-long hell of worry and toil."

Americans Adopt the Spanish System   Americans soon adopted the Spanish system as their own. Large-scale sheep raising spread from New Mexico across the Southwest. In California, the churro was crossed with the merino to produce a sheep with far better wool. As a result, between 1862 and 1880, U.S. wool production soared from 5 million to 22 million pounds a year.

17.6 Irrigated Farming

Americans coming to the Southwest knew as little about irrigated farming as they did about mining, cattle ranching, and sheep raising. In the East, enough rain fell year-round to water a farmer's crops. **Irrigation** was unnecessary and unknown. But in the Southwest, where six months could go by with no rain, irrigation was essential.

Mexican settlers in the Southwest brought with them irrigation techniques that had been developed centuries earlier in Spain and North Africa. They borrowed other techniques from the Pueblo Indians of New Mexico. When settlers first arrived, the Pueblos were irrigating between 15,000 and 25,000 acres of crop land in the arid Rio Grande Valley.

The Mexican System of Irrigation Bringing water to fields involved an enormous amount of work. First, farmers had to redirect water from local streams to their fields. They began by building a dam of rocks, earth, and brush across the stream. The water that backed up behind the dam was brought to the fields by irrigation ditches.

To keep from wasting this precious water, Mexicanos carefully leveled their fields. Then they divided the fields into squares. Each square was marked off by a wall of earth high enough to hold in water. When one square had been soaked with water, farmers made a hole in its wall. The water then flowed to the next square. The farmers continued in this way until the entire field was soaked. This method of irrigation was known as "the Mexican system."

America's Fruit Basket Using crops introduced by Mexicanos and the Mexican system of irrigation, American settlers turned the Southwest into America's fruit basket. Among the many fruits brought by Mexicanos to the Southwest were grapes, dates, olives, apples, walnuts, pears, plums, peaches, apricots, and quinces. Mexicano settlers also brought the first citrus fruits—lemons, limes, and oranges—to the region. Many of these fruits were unknown in the East, where the climate was too cold for them to grow. But they thrived in sunny Arizona and California. With the help of Mexicano farmworkers, American farmers transformed dry deserts into irrigated fruit orchards and citrus groves.

irrigation a system for bringing water to farmland by artificial means, such as using a dam to trap water and ditches to channel it to fields

The Mexicanos introduced a system of irrigation that allowed settlers in the Southwest to turn deserts into productive, fertile fields.

17.7 Mexican Food

In 1835, William Heath Davis became one of the first Americans to settle in California. There he got his first taste of Mexican food. Davis later wrote of the Californios:

> *Their tables were frugally [simply] furnished, the food clean and inviting, consisting mainly of good beef broiled on an iron rod, or steaks with onions, also mutton [sheep], chicken, eggs.... The bread was tortillas; sometimes made with yeast. Beans were a staple dish.... Their meat stews were excellent when not too highly seasoned with red pepper.*

Davis may not have known it, but the food he was enjoying in California brought together the best of two worlds.

Corn, a food of the native Indians, was a staple in the Mexicano diet. Here, a Mexicano woman is grinding corn that she will use to make a flat cornbread called *tortillas*.

A Food Revolution   The conquest of Mexico in 1521 began one of the great food revolutions in history. The Spanish came to Mexico in search of gold, but the greatest treasures they found were Indian foods unknown in Europe. These "New World" foods included corn, tomatoes, chocolate, peanuts, vanilla, beans, squash, avocados, coconuts, sunflower seeds, and chili peppers.

The Spanish shipped these new foods back to Spain. From there they spread throughout Europe, greatly expanding people's food choices.

In turn, the Spanish brought the foods of the "Old World" to Mexico. They introduced meats such as pork, beef, lamb, chicken, and goat. They brought nuts and grains such as almonds, walnuts, rice, wheat, and barley. They planted fruits and vegetables such as apples, oranges, grapes, olives, lettuce, carrots, sugarcane, and potatoes (which they discovered in Peru). And they introduced herbs and spices such as cinnamon, parsley, coriander, oregano, and black pepper.

A New Style of Cooking   Mexican cooks combined these Old and New World foods to create a rich and flavorful style of cooking that was neither Indian nor Spanish. It was distinctly Mexican.

As Americans settled the Southwest, they were introduced to Mexican food. Many of them liked the new tastes, and they borrowed recipes from Mexicano cooks. In Texas, the mingling of Mexican and American dishes resulted in a style of cooking known as "Tex-Mex." And across America, a spicy stew of beef and beans known simply as "chili" became as American as apple pie.

Courtyards, rounded arches, thick adobe walls, and red tile roofs are characteristics of Spanish-style architecture.

17.8 Spanish-style Architecture

Throughout the Southwest, the Mexicano contribution to architecture is easy to see. Many buildings can be found with the thick walls, red tile roofs, rounded arches, and courtyards that are typical of Spanish architecture.

Spanish architecture took root in Mexico during the colonial period. Mexican settlers brought their knowledge of this tradition to the Southwest. Their missions, homes, and other structures were simple and attractive. And they were ideally suited to the hot, dry climate of the Southwest.

Adobe Buildings Since wood was sparse in the Southwest, Mexicanos used adobe bricks as their main building material. *Adobe* is a mixture of earth, grass, and water that is shaped into bricks and baked in the sun. Mexicanos covered their adobe homes with colorful red clay tiles. Besides being attractive and fireproof, a tile roof kept the adobe walls from being washed away during heavy rains.

Many adobe buildings featured patios and verandas. A *patio* is a roofless inner courtyard, often located at the center of a home. A *veranda* is a roofed porch or balcony extending along the outside of a building. Patios and verandas allowed Mexicanos to spend much of their time outdoors while still protected from the hot sun and dry desert winds.

Newcomers Adopt the Spanish Style Americans moving to the Southwest quickly saw the advantages of building with adobe. Because of their thick walls, adobe structures stayed cooler in summer and warmer in winter than the wood buildings that Americans from the East were used to. Adobe structures could also be easily constructed from locally available materials.

American settlers used adobe to build not only homes, but also courthouses, trading posts, post offices, and other buildings. Later, builders adapted Spanish architecture to new materials such as concrete and stucco. By the 1930s, nearly a million Spanish-style homes had been built in California. "Who would live in a structure of wood and brick if they could get a palace of mud?" wrote an admiring easterner. "The adobes to me [make] the most picturesque and comfortable [homes]…and harmonize… with the whole nature of the landscape."

17.9 Mexican Laws

The Mexicanos of the Southwest were used to being governed by Mexican laws. These laws often differed from American law. For example, Mexico had outlawed slavery in 1829. Slaves from the American South sometimes ran away to find freedom in Mexican settlements. (Recall that Mexico's abolition of slavery was one of the issues that led Texans to fight for their independence from Mexico.)

In time, both Mexican and American legal traditions would shape laws in the West. Particularly important were Mexicano laws governing mining, water, and community property.

Mining Law   Before the discovery of gold in California, there was so little mining in the United States that Americans had no mining law. Once in the goldfields, the forty-niners desperately needed rules to keep order. With the help of Mexicano miners, Americans developed a "law of the mines" based on Mexican mining law. California miners later carried this law of the mines to other parts of the Southwest.

Water Law   The water law brought west by Americans worked well enough in the East, where rainfall was abundant. Under American law, water flowing across a field or farm belonged to the owner of that land. Landowners could use their water in whatever ways they wanted.

This principle did not work well in the West, where water was scarce and precious. Disputes over who controlled streams led to endless legal conflicts and even water wars.

To end these conflicts, settlers wrote new laws based on Mexican "pueblo law." Pueblo law said that water was too valuable to be owned or controlled by any one person. Instead, water belonged to an entire community and should be used for the benefit of all.

Community Property Law   For women, the most important legal principle borrowed from Mexican law was the idea of community property. In eastern states, married women had few property rights. Any property acquired by a married couple— such as a home, farm, or business—belonged solely to the husband.

In contrast, Mexican law said that all property acquired during a marriage was "community property." If a couple separated, half of that property belonged to the wife, half to the husband.

American settlers liked the idea of sharing the gains of marriage between husband and wife. Today, Texas, California, New Mexico, Arizona, Idaho, Nevada, Washington, Wisconsin, and Louisiana are all community property states.

The Mexicano legal principle of community property gave women property rights they did not have under British law. According to the Mexican principle, women were entitled to half of all property acquired during a marriage.

17.10 Mexicano Entertainments

The Californios, observed William Heath Davis, "were about the happiest and most contented people I ever saw." Californios worked hard. But they also knew how to entertain themselves with music, dance, and *fiestas* (celebrations). Americans settling the Southwest shared in these entertainments.

In the picture above, the couple is performing the fandango. During this popular Mexican dance, the man and the woman play castanets, which are small pieces of wood held in the palm of the hand and clicked together.

Music and Dancing   Mexicano music greatly influenced country and western music in the Southwest. The most important contribution was the *corrido,* or folk ballad. A corrido is a dramatic story sung to the accompaniment of guitars. The subjects of corridos ranged from exciting tales of heroes and bandits to sad songs of love and betrayal.

American settlers greatly admired the color and energy of traditional Mexicano dance. Dancing was an important part of any Mexicano fiesta. Favorite dances included the *jota*, the *fandango*, and *la bamba*. The last of these, the bamba, was danced by a young woman balancing a full glass of water on her head. Generations of schoolchildren learned another popular dance, the *jarabe tapatío*, or "Mexican hat dance," as part of their southwestern cultural heritage.

Fiestas and Rodeos   Throughout the year, Mexicanos held a variety of religious fiestas. One of the most important honored Our Lady of Guadalupe, the patron saint of Mexico. In San Antonio, Texas, Tejanos marked this day (December 12) with an elaborate procession to the cathedral. After attending church services, the Tejanos danced all night long in their homes.

Today, the most widely celebrated Mexicano holiday is *El Cinco de Mayo* (the Fifth of May). This holiday commemorates an important victory in Mexico's fight for independence from French rule in 1862. Cinco de Mayo fiestas bring together Mexican and non-Mexican Americans to enjoy Mexicano music, dance, and food.

For millions of Americans, rodeo is an exciting professional sport. Rodeo's roots go back to cattle roundups on Mexicano ranchos. During these get-togethers, Mexicano cowboys competed with each other in events such as calf roping, bull riding, and bronco busting. American cowboys joined in these contests, and soon rodeos became annual events in western cities. To its many fans, the rodeo, with its mixed Mexicano and American heritage, represents the best of the West.

17.11 Chapter Summary

In this chapter, you learned about Mexicano contributions to the culture of the Southwest. You used a matrix to organize your information. Movies and television often portray the settling of the West as a story of white pioneers taming the wilderness. As you have seen, the story is not that simple. Long before whites arrived, Mexicanos had learned to survive and even thrive in the harsh landscape of the Southwest. Although often mistreated by pioneers from the East, their knowledge would prove to be more valuable than gold to the newcomers.

American settlers learned about mining, cattle ranching, cowboy life, and sheep raising from Mexicanos. They adopted irrigation techniques that had been pioneered by Mexicanos and by Pueblo Indians. They learned to appreciate Mexicano food. They borrowed the Mexicanos' architectural styles and laws. And they learned to enjoy Mexicano entertainments.

Today, Mexicano culture survives in such American adaptations as the organization of ranches, Spanish-style homes, popular foods, and legal traditions regarding water and community property. The American language is enriched by Spanish and Mexican words like *patio, rodeo,* and *poncho*. From San Francisco to San Antonio, hundreds of place names in the West and Southwest echo the Spanish-Mexican heritage. Millions of Americans celebrate the Mexican holiday Cinco de Mayo. It is hard to imagine what the United States would be like without this rich legacy.

Mexicano contributions played a central role in turning the southwestern United States into a unique, prosperous section of the country.

239

LUCRETIA MOTT.

ELIZABETH CADY STANTON.

LUCY STONE.

JULIA WARD HOWE.

SUSAN B. ANTHONY.

MRS. MARTHA C. WRIGHT.
First President N. Y. State Suffrage
Association. Elected 1860.

MRS. JEAN BROOKS GREENLEAF.
Fourth President N. Y. State Suffrage
Assn. Served 6 years, 1890-96.

REV. ANNA H. SHAW.

MRS. ELIZABETH BOYNTON HAR-
BERT.

Rev. Anna H. Shaw

A. D. R.
C 1887
AC 6294/App.3

DOROTHEA LYNDE DIX.

This page, from a scrapbook kept by Mary S. Anthony, pictures women who led various reform movements.

An Era of Reform

18.1 Introduction

In 1851, a group of people gathered in a church to discuss the rights of women. A tall African American woman made her way through the crowd and sat down. Her name was Sojourner Truth. Back when she was a slave, she had learned to pay careful attention to white people. Now she listened as whites discussed whether women should have the same rights as men.

Sojourner heard one minister after another explain that women didn't need more rights because they weren't smart or strong enough to do much besides raise children. Women, they argued, needed help from men. One man summed it up by saying, "Women are weak."

With that, the former slave had heard enough. She rose slowly to her stately height of six feet and walked to the pulpit. The room grew quiet as everyone waited for her to speak.

"The man over there says women need to be helped into carriages and lifted over ditches and over puddles, and have the best places everywhere," she began. "Nobody helped me into carriages or over puddles, or gives me the best place."

Her voice rose to a thunderous pitch. "And ain't I a woman? Look at my arm! I have plowed and planted and gathered into barns, and no man could head [outdo] me—and ain't I a woman? I could work as much and eat as much as a man—when I could get it—and bear the lash as well! I have borne thirteen children, and seen most of 'em sold into slavery, and when I cried out with my mother's grief, none but Jesus heard me—and ain't I a woman?"

When she finished, people applauded. Some cried. One witness said, "She had taken us up in her strong arms and carried us safely."

As a woman and a former slave, Sojourner Truth represented two of the great reform movements in America in the 1800s. Between about 1820 and 1850, American **reformers** devoted themselves to such causes as ending slavery, promoting women's rights, and improving education. As you will read in this chapter, women like Sojourner Truth not only participated in these movements, but emerged as powerful leaders.

Graphic Organizer: Illustration
You will use this illustration to learn about the Era of Reform.

Preachers at religious meetings, such as the one pictured below, proclaimed that people could earn salvation by doing good works. This message encouraged many people to work to improve society.

18.2 The Spirit of Reform

It was fitting that the meeting attended by Sojourner Truth took place in a church. New religious movements played a key role in inspiring thousands of Americans to try to remake society.

The Second Great Awakening   A revival of religious feeling swept across the nation in the 1820s and 1830s. Church leaders called this period the **Second Great Awakening**. Day after day, people gathered in churches and big white tents to hear a message of hope. Preachers like Charles G. Finney, a leader of the movement, urged Christians to let themselves be "filled with the Spirit of God." Their listeners prayed, shouted, and sang hymns. Sometimes they cried for hours or fell down in frenzies.

Like the First Great Awakening during colonial days, this religious revival fired people's emotions. But the Second Great Awakening also offered something new. In the past, most Christian ministers had said that God had already decided who would be saved. Now preachers told their flocks that everyone could gain forgiveness for their sins. Many of them taught that one way to be saved was to do good works. Christians, they said, could build "heaven on Earth."

The Granger Collection, New York

This optimistic message attracted enthusiastic followers throughout the West and North. It gave men and women alike a reason to work for the improvement of society. Charles Finney's preaching, for example, inspired many people to actively oppose slavery.

Optimistic Ideas   Other optimistic ideas also inspired Americans during this time. In New England, Ralph Waldo Emerson, a former minister, was the central figure in a movement called **transcendentalism**. Emerson believed that every human being had unlimited potential. But to realize their godlike nature, people had to "transcend," or go beyond, purely logical thinking. They could find the answers to life's mysteries only by learning to trust their emotions and intuition.

Transcendentalists added to the spirit of reform by urging people to question society's rules and institutions. Do not conform to others' expectations, they said. If you want to find God—and your own true self—look to nature and the "God within."

Emerson's friend Henry David Thoreau captured this new individualism in a famous essay. "If a man does not keep pace with his companions," wrote Thoreau, "perhaps it is because he hears a different drummer. Let him step to the music which he hears."

Thoreau practiced what he preached. In 1845, he went into the woods near Concord, Massachusetts, to live alone and as close to nature as possible. Thoreau spent more than two years in solitude, recording his thoughts in a 6,000-page journal. Once he was jailed overnight for refusing to pay taxes to support the Mexican-American War.

Model Communities While Thoreau tried to find the ideal life in solitude, other transcendentalists tried to create perfect communities. In 1841, George Ripley started a community called Brook Farm near Boston. Residents at Brook Farm tried to live in "brotherly cooperation" instead of competing with each other, as people in the larger society did. They shared the labor of supporting themselves by farming, teaching, and making clothes.

Brook Farm was only one of hundreds of model communities started by reformers in the first half of the 19th century. Most of these experiments lasted only a few years. But they were a powerful expression of the belief that people of good will could create an ideal society.

In the book *Walden,* transcendentalist Henry David Thoreau wrote of building a cabin in the woods. There he meditated on the meaning of his life, society, nature, and the human spirit.

transcendentalism a philosophy which taught that people should "transcend" (go beyond) logical thinking to reach true understanding with the help of emotion and intuition

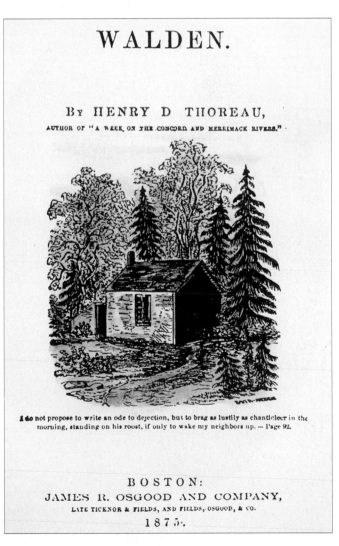

WALDEN.

By HENRY D THOREAU,

AUTHOR OF "A WEEK ON THE CONCORD AND MERRIMACK RIVERS."

I do not propose to write an ode to dejection, but to brag as lustily as chanticleer in the morning, standing on his roost, if only to wake my neighbors up. — Page 92.

BOSTON:
JAMES R. OSGOOD AND COMPANY,
LATE TICKNOR & FIELDS, AND FIELDS, OSGOOD, & CO.
1875.

18.3 Reforming the Treatment of Prisoners and the Mentally Ill

One day in 1841, a Boston woman named Dorothea Dix agreed to teach Sunday school at a jail. What she witnessed that day changed her life forever.

Dix was horrified to see that many inmates were bound in chains and locked in cages. Children accused of minor thefts were jailed with adult criminals. Were conditions this bad everywhere?

To find out, Dix visited hundreds of jails and prisons throughout Massachusetts. She also visited debtors' prisons, or jails for people who owed money. Most of the thousands of Americans in debtors' prisons owed less than 20 dollars. While they were locked up, they could not earn money to repay their debts. As a result, they remained imprisoned for years.

Horrified by what she saw during a visit to a local jail, Dorothea Dix worked tirelessly to improve conditions for prisoners and the mentally ill.

The Plight of the Mentally Ill What shocked Dix most of all was the way mentally ill people were treated. Most people who were judged "insane" were locked away in dirty, crowded prison cells. If they misbehaved, they were whipped.

Dix and other reformers believed that the mentally ill needed treatment and care, not punishment. Massachusetts had one private asylum, or hospital for the mentally ill. But only the wealthy could afford to send a family member there. Even so, the asylum was filled to overflowing. The state needed more mental hospitals.

Campaigning for Better Conditions For two years, Dix quietly gathered firsthand information about the horrors she had seen. Then she prepared a detailed report for the Massachusetts state legislature. "I come as the advocate of helpless, forgotten, insane, and idiotic men and women," she said. "I proceed, gentlemen, briefly to call your attention to the present state of insane persons, confined…in cages, closets, cellars, stalls, pens! Chained, naked, beaten with rods, and lashed into obedience!" Shocked by Dix's report, the lawmakers voted to create public asylums for the mentally ill.

Inspired by her success, Dix visited prisons in other states as well. After she prepared reports demanding justice for the mentally ill, those states also created special mental hospitals.

Dix continued campaigning for reform for the rest of her life. By the time she died in 1887, state governments no longer put debtors in prison. Most had created special justice systems for children in trouble. And many had outlawed cruel punishments, such as branding people with hot irons. Dix had shown that with enough courage and dedication, reformers—including women—could lead society to make significant changes.

18.4 Improving Education

A second reform movement that won support in the 1800s was the effort to make education available to more children. The man who led this movement was Horace Mann, "the father of American public schools."

The Need for Public Schools As a boy in Massachusetts in the early 1800s, Horace Mann attended school only ten weeks a year. The rest of the time, he had to work on the family farm.

Mann was lucky to have even this limited chance to attend school. In Massachusetts, Puritans had established town schools. Few other areas had **public schools**—schools paid for by taxes. Wealthy parents sent their children to private school or hired tutors at home. On the frontier, 60 children might attend a part-time, one-room school. Their teachers had limited education and received little pay. Most children simply did not go to school at all.

In the cities, some poor children stole, destroyed property, and set fires. Reformers believed that education would help these children escape poverty and become good citizens. Influenced by its big cities, New York set up public elementary schools in every town as early as the 1820s.

Meanwhile, in Massachusetts, Horace Mann became the state's supervisor of education. In towns and villages, he spoke out on the need for public schools. "Our means of education," he stated, "are the grand machinery by which the 'raw material' of human nature can be worked up into inventors and discoverers, into skilled artisans and scientific farmers."

Citizens in Massachusetts responded to Mann's message. They voted to pay taxes to build better schools, to pay teachers higher salaries, and to establish special training schools for teachers.

An Unfinished Reform By 1850, many states in the North and West used Mann's ideas. Soon most white children, especially boys, attended free public schools.

But America still did not offer education to everyone. Most high schools and colleges did not admit girls. States as far north as Illinois passed laws to keep African

> **public schools** schools that are paid for by taxes and managed by local government for the benefit of the general public

Prior to the reforms in public education led by Horace Mann, most children did not attend school. Those that did usually had to suffer overcrowded classrooms, like the one shown below, and poorly trained teachers.

abolitionists people who favored abolition, the ending of slavery

Americans out of public schools. When towns did allow African Americans to attend school, most made them go to separate schools that received less money. In the South, few girls and no African Americans could attend public schools.

Education for girls and women did make some progress. In 1837, Ohio's Oberlin College became the first college to admit women as well as men. When states started the first public universities in the 1860s, most accepted female students.

African Americans, however, had few options. When Prudence Crandall admitted an African American girl to her girls' school in Connecticut, white parents took their children out of the school. Crandall responded by having all African American students. Enraged, white people threw stones at the school and had Crandall jailed. After two years, she was forced to close her school.

Horace Mann realized that much more needed to be done to increase educational opportunity for women and African Americans. He became the first president of a new college for men and women, Antioch College in Ohio. There, he urged his students to become involved in improving society. "Be ashamed to die," he told them, "until you have won some victory for humanity."

Sojourner Truth, a former slave, gave speeches throughout the North against slavery and, later, in favor of women's rights.

18.5 Fighting Slavery

In 1835, a poster appeared on walls throughout Washington, D.C. The poster showed two drawings. One drawing, labeled "The Land of the Free," showed the founding fathers reading the Declaration of Independence. The other, labeled "The Home of the Oppressed," showed slaves trudging past the Capitol building, the home of Congress. The poster posed a challenging question: How could America, the "land of the free," still allow slavery? By the 1830s, growing numbers of people were asking this question. They were called **abolitionists**.

The Struggle Begins Some Americans had opposed slavery even in Revolutionary War times. Quakers stopped owning slaves in 1776. By 1792, every state as far south as Virginia had anti-slavery societies.

Once the slave trade ended in 1808, northern shipping communities had no more interest in slaves. Still, northern factory owners liked the cheap cotton that the South provided. Although slavery ended in the North by the early 1800s, many northerners still accepted southern slavery.

Unlike their neighbors, abolitionists wanted to end slavery. But they did not always agree about how to do it. Radicals tried to inspire slaves to rise up in revolt.

Others wanted to find a peaceful way to end slavery immediately. Moderates wanted to give slaveholders time to develop farming methods that didn't rely on slave labor.

From the early days, both blacks and whites worked in the abolition movement, sometimes together, sometimes separately. Black activists often maintained their independence. One African American journalist wrote, "As long as we let them think and act for us…they will outwardly treat us as men, while in their hearts they still hold us as slaves."

In 1831, a deeply religious white man, William Lloyd Garrison, started a fiery abolitionist newspaper, the *Liberator*. Braving the disapproval of many northerners, Garrison demanded the immediate freeing of all slaves. "I will be as harsh as truth," he wrote. "I will not retreat a single inch—and I will be heard." Angry pro-slavery groups destroyed Garrison's printing press and burned his house.

Frederick Douglass Speaks Out

One day, Garrison heard an escaped slave, Frederick Douglass, speaking to a meeting of abolitionists. Over six feet tall, Douglass spoke with a voice like thunder. When he described the cruel treatment of slave children, people cried. When he made fun of ministers who told slaves to love slavery, people laughed. When he finished, Garrison jumped up and cried, "Shall such a man be held a slave in a Christian land?" The crowd called out, "No! No! No!"

Frederick Douglass quickly became a leader in the abolitionist movement. His autobiography (the story of his life) became an instant best-seller. A brilliant, independent thinker, Douglass eventually started his own newspaper, *North Star*. Its motto read, "Right is of no sex—Truth is of no color—God is the father of us all, and we are all Brethren."

Women Get Involved

Many women were inspired by the religious reform movement to become involved in the fight against slavery. Like other abolitionists, they sometimes faced violence. When a young woman named Angelina Grimke spoke against slavery, an anti-abolition mob threw stones. When she kept speaking, they burned the building.

Angelina and her sister Sarah had been raised in a South Carolina slave-holding family. After traveling North and becoming Quakers, they saw slavery in a new way. The two sisters began speaking out about the poverty and pain of slavery. At first they spoke only to other women, but soon they were speaking to large groups of men and women throughout the North. The Grimkes led the way for other women to speak in public.

Some abolitionists, like Sojourner Truth, were former slaves. Truth had always been strongly spiritual and had preached throughout the North at religious meetings and on street corners. But when she met Douglass and Garrison, their enthusiasm inspired her to speak out about slavery. An outstanding speaker, Truth argued that God would end slavery peacefully.

Abolitionists were a minority, even in the North. But their efforts, and the violence directed against them, helped change northerners' attitudes toward slavery. In addition, the anti-slavery fight helped pave the way for the next great reform movement, the struggle for women's rights.

Wilson Chinn, a branded slave from Louisiana, poses with the irons used to chain him.

Theodore Weld, who once studied for the ministry, preached the sinfulness of slavery. As an organizer for the American Anti-Slavery Society, he wrote influential pamphlets and trained speakers who helped spread the abolitionist "gospel." In 1838, Weld married another anti-slavery activist, Angelina Grimke.

Photograph © 2003 Museum of Fine Arts, Boston.

In this painting, women are represented in traditional ways—shy, in the background, or serving men. During the Era of Reform, many women began to work to change and expand the way women were viewed.

18.6 Equal Rights for Women

Women abolitionists were in a strange position. They were trying to convince lawmakers to make slavery illegal, yet they themselves could not vote or hold office. They worked to raise money for the movement, yet their own money and property were controlled by their fathers and husbands. They spoke out against slave beatings, yet their husbands could discipline them whenever they wanted.

Even wealthy women like the Grimke sisters started to see that women and slaves had much in common. "What then can woman do for the slave," asked Angelina, "when she herself is under the feet of man and shamed into silence?"

The Struggle Begins   The organized movement for women's rights was sparked by the friendship between Lucretia Mott and Elizabeth Cady Stanton. The two women met in 1840 at the World Anti-Slavery Convention in London. When they arrived, they were outraged to discover that women were not allowed to speak at the meeting. The men who ran the convention even made women sit in the balcony, behind a curtain!

The men's decision may have backfired, because it was in the balcony that Mott and Stanton met. At first glance, the two women seemed quite different. Mott was 47 years old, the mother of four children, and an active reformer. Inspired by the Grimke sisters and her own Quaker faith, she had preached against slavery in both white and black churches. She had also helped Prudence Crandall try to find students for her school for black girls.

Stanton was 25 years old and newly married. She had never spoken in public. As a young girl, she had overheard women beg her father, a judge, to protect them from husbands who had beaten them. He had to tell them that there was no law against it. Later, she attended Troy Female Seminary, the nation's first high school for girls. She knew from her studies in history that America did not treat women fairly. When she met Lucretia Mott in London, she readily agreed that something had to be done about the injustices suffered by women.

Unequal Treatment of Women   Even a fine education like Stanton's did not assure women equal treatment. When Lucy Stone graduated from Oberlin College, the faculty invited her to write a speech. But a man would have to give the speech, since the school would not allow women to speak in public! Stone refused. After graduation, she spoke out for women's rights. Because women could not vote, she refused to pay property taxes. "Woman suffer taxation," she said, "and yet have no representation."

Stone's sister-in-law, Elizabeth Blackwell, wanted to be a doctor. She knew mathematics, science, and history. She had even been tutored by a helpful doctor. Yet she was rejected by 29 medical schools before one finally accepted her. She graduated at the top of her class, becoming the country's first female doctor. Still, no hospitals or doctors would agree to work with her.

To overcome such barriers, women would have to work together. By the time Elizabeth Cady Stanton and Lucretia Mott left London, they had decided "to hold a convention…and form a society to advocate the rights of women."

18.7 The Seneca Falls Convention and the Declaration of Sentiments

Eight years passed before Stanton and Mott met again. Over afternoon tea at the home of Mott's sister, they decided to send a notice to the local newspaper announcing a women's convention in Seneca Falls, New York. The organized movement for women's rights was about to begin.

The Declaration of Sentiments   On July 19, 1848, almost 300 people, including 40 men, arrived for the Seneca Falls Convention. Many were abolitionists, Quakers, or other reformers. Some were local housewives, farmers, and factory workers.

The convention organizers modeled their proposal for women's rights, the **Declaration of Sentiments,** on the Declaration of Independence. "We hold these truths to be self-evident," the document began, "that all men and women are created equal."

Just as the Declaration of Independence listed King George's acts of tyranny over the colonists, the new declaration listed acts of tyranny by men over women. Man did not let woman vote. He did not give her property rights, even to her own wages. He did not allow her to practice professions like medicine and law.

Elizabeth Cady Stanton was one of the organizers of the Seneca Falls Convention. The image below shows her reading the Declaration of Sentiments to the participants at the convention.

Elizabeth Cady Stanton and Women's Rights

An Era of Reform   **249**

Stanton's presentation of the declaration at the convention was her first speech. A few other women also summoned the courage to speak. One of them, Charlotte Woodward, was a 19-year-old factory worker. "Every fiber of my being," she said, "rebelled [against] all the hours that I sat and sewed gloves for a miserable pittance which, after it was earned, could never be mine."

Debate About the Right to Vote   The convention passed resolutions in favor of correcting these injustices. Then Stanton proposed that women demand the right to vote. For many, this step was too big. Even Mott cried, "Thou will make us ridiculous! We must go slowly."

At this point, Stanton received powerful support from another participant at the convention, Frederick Douglass. Everyone who believed that black men should have the right to vote, Douglass argued, must also favor giving black women the right to vote. And that meant all women should have this precious right. Inspired by Douglass's speech, the convention voted narrowly to approve this last resolution.

Elizabeth Cady Stanton (above) and Elizabeth Blackwell (below) were two leaders in the early struggle for women's rights.

The Legacy of Seneca Falls   The Seneca Falls Convention helped to create an organized campaign for women's rights. Sojourner Truth, who would later mesmerize an audience by asking defiantly, "Ain't I a woman?" became an active campaigner in the movement.

Elizabeth Cady Stanton didn't like speaking at conventions, but she could write moving speeches. Fortunately, she made friends with Susan B. Anthony, a refomer with a flair for public speaking.

While Stanton stayed in Seneca Falls to raise her children, Anthony traveled from town to town, speaking for women's rights. Of their lifelong teamwork, Stanton said, "I forged the thunderbolts, she fired them."

Slowly, reformers for women's rights made progress. New York gave women control over their property and wages. Massachusetts and Indiana passed more liberal divorce laws. Elizabeth Blackwell started her own hospital, including a medical school to train other female doctors.

Other reforms would take decades to become reality. Of all the women who signed the declaration at Seneca Falls, just one would live to vote for president legally—Charlotte Woodward.

18.8 Chapter Summary

In this chapter, you read about the reform movements that swept through the United States between about 1820 and 1850. You used an illustration of a protest march to learn about these reforms.

Many reformers were inspired by the Second Great Awakening, which taught Christians to perform good works in order to be saved. Others were inspired by transcendentalist writers like Ralph Waldo Emerson and Henry David Thoreau.

Dorothea Dix pioneered the reform of prisons and the treatment of the mentally ill. The movement to make education freely available to all was led by Horace Mann.

Inspired in part by religious revivalism, abolitionists braved violent opposition as they worked to end slavery. Women and former slaves played a key role in this movement.

The abolitionist campaign helped spark the struggle for women's rights. The organized movement for women's rights began with the Seneca Falls Convention and its Declaration of Sentiments.

These reform movements had their greatest effect in the North. In the next chapter, you will learn about the growing differences between the North and the South.

In 1998, Hilary Rodham Clinton spoke at the 150th anniversary of the Seneca Falls Convention. In her speech, she said, "Much of who women are…today can be traced to the courage, vision, and dedication of the pioneers who came together at Seneca Falls. Now it is our responsibility to finish the work they began."

251

In what ways was life different for people living in these two sections of the country?

19

The Worlds of North and South

19.1 Introduction

Eli Whitney, a young man from Massachusetts, listened politely to the Georgia planters' complaints. Tobacco prices were low, and rice and indigo prices weren't much better. Cotton grew well, but cleaning the seeds out of cotton fibers was a big problem. A slave picking out seeds by hand could clean only a few pounds a day. At that rate, even using cheap slave labor, there was no profit in raising cotton. Unless something changed, the future of farming in the South looked bleak.

As the planters talked, a solution to their problem began to take shape in Whitney's head. While growing up in Massachusetts, Whitney had revealed a gift for invention. As a boy, he had found a way to manufacture nails more quickly than by hand. From nails, he had gone on to hat pins and men's canes. After graduating from college in 1792, Whitney went to Georgia to work as a tutor. Instead of tutoring, however, he became intrigued by the problem of cotton cleaning and, he wrote, "struck out a plan of a machine in my mind."

The result, as you will read, was a simple but brilliant invention that changed life in both the North and the South—but in very different ways. This probably did not surprise Whitney. As a northerner living in the South, he had already noticed many differences between the two sections of the country.

Northerners and southerners shared the same language and worshipped in the same kinds of churches. They shared a fierce pride in their country and a faith in democracy. Yet their outlooks and attitudes about many things were quite different. The two sections also differed in other ways, including their economies, transportation systems, and societies. Between 1800 and 1850, these differences led to sharply conflicting views on many national issues—so much so that, at times, northerners and southerners seemed to be living in two separate worlds.

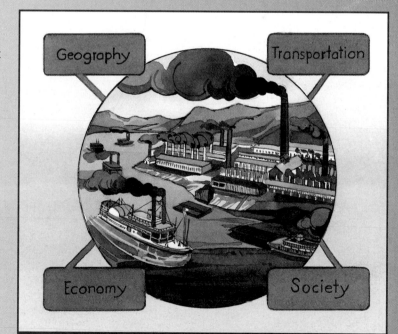

Graphic Organizer: Spoke Diagram
You will use spoke diagrams to learn about the worlds of the North and the South.

253

19.2 Geography of the North

From the rocky shores of Maine to the gently rolling plains of Iowa, the North included a variety of climates and natural features.

Northerners adapted to these geographical differences by creating different industries and ways of making a living.

Climate   All the northern states experienced four very distinct seasons, from frozen winters to hot, humid summers. But the most northerly states, such as Maine and Minnesota, had colder winters and shorter summer growing seasons than states farther south, such as Pennsylvania and Ohio.

Natural Features   Different areas of the North had distinctive natural features. The jagged New England coast, for example, had hundreds of bays and inlets that were perfect for use as harbors. Shipbuilding, fishing, and commerce flourished in this area, while towns such as Boston became busy seaports.

Inland from the sea lay a narrow, flat plain with a thin covering of rocky soil. Farming was never easy here. Instead, many people turned to trade and crafts. Others moved west in search of better farmland.

New England's hills rose sharply above V-shaped valleys carved by steep streams. The hillsides offered barely enough land for a small farm, but they were covered with thick forests of spruce and fir. New Englanders found that they could make money by harvesting timber. The wood was used for shipbuilding and in trade with other countries.

Farther south in New York, Pennsylvania, and New Jersey, broad rivers like the Hudson and the Delaware had deposited rich soil over wide plains. People living in these areas supported themselves by farming.

Across the Appalachians lay the Central Plains, a large, forested region drained by the Ohio and Mississippi Rivers. The Central Plains boast some of the best agricultural soil on Earth. From Ohio to Illinois, settlers cleared the forests to make way for farms.

Industrious northerners were thus changing the landscape. One result was **deforestation**, or the destruction of forests. By 1850, Americans had cleared about 177,000 square miles of dense forest. And with the growth of industry, the demand for coal and other minerals led to a big increase in mining after about 1820, especially in Pennsylvania.

deforestation the clearing away of forests

This photograph shows a section of New England coastline. What geographic features can you identify?

19.3 Geography of the South

The South extended from Maryland south to the tip of Florida, and from the Atlantic Coast west to Louisiana and Texas. This section's climate and natural features encouraged southerners to base their way of life on agriculture.

Climate   Compared to the North, the southern states enjoyed mild winters and long, hot, humid summers. Plentiful rainfall and long growing seasons made this a perfect place for raising warm-weather crops that would have withered and died farther north.

Natural Features   Wide coastal plains edged the southern shoreline from Chesapeake Bay to the Gulf of Mexico. These fertile lowlands stretched inland for as much as 300 miles in parts of the South.

Along the coast, the plains were dotted with swamps and marshes. These damp lowlands were ideal for growing rice and sugarcane, which thrived in warm, soggy soil. Indigo was grown on the dry land above the swamps, and tobacco and corn were farmed farther inland. A visitor to this section noted that "the planters, by the richness of the soil, live [in] the most easy and pleasant manner of any people I have met with."

Above the plains rose the Appalachian Mountains. Settlers who ventured into this rugged backcountry carved farms and orchards out of rolling hills and mountain hollows. Some backcountry farmers were said to "work on land so steep that they keep falling out of their cornfields."

Although most people in the South were farmers, southerners used natural resources in other ways as well. In North Carolina, they harvested thick pine forests for lumber. From Chesapeake Bay in Virginia and Maryland, they gathered fish, oysters, and crabs.

An especially important feature of the South was its broad, flat rivers. Many of the South's earliest towns were built at the mouths of rivers. As people moved away from the coast, they followed the rivers inland, building their homes and farms alongside these water highways. Oceangoing ships could even sail up southern rivers to conduct business right at a planter's private dock. Here, the ships were loaded with tobacco or other cash crops for sale in the Caribbean or Europe.

This photograph shows a southern waterway. What geographic features can you identify?

19.4 Economy of the South

The South's economy was based on agriculture, and southerners were proud of it. Most white southerners were **agrarians** who favored a way of life based on farming. This was especially true of rich **plantation** owners, who did not have to do the hard work of growing crops themselves.

Although most white southerners worked their own small farms, plantation owners used slaves to grow such cash crops as tobacco, rice, sugarcane, and indigo. By the early 1790s, however, the use of slaves had begun to decline. Europeans were unwilling to pay high prices for tobacco and rice, which they could purchase more cheaply from other British colonies. Cotton was a promising crop, but growers who experimented with it had a hard time making a profit. Until some way was found to clean the seeds out of its fiber easily, cotton was of little value. Discouraged planters were buying fewer slaves, and even letting some go free.

In 1793, a young Yale graduate named Eli Whitney took a job tutoring children on a Georgia plantation. There he saw his first cotton boll. Observing the way cotton was cleaned by hand, Whitney had an idea. "If a machine could be invented that would clean the cotton with expedition [speed]," he wrote his father, "it would be a great thing…to the country."

Whitney set to work. Six months later, he had a working machine that would change the face of the South.

The Granger Collection, New York

The economy of the South was based on agriculture. After the invention of the cotton gin in 1793, cotton quickly became the most important crop in the South.

King Cotton Whitney's "cotton engine," called the **cotton gin** for short, was a simple machine that used rotating combs to separate cotton fiber from its seeds. Using a cotton gin, a single worker could clean as much cotton as 50 laborers working by hand.

Across the South, planters began growing cotton. Within ten years, cotton was the section's most important crop. By 1860, sales of cotton overseas earned more money than all other U.S. exports combined. It was little wonder that many southerners liked to boast, "Cotton is King."

Expanding Demand for Land and Slaves Raising cotton in the same fields year after year soon wore out the soil. In search of fresh, fertile soil, cotton planters pushed west. By 1850, cotton plantations stretched from the Atlantic Coast to Texas.

Whitney had hoped that his invention would lighten the work of slaves. Instead, it made slavery more important than ever to the South. As cotton spread westward, slavery followed. Between 1790 and 1850, the number of slaves in the South rose from 500,000 to more than 3 million.

With white southerners putting all their money into land and slaves, they had little interest in building factories. As a result, wrote an Alabama newspaper, "We purchase all our luxuries and necessities from the North… the slaveholder dresses in Northern goods, rides in a Northern saddle, sports his Northern carriage, reads Northern books. In Northern vessels his products are carried to market."

One successful southern factory was the Tredegar Iron Works in Richmond, Virginia. Using mostly slave labor, the factory made ammunition and weapons for the U.S. army, as well as steam engines, rails, and locomotives. But the vast majority of white southerners made their living off the land.

19.5 Economy of the North

If cotton was king in the South, inventiveness seemed to rule the North. In colonial times, Americans created everything they needed—every shirt or gun—by hand. Beginning in the late 1700s, however, inventors started to devise machines to make products more quickly and cheaply. This shift from hand manufacturing to machines is called the **Industrial Revolution**. It created a new class of wealthy **industrialists** who owned large factories and other businesses based on machines.

Industrial Revolution The dramatic change in economies brought about by the use of machines to do work formerly done by hand. The Industrial Revolution began in England in the late 1700s and spread to America and the rest of Europe.

industrialist a person whose wealth comes from the ownership of industrial businesses and who favors government policies that support industry

The fast-flowing rivers of the North provided the power source for textile mills like the one in this painting.

Factories, such as the one shown above, produced more goods and made them more affordable. However, they also put many skilled craftspeople out of work.

The Growth of Industry   In 1810, Francis Cabot Lowell, a failing businessman from Boston, visited England. There he saw how mill owners were using machines to spin cotton into thread and weave the threads into cloth. To power these devices, they used fast-moving streams to turn a wheel, which in turn supplied energy to the machinery.

Lowell memorized the design of the British machines. When he returned to Massachusetts, he built even better ones. By 1815, he and his partners had built the first American textile factory, along the Merrimack River. This factory combined spinning and weaving machinery in the same building. One observer marveled that Lowell's mill "took your bale of cotton in at one end and gave out yards of cloth at the other, after goodness knows what digestive process."

To run his machinery, Lowell hired young farmwomen, who jumped at the chance to earn cash wages. The "Lowell girls" toiled 12 to 15 hours each day, with only Sundays off. Soon textile mills were springing up all along other northern rivers.

By the 1830s, inventors had learned to use steam engines to power machinery. With steam engines, businesspeople could build factories anywhere, not just along rivers. Meanwhile, the inventive Eli Whitney showed manufacturers how they could assemble products even more cheaply by making them from identical, interchangeable parts.

New inventions and manufacturing methods made goods cheaper and more plentiful. But they also shifted work from skilled craftspeople to less skilled laborers. When Elias Howe developed the sewing machine, for example, skilled seamstresses could not compete. Some took jobs in garment factories, but they earned much less money working the sewing machines than they had sewing by hand.

For northern industrialists, the new machines and production methods were a source of great wealth. Factory owners tended to favor a strong national government that could promote improvements in manufacturing, trade, and transportation. Southern agrarians, however, looked down on the newly rich industrialists and the laborers who worked for them. Proud southerners called factory workers "wage slaves." But they also worried that northern interests might grow too powerful and threaten the South's way of life.

Machines Make Agriculture More Efficient   The Industrial Revolution changed northern agriculture as well. In 1831, Virginia farmer Cyrus McCormick built a working model of "a right smart" machine called a *reaper*. A reaper could cut 28 times more grain than a single man using a scythe (a hand tool with a long, curved blade).

In 1847, McCormick built a reaper factory in Chicago. Using interchangeable parts, he was soon producing several thousand reapers a year. By making it easier to harvest large quantities of wheat, inventions like the reaper helped transform the Central Plains into America's "bread basket."

Thanks to the Industrial Revolution, the northern economy grew rapidly after 1800. By 1860, the value of manufacturing in the North was ten times greater than in the South.

19.6 Transportation in the North

Factory owners needed fast, inexpensive ways to deliver their goods to distant customers. South Carolina congressman John C. Calhoun had a solution. "Let us bind the republic together," he said, "with a perfect system of roads and canals." Calhoun called such projects "internal improvements."

Building Better Roads   In the early 1800s, most American roads were rutted boneshakers. In 1806, Congress funded the construction of a National Road across the Appalachian Mountains. The purpose of this highway was to tie the new western states with the East. With its smooth gravel surface, the National Road was a joy to travel.

As popular as the National Road was, in 1816 President James Monroe vetoed a bill that would have given states money to build more roads. Monroe argued that spending federal money for internal improvements within a state was unconstitutional.

Fast Ships and Canals   Even with better roads, river travel was still faster and cheaper than travel by land. But moving upstream, against a river's current, was hard work. To solve this problem, inventors experimented with boats powered by steam engines.

In 1807, Robert Fulton showed that steamboats were practical by racing the steamboat *Clermont* upstream on New York's Hudson River. Said Fulton, "I overtook many boats and passed them as if they had been at anchor." A Dutchman watching the strange craft from the shore shouted, "The devil is on his way up-river with a sawmill on a boat!" By the 1820s, smoke-belching steamboats were chugging up and down major rivers and across the Great Lakes.

Of course, rivers weren't always located where people needed them. In 1817, the state of New York hired engineers and workers to build a 363-mile canal from the Hudson River to Lake Erie. The Erie Canal provided the first all-water link between farms on the Central Plains and East Coast cities. It was so successful that other states built canals as well.

Overseas traders also needed faster ways to travel. Sailing ships sometimes took so long to cross the Pacific Ocean that the goods they carried spoiled. In the 1840s, sleek clipper ships were introduced that cut ocean travel time in half. The clipper ships spurred northern trade with foreign ports around the world.

Traveling by Rail   The future of transportation, however, lay not on water, but on rails. Inspired by the success of steamboats, inventors developed steam-powered locomotives. Steam-powered trains traveled faster than steamboats, and they could go wherever tracks could be laid—even across mountains.

So many railroad companies were laying tracks by the 1840s that railroads had become the North's biggest business. By 1860, more than 20,000 miles of rail linked northern factories to cities hundreds of miles away.

Many new and faster forms of transportation were put to use in the North. How many of them can you identify in the image below?

19.7 Transportation in the South

Most of the rail lines were in the North. In the South, people and goods continued to move on rivers. The slow current and broad channels of southern rivers made water travel easy and relatively cheap.

The most important southern product shipped by water was cotton. On plantation docks, slaves loaded cotton bales directly onto steam-powered riverboats. The riverboats then traveled hundreds of miles downstream to such port cities as Savannah, Georgia, or Mobile, Alabama. West of the Appalachians, most cotton moved down the Mississippi River, the mightiest of all the southern waterways. The cotton boom made New Orleans, the port at the mouth of the Mississippi, one of the South's few big cities. Once the cotton reached the sea, it was loaded onto sailing ships headed for ports in England or the North.

Because river travel was the South's main form of transportation, most southern towns and cities sprang up along waterways. With little need for roads or canals to connect these settlements, southerners opposed bills in Congress that would use federal funds to built internal improvements. Such bills, they believed, would benefit the North far more than the South.

Some railroads were built in the South, including lines that helped southern farmers ship their products to the North. Southerners were proud of the fact that the iron rails for many of their section's railroads came from Virginia's Tredegar Iron Works. Still, in 1860 the South had just 10,000 miles of rail, compared with over 20,000 miles in the North.

This photograph shows products being loaded onto steam-powered riverboats. What geographic feature of the South made riverboats the most practical way to transport goods?

Geography Challenge

Comparing the Worlds of North and South

Agriculture, 1860

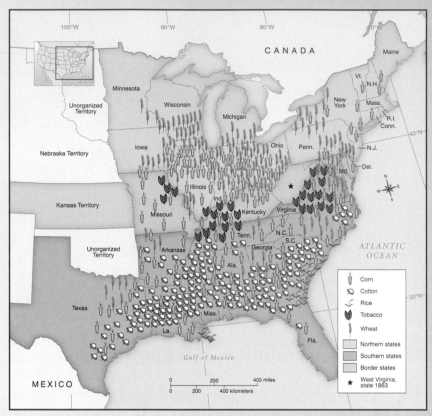

Railroads, 1860

Industry and Raw Material, 1860

Map labels:

CANADA

100°W · 90°W · 50°N · 80°W · 70°W

Minnesota
Wisconsin
Michigan
Maine
Vt.
N.H.
Mass.
New York
R.I.
Conn.
Pennsylvania
N.J.
Unorganized Territory
Iowa
Illinois
Indiana
Ohio
Del.
Md.
Nebraska Territory
Missouri
Kentucky
Virginia
Kansas Territory
North Carolina
Tennessee
Unorganized Territory
Arkansas
South Carolina
ATLANTIC OCEAN
Mississippi
Alabama
Georgia
Louisiana
Texas
Florida
Gulf of Mexico

40°N
30°N

Legend:
- Bituminous coal
- Iron ore
- Textiles
- ● Value of product over $100,000,000
- • Value of product over $10,000,000
- Northern states
- Southern states
- Border states
- ★ West Virginia, state 1863

0 · 200 · 100 miles
0 · 200 · 400 kilometers

Free and Slave Population, 1860

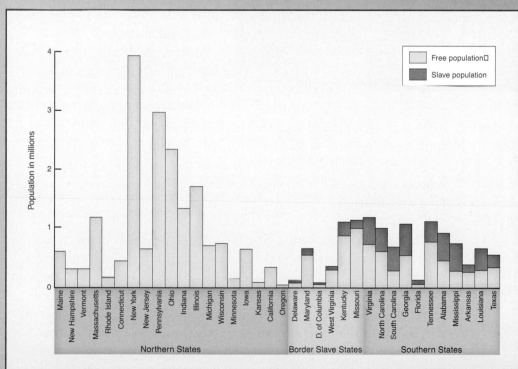

Population in millions

Free population
Slave population

Maine · New Hampshire · Vermont · Massachusetts · Rhode Island · Connecticut · New York · New Jersey · Pennsylvania · Ohio · Indiana · Illinois · Michigan · Wisconsin · Minnesota · Iowa · Kansas · California · Oregon · Delaware · Maryland · D. of Columbia · West Virginia · Kentucky · Missouri · Virginia · North Carolina · South Carolina · Georgia · Florida · Tennessee · Alabama · Mississippi · Arkansas · Louisiana · Texas

Northern States | Border Slave States | Southern States

19.8 Society of the South

For the most part, the South was not greatly affected by the Jacksonian spirit of equality and opportunity or the reform movements of the 1840s. Southerners in 1860 still measured wealth in terms of land and slaves. The result was a rigid social structure with a few rich plantation owners at the top, white farmers and workers in the middle, and African Americans—mostly slaves—at the bottom.

Slavery deeply affected the lives of all southerners, black and white. As long as the slave economy could be preserved, the South had little incentive to make progress economically or culturally. Even religion was affected. Southern church leaders defended the practice—taking a position that divided them from many churches in the North, whose leaders taught that slavery was un-Christian. In the words of one historian, "The South grew, but it did not develop."

White Southerners A small group of wealthy plantation owners dominated the economy and politics of the South. They treasured a leisurely way of life, filled with parties and social visits. While their sons often went to colleges and universities, their daughters rarely received much education. Instead girls were brought up to be gracious wives and hostesses.

Most white families owned some land, but only about one in four owned even one slave. The majority of white families worked their own fields and made most of what they needed themselves. About 10 percent of whites were too poor to own any land. They rented rugged mountain or forest land and paid the rent with the crops they raised. Since public schools were few and often inferior to those in the North, many white children were illiterate.

African Americans in the South A small minority of the African Americans in the South were free blacks. Resented by white southerners, free blacks were often forced to wear special badges, pay extra taxes, and live separately from whites. Most lived in towns and cities, where they found jobs as skilled craftspeople, servants, or laborers.

The great majority of African Americans in the South were slaves. Some worked as cooks, carpenters, blacksmiths, house servants, or nurse-maids. But most were field hands who labored from dawn until past dusk.

The Granger Collection, New York

Wealthy planters in the South modeled their homes and lives on European nobility. Their large mansions featured tall columns and fancy gardens. Most whites in the South, however, owned or worked on small farms with few of the luxuries enjoyed by the rich.

19.9 Society of the North

As in the South, most people in the North were neither wealthy nor powerful. But northerners believed that by hard work, ordinary people could acquire wealth and influence.

By 1860, about seven in ten northerners still lived on farms. But more and more northerners were moving to towns and cities. Between 1800 and 1850, the number of cities with populations of at least 2,500 had increased from 33 to 237. Except for a few cities around the Great Lakes, such as Chicago and Detroit, nearly all of the 50 largest urban areas were in the Northeast. (Only 12 were in the slave states of the South.) And northern cities were growing rapidly. Between 1840 and 1860, the populations of New York, Philadelphia, and Boston nearly tripled. By 1860, more than a million people crowded the streets of New York.

New or old, northern cities often lacked sewers and paved streets. In dirty and crowded neighborhoods, diseases spread rapidly. "The streets are filthy," wrote one observer about New York City, "and the stranger is not a little surprised to meet the hogs walking about in them, for the purpose of devouring the vegetables and trash thrown into the gutter."

African Americans in the North After the American Revolution, all of the northern states had taken steps to end slavery. Although African Americans in the North were free, they were not treated as equal to whites. In most states they could not vote, hold office, serve on juries, or attend white churches and schools.

In 1860, most people in the North still lived on farms, but more and more people were moving to towns and cities like the one shown below. These cities often sprang up near factories and railroad hubs.

African Americans responded by forming their own churches and starting their own businesses. Because few employers would give them skilled jobs, African Americans often worked as laborers or servants.

Immigrants Arrive in the North   Between 1845 and 1860, four million **immigrants**—most of them from Ireland and Germany—swelled the North's growing population. In Ireland, a potato famine drove thousands of families to America. In Germany, a failed revolution sent people fleeing overseas. Some immigrants had enough money to buy land and farm. But most settled in cities, where they found jobs in mills and factories.

Some northerners resented the newcomers. Anti-immigrant feeling occasionally exploded into riots. More often it was expressed in everyday discrimination, such as help-wanted signs with the words, "No Irish need apply." Still the immigrants came, attracted, said one German newcomer, by "a new society with almost limitless opportunities open to all."

19.10 Chapter Summary

In this chapter, you learned how the North and the South developed differently from each other in the first half of the 1800s. You used spoke diagrams to describe the geography, economy, transportation, and society of the two sections.

The Granger Collection, New York

immigrant A person who moves from one country to another. Such a movement is called *immigration*.

Look at the two images of the South (left) and the North (right). How many features of geography, economy, transportation, and society can you identify?

Geography was a principal reason why northerners and southerners developed different ways of life. In contrast to the variety of trades and businesses in the North, the South depended primarily on agriculture. Although only a minority of white southerners owned slaves, much of the South's economy depended on slave labor.

In the North, the new inventions of the Industrial Revolution led to the development of mills and factories. Increasing numbers of people went to work as wage earners. New machines such as Cyrus McCormick's reaper revolutionized agriculture.

Dramatic improvements in transportation made it easier for northerners to travel and to ship goods over long distances. In the South, however, people continued to travel by river, and rail lines were fewer.

Southern society was divided into ranks. The wealthy few enjoyed great influence and power. But even the poorest whites ranked above African Americans, whether free or slave.

The North, too, had its wealthy class. But farmers and laborers alike believed they could create comfortable lives for their families through hard work.

The different worlds of the North and South led to conflicting viewpoints on many issues, including internal improvements and trade. But the most divisive issue of all was slavery. In the next chapter, you will learn what life was like for African Americans, both free and slave, in 1850.

Why did quilts like this one made by a slave provide comfort for slaves?

African Americans at Mid-Century

20.1 Introduction

By 1850, the population of the United States had grown to just over 23 million. This figure included 3.6 million African Americans. The great majority of African Americans lived in slavery. Harriet Powers, the woman who created the quilt you see here, was one of them.

Like many slaves, Harriet Powers grew up hearing Bible stories. In her quilts, Powers used animals and figures from Africa and America to illustrate those stories, along with scenes from her life. Hidden in her images were messages of hope and freedom for slaves.

Not all African Americans were slaves. By mid-century, there were about half a million free blacks as well. Many were former slaves who had escaped to freedom.

Whether African Americans lived in slavery or freedom, racism shaped their lives. Everywhere, whites looked down on blacks. Whites ignored the great contributions blacks made to American life. They thought of the United States as "their country." Such racist thinking prompted African American scholar and reformer W.E.B. Du Bois to ask:

> *Your country? How came it to be yours? Before the Pilgrims landed we were here. Here we brought you our three gifts and mingled them with yours; a gift of story and song, soft, stirring melody in an...unmelodious land; the gift of sweat and brawn [physical strength] to beat back the wilderness...and lay the foundations of this vast economic empire...the third, a gift of the Spirit.*

In this chapter, you will explore the experience of African Americans at mid-century. As you read, you will learn more about the gifts that African Americans brought to America.

Graphic Organizer: Story Quilt
You will use a story quilt to learn about the life of African Americans in the 19th century.

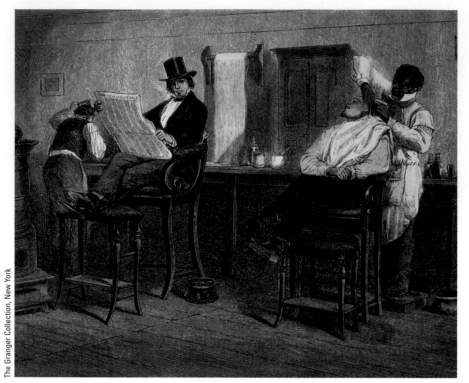

The Granger Collection, New York

Free African Americans usually held low-paying jobs. The barber pictured above is one example.

20.2 North and South, Slave and Free

The experiences of African Americans at mid-century depended on where they lived and whether they lived in slavery or freedom. Former slave Frederick Douglass toured the North talking to white audiences about slavery. To him, the biggest difference between slaves and free blacks was their legal status. Free blacks had some rights by law. Slaves did not.

Slaves' Legal Status   Douglass reminded his listeners that the law defined slaves as property, not human beings. Legally, slaveholders could do almost anything with their human property. They could buy and sell slaves. They could leave slaves to their children or heirs. They could give slaves away to settle a bet. But in many states, they could not set slaves free.

As property, slaves had none of the rights that free people took for granted. "In law, the slave has no wife, no children, no country, no home," Douglass said. "He can own nothing, possess nothing, acquire nothing."

Rural and Urban Slaves   Most slaves worked on farms and planta-tions across the South. By 1860, there were also about 70,000 urban slaves living in towns and cities. Most were "hired out," or sent to work in facto-ries, mills, or workshops. The wages they earned belonged to their owners. Often urban slaves were allowed to "live out" on their own, rather than under the watchful eyes of their owners. Because of such freedom, observed Douglass, "A city slave is almost a freeman compared to a slave on a plantation."

Free Blacks in the South   About half of all free African Americans lived in the South. Most worked as laborers, craftspeople, or household servants in towns and cities.

White southerners viewed free blacks as a dangerous group that had to be controlled so that, in the words of South Carolina slaveholders, they would not create "discontent among our slaves." Free blacks were forbidden to own guns. They could not travel freely from town to town or state to state. Blacks were not allowed to work at certain jobs. Such restric-tions led Douglass to conclude, "No colored man is really free in a slaveholding state."

Free Blacks in the North   African Americans in the North lived freer lives. But blacks experienced **discrimination,** or unequal treatment, everywhere they turned. In many states, African Americans were denied the right to vote. Everywhere they had trouble finding good jobs. In the 1850s, some 87 percent of free blacks in New York held low-paying jobs. "Why should I strive hard?" asked one young African American. "What are my prospects?... No one will employ me; white boys won't work with me."

In addition to unequal treatment, policies of **segregation** separated blacks from whites in nearly all public places. Black children were often denied entry into public schools. Those states that did educate black children set up separate schools for that purpose. A New Yorker observed:

> *Even the noblest black is denied that which is free to the vilest [worst] white. The omnibus, the [railroad] car, the ballot-box, the jury box, the halls of legislation, the army, the public lands, the school, the church, the lecture room, the social circle, the [restaurant] table, are all either absolutely or virtually denied to him.*

Frederick Douglass discovered how deeply rooted this racism was when he tried to join a church in New Bedford, Massachusetts, and was turned away. Douglass wrote, "I tried all the other churches in New Bedford with the same result."

African Americans responded to discrimination by organizing to help themselves. In 1816, Richard Allen, a former slave, became the first bishop of the African Methodist Episcopal Church (AME). The AME, which still exists today, quickly became a center of African American life. Allen also created organizations to improve the lives of blacks, such as the African Society for the Education of Youth.

Other northern blacks started their own churches, schools, and self-help organizations. In 1853, free blacks formed the National Council of Colored People to protest the unequal treatment they received. Such treatment, the council declared, "would humble the proudest, crush the energies of the strongest, and retard the progress of the swiftest." That African Americans were neither humbled nor crushed by prejudice and discrimination was evidence of their courage and spirit.

discrimination unequal treatment based on a person's race, gender, religion, place of birth, or other arbitrary characteristic

segregation the social separation of groups of people, especially by race

The Granger Collection, New York

Lemuel Haynes, shown here preaching from a pulpit, fought at Lexington during the Revolutionary War. He was the first African American minister of a white congregation.

20.3 The Economics of Slavery

As you read in Chapter 19, only wealthier planters could afford to buy slaves. The great majority of white southerners did not own slaves. Why, then, did the South remain so loyal to slavery? Part of the answer lies in the growth of the southern economy after the invention of the cotton gin in 1793.

The cotton gin made cotton a hugely profitable cash crop in the South. In 1790, the South produced just 3,000 bales of cotton. By the 1850s, production had soared to more than 4 million bales a year. Cotton brought new wealth to the South. Robert Fogel, a historian who has studied the economics of slavery, wrote:

> If we treat the North and South as separate nations, the South would stand as the fourth most prosperous nation of the world in 1860...more prosperous than France, Germany, Denmark, or any of the countries in Europe except England.

Whether they owned slaves or not, white southerners understood that their economy depended on cotton. They also knew that cotton planters depended on slave labor to grow their profitable crop. They dreamed that someday they would be able to buy slaves and join the powerful planter class. It mattered little to them that owning slaves became less and less likely as the demand for, and the price of, slaves rose.

High prices were both good and bad for the men and women trapped in slavery. As prices went up, slaves became more valuable to their owners. This may have encouraged slaveholders to take better care of their workers. At the same time, the rising value of their slaves made slaveholders less willing to listen to talk of ending slavery. In their eyes, freeing their slaves could only mean one thing—complete and utter financial ruin.

Cotton was the South's most valuable export. Most southerners knew that their economy depended upon slave labor to grow and harvest this crop.

Geography Challenge
The Slave System, 1801–1860

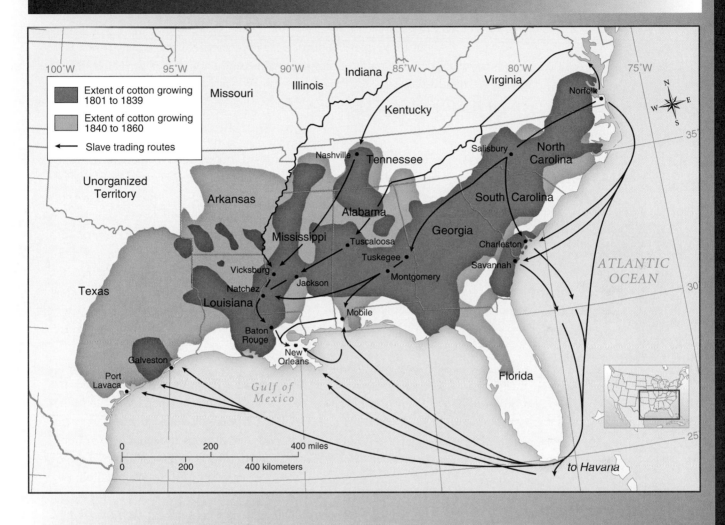

Legend:
- Extent of cotton growing 1801 to 1839
- Extent of cotton growing 1840 to 1860
- Slave trading routes

1. What does this map show?

2. How did the size of the area where cotton was grown change between 1801 and 1860?

3. Did the production of cotton increase or decrease between 1801 and 1860? What effect do you think this had on the use of slavery?

4. What invention accounts for the changes you can see on this map?

5. How might these changes have affected slaves? How might these changes have affected the economy of the South? Were these changes good or bad? Why do you think so?

20.4 Working Conditions of Slaves

Slaves worked on farms of various sizes. On small farms, owners and slaves worked side by side in the fields. On large plantations, planters hired overseers to supervise their slaves. Overseers were paid to "care for nothing but to make a large crop." To do this, they tried to get the most work possible out of slaves' tired bodies.

About three quarters of rural slaves were field hands who toiled from dawn to dark tending crops. An English visitor described a field hand's day:

Slaves who worked as field hands labored from dawn until well into the night. If they failed to pick their usual amount, they were beaten.

He is called up in the morning at day break, and is seldom allowed enough time to swallow three mouthfuls of hominy [boiled corn], or hoe-cake [cornbread], but is immediately driven out to the field to hard labor.... About noon...he eats his dinner, and he is seldom allowed an hour for that purpose.... Then they return to severe labor, which continues until dusk.

Even then, a slave's workday was not finished. After dark, there was still water to carry, wood to split, pigs to feed, corn to shuck, cotton to clean, and other chores to be done. One slave recalled:

I never knowed what it was to rest. I jes work all the time from morning late at night. I had to do everything.... Work in the field, chop wood, hoe corn, 'till sometime I feels like my back surely break.

Not all slaves worked in the fields. Some were skilled seamstresses, carpenters, or blacksmiths. Others worked in the master's house as cooks or servants. When asked about her work, a house slave replied:

What kind of work I did? Most everything, chile [child]. I cooked, then I was house maid, and I raised I don't know how many children.... I was always good when it come to the sick, so that was mostly my job.

No matter how hard they worked, slaves could not look forward to an easier life. Most began work at the age of six and continued until they died. As one old man put it, "Slave young, slave long."

20.5 Living Conditions of Slaves

Most masters viewed their slaves as they did their land—things to be "worn out, not improved." They provided only what was needed to keep their slaves healthy enough to work. Slaves lived crowded together in rough cabins. One recalled:

> We lodged in log huts, and on bare ground. Wooden floors were an unknown luxury. In a single room were huddled, like cattle, ten or a dozen persons, men, women, and children.... We had neither bed-steads, nor furniture of any description. Our beds were collections of straw and old rags, thrown down in the corners.

Slaves seldom went hungry. "Not to give a slave enough to eat," reported Frederick Douglass, "is regarded as...meanness [stinginess] even among slaveholders." Once a week, slaves received a ration of cornmeal, bacon, and molasses. Many kept gardens or hunted and fished to vary their diets. The owner described here fed his slaves well:

> Marse [master] Alec had plenty for his slaves to eat. There was meat, bread, collard greens, snap beans, 'taters, peas, all sorts of dried fruit, and just lots of milk and butter.

Slaves wore clothing made of coarse homespun linen or rough "Negro cloth." Northern textile mills made this cloth especially for slave clothes. Frederick Douglass reported that a field hand received a yearly allowance of "two coarse linen shirts, one pair of linen trousers...one jacket, one pair of trousers for winter, made of coarse negro cloth, one pair of stockings, and one pair of shoes." The shoes usually fit so badly that slaves preferred going bare-foot much of the time. Children too young to work received "two coarse linen shirts per year. When these failed them, they went naked until the next allowance-day."

While slaves were poorly housed and clothed compared to most white southerners, they were more likely to receive med-ical care. Slaveholders often hired doctors to treat sick or injured slaves. Given doctors' limited medical knowledge, this care probably did little to improve the health of slaves.

Most slave cabins consisted of a single room where the entire family lived. They had a fireplace for cooking and heat. The windows usually had no glass.

20.6 Controlling Slaves

Slavery was a system of forced labor. To make this system work, slaveholders had to keep their slaves firmly under control. Some slaveholders used harsh punishments—beating, whipping, branding, and other forms of torture—to maintain that control. But punishments often backfired on slaveholders. A slave who had been badly whipped might not be able to work for some time. Harsh punishments were also likely to make slaves feel more resentful and rebellious.

Slaveholders preferred to control their workforce by making slaves feel totally dependent on their masters. Owners encouraged such dependence by treating their slaves like grown-up children. They also kept their workers as ignorant as possible about the world beyond the plantation. Frederick Douglass's master said that a slave "should know nothing but to obey his master—to do as it is told to do."

Slaves who failed to learn this lesson were sometimes sent to slavebreakers. Such men were experts at turning independent, spirited African Americans into humble, obedient slaves. When he was 16, Douglass was sent to a slavebreaker named Edward Covey.

Covey's method consisted of equal parts violence, fear, and overwork. Soon after Douglass arrived on Covey's farm, he received his first whipping. After that, he was beaten so often that "aching bones and a sore back were my constant companions."

Covey's ability to instill fear in his slaves was as effective as his whippings. They never knew when he might be watching them. "He would creep and crawl in ditches and gullies," Douglass recalled, to spy on his workers. Finally, Covey worked his slaves beyond endurance. Wrote Douglass:

We worked in all weathers. It was never too hot or too cold; it could never rain, blow, hail, or snow too hard for us to work in the field. …The longest days were too short for him, and the shortest nights too long for him. I was somewhat unmanageable when I first got there, but a few months of this discipline tamed me…. I was broken in body, soul, and spirit…. The dark night of slavery closed in upon me.

Beating, or whipping, was slave owners' most common way of controlling their workers. However, most slave owners avoided savage beatings because injured slaves could not work, and lash marks reduced their resale value.

20.7 Resistance to Slavery

Despite the efforts of slaveholders to crush their spirits, slaves found countless ways to resist slavery. As former slave Harriet Jacobs wrote after escaping to freedom, "My master had power and law on his side. I had a determined will. There is power in each."

Day-to-Day Resistance For most slaves, resistance took the form of quiet acts of rebellion. Field hands pulled down fences, broke tools, and worked so sloppily that they damaged crops. House slaves sneaked food out of the master's kitchen.

Slaves pretended to be dumb, clumsy, sick, or insane to escape work. One slave avoided working for years by claiming to be nearly blind, only to regain his sight once freed.

Resistance turned deadly when house servants slipped poison into the master's food. So many slaves set fire to their owners' homes and barns that the American Fire Insurance Company refused to insure property in the South.

Open Defiance Quiet resistance sometimes flared into open defiance. When pushed too hard, slaves refused to work, rejected orders, or struck back violently. Owners often described slaves who reacted in this way as "insolent" [disrespectful] or "unmanageable."

Frederick Douglass reached his breaking point one day when the slave-breaker Covey began to beat him for no particular reason. Rather than take the blows, as he had so many times before, Douglass fought back. He wrestled Covey to the ground, holding him "so firmly by the throat that his blood followed my nails." For Douglass, this moment was "the turning point in my career as a slave."

The bloodiest slave uprising in the South was organized by Nat Turner, a black preacher, in 1831. This wood engraving, entitled *Nat Turner and His Confederates in Conference,* shows Turner leaning on a pole, speaking to his companions.

My long-crushed spirit rose, cowardice departed, bold defiance took its place; and I now resolved that, however long I might remain a slave in form, the day had passed when I could be a slave in fact. I did not hesitate to let it be known of me, that the white man who expected to succeed in whipping, must also succeed in killing me.

Covey knew this and never laid a hand on Douglass again.

THE RESURRECTION OF HENRY BOX BROWN AT PHILADELPHIA
Who escaped from Richmond Va in a Box 3 feet long 2½ ft deep and 2 ft wide

Slaves used many methods to try to escape bondage. Henry Brown, pictured above, shipped himself to freedom in a crate.

Running Away Some slaves tried to escape by running away to freedom in the North. The risks were enormous. Slaveholders hired professional slave catchers and their packs of howling bloodhounds to hunt down runaway slaves. If caught, a runaway risked being mauled by dogs, brutally whipped, or even killed. Still, Douglass and countless other slaves took the risk.

Slaves found many ways to escape bondage. Some walked to freedom in the North, hiding by day and traveling at night when they could follow the North Star. Others traveled north by boat or train, using forged identity cards and clever disguises to get past watchful slave patrols. A few runaways mailed themselves to freedom in boxes or coffins.

Thousands of runaways escaped to free states and to Canada with the help of the Underground Railroad, a secret network of free blacks and sympathetic whites. The members of the Underground Railroad provided transportation and "safe houses" where runaways could hide. A number of guides, or "conductors," risked their lives to help escaping slaves travel the "freedom train." One of the most successful was Harriet Tubman. Having escaped slavery herself, Tubman courageously returned to the South more than a dozen times between 1850 and 1860, guiding more than 200 men, women, and children to freedom.

Rebellion At times, resistance erupted into violent rebellion. Slave revolts occurred in cities, on plantations, and even on ships at sea. Fear of slave uprisings haunted slaveholders. Planters, wrote one visitor to the South, "never lie down to sleep without…loaded pistols at their sides."

In 1822 authorities in Charleston, South Carolina, learned that Denmark Vesey, a free black, was preparing to lead a sizable revolt of slaves. Vesey, along with more than 30 slaves, was arrested and hanged.

Nine years later, in 1831, a slave named Nat Turner led a bloody uprising in Virginia. Armed with axes and guns, Turner and his followers set out to kill every white person they could find. Before their reign of terror ended two days later, at least 57 people had been hacked to death.

Denmark Vesey's and Nat Turner's rebellions panicked white southerners. In response, southern states passed strict slave codes that tightened owners' control of their slaves and provided for harsher punishment of slaves by authorities. As one frightened Virginian remarked, "A Nat Turner might be in any family."

20.8 Slave Families and Communities

Slavery made community and family life difficult. Legally, slave families did not exist. No southern state recognized slave marriages. Legal control of slave children rested not with their parents, but with their masters. Owners could break up slave families at any time by selling a father, a mother, or a child to someone else. Along with being whipped, slaves most feared being sold away from their loved ones.

Most slaves grew up in families headed by a father and mother. Unable to marry legally, slaves created their own weddings that often involved the tradition of jumping over a broomstick. As one recalled:

> *The preacher would say to the man, "Do you take this woman to be your wife?" He says, "Yes." "Well, jump the broom." After he jumped, the preacher would say the same to the woman. When she jumped, the preacher said, "I pronounce you man and wife."*

Caring for children was never easy. Frederick Douglass's mother "snatched a few moments for our care in the early morning before her work began, and at night after the day's work was done." Still, parents found time to teach their children the lessons they would need to survive.

Silence around whites was one such lesson. Elijah Marrs recalled that "Mothers were necessarily compelled to be severe on their children to keep them from talking too much." Obedience was another lesson. William Webb's mother taught him "not to rebel against the men who were treating me like some dumb brute, making me work and refusing to let me learn."

Parents also taught their children other essential lessons about caring, kindness, pride, and hope. They taught them to respect themselves and other members of the slave community, especially older slaves. "There is not to be found, among any people," wrote Douglass, "a more rigid enforcement of the law of respect to elders."

These were the lessons that helped slaves, under the most difficult conditions, to create loving families and close communities. In doing so, they met the most basic of human needs—the need for a place to feel loved, respected, and safe.

This photograph shows five generations of a slave family on a plantation in South Carolina. Enslaved African Americans often found it difficult to keep their families together because Southern laws did not recognize slave marriages or families, and owners could split up families as they wished.

In this painting, black house servants are shown celebrating a wedding party in the kitchen. Dancing, singing, and telling tales allowed slaves to temporarily forget their harsh conditions.

20.9 Leisure Time Activities

Come day,
Go day,
God send Sunday.

These simple words capture the weariness of slaves. They toiled all week in fields that seemed to stretch "from one end of the earth to the other." But, on Saturday night and Sunday, their time was their own.

Saturday nights were a time for social events, like corn-husking or pea-shelling parties, that combined work and fun. One slave recalled:

I've seen many a corn huskin' at ole Major's farm when the corn would be piled as high as the house. Two sets of men would start huskin' from opposite sides of the heap. It would keep one man busy just getting the husks out of the way, and the corn would be thrown over the husker's head and filling the air like birds. The women usually had a quilting at those times, so they were pert and happy.

A quilting bee was one of the rare times when slave women could gather to work and talk. In those few precious hours, they were free to express themselves with needle and cloth. The quilts they created were not only beautiful, but very much needed as bedding for their families. Looking at a sunburst quilt she had sewn, one woman exclaimed, "It's poetry, ain't it?"

When the sewing was done, men joined the party for a "quilting feast" and dancing. Slaves made music out of almost anything. "Stretch cow-hides over cheese-boxes and you had tambourines," one former slave recalled. "Saw bones from a cow, knock them together and call it a drum. Or use broom straw on fiddle-strings and you had your entire band."

Sunday was a day for religion and recreation. Slaves spent their Sundays going to church, eating, hunting, fishing, dancing, singing, gambling, telling tales, naming babies, playing games, drinking whiskey, and visiting with friends. In New Orleans, hundreds of slaves gathered on Sunday afternoons in a public space known as "Congo Square" to dance, sing, and talk. All of these activities helped African Americans forget the sorrows of slavery.

20.10 Slave Churches

Many slaveholders encouraged their slaves to attend church on Sunday. Some read the Bible to their workers and prayed with them. Owners and white ministers preached the same message: "If you disobey your earthly master, you offend your heavenly Master."

Not surprisingly, this was not a popular lesson among slaves. "Dat ole white preacher just was telling us slaves to be good to our marsters," recalled Cornelius Garner. "We ain't kerr'd a bit 'bout dat stuff he was telling us 'cause we wanted to sing, pray, and serve God in our own way."

Instead, slaves created their own "invisible church" that brought together African roots and American needs. This invisible church met in slave quarters or secret forest clearings known as "hush arbors." One slave reported that

> When [slaves] go round singing, "Steal Away to Jesus" that mean there going to be a religious meeting that night. The masters...didn't like them religious meetings, so us naturally slips off at night, down in the bottoms or somewheres. Sometimes us sing and pray all night.

Rather than teach about obedience, black preachers told the story of Moses leading his people out of slavery in Egypt. Black worshipers sang spirituals that expressed their desire for freedom and faith in a better world to come. A black preacher wrote:

> The singing was accompanied by a certain ecstasy of motion, clapping of hands, tossing of heads, which would continue without cessation [stopping] about half an hour.... The old house partook of their ecstasy; it rang with their jubilant shouts, and shook in all its joints.

Whites sometimes criticized the "enthusiasm" of black worshipers, saying they lacked true religious feeling. Many slaves, however, believed that it was their masters who lacked such feeling. "You see," explained one man, "religion needs a little motion— specially if you gwine [going to] feel de spirit."

Religion helped slaves bear their suffering and still find joy in life. In their prayers and spirituals, they gave voice to their deepest longings, their greatest sorrows, and their highest hopes.

Biblical stories were frequently illustrated on quilts made by slaves.

20.11 African American Culture

Africans arrived in the United States speaking many languages and following many cultural traditions. To survive, they had to learn a new language—English—and adopt a new way of life. Yet they did not forget their African roots. Across the South, slaves combined their old traditions and new realities to create a distinctive African American culture.

You can see this combining of cultures in Harriet Powers' story quilt. In square after square, Powers used African and American animals to illustrate Bible stories that she learned as a slave on a Georgia

This watercolor, entitled *The Old Plantation,* shows one aspect of the rich culture slaves developed in spite of the bondage they endured. Slave dances, songs, quilts, and folk stories all reflected a combination of slaves' old African traditions and the new life they faced in America.

plantation. The doves in her quilt are symbols of a slave's yearning for freedom. As one spiritual said with sad longing, "Had I the wings of a dove, I'd fly away and be at rest."

You can also hear this combining of cultures in the songs and spirituals sung by slaves. These songs throb with the rhythms and harmonies of Africa. But they speak about the realities of slavery. Slaves sang about faith, love, work, and the kindness and cruelty of masters. They also expressed their **oppression,** as in this song recorded by Frederick Douglass:

> *We raise the wheat, dey gib [they give] us the corn;*
> *We bake the bread, dey gib us the cruss;*
> *We sif the meal, dey gib us the huss;*
> *We peel the meat, dey gib us the skin;*
> *And dat's the way dey takes us in.*

oppression the feeling of being weighed down or held back by severe and unfair force

Slave dances were based on African traditions as well. Dancing helped slaves to escape their cares, express their feelings, and refresh their spirits. According to one former slave, good dancers "could play a tune with their feet, dancing largely to an inward music, a music that was felt, but not heard."

African legends and folktales survived in the stories and jokes told by slaves. For example, Br'er Rabbit, the sly hero of many slave tales, was based on the African trickster Shulo the Hare. In these stories, the small but clever brother rabbit always managed to outwit larger, but duller, brother bear or brother fox—just as slaves hoped to outwit their more powerful masters.

20.12 Chapter Summary

In this chapter, you learned what life was like for African Americans during the 19th century. You looked at a story quilt made by a slave that gave you clues, or messages, about slavery.

African Americans had a great impact on the development of American life. The economy of the South was built on the labor of African American slaves. Some African Americans lived in freedom in both the North and South, but nowhere could they escape racism and discrimination.

Those who lived in slavery worked endlessly, either in the fields or as servants in the master's house. Most lived in simple, dirt-floor cabins with only straw and rags for beds. Many slaves lived in daily fear of harsh punishments. Their biggest fear was the threat of family members being sold to other farms. Many slaves learned to rebel in small ways. They might break a tool on purpose or pretend to be lame or blind. Some slaves fought back openly when the oppression became too much to bear. At great risk, many tried to run away. Some slaveholders would rather kill runaways than allow them to escape.

Slaves were encouraged to attend church, and Sunday was a day of rest for everyone. Slaves spent Saturday nights at social events and worshiped in their own secret churches on Sundays. They prayed and sang spirituals to help themselves find joy and hope in their hard lives.

In the next chapter, you will read about how different views on slavery in the North and the South threatened to divide the nation.

These cards show scenes of slavery in the United States, including abolition.

How did the people in the South and North respond to the news of civil war?

OUR MOTTO
SOUTHERN RIGHTS
EQUALITY of STATES
DONT TREAD ON ME

21

A Dividing Nation

21.1 Introduction

In 1860, after one of the strangest elections in the nation's history, a tall, plain-spoken Illinois lawyer named Abraham Lincoln was elected president. On learning of his victory, Lincoln said to the reporters covering the campaign, "Well, boys, your troubles are over. Mine have just begun."

Within a few weeks, it became clear just how heavy those troubles would be. By the time Lincoln took office, the nation had split apart over the issue of slavery and was preparing for war. The survival of the United States of America, and the fate of four million slaves, rested in Lincoln's large, strong hands.

The troubles Lincoln faced were not new. The issue dividing the nation could be traced back to 1619, when the first slave ship arrived in Virginia. Since that time, slavery had ended in half of the United States. The question was, could the nation continue half-slave and half-free?

For decades, Americans tried to avoid that troubling question. Many hoped that slavery would simply die out on its own. Instead, slavery began to expand into new territories, and the question could no longer be ignored.

Between 1820 and 1860, Americans tried to fashion several compromises on the issue of slavery. Each compromise, however, created new problems and new divisions.

Lincoln understood why. Slavery was not simply a political issue to be worked out through compromise. It was a deeply moral issue. As Lincoln wrote in a letter to a friend, "If slavery is not wrong, nothing is wrong."

In this chapter, you will learn how Americans tried to keep the United States united despite their deep divisions over slavery. And you will find out how they finally answered that most troubling question: Could a nation born in freedom endure half-slave and half-free?

Graphic Organizer: Visual Metaphor
You will use a visual metaphor of an unraveling flag to understand the compromises and decisions made to preserve the Union.

the Union The United States as one country, united under a single government. During the Civil War, "the Union" came to mean the government and armies of the North.

A traveler, heading west across the Appalachians after the War of 1812, wrote, "Old America seems to be breaking up and moving westward." It was true. By 1819, restless settlers had formed seven new states west of the Appalachians.

Congress had established a process for forming new states in the Northwest Ordinance of 1787. Besides outlining the steps leading to statehood, this law also banned slavery north of the Ohio River. As a result, the three western states that were formed north of the river—Ohio, Indiana, and Illinois—were free states. The four states that were formed south of the Ohio River—Kentucky, Tennessee, Louisiana, and Mississippi—all permitted slavery.

In 1819, Alabama and Missouri applied to Congress for statehood as slave states. No one in Congress questioned admitting Alabama as a slave state. Alabama was located far south of the Ohio River, and was surrounded by other slave states.

Congress had another reason for admitting Alabama with no debate. For years there had been an unspoken agreement in Congress to keep the number of slave states and free states equal. The admission of Illinois as a free state in 1818 had upset this balance. By accepting Alabama with slavery, Congress was able to restore the balance between slave and free states.

Missouri, however, was another matter.

In 1819, the number of slave states and free states stood at 11 apiece. This balance was threatened when Missouri applied for statehood as a slave state.

Slave States	Free States
Georgia	Pennsylvania
South Carolina	New Jersey
North Carolina	New York
Virginia	Connecticut
Maryland	Rhode Island
Delaware	Massachusetts
Kentucky (1792)	New Hampshire
Tennessee (1796)	Vermont (1791)
Louisiana (1812)	Ohio (1803)
Mississippi (1817)	Indiana (1816)
Alabama (1819)	Illinois (1818)

■ Original 13 States
■ States Entering the Union, 1791–1819

Questions about Missouri Some northerners in Congress questioned whether Missouri should also be admitted as a slave state. Most of Missouri, they observed, lay north of the point where the Ohio River flows into the Mississippi. On the eastern side of the Mississippi, slavery was banned north of that point. Shouldn't the same ban also be applied west of the Mississippi?

This question led to another one. If Missouri was allowed to enter **the Union** as a slave state, some asked, what would keep slavery from spreading across all of the Louisiana Territory? The vision of a block of new slave states stretching from the Mississippi to the Rocky Mountains was enough to give some northerners nightmares.

The Tallmadge Amendment When the bill to make Missouri a state came before Congress, Representative James Tallmadge of New York decided to keep that nightmare from coming true. Tallmadge proposed an amendment to the statehood bill. The amendment said that Missouri could join the Union, but only as a free state.

Southerners in Congress greeted Tallmadge's amendment with a roar of protest. What right, they asked, did Congress have to decide whether a new state should be slave or free? According to the theory of states' rights favored by many southerners, Congress had no power to impose its will on a state, old or new. Instead, the people of each state should decide whether to permit slavery. The fight over slavery thus involved a basic question about the powers of the federal and state governments under the Constitution.

A Deadlocked Congress   Southerners' protests were based on their fear that if Congress was allowed to end slavery in Missouri, it might try to end slavery elsewhere. The North already had more votes in the House of Representatives than the South. Only in the Senate did the two sections have equal voting power. As long as the number of free states and slave states remained equal, southern senators could defeat any attempt to interfere with slavery. But if Missouri entered the Union as a free state, the South would lose its power to block anti-slavery bills in the Senate. If that happened, southerners warned, it would be a disaster for the South.

In the North, the Tallmadge Amendment awakened strong feelings against slavery. Many towns sent petitions to Congress, condemning slavery as immoral and unconstitutional. Arguing in favor of the amendment, New Hampshire representative Arthur Livermore spoke for many northerners when he said:

> *An opportunity is now presented to prevent the growth of a sin which sits heavy on the soul of every one of us. By embracing this opportunity, we may retrieve the national character and, in some degree our own.*

The House voted to approve the Tallmadge Amendment. In the Senate, however, southerners were able to defeat it. The two houses were now deadlocked over the issue of slavery in Missouri. They would remain so as the 1819 session of Congress drew to a close.

An auctioneer holds a baby during a slave auction, while the child's mother begs not to be separated from her child. Scenes like this fueled the moral outrage many felt toward slavery.

21.3 The Missouri Compromise

secession the act of withdrawing from an organization or alliance, such as the withdrawal of the southern states from the Union

When Congress returned to Washington in 1820, it took up the question of Missouri statehood once again. By then, the situation had changed, for Maine was now asking to enter the Union as a free state.

For weeks, Congress struggled to find a way out of its deadlock over Missouri. As the debate dragged on and tempers wore thin, southerners began using such dreaded words as **"secession"** and "civil war."

"If you persist," Thomas Cobb of Georgia warned supporters of the amendment, "the Union will be dissolved. You have kindled a fire which only a sea of blood can extinguish."

"If disunion must take place, let it be so!" thundered Tallmadge in reply. "If civil war must come, I can only say, let it come."

A Compromise Is Reached   Rather than risk the breakup of the Union, Congress finally agreed to a compromise crafted by Representative Henry Clay of Kentucky. The compromise admitted Missouri to the Union as a slave state and Maine as a free state. In this way, it maintained the balance of power between slave and free states.

As a result of the Missouri Compromise, Missouri entered the Union as a slave state, while Maine entered as a free state. In addition, a line was drawn at the 36°30′ parallel, below which slavery would be allowed. Above this line, slavery was prohibited.

At the same time, Congress drew an imaginary line across the Louisiana Territory at latitude 36°30′. North of this line, slavery was to be banned forever, except in Missouri. South of the line, slaveholding was permitted.

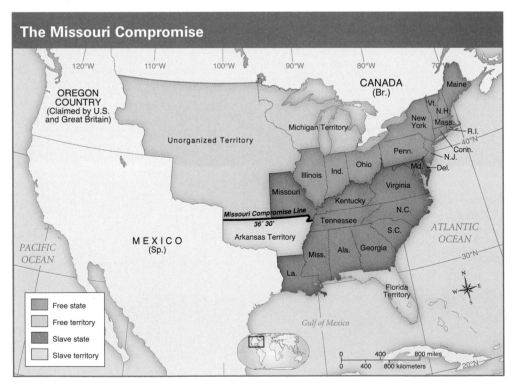

The Missouri Compromise

Legend:
- Free state
- Free territory
- Slave state
- Slave territory

Reactions to the Compromise   The Missouri Compromise kept the Union together. But it pleased no one. In the North, congressmen who voted to accept Missouri as a slave state were called traitors. In the South, slaveholders deeply resented the ban on slavery in part of the Louisiana Territory.

Meanwhile, as Secretary of State John Quincy Adams recognized, the compromise had not settled the future of slavery in the United States as a whole. "I have favored this Missouri compromise, believing it to be all that could be effected [accomplished] under the present Constitution, and from extreme unwillingness to put the Union at hazard [risk]," wrote Adams in his diary. "If the Union must be dissolved, slavery is precisely the question on which it ought to break. For the present, however, the contest is laid asleep."

21.4 The Missouri Compromise Unravels

As John Quincy Adams predicted, for a time the "contest" over slavery was laid to rest. But a powerful force was building that soon pushed the issue of slavery into the open again: the Second Great Awakening. As you read in Chapter 18, leaders of the religious revival of the 1820s and 1830s promised that God would grant salvation to those who did the Lord's work. And for some Americans, the Lord's work was the abolition of slavery.

The horrors of slavery were detailed in many northern newspapers and periodicals such as this one.

The "Gag Rule"   During the 1830s, abolitionists flooded Congress with anti-slavery petitions. Congress, they were told, had no power to interfere with slavery in the states. Then what about the District of Columbia? asked the abolitionists. Surely Congress had the power to ban slavery in the nation's capital.

Rather than face that question, Congress voted in 1836 to table all anti-slavery petitions. (To *table* means to set something aside indefinitely.) Outraged abolitionists called this action the "gag rule," because it gagged (silenced) all congressional debate over slavery.

In 1839, the gag rule prevented consideration of an anti-slavery proposal by John Quincy Adams, who was now a member of Congress. Knowing that the country would not agree on abolishing slavery altogether, Adams proposed a constitutional amendment saying that no one could be born into slavery after 1845. Congress, however, refused to consider his proposal.

Southern Fears   Abolitionists were far from silenced by the refusal of Congress to debate slavery. They continued to attack slavery in books, in newspapers, and at public meetings.

White southerners deeply resented the abolitionists' attacks as an assault on their way of life. After Nat Turner's slave rebellion in 1831, resentment turned to fear. Southern states adopted strict new laws to control the movement of slaves. Many states also tried to keep abolitionist writings from reaching slaves. Mississippi even offered a reward of $5,000 for the arrest and conviction of any person "who shall utter, publish, or circulate" abolitionist ideas.

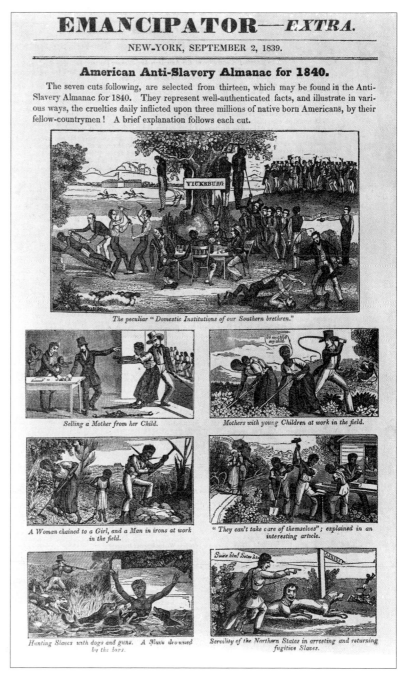

EMANCIPATOR—*EXTRA.*

NEW-YORK, SEPTEMBER 2, 1839.

American Anti-Slavery Almanac for 1840.

The seven cuts following, are selected from thirteen, which may be found in the Anti-Slavery Almanac for 1840. They represent well-authenticated facts, and illustrate in various ways, the cruelties daily inflicted upon three millions of native born Americans, by their fellow-countrymen! A brief explanation follows each cut.

The peculiar " Domestic Institutions of our Southern brethren."

Selling a Mother from her Child.

Mothers with young Children at work in the field.

A Woman chained to a Girl, and a Man in irons at work in the field.

" They can't take care of themselves"; explained in an interesting article.

Hunting Slaves with dogs and guns.   A Slave drowned by the dogs.

Servility of the Northern States in arresting and returning fugitive Slaves.

Fugitive Slaves   Nat Turner's rebellion was the last large-scale slave revolt. But individual slaves continued to rebel by running away to freedom in the North. These **fugitives** from slavery were often helped in their escape by sympathetic people in the North.

To slaveholders, these northerners were no better than bank robbers. A good slave was a valuable piece of property. Every time a slave escaped, it was like seeing five acres of land vanish into thin air. Slaveholders demanded that Congress pass a fugitive slave law to help them recapture their property.

Slavery in the Territories   The gag rule kept the slavery issue out of Congress for ten years. Then, in 1846, President James Polk sent a bill to Congress asking for funds for the war with Mexico. Pennsylvania representative David Wilmot added an amendment to the bill known as the Wilmot Proviso. (A *proviso* is a condition added to an agreement.) Wilmot's proviso stated that "neither slavery nor involuntary servitude shall ever exist" in any part of the territory that might be acquired from Mexico.

Southerners in Congress strongly opposed Wilmot's amendment. Congress had no right, they maintained, to decide where slaveholders could take their property. The Wilmot Proviso passed the House, but it was rejected by the Senate.

Statehood for California   For the next three years, Congress debated what to do about slavery in the territory gained from Mexico. Southerners wanted all of the Mexican Cession open to slavery. Northerners wanted all of it closed.

Nat Turner, pictured above, led the last major slave uprising in the United States. Following the Turner revolt, southerners tightened restrictions on slaves.

As a compromise, southerners proposed a bill that would extend the Missouri Compromise line all the way to the Pacific. Slavery would be banned north of that line and allowed south of it. Northerners in Congress rejected this proposal.

Then, late in 1849, California applied for admission to the Union as a free state. Northerners in Congress welcomed California with open arms. Southerners, however, rejected California's request. Making California a free state, they warned, would upset the equal balance between slave and free states. The result would be to make the slave states "a fixed, dreary, hopeless minority."

The year ended with Congress deadlocked over California's request for statehood. Once again, resentful southerners spoke openly of withdrawing from the Union. And once again, angry northerners denounced slavery as "a crime against humanity…a great evil."

21.5 The Compromise of 1850

On January 21, 1850, Henry Clay, now a senator from Kentucky, trudged through a Washington snowstorm to pay an unexpected call on Senator Daniel Webster of Massachusetts. Clay, the creator of the Missouri Compromise, had come up with a plan to end the deadlock over California. But to get his plan through Congress, Clay needed Webster's support.

Something for Everyone   Clay's new compromise had something to please just about everyone. It began by admitting California to the Union as a free state. That would please the North. Meanwhile, New Mexico and Utah would be organized as territories open to slavery, which would please the South.

In addition, Clay's plan ended the slave trade in Washington, D.C. Although slaveholders in Washington would be able to keep their slaves, human beings would no longer be bought and sold in the nation's capital. Clay and Webster agreed that this compromise would win support from abolitionists without threatening the rights of slaveholders.

Finally, Clay's plan called for passage of a strong fugitive slave law. Slaveholders had long wanted such a law, which would make it easier to find and reclaim their runaway slaves.

The Compromise Is Accepted   Hoping that Clay's compromise would end the crisis, Webster agreed to help push it through Congress. But despite his support, Congress debated Clay's proposals for nine frustrating months. As tempers frayed, southerners talked of simply leaving the Union peacefully.

Webster dismissed such talk as foolish. "Secession! Peaceable secession!" he exclaimed. "Your eyes and mine are never destined to see that miracle.... I see it as plainly as I see the sun in heaven—I see that secession must produce such a war as I will not describe."

A war over slavery? That was something few Americans wanted to face. In September 1850, Congress finally adopted Clay's plan.

Most Americans were happy to see the crisis end. Some southerners, however, remained wary of the Compromise of 1850. A North Carolina newspaper warned the North to "let this question of Slavery alone, take it out and keep it out of Congress; and respect and enforce the Fugitive Slave Law as it stands. *If not, we leave you!*"

The Compromise of 1850 admitted California as a free state and allowed the southwestern territories to be set up with no restriction on slavery.

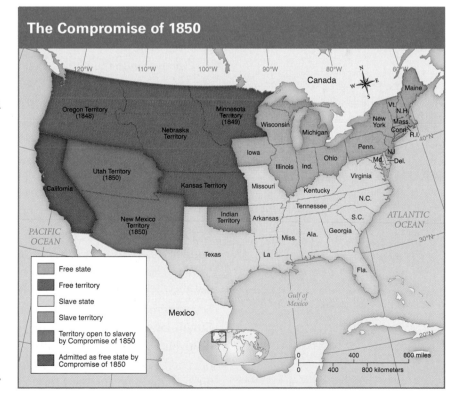

The Compromise of 1850

Free state
Free territory
Slave state
Slave territory
Territory open to slavery by Compromise of 1850
Admitted as free state by Compromise of 1850

21.6 The Compromise Satisfies No One

Clay and Webster hoped that the Compromise of 1850 would quiet the slavery controversy for years to come. In fact, it satisfied almost no one. Instead of quieting down, the debate grew louder each year.

In this painting, a group of fugitive slaves are helped as they make their escape from bondage. The assistance northerners gave to escaped slaves caused hard feelings among southern slaveholders.

The Fugitive Slave Law

Both sides were unhappy with the Fugitive Slave Law, though for different reasons. Northerners did not want to enforce the law. Southerners felt the law did not do enough to ensure the return of their escaped property.

Under the Fugitive Slave Law, any person arrested as a runaway slave had almost no legal rights. Many runaways fled to Canada rather than risk being caught and sent back to their masters. Others decided to stand and fight. Reverend Jarmain Loguen, a former slave living in New York, said boldly, "I don't respect this law—I don't fear it—I won't obey it…I will not live like a slave, and if force is employed to reenslave me, I shall make preparations to meet the crisis as becomes a man."

The Fugitive Slave Law also said that any person who helped a slave escape, or even refused to aid slave catchers, could be jailed. This provision, complained New England poet Ralph Waldo Emerson, made "slave catchers of us all."

Opposition to the law was widespread in the North. When slave catchers came to Boston, they were hounded by crowds of angry citizens shouting, "Slave hunters—there go the slave hunters." After a few days of this treatment, most slave catchers decided to leave.

Notherners' refusal to support the law infuriated slaveholders. It also made enforcement of the law almost impossible. Of the tens of thousands of fugitives living in the North during the 1850s, only 299 were captured and returned to their owners.

Uncle Tom's Cabin   Nothing brought the horrors of slavery home to northerners more than *Uncle Tom's Cabin,* a novel by Harriet Beecher Stowe. The novel grew out of a horrifying vision Stowe experienced while she was sitting in church on a wintry Sunday morning in 1851. The vision began with a saintly slave known as Uncle Tom and his cruel master, Simon Legree. In a furious rage, Legree had the old slave whipped to death. Just before Uncle Tom's soul slipped out of his bloodied body, he opened his eyes and whispered to Legree, "Ye poor miserable critter! There ain't no more ye can do. I forgive ye, with all my soul!"

Racing home, Stowe scribbled down what she had seen. Her vision of Uncle Tom's death became part of a much longer story that was first published in installments in an abolitionist newspaper. In one issue, terrified readers held their breath as the beautiful slave Eliza chose to risk death rather than be sold away from her young son. Chased by slave hunters and their dogs, Eliza dashed to freedom across the ice-choked Ohio River, clutching her child in her arms. Later, Stowe's readers wept as they read her account of how Uncle Tom died at the hands of Simon Legree.

In 1852, *Uncle Tom's Cabin* was published as a novel. Plays based on the book toured the country, thrilling audiences with Eliza's dramatic escape to freedom. No other work had ever aroused such powerful emotions about slavery. In the South, the novel and its author were scorned and cursed. In the North, *Uncle Tom's Cabin* turned millions of people against slavery.

The Ostend Manifesto and the Kansas-Nebraska Act

Northerners who were horrified by slavery were roused to fury by two events in 1854: the publication of the so-called Ostend Manifesto, and the Kansas-Nebraska Act.

The document known as the Ostend Manifesto was a message sent to the secretary of state by three American diplomats who were meeting in Ostend, Belgium. President Franklin Pierce had been trying to purchase the island of Cuba from Spain, but Spain had refused the offer. The message from the diplomats urged the U.S. government to seize Cuba by force if Spain continued to refuse to sell the island. When the message leaked to the public, angry northerners charged that Pierce's government wanted to grab Cuba in order to add another slave state to the Union.

Early that same year, Senator Stephen A. Douglas of Illinois introduced a bill in Congress that aroused an even greater furor. Douglas wanted to get a railroad built to California, and he thought the project was more likely to happen if Congress organized the Great Plains into Nebraska Territory and opened the region to settlers. Because this territory lay north of the Missouri Compromise, Douglas's bill said nothing about slavery. But southerners in Congress agreed to support the bill only if Douglas made a

UNCLE TOM'S CABIN

ELIZA'S ESCAPE

Perhaps no other novel in American history has had the political impact of *Uncle Tom's Cabin*. Upon meeting author Harriet Beecher Stowe, Abraham Lincoln said, "So you're the little woman who wrote the book that made this great war."

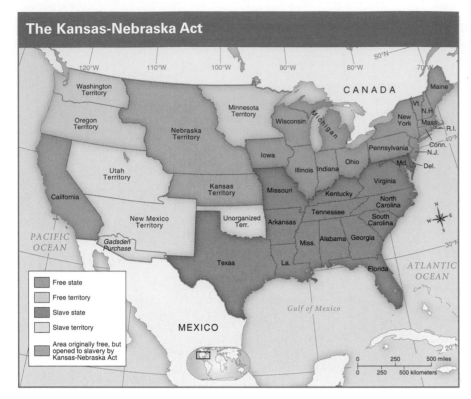

The Kansas-Nebraska Act

Free state
Free territory
Slave state
Slave territory
Area originally free, but opened to slavery by Kansas-Nebraska Act

The Kansas-Nebraska Act outraged northerners because it violated the Missouri Compromise.

few changes—and those changes had far-reaching consequences.

Douglas's final bill created two new territories, Kansas and Nebraska. It also scrapped the Missouri Compromise by leaving it up to the settlers themselves to vote on whether to permit slavery in the two territories. Douglas called this policy "popular sovereignty," or rule by the people.

Douglas's Kansas-Nebraska Act hit the North like a thunderbolt. Once again, northerners were haunted by nightmare visions of slavery marching across the plains. Douglas tried to calm their fears by saying that the climates of Kansas and Nebraska were not suited to slave labor. But when northerners studied maps, they were not so sure. Newspaper editor Horace Greeley charged in the *New York Tribune:*

The pretense of Douglas & Co. that not even Kansas is to be made a slave state by his bill is a gag [joke]. Ask any Missourian what he thinks about it. The Kansas Territory…is bounded in its entire length by Missouri, with a whole tier of slave counties leaning against it. Won't be a slave state!…Gentlemen! Don't lie any more!

Bloodshed in Kansas After the Kansas-Nebraska Act was passed, settlers poured into Kansas. Most were peaceful farmers looking for fertile soil. Some settlers, however, moved to Kansas either to support or to oppose slavery. In the South, towns took up collections to send their young men to Kansas. In the North, abolitionists raised money to send weapons to anti-slavery settlers. Before long, Kansas had two competing governments, one for slavery and one against it.

The struggle over slavery soon turned violent. On May 21, 1856, pro-slavery settlers and "border ruffians" from Missouri invaded Lawrence, Kansas, the home of the anti-slavery government. The invaders burned a hotel, looted several homes, and tossed the presses of two abolitionist newspapers into the Kaw River. As the invaders left Lawrence, one of them boasted, "Gentlemen, this is the happiest day of my life."

The raid on Lawrence provoked a wave of outrage in the North. Money was quickly raised to replace the destroyed presses. And more "free-soilers," as the anti-slavery settlers were called, prepared to move to Kansas.

Meanwhile, a fiery abolitionist named John Brown plotted his own revenge. Two days after the Lawrence raid, Brown and seven followers, including four of Brown's sons and his son-in-law, invaded the pro-slavery town of Pottawatomie. There they dragged five men they suspected of supporting slavery from their homes and hacked them to death with swords.

Violence in Congress   The violence in Kansas greatly disturbed Senator Charles Sumner of Massachusetts. To Sumner, it was proof of what he had long suspected—that Senator Stephen Douglas had plotted with southerners to make Kansas a slave state.

In 1856, Sumner voiced his suspicions in a passionate speech entitled "The Crime Against Kansas." Using harsh, shocking language, Sumner described the "crime against Kansas" as a violent assault on an innocent territory, "compelling it to the hateful embrace of slavery." He dismissed Douglas as "a noisome [offensive], squat, and nameless animal." Sumner also heaped abuse on many southerners, including the distinguished Senator Andrew P. Butler of South Carolina.

Just what Sumner hoped to accomplish was not clear. However, copies of his speech were quickly printed up for distribution in the North. After reading it, New England poet Henry Wadsworth Longfellow congratulated Sumner on the "brave and noble speech you made, never to die out in the memories of men."

Certainly it was not about to die out in the memories of enraged southerners. Two days after the speech, Senator Butler's nephew, South Carolina representative Preston Brooks, attacked Sumner in the Senate, beating him with his cane until it broke in half. By the time other senators could pull Brooks away, Sumner had collapsed, unconscious and bloody.

Reactions to the attack on Sumner showed how badly divided the country had become. Many southerners applauded Brooks for defending the honor of his family and the South. From across the South, supporters sent Brooks new canes to replace the one he had broken on Sumner's head.

Pro-slavery men from Missouri on their way to Lawrence, the "Free Soil" capital of Kansas. These "border ruffians" used violence and threats to frighten anti-slavery citizens.

Most northerners viewed the beating as another example of southern brutality. In their eyes, Brooks was no better than the pro-slavery bullies who had attacked the good people of Lawrence. One Connecticut student was so upset that she wrote to Sumner about going to war. "I don't think it is of very much use to stay any longer in the high school," she wrote. "The boys would be better learning to hold muskets, and the girls to make bullets."

The *Dred Scott* Case   In 1857, the slavery controversy shifted from the bloodied floor of Congress to the Supreme Court. The Court was about to decide a case concerning a Missouri slave named Dred Scott. Years earlier, Scott had traveled with his owner to Wisconsin, where slavery was banned by the Missouri Compromise. Upon his return to Missouri, Scott went to court to win his freedom. He argued that his stay in Wisconsin had made him a free man.

There were nine justices on the Supreme Court in 1857. Five of them, including Chief Justice Roger Taney, were from the South. Four were from the North. The justices had two key questions to decide. First, as a slave, was Dred Scott a citizen who had the right to bring a case before a federal court? Second, did his time in Wisconsin make him a free man?

Taney, however, hoped to use the *Scott* case to settle the slavery controversy once and for all. And so he asked the Court to consider two more questions: Did Congress have the power to make any laws at all concerning slavery in the territories? And, if so, was the Missouri Compromise a constitutional use of that power?

Preston Brooks savagely beats Charles Sumner on the U.S. Senate floor. It took Sumner three and a half years to recover from the beating.

21.7 The *Dred Scott* Decision

On March 6, 1857, Chief Justice Roger Taney prepared to deliver the most important decision of his career. Nearly 80 years old, the chief justice had long been opposed to slavery. As a young Maryland lawyer, he had publicly declared that "slavery is a blot upon our national character and every lover of freedom confidently hopes that it will be…wiped away."

True to his words, Taney had gone on to free his own slaves. Many observers wondered whether he and his fellow justices would now free Dred Scott as well.

Two Judicial Bombshells   The chief justice began by reviewing the facts of Dred Scott's case. Then he dropped the first of two judicial bombshells. By a vote of five to four, the Court had decided that Scott could not sue for his freedom in a federal court because he was not a citizen. Nor, said Taney, could Scott become a citizen. No African American, whether slave or free, was an American citizen—or could ever become one.

Next, Taney dropped bombshell number two. The Court had also rejected Scott's argument that his stay in Wisconsin had made him a free man. The reason was simple. The Missouri Compromise was unconstitutional.

Taney's argument went something like this. Slaves are property. The Fifth Amendment to the Constitution says that property cannot be taken from people without due process of law—that is, a proper court hearing. Banning slavery in a territory, Taney reasoned, is the same as taking property away from slaveholders who would like to bring their slaves into that territory. And that is unconstitutional. Rather than banning slavery, Congress has a constitutional responsibility to protect the property rights of slaveholders in a territory.

The *Dred Scott* decision delighted slaveholders. They hoped that, at long last, the issue of slavery in the territories had been settled—and in their favor.

Many northerners, however, were stunned and enraged by the Court's ruling. The *New York Tribune* called the decision a "wicked and false judgment." Another New York newspaper expressed outrage in its bold headlines:

Dred Scott's struggle for freedom hastened the beginning of the Civil War and, in the end, led to freedom for all slaves.

The *Dred Scott* Decision

As a result of the *Dred Scott* decision, slavery was allowed in all territories.

The Decision of the Supreme Court
Is the Moral Assassination of a Race and Cannot Be Obeyed!

21.8 From Compromise to Crisis

During the controversy over the Kansas-Nebraska Act, anti-slavery activists formed a new political organization called the Republican Party. The Republicans were united by their beliefs that "no man can own another man...that slavery must be prohibited in the territories...that all new states must be free states...that the rights of our colored citizen...must be protected."

In 1858, Republicans in Illinois nominated Abraham Lincoln to run for the Senate. In his speech accepting this honor, Lincoln pointed out that all attempts to reach compromise on the slavery issue had failed. Quoting from the Bible, he warned, "A house divided against itself cannot stand." Lincoln went on: "I believe this government cannot endure, permanently half-slave and half-free. I do not expect the Union to be dissolved—I do not expect the house to fall—but I do expect it will cease to be divided. It will become all one thing, or all the other."

Abraham Lincoln addresses an audience during one of the famous Lincoln-Douglas debates. Stephen Douglas is directly behind Lincoln on the platform.

The Granger Collection, New York

The Lincoln-Douglas Debates

Lincoln's opponent in the Senate race was Senator Stephen Douglas. The Illinois senator saw no reason why the nation could not go on half-slave and half-free. When Lincoln challenged him to debate the slavery issue, Douglas agreed.

During the debates, Douglas argued that the *Dred Scott* decision had put the slavery issue to rest. Lincoln disagreed. In his eyes, slavery was a moral, not a legal, issue. He declared, "The real issue in this controversy...is the sentiment of one class [group] that looks upon the institution of slavery as a wrong, and of the other class that does not look upon it as a wrong."

Lincoln lost the election. But the debates were widely reported, and they helped make him a national figure. His argument with Douglas also brought the moral issue of slavery into sharp focus. Compromise over slavery was becoming impossible.

John Brown's Raid
While Lincoln fought to stop the spread of slavery through politics, John Brown adopted a more extreme approach. Rather than wait for Congress to act, Brown planned to seize the federal arsenal (a place

where weapons and ammunition are stored) at Harpers Ferry, Virginia. He wanted to use the weapons to arm slaves for a rebellion that would destroy slavery forever.

It was an insane scheme. All of Brown's men were killed or captured during the raid on the arsenal. Brown himself was convicted of treason and sentenced to die. On the day of his hanging, he left a note that read, "I John Brown am now quite certain that the crimes of this guilty land will never be purged away but with blood."

Such words filled white southerners with fear. If a slave rebellion did begin, it was their blood that would be spilled. The fact that many northerners viewed Brown as a hero, rather than a lunatic, also left white southerners uneasy.

The Election of 1860   The 1860 presidential race showed just how divided the nation had become. While the Republicans were united behind Lincoln, the Democrats had split between northern and southern factions. Northern Democrats nominated Stephen Douglas. Southern Democrats supported John C. Breckinridge of Kentucky. The election became even more confusing when a group called the Constitutional Union Party nominated John Bell of Tennessee.

With his opposition divided three ways, Lincoln sailed to victory. But it was a strange sort of victory. Lincoln won with just 40 percent of the votes, all of them cast in the North. In ten southern states, he was not even on the ballot.

For white southerners, the election had an unmistakable message. The South was now a minority section. It no longer had the power to shape national events or policies. Sooner or later, southerners feared, Congress would try to abolish slavery. And that, wrote a South Carolina newspaper, would mean "the loss of liberty, property, home, country—everything that makes life worth living."

In the weeks following the election, talk of secession filled the air. Alarmed senators formed a committee to search for yet another compromise that might hold the nation together. They knew that finding one would not be easy. Still, they had to do something to stop the rush toward disunion and disaster.

JOHN BROWN, NOW UNDER SENTENCE OF DEATH FOR TREASON AND MURDER, AT CHARLESTOWN, VA.—FROM A PHOTOGRAPH TAKEN ONE YEAR AGO BY MARTIN M. LAWRENCE, 881 BROADWAY, N. Y.

John Brown was a hero to antislavery northerners and a villain to the slaveholding South.

The opening shots of the Civil War were fired at Fort Sumter on April 12, 1861. No one was killed in the 33-hour bombardment. It was a bloodless opening to the bloodiest war in American history.

21.9 Secession

The Senate committee held its first meeting on December 20, 1860. Just as the senators began their work, events in two distant cities dashed their hopes for a settlement.

In Springfield, Illinois, a reporter called on president-elect Abraham Lincoln. When asked whether he could support a compromise on slavery, Lincoln's answer was clear. He would not interfere with slavery in the South. And he would support enforcement of the Fugitive Slave Law. But Lincoln drew the line at letting slavery extend into the territories. On this question, he declared, "Let there be no compromise."

In Charleston, South Carolina, delegates attending a state convention voted that same day to leave the Union. The city went wild. Church bells rang. Huge crowds filled the streets, roaring their approval. A South Carolina newspaper boldly proclaimed, "THE UNION IS DISSOLVED!" Six more states soon followed South Carolina's lead.

Civil War On March 4, 1861, Lincoln became president of the not-so-United States. In his inaugural address, Lincoln stated his belief that secession was both wrong and unconstitutional. He then appealed to the rebellious states to return in peace. "In your hands, my dissatisfied fellow countrymen, and not in mine," he said, "is the momentous issue of civil war."

A month later, hotheads in Charleston, South Carolina, forced the issue. On April 12, they opened fire on Fort Sumter, a federal fort in Charleston Harbor. After 33 hours of heavy shelling, the defenders of the fort hauled down the Stars and Stripes and replaced it with the white flag of surrender.

The news that rebels had fired on the American flag unleashed a wave of patriotic fury in the North. All the doubts that people had about using force to save the Union vanished. A New York newspaper reported excitedly, "There is no more thought of bribing or coaxing the traitors who have dared to aim their cannon balls at the flag of the Union…. Fort Sumter is temporarily lost, but the country is saved."

The time for compromise was over. The issues that had divided the nation for so many years would now be decided by war.

21.10 Chapter Summary

In this chapter, you learned how a series of compromises failed to keep the United States from splitting in two over the issue of slavery. You used the metaphor of an unraveling flag to understand the compromises and decisions that were made in an effort to preserve the Union. In 1820, the Missouri Compromise resolved the first great crisis over slavery by admitting Missouri to the Union as a slave state and Maine as a free state. The compromise also drew a line across the Louisiana Territory. In the future, slavery would be permitted only south of that line.

The furor over slavery in new territories erupted again after the war with Mexico. The Compromise of 1850 admitted California as a free state while leaving the territories of New Mexico and Utah open to slavery. In addition, the compromise ended the slave trade in Washington, D.C., and included a fugitive slave law.

Once again, compromise failed. Northerners refused to honor the Fugitive Slave Law. Attitudes on both sides were hardened further by Harriet Beecher Stowe's powerful novel *Uncle Tom's Cabin,* the Kansas-Nebraska Act, and the Supreme Court's decision on the *Dred Scott* case.

In Illinois, the issue of slavery was the focus of well-publicized debates between Abraham Lincoln and Stephen Douglas. Tempers— and fears—rose even higher after John Brown's raid on Harpers Ferry.

For many southerners, Lincoln's election as president in 1860 was the last straw. Led by South Carolina, several southern states left the Union. When southerners fired on Fort Sumter, in Charleston Harbor, the time for compromise had passed. The nation was poised on the brink of war.

This broadside, printed in December 1860, boldly announces the secession of South Carolina from the Union.

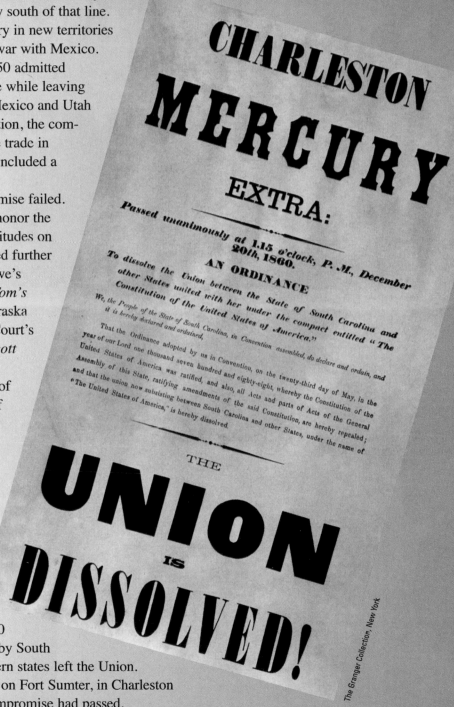

The Granger Collection, New York

301

How do you think people's attitudes toward the Civil War changed from the beginning of the war, pictured above, to later in the war, shown at the left?

The Civil War

22.1 Introduction

The cannon shells bursting over Fort Sumter ended months of confusion. The nation was at war. The time had come to choose sides.

For most whites in the South, the choice was clear. Early in 1861, representatives from six of the seven states that had seceded from the Union met to form a new nation called the Confederate States of America. Southerners believed that just as the states had once voluntarily joined the Union, they could voluntarily leave it now. The men who fought for the **Confederacy** were proud defenders of "Southern Rights" and "Southern Independence."

For many northerners, the choice was just as clear. "There can be no neutrals in this war," declared Stephen Douglas after Fort Sumter, "only patriots—and traitors." Most northerners viewed the secession of southern states as traitorous acts of rebellion against the United States. They marched off to war eager to defend "Our Union! Our Constitution! and Our Flag!"

Choosing sides was harder for the eight slave states located between the Confederacy and the free states. Four of these "border states"— Virginia, Arkansas, Tennessee, and North Carolina—joined the Confederacy. The western counties of Virginia, however, remained loyal to the Union. Rather than fight for the South, they broke away to form a new state called West Virginia. The other four border states—Delaware, Maryland, Kentucky, and Missouri— remained in the Union, although many of their citizens fought for the South.

As Americans took sides, they began to see why a **civil war**—a conflict between two peoples in one country—is the most painful kind of war. This conflict divided not only states, but also families and friends. In this chapter, you will learn how this "brothers' war" turned into the most destructive of all American wars. As you read, put yourself in the shoes of the men and women who were part of this long and tragic struggle.

Graphic Organizer: Annotated Illustration
You will use this illustration of a soldier's haversack to understand the events and effects of the Civil War.

This iron- and wireworks in Massachusetts was just one of many northern factories. Ninety percent of the nation's manufacturing was in the North.

22.2 Preparing for War

President Lincoln's response to the attack on Fort Sumter was quick and clear. He called for 75,000 volunteers to come forward to preserve the Union. At the same time, Jefferson Davis, the newly elected president of the Confederacy, called for volunteers to defend the South.

Both sides looked forward to a quick victory. "I cannot imagine that the South has resources for a long war or even a short one," said a Philadelphia lawyer. Southerners, on the other hand, believed they could easily whip any army Lincoln sent south. A North Carolina journalist boasted:

> *The army of the South will be composed of the best material that ever yet made up an army; while that of Lincoln will be gathered from the sewers of the cities...who will serve for pay and will run away as soon as danger threatens.*

Strengths and Weaknesses of the North   The North began the war with impressive strengths. Its population was about 22 million, compared to 9 million in the South. And the North was both richer and more technologically advanced than the South. About 90 percent of the nation's manufacturing, and most of its banks, were in the North.

The North had geographic advantages, too. It had more farms than the South to provide food for troops. Its land contained most of the country's iron, coal, copper, and gold. The North controlled the seas, and its 21,000 miles of railroad track allowed troops and supplies to be transported wherever they were needed.

The North's greatest weakness was its military leadership. At the start of the war, about one third of the nation's military officers resigned and returned to their homes in the South. During much of the war, Lincoln searched for effective generals who could lead the Union to victory.

Strengths and Weaknesses of the South

When the war began, southerners also had reasons to be confident of victory. To win the war, the North would have to invade and conquer the South. The sheer size of the South made this a daunting task. In addition, the North would need a much larger navy to seal off the long southern coastline and prevent the South from importing weapons and supplies from Europe.

In addition to geographic obstacles, the North faced the challenge of subduing people who believed they were defending their liberty, their homes, and their traditions. The South, in contrast, could win simply by defending its territory until northerners grew tired of fighting. But the South did have an important geographic disadvantage: if the Union could control the Mississippi River, it could split the Confederacy in two.

The South's great strength was its military leadership. Most of America's best military officers were southerners who chose to fight for the Confederacy. This was not an easy decision for many of them. Colonel Robert E. Lee, for example, was opposed to slavery and secession. But he decided that he could not fight against his native Virginia. Lee resigned from the U.S. Army to become the commander-in-chief of the Confederate forces.

The South's main weakness was an economy that could not support a long war. It had few factories to produce guns and other military supplies. Southerners could trade cotton for war material from Europe, but Union ships could sharply reduce this trade with blockades of Southern ports.

The Confederacy also faced serious transportation problems. The South lacked the railroad network needed to haul goods over long distances. Most rail lines were short and went only to seaport towns. Supplies had to be carried by wagon from the railroad to the troops. And as the war dragged on, horses and mules to draw these wagons were in short supply.

Money might have helped solve these problems. But most wealth in the South was invested in land and slaves. The Confederate government printed paper money to finance the war effort. But as these paper dollars flooded the South, their value quickly dropped.

Abraham Lincoln versus Jefferson Davis   The North's greatest

advantage was its newly elected president, Abraham Lincoln. Through even the darkest days of the war, Lincoln never wavered from his belief that the Union was "perpetual"—never to be broken. Confederate president Jefferson Davis was equally devoted to the secessionist cause. But he was

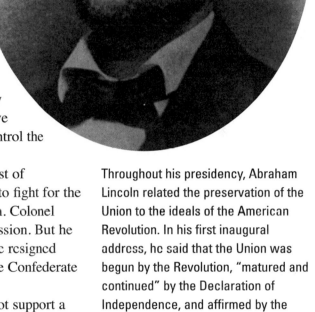

Throughout his presidency, Abraham Lincoln related the preservation of the Union to the ideals of the American Revolution. In his first inaugural address, he said that the Union was begun by the Revolution, "matured and continued" by the Declaration of Independence, and affirmed by the Constitution.

never able to form a strong, single nation out of 11 stubbornly independent states.

Abraham Lincoln was born in Kentucky on February 12, 1809. His family was poor, and his mother died while he was a young child. All in all, Lincoln figured that his schooling "did not amount to a year." It was enough, however, to excite a craving for knowledge. He read everything he could lay his hands on. "My best friend," he said, "is the man who'll get me a book I ain't read."

When Lincoln was 21, his family moved to Illinois. During the next few years, he held whatever jobs he could find—store clerk, rail-splitter, surveyor, postmaster. In the evenings, he read law books and eventually became a lawyer before entering politics.

At six feet four inches tall, Lincoln towered above most other men. His dark, sunken eyes gave him a sad but kind appearance. In this case, looks did not lie. Lincoln was patient, thoughtful, and tolerant of others. He also possessed a good sense of humor that often saved him from despair in moments of failure and frustration during the war. "I laugh," he once said, "because if I didn't I would weep."

Like Lincoln, Jefferson Davis was born in Kentucky in a log cabin. He grew up on a small plantation in Mississippi. As a young man, he attended the military academy at West Point, New York. Davis fought in the Mexican War and served as Secretary of War under President Franklin Pierce. At the time of the secession crisis, he was a U.S. senator representing Mississippi. A firm believer in states' rights, he resigned his seat in the Senate when Mississippi left the Union.

Tall, lean, and intense, Davis never really enjoyed politics. He served the Confederacy out of a sense of duty. The South, he believed, was fighting for the same freedom cherished by America's founders. After being sworn in as president of the Confederate States, he declared, "Our present condition...illustrates the American idea that government rests upon the consent of the governed."

Like Abraham Lincoln, Jefferson Davis often spoke of the American Revolution. When southerners formed their own government, he said, they "merely asserted a right which the Declaration of Independence of 1776 had defined to be inalienable."

Geography Challenge

The Civil War 1861–1865

Map Legend:
- Union states
- Border states
- Confederate states
- ✸ Union victory
- ✸ Confederate victory
- ✸ Indecisive or draw

0 200 400 miles
0 200 400 kilometers

CANADA

Maine
Vt.
N.H.
New York
Mass.
R.I.
Conn.
N.J.
Del.
Md.
W.V.
Pennsylvania
Washington, D.C.
Richmond
Va.
Appomattox Court House
Minnesota
Wisconsin
Michigan
Iowa
Illinois
Indiana
Ohio
Nebraska Territory
Colorado Territory
Kansas
Missouri
Kentucky
North Carolina
New Mexico Territory
Indian Territory
Arkansas
Tennessee
South Carolina
Atlanta
Georgia
Savannah
Miss.
Alabama
Texas
La.
Florida
MEXICO
Gulf of Mexico
ATLANTIC OCEAN

Battles:
- Gettysburg *July 1–3, 1863*
- Antietam *Sept. 17, 1862*
- 1st Bull Run *July 21, 1861*
- 2nd Bull Run *Aug. 29–30, 1862*
- Fredericksburg *Dec. 11-15, 1862*
- Chancellorsville *May 1–4, 1863*
- Hampton Roads *March 8-9, 1862*
- Seven Days' Battle *June 25–July 1, 1862*
- Petersburg *June 1864–April 1865*
- Ft. Sumter *April 12–14, 1861*
- Ft. Wagner *July 18-Sept. 7, 1863*
- Fort Henry *Feb. 6, 1862*
- Fort Donelson *Feb. 13-16, 1862*
- Shiloh *April 6–7, 1862*
- Chickamauga *Sept. 19–20, 1863*
- Vicksburg *May 19–July 4, 1863*

100°W 90°W 80°W 40°N 30°N

1. Identify four interesting details on this map.

2. Where did most battles take place: in Union states, in Confederate states, or in border states?

3. In the early part of the war (1861–1862), which side won more battles? Why do you think this side was more successful?

4. In the later part of the war (1863–1865), which side won more battles? Why do you think this side was more successful?

22.3 Bull Run: A Great Awakening

In the spring of 1861, President Lincoln and General Winfield Scott planned the Union's war strategy. Step one was to surround the South by land and sea to cut off its trade. Step two was to divide the Confederacy into sections so that one rebel region could not help another. Step three was to capture Richmond, Virginia, the capital of the Confederacy, and destroy the rebel government. Journalists called this strategy the "Anaconda Plan" because it resembled the crushing death grip of an anaconda snake.

Rose Greenhow's Dilemma   Most northerners, however, believed that the war could be won with a single Union assault on Richmond. In 1861, thousands of volunteers poured into

Rose Greenhow is shown here with her daughter. During her Washington parties, she collected valuable information about Union plans to attack Richmond. She passed this information on to Confederate leaders through coded messages such as the one below.

Washington, D.C., shouting, "On to Richmond!" These eager troops were watched carefully by an attractive young widow and Washington social leader named Rose O'Neal Greenhow.

Greenhow was a strong supporter of the southern cause. She used her friendship with government officials to learn just when and how the Union planned to attack Richmond. Her problem was to find some way to deliver this information to Confederate leaders without being discovered.

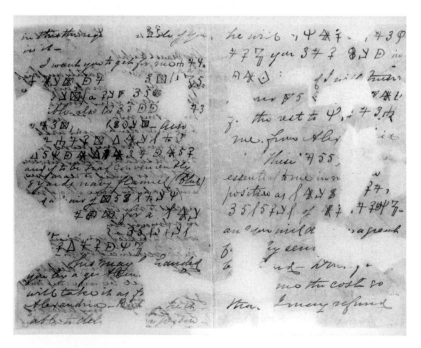

The Battle of Bull Run   On a hot July morning, long lines of soldiers marched out of Washington heading for Richmond. Their voices could be heard singing and cheering across the countryside. Parties of politicians and society folks followed the army, adding to the excitement. They had come along to see the end of the rebellion.

The troops would not have been so cheerful had they known what was waiting for them at Manassas, a small town on the way to Richmond. Rose Greenhow had managed to warn southern military leaders of Union plans. She had smuggled a coded note to them in the curls of a young girl. Southern troops were waiting for the Union forces as they approached Manassas. The two armies met at a creek known as Bull Run.

At first, Union victory looked certain. But Confederate general Thomas Jackson and his regiment of Virginians refused to give way. "Look," shouted South Carolina general Bernard Bee to his men, "there is Jackson with his Virginians, standing like a stone wall." Thus inspired by "Stonewall" Jackson's example, the rebel lines held firm until reinforcements arrived. Late that afternoon, Jackson urged his men to "yell like furies" as they charged the Union forces. The sound and fury of this charge unnerved the green (inexperienced) Union troops, who fled in panic back to Washington.

The Battle of Bull Run was a smashing victory for the South. For the North, it was a shocking blow. Lincoln and his generals now realized that ending the rebellion would not be easy. It was time to prepare for a long war.

Women Support the War   Over the next year, both the North and the South worked to build and train large armies. As men went off to war, women took their places on the home front. Wives and mothers supported their families by running farms and businesses. Many women went to work for the first time in factories. Others found jobs as nurses, teachers, or government workers.

Women also served the military forces on both sides as messengers, guides, scouts, smugglers, soldiers, and spies. Rose Greenhow was arrested for spying shortly after the Battle of Bull Run. Although she was kept under guard in her Washington home, she continued to smuggle military secrets to the Confederates. The following year, Greenhow was allowed to move to the South, where President Jefferson Davis welcomed her as a hero.

Women also volunteered to help tend sick and wounded soldiers. Dorothea Dix was already well known for her efforts to improve the treatment of the mentally ill. She was appointed director of the Union army's nursing service. Dix insisted that all female nurses be over 30 years old, plain in appearance, physically strong, and willing to do unpleasant work. Her rules were so strict that she was known as "Dragon Dix."

While most nurses worked in military hospitals, Clara Barton followed Union armies into battle, tending troops where they fell. Later generations would remember Barton as the founder of the American Red Cross. To the soldiers she cared for during the war, she was "the angel of the battlefield."

During the Civil War, many women went to work in factories such as this munitions plant. They replaced men who were in the army.

22.4 Antietam: A Bloody Affair

The Battle of Bull Run ended northerners' hopes for a quick victory. In the months that followed that sobering defeat, the Union began to put the Anaconda Plan into effect.

The Union Blockade   In 1861, the Union navy launched its blockade of southern ports. By the end of the year, most southern ports were closed to foreign ships. As the blockade shut down its ports, the Confederacy asked Britain for help in protecting its ships. The British, however, refused this request. As a result, the South could not export its cotton to Europe, nor could it import needed supplies.

For 12 hours, Confederate and Union forces fought at Antietam in what was the bloodiest day of the Civil War. Some of the 2,770 Confederate soldiers who died during this battle are shown in this photograph.

Dividing the Confederacy   Early in 1862, Union forces moved to divide the Confederacy by gaining control of the Mississippi River. In April, Union admiral David Farragut led 46 Union ships up the Mississippi River to New Orleans. This was the largest American fleet ever assembled. In the face of such overwhelming force, the city surrendered without firing a shot.

Meanwhile, Union forces headed by General Ulysses S. Grant began moving south toward the Mississippi from Illinois. In 1862, Grant won a series of victories that put Kentucky and much of Tennessee under Union control. A general of remarkable determination, Grant refused to accept any battle outcome other than unconditional (total) surrender. For this reason, U.S. Grant was known to his men as "Unconditional Surrender" Grant.

Attacking Richmond   That same year, Union general George McClellan sent 100,000 men by ship to capture Richmond. Again, a Union victory seemed certain. But despite being outnumbered, Confederate forces stopped the Union attack in a series of well-fought battles. Once more, Richmond was saved.

The Battle of Antietam   At this point, General Robert E. Lee, the commander of the Confederate forces, did the unexpected. He sent his troops across the Potomac River into Maryland, a slave state that remained in the Union. Lee hoped that this show of strength might persuade Maryland to join the Confederacy. He also hoped that a Confederate victory on Union soil would convince European nations to support the South.

On a crisp September day in 1862, Confederate and Union armies met near the little town of Sharpsburg along Antietam Creek. All day long,

McClellan's troops pounded Lee's badly outnumbered forces. The following day, Lee pulled back to Virginia.

McClellan claimed Antietam as a Union victory. But many who fought there saw the battle as "a defeat for both armies." Of the 75,000 Union troops who fought at Antietam, about 2,100 were killed. Another 10,300 were wounded or missing. Of the 52,000 Confederates who fought at Antietam, about 2,770 lost their lives, while 11,000 were wounded or missing. In that single day of fighting, more Americans were killed than in the War of 1812 and the Mexican War combined. The Battle of Antietam was the bloodiest day of the war.

The New Realities of War The horrifying death toll at Antietam reflected the new realities of warfare. In past wars, battles had been won in hand-to-hand combat using bayonets. During the Civil War, improved weapons made killing at a distance much easier. Rifles, which replaced muskets, were accurate over long distances. Improved cannons and artillery also made it easier for armies to rain down death on forces some distance away. As a result, armies could meet, fight, bleed, and part without either side winning a clear victory.

Unfortunately, medical care was not as advanced as weaponry. Civil War doctors had no understanding of the causes of infections. Surgeons operated in dirty hospital tents with basic instruments. Few bothered to wash their hands between patients. As a result, infections spread rapidly from patient to patient. The hospital death rate was so awful that soldiers often refused medical care. An injured Ohio soldier wrote that he chose to return to battle rather than see a doctor, "thinking that I had better die by rebel bullets than Union Quackery [unskilled medical care]."

As staggering as the battle death tolls were, far more soldiers died of diseases than wounds. Unsanitary (unclean) conditions in army camps were so bad that about three men died of typhoid, pneumonia, and other diseases for every one who died in battle. As one soldier observed, "these big battles [are] not as bad as the fever."

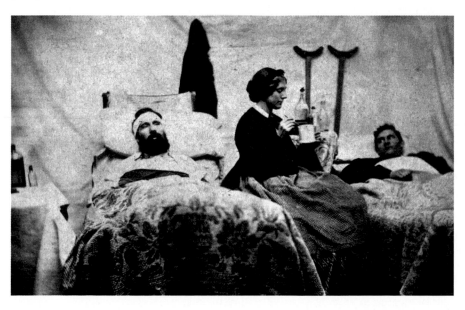

Medical care was shockingly poor during the Civil War. Surgeries were performed without anesthetics. Thousands of soldiers died from infections or disease. Nevertheless, nurses performed heroically as they cared for the sick and wounded.

22.5 Gettysburg: A Turning Point

While neither side won the battle of Antietam, it was enough of a victory for Lincoln to take his first steps toward ending slavery. When the Civil War began, Lincoln had resisted pleas from abolitionists to make **emancipation,** or the freeing of slaves, a reason for fighting the Confederacy. He himself opposed slavery. But the purpose of the war, he said, "is to save the Union, and is not either to save or destroy slavery."

In this illustration, slaves are pictured waiting for the Emancipation Proclamation. While the proclamation had little immediate effect, it meant the Union was now fighting to end slavery.

The Emancipation Proclamation   As the war dragged on, Lincoln changed his mind. Declaring an end to slavery, he realized, would discourage Europeans who opposed slavery from assisting the Confederacy. Freeing slaves could also deprive the Confederacy of a large part of its workforce.

On January 1, 1863, President Lincoln issued the Emancipation Proclamation. The proclamation, or formal order, declared slaves in all Confederate states to be free. This announcement had little immediate effect on slavery. The Confederate states simply ignored the document. Slaves living in states loyal to the Union were not affected by the proclamation.

Still, for many in the North, the Emancipation Proclamation changed the war into a crusade for freedom. The Declaration of Independence had said that "all men are created equal." Now the fight was about living up to those words.

emancipation the act of freeing people from slavery

draft a system for requiring citizens to join their country's armed forces

The Draft   Meanwhile, both the North and the South had run out of volunteers to fill their armies. In 1862, the Confederacy passed the nation's first **draft** law. This law said that all white men aged 18 to 35 could be called for three years of military service. A year later, the North passed a similar law that drafted men aged 20 to 45.

Under both laws, a drafted man could avoid the army by paying a substitute to take his place. This provision led to charges that the conflict was "a rich man's war and a poor man's fight."

The Battle of Gettysburg   The need to pass draft laws was a sign that both sides were getting tired of war. Still, in the summer of 1863, Lee felt confident enough to risk another invasion of the North. He hoped to capture a northern city and help convince the weary North to seek peace.

Union and Confederate troops met on July 1, 1863, west of Gettysburg, Pennsylvania. The Union troops, about 90,000 strong, were led by newly appointed General George C. Meade. After a brief skirmish, they occupied four miles of high ground along an area known as Cemetery Ridge. About a mile to the west, some 75,000 Confederate troops gathered behind Seminary Ridge.

The following day, the Confederates attempted to find weak spots in the Union position. But the Union lines held firm. On the third day, Lee ordered an all-out attack on the center of the Union line. Cannons filled the air with smoke and thunder. George Pickett led 15,000 Confederate soldiers in a charge across the low ground separating the two forces.

Pickett's charge marked the northernmost point reached by southern troops during the war. But as the rebels pressed forward, Union gunners opened great holes in their advancing lines. Those brave men who managed to make their way to Cemetery Ridge were struck down by Union troops in hand-to-hand combat.

The losses at Gettysburg were staggering. More than 17,500 Union soldiers and 23,000 Confederate troops were killed or wounded in three days of battle. Lee, who lost about a third of his army, withdrew to Virginia. From this point on, he would only wage a defensive war on southern soil.

Opposition on the Union Home Front   Despite the victory at Gettysburg, Lincoln faced a number of problems on the home front. One was opposition to the war itself. A group of northern Democrats were far more interested in restoring peace than in saving the Union or ending slavery. Republicans called these Democrats "Copperheads" after a poisonous snake with that name.

Other northerners opposed the war because they were sympathetic to the Confederate cause. When a pro-slavery mob attacked Union soldiers marching through Maryland, Lincoln sent in troops to keep order. He also used his constitutional power to suspend, or temporarily discontinue, the right of **habeas corpus**. During the national emergency, citizens no longer had the right to a trial before being jailed. People who were suspected of disloyalty were jailed without trial.

Draft Riots   The Union draft law was passed just two months after Lincoln issued the Emancipation Proclamation. It also created opposition to the war. Some northerners resented being forced to fight to end slavery. Others protested that the new law "converts the Republic into one grand military dictatorship."

When the federal government began calling up men in July 1863, a riot broke out in New York City. For four days, crowds of angry white New

habeas corpus a written order from a court that gives a person the right to a trial before being jailed

On July 3, 1863, General George Pickett led 15,000 Confederate troops in a charge against the Union lines. Row after row of Confederate soldiers fell under a rain of bullets until they finally retreated.

During the draft riots, white workers attacked free blacks. The whites feared African Americans would take their jobs and resented being forced to fight a war to end slavery. Almost 100 African Americans died during the four days of riots.

Yorkers burned draft offices and battled police. But their special targets were African Americans. Almost 100 black New Yorkers died as mobs attacked black boardinghouses, a black church, and a black orphanage. The rioting finally stopped when troops fresh from Gettysburg restored order.

Lincoln's Gettysburg Address   Four months after the draft riots, President Lincoln traveled to Gettysburg. Thousands of the men who died there had been buried in a new cemetery overlooking the battlefield. Lincoln was among those invited to speak at the dedication of this new burial ground.

After an hour-long talk by another speaker, Lincoln rose and spoke a few words. Many of the 15,000 people gathered on Cemetery Ridge could not hear what he had to say. But the nation would never forget Lincoln's Gettysburg Address.

The president deliberately spoke of the war in words that echoed the Declaration of Independence. The "great civil war," he said, was testing whether a nation "conceived in liberty, and dedicated to the proposition that all men are created equal…can long endure." He spoke of the brave men, "living and dead," who had fought to defend that ideal. "The world…can never forget what they did here." Finally, he called on Americans to remain

> *dedicated to the great task remaining before us—that from these honored dead we take increased devotion to that cause for which they gave the last full measure of devotion—that we here highly resolve that these dead shall not have died in vain— that this nation, under God, shall have a new birth of freedom—and that government of the people, by the people, for the people, shall not perish from the earth.*

22.6 Vicksburg: A Besieged City

The Civil War was a war of many technological firsts. It was the first American war to use railroads to move troops and to keep them supplied. It was the first war in which telegraphs were used to communicate with distant armies. It was the first conflict to be recorded in photographs. It was also the first to see combat between armor-plated steamships.

In 1862, the *Monitor* and the *Merrimac,* two ironclad ships, fought to a standstill. Nevertheless, the battle between the two signaled the end of wooden warships.

The *Merrimac* and the *Monitor* Early in the war, Union forces withdrew from the navy yard in Norfolk, Virginia. They left behind a warship named the *Merrimac*. The Confederacy began the war with no navy. They covered the wooden *Merrimac* with iron plates and added a powerful ram to its prow.

In response, the U.S. Navy built its own ironclad ship. Completed in less than 100 days, the *Monitor* had a flat deck and two heavy guns in a revolving turret. It was said to resemble a "cheese box on a raft."

In March 1862, the *Merrimac,* which the Confederates had renamed the *Virginia,* steamed into Chesapeake Bay. With cannonballs harmlessly bouncing off its sides, the iron monster destroyed three wooden ships and threatened the entire blockade fleet.

The next morning, the *Virginia* was met by the *Monitor.* The two ironclads exchanged shots for four hours before withdrawing. Neither could claim victory, and neither was harmed.

The battle of the *Merrimac* and the *Monitor* proved that "wooden vessels cannot contend with iron-clad ones." After that, both sides added ironclads to their navies. But the South was never able to build enough ships to threaten the Union blockade of southern harbors.

Control of the Mississippi Ironclads were also part of the Union's campaign to divide the South by taking control of the Mississippi River. After seizing New Orleans in 1862, Admiral Farragut moved up the Mississippi to capture Baton Rouge and Natchez. At the same time, other Union ships gained control of Memphis, Tennessee.

The Union now controlled both ends of the Mississippi. The South could no longer move men or material up and down the river. But neither could the North as long as the Confederates continued to control one key location—Vicksburg, Mississippi.

For more than a month, Union forces bombarded Vicksburg with an average of 2,800 shells a day. Forced to eat horses, mules, dogs, and rats, the defenders finally surrendered.

Vicksburg   The town of Vicksburg was located on a bluff above a hairpin turn in the Mississippi River. The city was easy to defend and difficult to capture. Whoever held Vicksburg could, with a few well-placed cannons, control movement on the Mississippi. But even Farragut had to admit that ships "cannot crawl up hills 300 feet high." An army would be needed to take Vicksburg.

In May 1863, General Grant battled his way to Vicksburg with the needed army. For six weeks, Union gunboats shelled the city from the river while Grant's army bombarded it from land. Slowly but surely, the Union troops burrowed toward the city in trenches and tunnels.

As shells pounded the city, people in Vicksburg dug caves into the hillsides for protection. To survive, they ate horses, mules, and bread made of corn and dried peas. "It had the properties of India rubber," said one Confederate soldier, "and was worse than leather to digest."

Low on food and supplies, Vicksburg surrendered on July 4, 1863. The Mississippi was a Union waterway, and the Confederacy was divided.

Problems on the Confederate Home Front   As the war raged on, life in the South became grim. Because of the blockade, imported goods disappeared from stores. What few items were available were extremely expensive.

Unable to sell their tobacco and cotton, farmers planted food crops instead. Still, the South was often hungry. Invading Union armies destroyed crops. They also cut rail lines, making it difficult to move food and supplies to southern cities and army camps.

As clothing wore out, southerners made do with patches and rough, homespun cloth. At the beginning of the war, Mary Boykin Chesnut had written in her journal of well-dressed Confederate troops. By 1863, she was writing of soldiers dressed in "rags and tags."

By 1864, southern troops were receiving letters like this one: "We haven't got nothing in the house to eat but a little bit o' meal. I don't want to you to stop fighting them Yankees...but try and get off and come home and fix us all up some." Many soldiers found it hard to resist such pleas, even if going home meant deserting their units.

22.7 Fort Wagner: African Americans Join the War

Early in the war, abolitionists had urged Congress to recruit African Americans for the army. But at first, most northerners regarded the conflict as "a white man's war." Congress finally opened the door to black recruits in 1862. About 186,000 African Americans, many of them former slaves, enlisted in the Union army. Another 30,000 African Americans joined the Union navy.

The Massachusetts 54th Regiment Massachusetts was one of the first states to organize black regiments. The most famous was the 54th Massachusetts Infantry, commanded by Colonel Robert Gould Shaw. Two of the 54th Infantry's 1,000 soldiers were sons of Frederick Douglass.

The men of the Massachusetts 54th were paid less than white soldiers. When the black soldiers learned this, they protested the unequal treatment by refusing to accept any pay at all. In a letter to Lincoln, Corporal James Henry Gooding asked, "Are we soldiers or are we laborers?…We have done a soldier's duty. Why can't we have a soldier's pay?" At Lincoln's urging, Congress finally granted black soldiers equal pay.

After three months of training, the Massachusetts 54th was sent to South Carolina to take part in an attack on Fort Wagner. As they prepared for battle, the men of the 54th faced the usual worries of untested troops. But they also faced the added fear that if captured, they might be sold into slavery.

African American soldiers demonstrated their courage during their attack on Fort Wagner. The 54th Massachusetts Infantry charged across 200 yards of open beach in their effort to reach the fort. The regiment withdrew after almost half of their men were lost.

African Americans at War The assault on Fort Wagner was an impossible mission. To reach the fort, troops had to cross 200 yards of open, sandy beach. Rifle and cannon fire poured down on them. After losing nearly half of their men, the survivors of the 54th regiment pulled back. But their bravery won them widespread respect.

During the war, 166 African American regiments fought nearly 500 battles. Black soldiers often received little training, poor equipment, and less pay than white soldiers.

They also risked death or enslavement if captured. Still, African Americans fought with great courage to save the Union and to end slavery forever.

22.8 Appomattox: Total War Brings an End

During the first years of the war, Lincoln had searched for a commander who was willing to fight the Confederates. The president finally found the leader he needed in General Grant. Grant's views on war were quite straightforward: "The art of war is simple enough. Find out where your enemy is. Get at him as soon as you can. Strike him as hard and as often as you can, and keep moving on."

Using this strategy, Grant mapped out a plan for ending the war. He would lead a large force against Lee to capture Richmond. At the same time, General William Tecumseh Sherman would lead a second army into Georgia to take Atlanta.

In 1864, Lincoln gave command of all Union forces to Ulysses S. Grant. Grant believed in using his larger army to wear down the enemy regardless of the casualties that his own forces suffered.

On to Richmond In May 1864, Grant invaded Virginia with a force of more than 100,000 men. They met Lee's army of 60,000 in a dense forest known as "The Wilderness." In two days of fierce fighting, Grant lost 18,000 men. Despite these heavy losses, Grant would not retreat. "I propose to fight it out along this line," he said, "if it takes all summer." He followed Lee's army to Cold Harbor, where he lost 7,000 men in 15 minutes of fighting.

By the time the two forces reached Petersburg, a railroad center 20 miles south of Richmond, Grant's losses almost equaled Lee's entire army. But he was able to reinforce his army with fresh troops. Lee, who had also suffered heavy losses, could not.

Total War Grant believed in total war—war on the enemy's will to fight and its ability to support an army. With his army tied down in northern Virginia, Grant ordered General Philip Sheridan to wage total war in Virginia's grain-rich Shenandoah Valley. "Let that valley be so left that crows flying over it will have to carry their rations long with them," ordered Grant.

In May 1864, General Sherman left Tennessee for Georgia with orders to inflict "all the damage you can against their war resources." In September, he reached Atlanta, the South's most important rail and manufacturing center. His army set the city ablaze.

The Reelection of Lincoln Any hope of victory for the South lay in the defeat of President Lincoln in the election of 1864. The northern Democrats nominated General George McClellan to run against Lincoln. Knowing that the North was weary of war, McClellan urged an immediate end to the conflict.

Lincoln doubted he would be reelected. Grant seemed stuck in northern Virginia, and there was no end in sight to the appalling bloodletting. Luckily for the president, Sheridan's destruction of the Shenandoah Valley and Sherman's capture of Atlanta came just in time to rescue his campaign. These victories changed northern views of Lincoln and his prospects for ending the war. In November, Lincoln was reelected.

Sherman's March Through Georgia

After burning Atlanta, Sherman marched his army toward Savannah, promising to "make Georgia howl." His purpose was to destroy the last untouched supply base for the Confederacy.

As they marched through Georgia, Sherman's troops destroyed everything they found of value. Fields were trampled or burned. Houses were ransacked (robbed). Hay and food supplies were burned. Roads were lined with dead horses, hogs, and cattle that his troops could not eat or carry away. Everything useful in a 60-mile-wide path was destroyed.

In December 1864, Sherman captured Savannah, Georgia. From there, he turned north and destroyed all opposition in the Carolinas. Marching 425 miles in 50 days, he reached Raleigh, North Carolina, by March 1865. There he waited for Grant's final attack on Richmond.

The End at Appomattox

For nine months, Grant's forces battered Lee's army at Petersburg, the gateway to Richmond. On April 1, 1865, the Union forces finally broke through Confederate lines to capture the city. Two days later, Union troops marched into Richmond.

Grant's soldiers moved quickly to surround Lee's army. Lee told his officers, "There is nothing left for me to do but go and see General Grant, and I would rather die a thousand deaths."

On April 9, 1865, General Lee, in full dress uniform, arrived at Wilmer McLean's house in the village of Appomattox Courthouse. He was there to surrender his army to General Grant. The Union general met him in a mud-splattered and crumpled uniform.

Grant's terms of surrender were generous. Confederate soldiers could go home if they promised to fight no longer. They could take with them their own horses and mules, which they would need for spring plowing. Officers could keep their swords and weapons. Grant also ordered that food be sent to Lee's half-starved men. Lee accepted the terms.

As Lee returned to his headquarters, Union troops began to shoot their guns and cheer wildly. Grant told them to stop celebrating. "The war is over," he said, "the rebels are our countrymen again."

General Sherman, a believer in total war, cut a path of destruction through Georgia. The photograph below shows the burned ruins of Atlanta.

General Lee surrendered to General Grant at Appomattox Courthouse in Virginia. Grant was generous to Lee's soldiers, sending food to the troops and allowing them to keep their horses and mules.

"Touched by Fire"   No one who fought in the Civil War would ever forget the intensity of the experience. "In our youths," wrote Oliver Wendell Holmes Jr., "our hearts were touched by fire."

The nation, too, had been touched by fire. Many compared the Civil War to a great furnace that burned away one country and forged a new one in its place. In this new country, neither slavery nor the right to secession had any place. Just as Lincoln had said, the Union was a single whole, not a collection of sovereign states. Before the war, Americans tended to say "the United States *are*." After the war, they said "the United States *is*."

These momentous changes came at a horrifying cost. Billions of dollars had been spent on the conflict. Almost every family had lost a member or a friend. More than 620,000 Union and Confederate soldiers lay dead. Thousands more came home missing an arm or a leg. It would take generations for the South to recover from the environmental destruction wrought by the war. Croplands lay in ruins. Two fifths of the South's livestock had been destroyed.

Many historians have called the Civil War the first truly modern war. It was the first war to reflect the technology of the Industrial Revolution: railroads, the telegraph, armored ships, more accurate and destructive weaponry. It also introduced "total war"—war between whole societies, not just uniformed armies.

As devastating as it was, the Civil War left many issues unsettled. The old society of the South had been destroyed, but the memory of it lingered. Thousands of white southerners clung to a romantic picture of the pre-war South. Decaying plantation houses became shrines. In the years to come, many in the South would try to re-create their vanished way of life. Secession and slavery were gone, but conflicts over states' rights and the status of African Americans would continue long into the future.

22.9 Chapter Summary

In this chapter, you read about the Civil War between the Union and the Confederacy. You used an annotated illustration of a soldier's haversack to help you understand the events and effects of the Civil War.

Both sides had advantages and disadvantages going into the war. The North had a larger population and more factories and railroads than the South, but it lacked strong military leadership. The South had serious economic problems, but it had capable generals and the advantage of fighting a defensive war.

New weapons and military tactics allowed soldiers to kill from greater distances. They also caused horrifying numbers of deaths and casualties. Unfortunately, medical knowledge was not as advanced as the weapons of war. Many more soldiers died of disease than from wounds.

After the Battle of Antietam, President Lincoln issued his Emancipation Proclamation, freeing all slaves in the Confederacy. The proclamation helped to make the war a crusade for freedom.

The battle of Gettysburg ended the South's last attempt to invade the North. It proved to be a turning point. Lincoln's speech dedicating the cemetery at Gettysburg gave the war a larger meaning by relating it to the ideals of the American Revolution.

The Union finally won the war under the leadership of General Grant. Grant began waging total war on the Confederacy. Union soldiers marched through the South, burning fields and houses and terrifying all those in their path. When the Union army surrounded General Lee's Confederate troops, Lee was forced to surrender. Grant was generous to the southern troops. He fed them and sent them home to rebuild their lives.

The Civil War has been compared to a furnace that forged a new country, one in which secession and slavery had no place. But the costs were enormous, and many issues remained. In the next chapter, you will read about how the nation tried to become whole again.

This painting, *End of the Rebellion in the United States,* 1865, celebrates the conclusion of the Civil War and the preservation of the Union.

What is this man doing?

How are the lives of these former slaves different now?

23

The Reconstruction Era

23.1 Introduction

By the end of the Civil War, Americans longed for peace. But what kind of peace? One that punished the South for its rebellion? A peace that helped rebuild the devastated region? A peace that helped the four million African Americans freed from slavery become full and equal citizens? In his second inaugural address, delivered in 1865, President Abraham Lincoln spoke of a healing peace.

With malice [hatred] toward none, with charity for all, with firmness in the right as God gives us to see the right, let us strive on to finish the work we are in, to bind up the nation's wounds, to care for him who shall have borne the battle and for his widow and orphan, to do all which may achieve and cherish [hold dear] a just and lasting peace.

The nation would never know how Lincoln planned to achieve such a peace. On April 14, 1865, just five days after the war ended, the president was assassinated (murdered) while attending a play at Ford's Theater in Washington, D.C. His murderer was an actor named John Wilkes Booth. Booth thought that killing Lincoln would somehow save the Confederacy.

With Lincoln dead, the task of healing the nation's wounds fell to Vice President Andrew Johnson. **Reconstruction,** or rebuilding the South and bringing the southern states back into the Union, would not be easy. For while the nation was united again, Americans remained deeply divided.

As you read about how Reconstruction was carried out, think about Lincoln's dream of "a just and lasting peace." Did the end of the war and of slavery lead to a peace based on liberty and justice for all? Or was Reconstruction just the first stage in a long and difficult struggle for equal rights for all Americans?

Graphic Organizer: Visual Metaphor
You will use this visual metaphor of a road to understand African Americans' struggle to gain full rights as citizens during Reconstruction.

23.2 Presidential Reconstruction

As the Civil War ended, people in the United States had sharply different views about how to treat the defeated Confederacy. For President Andrew Johnson, a southerner from Tennessee, Reconstruction had two main aims. First, southern states had to create new governments that were loyal to the Union and that respected federal authority. Second, slavery had to be abolished once and for all.

These goals left many issues to be resolved. For example, who would control the new state governments in the South—former rebels? Would the freed slaves have the same rights as other citizens? And what would the relations be between freed slaves and their former masters?

Many Republicans in Congress believed that strong measures would be needed to settle these issues. To them, Reconstruction meant nothing less than a complete remaking of the South based on equal rights and a free-labor economy. The stage was set for a battle over the control—and even the meaning—of Reconstruction.

President Johnson's Reconstruction Plan In May 1865, President Johnson announced his Reconstruction plan. A former Confederate state could rejoin the Union once it had written a new state constitution, elected a new state government, repealed its act of secession, canceled <u>its</u> war debts, and ratified the Thirteenth Amendment, which abolished slavery.

By the fall of 1865, every southern state had met the president's requirements, and the Thirteenth Amendment became part of the Constitution. Presidential Reconstruction had begun.

The Freedmen's Bureau For former slaves, called **freedmen,** the freedom guaranteed by the Thirteenth Amendment brought problems as well as opportunities. As Frederick Douglass wrote, the freedman

> was free from the individual master but a slave of society. He had neither money, property, nor friends. He was free from the old plantation, but he had nothing but the dusty road under his feet…. He was turned loose, naked, hungry, and destitute [penniless] to the open sky.

To assist former slaves, Congress established the Freedmen's Bureau in March 1865. Over the next four years, the bureau

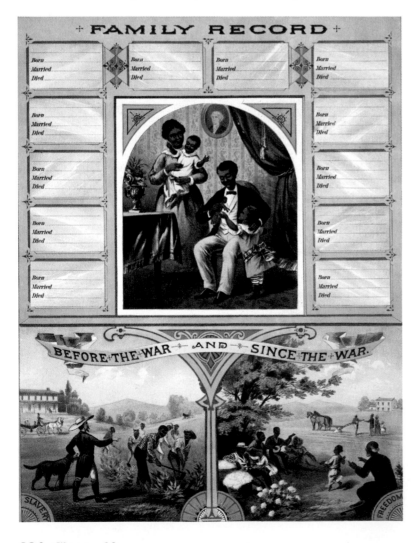

During Reconstruction, former slaves were granted the right to marry and live with family members from whom they had been separated. Forms, such as this one, allowed freedmen to keep a record of their marriage and family.

provided food and medical care to both blacks and whites in the South. It helped freedmen bargain for wages and good working conditions. It also distributed some land in forty-acre plots to "loyal refugees and freedmen." Resentful whites, however, attacked the bureau as an example of northern interference in the South. Ultimately, the hope of many freedmen for "forty acres and a mule" died when Congress refused to take land away from southern whites.

The most lasting benefit of the Freedmen's Bureau was in education. Thousands of former slaves, both young and old, flocked to free public schools built by the bureau. Long after the bureau was gone, such institutions as Howard University in Washington, D.C., continued to provide educational opportunity for African Americans.

The Black Codes   As new state governments took power in the South, many Republicans in Congress were alarmed to see that they were headed by the same people who had led the South before the war—wealthy white planters. Once in office, these leaders began passing laws known as *black codes* to control their former slaves.

The black codes served three purposes. The first was to limit the rights of freedmen. Generally, former slaves were given the right to marry, to own property, to work for wages, and to sue in court. But other rights of citizenship were denied them. Blacks, for example, could not vote or serve on juries in the South.

The second purpose of the black codes was to help planters find workers to replace their slaves. The codes required freedmen to work. Those without jobs could be arrested and hired out to planters. The codes also limited freedmen to farmwork or jobs requiring few skills. African Americans could not enter many trades or start businesses.

The third purpose of the black codes was to keep freedmen at the bottom of the social order in the South. Most codes called for the segregation of blacks and whites in public places. Black children were not allowed to attend public schools. A Louisiana lawmaker defended this ban by saying that it made no sense to spend tax money to educate "any but the superior race of man—the White race."

This political cartoon shows President Andrew Johnson using his veto to try to do away with the Freedmen's Bureau.

23.3 Congressional Reconstruction

As 1865 came to a close, President Johnson announced that Reconstruction was over. The southern states were ready to rejoin the Union. Republican leaders in Congress did not agree. These lawmakers believed that the South would not be reconstructed until freedmen were granted full rights of citizenship.

The following year, Congress enacted two bills designed to help freedmen. The first extended the life of the Freedmen's Bureau. The second was the **Civil Rights** Act of 1866. It struck at the black codes by declaring freedmen to be full citizens with the same rights as whites. Johnson declared both bills unconstitutional and vetoed them. An angry Congress overrode his vetoes.

civil rights the rights that are guaranteed by the Constitution to all people as citizens, especially equal treatment under the law

The Fourteenth Amendment To further protect the rights of African Americans, Congress approved the Fourteenth Amendment. This amendment declared former slaves to be citizens with full civil rights. "No state," it said, "shall…deny to any person…the equal protection of the laws." This meant that state governments could not treat some citizens as less equal than others.

President Johnson opposed the Fourteenth Amendment and called on voters to throw Republican lawmakers out of office. Instead, Republican candidates won a two-thirds majority in both houses of Congress in the 1866 election. From that point on, Congress controlled Reconstruction.

Military Reconstruction and the Readmission of the South

[date] = Date of readmission to the Union

Radical Republicans in Congress reorganized the South into the five military districts shown on this map.

Military Reconstruction Act Early in 1867, the new Congress passed its own Military Reconstruction Act. Once again, it did so over Johnson's veto. This plan divided the South into five military districts, each governed by a general who was backed by federal troops. The state governments set up under Johnson's Reconstruction plan were declared illegal. New governments were to be formed by southerners loyal to the United States—both black and white. Southerners who had supported the Confederacy were denied the right to vote.

Lawmakers also passed two acts designed to reduce Johnson's power to interfere with Congressional Reconstruction. The Command of the Army Act limited his power over the army. The Tenure of Office Act barred him from firing certain federal officials without the Senate's consent. President Johnson blasted both laws as unconstitutional. Then, to prove his point, he fired one of the officials protected under the Tenure of Office Act.

The Impeachment of Johnson   The House of Representatives responded to Johnson's challenge by voting to impeach the president. Besides violating the Tenure of Office Act, Johnson was charged with bringing "the high office of the President of the United States into contempt, ridicule, and disgrace, to the scandal of all good citizens."

During his trial in the Senate, the president's lawyers argued that Johnson's only "crime" had been to oppose Congress. If he were removed from office for that reason, they warned, "no future President will be safe who happens to differ with a majority of the House and Senate."

Two thirds of the Senate had to find the president guilty in order to remove him from office. Despite very heavy pressure to convict him, 7 Republicans and 12 Democrats voted "not guilty." Johnson escaped removal from office by one vote, but his power was broken.

Sharecropping   While Congress and the president battled over Reconstruction, African Americans in the South struggled to build new lives. Most former slaves desperately wanted land to farm but had no money to buy it. Meanwhile, their former owners desperately needed workers to farm their land but had no money to pay them. Out of the needs of both groups came a farming system called *sharecropping*.

Planters who turned to sharecropping divided their land into small plots. They rented these plots to individual tenant farmers (farmers who pay rent for the land they work). A few tenants paid the rent for their plots in cash. But most paid their rent by giving the landowner a share—usually a third or a half—of the crops they raised on their plots.

Sharecropping looked promising to freedmen at first. They liked being independent farmers who worked for themselves. In time, they hoped to earn enough money to buy a farm of their own.

However, most sharecroppers had to borrow money from planters to buy the food, seeds, tools, and supplies they needed to survive until harvest-time. Few ever earned enough from their crops to pay back what they owed. Rather than leading to independence, sharecropping usually led to a lifetime of poverty and debt.

Sharecroppers, such as these shown growing cotton, rented their land from plantation owners. In exchange, most paid one third to one half of their crops back to the landowners.

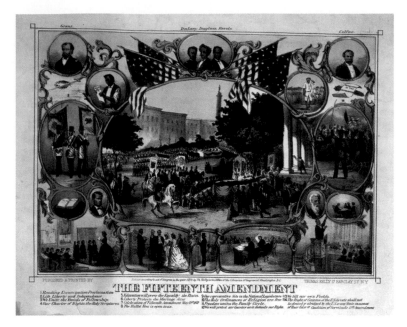

This poster celebrated the passage of the Fifteenth Amendment, which said that a citizen's right to vote could not be denied on account of race, color, or previous condition of servitude. The poster includes pictures of students, soldiers, preachers, teachers, and lawmakers.

scalawags white southerners who supported the federal government after the Civil War

carpetbaggers northerners who went to the South after the Civil War to gain money and political power

23.4 Southern Reconstruction

The U.S. Army returned to the South in 1867. The first thing it did was begin to register voters. Because Congress had banned former Confederates from voting, the right to vote in the South was limited to three groups—freedmen, white southerners who had opposed the war, and northerners who had moved south after the war.

The South's New Voters   African Americans made up the South's largest group of new voters. Most black voters joined the Republican Party—the party of Lincoln and emancipation.

White southerners who had not supported secession were the next largest group. Many were poor farmers who had never voted before. In their eyes, the Democratic Party was the party of wealthy planters and secession. As a result, they also supported the Republican Party. Southern Democrats were appalled. They saw any white man who voted Republican as a traitor to the South. Democrats scorned such people as **scalawags,** or worthless scoundrels.

The last group of new voters were northerners who had moved south after the war. Yankee-hating southerners called the newcomers **carpetbaggers** after a type of handbag used by many travelers. They saw carpetbaggers as fortune hunters who had come south "to fatten on our misfortunes."

The 1868 Election   These new voters cast their first ballots in the 1868 presidential election. The Republican candidate was former Union general Ulysses S. Grant. Grant supported Reconstruction and promised to protect the rights of African Americans in the South. His Democratic opponent, Horatio Seymour, promised to end Reconstruction and return the South to its traditional leaders—white Democrats.

Seymour won a majority of white votes. Grant, however, was elected with the help of half a million black votes. The election's lesson to Republicans was that if they wanted to keep control of the White House and Congress, they needed African American votes.

The Fifteenth Amendment   In 1869, at President Grant's urging, Congress passed the Fifteenth Amendment. This amendment said that a citizen's right to vote "shall not be denied…on account of race, color, or previous condition of servitude." Its purpose was to protect the right of African American men to vote.

With the passage of this amendment, most abolitionists felt their work was done. The American Anti-Slavery Society declared the Fifteenth Amendment to be "the capstone and completion of our movement; the fulfillment of our pledge to the Negro race; since it secures to them equal political rights with the white race."

New State Constitutions When the army finished registering voters, southern Reconstruction got underway. Across the South, delegates were elected to constitutional conventions. About a fourth of those elected were African Americans.

The conventions met and wrote new constitutions for their states. These constitutions were the most progressive, or advanced, in the nation. They guaranteed the right to vote to every adult male, regardless of race. They ended imprisonment for debt. They also called for the establishment of the first public schools in the South. The Georgia constitution stated that these schools should be "forever free to all the children of the state."

New State Governments
Elections were then held to fill state offices. To the dismay of southern Democrats, a majority of those elected were Republicans. About a fifth were African Americans.

The South's new state governments quickly ratified the Fourteenth and Fifteenth Amendments. By 1870, every southern state had finished this final step of Reconstruction and rejoined the Union.

Next, southern governments turned to the task of rebuilding. Work was begun on damaged roads, bridges, and railroads. Schools and hospitals were built. To pay for these projects, state legislatures raised taxes. Between 1860 and 1870, taxes in the South increased by up to 400 percent.

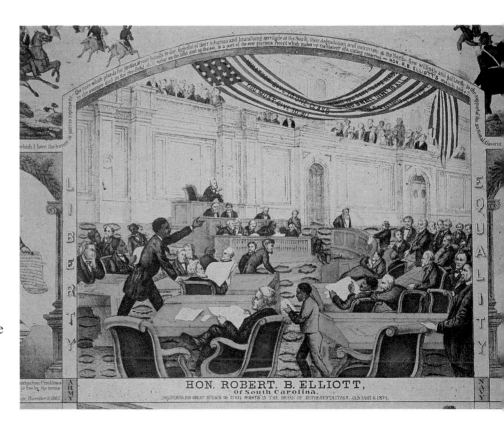

HON. ROBERT. B. ELLIOTT,
Of South Carolina,
DELIVERING HIS GREAT SPEECH ON CIVIL RIGHTS IN THE HOUSE OF REPRESENTATIVES, JANUARY 6, 1874.

Robert B. Elliott, African American congressman from South Carolina, delivers a speech in favor of civil rights. During Reconstruction, many African Americans were elected to the House of Representatives and the Senate.

African Americans in Office About a fifth of the South's new officeholders were African Americans. Blacks served in every southern legislature and held high offices in three states. Twenty-two African Americans represented their states in Congress—20 in the House, and 2 in the Senate. After watching these representatives, many of whom had been born slaves, Pennsylvania congressman James G. Blaine observed:

> *The colored men who took their seats in both the Senate and House did not appear ignorant or helpless. They were as a rule studious, earnest, ambitious men, whose public conduct...would be honorable to any race.*

TWO MEMBERS OF THE KU-KLUX KLAN IN THEIR DISGUISES.

Ku Klux Klan members, shown above, were determined to prevent African Americans from participating in politics. Using threats, beatings, and even murder, the Klan eventually reestablished white Democratic rule in the South.

23.5 The End of Reconstruction

Most whites in the South bitterly resented the southern Reconstruction governments. They hated the fact that these governments had been "forced" on them by the Yankees.

Many taxpayers also blamed their soaring tax bills on corruption (misuse of public office for personal gain) by the South's new leaders. One outraged Democrat called Republican rule in the South the "most stupendous system of organized robbery in history." While some southern officeholders did line their pockets with public funds, most, whether black or white, were honest, capable leaders. Still, when taxes increased, so too did opposition to the new state governments.

But what bothered southerners most about their Reconstruction governments was seeing former slaves voting and holding public offices. Across the South, Democrats vowed to regain power and return their states to "white man's rule."

White Terrorism At first, Democrats tried to win black voters away from the Republican Party. When that failed, they tried using legal tricks to keep blacks from voting or taking office. In Georgia, for example, the legislature refused to seat elected black lawmakers until forced to by the state supreme court. When legal tricks failed, whites turned to terrorism, or violence.

Throughout the South, whites formed secret societies to drive African Americans out of political life. The most infamous of these groups was the Ku Klux Klan. Dressed in long, hooded robes and armed with guns and swords, Klansmen did their work at night. They started by threatening black voters and officeholders. African Americans who did not heed their threats were beaten, tarred and feathered, and even murdered.

The Enforcement Acts In 1870 and 1871, Congress passed three laws to combat terrorism against African Americans. Known as the Enforcement Acts, these laws made it illegal to prevent another person from voting by bribery, force, or scare tactics.

President Grant sent troops into the South to enforce these acts. Hundreds of people were arrested for their terrorist activities. Those who were brought to trial, however, were seldom convicted. Few witnesses and jurors wanted to risk the Klan's revenge by speaking out against one of its members.

The Amnesty Act of 1872   By this time, however, most northerners were losing interest in Reconstruction and the plight of the freedmen. It was time, many people said, to "let the South alone." One sign of this changing attitude was the passage of the Amnesty Act of 1872. (*Amnesty* means forgiveness for past offenses.) This law allowed most former Confederates to vote once again.

The effects of the Amnesty Act were quickly seen. By 1876, Democrats had regained control of all but three states in the South. Republicans clung to power in South Carolina, Louisiana, and Florida, but only with the help of federal troops.

The Disputed Election of 1876   In 1876, Americans went to the polls to choose a new president. The Democrats nominated New York governor Samuel J. Tilden as their candidate. Rutherford B. Hayes was the Republican nominee. When the votes were tallied, Tilden won a majority of popular votes and 184 electoral votes, just one short of the 185 needed for election. Hayes received 165 electoral votes. Twenty electoral votes from four states were in dispute.

Congress, which was controlled by Republicans, appointed a commission to decide who should get the disputed votes. The commission awarded all 20 to Hayes, giving him exactly the 185 electoral votes he needed to win. Outraged Democrats in Congress threatened to block the election of anyone. Inauguration day drew near with no president in sight.

The Compromise of 1877   At the last moment, the two parties agreed to compromise. Democrats allow Hayes to become president. In return, Hayes agreed to give southern states "the right to control their own affairs."

Once in office, President Hayes withdrew all remaining federal troops from the South. After that, Democrats quickly took control of the last southern states. "This is a white man's country," boasted South Carolina senator Ben Tillman, "and white men must govern it."

Most white southerners cheered the end of Reconstruction. But for freedmen, the return of the South to "white man's rule" was a giant step backward. "The whole South— every state in the South," observed a Louisiana freedmen, "has got into the hands of the very men that held us as slaves."

Thomas Nast's political cartoon "Is This a Republican Form of Government?" condemns northern indifference to the violence that African Americans had to endure as Reconstruction ended.

The Granger Collection, New York

23.6 Reconstruction Reversed

With Reconstruction over, southern leaders talked of building a "New South" humming with mills, factories, and cities. Between 1880 and 1900, the number of textile mills in the South grew rapidly. Birmingham, Alabama, became a major iron-making center. Still, most southerners, black and white, remained trapped in an "Old South" of poverty.

Losing Ground in Education   During Reconstruction, freedmen had pinned their hopes for a better life on education provided by the South's first public schools. When southern Democrats regained control of states, however, they cut spending on education. "Free schools are not a necessity," explained the governor of Virginia. Schools, he said, "are a luxury…to be paid for, like any other luxury, by the people who wish their benefits."

As public funding dried up, many schools closed. Those that stayed open often charged fees. By the 1880s, only about half of all black children in the South attended school.

This painting shows a new South rising from the ashes of the Civil War. Although southern leaders hoped this would be the future of the South, most whites and African Americans continued to live in poverty.

Losing Voting Rights   Southern Democrats also reversed the political gains made by freedmen after the war. Many southern states passed laws requiring citizens who wanted to vote to pay a poll tax. The tax was set high enough that voting, like education, became a luxury that many black southerners could not afford.

Some southern states also required citizens to pass a literacy test to show that they could read before allowing them to vote. These tests were rigged (set up) to fail any African American, regardless of his education.

In theory, these laws applied equally to blacks and whites and, for that reason, did not violate the Fifteenth Amendment. In practice, however, whites were excused from paying poll taxes or taking literacy tests by a "grandfather clause" in the laws. This clause said the taxes and tests did not apply to any man whose father or grandfather could vote on January 1, 1867. Since no blacks could vote on that date, the grandfather clause applied only to whites.

African Americans protested that these laws denied them their Constitutional right to vote. The Supreme Court, however, ruled that the new voting laws did not violate the Fifteenth Amendment because they did not deny anyone the right to vote on the basis of race.

Drawing a "Color Line" During Reconstruction, most southern states had outlawed segregation in public places. When Democrats returned to power, they reversed these laws and drew a "color line" between blacks and whites in public life. Whites called the new segregation acts **Jim Crow laws**.

Not all white southerners supported segregation. When a Jim Crow law was proposed in South Carolina, the Charleston *News and Courier* tried to show how silly it was by taking segregation to ridiculous extremes.

> *If there must be Jim Crow cars on railroads, there should be Jim Crow cars on the street railways. Also on all passenger boats.... There should be Jim Crow waiting saloons [waiting rooms] at all stations, and Jim Crow eating houses.... There should be Jim Crow sections of the jury box, and a separate Jim Crow...witness stand in every court—and a Jim Crow Bible for colored witnesses to kiss.*

Instead of being a joke, as intended, most of these "silly" suggestions soon became laws.

Plessy v. Ferguson African Americans argued that segregation laws violated the Fourteenth Amendment's guarantee of "equal protection of the laws." Homer Plessy, who was arrested for refusing to obey a Jim Crow law, took his protest all the way to the Supreme Court. His case is known as *Plessy v. Ferguson.*

In 1896, the majority of Supreme Court justices ruled that segregation laws did not violate the Fourteenth Amendment as long as the facilities available to both races were roughly equal. Justice John Marshall Harlan, a former slaveholder, disagreed. "Our Constitution is color blind," he wrote, "and neither knows nor tolerates classes among citizens."

After the Supreme Court's decision in *Plessy v. Ferguson,* more Jim Crow laws were passed. Blacks and whites attended separate schools, played in separate parks, and sat in separate sections in theaters. But despite the Court's ruling that these separate facilities must be equal, those set aside for African Americans were almost always inferior to facilities labeled "whites only."

In the cartoon below, Thomas Nast attacks the Ku Klux Klan and other white supremacist groups. According to this cartoon, what did supremacist groups do to African Americans? What does the label "Worse Than Slavery" mean?

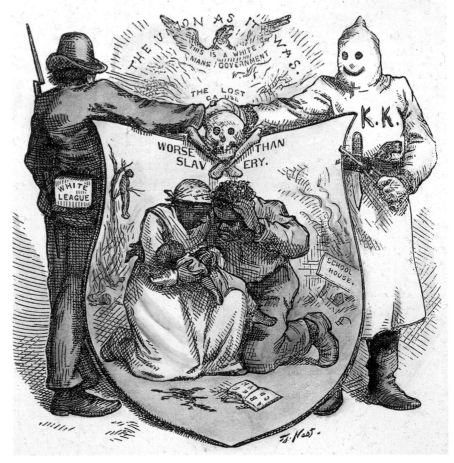

The Granger Collection, New York

23.7 Responding to Segregation

African Americans responded to segregation in many ways. The boldest protested openly. Doing so, however, was dangerous. Blacks who spoke out risked being attacked by white mobs. Some were even lynched, or murdered (often by hanging), for speaking out against "white rule." During the 1890s, there was an African American lynched somewhere in the United States almost every day.

Two units of African American cavalrymen, the Ninth and Tenth U.S. Cavalry, fought in the Indian wars that followed the end of the Civil War. Dubbed "Buffalo Soldiers" by Native Americans, the black cavalrymen served loyally but were often mistreated by the white settlers they were supposed to protect. Twenty-three Buffalo Soldiers earned the Medal of Honor for heroism.

Migration   Thousands of African Americans responded to segregation by leaving the South. A few chose to return to Africa. In 1878, some 200 southern blacks chartered a ship and sailed to Liberia, a nation founded by freed American slaves on the coast of West Africa.

Many more African Americans migrated to other parts of the United States. Not only were they "pushed" from the South by racism and poverty, but they were "pulled" by the lure of better opportunities and more equal treatment. Some sought a new life as wage earners by migrating to cities in the North. There they competed for jobs with recent immigrants from Europe and often faced racism, if not southern-style segregation. Others headed to the West, where they found work as cowboys and Indian fighters. Two all-black U.S. Cavalry units known as the Buffalo Soldiers fought on the front lines of the Indian wars. Ironically, some blacks found new homes with Native American nations.

Thousands of black families left the South for Kansas in the "Exodus of 1879." The "exodusters," as the migrants were known, faced many hardships on their journey west. Bands of armed whites patrolled roads in Kansas in an effort to drive the migrants away. Still, the exodusters pushed on, saying, "We had rather suffer and be free."

Self-Help   Most African Americans, however, remained in the South. They worked hard as families, churches, and communities to improve their lives. While most blacks farmed for a living, a growing number started their own businesses. Between 1865 and 1903, the number of black-owned businesses in the South soared from about 2,000 to 25,000.

Families, churches, and communities also banded together to build schools and colleges for black children. Because of these efforts, literacy among American Americans rose rapidly. When slavery ended in 1865, only 5 percent of African Americans could read. By 1900, more than 50 percent could read and write.

23.8 Chapter Summary

In this chapter, you read about the events of Reconstruction in the South after the Civil War. You used a visual metaphor to understand African Americans' struggle to achieve full rights as citizens during the five phases of Reconstruction.

In the first phase, the Thirteenth Amendment became part of the Constitution, and slavery became illegal. However, freedmen still could not vote and were allowed to work only at unskilled jobs. African Americans were kept separate from whites in public. Black children could not attend public schools.

Congressional Reconstruction was an attempt to give African Americans all the rights of citizens. The Fourteenth Amendment granted full citizenship to all people born in the United States.

Congress sent federal troops back to the South to begin Southern Reconstruction. The Fifteenth Amendment guaranteed the right to vote to eligible citizens of all races. Many African Americans were elected to state government offices during this third phase of Reconstruction.

During the fourth phase of Reconstruction, President Hayes withdrew federal troops from the South. Throughout the South, the men who had held African Americans in slavery before the war were again in charge of their lives and livelihoods.

During the final stage of Reconstruction, southern state governments began reversing the gains that African Americans had made. Education and the right to vote in the South became luxuries that only white southerners could afford. Jim Crow laws quickly reestablished segregation.

African Americans were free to leave the South, and many did. They migrated to the North and the West, or returned to Africa. But most remained in the South, where they formed communities to help themselves build better lives.

In the next chapter, you will read about the tensions that arose as Americans settled the West.

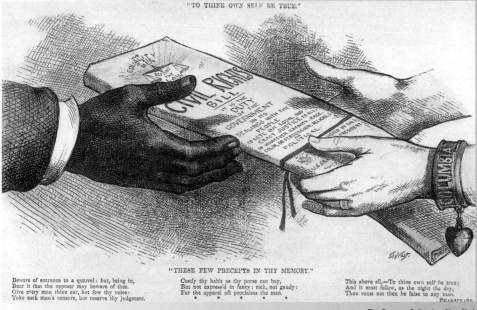

This Thomas Nast cartoon celebrates the Civil Rights Bill of 1875. This bill and other Reconstruction legislation tried to give full citizenship rights to African Americans.

The Granger Collection, New York

Why is this soldier fighting on foot?

What country's army does this soldier belong to?

What group does this soldier belong to? Why is he fighting?

Tensions in the West

24.1 Introduction

In the spring of 1889, two women arrived at the Nez Percé **reservation** in Lapwai, Idaho. One of them, Jane Gay, had nursed soldiers during the Civil War. The other, Alice Fletcher, had been a leader in the growing movement for women's rights. Now a new cause had brought these women west. They wanted to improve the lives of Native Americans.

Gay and Fletcher were just two of the thousands of Americans who moved west after the Civil War. As you read in the last chapter, during this period politicians in the East were arguing over Reconstruction. Meanwhile, railroad builders, miners, ranchers, and farmers continued to push westward. In this chapter, you will read about how the settlers' dreams of freedom and opportunity clashed with the dreams of the Native Americans who already lived in the West.

The conflict between settlers and Indians was not just a fight over land. It was a conflict between two very different cultures and ways of seeing the world.

Jane Gay and Alice Fletcher discovered these deep differences soon after they arrived at Lapwai. Like other Indians, the Nez Percé had already been forced onto reservations to make way for new settlers. Now Fletcher told the Indians that the government wanted to divide the Lapwai Reservation into farm plots. Each family would receive one plot. Then the Nez Percé could live like other Americans.

The Indians listened in stony silence. Settlers might think of owning a plot of land as a way to be free. But to a Nez Percé, being tied to one spot of earth would be like being in jail.

Finally, one man spoke. "We do not cut up our land in little pieces," the Indian said. "We have not told you to do it. We are content to be as we are."

The Indian's words show why tensions were bound to develop between settlers and Native Americans. As you read about the Nez Percé and other Indian groups, you will see how the progress of the settlers meant the end of the Indians' ways of life.

Graphic Organizer: Annotated Illustration
You will use an annotated illustration of a buffalo hide to record information about four groups of settlers and their impact on native peoples.

337

24.2 The Nez Percé

For centuries, the Nez Percé freely roamed the lush mountains and valleys where Oregon, Washington, and Idaho come together today. Their name, which means "pierced nose" in French, was given to them by French explorers. The French had confused the Nez Percé with other Indians who decorated their noses with pieces of shell. In reality, the Nez Percé did not usually pierce their noses or wear nose ornaments.

When horses arrived in the Northwest in the 1700s, the Nez Percé became expert riders and horse breeders. They developed their own special breed known as the Appaloosa. These beautiful, spotted horses were fast, strong, and brave. The Nez Percé trained them to ride into stampeding buffalo herds and single out one animal for the kill.

The Nez Percé treasured their homeland and way of life. But in the years after the Civil War, more and more strangers arrived from the East to settle in the Pacific Northwest. The world of the Nez Percé would never be the same.

Friendship with Whites For decades the Nez Percé were among the friendliest of all western Indians toward whites. In 1805, they saved Lewis and Clark and their expedition from starvation. They were also friendly with the first trappers, traders, and missionaries who came to the Northwest. The Nez Percé had never killed a white person.

The friendship was finally broken by Americans' hunger for land and riches. In the 1860s, miners swarmed over Nez Percé land, looking for gold. Settlers followed. Some Nez Percé bands signed treaties in which they agreed to give up their land and move to the Lapwai Reservation in Idaho. Other bands refused to sign any treaty.

One of these "no treaty" bands lived in the Wallowa Valley of eastern Oregon. It was led by a man whose Indian name meant "Thunder Rolling in the Mountains." The newcomers called him Chief Joseph. In 1877, representatives of the United States government presented Chief Joseph with a terrible choice. You can give up your land peacefully and move to Lapwai, they told him, or else army troops will come and force you out.

Fearing a war he could not win, Chief Joseph agreed to

Hurricane Creek runs majestically through the Wallowa Valley, home to the Nez Percé Indians. In the background is Chief Joseph Mountain.

move. "I would give up my country," he said, "rather than have the blood of white men upon the hands of my people."

Blood Is Shed   That summer, 700 Nez Percé left the Wallowa Valley, their hearts filled with bitterness. One night, a group of angry young warriors slipped out of camp and murdered several whites. Chief Joseph knew that the killings would bring soldiers to punish his people. For the first time, the Nez Percé would be at war with whites.

The soldiers came. Still hoping to avoid war, Indians carrying the white flag of peace came forward to talk. Foolishly, the troops opened fire anyway. Minutes later, 34 soldiers were dead. "I have been in lots of scrapes," reported a survivor, "but I never went up against anything like the Nez Percé in all my life."

The Flight to Canada   In desperation, the Nez Percé headed for the one place where they might still live free—Canada. For the next three months, Chief Joseph led the U.S. Army on a chase of more than 1,000 miles through rugged mountain country. Although greatly outnumbered, his warriors won several battles.

The chase ended less than 40 miles from the Canadian border. Forced to surrender, Chief Joseph spoke his heart in these words:

> *I am tired of fighting. Our chiefs are killed…. The old men are all dead…. It is cold and we have no blankets. The little children are freezing to death. My people, some of them, have run away to the hills, and have no blankets, no food; no one knows where they are…. Hear me, my chiefs. I am tired; my heart is sick and sad. From where the sun now stands I will fight no more forever.*

After their surrender, Chief Joseph and his followers were sent to a barren reservation in Oklahoma. There they began to fall sick and die. Soon they had a cemetery just for babies, with more than a hundred graves.

Chief Joseph begged the government to allow his people to join the rest of the Nez Percé in Lapwai. Although some did go to Lapwai, others, including Chief Joseph, were sent to the Colville Reservation in Washington. They never went back to their homeland. When the chief died in 1904, the doctor listed the cause of death as "a broken heart."

Chief Joseph was a great leader among the Nez Percé. He promised his dying father that he would not sell or give away his people's land. Tragically, white settlers and government troops drove the Nez Percé from their homes in the 1870s. Chief Joseph died of a "broken heart" on a remote Indian reservation in 1904.

homesteader a farmer who is given a plot of public land (called a *homestead*) in return for cultivating it

transcontinental railroad a railroad that crosses a continent (*trans* means "across")

subsidy money or other things of value (such as land) that a government contributes to an enterprise

Settlers had been gradually forcing Native Americans from their land ever since the first colonists arrived in North America. Still, by the start of the Civil War, the West was populated mostly by roaming Indians and huge herds of buffalo. Then, in 1861 and 1862, Congress passed two laws that stirred new interest in the West—the Homestead Act and the Pacific Railroad Act.

The Homestead Act The Homestead Act offered farmers 160 acres of public land in the West for free. All the farmer, or **homesteader,** had to do was clear the land and farm it for five years. At the end of that time, the homesteader was given ownership of the land.

The impact of the new law was enormous. Year after year, the promise of free land drew hopeful homesteaders west. Between 1860 and 1910, the number of farms in the United States tripled from 2 million to more than 6 million.

As settlers moved west, they seized more and more land from the Native Americans who lived and hunted there. Below we see a Native American village near Fort Laramie, in what is now Wyoming.

The Pacific Railroad Act The Pacific Railroad Act called for the building of a **transcontinental railroad** to link the Atlantic and Pacific coasts. This huge construction project was given to two railroad companies, the Union Pacific and the Central Pacific.

To help the railroad companies pay for the project, Congress gave them **subsidies** in the form of sections of free land for every mile of track they

laid. Later, the railroads could sell this land to settlers. The government also loaned the two companies more than $60 million.

The Pacific Railroad Act kicked off the greatest period of railroad construction in the nation's history. By 1900, the railroads had laid 170,000 miles of track, much of it in the West. "Rail barons" like the Central Pacific's Leland Stanford and Charles Crocker made vast fortunes.

Railroads opened the West to a flood of new settlers. The newcomers included farmers and ranchers, prospectors and preachers, schemers and dreamers, and more than a few crooks. But most were ordinary folk who dreamed of a new start. For them, the West was a place where a lot of hard work and a little luck could make their dreams come true.

24.4 The Railroad Builders

The plan for building a transcontinental railroad looked simple enough on paper. The Union Pacific would start in Nebraska and build tracks westward across the Great Plains and the Rocky Mountains. Meanwhile, the Central Pacific would start in California and lay tracks eastward across the Sierra Nevada mountains and the Great Basin. The two lines would meet somewhere in between the starting points. The company that laid the most track would get more land, more loans, and more profits.

Laying track was hard work. First the surveyors studied the land and chose the route for the tracks. They were followed by the graders, who prepared the land. Armed with picks and shovels, the graders cut through hills and filled up valleys to make the route as level as possible.

Next came the tracklayers. They put down wooden ties and hauled in heavy iron rails. One rail weighed 700 pounds, and there were 400 rails in each mile of track. Last came the spikers. The spikers nailed the rails to the ties with spikes—ten spikes per rail, three hammer blows for every spike.

The Union Pacific Builds West   The Union Pacific got off to a slow start. Then, in 1866, a former Civil War general named Grenville Dodge took charge of construction. Dodge had built railroads before the war, and, as a military officer, he knew how to lead men. Now he commanded an army of 10,000 workers. Most of them were Irish immigrants who were fleeing the slums of eastern cities. They were joined by other immigrants, ex-soldiers, Mexicans, and freed slaves. All were young men who needed jobs and craved adventure. Most of all, they hoped to start new lives in the open spaces of the West.

Chinese laborers were recruited to do the backbreaking work required to lay rails across the Sierra Nevada mountains. They were paid one dollar a day for their labor.

Native Americans depended heavily on the buffalo for food, shelter, and clothing. As the railroad moved west, bored passengers and hunters shot buffalo out the windows of trains. Between 1872 and 1874, nine million buffalo were killed. By 1900, there were fewer than 50 buffalo left in the United States.

By 1867, Dodge's crews were laying as much as seven miles of track a day across the plains. The workers lived in tent cities that followed the tracks west. These portable towns were tough, often dangerous places. A reporter wrote, "Not a day passes but a dead body is found somewhere in the vicinity with pockets rifled of their contents."

For the Plains Indians, the railroad was an invasion of their homeland. They watched in anger as millions of buffalo were slaughtered, destroying their main source of food. Warriors attacked the work crews and derailed supply trains by prying up sections of track. Grenville Dodge demanded military help, and soon he had 5,000 troops guarding his crews as they inched their way west.

The Central Pacific Builds East   In California, the Central Pacific Railroad faced different problems. Soon after the company began laying track, many of the workers dashed off to newly discovered silver mines in Nevada. Construction practically stopped.

In desperation, Charles Crocker, the head of construction, hired 50 Chinese workers. He doubted that the Chinese were big enough to do heavy construction. On average, they weighed just 110 pounds. But the Chinese surprised him. They could do as much work in a day as any other crew, and often more.

Crocker was so impressed that he sent agents to China to hire more Chinese workers. The agents were lucky. War and unrest had driven millions of Chinese into poverty and debt. Young men jumped at the chance of going to America to build a railroad. Most of them planned to save their money and return to China as wealthy men.

More than 12,000 Chinese laborers worked for the Central Pacific. They cleared trees, shoveled dirt, blasted tunnels, and laid tracks. At least 1,000 Chinese workers lost their lives in explosions, snow slides, and other accidents. Despite these losses, the workers managed to lay up to ten miles of track in a day.

The Two Lines Meet   On May 10, 1869, the two lines met at Promontory Point, Utah. A golden spike was driven in to complete the 1,800 miles of track. In time, a network of railroads would bring new settlers, encourage construction of towns and cities, and allow mail and supplies to be shipped clear across the country.

The Chinese workers, who had contributed so much to building the railroad, were not acknowledged at the celebration. Their reward for years of hard work was to lose their jobs. A few of them fulfilled their dream of returning to China. But most stayed on in America, helping to build new farms and businesses across the West.

24.5 The Miners

A second group of pioneers—the miners—dreamed of striking it rich. The discovery of gold in California in 1848 set off a great treasure hunt in the mountains and deserts of the West. By 1874, gold or silver had been found in California, Oregon, Washington, Nevada, Montana, Colorado, Arizona, and New Mexico.

Boomtowns and Ghost Towns   Mining in the West followed a predictable pattern. First came the discovery of gold or silver. Soon fortune seekers from around the world flocked to the site. Almost overnight, mining camps mushroomed into fast-growing settlements called *boomtowns*.

The discovery of gold or silver often resulted in instant "boomtowns" throughout the West. Pictured here is Leadville, Colorado, in the 1870s. After mining was finished, ghost towns quickly replaced the boomtowns.

Heavy machinery, used to remove gold and silver buried deep in rocks, badly damaged the land.

Newspaper reporter J. Ross Browne described the birth of one such town, Gila City, in present-day Arizona:

Enterprising men hurried to the spot with barrels of whiskey and billiards tables…. Traders crowded in with wagons of pork and beans. Gamblers came with cards…. There was everything in Gila City within a few months but a church and a jail.

These instant towns had no government, no law, and little order. Robbery and murder were common. Honest miners fought back by forming "vigilance committees" to control crime. The members of these committees, called *vigilantes,* handed out quick justice. A suspected murderer might be arrested, tried, convicted, and hanged all in the same day. If asked about their methods, the vigilantes pointed out that there were no courts or jails nearby. And no miner had time to waste guarding criminals.

When the easy-to-find gold or silver was gone, most miners moved on. Just seven years after its birth, Gila City was a ghost town. All that remained, wrote Browne, were "three chimneys and a coyote."

Mining Changes the West   In many ways, mining was destructive. It damaged the land and displaced many Native Americans. But most Americans saw mining as a source of wealth and opportunity. Some boomtowns, like Reno and Denver, survived to become prosperous cities. Mining also opened up the West's mountains and deserts to other settlers. Some were businesspeople who invested in the heavy equipment needed to extract hard-to-find ore from western mountains. Others were farmers and ranchers. These were the people who would turn lonely territories into new western states.

24.6 Ranchers and Cowboys

A third group of settlers in the West consisted of ranchers and the cowboys who tended their herds of cattle. At the end of the Civil War, millions of longhorn cattle roamed the plains of Texas. The longhorns got their name from their impressive horns, which could measure more than seven feet from tip to tip. The market for all this beef was the crowded cities of the East. Cattle worth $3 a head in Texas might be sold for $50 in New York or Chicago. The problem was how to transport the cattle to the cities. This challenge was complicated by the presence of angry Indians and stampeding buffalo herds.

The Extermination of the Buffalo The railroads made the ranchers' task much easier. As the railroads moved onto the Great Plains, buffalo hunters followed. The hunters killed huge numbers of buffalo for their hides and bones, which were shipped by rail for sale in the East.

The Plains Indians depended on the buffalo for food. They were horrified by the slaughter. So were some other Americans. In 1874, Congress passed a bill outlawing the killing of more buffalo than could be used for food. But President Grant refused to sign the bill into law. General Philip Sheridan supported Grant's decision. "You ought to give each hunter a medal," he said. "Let them kill, skin and sell until the buffalo are exterminated [wiped out]. Then your prairies can be covered with cattle and the cowboy."

By 1880, the buffalo had all but vanished. With their food gone, the Plains Indians had little choice but to move to reservations. The plains were now open to ranchers and their cattle.

The "Long Drive" The railroads also solved the ranchers' transportation problem. In 1867, Joseph McCoy built a stockyard next to the railroad in Abilene, Kansas. A *stockyard* is a large holding pen where cattle are kept temporarily. That summer, cowboys herded a few thousand cattle from Texas to the Abilene stockyard, in what they called the "long drive." There the cattle were loaded into boxcars and shipped east. Over the next 20 years, cowboys drove more than 5 million cattle to Abilene and other "cow towns" beside the rails.

Being a cowboy was dangerous and low-paying work. Still, life on the trail attracted many young adventurers. Most were Texans. About a third were of Mexican or African American heritage. Rarely, however, were black cowboys promoted to trail boss. Jim Perry, for example, was an expert rider, roper, and trail cook. He once said, "If it weren't for my damned old black face, I'd have been a boss long ago."

During the long drive, cowboys worked 17 hours a day, seven days a week, for three to four months. Much of the work was boring—except for moments of terror when a herd stampeded. By the time they reached the end of the trail, most cowboys were ready for rowdy fun, including drinking, gambling, and brawling. That made the cow towns wild, noisy, and often dangerous places.

The most notorious cow town was Dodge City in Kansas. An eastern

Cowboys, like Isom Dart (pictured below), moved out west to herd cattle. Many cowboys dreamed of getting their own herd and making their fortune in the rapidly growing cattle empire.

Dodge City, Kansas, shown above, was a wild cow town. When cowboys reached the end of the drive, they were ready for fun.

newspaper described it as "a wicked little town." Between 1872 and 1878, 64 victims of gunfights were buried on the hill above the town. Later, several graves were dug up to make way for a new school. The gravediggers turned up a fine collection of skeletons, most still wearing their cowboy boots. To this day, the Dodge City cemetery is known as Boot Hill.

The End of the "Long Drive" After growing rapidly for 20 years, the cattle industry collapsed in 1887. The winter of 1886–1887 was the worst that anyone could remember. January was so cold that one cowboy described his life as "hell without the heat." Whole herds of cattle froze to death. Ranchers called that terrible winter the "Great Die-Up." Many of them lost everything. The survivors reduced their herds and fenced their grazing lands. They built barns and raised hay so that they could shelter and feed their animals in winter. The days of the long drive were over. Wild cow towns became civilized ranching centers. Adventuresome cowboys settled down to work as ranch hands.

The cattlemen's glory years faded into the past. Still, they had much to be proud of. They had opened the Great Plains to settlement. And they had created an industry that remains an important part of life in the West today.

24.7 The Homesteaders

Farmers followed the ranchers onto the Great Plains. For half a century, the plains had been viewed as too dry for farming. Mapmakers labeled the area the "Great American Desert." Then in the 1870s, a few homesteaders plowed and planted the grassland. They were lucky. These were years of plentiful rain, and their fields yielded fine crops.

The western railroads and land dealers made the most of this good luck. Maybe the plains used to be too dry for farming, they said, but not any more. Some even said that rain had followed the rails west. "The increase of railroads," wrote a Colorado journalist, "has the…effect of producing more showers." Others gave farming the credit for the wet years, claiming that "rain follows the plow."

The Homesteaders Arrive   Rain might not follow the rails or the plow, but a rush of new settlers did. By 1900, some 500,000 homesteaders had moved onto the Great Plains. Many were farm families from the East who were lured west by the promise of free or cheap land. Some were former slaves looking for a new start in freedom. Tens of thousands of European immigrants also settled the plains. While most of them were seeking land, one group, Russian Mennonites, came looking for religious freedom.

Farming the Dry Plains   The homesteaders faced huge challenges as they struggled to turn grasslands into grain fields. Rain was unreliable. Some years their crops withered under the hot prairie sun. Other years clouds of locusts, or large grasshoppers, swept across the plains, eating everything in their path. In addition, the plains had few trees, so there was little wood for homes.

Over time, the homesteaders solved these problems. Instead of using wood, they built houses out of chunks of sod (mats of soil held together by grassy roots). They used windmills to pump water from deep in the ground. They learned how to plow deeply to reach moist soil. The Mennonites introduced a type of winter wheat that thrived on the plains. With hard work and the right crop, homesteaders made the Great Plains the most productive wheat-growing region in the world.

The plains greeted newcomers with miles and miles of treeless grassland. Since lumber was expensive or unavailable, farmers built homes out of sod, or mats of soil. Sod houses proved to be cool in the summer and warm in the winter.

Tensions in the West   **347**

Geography Challenge

Land Losses of Native Americans

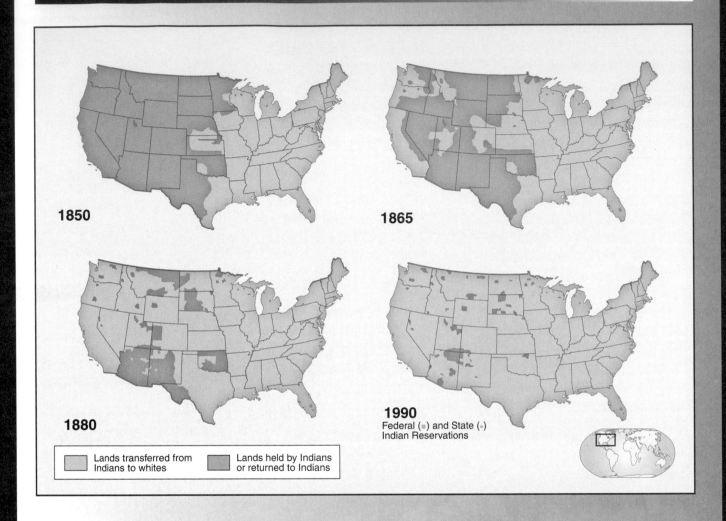

1850

1865

1880

1990
Federal (▪) and State (•)
Indian Reservations

Lands transferred from Indians to whites

Lands held by Indians or returned to Indians

1. Identify at least four interesting details on these maps.

2. Approximately what percentage of the land in the continental United States was held by Native Americans in 1850? 1865? 1880? 1990?

3. What are some of the reasons Native Americans lost so much land between 1850 and 1990?

4. How do you think Native Americans responded to this loss of land?

24.8 War on the Plains

The flow of miners, ranchers, and farmers to the West compelled a change in federal policy toward Native Americans. Under the Indian Removal Act of 1830, Native Americans had been promised lands in the Great Plains in exchange for giving up their homelands in the East. By the mid-1800s, whites were pushing deep into this "Indian Territory." A number of small wars raged as Indians resisted the tide of settlement. More and more, government officials saw Indians as standing in the way of the agricultural and industrial development of the West.

In 1867, Congress tried to separate Indians and settlers by moving the Indians onto reservations. In exchange for their land, the Native Americans were promised food, farm tools, and schools where their children would learn to "live like whites."

The new policy was backed up by force. The U.S. Army was authorized to round up Indians and keep them on reservations.

Many Native Americans fought this effort to take away their land and change their way of life. In the 1870s, the wars on the plains would settle the issue once and for all.

Reservation Life The nomadic Plains peoples hated the idea of being penned up on a reservation. A Sioux chief named Sitting Bull spoke for many Indians when he said:

> *I will remain what I am until I die, a hunter, and when there are no buffalo or other game I will send my children to hunt and live on prairie mice, for when an Indian is shut in one place, his body becomes weak.*

Sitting Bull's Indian name was Tatanka Iyotaka. This Sioux chief resisted white settlement with passion and courage. Nevertheless, his leadership was not enough to stop the tide of newcomers.

Despite Sitting Bull's words, the buffalo were disappearing, and most Plains Indians had little choice but to move to reservations. Once they did, however, the promised food often failed to arrive. Sometimes dishonest Indian agents sold it to settlers instead. Often the food was spoiled by the time it reached the Indians.

Hungry and unhappy with reservation life, many warriors left the reservations to look for game or to attack settlers. When they did, they were hunted down by army troops.

General George Crook sympathized with the Indians. "I do not wonder that when these Indians see their wives and children starving they go to war," he wrote. "And then we are sent out to kill. It is an outrage."

The Granger Collection, New York

This artist's depiction of Custer's Last Stand, or the Battle of the Little Big Horn, shows Sioux warriors overwhelming Custer's troops. Custer himself was killed by a gunshot to the head. The battle lasted only half an hour.

The Battle of the Little Big Horn   The most famous battle in this long struggle was fought near the Little Big Horn River in present-day Montana. The Battle of the Little Big Horn soon came to be known by another name—Custer's Last Stand.

The trouble began when soldiers led by Indian fighter George Custer found gold in the Black Hills of Dakota Territory. Within months, 15,000 gold-hungry whites were swarming over Sioux land. Rather than remove the miners, the government demanded that the Sioux sell the Black Hills. The Sioux refused. "I never want to leave this country," a leader named Wolf Necklace told the government agents. "All my relatives are lying here in the ground, and when I fall to pieces I am going to fall to pieces here."

The army was ordered to force the Indians out. In June 1876, army scouts reported that several thousand Sioux and Cheyenne were camped beside the Little Big Horn River. Custer was ordered to locate the camp and then wait for reinforcements.

Once Custer spotted the Indian camp, however, he decided to attack at once. The attack ended in disaster. Custer split up his troops, and the group that he led suddenly found itself surrounded by angry warriors.

The battle, one warrior said, lasted no longer than a hungry man needs to eat his dinner. In those few minutes, Custer and all his men—about 260 soldiers—were killed.

Angry whites called the battle a massacre. Over the next few months, the army tracked down the Sioux and Cheyenne and forced them onto reservations. Ignoring earlier treaties, Congress took the Black Hills and another 40 million acres of land away from the Sioux.

By 1887, most Native American peoples had been moved onto reservations. Never again would Indians roam freely across the West.

24.9 Chapter Summary

In this chapter, you read about the tensions that developed between settlers and Native Americans in the West after the Civil War. You used an illustration of a buffalo hide to record information about four groups of settlers and their impact on the West's native peoples.

As settlers moved west, Native Americans were pushed off their lands and onto reservations. When Indians like the Nez Percé resisted, soldiers were sent to move them by force.

During the Civil War, the Homestead Act and the Pacific Railway Act aroused new interest in the West. The completion of the first transcontinental railroad in 1869 opened the West to a flood of new settlers.

Much of the West was first explored by miners seeking gold and silver. The railroads helped ranchers and cowboys introduce large-scale cattle ranching to the Great Plains. Homesteaders turned the Great Plains into the most productive wheat-producing region in the world.

The wars between settlers, soldiers, and Plains Indians came to a head in the Battle of the Little Big Horn. The Indians won the battle, but soon afterward the Sioux and Cheyenne were forced onto reservations.

The settling of the West helped to make the United States one of the world's largest and wealthiest countries. In the next chapter, you will learn how the rise of big business created new opportunities and problems for workers, immigrants, and politicians from east to west.

Settlers rush to claim land in the Oklahoma Territory in 1893.

What do you think this man's job is?

How do you think this woman feels about her job?

25

The Rise of Industry

25.1 Introduction

The tragedy started late in the afternoon on March 25, 1911. The quitting bell had just sounded in New York City's Triangle Shirtwaist Factory. Nearly 500 employees, most of them young immigrant women, headed toward the exit. It was Saturday, and they were looking forward to a day off with family and friends.

One woman sniffed the air. Something was burning! Another spotted flames leaping out of a pile of cloth scraps. Before she could react, the wooden table above the fabric was ablaze. From there the flames jumped to the paper fabric patterns hanging above the table. Flaming bits of paper and fabric whirled around the room, setting other tables on fire.

The room filled with smoke, and the air became so hot that it burst the windows. Fresh air poured into the room, sending the flames even higher. Fingers of the blaze started to scorch workers' clothing and hair.

"I heard somebody cry, 'Fire!' I left everything and ran for the door," recalled one woman. "The door was locked and immediately there was a great jam of girls before it." She could see at once that, "If we couldn't get out, we would all be roasted alive."

Such factories and their dangers were a relatively new part of life in the United States. You read in Chapter 19 how the Industrial Revolution began. After the Civil War, new inventions and business methods allowed Americans to create industry on a much larger scale than ever before. Unfortunately, this industrial progress brought not only economic benefits, but also tragedies to the United States. The nation's new mills and factories produced a wondrous assortment of goods that made life better for many. But the people who were employed in these new industries often lived and worked in the most miserable, even dangerous, conditions.

In this chapter, you will read the rest of the story of the Triangle Shirtwaist Factory fire. You will also find out how, by 1900, the United States became the world's leading industrial nation.

Graphic Organizer: Illustration
You will use an illustration of factory workers to learn more about the expansion of industry and the effects of this expansion on workers.

industrialization the birth and growth of businesses that make and distribute products through the use of machinery

entrepreneur someone who starts a business and is good at making money

laissez-faire the theory that economies work best when governments do not interfere with them. (*Laissez-faire* is French for "leave alone.")

25.2 Overview: A Nation Transformed

On March 26, 1883, Mrs. William Kissam Vanderbilt threw a party to show off her family's new home in New York City. It wasn't just a party, it was a grand ball—the most dazzling social event in the city's history. And it wasn't just any home. The Vanderbilts had built a mansion in the style of a European castle, complete with medieval furniture, tapestries, and armor.

But then, the Vanderbilts weren't just any family. Mrs. Vanderbilt's husband, a railroad tycoon, was the grandson of Cornelius Vanderbilt, who had made a fortune in banking and shipping. The Vanderbilt clan was one of America's wealthiest and most powerful families.

More than 1,200 of New York's social elite flocked to Mrs. Vanderbilt's ball, dressed in glittering costumes. Many of the guests came as kings and queens. But Mrs. Vanderbilt's sister-in-law decided to be more modern. She came dressed as The Electric Light.

Mrs. Vanderbilt's party reflected the way rapid **industrialization** was transforming American life in the decades after the Civil War. Cities like New York were booming. **Entrepreneurs** in banking, commerce, and industry were amassing enormous wealth. And technological marvels like electric light were changing how Americans lived and worked. But as the workers in the Triangle Shirtwaist Factory knew, not everyone benefited from this progress.

Industrialization produced a wide range of affordable consumer goods. Giant catalogs like this one offered American families everything from pots and pans to pianos.

The Growth of Big Business Families like the Vanderbilts made huge profits from the growth of big business after the Civil War. Businesses got bigger in part because of new technology and manufacturing practices. They also grew because there was more money to invest in them. Bankers and investors were happy to provide the necessary funds in hopes of earning large returns. Some of the money that fueled industrialization came from the large-scale mining of gold and silver in the West.

Government policies also contributed to the boom in big business. According to the doctrine of **laissez-faire,** economies worked best when governments did not meddle in them. To business tycoons and their politician allies, laissez-faire meant that government should not regulate the price or quality of goods, the working conditions of laborers, or the business practices of bankers and industrialists—even when those practices were ruthless.

But businesses were only too happy to accept the kind of "meddling" that protected and increased their wealth. Federal, state, and local governments all actively helped business through favorable laws and subsidies, such as the land grants given to railroads and farmers. Congress passed higher and higher tariffs. These made imported goods more expensive, and therefore less competitive with those produced in the United States.

The business boom fed the growth of American cities. For 100 years, Americans had been going West to seek their fortunes. In 1890, the Census Bureau said that it could no longer draw a line to show the farthest limit of westward migration. The frontier was closed. The new "land of opportunity" was located in the cities of the Northeast and around the Great Lakes, where factories provided thousands of new jobs.

Outside the cities, even farming was getting to be big business. In the Midwest, commercial farmers used new machinery and techniques to grow crops on a larger scale than ever before. "The wildest dream has become reality," marveled one writer in 1887. "Nothing is too large for belief. Twenty and even thirty thousand acre farms, and a hundred bushels to the acre…The New West…is a veritable 'Wonderland.'"

The Gilded Age As businesses got bigger, so did the fortunes of those who owned or invested in them. Between 1860 and 1892, the number of millionaires in the United States grew from 400 to more than 4,000. The newly rich filled their palace-like homes with gaudy decorations and European art and antiques. In 1873, the great American writer Mark Twain scornfully dubbed this time of showy wealth "the Gilded Age."

Twain's name stuck, but it did not describe the lives of most Americans. While wealthy capitalists lived like royalty, many workers lived in dire poverty. Those who were immigrants often faced prejudice and discrimination. During business downturns many workers lost their jobs. People were angry about the cozy relationships between tycoons and politicians which resulted in widespread corruption. As you will learn, these conditions eventually sparked protests and calls for reform.

This lavish dining room in the summer home of the powerful Vanderbilt family is typical of the showy wealth of the Gilded Age.

25.3 Improved Technology

By the 1860s, many of the factors necessary for the rapid industrialization of the United States were already in place. Machines had taken over much of the work once done by hand. Work had moved from homes to factories. Railroads had begun to connect customers and manufacturers with an efficient transportation system.

After the Civil War, new inventions and improved technology prompted the growth of new industries. Some of these innovations, or new ideas, helped businesses to grow and become more efficient. Others made daily life easier for many Americans.

Sparks fly in a steel-manufacturing plant as molten metal meets cold air in the Kelly-Bessemer process. The process cleaned the steel of impurities.

The Age of Steel Before the Civil War, the nation's railroads ran on iron rails that wore out quickly. Railroad owners knew that rails made of steel—a mixture of iron, carbon, and sometimes other metals—were stronger and would last longer. Steel, however, was difficult and costly to make.

In 1872, a Scottish immigrant named Andrew Carnegie went to England to study a less expensive method of making steel, invented by Henry Bessemer. Carnegie owned a company that made iron bridges for railroads. But he knew that his bridges would be better if made out of steel. Carnegie was so impressed by the Bessemer process that he brought it back to the United States. "The day of iron has passed," he announced. "Steel is king!"

Carnegie was right. Within a decade, steel was replacing iron in rails, locomotives, and bridges. Other industries also took advantage of less expensive steel. Steel nails, needles, and knives became common household items.

Many steel companies competed fiercely to supply steel for such products. To remain the leader, Carnegie hired scientists to improve the quality of his company's steel. He employed good managers to make his steel mills run efficiently. His recipe for success was, "Adopt every improvement, have the best machinery, and know the most."

To keep costs low, Carnegie set out to control every step in the steel-making process. He purchased iron mines to supply his ore, coal fields to fire his furnaces, and railroads to ship his finished steel to customers.

To reduce his competition, Carnegie also bought up several rival steel companies. He then combined them all to form the giant Carnegie Steel Company. By 1900, Carnegie Steel produced a quarter of the nation's steel.

Electric Power   In 1876, Thomas Edison opened an "invention factory" in New Jersey. With a team of workers, he set out to create a "minor" invention every ten days and a major one "every six months or so."

Edison succeeded brilliantly. More than any other inventor, he helped turn electricity into an everyday source of light and power. His workshop turned out the first practical electric lightbulb, the phonograph, the motion picture projector, and many other inventions.

In 1882, Edison built the first electrical power station and distribution system in New York City. His team invented everything the system required, including generators, regulators, meters, switches, light sockets, fuse boxes, and underground electric cables. When he finally turned the generator on, electricity began to flow to homes, stores, and factories. The age of electricity had begun.

By 1900, some 25 million lightbulbs were glowing across the country. Many factories were replacing waterwheels and steam engines with electric motors. Streetcars powered by electricity carried workers and shoppers along city streets. New electric-powered devices, such as washing machines and vacuum cleaners, were making housework easier.

The Collection of the New-York Historical Society, negative number 2946

Electric lines form a crisscross canopy over this city street. Thomas Edison's invention of the lightbulb in the 1880s spurred tremendous growth in the electric industry.

The Telephone   The telephone was invented by a Scottish immigrant named Alexander Graham Bell. In 1876, as he was getting ready to test his "talking machine," Bell spilled acid on himself. "Watson, come here, I want you," he commanded his assistant. Watson, who was in another room, heard every word over a telephone.

Bell's invention worked so well that, by 1915, Americans were communicating with one another over nine million telephones. All these telephones made American industry more efficient and competitive by allowing producers, sellers, and customers to communicate quickly and easily.

New Production Methods   New methods of organizing work were also making business more efficient. Factory owners adopted Eli Whitney's idea of assembling a wide variety of products from interchangeable parts. They also used the assembly line. In a shoe factory, for example, one worker operated a heel-cutting machine. Another operated a sole-cutting machine. Another made shoelaces. Still other workers assembled, labeled, and packaged the shoes.

These techniques of **mass production** enabled workers to produce more goods per day at less cost. As prices dropped, more Americans could afford to buy manufactured products. More customers meant more factories. By 1900, almost four times as many Americans worked in factories as had a generation earlier.

> **mass production** the use of interchangeable parts and assembly lines to make large quantities of identical goods

The Triangle Factory

The Triangle Shirtwaist Factory was just one of many new businesses that took advantage of improved technology to mass-produce a quality product at a good price. The Triangle Factory specialized in a style of women's blouse known as a *shirtwaist*. A shirtwaist had puffy sleeves, a neat collar, front buttons, and a snug waist. Women liked shirtwaists so much that by 1909, New York City had more than 500 factories that made only such blouses.

Sam Bernstein, the production manager at the Triangle Shirtwaist Factory, loved watching his workers use up-to-date tools and production methods. Each person at the cutting tables had a special steel knife. This knife could slice through many layers of fabric at a time, cutting dozens of sleeves, then fronts, then backs. That was the way to get things done in a modern factory!

From the next floor of the building, Bernstein could hear the whirring of 240 sewing machines. The machines were neatly laid out in 16 tightly packed rows. Flexible belts connected each machine to a rotating axle running down each row just above the floor. This axle, which was spun by an electric motor, delivered power to each machine. The machines clattered loudly as women sewed the pieces of shirtwaists together.

Piles of finished blouses were then lifted to the floor above by electric freight elevators. There, two rows of workers gave the shirtwaists a final pressing. Finally, shipping clerks packed the shirtwaists into boxes for shipment.

Usually, the factory almost ran itself. But if a problem occurred, the company's switchboard operator could reach Bernstein by telephone on any of the three floors of the factory.

Sewing machines, shirtmakers, bobbins, and piles of cloth crowd this factory. Imagine working here in the heat of summer.

25.4 The Rise of Big Business

When Carnegie opened his first factory in 1865, most businesses were still owned by one person or a few partners. Because the owners' funds were limited, businesses were small. Owners knew their employees and often treated them like family.

Growth of Corporations A partnership might work well for a garment, or clothing, factory. But big businesses, such as railroads, needed much more capital (money to start a business) than a few partners could provide. To raise larger sums, entrepreneurs set up **corporations**. A corporation is a business that is owned by many investors, or people who help pay its initial expenses.

A corporation raises funds by selling stock, or shares in a business. The investors who buy the stock are known as *stockholders*. In return for their investment, stockholders hope to receive dividends, or a share of the corporation's profits.

The money invested by the stockholders is used to build the business. To make sure their money is used properly, stockholders elect a board of directors. The people on the board of directors oversee the running of the corporation.

After the Civil War, corporations attracted large amounts of money from investors. By the 1880s, thousands of corporations were doing business across the United States.

Rockefeller's Oil Trust A giant in the oil business, John D. Rockefeller introduced another form of business organization known as the **trust**. A trust is a group of corporations run by a single board of directors.

Rockefeller invested in his first oil refinery in 1862, at the age of 23. At that time, petroleum, or oil found underground, was just becoming a valuable resource. Oil refineries purify petroleum into fuel oil. During the 19th century, oil was used to light homes, cook food, and run engines and generators.

Before long, many small refineries were competing fiercely in the oil business. The amount of oil produced by these firms rose and fell wildly, along with prices. Rockefeller saw this as wasteful and inefficient. To reduce competition, he did everything he could to drive his rivals out of business. Those companies he could not destroy, he bought.

Like Carnegie, Rockefeller took control of every step of his business. He bought oil fields along with railroads, pipelines, and ships to move his oil. He built his own warehouses and even made his own oil barrels for storing oil products. By 1880, Rockefeller controlled 95 percent of the nation's oil refining.

To manage his many businesses, Rockefeller combined them into the Standard Oil Trust. The trust made the oil industry more efficient than ever before. But, as a **monopoly,** it had the power to control oil prices. This worried people who depended on oil in their homes and businesses.

Following Rockefeller's example, entrepreneurs created trusts in other businesses such as railroads, meatpacking, sugar, whiskey, and tobacco.

corporation a business that is owned by many investors

trust a group of corporations that unite in order to reduce competition and control prices in a business or an industry

monopoly a company that controls all production and sales of a particular product or service

J. P. Morgan, pictured above, was to banking and finance what Carnegie and Rockefeller were to steel and oil. In 1901, Morgan used his financial resources to buy Carnegie's steel company. Morgan founded U.S. Steel, America's first billion-dollar corporation.

The "people's entrance" to the United States Senate is "closed" in this turn-of-the-century cartoon. According to the cartoonist, the Senate was controlled by business trusts, depicted here as giant, bloated moneybags.

The business leaders who controlled these huge trusts became fabulously wealthy. Because most had made their fortunes by crushing their competitors, critics called them "robber barons."

The Evils of Trusts   The growth of trusts alarmed many Americans. They saw these monopolies as a threat to the free-enterprise system. This system depends on free competition among businesses to provide the public quality products at fair prices. A monopoly, people argued, has little reason to improve its products or to keep prices low because it has no competition.

People also worried about the influence of trusts on the political process. Wealthy entrepreneurs, they complained, were using their enormous wealth to buy elections and corrupt public officials. As the *Chicago Tribune* warned, "liberty and monopoly cannot live together."

The Triangle Factory

The Triangle Shirtwaist Factory would never be the size of U.S. Steel or Standard Oil. However, it was the largest shirtwaist factory in the country. The two men who owned the factory, Max Blanck and Isaac Harris, were known in the garment industry as "the shirtwaist kings."

The owners worked well together. While Max Blanck entertained buyers from stores to convince them to carry Triangle products, Isaac Harris ran the factory. Harris kept up with garment production, machinery maintenance, and work flow. He did not, however, try to keep up with his workforce. The factory had too many workers for him to get to know them all personally.

The shirtwaist business made Blanck and Harris very wealthy. They drove fancy cars and enjoyed comforts that their workers could only dream about. Both had worked hard in a competitive business and probably felt that they had earned their success.

25.5 The Growth of Cities

Industrialization brought with it **urbanization**, or city growth. Most of the nation's new industries were located in cities. Immigrants and rural Americans flocked to these industrial centers looking for jobs. Chicago, for example, more than tripled its population between 1880 and 1900.

Urban Tenements   As cities swelled with workers, demand for cheap housing exploded. To meet this demand, developers threw up cheap apartment buildings called *tenements*. One person described tenements as "great prison-like structures of brick, with narrow doors and windows, cramped passages and steep, rickety stairs." By 1900, about two thirds of New Yorkers lived in such buildings.

A poor family might occupy just one or two rooms in a tenement, usually with no heat or water. Friends or family often took in newcomers who arrived in cities without money for rent. As a result, tenement neighborhoods were some of the most heavily populated areas on Earth.

Tenements were unclean and even dangerous places to live. Only a few rooms had windows to provide light and fresh air. The rest were dark and airless. In some tenements, the only source of water was a single faucet in a courtyard. Many lacked sewer services. In such conditions, diseases such as typhoid and cholera spread quickly, killing infants and young children. Fire was another constant worry.

Cities Expand Upward   As cities expanded, urban land costs shot up. In New York, land that had sold for $80 in 1804 was selling for $8,000 by 1880. Such prices inspired builders to construct more building space on less land by going upward. Using lightweight steel beams to support walls and ceilings, builders constructed skyscrapers that rose ten or more stories into the air. Electric elevators whisked people and freight effortlessly from floor to floor.

A family in a New York City tenement in the early 1900s. Cramped, dirty, dark, and crowded, tenements spread disease and misery among their inhabitants.

Businesspeople rented space in city skyscrapers for their offices and factories. Factory owners preferred the top floors. Rents were cheaper higher up, and the natural light was better, saving owners money on electric lighting. The cost of insurance was low as well because steel buildings were thought to be fireproof. By the early 1900s, more than half of New York City's workers labored above the seventh floor.

City Excitement   For all their problems, cities were also exciting places to live. City stores were filled with products never seen on a farm. City dwellers enjoyed all sorts of entertainment, from operas and art museums to dance halls and sporting events. When writer Hamlin

The ten-story Asch Building in New York City had only two staircases, even though the city required at least three for safety reasons.

Garland came to Chicago with his brother, he found that, "Everything interested us…. Nothing was commonplace; nothing was ugly to us."

The Triangle Factory

Blanck and Harris located their thriving shirtwaist business on the top three floors of the ten-story Asch Building in New York City. They chose this space partly because of the morning sunlight that streamed in through its large windows. Their landlord, Joseph Asch, boasted that when construction was completed in 1901, "the architects claimed my building was ahead of any other building of its kind which had previously been constructed."

It may have been ahead of other buildings, but the Asch Building was not perfect. It had only two staircases, even though the city building code required three. The city had agreed to count the building's fire escape as the third staircase. But the fire escape ended at the second floor. Nor was the Asch Building well designed for evacuation during an emergency. Its staircases were narrow. Instead of opening outward to let people escape easily, the building's doors opened inward. Despite scares from several small fires in the building, Asch had not bothered to fix these problems.

The Triangle Factory's workforce was made up mainly of young immigrant women, most of them Italians and Jews from Eastern Europe. Even if they had been aware of these safety problems, they would have hesitated to demand improvements for fear of being fired. Often their jobs provided their family's only income.

Like most factory workers, Triangle employees could only afford housing in crowded slums. "I lived in a two-room tenement with my mother and two sisters and the bedroom had no windows," recalled one employee. "There was nothing to look forward to."

Geography Challenge
United States Industry and Agriculture in 1900

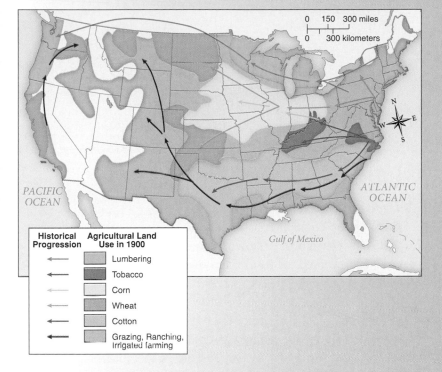

Agricultural Regions, 1900

Historical Progression	Agricultural Land Use in 1900
←	Lumbering
←	Tobacco
←	Corn
←	Wheat
←	Cotton
←	Grazing, Ranching, Irrigated farming

PACIFIC OCEAN

ATLANTIC OCEAN

Gulf of Mexico

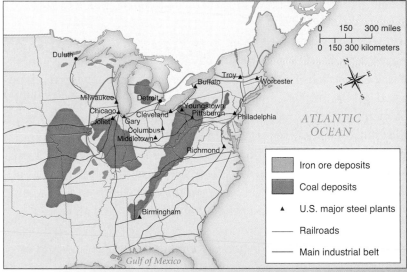

Iron and Steel Production, 1900

Duluth

Milwaukee
Chicago
Joliet
Detroit
Cleveland
Gary
Columbus
Middletown
Youngstown
Pittsburgh
Buffalo
Troy
Worcester
Philadelphia
Richmond
Birmingham

ATLANTIC OCEAN

Gulf of Mexico

- Iron ore deposits
- Coal deposits
- ▲ U.S. major steel plants
- — Railroads
- — Main industrial belt

1. What do these two maps show?
2. Which direction is agricultural development moving? How might weather present a problem for farmers settling in some parts of the West? Judging from the map, how do they solve their problems?
3. Where are iron ore and coal deposits? Where is iron and steel production located? Where are railroads located? What is the relationship between the location of raw materials, transportation, and industry?

A young girl stands between looms in a textile factory. At the turn of the century, millions of children worked long hours in mines, mills, and factories.

25.6 Working Conditions

Working conditions in most industries were appalling. Gone were the days when business owners knew and cared about the people who worked for them. Men like Carnegie and Rockefeller knew little about their workers.

Working Families   Gone too were the days when factory workers could expect decent pay. With so many people looking for jobs, business owners could pay low wages. Many wages were so low that men could not support their families. To get by, wives and children had to work as well, usually at even lower wages.

Most factory women earned about $1 to $3 per day. If business was slow, wages dropped. A boss might not pay a new worker anything until she had learned her job. Then he would charge her for the sewing machine she worked on. If a worker complained, she could easily be replaced with a new one, perhaps for less money.

Millions of young children worked in mines, mills, and factories. A newspaper reported that young boys hired by coal miners to separate lumps of coal from rocks, "go to work...at seven o'clock in the morning and work till it is too dark to see any longer. For this they get $1 to $3 a week." They also got curved spines from bending over piles of coal all day.

Inside Factories   Mills and factories were hot in summer and cold in winter. To keep costs low, owners crowded workers together.

Of all working dangers, fire claimed the most lives. In New York, tall buildings often lacked fire escapes. New York City's fire chief wanted buildings to have fire escapes and sprinkler systems that could put out fires quickly. But factory owners objected to such added expenses.

New York City did require that factory doors "open outwardly" and "shall not be locked" so workers might escape quickly in case of fire. The law was not enforced, however. In 1910, some 94 percent of all factory doors in the city opened inward instead of outward.

The Triangle Factory

Saturday was payday at the Triangle Shirtwaist Factory. Most workers earned only $9 per week, with the most experienced making up to $12. The younger workers, some only 13 years old, earned just $6 per week for sewing on buttons all day. The very youngest earned even less. Worker Pauline Newman recalled:

> We were young, eight, nine, ten years old.... The hours were from 7:30 in the morning to 6:30 at night when it wasn't busy. When the [busy] season was on we worked until 9 o'clock. No overtime pay, not even supper money.... My wages were $1.50 for a seven-day week.

Of course, these pay rates were what workers earned before deductions. The company charged its employees for the thread and electricity they used, for the chairs they sat on, and even for using Triangle's coat lockers.

Everybody was expected to work at least 59 hours a week. This included every Saturday, plus occasional Sundays. To keep workers from claiming overtime pay, the managers sometimes set the clock back. To keep workers from being "interrupted," the heavy steel doors to the hall and stairs remained locked until closing time.

To make sure workers didn't steal any shirtwaists, fabric, or lace, the factory built a narrow corridor leading to the elevators. Every day at quitting time, employees filed through this corridor one at a time so that a watchman could inspect each woman's handbag.

Working at Triangle was unhealthy, uncomfortable, and unsafe. Managers seldom let workers leave the factory floor to use the toilet or drink from the dirty tap in the hallway. In the crowded sewing room, women could barely squeeze by each other's machines. The wooden chairs behind the machines often lacked backs to support the sewers while they worked. When all the machines were in use, the noise could be deafening.

Fire hazards abounded. Even though the city prohibited smoking, the factory rarely enforced that rule. Workers stuffed leftover fabric into wooden bins where it sat for months just waiting for a misplaced spark to set it ablaze. The Asch Building's only fire protection was a few hundred pails of water scattered throughout its ten floors.

An inspector points to a bolted door in the Triangle Shirtwaist Factory. The inspection came too late for the women who lost their lives in the fire. Tragically, the factory owners had locked the door to keep workers on the job.

25.7 Labor Unions

As a teenager, Rose Schneiderman found work in a cap factory. After three years, she later wrote, "it began to dawn on me that we girls needed an organization. We were helpless; no one girl dared stand up for anything alone."

Workers like Rose Schneiderman had been forming unions since the 1830s. These early labor organizations were **trade unions**. They organized workers in the same trade, or job, to fight for better wages and working conditions. Sometimes these unions went out on strike, refusing to work until their employers agreed to meet their demands.

Knights of Labor In 1869, Uriah Stephens organized a new union known as the Knights of Labor. Stephens hoped to unite "men and women of every craft, creed, and color" into "one common brotherhood." The Knights led several successful strikes against telegraph and railroad companies. With such victories, the union grew to over 700,000 members.

In 1886, nearly 200,000 workers went on strike nationwide to demand an eight-hour workday. During a rally at Haymarket Square in Chicago, someone threw a bomb at police. The police shot back, injuring many workers. Four workers were sentenced to death for the bombing, even though no evidence tied them to the bomb.

Fearing more violence, employers fired anyone associated with the Knights. Membership dropped quickly, and the organization faded away.

American Federation of Labor As the Knights declined, a group of local trade unions formed the American Federation of Labor (AFL). Led by Samuel Gompers, the AFL used **collective bargaining** to reach its goals. Instead of striking, union representatives tried to negotiate agreements with employers on such issues as wages.

Despite the AFL's peaceful approach, many employers made their workers sign pledges not to join unions. They also fired union members and exchanged lists of such "troublemakers" with other employers.

trade unions early labor organizations that brought together workers in the same trade, or job, to fight for better wages and working conditions

collective bargaining a method for negotiating labor issues in which union representatives bargain with employers on behalf of the union's members

The Granger Collection, New York

Strikes often pitted the police against labor organizers. This image shows a policeman being shot on Haymarket Square in Chicago during a strike of the Knights of Labor in 1886. A short time later, a dynamite bomb killed or injured several dozen persons, including police.

The Homestead Strike   Some bosses used force to defeat unions. When workers struck at a Carnegie steel plant in Homestead, Pennsylvania, Henry Clay Frick, Carnegie's partner, refused to talk about their demands. Instead Frick made plans to reopen his plant with non-union workers. To protect these strikebreakers, he hired 300 armed guards.

When the guards arrived in Homestead, they faced an angry crowd of strikers. A battle broke out in which both guards and strikers died. Still Frick went ahead with his plan. When the Homestead plant reopened with strikebreakers, the union collapsed in defeat.

Women Organize   Such tactics kept many women from joining unions, but not Rose Schneiderman. Upset by pay cuts, Schneiderman organized the women in her factory as part of the National Board of United Cloth Hat and Cap Makers. Soon after she joined the union, she wrote,

> *A strike was declared in five of the biggest factories. There are 30 factories in the city. About 100 girls went out. The result was a victory, which netted us—I mean the girls—$2 increase in our wages on the average…. But all was not lovely by any means, for the bosses were not at all pleased with their beating and had determined to fight us again.*

The largest women's union was the International Ladies' Garment Workers' Union (ILGWU), which represented women in clothing factories. In 1909, thousands of New York City garment workers walked off their jobs to protest poor working conditions and low pay. As the strike grew, so did public sympathy for the young women. The newspapers called this movement "The Uprising of the 20,000."

The strike ended months later when employers agreed to a shorter workweek and better pay. They also ended fees for the use of factory equipment. The employers refused, however, to meet the workers' demands for safety improvements. Most garment factories remained unsafe.

Shirtwaist workers display strike leaflets for a newspaper photographer. Strikers wanted shorter hours, higher pay, and safer working conditions.

The Triangle Factory

About 5,000 workers from the Triangle Shirtwaist Factory were part of the ILGWU strike of 1909. Their demands included unlocked doors during working hours and safer fire escapes in the Asch Building.

Rather than meet those demands, Blanck and Harris responded by locking the strikers out of the factory and advertising for replacements. "If the union had won, we would have been safe," said striker

Rose Safran. "But the bosses defeated us and we didn't get the open doors or the better fire escapes." Because of that defeat, 146 workers would die needlessly.

The cause of the fire that swept through the Triangle Shirtwaist Factory in 1911 was never known. But suddenly people on the eighth floor began to cry, "Fire!" Within minutes, the entire floor was a "mass of flames." Escaping workers rushed to the stairs or pushed their way into the two small elevators. The stairs, however, were soon ablaze, and the elevators stopped running.

On the tenth floor, Mary Alter was warned of the fire by telephone. Harris and Bernstein led everyone out onto the roof. People from neighboring buildings stretched ladders between the rooftops to help the workers on the roof escape.

Workers on the ninth floor had no warning. The fire just appeared. Some women died immediately. Firemen later found them as "skeletons bending over sewing machines." Those who had time to escape found themselves trapped by the locked factory door. In desperation, they rushed to the windows and began to jump.

The crowd that gathered outside the Asch Building watched in horror as girls began to fall out of the sky—"fire streaming back from their hair and dresses." Their bodies hit the pavement with sickening thuds.

Firefighters arrived quickly, but had trouble bringing their equipment close to the building because of the bodies on the pavement. Not that it mattered. There was little the firemen could do. Their ladders were not tall enough to reach beyond the sixth floor. Their safety nets were just as useless. The workers fell with such force, said one fireman, that they "went right through the life nets."

At the public funeral for the Triangle victims, garment workers marched under a banner proclaiming, "We demand fire protection." As she marched, Rose Schneiderman glanced up at the buildings lining the funeral procession. "There they were. Girls right at the top of hundreds of Buildings, looking down on us," she recalled. "The structures were no different from the Asch Building…many were in a far worse condition."

Honoring the Triangle Victims

Mourners stand shoulder to shoulder in the rain to honor the women who died in the Triangle Shirtwaist Factory fire. One hundred forty-six girls and women were killed or fell to their deaths in the preventable tragedy.

25.8 Chapter Summary

In this chapter, you read about the rapid industrialization of the United States and how this progress influenced the way average people earned their livings. You also read a detailed account of an infamous event in history—the Triangle Shirtwaist Factory fire. You used an illustration to learn about the expansion of industry and the effects of this expansion on workers.

New inventions and ideas made it possible for businesses to grow in size and efficiency. While these innovations allowed more Americans to afford manufactured items, there was a hidden price to pay. With the rise of big business through corporations, trusts, and monopolies, the wealthy got wealthier and the poor got poorer.

As cities grew, factories rose ten or more stories above the ground, and people from all over came looking for jobs. People lived in crowded, unclean, and dangerous tenement buildings. Men, women, and children worked long hours for low wages in crowded, unsafe factories. Doors were kept locked, and workers could not leave their stations without permission. Most worked in miserable conditions.

Workers didn't dare speak up for fear of losing their jobs. By joining trade unions, they could fight as a group for better wages and working conditions. When organized workers went on strike, factory owners often responded with violence or by simply hiring other workers. Unfortunately, it took the horrors of the Triangle Factory fire to make the dangers of factory life real to the American public.

In the next chapter, you will read about the many immigrants who worked in these factories and how they viewed their lives in America.

This cartoon shows the women of the Triangle Shirtwaist Factory desperately trying to open one of the few exit doors. A man dressed in a suit decorated with dollar signs holds the door closed. The cartoonist believes that the women died because of the greed of factory owners.

What might these people be thinking?

What does this statue symbolize?

26

The Great Wave of Immigration

26.1 Introduction

In the early 1880s, a young American Jew named Emma Lazarus saw a boatload of Jewish immigrants who had just arrived in New York City. The Jews crowded on the boat were fleeing a religious massacre in Russia. Inspired by their suffering, Lazarus wrote a poem in which the Statue of Liberty welcomes immigrants. The poem begins:

Give me your tired, your poor,
Your huddled masses yearning to breathe free.

In 1903, a plaque inscribed with Lazarus's poem was attached to the base of the famous statue. Her words expressed the hopes of the millions of people who made their way to the United States during a great wave of immigration between 1880 and 1920. During those 40 years, more than 23 million immigrants arrived in America. Many were escaping poverty, political violence, and religious persecution. Others came seeking economic opportunity in a land of seemingly boundless promise.

Most of the newcomers flocked to cities, where industry was booming and jobs were plentiful. The sheer number of immigrants changed the face of America. The newcomers often clustered in rapidly growing ethnic neighborhoods. In both New York and San Francisco, for example, "Little Italy" districts grew up alongside "Chinatowns."

The new arrivals spurred the growth of the nation's cities and industries. Their languages, customs, music, and food made cities like New York, Chicago, and San Francisco more diverse and exciting places. Yet many native-born Americans responded to them with suspicion and prejudice. For immigrants, these attitudes added to the challenge of starting life in a new country.

In this chapter, you will learn about the experiences and contributions of immigrant groups from around the world. You will also find out how Americans' attitudes toward immigration changed by the 1920s. Never again would the United States hold open its doors so wide to people from other lands.

Graphic Organizer: Illustration
You will use an illustration to record information about four different immigrant groups.

26.2 Immigration from Around the Globe

Patterns of immigration to the United States changed in the 1880s. Before this time, most immigrants came from northern Europe, particularly Ireland and Germany. By 1890, most were coming from countries in southern and eastern Europe, such as Italy, Greece, Russia, and Poland. Others came from China, Japan, Korea, and the Philippines. Still others crossed the borders from Canada and Mexico.

Many of these newcomers were **refugees** escaping from violence or poverty in their homelands. Compared to earlier arrivals, they tended to be poorer, less well educated, and less likely to speak English. Among them were many Jews and Catholics, as well as Buddhists and Confucianists—a major change for a country that had always been largely Protestant.

refugees people who flee their homes or countries because of war, persecution, or other causes

assimilation the process by which immigrants or other newcomers acquire the attitudes, behaviors, and cultural patterns of the society around them

Between 1880 and 1920, more than 20 million people came to the United States in search of a better life. The hardships of their journey were only the beginning of the challenges they would face as they tried to build a new life in America.

The Struggle for Acceptance Americans wondered how the throngs of immigrants would affect the country. Most favored the **assimilation** of foreign-born people into the culture of their new homeland. They expected immigrants to become "Americanized"—to talk, dress, and act like their native-born neighbors. Others believed that the new immigrants, especially nonwhites, were too "different" to be assimilated. Their prejudices were reinforced when ethnic groups clustered in their own towns or neighborhoods, in part for mutual support and in part because they were not accepted elsewhere.

In fact, many immigrants were eager to adopt American ways. Others had little choice. Public schools taught in English, and most stores sold only American-style clothes, food, and other goods. Many employers demanded that their workers speak English on the job.

Some immigrants did cling to their own language and way of life. But even those who tried hardest to assimilate often met with abuse and discrimination. Immigrants also faced resentment from workers who saw them as competing for jobs.

Contributions of Immigrants The new immigrants made vital contributions to America's rapidly industrializing society. As one historian has written, "They and their fellow workers built the railroad…mined the gold and silver…labored in the oilfields, steel mills, coal pits, packing plants, and factories…." Without the immigrants' skills and labor, the nation's cities and industries would not have grown nearly as fast as they did.

Immigrants also brought a vibrant diversity to their adopted land. America became a truly multicultural society, enriched by the customs, crafts, languages, and faiths of people from around the globe.

Geography Challenge

Immigration to the United States, 1820–1990

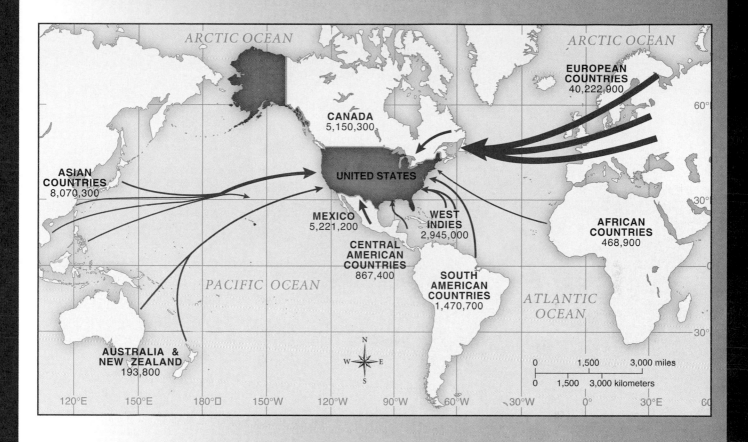

1. Identify at least four interesting details on this map.

2. What do the arrows on the map indicate?

3. Between 1820 and 1990, where did the greatest number of immigrants come from? Where did the least number of immigrants come from? How do you know?

4. Which of the arrows on the map shows where your family or ancestors came from?

5. What are or were some of the effects on the United States of the immigration patterns shown on this map?

26.3 Italian Immigrants

When Pascal D'Angelo heard that his father was leaving their poor Italian village to work overseas, he was angry. "America was stealing my father from me," he later said. His mother tried to soothe him, saying that soon Papa would return, "laden with riches." But Pascal begged his father to take him along. His father agreed, and the two of them boarded a steamship bound for the United States.

From Italy to America   Like millions of other Italians, Pascal and his father came to America to escape poverty. In the late 1800s, much of Italy, and especially mountainous southern Italy, could not support the country's rapidly growing population. Farmers struggled to eke out a living on worn-out, eroded land where crops too often failed. There were few factories to provide other jobs.

Poor immigrants like Pascal and his father usually made the ocean passage in "steerage." Steerage was a deck, deep in the ship, that was reserved for the passengers who paid the lowest fares. These passengers were given narrow beds in crowded compartments that smelled of spoiled food, human waste, and sweating people who had nowhere to bathe.

Steerage passengers were allowed on deck only once a day. The rest of the time, they tried to amuse themselves by playing games, singing, and making music with accordions, mandolins, and other instruments.

After almost two weeks, the weary travelers arrived at the immigration station on Ellis Island in New York Harbor. There they had to pass medical examinations and answer questions about how they planned to support themselves in the United States. People who did not pass these inspections could be sent home, even if other family members were allowed to enter. So many families were forced to separate that Italians started calling Ellis Island "The Island of Tears."

Millions of Italians, anxious to escape the poverty of their homeland, journeyed by ship to America. During the long voyage, they endured crowded, smelly conditions and poor food.

Starting a New Life   Judged healthy and ready to work, Pascal and his father entered New York City. A fellow Italian, a work agent called a padrone, helped them to find jobs building roads. Padrones helped many Italian immigrants get unskilled work building sewers, subways, and roads, cleaning streets, and laying bricks for new **tenement buildings**. By 1890, Italians made up 90 percent of New York's public works employees and 99 percent of Chicago's street workers.

tenement buildings
crowded and usually run-down buildings with many small, cheap apartments

Many Italian immigrants were "birds of passage"—young men who came to America to earn some money and then went back home. When several co-workers died in a work accident, Pascal's father decided to return to Italy as well. "We are not better off than when we started," he said.

Pascal, however, decided to stay in his new country. He settled in a poor Italian neighborhood in New York, one of the many "Little Italys" that sprang up in American cities. These mostly Italian neighborhoods bulged with residents who could afford only the cheapest tenement housing. Crowded together in tiny apartments, most families had no privacy. The difficulties of their new life led some immigrants to depression and despair.

Fortunately, Italian neighborhoods also offered opportunities for fun. Most Italians were Catholics who celebrated saints' days as they had in Italy. They strung colored lights, flags, and streamers along the shops and streets. Children dashed among booths that offered food and games. Fireworks, music, and dancing reminded everyone of life back home.

Above everything else, Italians valued family closeness. Some Italian parents didn't send their children to school because they feared that learning English would distance their children from the family. Besides, a child in school wasn't earning money to help the family. As a result, many immigrant children never learned the skills they needed for better jobs.

Italian immigrants often moved to "Little Italys" such as Mulberry Street in New York City, shown in the photograph. Here, rents were cheap and living conditions crowded.

Because many Italian newcomers were poor and uneducated, Americans tended to look down on them. When a few Italians turned to crime and became notorious gangsters, some people started thinking of all Italians as criminals. As a group, however, Italian immigrants were generally more law-abiding than average Americans.

Some Americans feared that immigrants from Italy would always be poor and illiterate. Pascal D'Angelo was one of many who proved them wrong. After arriving in America, Pascal bought himself a dictionary and learned to read and write English. In time, he became a well-known poet whose work was published in national magazines.

When immigrants arrived at Ellis Island, they faced the dreaded medical inspection. Those judged to be in poor health had to stay on Ellis Island until they were well. Those who never improved were sent home.

pogroms Organized and often violent persecutions of minority groups. The word *pogrom* comes from Russian words meaning "like thunder."

26.4 Jewish Immigrants from Eastern Europe

Maryusha Antonovksy was no more. In her place stood Mary Antin, the same immigrant Jewish girl but with a new, "American," name. Mary had also bought "real American machine-made garments" to replace her "hateful" homemade European-style clothes. "I long to forget," she said. "It is painful to be conscious of two worlds."

Fleeing Persecution   Mary Antin's first world had been a Jewish village in Russia. For centuries, Russians had resented Jews, who dressed, worshiped, and ate differently from their Christian neighbors. By the 1800s, Russia had hundreds of anti-Jewish laws. Jews could live only in certain areas. They couldn't live in big cities or own land.

In 1881, assassins killed the Russian monarch Czar Alexander II. Nervous government leaders blamed Jews for his murder, even though the assassin wasn't Jewish. Angry Russians raged through Jewish villages, burning, looting, and killing. These attacks, called **pogroms,** happened repeatedly for more than 30 years.

Many Jews fled these terrors, hoping to find refuge in America. Between 1881 and 1924, some 2.4 million Jews came to the United States from Russia and other countries in eastern Europe. Mary Antin's father was one of them.

Mary's father left for America in 1891, hoping to earn enough money to send for his family. In his first letter home, Mary sensed "an elation [joy], a hint of triumph…. My father was inspired by a vision. He saw something—he promised us something. It was this 'America.'"

When Antin sent a steamship ticket for his family to join him, the people in Mary's village gathered, filled with longing. "They wanted to handle the ticket," Mary remembered, "and mother must read them what is written on it."

After long rides in overcrowded trains and weeks of delay, Mary's family finally boarded a ship in Hamburg, Germany. Although richer immigrants enjoyed comfortable cabins, the Antins were crowded together with hundreds of other passengers deep down in the ship. Seasick at first, they frequently came up on deck for fresh air, where "sailors and girls had a good many dances."

Like most European immigrants, the Antins entered the United States via New York Harbor. Wealthier passengers in first-class and second-class cabins were questioned briefly before being admitted to their new country. But the majority of arrivals were taken on crowded barges to the immigration station on Ellis Island. Often they had to wait for hours while inspectors and doctors examined each person. Fortunately, most new arrivals spent less than a day on the island before proceeding to shore and the beginning of their new life in America.

Jewish Life in America   From Ellis Island, Jews headed for New York City's Lower East Side neighborhood. There they established shops, newspapers, religious schools, and synagogues (community centers and places of worship). The Lower East Side became the most densely populated neighborhood in the city. People lived packed into cheap tenements, often sleeping three or four to a room.

Some Jews worked as street vendors, using a pushcart to sell everything from coal to second-hand clothes. Pushcart vendors saved their money to buy horse-drawn carts and then little stores. Although most Jews were poor, they arrived in America with a wide range of skills. Jews worked as cobblers, butchers, carpenters, and watchmakers. Almost half found jobs in the city's garment factories.

Jewish immigrants did whatever they could to keep their children in school. In Europe, Jews had honored educated people, but schooling had cost money. As a result, many Jews had never learned to read and write. In America, Mary Antin wrote, "Education was free…. It was the one thing that [my father] was able to promise us when he sent for us: surer, safer than bread or shelter."

Immigrants were often forced to take jobs in sweatshops, such as the one shown here, where most of the work was done by women and children. Workers were usually paid 25 to 40 cents a day.

Parents who made a little money often sent their sons, and sometimes their daughters, to the city's inexpensive public colleges. By 1910, more Jewish youths over 16 were still in school than were young people of any other ethnic group.

Like other immigrant groups, Jews faced prejudice and discrimination. Most private schools and clubs refused to accept Jews. Hospitals would not hire Jewish doctors; the New York Bar Association would not admit Jews (as lawyers). Many ads for jobs stated simply, "Christians only."

Still, eastern European Jews were grateful to be in their new country. One immigrant recalled, "There were markets groaning with food and clothes…. There was no military on horseback and no whips."

Chinese immigrants were sometimes detained for several months on Angel Island before they were allowed to enter the United States. In their crowded barracks, some carved poems on the wooden walls, expressing despair over their condition.

26.5 Chinese Immigrants

As you read in earlier chapters, the first Chinese immigrants came to the United States to seek gold in California. Later, many helped to build the first transcontinental railroad. Some of these immigrants returned to China with money they had made in America. Their good fortune inspired Lee Chew to leave his poor village for the United States in 1882.

Traveling to California Lee paid 50 dollars for a bunk on a crowded steamship making the month-long voyage to San Francisco. On the ship, he got his first taste of foreign food and marveled at machinery he had never seen before. "The engines that moved the ship were wonderful monsters," he wrote, "strong enough to lift mountains."

Lee arrived just in time. In the United States, anti-Chinese sentiment (feeling) had been building ever since whites had pushed Chinese off their mining claims. As the number of Chinese immigrants increased, labor leaders warned of hordes of Chinese workers who would work for less pay than whites and take away their jobs. In 1882, Congress passed an Exclusion Act that banned Chinese laborers from immigrating to the United States. The law also denied Chinese immigrants the right to become citizens.

As a result of the Chinese Exclusion Act, Chinese immigration slowed to almost nothing. Then, in 1906, an earthquake and fire destroyed much of San Francisco, including most birth records. Suddenly, many Chinese men could claim to be native-born citizens. As citizens, they were allowed to bring their wives and children to the United States.

Chinese claiming American birth started arranging for people in China to immigrate to the United States as their relatives. On the long ship voyage, the newcomers studied hundreds of pages describing their "families." When they reached San Francisco Bay, they threw the papers overboard.

These "paper relatives" landed at Angel Island in San Francisco Bay. Government immigration officials "locked us up like criminals in compartments like the cages in zoos," said one Chinese immigrant. Chinese usually remained on the island for three to four weeks, but sometimes they spent months or even years there. To pass the time, they carved poems on the wooden walls with silverware smuggled from the dining halls. One wrote,

Why do I have to sit in jail? It is only because my country is weak and my family is poor. My parents wait at the door in vain for news. My wife and child wrap themselves in their quilt, sighing with loneliness.

Before being allowed to leave the island, each immigrant faced detailed questioning by suspicious officials. "How many steps are there in your house?" "Where do you sleep in your house?" "Who lives next door?" Then they asked a "family" witness from San Francisco the same questions. If the answers didn't match, officials could deport the newcomer. Nearly one in ten Chinese who came to America was sent back to China.

Chinese Life in the United States   When Lee Chew arrived, he worked first as a servant, and then set up his own laundry. Many Chinese started laundries because, as Lee explained, "It requires little capital [money] and is one of the few opportunities that are open. Men of other nationalities who are jealous of the Chinese…have shut him out of working on farms or in factories or building railroads."

Like Lee, most Chinese settled in city neighborhoods like San Francisco's bustling Chinatown. Here, they could find work at Chinese laundries, restaurants, and stores. Chinese newspapers, herbal medicines, foods, and festivals provided comfort and support.

For many years, most Chinese immigrants were men. In 1900, only about 1 in 20 Chinese on the United States mainland was female. With so few women and families, the Chinese population in America began to decline. In 1880, about 105,000 Chinese lived in the United States. By 1920, just 61,600 remained.

Gradually, more women and children arrived, especially in San Francisco. Housing was closed to Chinese in most areas, so Chinatown became more and more crowded.

For white Americans, Chinatown became a tourist attraction, a "mysterious" place to see "strange faces" and eat new foods. To most Chinese immigrants, however, Chinatown was home.

Chinese immigrants settled in Chinatowns like this one in San Francisco. There they preserved the culture they had left behind.

By 1900, railroad lines linked the United States and Mexico. Trains provided convenient transportation for Mexicans, who were free to enter the United States without passports.

passport a document issued by a citizen's home government that identifies a person and permits him or her to travel to other countries

26.6 Mexican Immigrants

Soldiers were shooting all around. A flying bullet almost hit him. That was when Pablo Mares decided he had to get out of Mexico. "I had to come to the United States," he said later, "because it was impossible to live down there with so many revolutions."

Mares had been caught in the middle of a bloody civil war. The conflict began when Mexico's president allowed wealthy landowners to take over the lands of 6 million Indians and 8 million poor farmers. In 1910, landless farmers rebelled, breaking up large landholdings and giving the land to poor families. In response, soldiers attacked villages, killing thousands of peasants.

Crossing the Border   The Mexican Revolution dragged on for 10 terrible years. Between 1910 and 1920, about 500,000 Mexicans entered the United States. They entered freely, without **passports** or money.

Many Mexicans walked hundreds of miles to reach the border, carrying all they owned on their backs. In just one day, a Texas reporter saw "hundreds of Mexicans, all journeying northward on foot, on burroback and in primitive two-wheel carts." Others traveled north by rail. By 1900, railroad lines connected American and Mexican cities. Railroads provided both transportation and jobs for Mexican immigrants. One Mexican newspaper reported, "There is not a day in which passenger trains do not leave for the border, full of Mexican men who are going in gangs to work on railroad lines in the United States."

Mexicans in America   Many American employers welcomed the Mexicans. Expanding railroads and large-scale farms and ranches in the Southwest depended on laborers who were willing to work hard for little pay. After Congress banned Chinese immigration in 1882, these employers looked to Mexico for new workers. "Where I came from," said one Mexican construction worker, "I used to work ten hours for $1.25.... Then I came here and they paid $1.25 for eight hours—it was good."

Some Mexican immigrants found jobs with railroads, mines, factories, and canneries. But most found work in agriculture. Mexican farmworkers moved from region to region, harvesting crops as they ripened. They picked oranges in southern California, almonds in central California, and then apples in Oregon. They harvested cotton in Texas and Arizona, and then moved on to sugar beets in Colorado.

Farmwork paid very little. One Texas farmer said, "I was paying Pancho and his whole family 60 cents a day.... He worked from sun to sun." Children worked in the fields beside their parents to help support their families. Few of these children had a chance to attend school.

Farmworkers often lived in camps that they built near the fields. "Shelters were made of almost every conceivable thing—burlap, canvas, palm branches," said one visitor. Some farms and ranches provided housing for their workers. Either way, these temporary homes usually lacked running water and basic sanitation.

After harvest season, farmworkers sometimes moved to nearby towns. *Barrios,* or Mexican neighborhoods, sprang up on the edges of cities near such farming areas as Los Angeles, California, and San Antonio, Texas. Food stands and grocery stores in the barrio offered familiar tastes and smells. Residents helped each other take care of the sick and find jobs. On Mexican religious holidays, Catholic churches held special ceremonies. On those days, the barrio was filled with singing, dancing, and fireworks.

Many Mexican immigrants originally planned to return to Mexico once the revolution was over. Whites who believed that Mexicans were taking their jobs encouraged such returns. One wrote, "I wish the Mexicans could be put back in their country."

Mexicans who remained in the United States often faced strong prejudice. Compared to whites, they earned very low wages, and they had little say in their working conditions. In schools, white children were sometimes taught to "boss" their Mexican classmates, as they were expected to do when they grew up.

Despite these problems, many Mexican immigrants chose to stay. Like Isidro Osorio, a farm and railroad worker, they hoped for a better future in their new homeland. "I have worked very hard to earn my $4.00 a day," reported Osorio. "That is why I want to give a little schooling to my children so that they won't stay like I am."

Some Mexicans, such as those in this photograph, found jobs in mines. Most, however, were employed as agricultural workers.

Immigrants like the Chinese man in the cartoon above often faced discrimination and lack of acceptance in their new country.

nativism an attitude of superiority and resentment toward the foreign-born.

quota a limit based on numbers or proportions—for example, the proportion of a country's population allowed to immigrate to the United States

visas government documents that allow people from other nations to enter the country for a limited period of time

26.7 Closing the Door on Immigration

In 1920, a mob stormed through the Italian neighborhood of West Frankfort, a small Illinois town. The crowd was frustrated by a mining strike and angered by bank robberies that Italian criminals were rumored to have committed. For three days, mobs beat up Italian immigrants and burned their homes. This attack reflected a surge of **nativism,** or anti-immigrant feeling, that peaked in the United States around this time.

The Tide Turns Against Immigrants The United States has always been a nation of immigrants, yet time and again nativism has sparked actions and policies directed against newer arrivals. Sometimes nativism is rooted in economic competition. Sometimes it stems from ethnic, religious, and other differences. In the 1830s, for example, Protestant nativists charged that Catholic immigrants were enemies of democracy because they owed their primary loyalty to the Pope in Rome.

The surge in immigration that began in the 1880s fueled another rise in nativism. Native-born Americans blamed immigrants for everything from slums and crime to hard times. Fearing competition for jobs, many labor leaders stoked the fires of prejudice, especially against nonwhites. In 1909, the president of the United Mine Workers wrote of Asians that "as a race their standard of living is extremely low, and their assimilation by Americans impossible."

Restricting Immigration Politicians responded to the growing clamor against immigrants. As you have read, in 1882 Congress banned further immigration by Chinese laborers. In 1907, Japanese immigrants were forbidden entry to the United States. In 1917, Congress required immigrants to prove that they could read and write before they would be allowed into the United States.

To further limit immigration, Congress established a **quota** system in 1921 and refined it in 1924. Under this system, by 1927 only 150,000 immigrants were allowed to enter the United States each year. East Asians were completely excluded. In addition, quotas limited immigration from any one country to 2 percent of the number of people from that country who lived in the United States in 1890. Most eastern and southern Europeans had arrived after that year. As a result, most of the quota spaces were reserved for immigrants from England, Ireland, and Germany.

The new laws did not limit Mexican immigration. However, Mexicans now needed passports and **visas** to enter the United States. For the first time, America was closing its doors.

26.8 Chapter Summary

In this chapter, you read about the great wave of immigration to the United States between 1880 and 1920. You used an illustration to learn about the experiences of four immigrant groups from around the world who built new lives in America.

The immigrants of this period were far more diverse than earlier arrivals. Many were escaping from poverty, wars, or persecution. Others were drawn to America by the promise of economic opportunity. With their skills and labor, these new immigrants helped build the nation's booming cities and industries. But they also faced many challenges, including the tension between assimilation and preserving their way of life.

Each group of immigrants faced its own challenges in journeying to America. Once they arrived, most had to pass inspection at immigration stations like those on Ellis Island in New York Harbor and Angel Island in San Francisco Bay. There they could be denied entry and sent home.

The immigrants who did enter the country often experienced prejudice and discrimination. In cities, they crowded into their own neighborhoods and worked at lower-paying jobs. In the West and the Southwest, Mexican farmworkers labored long hours in the fields and followed the crops from region to region.

In the 1920s, anti-immigrant feeling led Congress to limit the number of people who would be allowed into the United States. These immigration-restriction laws brought an end to the great wave of immigration. But by then, the United States had become a far more diverse country. Only time would tell whether Americans would embrace this diversity and extend the promise of equal opportunity to all the nation's people.

The great wave of immigration during the late 19th century created a nation of rich, diverse cultures. People from many backgrounds came together and became Americans. In this photograph, a mix of immigrants are in class together learning English.

What does the scientist think he will find as he tests the milk and the sugar?

The Progressive Era

27.1 Introduction

"The men who start the great new movements in the world are enthusiasts," said Sam McClure at his college graduation, "whose eyes are fixed upon the end they wish to bring about."

Some of his fellow students may have brushed off McClure's words as mere speech making. They shouldn't have. This immigrant from Ireland was serious about starting "great new movements." And he had just the enthusiasm to do it. But how?

McClure's answer was to start a journal called *McClure's Magazine*. McClure prided himself on knowing what people wanted to read about. "If I like a thing," he said, "then I know that millions will like it."

In 1900, McClure decided that Americans wanted to know the truth about trusts, those giant business monopolies that worked to reduce competition. He hired a reporter named Ida Tarbell to write a history of one of the biggest trusts—John D. Rockfeller's Standard Oil. McClure ran Tarbell's report as a serial, printing one part at a time in issue after issue. The report told about unfair pricing putting Standard Oil's competitors out of business. McClure's popularity soared.

McClure began hiring more journalists to uncover the truth about other evils in America. Some people called his journalists *muckrakers* because they spent so much effort stirring up dirt and filth. Writers like Tarbell adopted this name with pride.

McClure and his muckrakers were part of a larger reform effort known as the **Progressive movement.** Looking back at the century just ended, Progressives could see great progress. Slavery had ended. The United States had become an industrial giant. Still, huge problems remained to be solved.

Progressives did not work as a single group. Some fought railroad monopolies, while others marched with child factory workers. Some worked for equal rights for African Americans, and others to protect forests. Whatever their cause, most Progressives wanted government to play a larger role in helping to cure the nation's ills. And all of them believed that ordinary people could start "great new movements" that would improve American life.

Graphic Organizer: Panel of Historical Figures
You will use this panel to help you understand the views and work of social leaders during this time.

27.2 Sowing the Seeds of Reform

The Progressives of the early 20th century rebelled against economic and social injustice, the power of big business, and political corruption. But they were not the first to criticize these conditions and propose far-reaching reforms.

As you have learned, industrialization began remaking American society shortly after the Civil War. To some, the rise of big industry meant endless progress and prosperity. Others, however, felt left behind. As early as the 1870s, some of these "have-nots" began organizing mass movements to work for political and social change. These **populist** revolts sowed the seeds of Progressive reform.

The Farmers Revolt Organized protest against the power of big business began on the farms of the Midwest. After the Civil War, many midwestern farmers were caught between rising costs and falling prices for their crops. Farmers felt victimized. Banks made it hard for people to get cash loans to keep their farms going in lean times. Railroads and grain storage companies charged high rates to transport and store crops. And merchants paid too little for what farmers produced.

In 1867, Oliver Kelley, a clerk in the U.S. Department of Agriculture, began organizing self-help clubs for farmers called Granges. The movement spread rapidly through the Midwest. By the mid 1870s, the Grange had grown into a political force. Farmers used the Grange to protest unfair practices by the railroads. Grangers banded together to negotiate better prices and started their own banks. They campaigned for political candidates and worked for reforms such as an income tax and laws against trusts.

populist devoted to the needs and interests of common people

In the 1870s, angry farmers attacked the power of the railroads to set whatever rates they wanted. This cartoon shows wealthy "rail barons" carving up the country for their own profit.

Pressure from the Grangers led some states to pass laws that limited railroad shipping rates and prices for grain storage. Big businesses protested this interference with their "rights." In 1877, the U.S. Supreme Court sided with the Grangers. In a series of cases, the Court ruled that states had the right to regulate private property when it is used in the public interest. The Grangers had won a key victory for the idea that government had a responsibility to help protect the common good.

Membership in the Granges dropped in the 1880s as conditions improved for midwestern farmers. The farmers' revolt continued, however, in the South and West, where organizations called Farmers' Alliances took up the cause of reform.

The Farmers' Alliances angrily challenged the influence of eastern bankers and industrialists. A favorite target was Wall Street in New York City, the nation's financial capital. Mary Elizabeth Lease of Kansas charged:

> *It is no longer a government of the people, by the people, and for the people, but a government of Wall Street, by Wall Street, and for Wall Street. The great common people of this country are slaves and monopoly is the master.*

The People's Party In the 1890s, the Farmers' Alliances took the lead in forming a new People's Party (often called the Populist Party). The party's leaders hoped to forge an alliance between farmers and industrial workers. Such a mass movement, they believed, could break the power of big business to dictate government policy.

In 1892, the People's Party adopted a **platform** calling for such reforms as an eight-hour working day and government ownership of railroads. That fall, Populist candidates won election to hundreds of state and local offices. The Populist candidate for president, James B. Weaver of Iowa, received over a million votes, winning six of the Mountain and Plains states. But that was the high point for the People's Party.

Four years later, the Democratic Party adopted some Populist ideas as part of its platform. The Populists decided to support the Democratic presidential candidate, William Jennings Bryan. The Republican candidate, William McKinley, drew heavy support from business and financial interests. The battle lines were drawn between eastern capitalists and the reform-minded farmers of the South and West.

McKinley won the election handily. His victory was a triumph for those who were opposed to radical change. The People's Party, which had lost its identity after fusing with the Democrats, soon dissolved.

For the moment, big business and its allies reigned supreme. It would be up to other reformers to continue the fight begun by the Grangers and the Populists.

Wealthy industrialists gave huge sums of money to help elect Republican William McKinley to the presidency in 1896.

platform a statement of the policies favored by a political party

The Granger Collection, New York

Andrew Carnegie made a huge fortune in the steel industry. When he retired, he began to give away most of his money. Here we see him carrying libraries like gifts, symbolizing the money he gave to thousands of communities for libraries.

27.3 Andrew Carnegie and John D. Rockefeller: Captains of Industry

When business leaders like Andrew Carnegie and John D. Rockefeller looked at the United States in 1900, they saw progress everywhere. Railroads linked towns and cities across the nation. The increased ease of delivering goods by rail had nourished countless new industries, including their own. Both men were proud to be "captains of industry," leading the way in this growth. "Mere money-making has never been my goal," wrote Rockefeller. "I had an ambition to build."

Industry Brings Progress   New industries meant more jobs for a growing nation. With immigrants pouring into the country, the population of the United States tripled between 1850 and 1900. Every new factory or mill created jobs for the newcomers. Carnegie Steel alone employed more than 20,000 workers, many of them immigrants.

The nation's new industries turned out a wealth of new products at prices ordinary Americans could afford. "The home of the laboring man in our day boasts luxuries which even in the palaces of monarchs as recent as Queen Elizabeth were unknown," wrote Carnegie. "What were luxuries for some," he noted, "are now necessities for all."

The Benefits of Bigness   What made such progress possible? The growth of big business, answered the captains of industry! Only big business enterprises could deliver quality goods at prices everyone could afford. As Carnegie explained in an article defending big business to its critics:

> [The] cheapness [of goods] is in proportion to the scale of production…. The larger the scale of operation the cheaper the product…. Instead of attempting to restrict [bigness], we should hail every increase as something to be gained, not for the few rich, but for the millions of poor.

Bigness, in Carnegie's view, was the inevitable result of competition. When many small companies compete in the same industry, some are more likely to do well than others. Those that are run most efficiently will thrive from competition and grow larger. Those that are not well run will perish. "The law of competition," Carnegie argued, "may be sometimes hard for the individual, [but] it is best for the race, because it ensures the survival of the fittest in every department."

When Carnegie wrote about "the law of competition" in business, he was borrowing an idea from the British naturalist Charles Darwin. Darwin had observed that, in nature, animals and plants compete for food and living space. Those that are best adapted to their environments are the most likely to survive. This idea was popularized as "survival of the fittest."

Before long, some people began to apply Darwin's idea to human society. The result was **Social Darwinism**. According to this theory, people and societies competed for survival just as plants and animals did. The most fit became wealthy and successful. The least fit struggled just to survive.

Social Darwinism seemed to provide a "scientific" justification for huge differences in people's wealth and power. It also lent support to the idea of laissez-faire. Let businesses compete without restraint, argued corporate leaders. Then the best possible economy will emerge naturally. By this line of thinking, it was misguided for government to try to correct such problems as child labor, poor working conditions, or cutthroat business practices.

Giving Away Wealth   In 1901, Carnegie sold his steel company for $250 million. Then he retired to devote his life to philanthropy, or generosity to charities. Rich people, he believed, have a responsibility to use their wealth to help others. "The man who dies rich," he wrote, "dies disgraced."

Carnegie used his wealth to build concert halls, universities, and hospitals. Most of all, he loved building libraries. A library, he said, "outranks any other one thing that a community can do to benefit its people." Before 1880, few Americans had access to free public libraries. Just one generation later, 35 million people a day were using libraries that Carnegie had helped to build.

"Your example will bear fruits," Rockefeller wrote to Carnegie. "The time will come when men of wealth will more generally be willing to use it for the good of others."

Rockefeller used his own fortune to fund universities, medical research, the arts, and education for all. During his lifetime, he contributed about $182 million to the Rockefeller Foundation, a charitable organization he established to promote "the well-being of mankind throughout the world."

Social Darwinism the idea that people and societies compete for survival, with the fit becoming wealthy and successful while the weak struggle to survive

John D. Rockefeller's Standard Oil Company controlled 90% of the oil refined in the United States at the turn of the century. His business methods were deemed ruthless by his critics and brilliant by his supporters.

27.4 Theodore Roosevelt: Trust-Busting President

Not everyone admired big business the way Rockefeller and Carnegie did. Many thought big businesses took unfair advantage of workers and consumers. In 1890, Congress passed the Sherman Antitrust Act to outlaw any form of business monopoly. The law was so vague and big business so powerful, however, that for years the law was not enforced. The Sherman Antitrust Act got its first real test only after Theodore Roosevelt became president in 1901.

Breaking a Railroad Trust Roosevelt came into the White House with a reputation as a reformer. As president, he attacked business monopolies with great energy. "We do not want to destroy corporations," he assured the public, "but we do wish to make them [serve] the public good."

Roosevelt's first target was a railroad monopoly called the Northern Securities Company. This company controlled nearly every rail line between Chicago and the Pacific Northwest. Roosevelt had the Justice Department sue Northern Securities for violating the Sherman Antitrust Act. The justices of the Supreme Court ordered the monopoly to be broken up into smaller railroad companies.

"Trust-busting" Teddy Roosevelt is shown here vigorously shaking the railroad trust. Roosevelt tried to break up monopolistic trusts in order to make American business fair for all.

Trust-Busting Expands Just after Roosevelt filed suit against Northern Securities, *McClure's Magazine* began publishing Ida Tarbell's history of the Standard Oil Trust. In her report, Tarbell documented how Rockefeller had driven his competitors out of business. She told about secret deals he had made with railroads to ship his oil at lower prices than other oil companies paid. She explained how Rockefeller had cut his oil prices below what the oil cost to produce. This attracted customers away from other oil companies. After his competitors went out of business, he raised prices again.

A shocked public demanded action. Roosevelt filed suit against not only Standard Oil, but against 44 other trusts as well. In 1911, Standard Oil was "busted"—broken up into five major oil companies and several smaller ones.

Roosevelt thought that government **regulation,** or enforcement of laws, was a good long-term solution to bad business behavior. "The great development of industrialism," he said, "means that there must be an increase in the supervision exercised by the Government over business enterprise."

27.5 Robert La Follette: Fighter for Political Reform

In 1890, Robert La Follette of Wisconsin ran for reelection to Congress and lost. Still a young man, he returned to his work as a laywer. Then something happened. Senator Philetus Sawyer, a powerful Republican Party boss, offered La Follette a bribe to "fix" a court case. Sawyer thought that he could pay La Follette to guarantee that he would win the case. An insulted La Follette reported the bribery attempt to the newspapers.

An equally insulted Sawyer decided to crush La Follette. But "Battling Bob" was not an easy man to put down. Sawyer had made him so mad that La Follette decided to run for governor of Wisconsin. As governor, he could put the party bosses out of business.

In Wisconsin and other states, political machines, or groups run by party bosses, controlled local and state governments. To make sure that their candidates were elected, corrupt bosses were known to bribe voters and "stuff" ballot boxes with fake votes.

Thus, the bosses, not the people, chose each party's candidates for office. The candidates, men like lumber millionaire Sawyer, usually represented powerful business interests. Without the party's support, upstart reformers like La Follette had little chance of reaching voters. La Follette was defeated twice by Wisconsin's powerful Republican "machine," but finally won election as governor in 1900.

Once elected, La Follette pushed reforms that put the people in charge of politics. Wisconsin became the first state to adopt the direct primary. This election system allowed party members, not bosses, to chose party candidates. By 1916, over half the states had adopted the "Wisconsin Idea." With the people choosing their leaders in primary elections, reform governors swept into office across the nation.

Oregon introduced three other reforms that put political power into the hands of the people. The *initiative* allowed citizens to enact laws by a popular vote. The *referendum* allowed voters to overturn an existing law. The *recall* allowed voters to remove an elected official from office.

What all these reforms had in common, wrote La Follette, was a belief that each state could become a place where "the opportunities of all its people are more equal... [and] human life is safer and sweeter."

Party bosses controlled the American political system through a corrupt system of bribery. Reformers like Robert La Follette sought to take power out of the hands of the bosses and return it to the people.

27.6 Mother Jones: Champion of Workers' Rights

In 1903, labor leader Mary Harris Jones—known as Mother Jones—went to Pennsylvania to support a strike by 75,000 textile workers. About 10,000 of the strikers were children. Jones wrote of these young workers:

> *Every day little children came into Union Headquarters, some with their hands off, some with the thumb missing, some with their fingers off at the knuckle. They were stooped little things, round shouldered and skinny. Many of them were not over ten years of age.*

Child Labor Laws   The situation Mother Jones found in Pennsylvania was not unusual. In the early 1900s, more than 1 million children under the age of 16 worked in mines and factories for up to 13 hours a day. To publicize their plight, Jones led a "March of the Mill Children" from Pennsylvania all the way to Oyster Bay, New York, to petition President Roosevelt to support child labor laws.

The children's march prompted stories and photographs of child workers in newspapers and magazines. Across the country, reformers demanded an end to child labor. Employers claimed that abolishing child labor would produce "a nation of sissies." But, by 1909, 43 states had passed laws that outlawed the hiring of children.

Improving Working Conditions   Progressive reformers also worked to improve the lives of adult workers. In 1903, for example, Oregon passed a law that limited women workers to a ten-hour workday. Maryland set up a program to assist workers who had been injured on the job.

New York responded to the tragic 1911 Triangle Shirtwaist Factory fire by setting up a state committee to investigate conditions in factories. Based on the committee's work, the state legislature passed 56 worker-protection laws. Many of these laws called for improvements in factory safety. One permitted women workers to take pregnancy leaves. (A *leave* is time away from work.) Another required employers to provide garment workers with chairs that had backs, rather than simple stools.

Mother Jones saw progress for the worker in such reforms. "Slowly his hours are shortened, giving him leisure to read and to think," she wrote. "Slowly the cause of his children becomes the cause of all."

At the turn of the century, school-age children worked long hours for meager wages in America's mines and factories.

27.7 John Muir: Protector of the Environment

John Muir was so clever with machines that he might have been a great inventor. But one day in 1867, a file slipped from his hand and hit him in the eye. This accident sent Muir's life down a different path. After recovering from his injury, Muir decided to spend his life roaming wild places. "I might have been a millionaire," he said. "I chose to become a tramp."

Muir found his wilderness home in Yosemite Valley, a place of great natural beauty in California's Sierra Nevada mountains. "God seems to be doing his best here," he wrote of Yosemite.

Humans, in contrast, seemed to be doing their worst. Loggers were felling Yosemite's ancient redwood trees. Herds of sheep were stripping its meadows and hillsides bare. "To let sheep trample so divinely fine a place seems barbarous!" wrote Muir.

Theodore Roosevelt and John Muir are pictured high on a cliff in Yosemite National Park. Muir (on the right) founded the Sierra Club, an organization committed to the preservation of the environment.

Yosemite was not the only wild place threatened by human activity. Rapid industrial growth and urbanization were causing massive environmental changes. Loggers were felling the nation's forests at an alarming rate. Miners were scarring mountains and polluting rivers. Many species of birds and animals were near extinction or already lost forever.

Concerns over such changes had given birth to a small but growing **conservation** movement. Some conservationists worried most about dwindling natural resources. They advocated careful development of the wilderness. Others, like Muir, wanted to preserve wonders like Yosemite in their natural state.

To rally the public to his cause, Muir started publishing articles urging the passage of laws to protect wilderness. By 1890, his writings had attracted enough support to convince Congress to create Yosemite National Park.

Conservationists found an ally in President Theodore Roosevelt. While Roosevelt was in office, he increased the amount of land set aside as national forest from 47 million to 195 million acres. He also doubled the number of national parks. To Muir's delight, the president also prohibited logging and ranching in Yosemite and other national parks.

"Wilderness is a necessity," said Muir. "Mountain parks and reservations are useful not only as fountains of timber and irrigating rivers, but as fountains of life."

conservation the effort to protect something valuable from being destroyed or used up

In 1917, the NAACP, which W. E. B. Du Bois helped form, organized this silent protest parade against lynching.

27.8 W. E. B. Du Bois: Spokesman for Equal Rights

In 1897, a black sociologist named W. E. B. Du Bois joined the faculty of Atlanta University. His plan was to study social problems "in the light of the best scientific research."

Everywhere he looked, Du Bois saw the terrible effects of racism on African Americans. In the South, Jim Crow laws segregated schools, trains, parks, and other public places. These laws also banned blacks from voting in most states. Blacks in the North were not legally segregated, but they still faced discrimination, particularly in housing and jobs.

African Americans who fought these injustices risked being lynched, or brutally attacked and killed. Between 1892 and 1903, almost 3,000 African Americans were lynched across the South. "One could not be a calm, cool, and detached scientist," Du Bois found, "while Negroes were lynched, murdered, and starved."

Du Bois wanted to do something, but what? Booker T. Washington, the best-known black leader of that time, advised African Americans to make the best of segregation. Washington was a former slave who had founded Tuskegee Institute, a vocational school for blacks. He believed that job skills for African Americans would lead to economic progress and eventual acceptance. "The wisest among my race understand that the agitation of questions of social equality is the extremest folly," he said.

Du Bois could not accept such thinking. In 1905, he gathered influential African Americans at Niagara Falls to push directly for voting rights. He wanted to see an end to discrimination, or unfair treatment based on race. "We want the Constitution of the country enforced," they declared. "We are men! We will be treated as men."

This group, known as the Niagara Movement, continued to meet each year. In 1909, they joined a group of white reformers who were also dissatisfied with Booker T. Washington's cautious approach. Together, they formed the National Association for the Advancement of Colored People (NAACP). The new organization pledged to work for equal rights and opportunities for all African Americans. By 1920, the NAACP had over 90,000 members. Their goal was to make 11 million African Americans "physically free from peonage [servitude], mentally free from ignorance, politically free from disenfranchisement [denial of rights], and socially free from insult."

27.9 Upton Sinclair: Truth Writer

When Upton Sinclair wrote a novel about the horrors of slavery, few people bought it. Then a publisher asked if Sinclair would write a book about factory workers who were treated like slaves. Sinclair jumped at the chance. Workers at a Chicago meatpacking plant had just been brutally defeated in a labor dispute. Sinclair would write about them.

Meatpacking Horrors   In 1900, Chicago was the home of the nation's biggest meatpacking companies. Disguised as a worker, Sinclair spent seven weeks in the slaughterhouses. There he observed how cattle and hogs became steaks and sausages. He observed employees with missing thumbs, and fingers eaten away by acid. He heard stories of deadly falls into cooking vats.

Based on his research, Sinclair wrote a tragic story of poor immigrants trapped in poverty by greedy meatpackers. In his novel *The Jungle,* he described the horrors of the meatpacking plants in great detail. He told of sick animals being processed into food. He described sausage made from old, rotten meat mixed with everything from sawdust to rodents. "Rats were nuisances," he wrote, "and the packers would put poisoned bread out for them; they would die, and then rats, bread, and meat would go into the hoppers together."

The Jungle became America's biggest bestseller since *Uncle Tom's Cabin.* But readers were more upset about the contents of their sausage than the treatment of the "wage slaves." "I aimed at the public's heart," said Sinclair, "and by accident I hit it in the stomach."

Safer Food and Drugs   After reading *The Jungle,* President Roosevelt ordered an investigation of the meatpacking industry. When his investigators confirmed that conditions were as bad as Sinclair had claimed, Congress passed the Meat Inspection Act. This set health standards for meatpacking and ordered federal inspection of meat.

Other muckrakers revealed similar problems in the food-canning and drug industries. Congress passed the Pure Food and Drug Act. This law requires manufacturers to use safe ingredients in their products and to advertise them truthfully. Future decades would bring more laws protecting American consumers.

Upton Sinclair shocked readers with his description of conditions inside meatpacking plants such as this one. The unsanitary conditions prompted the government to begin meat inspections.

27.10 Alice Paul: Heroine of Women's Rights

By 1900, women had won their fight for **suffrage,** or the right to vote, in four western states. Elsewhere, the drive for voting rights seemed stalled. The Progressive movement, however, breathed new life into the campaign begun at Seneca Falls in 1848. Many Progressives believed that their reforms would be adopted more quickly if women had the right to vote.

A New Suffrage Movement   In 1916, a young reformer named Alice Paul formed what came to be known as the National Woman's Party. Older women's groups had worked to win the right to vote state by state. Paul and her supporters were determined to win the vote by a constitutional amendment.

To build momentum for a suffrage amendment, Paul organized a parade in Washington, D.C. More than 5,000 women marched amidst jeers and insults from onlookers. Newspapers applauded the courage of the "suffragettes," as the activists came to be known.

Women across the country made banners, marched, and banded together to demand the right to vote.

Passing the Nineteenth Amendment   By 1918, women could vote in 12 states, but they had made little progress on the suffrage amendment. The Woman's Party began holding silent vigils outside the White House. The protesters held banners that read, "Mr. President, What Will You Do for Woman Suffrage?" and "How Long Must Women Wait for Liberty?"

Police arrested 200 women for blocking the sidewalk. While in jail, Paul and her supporters went on a hunger strike. When the jailers tried to force-feed them, the public became enraged. The women were released to a hero's welcome.

Less than two months later, a suffrage amendment was approved by the House of Representatives by just one vote more than the two-thirds majority required. The amendment had been introduced by Jeanette Rankin of Montana, the first woman elected to Congress. Senate approval took another 18 months. The states finally ratified the Nineteenth Amendment on August 26, 1920. That year, women across the country voted in their first national election.

Paul went on to draft another amendment guaranteeing equal rights to women. "I never doubted that equal rights was the right direction," she said, even though the amendment was never ratified. "Most reforms, most problems are complicated. But to me there is nothing complicated about ordinary equality."

27.11 Chapter Summary

In this chapter, you learned about the Progressive movement of the early 20th century. You used a panel of historical figures to help understand the views and work of social leaders during this time.

As early as the 1870s, farmers had organized in protest against government's laissez-faire policies and the growing power of big business. The Granger and Populist movements championed the cause of the "common man." Their ideas helped sow the seeds of Progressive reform.

To men of industry like Rockefeller and Carnegie, calls for reform were misguided. All of America, they argued, had benefited from industrialization. They saw a country that was growing in wealth. Ordinary Americans enjoyed luxuries that were unheard of just a short time before.

Progressives agreed that many industrial advances were good for the country. But they also saw continuing problems in American society. They used newspapers, magazines, and books to draw attention to such issues as child labor, fair business practices, conservation, and equal rights. Government regulation, they said, was needed to soften the negative effects of the industrial age.

Progressives fought for many different causes, such as the rights of workers, women, African Americans, and consumers. Their efforts convinced many people that government had a role to play in correcting social problems.

The work of Progressives gave hope for a better future for millions of Americans. In the next chapter, you will read about how America's successes helped the country to become a powerful world leader.

The Progressive Era was characterized by a spirit of reform. Americans faced a host of serious problems and tried to correct them. Did they succeed, or are some of the problems still evident today?

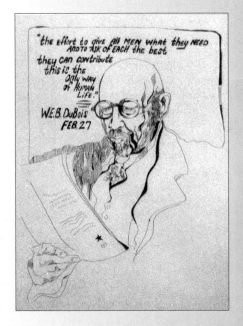

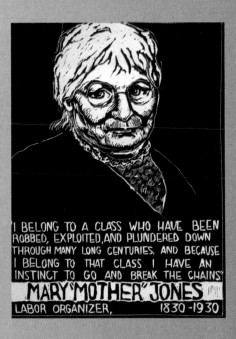

How would you describe the expression on the eagle's face?

Why is the American flag placed here?

CHAPTER

28

America Becomes a World Power

28.1 Introduction

William McKinley owed Theodore Roosevelt a big favor. Roosevelt had just helped him get elected president. The fiery Roosevelt had spoken all over America in 1896, promoting McKinley's support of business and industry. With energy and inspiration, he attacked the supporters of McKinley's opponent, like farmers and workers who felt left out of industry's great profits. These opponents, Roosevelt cried, planned nothing less than "revolution."

Now Roosevelt wanted McKinley to appoint him to be assistant secretary of the navy. McKinley, who favored peace, feared that Roosevelt was too warlike. Still, he gave Roosevelt the job. As he took office, Roosevelt said, "No triumph of peace is quite so great as the supreme triumphs of war.... It is through strife, or the readiness for strife, that a nation must win greatness."

Some newspapers called Roosevelt patriotic. Others worried that he would push the country into war. Americans had mixed feelings about getting involved in international affairs. Expanding across the continent had given America enough territory to move into for decades. Recovery from the Civil War, followed by industrial expansion, had also given Americans plenty to focus on at home.

Now, the West was more settled, and the United States had become an industrial and agricultural leader. To keep the economy growing, business leaders wanted overseas markets. Seeing European countries controlling foreign lands, they didn't want to be left out. The national pride that had inspired Manifest Destiny was calling for new challenges.

Roosevelt agreed. He allied himself with American **expansionists**—people who wanted to extend the nation's power within the Western Hemisphere and around the world. In this chapter, you will learn how the expansionists achieved their goals. As it flexed its muscles overseas, the United States acquired new territories and became a world power. Before long, it would be drawn into a global war—and a difficult struggle to restore the peace.

Graphic Organizer: Front Page Headline
You will use this front page headline to summarize key information about U.S. foreign policy from the late 1800s to 1920.

399

imperialism the policy of extending a nation's power by gaining political and economic control over other countries

28.2 America Stretches Its Wings

In 1867, Secretary of State William Seward arranged for the United States to purchase Alaska from Russia. At the time, few people thought that acquiring this vast wilderness was a good idea. Even at a price of just two cents an acre, many labeled the deal "Seward's Folly."

But the "arctic wasteland" turned out to have thick forests, plentiful fish and wildlife, and mild coastal climates. Eventually settlers would discover gold, copper, coal, and other minerals there. With such potential treasures at stake, expansionists felt that America should gain control over other areas of the world as well.

The Granger Collection, New York

In this political cartoon, Secretary of State William Seward is pictured pulling a wheelbarrow containing a useless block of ice. President Andrew Johnson is pushing the wheelbarrow. What do you think this cartoonist thought about the purchase of Alaska?

Rise of Expansionism Some Americans objected to expansionism, saying that it was contrary to American values. Taking over other lands, declared former senator Carl Schurz, would mean that "our old democratic principle that governments derive their just powers from the consent of the people will have to go overboard."

Others warned that such takeovers would cause revolutions abroad. Some raised racist objections, arguing that nonwhites in other countries could never learn American values.

William Jennings Bryan, who had run for president against McKinley, believed that the United States could be powerful without taking over other lands. He said that America "has exerted upon the human race an influence more potent than all the other nations of the earth combined, and it has exerted that influence without the use of the sword or Gatling [machine] gun."

By the 1890s, however, American business leaders were eager to dig mines and establish plantations in new places. Others wanted new markets for finished products. For years, European countries had been practicing **imperialism,** building empires by taking control of the governments and economies of other countries. American expansionists wanted to follow their example. Senator Henry Cabot Lodge declared, "Commerce follows the flag.... As one of the great nations of the world, the United States must not fall out of the line of march."

Expansion in Asia and the Pacific America's foreign expansionism started with measures to protect profitable overseas trading. In Asia, several European countries had made efforts to control trade with China. The

United States announced that American companies would trade anywhere in China they wanted. The government also established trade treaties with Japan.

To reach such Asian ports, ships crossing the Pacific needed to be able to stop at strategically located islands for fuel and food. To keep European countries from claiming all these places for themselves, the United States occupied the Midway Islands, which were located in the Pacific between California and Asia.

Annexing Hawaii   Closer to California lay a larger, more fertile group of islands that Americans found even more attractive—Hawaii. Americans had first come to these islands in the 1820s as missionaries. Their goal was to convert the native Hawaiians to Christianity. The Hawaiians, whose ancestors had come from the South Pacific, had lived on these islands for more than a thousand years. They were ruled by their own kings and queens.

In 1835, a Boston merchant established a large sugar plantation in Hawaii. Before long, American-owned sugar and pineapple plantations dotted the islands. The planters brought laborers to Hawaii from China and Japan to work in their vast fields. Under pressure from the planters, the Hawaiians agreed in 1887 to let the United States establish a naval base at Pearl Harbor, on the island of Oahu. The planters also persuaded Congress to allow Hawaiian sugar to be imported into the United States without paying any tariff (import tax).

U.S. sugar growers objected that the law now favored Hawaiian sugar over domestically grown sugar. They convinced Congress to give a bonus to growers in the United States. Hawaiian planters wanted that bonus, too. So they asked the United States to annex Hawaii.

Meanwhile, native Hawaiians increasingly resented being pushed around by Americans. When Queen Liliuokalani took the throne in 1891, people rallied around her call of "Hawaii for Hawaiians." Americans in Hawaii feared that they would lose their land. With help from U.S. marines, planters forced Queen Liliuokalani to give up her throne and established a new government for the islands.

Despite the planters' wishes, President Grover Cleveland refused to support the annexation of Hawaii. Cleveland, who opposed imperialism, said that Hawaii should be ruled by Hawaiians. But in 1898, under President McKinley, the United States did annex Hawaii.

Queen Liliuokalani, the last reigning monarch of Hawaii, insisted that native Hawaiians should control the islands. American planters, fearing they would lose their land, organized a revolt that dethroned her.

The Granger Collection, New York

When an explosion sunk the battleship *Maine* and killed 260 men, Americans immediately accused Spain of causing the tragedy, and demanded war. In 1976, Admiral H. G. Rickover, acting for the U.S. Navy, presented evidence that the explosion was probably caused by spontaneous combustion in one of the coal containers.

yellow journalism the practice of publishing sensational and often exaggerated news stories in order to attract readers

28.3 "A Splendid Little War"

Americans also established huge sugar plantations on the Caribbean island of Cuba, only 90 miles from Florida. Like nearby Puerto Rico, Cuba was still a Spanish colony.

By the 1890s, American expansionists wanted to annex both of these islands. To support their ambitions, they argued that it was time for the United States to enforce the Monroe Doctrine. No European country, they said, should control territory in the Western Hemisphere.

Cubans Struggle for Independence

The Cubans themselves had staged an unsuccessful revolt against Spain in 1868. In 1895, under the inspiring leadership of José Martí, Cubans again tried to win their independence.

To crush this movement, the Spanish herded men, women, and children into "reconcentration camps." Forced to live with inadequate food, beds, toilets, and medical care, tens of thousands died.

American newspapers jumped at the chance to report stories of Cuban suffering. Competing fiercely for customers, some newspapers resorted to **yellow journalism,** offering sensational and shocking reports. Some of these stories were based on rumors and untruths. One said that a Spanish general was "feeding prisoners to sharks."

As sympathy for Cubans grew, more and more Americans were willing to go to war for Cuba. To help Americans in Cuba in case of trouble, President McKinley sent the new battleship *Maine* to the island's capital city, Havana.

The Spanish-American War   Trouble soon erupted in Havana. On February 15, 1898, an explosion shook the *Maine,* sinking the battleship and killing 260 American sailors. No one knew whether the explosion was caused by an accident or a mine (bomb). But many Americans were quick to blame Spain. Said Theodore Roosevelt, "The *Maine* was sunk by an act of dirty treachery on the part of the Spaniards!"

Young men rushed to join the army, raising the battle cry "Remember the *Maine*!" Senators shouted "Free Cuba!" Hoping to avoid war, McKinley offered to work out a solution between the Spanish and the Cubans. But the Spanish did not respond.

Faced with newspapers and members of Congress calling him a coward, McKinley asked Congress to declare war. Congress quickly agreed, and on

April 19 voted to go to war with Spain to free Cuba. At the same time, Congress approved a resolution stating that the United States intended "to leave the government and control of the Island [Cuba] to its people."

The American army quickly grew from 30,000 to over 274,000 men. Roosevelt resigned from his position as assistant secretary of the navy and put together his own regiment. A mixture of powerful, wealthy men and seasoned ranch hands, it came to be called the Rough Riders.

After long preparations, the Rough Riders and 17,000 other Americans arrived in Cuba. Seeing that Cuban fighters lacked the strength or the weapons to force the Spanish out of fortified cities and harbors, Roosevelt and his Rough Riders decided to capture Santiago, a major city. To do this, they had to capture nearby San Juan Hill, from which Spanish forces were able to defend the city.

The attacking force included the Rough Riders and African American troops from several regiments. Up the hill they charged, braving Spanish fire. "They walked to greet death at every step, many of them, as they advanced, sinking suddenly or pitching forward...but others waded on... creeping higher and higher up the hill," wrote an American reporter. "It was a miracle of self-sacrifice, a triumph of bull-dog courage."

The Americans captured San Juan Hill. Realizing that Santiago was lost, the Spanish tried to save their ships, sending them steaming out of the harbor. But Americans sank or captured every ship. The Spanish soon surrendered.

The Spanish-American War lasted just four months. Only 345 Americans died in combat, although 5,500 died of disease. Many Americans agreed with Secretary of State John Hay that it had been "a splendid little war."

In the peace treaty with Spain, Cuba gained its independence, while Puerto Rico came under American rule. The United States agreed to remove all of its troops from Cuba. However, Cuba was forced to agree that American troops could return if necessary to preserve law and order as well as defend the island's independence. The United States was also allowed to keep naval bases in Cuba. Despite a revolution that forced American businesses out of Cuba in the 1950s, the naval bases still remain today.

The African American 10th Calvary provided strong support to Theodore Roosevelt's Rough Riders as they charged up San Juan Hill. The capture of the hill allowed American guns to bombard Santiago Harbor. When the Spanish fleet attempted to escape, it was completely destroyed, and Spain sued for peace.

28.4 The Philippines

After the *Maine* exploded in Cuba, Assistant Naval Secretary Theodore Roosevelt sent a telegram to the head of America's Pacific fleet, Admiral George Dewey. "In the event of declaration of war," the telegram ordered, "[begin] offensive operations in Philippine Islands."

Battle at Manila Bay The Philippines provided Spain's main base in the Pacific. The islands' people, called Filipinos, had tried many times to throw off Spanish colonial rule. In 1898 they were trying again. Led by General Emilio Aguinaldo, they had begun attacking the Spanish army and government officials. Now their struggle was about to become part of the war between the United States and Spain.

Dewey's fleet arrived in Manila, the Philippine capital, just five days after war with Spain was declared. At dawn on May 1, American battleships faced Spanish gunships. As naval bands struck up "The Star-Spangled Banner," sailors stood on deck and saluted the flag. These men were about to engage in the first battle of the Spanish-American War.

By 11 A.M., the entire Spanish fleet was burning, sunk, or sinking. Spain's old wooden ships were no match for the modern steel American ships with well-trained crews. Only one American had died in the battle.

General Emilio Aguinaldo believed that the United States would help the Philippines gain independence from Spain. When the United States annexed the Philippines, he fought for Filipino freedom.

Defeating the Spanish Dewey blockaded Manila's port until American troops could arrive to take the city. Filipino fighters, allied with Dewey, surrounded Manila. The Filipinos believed that the coming Americans would help them gain independence. While they waited, Aguinaldo issued the Philippine Declaration of Independence, formed a national government, and designed a national flag.

Once U.S. reinforcements showed up, the Spanish agreed to "lose" a fake battle in order to surrender to the Americans. They didn't want to give themselves up to the Filipinos, who resented Spanish rule so intensely.

Fighting the Filipinos In a treaty negotiated after the surrender, the United States "bought" the Philippines from Spain for $20 million. Then, in 1899, Congress voted to annex the Philippines.

Aguinaldo's government felt betrayed. Angrily, the Filipino leader called for "war without quarter to the false Americans who have deceived us! Either independence or death!"

For three years, over 80,000 Filipino fighters fought off better-trained and better-armed American troops. Soldiers on both sides tortured prisoners. Americans became increasingly cruel, harming civilians and destroying villages.

Some Americans protested that denying independence to the Philippines violated American ideals. Carl Schurz was a leader among these anti-imperialists. Said Schurz, "We shall, for the first time since the abolition of slavery, again have two kinds of Americans: first-class Americans, who have the privilege of taking part in government, and second-class Americans, who are to be ruled by the first-class Americans."

But expansionists won the day. Senator Henry Cabot Lodge argued that "Manila with its magnificent bay…will keep us open to the markets of China." President McKinley himself believed that the Philippines could become "a land of plenty… a people redeemed from savage and indolent [lazy] habits…set…in the pathway of the world's best civilization."

More than 20,000 Filipinos and about 4,000 Americans died in the struggle. When the revolt was finally put down, the Americans set up a nonmilitary government to "prepare Filipinos for independence." Americans built roads, hospitals, and schools. But the United States did not grant the Philippines independence until 1947.

A long war between the United States and the Filipinos who resisted U.S. control resulted in heavy casualties. More than 20,000 Filipinos were killed before the Philippines became independent in 1947.

28.5 Panama and the Canal

By 1901, America's favorite hero from the Spanish-American War, Theodore Roosevelt, had become vice president. "We stand on the threshold of a new century," Roosevelt declared. "Is America a weakling, to shrink from the work of the great powers? No. The young giant of the West stands on a continent and clasps the crest of an ocean in either hand."

Dreaming of a Canal   Roosevelt wanted to join those two oceans with a canal. If ships could move quickly between the Atlantic and the Pacific, the navy would be better able to defend America's new territories. And businesses would gain from lower shipping costs.

In September 1901, President McKinley was shot and killed by an assassin, and Roosevelt became president. In his first speech to Congress, Roosevelt argued for the canal. "No single great material work which remains to be undertaken on this continent is of such consequence to the American people," he told the nation.

Congress soon approved funding. In 1903, Roosevelt offered Colombia $10 million for land in their province of Panama, the narrowest part of Central America. The Colombian senate refused, feeling that the United States was trying to take a weaker country's valuable resources.

Furious, Roosevelt sent an American warship to Panama. Roosevelt knew that Panamanians wanted independence. The day after the ship arrived, a revolution started in Panama. With American marines keeping Colombian soldiers from reaching Panama's harbors, the rebels quickly won.

The new country of Panama agreed to accept $10 million in exchange for giving the United States control over a "canal zone" ten miles wide. Some American senators and newspapers, and countries all over the world, objected to America's "gunboat diplomacy." But most of the public supported the president. He was living out his personal motto, "Speak softly and carry a big stick."

The Culebra Cut, shown here, was one of the engineering miracles that allowed engineers to complete the Panama Canal in ten years. Millions of pounds of dynamite blasted apart the mountain. The earth was then used to construct dams to form lakes.

Building "The Big Ditch"

Construction on the canal began in 1904. Workers faced terrible conditions. "We had to bathe, wash our clothes in the same river; drink the same river water and cook with it," said one. A year later, three quarters of American workers had quit the project.

The majority of employees were workers from the West Indies who couldn't afford to go home. To prevent deadly yellow fever and malaria, crews worked to eliminate the mosquitoes that carried these diseases. They drained ditches, spread oil on swamps, and screened doors and windows. Within two years, canal workers were no longer dying from these diseases.

A new chief engineer improved housing and strictly organized the huge project. Using dynamite and huge steam shovels, men made a wide, deep cut through Panama's mountains. The excavated dirt was moved by railroad car to lower elevations. Here workers created earthen dams to form three giant lakes. Engineers supervised the construction of locks, a type of gate that would allow water levels to be raised and lowered along the canal.

By the time the 51-mile-long canal opened in 1914, Roosevelt had left office. His influence in the Panamanian revolution continued to be controversial. Roosevelt himself admitted, "I took the Canal Zone." In 1921, Congress apologized to Colombia and gave it $25 million. But anti-American feelings remained high in Latin America, and Panamanians increasingly resented American control of the Canal Zone. In 2000, the United States returned the zone to Panama.

Geography Challenge

U.S. Expansion Around the World, 1867–1903

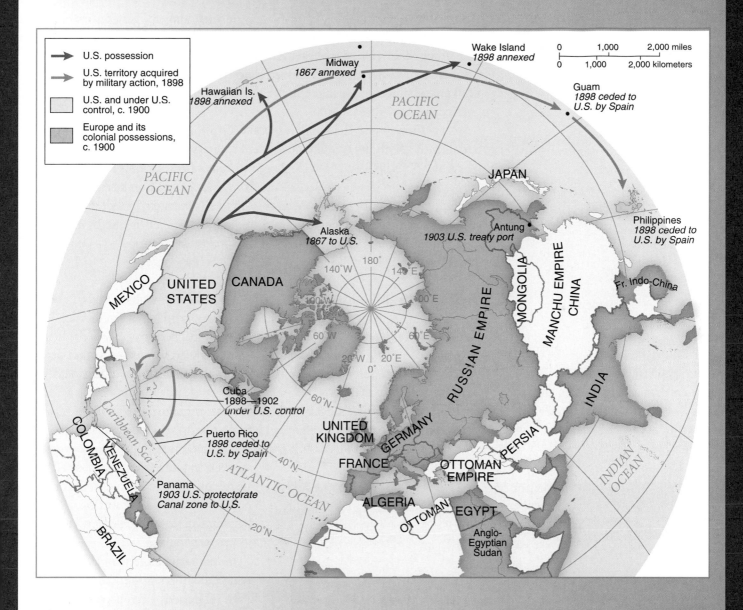

Legend:

→ U.S. possession

→ U.S. territory acquired by military action, 1898

U.S. and under U.S. control, c. 1900

Europe and its colonial possessions, c. 1900

Scale: 0 — 1,000 — 2,000 miles
0 — 1,000 — 2,000 kilometers

Wake Island
1898 annexed

Midway
1867 annexed

Hawaiian Is.
1898 annexed

Guam
1898 ceded to U.S. by Spain

PACIFIC OCEAN

PACIFIC OCEAN

JAPAN

Antung
1903 U.S. treaty port

Philippines
1898 ceded to U.S. by Spain

Alaska
1867 to U.S.

MEXICO

UNITED STATES

CANADA

180°

140°W

140°E

100°W

100°E

60°W

60°E

20°W

20°E

0°

RUSSIAN EMPIRE

MONGOLIA

MANCHU EMPIRE

CHINA

Fr. Indo-China

INDIA

Cuba
1898—1902 under U.S. control

Puerto Rico
1898 ceded to U.S. by Spain

Caribbean Sea

60°N

UNITED KINGDOM

GERMANY

FRANCE

PERSIA

OTTOMAN EMPIRE

Panama
1903 U.S. protectorate Canal zone to U.S.

ATLANTIC OCEAN

40°N

COLOMBIA

VENEZUELA

BRAZIL

20°N

ALGERIA

OTTOMAN

EGYPT

Anglo-Egyptian Sudan

INDIAN OCEAN

nationalism: devotion to a national or ethnic identity, including the desire for independence from rule by foreign countries

militarism: a policy of glorifying military power and military ideas and values

28.6 The Outbreak of World War I

By the time the first ship sailed through the Panama Canal, the world's attention was not on Panama, but on far-off Europe. In August 1914, German troops poured across Belgium, on their way to try to conquer France. Europe was at war.

Tensions in Europe   European countries had long competed with each other for colonies, trade, and territory. By the early 1900s, **nationalism** was complicating these rivalries. Austria-Hungry had built an empire by taking over smaller countries in the part of eastern Europe known as the Balkans. Nationalism inspired in the Balkan people a burning desire to be independent of Austrian rule.

As tensions grew, European leaders looked for safety in **militarism,** a policy of glorifying military power and military ideas and values. When Germany built up its navy to challenge Britain's fleet, Britain constructed more battleships. As Germany's army grew, France built up its own army.

European countries also looked for safety in alliances. In secret treaties, Germany and Austria-Hungary agreed to help each other in case of attack. Britain, Russia, and France made similar agreements. Europe was dividing into armed camps.

Assassination Leads to War   An outburst of nationalism lit the fuse of war. On June 28, 1914, the heir to the Austro-Hungarian throne, Archduke Franz Ferdinand, was visiting the city of Sarajevo in the province of Bosnia. Many Bosnians were Serbs who wanted to be part of nearby Serbia. A Serbian nationalist jumped out of a crowd and fatally shot the archduke and his wife.

Outraged, Austria-Hungary accused Serbia of having a hand in the assassinations and pressured Serbia to give up most of its independence. When the Serbs refused, Austria-Hungary declared war. The Russians stepped in to defend the Serbs. The Germans came to the aid of Austria-Hungary by declaring war on Russia. Russia's ally, France, began to prepare for war.

Eventually, more than a dozen countries took sides in the "Great War." (Decades later, people called the conflict World War I.) Austria-Hungary and Germany headed the Central Powers. France, Russia, and Britain led the Allied Powers.

Like most Americans, President Woodrow Wilson wanted to stay out of the war. Declaring that the United States would remain neutral, Wilson begged citizens to be "impartial in thought as well as deed."

The Archduke Franz Ferdinand and his wife are shown here shortly before they were assassinated by a Serbian nationalist. The assassination triggered World War I.

28.7 A New Kind of Warfare

By September 1914, six million soldiers were on the march across Europe. On Germany's Eastern Front, German troops fought Russians. On the Western Front, German forces advanced quickly before being stopped by French and British troops at the Marne River, about 40 miles outside Paris.

With neither army able to advance, both sides dug long, narrow ditches called *trenches* to protect their soldiers. A new kind of warfare was beginning.

Trench Warfare For the next three years, the war in the west was fought from two parallel lines of trenches. Men ate, slept, fought, and died in these miserable ditches. Eventually, the lines of trenches stretched for 600 miles across France.

Each side protected its front trench with barbed wire and booby traps. Between the opposing trenches lay a deadly "no-man's land." Attacking soldiers came under intense fire from the men in the trenches. Thousands upon thousands of soldiers died trying to advance their line of trenches a few yards.

The trenches were wretched places, infested with rats, lice, and disease. "We are not leading the life of men at all," wrote an American who had volunteered to fight with the British forces, "but that of animals, living in holes in the ground, and only showing outside to fight and to feed."

New Weapons New weapons added to the horror of trench warfare. "We never got anywhere near the Germans," one English corporal remembered. "The machine-guns were just mowing the top of the trenches." These new machine guns fired hundreds of bullets a minute. By the end of 1914, the French had lost 300,000 men. Germany lost more than 130,000 soldiers in a single battle.

The next spring, a green cloud floated over the Allied lines. Soldiers gasped and died, their throats and noses burning. The Germans had invented poison gas. Soon both sides were using chemical weapons.

The armies' new technology and strategies were effective for defense, but not for decisive attack. At one point, the British tried for six months to

During World War I, a new kind of war called *trench warfare* began. Hundreds of miles of trenches, like this trench for British soldiers, provided protection for infantrymen and allowed supplies and reinforcements to be safely delivered to the front.

The American public was furious when a U-boat sank the *Lusitania,* which the Germans suspected of carrying weapons to the Allies. Germany apologized and promised to stop sinking passenger ships without warning. However, Germany broke its promise and continued its attacks.

advance their lines. They gained only five miles, and lost 420,000 men. "The deadlock here is permanent," wrote an American volunteer.

War at Sea To supply soldiers in the trenches with food, ammunition, and other supplies, the warring nations bought goods from neutral countries. Each side tried to cut off the flow of supplies to its enemy.

Most trade, especially with the United States, was by sea. Britain had the world's greatest fleet and numerous ocean ports. Germany had a strong navy, but its only access to the ocean was through the North Sea. To close German ports, Britain mined the North Sea. This blockade stopped most of the neutral shipping and kept the German fleet bottled up in harbors for most of the war.

Unable to use its surface ships, the German navy tried to blockade Britain using submarines, called *U-boats* (for "underwater boats"). Fearing that the British would try to disguise their ships as neutrals, Germany announced that it might sink vessels flying the flags of neutral countries. Because submarines on the surface were easy targets for enemy fire, German submarines began sinking vessels on sight, instead of rising to the surface to give warning, as was traditional.

Germany Sinks the *Lusitania* The German embassy in the United States placed newspaper ads warning passengers not to sail to Britain, and specifically not to take the *Lusitania,* a British luxury liner. On May 7, 1915, six days after leaving New York, the *Lusitania* neared the coast of Ireland. Suddenly a ship's lookout shouted, "Torpedo coming on the starboard side!" Within moments, the ship exploded and quickly sank, killing 1,198 people, including 128 Americans.

Americans were outraged. One newspaper called the German attack "wholesale murder." When President Wilson protested, Germany said that the *Lusitania* had been carrying arms. Still, Germany apologized and offered to pay for damages. Hoping to keep the United States out of the war, Germany also promised not to attack merchant and passenger ships without warning in the future.

Protected by this promise, U.S. manufacturers increased their trade with the Allies. Trade with Allied countries swelled to $3.2 billion in 1916, while trade with the Central Powers dropped to $1 million. Americans weren't fighting in the war, but they had definitely taken sides.

28.8 To Make the World Safe for Democracy

After the sinking of the *Lusitania,* Wilson decided that the United States needed to prepare in case war became necessary. He worked with Congress to get money to improve the army and navy. Still, neither Wilson nor the country wanted war. In 1916, Wilson won reelection under the slogan, "He Kept Us out of War."

Wilson also tried to start peace talks. But European leaders, having lost so many soldiers, rejected Wilson's call for "peace without victory."

America Enters the War   The Germans soon risked war with the United States again. Even though U-boats were sinking 50 to 100 British merchant ships per month, enough were getting through to keep the Allies going. Desperate to prevent an Allied victory, the Germans decided to cut off British supplies before their own ran out. In February 1917, Germany resumed sinking merchant ships from other countries without warning.

In March, U-boats torpedoed three U.S. merchant ships, killing many Americans. In fact, these ships had been carrying weapons to the Allies. The Germans knew that this attack might bring the United States into the war, but they hoped to win before America was ready to fight.

It was a fatal mistake. Addressing a special session of Congress, Wilson urged a declaration of war. America would fight alongside the Allies, he said, not just to protect neutral shipping, but because "the world must be made safe for democracy."

Congress greeted Wilson's speech with applause. Later, Wilson reflected, "My message today was a message of death for our young men. How strange it seems to applaud that."

In the photograph below, Woodrow Wilson appears before Congress to ask for a declaration of war against Germany. Although Wilson tried to avoid war, continued U-boat attacks on merchant ships gave him no choice.

To recruit the necessary men for an army to send to Europe, the United States resorted to the draft. All men between the ages of 18 and 45 had to register. Within a few months, the army grew from 200,000 men to over 4 million.

Americans Prepare to Fight   On April 6, 1917, Congress declared war. The Allies rejoiced, hoping for American supplies—and soldiers. Allied ships were sinking faster than they could be replaced. To get U.S. supplies delivered safely, convoys of American warships started escorting cargo vessels, protecting them from attack. American destroyers also helped the British navy assault U-boats. These strategies dramatically reduced shipping losses.

When the United States entered the war, it had only 200,000 soldiers, and most of those had limited training. Congress quickly authorized a national draft. Soon, 3 million men were drafted. Another 2 million volunteered.

Fighting and Winning   American troops who sailed overseas were called the American Expeditionary Force (AEF). As they began arriving in Europe in June 1917, AEF soldiers soon learned from the Allies about trench warfare. The American commander, General John J. Pershing, hated these terrible conditions for soldiers. He also realized that trench warfare wasn't winning the war. He worked on a plan for driving the Germans out of the trenches and forcing them to retreat into open country.

Meanwhile, Russia had dropped out of the war. With millions of soldiers dead and starvation spreading across the country, Russians had revolted against their ruler, the czar. Russia's new government made peace with the Germans. This enabled Germany to bring soldiers back from the east, swelling their western forces to 3,500,000 men.

The German forces rushed to capture Paris before large numbers of Americans could arrive from overseas. They pushed quickly through the village of Chateau-Thierry and a nearby forest called Belleau Wood. They were within 50 miles of Paris when Americans reinforced the exhausted French. Gradually, American machine guns and artillery enabled the Allies to push the Germans back.

By the summer of 1918, more than a million Americans were in Europe. Pershing set his Allied offensive into motion. His plan took advantage of several offensive capabilities that had been developed during the war. Tanks could advance through trenches. Airplanes could deliver machine-gun fire and drop bombs. Carefully coordinating huge numbers of soldiers, tanks, airplanes, and artillery, the Allies forced the weakened Germans back to their own border.

To avoid the invasion of their own country, German leaders agreed to an armistice, or cease-fire. On November 11, 1918, for the first time in four years, the guns were silenced.

The costs of the war horrified the world. More than 9 million people had died. Entering the war late, the United States lost 116,000 lives. Throughout the warring nations, people mourned the loss of so many of their young men.

28.9 The Struggle for Peace

Less than two months after the fighting ended in Europe, President Wilson traveled to Paris to take part in peace talks. He was cheered by huge crowds. The United States had saved the French from endless war. And many Europeans welcomed Wilson's eagerness to prevent future wars.

Fourteen Points for World Peace

Months earlier, Wilson had presented to Congress a 14-point proposal for a postwar agreement. The first five points aimed to prevent conflict. Nations were asked to avoid secret treaties, to practice free trade, and to reduce their weapon supplies. Wilson asked that new borders be drawn based on self-determination, or the will of the people in each area.

Points 6 through 13 described new boundaries for many European countries. Finally, the ambitious fourteenth point called for nations to join a general association of countries to protect each other's independence. With this League of Nations, Wilson believed, the world could achieve a lasting peace.

Germany had surrendered, believing that Wilson's "Fourteen Points" would be the basis for a fair and just peace. But after years of fighting and dreadful losses, some Allied leaders weren't satisfied with a just peace.

The Treaty of Versailles

On January 18, 1919, delegates from dozens of countries assembled at a gorgeous French palace outside Paris called Versailles. In addition to Wilson, three Allied leaders dominated the treaty talks. They were David Lloyd George of England, Georges Clemenceau of France, and Vittorio Orlando of Italy.

The German representatives were not allowed to speak. This was a clue to the Allies' anger and their determination to punish Germany and remove it as a future threat. They created a treaty that forced Germany to disband almost all of its armed forces, give up its colonies, and surrender territory in Europe. In addition, they called on Germany to pay **reparations,** or money to make up for damages and war deaths. The amount of these reparations was later set at $33 billion.

President Wilson opposed such harsh treatment of Germany. However, he eventually accepted the Allied leaders' demands for punishment in order to win their support for his Fourteen Points.

The Allies rejected some of Wilson's points, including freedom of the seas. But the peace conference did create new national boundaries in

This painting shows the signing of the peace treaty that ended World War I at the Hall of Mirrors in Versailles. The treaty dealt harshly with Germany and planted the seeds of hatred that would lead to World War II.

reparations debts imposed on a defeated nation to pay for the harm done during a war

Europe based on self-determination. Most important to Wilson, the Treaty of Versailles established a League of Nations. Wilson thought that this agreement would make the peace treaty successful. The League of Nations, he believed, could fix any problems created by the treaty.

Struggling for Senate Ratification

Wilson needed the approval of two thirds of the U.S. Senate to ratify the peace treaty. He quickly ran into opposition, especially to the League of Nations. Some senators worried that other countries would force American soldiers to fight in international conflicts. They argued that only Congress had the Constitutional power to send Americans to war. Many didn't want the United States involved in messy European problems anyway.

Woodrow Wilson toured the country seeking public support for the League of Nations, which was opposed by Congress. On his tour, he suffered from a massive stroke. He was unable to continue his fight with Congress, and the Senate refused to approve the Treaty of Versailles.

The struggle over the treaty became a fight between political parties. Republicans had a majority in the Senate. They felt that Wilson, a Democrat, had made his Fourteen Points a political issue by not appointing any Republicans to his negotiating team.

Anxious to increase public support for the League of Nations, Wilson undertook an intense speaking tour. In 22 days, he toured 29 cities, speaking up to four times a day, with hardly any rest. Finally, he collapsed with severe headaches. He rushed back to Washington, D.C., where he suffered a massive stroke.

Recovering slowly, Wilson was less willing or able to compromise with opposition senators. In March 1920, the Senate rejected the Treaty of Versailles.

A Return to Isolationism

Once again, America was heading toward isolationism. When the League of Nations opened in Geneva, Switzerland, the United States did not participate. In later years, when big crises developed in Europe, the League lacked the power that Wilson hoped it would have.

In Germany, the Treaty of Versailles left a bitter legacy. Germans felt betrayed by the treaty—especially Adolf Hitler, a corporal who had been temporarily blinded by gas during the war. Hitler's rise to power in the 1930s would pose a fresh challenge to American isolationism. Only after a second world war would the United States take on the role of world power that it continues to fill today.

28.10 Chapter Summary

In this chapter, you read about American expansionism and the nation's involvement in World War I. You used a front-page headline to summarize key information about U.S. foreign policy from the late 1800s to 1920.

America's first great expansion after the Civil War was the purchase of Alaska. The United States also expanded westward by taking over the Midway Islands in the Pacific and annexing Hawaii.

As a result of the Spanish-American War, the United States gained two new possessions—Puerto Rico and the Philippines. Although the United States did not take over Cuba, it did keep the right to send troops to the island and to maintain naval bases there.

In Central America, the United States encouraged revolution in Panama, and then purchased a strip of land from the new country in order to build the Panama Canal. The United States maintained its control over the Canal Zone for the rest of the 20th century.

By the time World War I broke out, the United States was becoming a world power. America remained neutral until late in the war, and then entered the conflict on the side of the Allied Powers. President Wilson described the war as a fight to make the world safe for democracy.

Americans helped to win the war, but Wilson was unable to get all of his peace plan adopted. The U.S. Senate refused to ratify the peace treaty, preventing the United States from joining the League of Nations. In Europe, the harsh terms imposed by the victorious Allies caused great bitterness in Germany.

Meanwhile, the United States turned back toward isolationism. After World War II, however, America would remain engaged in world affairs.

Other big changes were also in store for Americans. In the final chapter of this book, you will explore some of these changes.

Does this political cartoon support or oppose U.S. expansion?

In Philadelphia, the past and the present sit side by side.

What significant events occurred in Philadelphia more than 200 years ago?

Do those events and the ideas they promoted still matter today?

Linking Past to Present

29.1 Introduction

Imagine that you were a 13-year-old living in the United States in 1914. How different would your life be, compared to your life today? Consider these facts. In 1914, you would be one of 99 million people in 48 states. Half of all Americans live on farms. Three out of four end their education in the eighth grade. Very few people own cars. If you want to make a telephone call, you have to dial an operator to place the call for you. If you want to travel from New York to California, you have to go by train. The trip will take five days. Nobody has ever seen a television or a computer.

In the South, laws segregate African Americans from whites. Blacks cannot live in certain neighborhoods or use the same swimming pools as whites. Throughout the country, very few women work outside the home. None of them can vote in a presidential election.

Now think about what life is like in the United States today. There are more than 280 million people in the nation's 50 states. Most of them live in cities or suburbs. More than 90 percent of young people will finish high school, and half will graduate from college. There are 226 million cars and trucks, and more than 46,000 miles of interstate highways. Commercial jets take passengers across the country in five hours. Nearly every home has a television, and half have at least one computer. People use the Internet every day to connect with individuals and sources of information around the world.

In the 21st century, the nation's population is more diverse than ever before. Throughout the country, laws forbid segregation and discrimination. Women not only vote, but are elected to Congress and run for president.

These changes, and many more, stem from the eventful years since 1914. In this chapter, you will learn how American society was transformed during these years. Along the way you will meet some of the individuals who helped to shape the world you live in today.

Before 1914

1600

1700

1800

1900

2000

1860s: Americans fight for equality during the Civil War.

54th Massachusetts Regiment

After 1914

1960s: Americans fight for equality during the civil rights era.

Civil Rights for All!

Civil Rights Now!

Graphic Organizer: Illustrated Timeline
You will use an illustrated timeline to see the connections between events before and after 1914.

29.2 Many Americans Struggled for Equality

The 20th century was a time of "firsts" for many Americans. Women, African Americans, and religious minorities all improved their social and economic status.

As you have learned, women first won the right to vote in national elections in 1920. Women, however, still strive for full equality with men. For example, women play a larger role in the work force than ever before. One hundred years ago, only 6 percent of American women worked outside the home. By 2002, 61 percent of women had paying jobs. Yet in 2003, women earned only 79 percent as much as men did.

Throughout the century, African Americans struggled to achieve equal rights with whites. In the 1950s, black Americans' fight for civil rights began to win the hearts and minds of people throughout the nation. On December 1, 1955, a black seamstress named Rosa Parks refused to give up her seat on a bus in Birmingham, Alabama. She was jailed because of a Jim Crow law that said blacks on a crowded bus had to give their seats to whites. In response, the city's black community organized a boycott of Birmingham buses. The boycott drew national attention to the injustice of segregation. It also brought nationwide fame to one of its leaders, the Reverend Martin Luther King Jr.

King became one of the most admired leaders of the civil rights movement. In 1963, during a rally called the March on Washington, he gave his eloquent "I have a dream" speech. King's words and actions helped win support for new laws that prohibit discrimination on the basis of race. African Americans, however, still face inequalities in social and economic opportunity. For example, blacks are twice as likely as whites to be poor.

Members of religious minorities also gained greater acceptance during the 20th century. The majority religion in America has always been Protestant Christianity. Members of other faiths have often faced prejudice. One sign of changing times was the 1960 election of John F. Kennedy, the first Roman Catholic to serve as president. In 2000, Democrat Joseph Lieberman became the first Jew to run for vice president on the ticket of a major party. Still, members of religious minorities sometimes feel the bite of prejudice even today.

More than 200,000 people demonstrated for civil rights during the March on Washington in 1963. The marchers heard Martin Luther King Jr. declare, "I have a dream that one day this nation will rise up and live out the true meaning of its creed: 'We hold these truths to be self-evident, that all men are created equal.'"

29.3 Education Improves Social and Economic Opportunity

Education has always served several purposes in American life. Americans have looked to schools to teach the rights and responsibilities of citizenship. Schools help to integrate the diverse groups that make up American society. Schooling also improves people's economic opportunities. That has never been more certain than it is today.

Early in the 20th century, schools helped students gain the basic skills needed at the time. Less than 25 percent of youths of high school age went to school beyond the eighth grade. Many rural teens became farmers. Young people in cities could find factory work or other jobs that did not require a high school diploma.

In the 1930s, the United States was hit by a long economic downturn called the **Great Depression**. Farms and businesses failed across the nation. The lack of opportunity sent many youths back to the classroom. As a result, school attendance grew dramatically. By 1940, 75 percent of young people were enrolled in high school.

Enrollment in colleges and universities mushroomed after World War II. On June 22, 1944, President Franklin D. Roosevelt signed the Servicemen's Readjustment Act. This law provided funds for military veterans to continue their education. Better known as the GI Bill ("GI" was a nickname for a member of the military), the law helped millions of veterans go to college. With more education, workers increased their earning power.

In the 1960s and 1970s, **feminists** encouraged women to seek equal opportunity with men. Increasingly, women joined men in seeking the advantages of education. By the 1980s, women college students outnumbered men for the first time in the nation's history.

As the 21st century began, well over 90 percent of American teens attended high school. About 69 percent graduated. Those young people who dropped out of school had a harder time finding and keeping a job later in life. Because of new technologies, there were fewer jobs for unskilled, uneducated workers. Today, most good-paying jobs require the knowledge and skills gained through high school, vocational training, or college. In 2000, full-time workers with a high school education earned about 30 percent more than workers who never finished high school.

Great Depression a drastic decline in the economy that led to widespread unemployment and poverty in the 1930s

feminist a person who is actively concerned with achieving social, political, and economic equality for women

Middle school students like these are more likely to earn high wages and have better jobs if they study hard and stay in school.

29.4 Innovation and Technology Transform the American Economy

New ideas and technologies have always helped to shape the American economy. In the 20th century, change came faster than ever before.

Early in the century, new techniques made manufacturing more efficient. Automaker Henry Ford introduced the *moving* assembly line and kept working to improve it. By the end of 1914, Ford had reduced the time it took to make one car from more than 12 hours to just 93 minutes. Other industries adopted his methods. Less time spent in production meant lower costs. When factories could produce goods more cheaply, prices could be lowered, and manufacturers could pay workers more. With wages rising, more and more families entered the middle class.

An even bigger change was the shift to an "information economy" after about 1970. By 1990, only one in five workers were manual laborers who made or moved things. Increasingly, Americans were "knowledge workers" who created and used information or ideas. Examples include engineers, lawyers, managers, and computer programmers.

This shift was made possible by the computer revolution. With computers, businesses could work with information more efficiently than ever before. In 1981 the IBM company began selling its first "personal computer." These desktop machines soon changed millions of jobs. Computers also became a consumer good. People began using them at home for both work and play, and to connect with one another over the Internet. Created in the 1960s, the **Internet** soared in popularity after the World Wide Web was developed in 1989.

Despite a growing middle class, millions of Americans were left behind in the changing economy. In 2002, about one in eight Americans lived in poverty. The rate of poverty was twice as high for African Americans and Hispanics as for whites. Immigrants were poorer, on average, than American citizens.

Immigrants confronted other challenges as well. Even legal immigrants did not enjoy all the same rights as citizens. For instance, they could not vote or hold many government jobs. Life was even more challenging for **undocumented immigrants**—people who entered the United States without official permission from the government. By law, these immigrants could not hold a job, though millions did. Most of these jobs, such as farm work, were very low paying. Undocumented immigrants could be forced to leave the country at any time.

Despite these challenges, newcomers continued to flock to America in search of a better life. By 1998, one in ten people in the country were immigrants.

Internet a network that allows computers in locations around the world to share information

undocumented immigrants people living in the United States without official permission from the government

The Information Age put a computer on nearly every desk and created a demand for "knowledge workers," people who work with ideas, information, and technology.

29.5 The Constitution Guarantees Individual Rights

You have learned that the U.S. Constitution is a "living document" that changes with the times. Since 1914, amendments and court rulings have broadened the Constitution's protection of individual rights.

One key Supreme Court decision concerned segregation. The Fourteenth Amendment guarantees all Americans "equal protection of the laws." In 1896 the Supreme Court had allowed segregation as long as the facilities for blacks and whites were "equal." The Court revisited this issue in *Brown v. Board of Education* in 1954. This case challenged racial segregation in schools. The Court ruled that separate educational facilities were inherently (by nature) unequal. This decision ended segregation in schools, but not in other aspects of American life. It wasn't until the Civil Rights Act of 1964 that segregation based on race, gender, religion, or nationality was outlawed in all public facilities.

The Sixth Amendment guarantees the right to a fair trial for anyone accused of a crime. But what if an accused person can't afford a lawyer? In 1963, the Supreme Court ruled in *Gideon v. Wainwright* that all accused persons have the right to a lawyer. If they cannot afford to pay a lawyer, the government must provide one.

One of Americans' most precious rights is the right to vote. In 1920, the Nineteenth Amendment guaranteed this right to women in federal elections. Voting rights remained an issue for other groups, however. Recall that after Reconstruction, some southern states made voters pay poll taxes. These taxes were used to keep poor people, especially African Americans, from voting. The Twenty-fourth Amendment, ratified in 1964, prohibits poll taxes in federal elections.

Until 1971, citizens had to be 21 years old to vote. That year, the Twenty-sixth Amendment guaranteed the vote to citizens who were at least 18. The amendment was ratified at the height of the Vietnam War. Hundreds of thousands of young soldiers risked their lives in this conflict. Many Americans felt that youths who were old enough to fight and die for their country were old enough to vote.

The Constitution is more than a historical document. It grows and changes through amendments and court decisions.

29.6 Individuals Can and Do Make a Difference

Ever since the Revolution, individual Americans have worked for a just society in which all people enjoy equal rights. Let's meet several people who took on this challenge during the 20th century.

It was 1954 when the Supreme Court ruled against segregation in schools. In 1957, a federal judge ordered desegregation in the public schools of Little Rock, Arkansas. That year, nine African Americans enrolled in the city's all-white Central High School. An angry mob threatened to lynch them. Federal troops were sent to protect the "Little Rock Nine." The example of these brave students inspired many Americans to support the cause of civil rights.

In the 1960s and 1970s, millions of Americans joined in a new women's movement. Much of the credit for sparking this movement went to Betty Friedan. Her 1963 book *The Feminine Mystique* challenged the notion that women should be content to be just wives and mothers. This idea, she argued, was used to keep women from competing on equal terms with men. In 1966 Friedan founded the National Organization for Women (NOW). Today, NOW is the nation's largest feminist group.

In the 1960s, farm workers found a champion in César Chávez. For decades, migrant farm workers like Chávez had suffered from low wages and poor working conditions. To strengthen the workers' power in bargaining with employers, Chávez began the United Farm Workers union. In 1968 he led a nationwide boycott of California table grapes to put pressure on grape growers to deal with the union. The boycott made Americans around the country aware of the farm workers' plight.

César Chávez used peaceful protest to call the nation's attention to the plight of migrant farm workers.

In the 1980s, a new and terrifying disease, AIDS, emerged. At first, little was known about how AIDS spread. People with AIDS often faced fear and prejudice.

A teenager named Ryan White was diagnosed with AIDS in 1984. While ill, White had been given blood infected with the virus that causes AIDS. In December, school officials refused to let him come back to school. He faced threats from students, parents, and even teachers. Bravely, White spent the next five years educating the nation about AIDS. He died in 1990 at the age of 18. That same year, Congress passed a law named after Ryan White to help pay for the care of people with AIDS.

29.7 Chapter Summary

In this chapter, you learned about some of the major changes in American life since 1914. You used a timeline as you made links between 20th century events and those of earlier times.

A major issue in the 20th century was the continuing struggle for equality. Several groups made important progress. Women won the right to vote. African Americans led the fight for civil rights and against segregation and discrimination. Religious minorities won greater acceptance. Yet inequalities remain an issue today.

More than ever before, education became a key to advancing in American society. Today's economy requires educated, skilled workers. Students who lack high school diplomas enjoy much less success than high school and college graduates.

The economy continues to change because of innovation and new technology. In recent decades, the computer revolution has reshaped American life both at work and at home. Despite economic progress, however, millions of people continue to live in poverty. African Americans, Hispanics, and immigrants are more likely to be poor than white Americans.

Since 1914, court decisions and constitutional amendments have broadened the protection of individual rights. The Supreme Court ended segregation in public schools and guaranteed the right of all accused persons to a lawyer. Constitutional amendments ended poll taxes and gave 18-year-olds the right to vote. These changes help meet the national promise of liberty and justice for all.

Individual Americans also worked for a more just society. The Little Rock Nine, Betty Friedan, César Chávez, and Ryan White all took action to make life better for Americans. They showed that ordinary people can make a big difference.

In this book you have learned about many individuals who have helped to nurture the American dream of freedom and equality. That dream connects all of us living today with those who have come before us. Some day, Americans will write the history of our own time. What part will you play in that history? What actions will you take to make a better world for the Americans of tomorrow?

Individuals making a difference: These teen volunteers are helping to build homes for people in need.

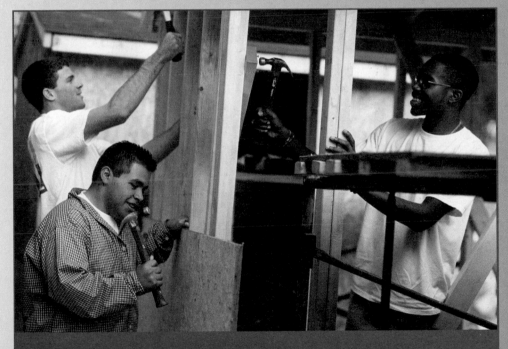

"Never doubt that a small group of thoughtful, committed citizens can change the world. Indeed, it's the only thing that ever has."

— Margaret Mead

423

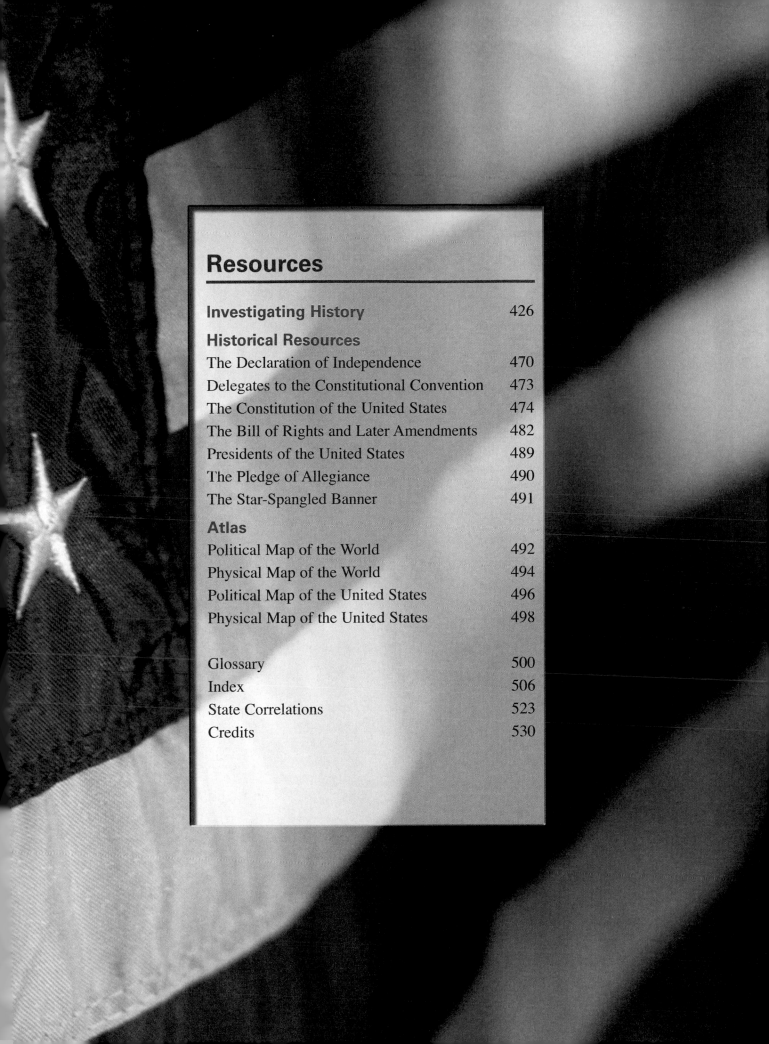

Resources

Investigating History   426

Historical Resources

The Declaration of Independence   470

Delegates to the Constitutional Convention   473

The Constitution of the United States   474

The Bill of Rights and Later Amendments   482

Presidents of the United States   489

The Pledge of Allegiance   490

The Star-Spangled Banner   491

Atlas

Political Map of the World   492

Physical Map of the World   494

Political Map of the United States   496

Physical Map of the United States   498

Glossary   500

Index   506

State Correlations   523

Credits   530

Investigating History

Investigating Literature

The World of the Native Americans

Native Americans lived on a vast and varied continent. In the Great Basin, it was hot and dry most of the year, but in the Eastern Woodlands, water was plentiful in most seasons and winter snows blanketed the land. Wherever they lived, Native Americans had to adapt to their surroundings. The environment affected everything from building materials to clothing choices. It is not surprising that Native Americans developed such a strong respect for nature. All parts of nature, including the people, were viewed as one community.

A traditional prayer of the Diné (Navajo), who lived in the Southwest, celebrates that community of nature and people. In this prayer, the author uses the word *beauty* to describe the world. What does *beauty* mean for the author? How does this compare with the way you see your world?

> **As I Walk with Beauty**
> As I walk, as I walk
> The universe is walking with me
> In beauty it walks before me
> In beauty it walks behind me
> In beauty it walks below me
> In beauty it walks above me
> Beauty is on every side
> As I walk, I walk with Beauty.

Assignment

Create an illustrated dictionary entry for the term *beauty* as used by the Diné in the prayer "As I Walk with Beauty." Include these elements:

- A definition of the term beauty in your own words
- A synonym (a word similar to the meaning of *beauty*)
- An antonym (a word opposite to the meaning of *beauty*)
- An illustration that represents the term *beauty*

Christopher Columbus Experiences a New World

When Christopher Columbus landed on the island of San Salvador in 1492, he thought he had found a new route to Asia. He didn't realize that he had stumbled upon two entirely different continents: North and South America. These two continents were truly a "New World" to Columbus and to the other Europeans who came after him.

On his return voyage, Columbus wrote to Luis de Sant Angel, Treasurer of Aragon. De Sant Angel had given Columbus significant help for his expedition. In the letter, Columbus records his impressions of the island he called Hispaniola and its people. Following is part of that letter. What do you think this experience must have been like for Columbus?

> Hispaniola is a marvel. Its hills and mountains, fine plains and open country, are rich and fertile for planting and for pasturage, and for building towns and villages. The seaports there are incredibly fine, as also the magnificent rivers, most of which bear gold…There are many spices and vast mines of gold and other metals in this island. They have no iron, nor steel, nor weapons, nor are they fit for them, because although they are well-made men of commanding stature, they appear extraordinarily timid. The only arms they have are sticks of cane, cut when in seed, with a sharpened stick at the end, and they are afraid to use these. Often I have sent two or three men ashore to some town to converse with them, and the natives came out in great numbers, and as soon as they saw our men arrive, fled without a moment's delay although I protected them from all injury.

Letter of Columbus to Luis de Sant Angel
Announcing His Discovery (1493)

Assignment

Columbus fought for years to obtain financing for his voyage in 1492. Of course, he wanted to prove to his investors that their money had been well spent. Is Columbus telling the whole truth in his letter? You be the judge. Read the letter again and assess its credibility by answering these questions:

1. Who did Columbus write this letter to?
2. Do any statements in the letter seem exaggerated? Which ones?
3. Which statements in the letter are definitely facts? (Facts are things that actually exist or have actually happened.) List at least three facts.
4. Which statements in the letter are opinions? (An opinion is a view or judgment that may or may not be factual). Write down one statement that you think is Columbus's opinion.
5. How would you rate the truthfulness of this letter on a scale of 1 to 10?
6. Why do you think Columbus chose to write this letter? What were his motives?

Investigating Primary Sources

Investigating Primary Sources

The Mayflower Compact

In Chapter 3, you read about the voyage of the *Mayflower* to America. Many of the passengers on the tiny ship were Separatists, people who wanted to break away from the Church of England. We know these people as the Pilgrims, but they called themselves the Saints. The other passengers, whom the Saints called Strangers, were not members of the Saints' congregation. Some of the Strangers were still loyal to the English church.

Could this diverse group of Saints and Strangers live and work together? Even before the *Mayflower* reached landfall, there had been tension between them. Keeping peace and order in a challenging new environment would be essential to their survival.

While still on board the ship, 41 men signed what later became known as The Mayflower Compact. This famous document appears below. What promises do the colonists make? To whom do they promise "obedience and submission"?

> In the name of God, Amen. We, whose names are underwritten, the loyal subjects of our dread sovereigne Lord, King James, by the grace of God, of Great Britaine, France, and Ireland king, defender of the faith, etc., having undertaken, for the glory of God, and advancement of the Christian faith, and honour of our king and country, a voyage to plant the first colony in the Northerne parts of Virginia, doe, by these presents, solemnly and mutually in the presence of God, and one another, covenant and combine ourselves together into a civil body politick [form a government], for our better ordering and preservation and furtherance of the ends aforesaid; and by virtue hereof to enact, constitute, and frame such just and equall laws, ordinances, acts, constitutions, and offices, from time to time, as shall be thought most meete and convenient for the generall good of the Colonie unto which we promise all due submission and obedience. In witness whereof we have hereunder subscribed our names at Cap-Codd the 11 of November, in the year of the raigne of our sovereigne lord, King James, of England, France, and Ireland, the eighteenth, and of Scotland the fiftie-fourth. Anno. Dom. 1620.

Governor William Bradford
Of Plimoth Plantation (1647)

Assignment

Many historians believe that the Mayflower Compact is directly related to the Magna Carta, the English Bill of Rights, the Declaration of Independence, and the U.S. Constitution. You can use the index of this book to find information about these important documents. Use that information to create a timeline that includes all five documents. Show the year each document was completed. Then write a paragraph explaining what type of government was proposed in all five documents. Your paragraph should show how these documents are related.

The First Great Awakening and Revolutionary Thinking

In Chapter 4 you read about the First Great Awakening, a religious revival that swept across the colonies in the 1730s. Historians argue that this "awakening" helped prepare the way for the American Revolution.

The following readings are from two sermons that support this argument. Both sermons were written long before the Revolution. Neither minister set out to cause rebellion. What ideas can you find in these sermons that might encourage colonists to challenge the King of England?

Investigating Primary Sources

> The wrath of kings is very much dreaded, especially of absolute monarchs, who have the possessions and lives of their subjects wholly in their power, to be disposed of at their mere will.... But the greatest earthly potentates [rulers] in their greatest majesty and strength, and when clothed in their greatest terrors, are but feeble, despicable worms of the dust, in comparison of the great and almightly Creator and King of heaven and earth. It is but little that they can do, when most enraged, and when they have exerted the utmost of their fury.... The wrath of the great King of Kings, is as much more terrible than theirs, as his majesty is greater. Luke 12:4, 5 [states] "And I say unto you, my friends, Be not afraid of them that kill the body, and after that, have no more that they can do. But I will forewarn you whom you shall fear: fear him, which after he hath killed, hath power to cast into hell: yea, I say unto you, Fear him."
>
> Jonathan Edwards
> *Sinners in the Hands of an Angry God* (1741)

> The essence of government (I mean *good* government...) consists in the *making* and *executing of good laws*—laws [that provide for] the common [welfare] of the *governed*.... We may very safely assert these two things in general, without undermining government: One is, That no civil rulers are to be obeyed when they [make laws] inconsistent with the commands of God.... All commands running counter to the declared will of the supreme legislator of heaven and earth, are null or void: And therefore disobedience to them is a duty, not a crime.—Another thing may be [argued] with equal truth and safety, is, That no government is to be submitted to, at the expense of that which is the sole end of all government, —the common good and safety of society.
>
> Jonathan Mayhew
> *A Discourse Concerning Unlimited Submission*
> *and Non-Resistance to the Higher Powers* (1750)

Assignment

Historians believe there is a connection between the First Great Awakening and the American Revolution. From your reading of the sermon excerpts, list at least two ways in which these major events might be related. Then write a paragraph that answers the following question: How might these sermons promote rebellion against a king?

Investigating Primary Sources

Independence Is "Common Sense"

In Chapter 5, you read that the first shots of the American Revolution were fired on Lexington Green, in Massachusetts, in April 1775. War had started, but many colonists were still uncertain about declaring independence from Britain.

For several months, there was little fighting outside of Massachusetts. Then, early in 1776, revolutionary feelings received a boost when a Patriot named Thomas Paine published a fiery pamphlet called *Common Sense*. In it, Paine made a strong case for independence. England, he stated, had lost touch with its American colonies. Furthermore, Britain had dragged the colonies into unnecessary wars with Britain's enemies. And, Paine wrote, American trade had suffered under British control.

Paine's arguments won thousands of colonists to the revolutionary cause. Below is an excerpt from *Common Sense*. What words and phrases does Paine use to convince people that independence is the right path? Which events in the 1760s and 1770s made Paine's ideas even more powerful?

> As a long and violent abuse of power, is generally the Means of calling the right of it in question (and in matters too which might never have been thought of, had not the Sufferers been aggravated into the inquiry) and as the King of England had undertaken in his own Right, to support the Parliament in what he calls Theirs, and as the good people of this country are grievously oppressed by the combination, they have an undoubted privilege to inquire into the pretensions of both, and equally to reject the usurpation of either....
>
> The cause of America is in a great measure the cause of all mankind. Many circumstances hath, and will arise, which are not local, but universal, and through which the principles of all Lovers of Mankind are affected, and in the Event of which, their Affections are interested. The laying of a Country desolate with Fire and Sword, declaring war against the natural rights of all Mankind, and extirpating the Defenders thereof from the Face of the Earth, is the Concern of every Man to whom Nature hath given the Power of feeling....
>
> Thomas Paine, *Common Sense* (1776)

Assignment

Design a cover for Thomas Paine's pamphlet *Common Sense*. On the front, include
- the title
- the author's name
- the date of publication
- a simple drawing that reflects the theme of the pamphlet

On the back cover, include
- a two-sentence description of the author
- a quotation from *Common Sense*
- one sentence explaining what the quotation means
- a list of events in the 1760s and 70s that make Paine's ideas about revolutionary behavior seem to be "common sense" (for example, the Boston Massacre)

New Information Changes Views of the Past

Interpretations of history often change. That's because historians are always finding new facts and interpreting the past in new ways. For example, histories of the American Revolution for decades focused on the participation of European Americans. Often the involvement of African Americans, women, and others was ignored.

In the last 30 years, however, historians have worked hard to paint a more complete picture of the Revolution. History has changed as a result. Below is a part of an article by Jon Swan that sheds light on some of the "Forgotten Patriots" of the Revolution. Who are the Forgotten Patriots that Swan talks about?

America's Forgotten Patriots

...When I was growing up, I had never heard a teacher mention the role blacks played in the Revolution. In fact, I suspect my ignorance on this score would have remained intact if I had not looked into the story of a black woman who sued for her freedom in 1780—and won.

... Black Americans—in and out of uniform, on land and at sea, and on both sides of the conflict—played a significant part during the struggles that would separate the colonies from England. Crispus Attucks, part black, part Natick Indian, and a towering six feet two inches tall, was among the five Americans killed by British soldiers in the Boston Massacre, which took place five years before the Battle of Lexington. In the words of a nineteenth-century memoirist, Attucks was "the first to defy, and the first to die." Similarly, on April 19, 1775, among the first to take a bullet at Concord Bridge was Prince Easterbrooks, a Lexington slave who had been enrolled in Captain John Parker's company, which was the first to engage the British. But Easterbrooks survived to fight in nearly every major campaign of the war.

Among the other black Minutemen who fought at Concord was Peter Salem, from Framingham, Massachusetts, a slave whose owners had freed him so he could enlist. Two months after the Battle of Concord, Salem was among the two dozen or so blacks to see action, and plenty of it, at the Battle of Bunker Hill. Several early accounts of the battle credited Salem with having fired the shot that killed Royal Marine Major John Pitcairn, who had led British Regulars into battle against the Patriots at Lexington and Concord. As historian Benjamin Quarles pointed out, however, "The story that Salem fired the shot that felled...Pitcairn is not easy to substantiate." In any event, the freed slave from Framingham appears to have won renown for his marksmanship because his musket, which saw further use at Saratoga and Stony Point, may be seen in a display case, bearing his name, at the Bunker Hill Monument.

Source: Jon Swan, "America's Forgotten Patriots," *MHQ: The Quarterly Journal of Military History*, Autumn 2000. Reprinted by permission.

**Chapter 6
The Declaration of Independence**

Investigating Literature

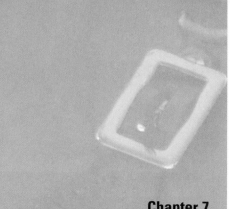

Assignment

After you have read the excerpt from "America's Forgotten Patriots," answer the following questions:

1. Who are the "Forgotten Patriots" that the author refers to?
2. What are some accomplishments of the men mentioned in the reading?
3. Why do you think these men were "forgotten"?
4. Why is it important for historians to uncover new facts and make new interpretations of the past?

Life in the Continental Army

In Chapter 7 you learned about the difficulties the Continental Army faced while fighting the British. The colonists began the American Revolution at an obvious disadvantage. Few men were trained to fight in a war against a professional army. Men enlisted for short periods of time—six months or a year. Necessities like guns, gunpowder, food, and shoes were in short supply. The winter of 1777–78 at Valley Forge was especially difficult. As one soldier, Joseph Martin, noted, "The greatest part were not only shirtless and barefoot, but destitute of all other clothing, especially blankets."

The Americans did have some advantages. Their army was fighting on home ground. The army's commander, General George Washington, was experienced and inspiring. Finally, the people were patriotic.

Joseph Plumb Martin was only 15 when he enlisted in 1776. He served until the war ended in 1783. Below is an excerpt from a book Martin wrote about his experiences. Published in 1830, this book is one of the most informative pieces on life in the Continental Army. What was daily life like for these early American soldiers?

> *May 1780* ...we got a little musty bread and a little beef, about every other day, but this lasted only a short time and then we got nothing at all. The men were now exasperated beyond endurance. They could not stand it any longer. They saw no alternative but to starve to death, or break up the army, give all up and go home. This was a hard matter for the soldiers to think upon. They were truly patriotic, they loved their country, and they had already suffered everything short of death in its cause. And now, after such extreme hardships to give up all was too much, but to starve to death was too much also. What was to be done? Here was the army starved and naked, and there their country sitting still and expecting the army to do notable things while fainting from sheer starvation.
>
> Joseph Plumb Martin
> *Narrative of Some of the Adventures, Dangers, and Sufferings of a Revolutionary Soldier* (1830)

Assignment

Joseph Plumb Martin, who wrote vividly about life as a soldier, was among the troops camped at Valley Forge for the winter. Review the information about Valley Forge in Chapter 7 (see page 94).

Based on what you have read, write two fictitious but realistic journal entries that tell about Valley Forge from a soldier's perspective. Include appropriate dates as well as the following terms: *farmers, von Steuben, drill, training,* and *stronger*. Also mention at least three hardships that you read about in the excerpts from Martin's book on pages 94–95 of your text. Use vivid and accurate details in your writing. Well-chosen details will help you clearly convey the situation at Valley Forge.

The Importance of State Constitutions

Americans declared their independence from Great Britain in 1776. By 1781, most states had adopted new state constitutions.

Early state constitutions reflected republican principles. They based the government's right to rule on the will of the people. They established legislatures in which the people's will could be represented. The constitutions of Vermont, Massachusetts, and New Hampshire abolished slavery in those states. Some constitutions took steps to separate church and state. And state constitutions were the first to include a bill of rights.

When delegates gathered for the Constitutional Convention in the summer of 1787, they brought with them their experience with state constitutions. Not surprisingly, some of the language and many of the ideas of the U.S. Constitution come directly from the state constitutions. Below are the preambles to the Massachusetts Constitution and to the U.S. Constitution. What principles and concepts do they contain? How are they similar? How are they different?

Preamble to the Constitution of Massachusetts (1780)

We, therefore, the people of Massachusetts, acknowledging, with grateful hearts, the goodness of the great Legislator of the universe, in affording us, in the course of His providence, an opportunity, deliberately and peaceably, without fraud, violence, or surprise; of entering into an original, explicit, and solemn compact with each other; and of forming a new constitution of civil government, for ourselves and posterity, and devoutly imploring His direction in so interesting a design, do agree upon, ordain, and establish, the following *Declaration of Rights, and Frame of Government,* as the Constitution of the Commonwealth of Massachusetts.

Preamble to the United States Constitution (1789)

We the People of the United States, in Order to form a more perfect Union, establish Justice, insure domestic Tranquility, provide for the common defence, promote the general Welfare, and secure the Blessings of Liberty to ourselves and our Posterity, do ordain and establish this Constitution for the United States of America.

Assignment

Set up a T-chart to compare the preamble to the Massachusetts Constitution with the preamble to the United States Constitution. On one side of the T-chart, record three differences you see. On the other side, record three similarities.

Chapter 8
Creating the Constitution

Investigating Primary Sources

"We" the People?

The framers of the Constitution resolved many questions when they formed the American system of government. How should states be represented in the new government? How should the chief executive be elected? How will power be balanced? Unfortunately, other questions were left unsettled. For example, as you learned in Chapter 8, the founders compromised on the issue of slavery. Eventually, Americans would have to come to grips with that explosive issue. As you will learn, it would contribute to the outbreak of Civil War in 1861.

Another question left unresolved was the status of women. Women made up nearly half of the population. Women provided essential support during the American Revolution. But common practice did not allow women to vote or to hold office. The Constitution did not change women's status.

Abigail Adams, wife of John Adams, was a strong supporter of women's rights. She believed in equal education for boys and girls, and she made sure her own daughter received a good education. Below are excerpts from letters between Abigail and John when John was serving in the Continental Congress in 1776. In the first excerpt, Abigail urges her husband to remember women. In the second excerpt, he reacts to her advice.

What does Abigail warn will happen if women are not included in the new government? How are her views and John's different? What do you think explains their different points of view?

> I long to hear that you have declared an independency—and by the way in the new Code of Laws which I suppose it will be necessary for you to make I desire you would Remember the Ladies, and be more generous and favourable to them than your ancestors. Do not put such unlimited power into the hands of the Husbands. Remember all Men would be tyrants if they could. If particular care and attention is not paid to the Ladies we are determined to foment [start] a Rebellion, and will not hold ourselves bound by any Laws in which we have no voice, or Representation [say].
>
> Abigail Adams
> *Letter to her husband* (1776)

> As to your extraordinary Code of Laws, I cannot but laugh. We have been told that our Struggle has loosened the bands of Government every where...But your Letter was the first Intimation [sign] that another Tribe [women] more numerous and powerful than all the rest were grown discontented.
>
> John Adams
> *Reply to Abigail* (1776)

Assignment

Pretend you are a woman living in the late 18th century. You agree with Abigail Adams, and you want to promote women's rights. Write a passionate letter to the editor of your local newspaper, trying to persuade people to adopt your views. Make sure your letter includes a well-defined thesis (one that states a clear and knowledgeable judgment). Give detailed examples and reasoning to support your argument. For example, your thesis might be, "Women can do everything men can do and should have all the same rights as men." As an example to support this thesis, you could mention the capable leadership of Elizabeth I, who served as queen of England long before the colonies declared their independence. How could men dutifully follow a queen for decades, yet then say that women are not capable of exercising the most basic political rights?

Separation of Church and State

The interaction between government and religion has often caused hard feelings in the United States. In colonial America, the church and the state were tied closely together. In fact, most citizens paid taxes to support a state-established church. For example, in Virginia, Baptists were forced to pay the salaries of Anglican ministers. Anglicans were happy. Understandably, most Baptists were not.

The American Revolution forced people to rethink state-established churches. Was it fair for the government to single out one church to receive tax dollars? Many said yes. Others, including George Washington and Patrick Henry, believed that the state should support all Christian churches, not just one. Still others argued that no church should have government support.

Thomas Jefferson believed that both institutions would be healthier if they were separate. In his view, separating church and state was the only way to truly preserve religious freedom. Otherwise, he argued, the government would always have some control over people's religious beliefs.

In 1786 the Virginia legislature passed a law called the *Statute for Religious Freedom.* This law, written by Thomas Jefferson, laid the foundation for the separation of church and state in Virginia. A few years later, drafters of the Bill of Rights drew on Jefferson's ideas when they wrote the First Amendment to prohibit government support for religion.

Following is a long, wordy sentence from Jefferson's statute. What one simple, yet important idea does he communicate in this sentence?

> Be it enacted by the General Assembly [of Virginia], That no man shall be compelled to frequent [attend] or support any religious worship, place, or ministry whatsoever, nor shall be enforced, restrained, molested, or burthened in his body or goods [hassled by others], nor shall otherwise suffer, on account of his religious opinions or belief; but that all men shall be free to profess, and by argument to maintain [hold], their opinions in matters of religion, and that the same shall in no wise diminish, enlarge, or affect their civil capacities [civil rights].
>
> Thomas Jefferson
> *Statute for Religious Freedom* (1786)

Assignment

Examine Jefferson's long sentence from the *Statute for Religious Freedom.* Many bills or acts of government are written in this style. The language is broad and tries to cover all kinds of circumstances. Could Jefferson have shortened this statement?

Decide which language is *essential* (absolutely necessary) to communicate his message, and which offers only *incidental* information (not necessary to communicate his ideas).

1. Write down one phrase from the passage that you think is essential.
2. Write down several words or phrases that you think might be incidental.
3. Finally, rewrite Jefferson's statement in a simple sentence that a typical middle school student could understand.

Investigating Primary Sources

A Policy of Peaceful Transition

The presidential election of 1800 was an important test for the young nation. The race between John Adams and Thomas Jefferson was close and hard fought. Both sides did some nasty campaigning to make the other side look bad. Jefferson was accused of robbing a widow of her trust funds and of being an atheist. Adams was roasted for backing a military buildup. In many countries, the tension might have led to open warfare. Fortunately, the United States had a model for a peaceful, democratic transfer of power. The elective process, though somewhat flawed, worked. Jefferson, the Republican, defeated Adams, the Federalist—and the United States was still one country.

Below is a passage from Jefferson's inaugural address. His intent is to unite the country. Jefferson's ideas continue to influence American politics today. What does Jefferson mean when he states, "We are all Republicans, we are all Federalists"?

> [The election] being now decided by the voice of the nation, announced according to the rules of the Constitution, all will, of course, arrange themselves under the will of the law, and unite in common efforts for the common good... Let us, then, fellow citizens unite with one heart and one mind... And let us reflect that...we have yet gained little if we countenance [allow] a political intolerance as despotic [tyrannical], as wicked, and capable of as bitter and bloody persecutions... But every difference of opinion is not a difference of principle. We have been called by different names brethren of the same principle. We are all Republicans, we are all Federalists... I believe this [to be]...the strongest Government on earth.

Thomas Jefferson
First Inaugural Address (1801)

Assignment

President Thomas Jefferson called the election of 1800 "The Revolution of 1800." Why would he make such a claim?

Set up a table to show all the presidential elections up to and including the election of 1800. Make three columns: one for the names of the presidents, one for the dates they were elected, and one for the states they came from. Then answer the following questions:

1. How many elections were held before 1800?
2. How old was the Constitution in 1800?
3. Why was it important to have a peaceful election in 1800 that followed the rules set out in the Constitution?
4. What was the significance of Jefferson's inaugural address?

Isolationism or Involvement?

As you learned in Chapter 12, Spain controlled much of Latin America in the early 1800s. About that time, an independence movement swept through that part of the world. Country after country separated from Spain. By 1825, the last Spanish troops were driven from South America. Many people in the United States pressured the president to back the new, independent Latin American nations.

Following is part of a speech that Secretary of State John Quincy Adams delivered to the House of Representatives on July 4, 1821. People continue to refer to Adams's famous words in debates about foreign policy today. According to Adams, how should the United States act? What does he say the United States stands for? How does his speech compare with the Monroe Doctrine of 1823?

Fourth of July Address, 1821

She [the United States] has, in the lapse [period] of nearly half a century, without a single exception, respected the independence of other nations while asserting and maintaining her own. She has abstained from interference in the concerns of others, even when conflict has been for principles to which she clings… But she goes not abroad [overseas], in search of monsters to destroy. She is the well-wisher to the freedom and independence of all… She well knows that by once enlisting under other banners than her own [joining in other country's battles], were they even banners of foreign independence…she might become the dictatress [single ruler] of the world. [America's] glory is not dominion [control over others], but liberty.

John Quincy Adams
Warning Against the Search for Monsters to Destroy (1821)

Assignment

Draw a political cartoon that illustrates the arguments Adams made in the speech quoted above. Include images that represent the United States, Europe, and Latin America. Add a caption. Show your cartoon to an adult and explain the historical background. Then, have the adult write a paragraph that explains your cartoon.

**Chapter 12
Foreign Affairs in the Young Nation**

Investigating Primary Sources

Investigating Literature

Defining America Through Literature

What is America? By the early 1800s, many events had defined the new nation politically: Independence had been declared in 1776. The American Revolution had been won. The Constitution had been written. The War of 1812 reaffirmed America's independence. America was a free and democratic nation.

Two men attempted to define America in a different way—through literature. Authors Washington Irving and James Fenimore Cooper helped to shape the identity of early America.

Washington Irving (1783–1859)

As a writer, Irving had a keen eye for the American landscape and the people who lived in it. He wrote about the New Yorkers he knew, often with humor. And he wrote sympathetically about the Native Americans who, he believed, were being ill treated by white settlers. For his charming tales in *The Sketch Book of Geoffrey Crayon, Gent.* (1819–20), Irving would later be called the father of the American short story. Following is a passage from one of his best-loved stories.

> It was toward evening that Ichabod arrived at the castle [house] of the Heer Van Tassel, which he found thronged with…farmers, a spare leathern-faced race, in homespun [homemade] coats and breeches, blue stockings, huge shoes, and magnificent pewter buckles. Their brisk, withered little dames [wives], in close crimped caps, long waisted short-gowns, homespun petticoats, with scissors and pin-cushions, and gay calico pockets hanging on the outside. Buxom lasses, almost as antiquated as their mothers, excepting where a straw hat, a fine ribbon, or perhaps a white frock, gave symptoms of city innovation. The sons, in short square-skirted coats, with rows of stupendous brass buttons, and their hair generally queued in the fashion of the times, especially if they could procure an eelskin for the purpose, it being esteemed throughout the country as a potent nourisher and strengthener of the hair.
>
> Washington Irving
> *The Legend of Sleepy Hollow* (1819)

James Fenimore Cooper (1789–1851)

Cooper was one of the first authors to use an entirely American setting for his stories. He featured the frontier—a setting that could not be mistaken for any place in Europe. His white, Native American, and black characters reflected the country's diversity.

> The frame of the white man…was like that of one who had known hardships and exertion from his earliest youth…. He wore a hunting shirt of forest-green, fringed with faded yellow, and a summer cap of skins which had been shorn [shaved] of their fur. He also bore a knife…but no tomahawk. His moccasins were ornamented after the gay fashion of the natives…. A pouch and horn completed his personal accouterments [accessories], though a rifle of great length, which the theory of the more ingenious whites had taught them was the most dangerous of all firearms, leaned against a neighboring sapling [young tree]. The eye of the hunter, or scout, whichever he might be, was small, quick, keen, and restless,

roving while he spoke, on every side of him, as if in quest of game, or distrusting the sudden approach of some lurking enemy. Notwithstanding the symptoms of habitual suspicion, his countenance was not only without guile [deceit], but at the moment at which he is introduced, it was charged with an expression of sturdy honesty.

James Fenimore Cooper
The Last of the Mohicans (1826)

Assignment

Draw a caricature of an American in the early 1800s as described by Irving or Cooper. Your drawing should include specific details of clothing, possessions, and background setting. Label parts of your drawing to explain key details. For example, you might draw a line from your person's shirt and write a short caption explaining why an American might have worn a homespun cotton shirt.

Note that your caricature may not represent the "average" American of that era. Cooper and Irving were describing colorful literary characters. In fact, by the time Irving wrote *The Legend of Sleepy Hollow*, many Americans were wearing industrially produced (rather than homespun) fabric and clothing.

Native American Policies Leave a "Trail of Tears"

White settlers wanted land and opportunity in America. As settlers moved west, their gains almost always came at the expense of Native Americans. On the frontier, tensions between settlers and natives were a constant source of difficulty for American policymakers. Early American presidents negotiated treaties with various Indian groups. These treaties had four goals: to end hostilities, to promote trade, to acquire land, and to keep tribes allied with the United States—not with European powers.

During George Washington's presidency, the United States negotiated the Treaty with the Six Nations in 1789. This treaty was supposed to "remove all causes of controversy, regulate trade, and settle boundaries." Six years later, a second major treaty, the Treaty of Greenville, was signed. This agreement ended a war with Indians in the West and secured some western lands for white settlers.

Native Americans hoped to maintain their hold of other lands. White settlers, however, were hungry for property. By 1805, as many as 100,000 settlers lived in Ohio. Most of them hoped to acquire fertile Indian lands.

President Thomas Jefferson promoted a program to "civilize" Native Americans. Jefferson admired Indians, but he also believed that if they would not join white civilization, they should be moved west of the Mississippi.

Some Native Americans did adopt white ways. The Creek and Cherokee nations built towns and plantations. Some even held slaves. Others rejected the effort to "civilize" them. During the Madison administration, warfare with Indians broke out before and during the War of

Investigating Primary Sources

1812. Madison signed the Treaty of Ghent to end hostilities not only with the British but also with Indian groups.

As you learned in Chapter 14, Andrew Jackson often ignored treaties with Native Americans. His policy of "forced removal" became a reality under President Van Buren, when more than 17,000 Cherokee were marched about a thousand miles to the west in the winter of 1838–39. They traveled by foot through Tennessee, Kentucky, Illinois, Missouri, and Arkansas, into Indian Territory. Several thousand died, many from hunger, disease, and exhaustion. Accounts of the "Trail of Tears" are heartbreaking. Following are portions of several eyewitness reports.

> I saw the helpless Cherokees arrested and dragged from their homes, and driven at the bayonet point into the stockades. And in the chill of a drizzling rain on an October morning I saw them loaded like cattle or sheep into six hundred and forty-five wagons and started toward the west.... On the morning of November the 17th we encountered a terrific sleet and snow storm with freezing temperatures and from that day until we reached the end of the fateful journey…the sufferings of the Cherokees were awful. The trail of the exiles was a trail of death. They had to sleep in the wagons and on the ground without fire. And I have known as many as twenty-two of them to die in one night of pneumonia due to ill treatment, cold and exposure...
>
> Private John G. Burnett

Source: The birthday story of Private John G. Burnett, Captain Abraham McClellan's Company, 2nd Regiment, 2nd Brigade, Mounted Infantry, Cherokee Indian Removal, 1838–39; written to his children on December 11, 1890.

> Long time we travel on way to new land. People feel bad when they leave Old Nation. Womens cry and make sad wails. Children cry and many men cry . . . but they say nothing and just put heads down and keep on go towards the West. Many days pass and people die very much. We bury close by Trail.
>
> Unnamed Cherokee survivor of the trail

> The sick and feeble were carried in waggons—about as comfortable for traveling as a New England ox cart with a covering over it—a great many ride on horseback and multitudes go on foot—even aged females, apparently nearly ready to drop into the grave, were traveling with heavy burdens attached to the back—on the sometimes frozen ground, and sometimes muddy streets, with no covering for the feet except what nature had given them.
>
> Unnamed white traveler observing the forced march

Source: "The Trail of Tears in the Southeast Missouri Region," a Web site hosted by Rose City Net.

Assignment

Some Americans were angered by Jackson's policy of forced removal of Native Americans from their lands. Take the position of one such American in 1839. Write an editorial for the *Washington Times*,

protesting the removal of the Cherokee along the Trail of Tears. Your editorial should
- be addressed "Dear Editor" and dated January 27, 1839.
- describe the physical and emotional hardship along the Trail of Tears.
- use supporting evidence from the chapter readings, including eyewitness reports.
- include a thesis designed to persuade the president to change his policy toward Native Americans.
- contain at least three paragraphs, free of errors in spelling, punctuation, capitalization, and grammar.

By Land or by Sea: Settling an Immense Land

There were three ways to get to California and Oregon from the eastern United States in the mid-19th century. One way was by ship around Cape Horn at the tip of South America. This journey took several months. It was the longest way to get to California, but often the easiest—if you survived the often stormy, icy, treacherous Cape.

Another way to travel west was also by ship. Travelers took a boat to Panama, crossed the land to the western coast, then boarded another vessel in the Pacific and sailed north. It was the fastest, but also the most dangerous way to go. Diseases were more common on this sea route. The cost of traveling by sea was between $600 and $1200 per person.

The third way to travel west was overland—also a long and dangerous trek. Many people spent months on the trail. Disease (with no doctors) and lack of water were major dangers, as was drowning in river crossings. To counter the perils along the trail, people organized wagon trains. A good variety of occupations and supplies among the members would make the journey more comfortable. Traveling by land was the least expensive way to go. For a family of four, the cost was around $700. This route was the most popular.

Following are excerpts from the letters and papers of four travelers who ventured west.

Around the Horn

We had head winds a great deal of the time, a great many days no wind at all, and sometimes blowing so hard, & the sea so rough we could not sail much. We were 70 days from Boston to Cape Horn and 3 weeks getting round the cape these 3 weeks it was blowing a Gale of wind nearly all the time, & the sea so rough, that the waves were continually washing over the vessel, keeping us wet all the time.

Thomas Boyd
Papers of Thomas Boyd 1852–1854 (1852)

Dear Mama, We are nearly around Cape Horn—I was only sea sick one day and Uncle Charlie laughed at me.—I have had two of my teeth pulled—I have sewed five strips of patch work.

Maud Maxson
Letter to her mother (1870)

Investigating Primary Sources

The Overland Journey

One morning, a piece of plank, standing upright on the summit of a grassy hill, attracted our notice, and riding up to it, we found the following words roughly traced upon it, apparently by a red-hot piece of iron: MARY ELLIS DIED MAY 7TH, 1845 AGED TWO MONTHS. Such tokens were of common occurrence…

Francis Parkman
The Oregon Trail (1849)

November 18 – My husband is sick. It rains and snows. We start this morning around the falls with our wagons. We have 5 miles to go. I carry my babe and lead, or rather carry, another through the snow, mud and water, almost to my knees. It is the worst road that a team could possibly travel. I went ahead with my children, and I was afraid to look behind me for fear of seeing the wagons turn over into the mud and water with everything in them. My children gave out with cold and fatigue and could not travel, and the boys had to unhitch the oxen and bring them and carry the children on to camp. I was so cold and numb that I could not tell by the feeling that I had any feet at all.

Elizabeth Dixon Smith Greer
Journal, 1847–1850

Assignment

Pretend that you are a traveler making the journey west in the mid-1800s. You may choose to travel by sea or by land. Write a postcard to a friend describing the journey. Write your message on one side of the postcard and sketch a picture on the other side. Your postcard must have

- a proper salutation and closing.
- a brief overview of the type of journey you are taking (by sea or by land).
- at least two reasons why you did not travel the other way.
- a description of at least one experience you have had on the journey.
- proper spelling and grammar.
- a colorful picture of one thing you have seen on your journey.

**Chapter 16
Life in the West**

Investigating Primary Sources

Women Meet the Challenge of the West

Women on the frontier had to be resourceful. Their roles were varied and often broke the traditional mold. Some of these roles were born out of necessity, since there was so much to do in settling a new place. Other roles resulted from the opportunities and independence the frontier offered.

In Chapter 16 you read about Annie Bidwell, who settled in California in the 1860s. She took an active role in many social causes in her community. You also read about Biddy Mason, who was brought west as a slave but won her freedom in a California court. Mason found a role in business and real estate, where she made a fortune. She also worked for social change, and spent much of her wealth helping the poor of all races.

Wyoming granted women a role in politics when, before any other state, it gave them the right to vote. In 1924, Wyoming elected Nellie Tayloe Ross the first woman governor in the United States. Ross would spend the rest of her life defending the place of women in politics.

Wherever they went and whatever they did, many women wrote about their lives. Laura Ingalls Wilder settled with her family in Dakota Territory and became a teacher. She later wrote about growing up on the midwestern prairies in the 1870s and 1880s. Her classic "Little House" books bring to life the hardships and simple joys of pioneer life.

Following are excerpts from writings by several pioneer women who are less well known. They speak matter-of-factly about their roles in the West.

One day [in 1891] three men came riding down the road—two of them stopped at our gate, the third one came up to my door. He had a terrible wound on his hand.… I started to wrap it with a clean white cloth when he told me to put something on it so the bandage would not stick.… Bill and May were clinging to my skirts and crying.… He took the grease and rubbed it all over his hand. When I was through bandaging it and started to tie it up, he said, "don't tie it—I want you to sew it on so it can't come off".… I sewed it on good and tight. He thanked me and the three men rode off down the road.

Diana Lucina Spicer Block

Source: "Her Story" as recorded by Devona Bezzant Block, from "Notable Women Ancestors," a Web site hosted by RootsWeb.

From Sacramento we went up the river by boat to Marysville… and to each of the other new mining camps as they were formed. I sluiced [mined for gold in the streams] many and many a day.… There were no bakeshops in those early days [1849], and I made many an apple pie, just of common dried apples, and sold them for a dollar apiece. The women helped in that way to support the families, for mining was not always a certain means of livelihood.

Mrs. Noble Martin

Source: From "Gold Rush Stories of Women Pioneers," a Web site hosted by the Museum of the City of San Francisco.

The pioneer Kansas woman shared her husband's work and interest in the garden, the orchard, the crops and animals of the farm; she worked in the garden and gathered its products. She knew just how each vineyard or tree in the young orchard was coming in. She shared in the hopes for a bountiful crop as the field things sprouted and grew green and tall. Did a horse, dog or other farm animal get badly gored, cut or wounded, hers was the task to cleanse the wound and take the stitches that drew the torn edges together.

Clara Hildebrand

Source: From the Lilla Day Monroe Collection of Pioneer Stories, quoted in Joanna L. Stratton, *Pioneer Women: Voices from the Kansas Frontier* (New York: Simon & Schuster, 1981), page 61.

Assignment

To better understand the past, historians keep asking questions. In fact, the best historians are usually the ones who ask the best questions. Write at least six questions about the women of the western frontier. Your questions may focus on a single woman, such as Laura Ingalls Wilder, or they may address pioneer women in general. Base at least two of your questions on the passages you just read. Then go to the library or the Internet to find the answers to your questions. Write and edit a research report about a pioneer woman. Your report should be one to two pages long and have

- a clever title
- the answers to your questions
- a page of illustrations or images that show what life was like for women in the West
- a bibliography

Chapter 17
Mexicano Contributions to the Southwest

Investigating Primary Sources

The Importance of Great Rivers and the Conflicts over Them

You read in Chapter 17 that Mexicano settlers developed irrigation systems essential to life in the Southwest. Without great rivers like the Colorado, Columbia, Rio Grande, or the Snake, many western areas would not have been habitable. Like Mexicanos, Anglo settlers tapped the great rivers to irrigate their farms and ranches.

As more settlers arrived, conflicts developed over this precious resource. People sometimes resorted to trickery and even violence to gain access to water. Upstream users sometimes cut off the supply of water to those downstream. Called the "water wars," these conflicts over water rights plagued the West throughout the 19th century. In some places, the conflicts continue today.

People can get downright nasty about water. In the 1800s, cattle ranchers asked cowboys to pose as homesteaders seeking land. Homesteaders were farmers who were given land by the government in return for cultivating it. The cowboys, known as "dummy" homesteaders, filed a claim of ownership on lands with water. When these "dummy" homesteaders were awarded the land, they transferred ownership to the cattle rancher. In this way, cattle ranchers did not have to pay for desirable land.

Even in Utah, where farmers had community irrigation systems, there was still conflict. One man felt he had to sit in the dark near the ditch that provided water for his farm. With a rock in hand, he hid waiting for any neighbor who might try to drop the gate to the ditch before his watering was completed.

John Wesley Powell, a geologist and explorer of the Southwest, suggested to Congress that reforms were needed. In 1878, Powell presented the Report on the Lands of the Arid Region of the United States. He recommended that lawmakers modify land laws to make settlement a more cooperative process. Powell was passionate about water. In 1869, he and a crew of nine men braved the wilds and rapids of the Colorado and Green Rivers. Below is an excerpt from Powell's book, *Canyons of the Colorado.* Written in 1895, the book recalls Powell's first expedition. Would you volunteer to join Powell on a similar expedition?

August 21 – We start early this morning, cheered by the prospect of a fine day and encouraged also by the good run made yesterday. A quarter of a mile below camp the river turns abruptly to the left, and between camp and that point is very swift.... From around this curve there comes a mad roar, and down we are carried with a dizzying velocity to the head of another rapid. On either side high over our heads there are overhanging granite walls, and the sharp bends cut off our view, so that a few minutes will carry us into unknown waters. Away we go on one long, winding chute. I stand on deck, supporting myself with a strap fastened on either side of the gunwale. The boat glides rapidly where the water is smooth, then, striking a wave, she leaps and bounds like a thing of life, and we have a wild, exhilarating ride for ten miles, which we make in less than an hour. The excitement is so great that we forget the danger until we hear the roar of a great fall below; then we back on our oars and are carried slowly toward its head and succeed in landing just above and find that we have to make another portage. At this we are engaged until some time after dinner.

John Wesley Powell, Canyons of the Colorado (1895)

Assignment

Historians examine the past very carefully to record an accurate record of historical events. But they also want to explain the importance of the past. The following terms help historians do just that.

Cause: reason for an action, event, or behavior
Effect: result of an action, event, or behavior
Sequence: the order of events.
Correlation: the relationship between two events
Short-term effect: effect seen shortly after an event, action, or behavior has occurred
Long-term effect: effect seen long after an event, action, or behavior has occurred

Look back over the entire reading. Record one example for each term listed above. Then write a short paragraph explaining how these six terms help historians study the past.

Women Speak Out for Equal Rights

Many individuals contributed to the growth of the women's movement in the first half of the 19th century. Four notable examples are Susan B. Anthony, Elizabeth Cady Stanton, Lucretia Mott, and Margaret Fuller. Below is a brief biographical sketch of each woman, along with an excerpt from her writings. What is each woman's message?

Susan B. Anthony (1820–1906)

Susan B. Anthony was born in Adams, Massachusetts. As a young woman, her Quaker family encouraged her work in the fight against slavery. She was angry, though, that she was not allowed to speak at any public meetings.

**Chapter 18
An Era of Reform**

Investigating Biographies

Anthony believed that women would not be able to improve society until they could vote. She dedicated her life to the cause of women's rights. Working with Elizabeth Cady Stanton, she organized the National Woman Suffrage Association in 1869.

When Anthony tried to vote in 1872, she was arrested and fined $100. Her death in 1906 came before women achieved the right to vote. In 1979, the United States government honored her life's work by making her the first woman to be featured on an American coin—the Susan B. Anthony silver dollar.

It is said women do not need the ballot for their protection because they are supported by men. Statistics show that there are 3,000,000 women in this nation supporting themselves. In the crowded cities of the East they are compelled [forced by circumstances] to work in shops, stores and factories for the merest pittance [small sum]. In New York alone, there are over 50,000 of these women receiving less than fifty cents a day.

Susan B. Anthony
Women Want Bread, Not the Ballot
(speech delivered in many cities, 1870–1880)

Elizabeth Cady Stanton (1815–1902)

Born to a wealthy New York family, Elizabeth Cady Stanton had the best education a woman could get at the time. As a young woman, she married an abolitionist. At the World Anti-Slavery Convention in London, Stanton and other women were forced to sit upstairs behind a screen. There she met another delegate, Lucretia Mott, and the two banded together to fight for women's rights.

Stanton and Mott organized the first women's rights convention at Seneca Falls, New York, in 1848. Stanton also helped Susan B. Anthony found the National Woman Suffrage Association. Like Anthony, she did not live to see women vote. She died in 1902, nearly two decades before the Nineteenth Amendment (granting women the right to vote) was approved.

If we consider her [woman] as a citizen, as a member of a great nation, she must have the same rights as all other members, according to the fundamental principles of our Government.... The strongest reason why we ask for woman a voice in the government under which she lives; in the religion she is asked to believe; equality in social life, where she is the chief factor; a place in the trades and professions, where she may earn her bread, is because of her birthright to self-sovereignty [self-rule]; because, as an individual, she must rely on herself.

Elizabeth Cady Stanton
Solitude of Self (1892)

Lucretia Mott (1793–1880)

Lucretia Mott was born in Nantucket, Massachusetts. As a child she attended a coeducational Quaker school. In adulthood, she worked with her husband in the abolitionist movement. She refused to buy cotton cloth or cane sugar, products that were made by slave labor.

Like Stanton, Mott realized the need to work for women's rights when she was prevented from participating in the World Anti-Slavery Convention in London. She helped Stanton organize the convention at Seneca Falls in 1848. She spent her life speaking on topics of social reform: abolition, women's rights, temperance, and world peace. In 1866 Mott became the first president of the Equal Rights Association, a group committed to African-American and woman suffrage. She was active in such causes up to the time of her death at age 87.

> Thou wilt [will] have hard work to prove the intellectual equality of Woman with man—facts are so against such an assumption, in the present stage of woman's development. We need not however admit inferiority, even tho' we may not be able to prove equality.
>
> Lucretia Mott
> *Letter to Elizabeth Cady Stanton* (1855)

Margaret Fuller (1810–1850)

Margaret Fuller was born in Cambridge, Massachusetts. She could not attend Harvard, which was at that time a school for men only. But she was well educated in classic and modern literature by her father. Fuller became one of the first professional women journalists in America. She wrote mostly about social issues, such as the treatment of women prisoners and the insane. In her most important work, *Woman in the Nineteenth Century* (1845), she discussed the unequal treatment of women and offered suggestions for improvement. Fuller was only 40 when she died tragically in a shipwreck.

> It should be remarked that, as the principle of liberty is better understood, and more nobly interpreted, a broader protest is made in behalf of Woman. As men become aware that few men have had a fair chance, they are inclined to say that no women have had a fair chance.... What Woman needs is not as a woman to act or rule, but as a nature to grow, as an intellect to discern [figure out], as a soul to live freely and unimpeded [not controlled], to unfold such powers as were given her when we left our common home.
>
> Margaret Fuller
> *Woman in the Nineteenth Century* (1845)

Assignment

Write a eulogy for one of these four women's rights leaders: Susan B. Anthony, Elizabeth Cady Stanton, Lucretia Mott, or Margaret Fuller. Your eulogy should

- include important biographical details in the life of the chosen individual.
- summarize her significant contributions to the women's rights movement.
- include brief quotation from her writing and a one- to two-sentence interpretation of what you think the quote means.
- explain how this individual's actions have affected the world today.
- be free of errors in spelling, punctuation, capitalization, and grammar.

**Investigating Literature and
Primary Sources**

Working Conditions in the Northeast

Factories and mills brought huge changes to life in the Northeast in the early 1800s. Below are two documents that reveal something about conditions in textile mills in Lowell, Massachusetts, at that time.

The first document is from *American Notes* by Charles Dickens. As a child, Dickens was treated harshly while working in English factories. Later, his writings were critical of the factory system there. The second document is excerpted from a letter by Mary Paul, a young girl who worked in the textile factories in Lowell. Paul started working when she was just 15. As you will see, the factories brought both positive and negative changes to the people of the Northeast.

American Notes

I happened to arrive at the first factory just as the dinner hour was over, and the girls were returning to their work.... These girls...were all well dressed.... They had serviceable [usable] bonnets, good warm cloaks and shawls.... They were healthy in appearance, many of them remarkably so, and had the manners and deportment [conduct] of young women.... The rooms in which they worked were as well ordered as themselves.... I am now going to state three facts, which will startle a large class of readers on this side of the Atlantic [in England], very much.

Firstly, there is a...piano in a great many of the boarding-houses. Secondly, nearly all these young ladies subscribe to circulating libraries. Thirdly, they have got up among themselves a periodical called *The Lowell Offering*, "A repository [set] of original articles, written exclusively by females actively employed in the mills."

The large class of readers, startled by these facts, will exclaim, with one voice, "How very preposterous!" On my deferentially inquiring why, they will answer, "These things are above their station." In reply to that objection, I would beg to ask what their station is.

It is their station to work. And they *do* work. They labour in these mills, upon an average, twelve hours a day, which is unquestionably work, and pretty tight work too. Perhaps it is above their station to indulge in such amusements, on any terms. Are we quite sure that we in England have not formed our ideas of the "station" of working people, from accustoming ourselves to the contemplation of that class as they are, and not as they might be? I think that if we examine our own feelings, we shall find that the pianos, and the circulating libraries, and even the *Lowell Offering,* startle us by their novelty, and not by their bearing upon any abstract question of right or wrong.

Charles Dickens
American Notes (1842)

Letter from a Young Factory Worker

Lowell, Dec 21st 1845

Dear Father,

I received your letter on Thursday the 14th with much pleasure. I am well which is one comfort. My life and health are spared while others are cut off. Last Thursday one girl fell down and broke her neck which caused instant death. She was going in or coming out of the mill and slipped down it being very icy, the same day as a man was killed by the cars, another had nearly all of his ribs broken, another was nearly killed by falling down and having a balc of cotton fall on him. Last Tuesday we were paid. In all I had six dollars and sixty cents paid $4.68 for board, with the rest I got me a pair of rubbers and a pair of 50 cts shoes. Next payment I am to have a dollar a week besides my board [costs for housing and food]. We have not had much snow, the deepest being not more than 4 inches. It has been very warm for winter. Perhaps you would like something about our regulations about going in and coming out of the mill. At 5 o'clock in the morning the bell rings for the folks to get up and get breakfast. At half past six it rings for the girls to get up and at seven they are called into the mill. At half past 12 we have dinner are called back again at one and stay till half past seven. I get along very well with my work. I can doff as fast as any girl in our room. I think I shall have frames before long. The usual time allowed for learning is six months but I think I shall have frames before I have been in three as long as I get along so fast. I think that the factory is the best place for me and if any girl wants employment I advise them to come to Lowell....

Mary Paul
Letter to her father (1845)

Source: Transcript of a letter in the collection of the Vermont Historical Society. Reprinted by permission.

Assignment

Analyze the two documents that address the working conditions in Lowell by answering these questions:

1. When were these two documents written?
2. Who are the authors?
3. Who is the audience for these writings?
4. How would your view of Lowell be different if you had read only *American Notes* by Dickens and not the letter written by Mary Paul?
5. Why is it important to examine many sources when reconstructing the past?
6. Based on what you learned from these documents, would you say the American factory system was an overall positive or negative force for the workers? For the American economy?
7. Would these two documents give you enough evidence to write with certainty about the factory system, or would you want to look at other sources? Explain.

Investigating Primary Sources

Voices of Opposition to Slavery

In Chapter 20 you read about people who resisted slavery through acts of rebellion. Another form of resistance was verbal: through books, pamphlets, newspapers, and speeches. In an age without television or radio, the written word and public speeches took on greater importance. Those who hated slavery wrote and spoke with great passion. Following are examples of some of the eloquent voices raised against slavery.

Fanny Kemble (1809–1893)

Fanny Kemble, actress and writer, was a strong-minded woman. She was married to a man who owned hundreds of slaves. Kemble hated slavery and hoped to persuade her husband to free those he kept on his Georgia plantation. The following excerpt is from Kemble's journal, which was later published.

> You will see how miserable the physical conditions of many of these poor creatures is.... Judge from the details I now send you; and never forget, while reading them, that the people on this plantation are well off, and consider themselves well off, in comparison with the slaves on some of the neighboring [communities].... Sophy, Lewis's wife, came to beg for some old linen. She is suffering fearfully; has had ten children, five of them are dead. The principal favor she asked was a piece of meat, which I gave her.
>
> Frances Anne Kemble
> *Journal of a Residence of a Georgian Plantation in 1838–1839*

Harriet Beecher Stowe (1811–1896)

The next excerpt is from *Uncle Tom's Cabin,* a novel by northern writer Harriet Beecher Stowe. As you will read in Chapter 21, *Uncle Tom's Cabin* had a dramatic effect on the country's attitudes toward slavery. It sold over half a million copies in the United States in just five years. It was also translated into 37 languages. The following is from the final chapter of Stowe's book, where she makes a strong appeal to her readers.

> And now, men and women of America, is this [slavery] a thing to be trifled with, apologized for, and passed over in silence? Farmers of Massachusetts, of New Hampshire, of Vermont, of Connecticut, who read this book by the blaze of your winter-evening fire,—strong-hearted, generous sailors and ship-owners of Maine,—is this a thing for you to countenance and encourage? Brave and generous men of New York, farmers of rich and joyous Ohio, and ye of the wide prairie states,— answer, is this a thing for you to protect and countenance? And you, mothers of America,—you who have learned, by the cradles of your own children, to love and feel for all mankind,—by the sacred love you bear your child;...pity those mothers that are constantly made childless by the American slave-trade! And say, mothers of America, is this a thing to be defended, sympathized with, passed over in silence?
>
> Harriet Beecher Stowe
> *Uncle Tom's Cabin* (1852)

William Lloyd Garrison (1805–1879)

In Chapter 18 you read about William Lloyd Garrison, who used his abolitionist newspaper, *The Liberator,* to speak out for the rights of black Americans for more than three decades. The newspaper's motto was: "Our country is the world—our countrymen are mankind." In the very first issue, Garrison wrote an editorial "To the Public" that set forth his goals. The following is from that piece.

> Assenting [agreeing] to the "self-evident truth" maintained in the American Declaration of Independence, "that all men are created equal, and endowed by their Creator with certain inalienable rights—among which are life, liberty and the pursuit of happiness," I shall strenuously [strongly] contend for the immediate enfranchisement [granting citizenship rights such as voting] of our slave population.... I am aware, that many object to the severity [strength] of my language; but is there not cause for severity? I will be as harsh as the truth, and as uncompromising as justice. On this subject, I do not wish to think, or speak, or write, with moderation.... I am in earnest—I will not equivocate—I will not excuse—I will not retreat a single inch—AND I WILL BE HEARD.
>
> William Lloyd Garrison
> *The Liberator* (January 1, 1831)

Theodore Dwight Weld (1803–1895)

Theodore Dwight Weld was a writer and active speaker against slavery. He led a campaign that sent many anti-slavery petitions to Congress. In his book, *American Slavery As It Is: Testimony of a Thousand Witnesses,* Weld wrote about the evils of slavery. His name is not widely known today. However, many historians believe that Weld was the most important figure in the abolitionist movement.

> We repeat it, every man knows that slavery is a curse. Whoever denies this, his lips libel his heart. Try him; clank the chains in his ears, and tell him they are for him. Give him an hour to prepare his wife and children for a life of slavery. Bid him make haste and get ready their necks for the yoke, and their wrists for the coffle chains, then look at his pale lips and trembling knees, and you have nature's testimony against slavery.
>
> Two millions seven hundred thousand persons in these States are in this condition. They were made slaves and are held such by force, and by being put in fear, and this for no crime! Reader, what have you to say of such treatment? Is it right, just, benevolent? Suppose I should seize you, rob you of your liberty, drive you into the field, and make you work without pay as long as you live, would that be justice and kindness, or monstrous injustice and cruelty?
>
> Theodore Dwight Weld
> *American Slavery As It Is: Testimony of a Thousand Witnesses* (1839)

David Walker (c. 1785–1830)

The son of a slave father and free mother, David Walker was a free black who left the South for Boston. In 1829 he published *An Appeal to the Colored Citizens of the World,* a powerful and controversial anti-slavery pamphlet. He called for slaves to rise up and free themselves.

Frederick Douglass said that Walker's *Appeal* "startled the land like a trump [trumpet] of coming justice."

> Having travelled over a considerable portion of these United States, and having, in the course of my travels, taken the most accurate observations of things as they exist, the result of my observations has warranted the full and unshaken conviction, that we (coloured people of these United States,) are the most degraded, wretched, and abject set of beings that ever lived since the world began; and I pray God that none like us ever may live again until time shall be no more.
>
> ...to my no ordinary astonishment, [a] Reverend gentleman got up and told us (coloured people) that slaves must be obedient to their masters— must do their duty to their masters or be whipped—the whip was made for the backs of fools, &c. Here I pause for a moment, to give the world time to consider what was my surprise, to hear such preaching from a minister of my Master, whose very gospel is that of peace and not of blood and whips.... They have newspapers and monthly periodicals...but on the pages of which, you will scarcely ever find a paragraph respecting slavery, which is ten thousand times more injurious [harmful] to this country than all the other evils put together; and which will be the final overthrow of its government, unless something is very speedily done; for their cup is nearly full. Perhaps they will laugh at or make light of this; but I tell you Americans! that unless you speedily alter your course, you and your Country are gone! ! ! ! !

David Walker
An Appeal to the Colored Citizens of the World (1829)

Frederick Douglass (c. 1817–1895)

After his escape from slavery in 1838, Frederick Douglass became a leading spokesman for the abolitionist movement. Douglass was a brilliant speaker. He gave a stirring speech to the Massachusetts Anti-Slavery Society in Boston in April of 1865. In it, he spoke about racial injustice.

> What is freedom? It is the right to choose one's own employment. Certainly it means that, if it means anything; and when an individual or combination of individuals undertakes to decide for any man when he shall work, where he shall work, at what he shall work, and for what he shall work, he or they practically reduce him to slavery.... No class of men can, without insulting their own nature, be content with any depriva-tion [taking away] of their rights. We want it again, as a means of educating our race.... By depriving us of suffrage [voting rights], you affirm our incapacity [inability] to form an intelligent judgment respect-ing public men and public measures; you declare before the world that we are unfit to exercise the elective franchise [voting], and by this means lead us to undervalue ourselves, to put a low estimate upon ourselves, and to feel that we have no possibilities like other men.

Frederick Douglass
What the Black Man Wants (1865)

Assignment

Powerful speeches and printed pieces played a large role in the abolitionist movement. Following the example of the arguments you have just read, write a persuasive speech convincing your audience that slavery is wrong. Your speech should contain at least four paragraphs and include

- an introduction that states a clear position.
- a body paragraph that supports your position with organized and relevant evidence. Include quotes from at least two of the primary sources above.
- a body paragraph that both anticipates counterarguments (why slavery is not wrong) and explains why your position is correct.
- a conclusion that restates your position and summarizes your main points.
- proper spelling, punctuation, and grammar.

Daniel Webster and John C. Calhoun Debate the Future

Tensions between the North and the South reached a crisis in 1850. During the lengthy debates over the Compromise of 1850, Southerners wondered aloud about leaving the Union. Secession—separating from the Union—was on their lips.

Right in the middle of the debates were two senators: Daniel Webster of Massachusetts and John C. Calhoun of South Carolina. Calhoun believed that federal authority over the states should be limited. In his Southern Address of 1849 Calhoun stated, "So far from maintaining the doctrine, which the issue implies, we hold that the Federal Government has no right to extend or restrict slavery, no more than to establish or abolish it." Webster, on the other hand, believed strongly in the supremacy of the federal government. In a famous 1830 speech, Webster argued against the idea of "Liberty first and Union afterwards." He said such statements were "words of delusion and folly." Following are excerpts from speeches given by Webster and Calhoun in 1850, at a very tense moment in American history.

John C. Calhoun (1782–1850)

… Is it, then, not certain that if something is not done to arrest it [Northern attacks on slavery], the South will be forced to choose between abolition [ending slavery] and secession?…

It is a great mistake to suppose that disunion can be effected by a single blow. The cords which bind these States together in one common Union are far too numerous and powerful for that. Disunion must be the work of time. It is only through a long process, and successively [one step at a time], that the cords can be snapped until the whole fabric falls asunder [secession breaks the Union apart]. Already the agitation [angry debate] of the slavery question has snapped some of the most important, and has greatly weakened all the others. If the agitation goes on, the same force, acting with increased intensity, as has been shown, will finally snap every cord, when nothing will be left to hold the States together except force.

The Clay Compromise Measures (March 4, 1850)

Investigating Primary Sources

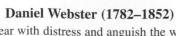

Daniel Webster (1782–1852)

Mr. President,...I hear with distress and anguish the word "secession," especially when it falls from the lips of those who are patriotic, and known to the country, and known all over the world, for their political services. Secession! Peaceable secession! Sir, your eyes and mine are never destined to see that miracle.... Is the great Constitution under which we live, covering this whole country, is it to be thawed and melted away by secession, as the snows on the mountain melt under the influence of a vernal [spring] sun, disappear almost unobserved, and run off? No, Sir! No, Sir! I will not state what might produce the disruption of the Union; but, Sir, I see as plainly as I see the sun in heaven what that disruption itself must produce; I see that it must produce war, and such a war as I will not describe.

The Seventh of March Speech (March 7, 1850)

Assignment

Complete an analysis of this discussion by answering the following questions:

1. What states did Webster and Calhoun represent in Congress?
2. In what key ways were their states different?
3. In what ways are their views different? The same?
4. To whom were these men speaking?
5. What events caused these men to write these speeches?
6. Why do you think these two men, with such different backgrounds and views, reached a very similar prediction—that war may result from the tensions between state and federal authority?

**Chapter 22
The Civil War**

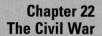

Investigating Biographies and Primary Sources

Generals and Soldiers of the Civil War

The Civil War was a tragedy for the men who served on both sides. More than 3 million soldiers wore the uniforms of the Blue and Gray. They fought in over 10,000 engagements. Horribly, 620,000 died. It was the bloodiest war in American history.

Following are brief biographies and statements of four men who served. Two were generals—the most famous of the war. Two were men that few have heard of, but whose words speak for countless others. As you read, ask yourself what motivated these men to fight in such a terrible conflict.

Robert E. Lee (1807–1870)

The commander in chief of the Confederate armies was Robert E. Lee. He was born in Virginia, the son of a Revolutionary War hero. Lee followed in his father's footsteps and joined the military. He graduated from West Point in 1829 and distinguished himself in battle during the Mexican War. Some of his fellow soldiers were men who would become generals—Grant, Meade, McClellan, Hooker, Burnside, Beauregard, and Johnston. They would all meet again in war—but not all would be on the same side.

Lee was serving in Texas when he was called to Washington, D.C., in early 1861. When Virginia seceded, Lee faced a terrible choice—to serve his nation or protect his state. After agonizing over the decision, he resigned from the army and went home to Virginia to command Confederate troops. By 1862, Lee was commanding the entire Army of Northern Virginia. His skillful leadership was admired in the North and South alike. He wrote about his choice to defend the South in a letter to his sister in 1861.

> With all my devotion to the Union and the feeling of loyalty and duty of an American citizen, I have not been able to make up my mind to raise my hand against my relatives, my children, my home. I have therefore resigned my commission in the Army, and save in defense of my native State, with the sincere hope that my poor services may never be needed, I hope I may never be called on to draw my sword....
>
> Robert E. Lee
> *Letter to his sister* (April 20, 1861)

Ulysses S. Grant (1822–1885)

Ulysses S. Grant was born in Ohio. He graduated from West Point in 1843. Like Lee, he served during the Mexican War. Later, after Grant had married and had children, he was assigned to lonely military outposts in the West. He began drinking and eventually resigned from the army. Afterward, he struggled to make a living in business.

When the Civil War broke out, Grant immediately offered his services. At first he was turned down. But with the help of a congressman, he took commands in Missouri and Tennessee. Grant's success in battle caught the attention of President Lincoln. Late in the war, Lincoln turned to Grant to command the largest Union army and end the war.

Grant's fame as a general helped him win election as president in 1868. In his memoirs, Grant made the following statement about why he chose to serve the Union.

> The 4th of March, 1861, came, and Abraham Lincoln was sworn to maintain the Union against all its enemies. The secession of one State after another followed, until eleven had gone out. On the fifth of April Fort Sumter, a National fort in the harbor of Charleston, South Carolina, was fired upon by the Southerners and a few days after was captured. The Confederates proclaimed themselves aliens, and thereby debarred [excluded] themselves of all right to claim protection under the Constitution of the United States. We did not admit the fact that they were aliens, but all the same, they debarred themselves of the right to *expect* better treatment than people of any other foreign state who make war upon an independent nation. Upon the firing on Sumter President Lincoln issued his first call for...75,000 volunteers.... There was not a state in the North of a million of inhabitants that would not have furnished the entire number faster than arms could have been supplied to them, if it had been necessary.
>
> Ulysses S. Grant
> *Personal Memoirs* (1885)

A Confederate Soldier

Robert W. Banks served in the Confederacy during the Civil War. This excerpt from a letter to his sister reveals something about his motives for fighting.

Dear Sister Mat [Martha Jane Banks],

... I dread this winter very much—Many a poor fellow in our company will "yield his carcass to the dust" before 'tis over—I can stand it as well as any of them—I believe that 'twill be no child's play for any of us. Infantry have an easy time in camp, but it is fully compensated for when, after a heavy march of a hundred or two miles, the bloody conflict comes on—I do not regret one particle, enlisting, if 'twere to do over I would volunteer again, but would not go as a private—But enough of this, I will not repine at the past, but hope that before another moon shall have passed to strike a blow for my country that will tell. Although, we have so many hardships to undergo, if I am but able to render any assistance to the land of my nativity either by sending a Yankee home with a "bug in his ear" or merely by following General Price on another "wild goose chase", then all of my tolls will be repaid—Cannot write more now—remember I write under very disparaging circumstances, i.e. soiled paper, nothing but my knee to write upon, and lastly with the certainty of a hard day's march before me.

Robert W. Banks
Letter to his sister written near Ripley, Mississippi (October 1, 1862)

Source: Marszalek, John F. and Williams, Clay. "Mississippi Soldiers in the Civil War," *Mississippi History Now,* the online publication of the Mississippi Historical Society, 2001. Reprinted by permission.

A Yankee Soldier

Sullivan Ballou served in the Rhode Island Volunteers. By the time the Civil War began, Ballou had risen from poverty to become a lawyer. He and his wife, Sarah, looked forward to raising their two sons, Edgar and Willie. Ballou was a strong Republican who had voted for Lincoln. He was killed at the Battle of Bull Run shortly after this letter was written.

My very dear Sarah:

The indications are very strong that we shall move in a few days—perhaps tomorrow. Lest I should not be able to write you again I feel impelled to write a few lines that may fall under your eye when I shall be no more.

I have no misgivings about, or lack of confidence in the cause in which I am engaged, and my courage does not halt or falter. I know how strongly American Civilization now leans upon the triumph of the Government and how great a debt we owe to those who went before us through the blood and suffering of the Revolution. And I am willing—perfectly willing—to lay down all my joys in this life, to help maintain this Government, and to pay that debt ....

Sarah, my love for you is deathless, it seems to bind me to you with mighty cables that nothing but Omnipotence could break; and yet my love of Country comes over me like a strong wind and bears me irresistibly on with all those chains to the battle field.

The memories of the blissful moments I have spent with you come creeping over me, and I feel most gratified to God and to you, that I have enjoyed them for so long. And how hard it is for me to give them up and burn to ashes the hopes of future years, when, God willing, we might still have lived and loved together, and seen our sons grown up to honorable manhood around us.

… If I do not [return], my dear Sarah, never forget how much I love you, and when my last breath escapes me on the battle field, it will whisper your name...

Sullivan Ballou
Letter to his wife (July 14, 1861)

Assignment

Imagine that you are a young man living in the South or the North in April 1861, when the Civil War began. Write a statement that expresses why you are willing to die for what you believe is right. Refer to the arguments made by Southerners like Robert E. Lee and Robert W. Banks or Northerners like Ulysses S. Grant and Sullivan Ballou. Select from the following forms of writing: a personal letter to a family member or friend, a letter to the editor of a wartime newspaper, or a report to your commanding officer. Your completed piece must be at least three paragraphs long and free of errors in spelling, punctuation, capitalization, and grammar.

Jim Crow Laws: A Legacy of the Reconstruction Era

In Chapter 23 you read that after the slaves were freed, Southern states passed laws known as black codes, denying recently freed blacks their rights. During the Reconstruction era, some of these codes were struck down. However, when the election of 1876 ended Northern occupation of the South, a new rash of segregation laws were passed.

From the 1880s to the 1960s, many states enforced segregation (the separation of whites and African Americans) through such "Jim Crow" laws. With these laws, states punished people for mixing with those of another race.

Below are examples of Jim Crow laws passed by various states. When these laws were written, many people accepted discrimination and commonly used terms such as *Negro* and *colored* that are now considered inappropriate or offensive. Fortunately these terms, like Jim Crow laws themselves, are now a part of our nation's past. As you read the laws below, imagine what it might have been like to be African American in the days of Jim Crow laws.

> *Education:* [The County Board of Education]: shall provide schools of two kinds; those for white children and those for colored children....

**Chapter 23
The Reconstruction Era**

Investigating Primary Sources

Pool and Billiard Rooms: It shall be unlawful for a Negro and white person to play together or in company with each other at any game of pool or billiards....

Toilet Facilities: Every employer of white or Negro males shall provide for such white or Negro males reasonably accessible and separate toilet facilities....

Barbers: No colored barber shall serve as a barber [to] white women or girls....

Burial: The officer in charge shall not bury, or allow to be buried, any colored persons upon ground set apart or used for the burial of white persons....

Amateur Baseball: It shall be unlawful for any amateur white baseball team to play baseball on any vacant lot or baseball diamond within two blocks of a playground devoted to the Negro race....

Parks: It shall be unlawful for colored people to frequent any park owned or maintained by the city for the benefit, use and enjoyment of white persons....

Intermarriage: The marriage of a white person with a Negro or mulatto or person who shall have one-eighth or more of Negro blood, shall be unlawful and void....

Fishing, Boating, and Bathing: The [Conservation] Commission shall have the right to make segregation of the white and colored races as to the exercise of rights of fishing, boating and bathing....

Jackson Sun
"The Untold Story of Jackson's
Civil Rights Movement" (October 1960)

Assignment

Write a letter from the perspective of an African American citizen of Mississippi in the late 19th century. Your letter should

- be addressed to an elected or appointed official, such as a Supreme Court justice or a governor of a southern state, and be dated April 25, 1897.
- describe how Jim Crow laws have affected you (the letter writer) personally.
- attempt to persuade the official why the laws must be changed.
- contain at least three paragraphs that are free of errors in spelling, punctuation, capitalization, and grammar.
- include historically appropriate emotional details and imaginary touches.

The Immigrant Experience in the West: Two Novels

Many writers have been attracted to the drama of the immigrant experience in the West. Willa Cather and Ole E. Rolvaag are two such writers.

Willa Cather (1873–1947)

Cather was not herself an immigrant. However, she met a lot of them when, as a girl, she moved with her family to Nebraska in 1883. Years later, she wrote *My Ántonia* about a Bohemian family in Nebraska. The novel traces the joys and tragedies of Ántonia Shimerda, the eldest daughter.

> While the autumn colour was growing pale on the grass and cornfields, things went badly with our friends the Russians. Peter told his troubles to Mr. Shimerda: he was unable to meet a note which fell due on the first of November; had to pay an exorbitant [huge] bonus on renewing it, and to give a mortgage on his pigs and horses and even his milk cow. His creditor was Wick Cutter, the merciless Black Hawk money-lender, a man of evil name throughout the county, of whom I shall have more to say later. Peter could give no very clear account of his transactions with Cutter. He only knew that he had first borrowed two hundred dollars, then another hundred, then fifty—that each time a bonus was added to the principal, and the debt grew faster than any crop he planted. Now everything was plastered with mortgages.
>
> Soon after Peter renewed his note, Pavel strained himself lifting timbers for a new barn, and fell over among the shavings with such a gush of blood from the lungs that his fellow workmen thought he would die on the spot. They hauled him home and put him into his bed, and there he lay, very ill indeed. Misfortune seemed to settle like an evil bird on the roof of the log house, and to flap its wings there, warning human beings away. The Russians had such bad luck that people were afraid of them and liked to put them out of mind.
>
> *My Ántonia* (1918)

Ole E. Rolvaag (1876–1931)

Unlike Cather, Rolvaag actually was an immigrant. He came from Norway in 1896 and settled in South Dakota. His novel *Giants in the Earth* is an account of immigrant pioneer life on the Dakota prairies in 1870s.

> Between the heads of the two oxen a yellow eye seemed to be gleaming through the curtain of the driving snow. "It must be my death signal" thought Per Hansa. He trembled so violently that he could hardly keep his feet. He saw now that the eye shining through the drifting snow was in reality the light from a small window.... He found his way around the house corner, came to a door, flung it open without ceremony and stumbled in.... The heat of the room seemed to flow over him in a great wave, deadening all his senses. The light blinded him, he could not open his eyes beyond a narrow slit, his face was crusted with snow and ice: his eyelashes were frozen together.... Out of the jaws of death he had walked in a single step into warmth and life and safety.
>
> *Giants in the Earth* (1927)

Investigating Literature

Assignment

Historians study a great number of sources in order to piece together an accurate picture of the past. They must learn to identify the most important details to help them discover what is most significant in a historical narrative or story. The following terms are handy labels to use for pieces of information while studying historical documents:

Relevant: information important to solving a problem or reaching a conclusion

Irrelevant: information not important to solving a problem or reaching a conclusion

Essential: information absolutely necessary to solving a problem or reaching a conclusion

Incidental: information absolutely not necessary to solving a problem or reaching a conclusion.

Verifiable: information that can be proven by examining other sources

Unverifiable: information that cannot be proven by examining other sources.

Imagine that you are a historian studying the West. You want to write a book about the life of immigrants in the West that proves the following statement: *The life of the immigrant farmer was dangerous and challenging.* What important information about this statement can be drawn from these two literary excerpts? Make a chart that lists the six terms, along with examples that you find in *My Ántonia* or *Giants in the Earth.* You may use the same fact or information in more than one place on the chart.

**Chapter 25
The Rise of Industry**

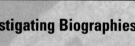

Investigating Biographies

Inventions Improve Life for Many

America experienced an explosion of industry and innovation at the turn of the 20th century. New technologies arose in many fields, from farming to films. Edison's electrical inventions and Bell's telephone ushered in a new age. Below are biographies of five individuals who made other innovations during this time. How did each of these people improve American life in the short term? What long-term effects might their ideas have—both good and bad?

Friend of the Farmer: George Washington Carver (1864–1943)

George Washington Carver was born a slave on a Missouri farm near the end of the Civil War. As a baby, he was separated from his mother, and his former owners brought him up like a son. Carver grew up learning about the plants and flowers that grew in the fields around their farm.

After studying horticulture (the science of plants) at Iowa State College, Carver became a professor at the Tuskegee Institute, a college dedicated to the education of African Americans. Many blacks in the South earned their living by farming. They grew almost nothing but cotton, and the cotton crops were ruining the soil. Every year, they had less to sell. Carver taught these farmers the idea of "crop rotation." He pointed out that planting a different crop in alternate years would help the soil recover. Certain crops were better for the soil than others: black-eyed peas, sweet potatoes, pecans, and peanuts.

While there was a big market for cotton, there wasn't much demand for a crop like peanuts. Carver turned to his labs to find new uses for these crops, to create a market for them. Through research, Carver developed more than 350 products from sweet potatoes, pecans, and especially peanuts. He turned these crops into such varied products as cooking oil, printer's ink, bleach, dyes, face powder, shaving cream, metal polishes, shampoo, and road paving material. Peanut butter was perhaps his most popular product.

Carver didn't try to patent most of his ideas. His goal was simply to help the poor farmers who depended on the red soil of the South, worn out by years of growing cotton. His products and his teachings about farming brought them new markets and new hope.

Carver's innovations were part of a wave of new ideas that improved farming production in the period from 1877 to 1920. Earlier inventions, such as John Deere's steel plow or Cyrus McCormick's mechanical reaper, paved the way. Now horse-drawn plows and combines were replaced by kerosene and gas-powered machines that could cover far more ground than a single farmer using livestock. These new ideas transformed the rural American landscape, just as industrialization and mechanization changed life in America's cities.

The Dishwashing Machine: Josephine Cochrane (1839–1913)

Josephine Cochrane was married to an Illinois politician. They were a wealthy couple who gave many dinner parties. Cochrane had plenty of servants to wash the fancy china dishes after these parties, but she was upset by the number of dishes they chipped or broke. She is reported to have said, "If nobody else is going to invent a dishwashing machine, I'll do it myself."

In 1886, Cochran began her invention by designing wire racks to hold the dishes. The racks were positioned inside a wheel that was turned by a motor. When the wheel turned, jets of hot soapy water would squirt up and over the dishes. Josephine Cochrane had invented a dishwasher.

As word spread of Cochrane's invention, hotels and restaurants ordered many of these dishwashing machines. Such businesses had to wash large numbers of dishes in a short period of time. Breakage was also an expensive problem. The dishwasher cut costs and improved efficiency for hotels and restaurants. Cochrane's invention was so impressive it won the highest award at the 1893 Chicago World's Fair.

The Affordable Automobile: Henry Ford (1863–1947)

At age 16, Henry Ford left his family farm to become an apprentice machinist in the city of Detroit. In 1891, the Edison Illuminating Company hired him as an engineer. Ford experimented with the idea of a self-propelled vehicle—an "automobile" that he called the Quadricycle. It had four wheels and a tiller (like a boat has) for steering. It went forward in two speeds, but did not go in reverse. It ran on gasoline.

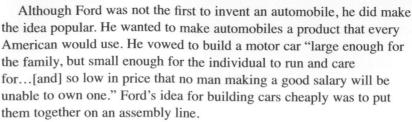

Although Ford was not the first to invent an automobile, he did make the idea popular. He wanted to make automobiles a product that every American would use. He vowed to build a motor car "large enough for the family, but small enough for the individual to run and care for...[and] so low in price that no man making a good salary will be unable to own one." Ford's idea for building cars cheaply was to put them together on an assembly line.

In 1908, Ford Motor Company introduced the Model T to a world dominated by horses and trains. It was reasonably priced and reliable. This car was easy to operate, simple to maintain, and strong on rough roads. Everybody wanted one. The Model T was a big success, as it greatly improved personal transportation. By 1918, half of all the cars sold in the United States were Model Ts.

A Sturdier Pair of Pants: Levi Strauss (1829–1902)

At 18 years of age, Levi Strauss immigrated to New York from Bavaria (part of modern-day Germany). Six years later, he moved to San Francisco to make his fortune in the California gold rush. Struass did not pan for gold, however, but opened a store to sell supplies to the miners. Customers wore out their trousers very quickly, working hard in the gold fields. Strauss sold them many pairs of overalls.

In 1873, Strauss formed a partnership with another European immigrant, tailor Jacob Davis. The two men patented an idea for using copper rivets (metal fasteners) in work pants. With rivets placed at key seams, the pants would not rip so easily.

That was the birth of "blue jeans": riveted, made of denim, dyed indigo blue. The new, stronger pants were an immediate success. Demand was so great, Strauss soon opened a factory in San Francisco that made nothing else. Today, Levi Strauss's blue jeans are a multimillion-dollar, worldwide industry.

The Fantastic Flying Machine:
Wilbur Wright (1867–1912) and Orville Wright (1867–1912)

As children, Orville and Wilbur Wright were encouraged to experiment with the world around them. Orville wrote of his childhood, "We were lucky enough to grow up in an environment where there was always much encouragement to children to pursue intellectual interests; to investigate whatever aroused curiosity."

The Wrights kept this outlook into their adulthood. The brothers were fascinated with the idea of a flying machine. They watched buzzards to learn about flight. They read a number of books. Unfortunately, many of those books contained inaccurate information, so they learned what worked—and what didn't—mostly by trial and error.

At first they experimented with gliders, which simply rode the wind. In 1903, the Wright brothers announced they would attempt to fly the world's first machine-powered airplane, the Wright Flyer. Only five people showed up at a beach in Kitty Hawk, North Carolina, to witness the famous flight. It lasted 12 seconds. Three years later, the Wrights obtained a patent for a flying machine—an airplane. In 1908, Wilbur Wright recorded a flight of 1 hour and 31 minutes. For a country as large as the United States, the airplane would greatly improve transportation and communication for years to come.

Assignment

Social scientists studying economics and politics often perform a cost-benefit analysis to judge if a particular idea or change has more costs (negative effects) or benefits (positive effects). Complete a cost-benefit analysis of the innovations you read about: Carver's ideas for southern farming, Cochrane's dishwasher, Ford's automobile, Strauss's blue jeans, and the Wright brothers' "flying machine."

Make a T-chart. List all the benefits on one side, and all the possible costs on the other. For example, Henry Ford developed an automobile that everyone could afford. One benefit is faster transportation. One cost is air pollution. Think about both the short term and the long term. You may not always find clear costs. List as many costs and benefits as you can. Then, write a short paragraph that answers this question: Were turn-of-the-century innovations good for the country?

Immigrants from Distant Shores

Millions of immigrants came to America between 1880 and 1920. Mary Antin was one of these. She left Russia in 1894 to join her father, who was already in America. She was eager to leave her homeland, where she faced prejudice and persecution because she was a Jew. In 1912, she published her autobiography, *The Promised Land*. Below are some excerpts in which Antin recalls her days at school. She was only 12 when she arrived in the United States. What challenges did Antin and her immigrant classmates face in their new country?

> I remember to this day what a struggle we had over the word, "water,"
> Miss Dillingham and I. It seemed as if I could not give the sound of w;
> I said "vater" every time. Patiently my teacher worked with me, inventing
> mouth exercises for me, to get my stubborn lips to produce that w; and
> when at last I could say "village" and "water" in rapid alternation, without misplacing the two initials, that memorable word was sweet on my
> lips. For we had conquered, and Teacher was pleased.
>
> • • •
>
> The class was repeating in chorus the Lord's Prayer, heads bowed on
> desks. I was doing my best to keep up by the sound; my mind could not
> go beyond the word, "hallowed," for which I had not found the meaning.
> In the middle of the prayer a Jewish boy across the aisle trod [stepped] on
> my foot to get my attention. "You must not say that," he admonished
> [warned] in a solemn [serious] whisper; "it's Christian." I whispered back
> that it wasn't, and went on to the "Amen." I did not know but what he
> was right, but the name of Christ was not in the prayer, and I was bound
> to do everything that the class did.
>
> Mary Antin
> *The Promised Land* (1912)

Chapter 26
The Great Wave of Immigration

Investigating Literature

Assignment

Immigration to the United States continues today. In 2000, almost 2 million persons came to the United States from countries all over the world. Pick one group of present-day immigrants and do some research to learn more about their experience. Use your research to answer these questions:

- In what ways is the immigrant group's experience different from that of Antin?
- What new patterns have emerged that makes the immigrant experience different from the past? What factors might explain these changes?
- In what ways is the immigrant group's experience similar to that of Antin?
- What do you think explains these similarities with the past?

Investigating Primary Sources

Life in the Slums

Jacob Riis came to the United States from Denmark in 1870. He settled in New York City, where he lived in poverty for several years. Finally he found a job as a police reporter for a newspaper. This job took him into the worst neighborhoods of the city. One such spot was the Five Points slum, notorious for its brutal living conditions. Riis was saddened by what he saw and set out to do something about it. The result was a book, *How the Other Half Lives* (1890). In his book, Riis used both pictures and words to describe the terrible conditions of New York City's poor. Examine the following picture and excerpt from that book. What must it have been like to live in New York's tenement housing?

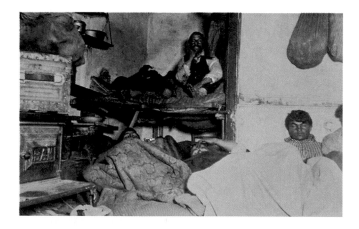

Of one thing New York made sure…the boundary line of the Other Half lies through the tenements…. It is ten years and over, now, since that line divided New York's population evenly. To-day three-fourths of its people live in the tenements, and the nineteenth century drift of the population to the cities is sending ever-increasing multitudes to crowd them. The fifteen thousand tenant houses that were the despair of the sanitarian in the past generation have swelled into thirty-seven thousand, and more than twelve hundred thousand persons call them home…. Where two families had lived ten moved in….

When once I asked the agent of a notorious Fourth Ward alley how many people might be living in it I was told: One hundred and forty families, one hundred Irish, thirty-eight Italian, and two that spoke the German tongue. Barring the agent herself, there was not a native-born individual in the court. The answer was characteristic of the cosmopolitan character of lower New York, very nearly so of the whole of it, wherever it runs to alleys and courts. One may find for the asking an Italian, a German, a French, African, Spanish, Bohemian, Russian, Scandinavian, Jewish, and Chinese colony.

Jacob Riis
How the Other Half Lives (1890)

Assignment

Historians use a variety of sources to examine the past. Text and photographs like those Riis put in his book are windows on America's past. From such documents, historians pull out information about both the physical features of the past (things you can touch, feel, or see) and the cultural features (ways that people live in their physical environment).

Make a list of at least 10 physical and cultural features that Riis mentions. Then answer the following questions:

1. Why do you think people moved from Europe to neighborhoods like the ones Riis describes?
2. How do you think immigrants might have contributed to the growth of the American economy?

The Sinking of the Maine: Two Different Views

You read in Chapter 28 that the sinking of the battleship *Maine* pushed America toward war. Angry citizens blamed the Spanish for the deaths of some 260 American sailors. Many members of the "yellow press" fueled anti-Spanish feelings by printing exaggerated stories about the brutality of Spanish rule in Cuba.

Strangely, recent evidence strongly suggests that Spain was not responsible for sinking the *Maine*. In 1976, Admiral Hyman Rickover presented convincing evidence that the *Maine*'s sinking was probably an accident caused by a faulty boiler.

Within two days of the sinking, two New York newspapers printed editorials on the subject. Working with very little evidence about the event—no eyewitness reports, no expert testimony, nothing from on-site journalists—the writers of these editorials developed two different historical points of view. One editorial clearly wants to place blame. The other is reserving judgment, waiting for more evidence. These editorials show how difficult it is for observers of history to develop an accurate view of the past. Sometimes important information is ignored, or people just get it wrong. For students of history, it is important to remember that history is not just a series of facts. Instead, history is a combination of fact and opinion. Keep that in mind as you read the editorials.

**Chapter 28
America Becomes a World Power**

Investigating Primary Sources

"Shameful Treachery": The *Journal* Blames Spain

To five hundred thousand Cubans starved or otherwise murdered have been added an American battleship and three hundred American sailors lost.... Two days ago we had five battleships in the Atlantic. Today we have four.... All the circumstances of the case fix the burden of proof [on Spain]. The *Maine* was lying in one of her harbors, under the guns of her fortresses, with the warships at hand. The removal [sinking] of the *Maine* meant a tremendous reduction in the odds against her in the event of the conflict that all Spanish Havana desired. The chances against such a removal by accident were millions to one, and yet the removal occurred. In such circumstances polite expressions of regret count for nothing. The investigations must clearly disclose Spain's innocence or her guilt will be assumed.... But while we must wait for definite evidence before formally charging Spain with the shameful treachery, which all the world is ready to suspect her, we need wait for nothing before instituting such a change of policy it will relieve us of the fear of future troubles.

New York Journal (February 17, 1898)

A Times Editorial on the *Maine* Tragedy

Nothing has been learned of the cause of the loss of the battle ship *Maine.* She is a burned and broken wreck, resting on the bottom of Havana Harbor, and two officers and 251 sailors have perished. There is no evidence to prove or disapprove treachery. Naval men tell of many ways in which the disaster could have been caused by accident which could not have been guarded against.... Of course, nobody is so foolish to believe that the *Maine* was destroyed by Spaniards with the knowledge and [support] of their Government.... Spain has just now too many reasons for avoiding cause of offense to us to make it permissible to suppose that she would not exercise due diligence to protect a ship of our navy visiting her waters. [The *Times* urges the people of both countries not to allow] themselves to become excited by criminally sensational newspapers or otherwise.

New York Times (February 17, 1898)

Assignment

After reading the two editorials on the sinking of the *Maine*, answer these questions:

1. What question is each of these editorials trying to answer?
2. What was the attitude of many Americans toward Spain when these editorials were written?
3. Whom does the *Journal* blame for the sinking of the *Maine?* Why?
4. Why does the *Times* believe the Spanish government was not responsible?
5. Given the fact that so little was known about the true cause of the sinking, which editorial better served the public?

Economic Changes in the Twentieth Century

Chapter 29 explores how the past is linked to the present. In order to better understand such links, historians closely examine economic data. Economic indicators such as unemployment rates and economic growth have a direct connection to how Americans live. As you examine the data in the graphs, think about how much life changed in the century just passed. What does the next century hold?

Investigating Graphic Information

United States Real Gross Domestic Product
1999 dollars per capita

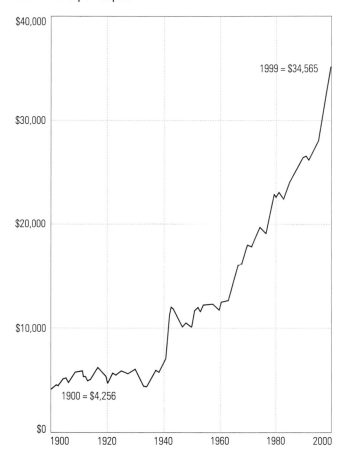

1999 = $34,565

1900 = $4,256

Note: Gross Domestic Product (GDP) is the value of all products and services produced. This graph shows GDP for each person (per capita).

Assignment
1. What does this graph show?
2. How much more productive were Americans in 2000 than in 1900?
3. What do you think accounts for the dramatic change in productivity?

Source: Nine graphs adapted from *The First Measured Century: An Illustrated Guide to Trends in America, 1900–2000* by Theodore Caplow, Louis Hicks, and Ben J. Wattenberg (Washington, DC: The AEI Press, 2001.) Reprinted with the permission of The American Enterprise Institute for Public Policy Research, Washington, D.C.

Changes in the American Home
Percentage of occupied housing units with each item

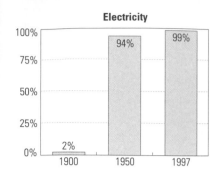

Electricity

100% | 75% | 50% | 25% | 0%

2% (1900) | 94% (1950) | 99% (1997)

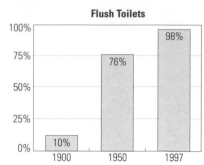

Flush Toilets

100% | 75% | 50% | 25% | 0%

10% (1900) | 76% (1950) | 98% (1997)

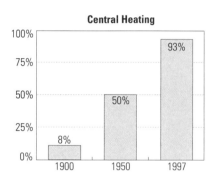

Central Heating

100% | 75% | 50% | 25% | 0%

8% (1900) | 50% (1950) | 93% (1997)

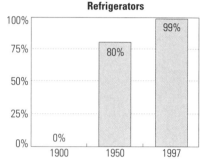

Refrigerators

100% | 75% | 50% | 25% | 0%

0% (1900) | 80% (1950) | 99% (1997)

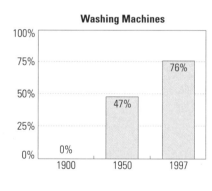

Washing Machines

100% | 75% | 50% | 25% | 0%

0% (1900) | 47% (1950) | 76% (1997)

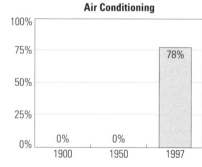

Air Conditioning

100% | 75% | 50% | 25% | 0%

0% (1900) | 0% (1950) | 78% (1997)

Assignment

1. Record at least five conclusions that can be drawn from these graphs.
2. Analyze the data. Historians often conduct a cost-benefit analysis to evaluate a political or economic trend or change. Costs are negatives. Benefits are positives. Set up a T-chart with "Costs" on one side and "Benefits" on the other. What are three costs of the changes shown by these graphs? What are three benefits?

   For example, in 1900, most homes had no electricity. In 2000, most did. On the "Benefit" side you might write, "In 2000, American homes had better lighting than in 1900." On the "Cost" side you might write, "In order to provide all Americans with electricity, dams had to be built. Fish populations suffered."

Workers' Pay for Manufacturing Work
Average hourly pay of production workers in 1999 dollar

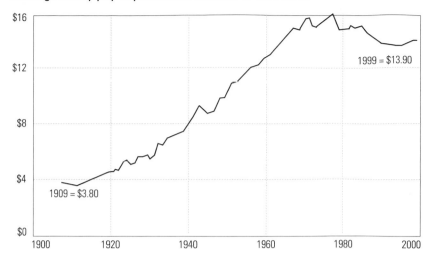

1999 = $13.90

1909 = $3.80

Assignment
1. What does this graph show?
2. How much more did workers earn in 2000 than in 1900?
3. What do you think accounts for the rise in wages?

Energy Use Per Person
Millions of Btu per year

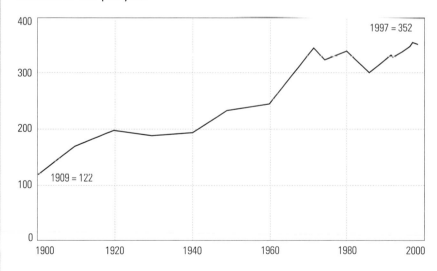

1997 = 352

1909 = 122

Assignment
1. What does this graph show?
2. How much more energy do Americans use now as compared to 1900?
3. Why do you think Americans use so much more energy in 2000 than in 1900?
4. Should American political leaders be concerned by this trend? Explain.

The Declaration of Independence

The unanimous Declaration of the thirteen united States of America

Preamble (Introduction)
The Preamble explains why the Declaration was written. The Declaration is a statement to the world that explains why the colonies believe they should be independent.

When in the Course of human events it becomes necessary for one people to dissolve the political bands which have connected them with another, and to assume among the powers of the earth, the separate and equal station to which the Laws of Nature and of Nature's God entitle them, a decent respect to the opinions of mankind requires that they should declare the causes which impel them to the separation.

Statement of Human Rights
This section boldly states that all people have rights that no government can take away. Three of these rights are life, liberty, and the pursuit of happiness. If a government does not respect these rights, the people have the right to change the government. By his actions, the king has failed to respect the colonists' rights.

We hold these truths to be self-evident, that all men are created equal, that they are endowed by their Creator with certain unalienable Rights, that among these are Life, Liberty and the pursuit of Happiness. —That to secure these rights, Governments are instituted among Men, deriving their just powers from the consent of the governed, — That whenever any Form of Government becomes destructive of these ends, it is the Right of the People to alter or to abolish it, and to institute new Government, laying its foundation on such principles and organizing its powers in such form, as to them shall seem most likely to effect their Safety and Happiness. Prudence, indeed, will dictate that Governments long established should not be changed for light and transient causes; and accordingly all experience hath shewn, that mankind are more disposed to suffer, while evils are sufferable, than to right themselves by abolishing the forms to which they are accustomed. But when a long train of abuses and usurpations, pursuing invariably the same Object evinces a design to reduce them under absolute Despotism, it is their right, it is their duty, to throw off such Government, and to provide new Guards for their future security. —Such has been the patient sufferance of these Colonies; and such is now the necessity which constrains them to alter their former Systems of Government. The history of the present King of Great Britain is a history of repeated injuries and usurpations, all having in direct object the establishment of an absolute Tyranny over these States. To prove this, let Facts be submitted to a candid world.

Statement of Charges against the King
This section lists more than 20 ways that the king has violated the colonists' rights. By interfering with laws, the king has taken away the colonists' right to govern themselves. Some of his laws have prevented the colonists from pursuing happiness in their own way. And by sending soldiers to fight the colonists, he has even threatened their right to life.

He has refused his Assent to Laws, the most wholesome and necessary for the public good.

He has forbidden his Governors to pass Laws of immediate and pressing importance, unless suspended in their operation till his Assent should be obtained; and when so suspended, he has utterly neglected to attend to them.

He has refused to pass other Laws for the accommodation of large districts of people, unless those people would relinquish the right of Representation in the Legislature, a right inestimable to them and formidable to tyrants only.

He has called together legislative bodies at places unusual, uncomfortable, and distant from the depository of their Public Records, for the sole purpose of fatiguing them into compliance with his measures.

He has dissolved Representative Houses repeatedly, for opposing with manly firmness his invasions on the rights of the people.

He has refused for a long time, after such dissolutions, to cause others to be elected, whereby the Legislative Powers, incapable of Annihilation, have returned to the People at large for their exercise; the State remaining in the mean time exposed to all the dangers of invasion from without, and convulsions within.

He has endeavoured to prevent the population of these States; for that purpose obstructing the Laws for Naturalization of Foreigners; refusing to pass others to encourage their migrations hither, and raising the conditions of new Appropriations of Lands.

He has obstructed the Administration of Justice, by refusing his Assent to Laws for establishing Judiciary Powers.

He has made Judges dependent on his Will alone, for the tenure of their offices, and the amount and payment of their salaries.

He has erected a multitude of New Offices, and sent hither swarms of Officers to harass our people and eat out their substance.

He has kept among us, in times of peace, Standing Armies without the Consent of our legislatures.

He has affected to render the Military independent of and superior to the Civil Power.

He has combined with others to subject us to a jurisdiction foreign to our constitution, and unacknowledged by our laws; giving his Assent to their Acts of pretended Legislation:

For Quartering large bodies of armed troops among us:

For protecting them, by a mock Trial, from punishment for any Murders which they should commit on the Inhabitants of these States:

For cutting off our Trade with all parts of the world:

For imposing Taxes on us without our Consent:

For depriving us in many cases, of the benefit of Trial by Jury:

For transporting us beyond Seas to be tried for pretended offences:

For abolishing the free System of English Laws in a neighbouring Province, establishing therein an Arbitrary government, and enlarging its Boundaries so as to render it at once an example and fit instrument for introducing the same absolute rule into these Colonies:

For taking away our Charters, abolishing our most valuable Laws, and altering fundamentally the Forms of our Governments:

For suspending our own Legislatures, and declaring themselves invested with power to legislate for us in all cases whatsoever.

He has abdicated Government here, by declaring us out of his Protection and waging War against us.

He has plundered our seas, ravaged our Coasts, burnt our towns, and destroyed the lives of our people.

He is at this time transporting large Armies of foreign Mercenaries to compleat the works of death, desolation and tyranny, already begun with circumstances of Cruelty & perfidy scarcely paralleled in the most barbarous ages, and totally unworthy the Head of a civilized nation.

He has constrained our fellow Citizens taken Captive on the high Seas to bear Arms

The Government's Failure to Answer the Colonists' Complaints

This section states that the colonists have tried many times to solve their problems with Britain peacefully. Both the king and the British government have failed to answer their complaints. For this reason, the colonists have no choice except to break away from Britain.

Statement of Independence

This section declares the colonies' independence. The writers of the Declaration emphasize that they are acting as the representatives of the people. As the Preamble stated, it is the people who have the right to form a new government. The colonies are now separate countries that have all the powers and rights of other nations.

against their Country, to become the executioners of their friends and Brethren, or to fall themselves by their Hands.

He has excited domestic insurrections amongst us, and has endeavoured to bring on the inhabitants of our frontiers, the merciless Indian Savages, whose known rule of warfare, is an undistinguished destruction of all ages, sexes and conditions.

In every stage of these Oppressions We have Petitioned for Redress in the most humble terms: Our repeated Petitions have been answered only by repeated injury. A Prince whose character is thus marked by every act which may define a Tyrant, is unfit to be the ruler of a free people.

Nor have We been wanting in attentions to our British brethren. We have warned them from time to time of attempts by their legislature to extend an unwarrantable jurisdiction over us. We have reminded them of the circumstances of our emigration and settlement here. We have appealed to their native justice and magnanimity, and we have conjured them by the ties of our common kindred, to disavow these usurpations, which, would inevitably interrupt our connections and correspondence. They too have been deaf to the voice of justice and of consanguinity. We must, therefore, acquiesce in the necessity, which denounces our Separation, and hold them, as we hold the rest of mankind, Enemies in War, in Peace Friends.

We, therefore, the Representatives of the united States of America, in General Congress, Assembled, appealing to the Supreme Judge of the world for the rectitude of our intentions, do, in the Name, and by Authority of the good People of these Colonies, solemnly publish and declare, That these United Colonies are, and of Right ought to be Free and Independent States; that they are Absolved from all Allegiance to the British Crown, and that all political connection between them and the State of Great Britain, is and ought to be totally dissolved; and that as Free and Independent States, they have full Power to levy War, conclude Peace, contract Alliances, establish Commerce, and to do all other Acts and Things which Independent States may of right do. —And for the support of this Declaration, with a firm reliance on the protection of divine Providence, we mutually pledge to each other our Lives, our Fortunes and our sacred Honor.

The foregoing Declaration was, by order of Congress, engrossed on parchment, and signed by the 56 members.

New Hampshire: Josiah Bartlett, William Whipple, Matthew Thornton

Massachusetts: John Hancock, Samuel Adams, John Adams, Robert Treat Paine, Elbridge Gerry

Rhode Island: Stephen Hopkins, William Ellery

Connecticut: Roger Sherman, Samuel Huntington, William Williams, Oliver Wolcott

New York: William Floyd, Philip Livingston, Francis Lewis, Lewis Morris

New Jersey: Richard Stockton, John Witherspoon, Francis Hopkinson, John Hart, Abraham Clark

Pennsylvania: Robert Morris, Benjamin Rush, Benjamin Franklin, John Morton, George Clymer, James Smith, George Taylor, James Wilson, George Ross

Delaware: Caesar Rodney, George Read, Thomas McKean

Maryland: Samuel Chase, William Paca, Thomas Stone, Charles Carroll of Carrollton

Virginia: George Wythe, Richard Henry Lee, Thomas Jefferson, Benjamin Harrison, Thomas Nelson, Jr., Francis Lightfoot Lee, Carter Braxton

North Carolina: William Hooper, Joseph Hewes, John Penn

South Carolina: Edward Rutledge, Thomas Heyward, Jr., Thomas Lynch, Jr., Arthur Middleton

Georgia: Button Gwinnett, Lyman Hall, George Walton

Delegates to the Constitutional Convention, 1787

New Hampshire
John Langdon
Nicholas Gilman

Massachusetts
Caleb Strong*
Elbridge Gerry*
Nathanial Gorham
Rufus King

Connecticut
Oliver Ellsworth*
Roger Sherman
William Samuel Johnson

New York
Alexander Hamilton
John Lansing, Jr.*
Robert Yates*

New Jersey
David Brearley
Jonathan Dayton
William Churchill Houston*
William Livingston
William Paterson

Pennsylvania
Benjamin Franklin
George Clymer
Gouverneur Morris
James Wilson
Jarod Ingersoll
Robert Morris
Thomas Fitzsimons
Thomas Mifflin

Delaware
George Read
Gunning Bedford, Jr.
Jacob Broom
John Dickinson
Richard Bassett

Maryland
Daniel Carroll
Daniel of St. Thomas Jenifer
James McHenry
John Francis Mercer*
Luther Martin*

Virginia
Edmund Randolph*
George Mason*
George Washington
George Wythe*
James Madison
James McClurg*
John Blair

North Carolina
Alexander Martin*
Hugh Williamson
Richard Dobbs Spaight, Sr.
William Blount
William Richard Davie*

South Carolina
Charles Cotesworth Pinckney
Charles Pinckney
John Rutledge
Pierce Butler

Georgia
Abraham Baldwin
William Few
William Houston*
William Pierce*

* indicates delegates who did not
  sign the Constitution

The Constitution of the United States

Preamble

The Preamble says that the Constitution receives its authority from the people of the United States. The people agree to form a government to protect their rights and provide for safety and order.

Article I: The Legislative Branch

The government's lawmaking branch is Congress, made up of a Senate and a House of Representatives. The margin notes that follow point out some of the specific powers of this branch.

Representation in the House: In the House, the number of representatives for each state depends on the number of people who live in the state. There are 435 representatives in the House.

Checks and balances: Impeachment. Only the House has the power to impeach federal officials.

Representation in the Senate: Each state is represented by two senators. Since there are 50 states, there are 100 senators.

We the People of the United States, in Order to form a more perfect Union, establish Justice, insure domestic Tranquility, provide for the common defence, promote the general Welfare, and secure the Blessings of Liberty to ourselves and our Posterity, do ordain and establish this Constitution for the United States of America.

ARTICLE I

Section 1. All legislative Powers herein granted shall be vested in a Congress of the United States, which shall consist of a Senate and House of Representatives.

Section 2. The House of Representatives shall be composed of Members chosen every second Year by the People of the several States, and the Electors in each State shall have the Qualifications requisite for Electors of the most numerous Branch of the State Legislature.

No Person shall be a Representative who shall not have attained to the Age of twenty five Years, and been seven Years a Citizen of the United States, and who shall not, when elected, be an Inhabitant of that State in which he shall be chosen.

[Representatives and direct Taxes[1] shall be apportioned among the several States which may be included within this Union, according to their respective Numbers, which shall be determined by adding to the whole Number of free Persons, including those bound to Service for a Term of Years, and excluding Indians not taxed, three fifths of all other Persons.][2] The actual Enumeration shall be made within three Years after the first Meeting of the Congress of the United States, and within every subsequent Term of ten Years, in such Manner as they shall by Law direct. The Number of Representatives shall not exceed one for every thirty Thousand, but each State shall have at Least one Representative; and until such enumeration shall be made, the State of New Hampshire shall be entitled to chuse [choose] three, Massachusetts eight, Rhode-Island and Providence Plantations one, Connecticut five, New-York six, New Jersey four, Pennsylvania eight, Delaware one, Maryland six, Virginia ten, North Carolina five, South Carolina five, and Georgia three.

When vacancies happen in the Representation from any State, the Executive Authority thereof shall issue Writs of Election to fill such Vacancies.

The House of Representatives shall chuse [choose] their Speaker and other Officers; and shall have the sole Power of Impeachment.

Section 3. The Senate of the United States shall be composed of two Senators from each State, [chosen by the Legislature thereof,][3] for six Years; and each Senator shall have one Vote.

Immediately after they shall be assembled in Consequence of the first Election, they shall be divided as equally as may be into three Classes. The Seats of the Senators of the first Class shall be vacated at the Expiration of the second Year, of the second Class at the Expiration of the fourth Year, and of the third Class at the Expiration of the sixth Year, so that one third may be chosen every second Year; [and if Vacancies

1. Changed by the Sixteenth Amendment
2. Changed by Section 2 of the Fourteenth Amendment
3. Changed by the Seventeenth Amendment

happen by Resignation, or otherwise, during the Recess of the Legislature of any State, the Executive thereof may make temporary Appointments until the next Meeting of the Legislature, which shall then fill such Vacancies.]4

No Person shall be a Senator who shall not have attained to the Age of thirty Years, and been nine Years a Citizen of the United States, and who shall not, when elected, be an Inhabitant of that State for which he shall be chosen.

The Vice President of the United States shall be President of the Senate, but shall have no Vote, unless they be equally divided.

The Senate shall chuse [choose] their other Officers, and also a President pro tempore, in the Absence of the Vice President, or when he shall exercise the Office of President of the United States.

The Senate shall have the sole Power to try all Impeachments. When sitting for that Purpose, they shall be on Oath or Affirmation. When the President of the United States is tried, the Chief Justice shall preside: And no Person shall be convicted without the Concurrence of two thirds of the Members present.

Judgment in Cases of Impeachment shall not extend further than to removal from Office, and disqualification to hold and enjoy any Office of honor, Trust or Profit under the United States: but the Party convicted shall nevertheless be liable and subject to Indictment, Trial, Judgment and Punishment, according to Law.

Section 4. The Times, Places and Manner of holding Elections for Senators and Representatives, shall be prescribed in each State by the Legislature thereof; but the Congress may at any time by Law make or alter such Regulations, except as to the Places of chusing [choosing] Senators.

The Congress shall assemble at least once in every Year, and such Meeting shall be [on the first Monday in December,]5 unless they shall by Law appoint a different Day.

Section 5. Each House shall be the Judge of the Elections, Returns and Qualifications of its own Members, and a Majority of each shall constitute a Quorum to do Business, but a smaller Number may adjourn from day to day, and may be authorized to compel the Attendance of absent Members, in such Manner, and under such Penalties as each House may provide.

Each House may determine the Rules of its Proceedings, punish its Members for disorderly Behaviour, and, with the Concurrence of two thirds, expel a Member.

Each House shall keep a Journal of its Proceedings, and from time to time publish the same, excepting such Parts as may in their Judgment require Secrecy; and the Yeas and Nays of the Members of either House on any question shall, at the Desire of one fifth of those Present, be entered on the Journal.

Neither House, during the Session of Congress, shall, without the Consent of the other, adjourn for more than three days, nor to any other Place than that in which the two Houses shall be sitting.

Section 6. The Senators and Representatives shall receive a Compensation for their Services, to be ascertained by Law, and paid out of the Treasury of the United States. They shall in all Cases, except Treason, Felony and Breach of the Peace, be privileged from Arrest during their Attendance at the Session of their respective Houses, and in going to and returning from the same; and for any Speech or Debate in either House, they shall not be questioned in any other Place.

Checks and balances: Impeachment. Only the Senate has the power to put impeached officials on trial.

4. Changed by the Seventeenth Amendment
5. Changed by Section 2 of the Twentieth Amendment

No Senator or Representative shall, during the Time for which he was elected, be appointed to any civil Office under the Authority of the United States, which shall have been created, or the Emoluments whereof shall have been encreased during such time; and no Person holding any Office under the United States, shall be a Member of either House during his Continuance in Office.

Section 7. All Bills for raising Revenue shall originate in the House of Representatives; but the Senate may propose or concur with Amendments as on other Bills.

Proposing laws: Either house of Congress can propose and vote on new laws. Only the House can propose new taxes.

Every Bill which shall have passed the House of Representatives and the Senate, shall, before it become a Law, be presented to the President of the United States; If he approve he shall sign it, but if not he shall return it, with his Objections to that House in which it shall have originated, who shall enter the Objections at large on their Journal, and proceed to reconsider it. If after such Reconsideration two thirds of that House shall agree to pass the Bill, it shall be sent, together with the Objections, to the other House, by which it shall likewise be reconsidered, and if approved by two thirds of that House, it shall become a Law. But in all such Cases the Votes of both Houses shall be determined by Yeas and Nays, and the Names of the Persons voting for and against the Bill shall be entered on the Journal of each House respectively. If any Bill shall not be returned by the President within ten Days (Sundays excepted) after it shall have been presented to him, the Same shall be a Law, in like Manner as if he had signed it, unless the Congress by their Adjournment prevent its Return, in which Case it shall not be a Law.

Checks and balances: Overriding the president's veto. Bills passed by Congress become laws when the president signs them. If the president vetoes (rejects) a bill, Congress can overrule the president's veto by a two-thirds vote of both houses.

Every Order, Resolution, or Vote to which the Concurrence of the Senate and House of Representatives may be necessary (except on a question of Adjournment) shall be presented to the President of the United States; and before the Same shall take Effect, shall be approved by him, or being disapproved by him, shall be repassed by two thirds of the Senate and House of Representatives, according to the Rules and Limitations prescribed in the Case of a Bill.

Section 8. The Congress shall have Power To lay and collect Taxes, Duties, Imposts and Excises, to pay the Debts and provide for the common Defence and general Welfare of the United States; but all Duties, Imposts and Excises shall be uniform throughout the United States;

Creating and collecting taxes: Congress has the power to create and collect taxes.

To borrow Money on the credit of the United States;

To regulate Commerce with foreign Nations, and among the several States, and with the Indian Tribes;

To establish an uniform Rule of Naturalization, and uniform Laws on the subject of Bankruptcies throughout the United States;

To coin Money, regulate the Value thereof, and of foreign Coin, and fix the Standard of Weights and Measures;

Creating a system of money: Congress has the power to create a national currency (system of money).

To provide for the Punishment of counterfeiting the Securities and current Coin of the United States;

To establish Post Offices and post Roads;

To promote the Progress of Science and useful Arts, by securing for limited Times to Authors and Inventors the exclusive Right to their respective Writings and Discoveries;

Creating federal courts: Congress has the power to create new federal courts.

To constitute Tribunals inferior to the supreme Court;

To define and punish Piracies and Felonies committed on the high Seas, and Offenses against the Law of Nations;

To declare War, grant Letters of Marque and Reprisal, and make Rules concerning Captures on Land and Water;

Declaring war: Only Congress can declare war on another country.

To raise and support Armies, but no Appropriation of Money to that Use shall be for a longer Term than two Years;

Creating and paying for armed forces: Congress has the power to create an army and navy, and to raise the money to pay for them.

To provide and maintain a Navy;

To make Rules for the Government and Regulation of the land and naval Forces;

To provide for calling forth the Militia to execute the Laws of the Union, suppress Insurrections and repel Invasions;

To provide for organizing, arming, and disciplining, the Militia, and for governing such Part of them as may be employed in the Service of the United States, reserving to the States respectively, the Appointment of the Officers, and the Authority of training the Militia according to the discipline prescribed by Congress;

To exercise exclusive Legislation in all Cases whatsoever, over such District (not exceeding ten Miles square) as may, by Cession of particular States, and the Acceptance of Congress, become the Seat of the Government of the United States, and to exercise like Authority over all Places purchased by the Consent of the Legislature of the State in which the Same shall be, for the Erection of Forts, Magazines, Arsenals, dock-Yards and other needful Buildings;—And

To make all Laws which shall be necessary and proper for carrying into Execution the foregoing Powers, and all other Powers vested by this Constitution in the Government of the United States, or in any Department or Officer thereof.

Making other laws: Congress has the power to make all laws that are needed to carry out the government's powers under the Constitution.

Section 9. The Migration or Importation of such Persons as any of the States now existing shall think proper to admit, shall not be prohibited by the Congress prior to the Year one thousand eight hundred and eight, but a Tax or duty may be imposed on such Importation, not exceeding ten dollars for each Person.

The Privilege of the Writ of Habeas Corpus shall not be suspended, unless when in Cases of Rebellion or Invasion the public Safety may require it.

No Bill of Attainder or ex post facto Law shall be passed.

No Capitation, or other direct, Tax shall be laid, unless in Proportion to the Census or Enumeration herein before directed to be taken.[6]

No Tax or Duty shall be laid on Articles exported from any State.

No Preference shall be given by any Regulation of Commerce or Revenue to the Ports of one State over those of another; nor shall Vessels bound to, or from, one State, be obliged to enter, clear, or pay Duties in another.

No Money shall be drawn from the Treasury, but in Consequence of Appropriations made by Law; and a regular Statement and Account of the Receipts and Expenditures of all public Money shall be published from time to time.

No Title of Nobility shall be granted by the United States: And no Person holding any Office of Profit or Trust under them, shall, without the Consent of the Congress, accept of any present, Emolument, Office, or Title, of any kind whatever, from any King, Prince, or foreign State.

6. See Sixteenth Amendment

Section 10. No State shall enter into any Treaty, Alliance, or Confederation; grant Letters of Marque and Reprisal; coin Money; emit Bills of Credit; make any Thing but gold and silver Coin a Tender in Payment of Debts; pass any Bill of Attainder, ex post facto Law, or Law impairing the Obligation of Contracts, or grant any Title of Nobility.

No State shall, without the Consent of the Congress, lay any Imposts or Duties on Imports or Exports, except what may be absolutely necessary for executing it's inspection Laws: and the net Produce of all Duties and Imposts, laid by any State on Imports or Exports, shall be for the Use of the Treasury of the United States; and all such Laws shall be subject to the Revision and Controul of the Congress.

No State shall, without the Consent of Congress, lay any Duty of Tonnage, keep Troops, or Ships of War in time of Peace, enter into any Agreement or Compact with another State, or with a foreign Power, or engage in War, unless actually invaded, or in such imminent Danger as will not admit of delay.

Article II: The Executive Branch

The head of the executive branch is the president. The margin notes that follow point out some of the specific powers of this branch.

ARTICLE II

Section 1. The executive Power shall be vested in a President of the United States of America. He shall hold his Office during the Term of four Years, and, together with the Vice President, chosen for the same Term, be elected, as follows:

Each State shall appoint, in such Manner as the Legislature thereof may direct, a Number of Electors, equal to the whole Number of Senators and Representatives to which the State may be entitled in the Congress: but no Senator or Representative, or Person holding an Office of Trust or Profit under the United States, shall be appointed an Elector.

[The Electors shall meet in their respective States, and vote by Ballot for two Persons, of whom one at least shall not be an Inhabitant of the same State with themselves. And they shall make a List of all the Persons voted for, and of the Number of Votes for each; which List they shall sign and certify, and transmit sealed to the Seat of the Government of the United States, directed to the President of the Senate. The President of the Senate shall, in the Presence of the Senate and House of Representatives, open all the Certificates, and the Votes shall then be counted. The Person having the greatest Number of Votes shall be the President, if such Number be a Majority of the whole Number of Electors appointed; and if there be more than one who have such Majority, and have an equal Number of Votes, then the House of Representatives shall immediately chuse [choose] by Ballot one of them for President; and if no Person have a Majority, then from the five highest on the List the said House shall in like Manner chuse the President. But in chusing the President, the Votes shall be taken by States, the Representation from each State having one Vote; A quorum for this Purpose shall consist of a Member or Members from two thirds of the States, and a Majority of all the States shall be necessary to a Choice. In every Case, after the Choice of the President, the Person having the greatest Number of Votes of the Electors shall be the Vice President. But if there should remain two or more who have equal Votes, the Senate shall chuse from them by Ballot the Vice President.][7]

The Congress may determine the Time of chusing the Electors, and the Day on which they shall give their Votes; which Day shall be the same throughout the United States.

No Person except a natural born Citizen, or a Citizen of the United States, at the time of the Adoption of this Constitution, shall be eligible to the Office of President; neither shall any person be eligible to that Office who shall not have attained to the Age of thirty five Years, and been fourteen Years a Resident within the United States.

7. Changed by the Twelfth Amendment

[In Case of the Removal of the President from Office, or of his Death, Resignation, or Inability to discharge the Powers and Duties of the said Office, the Same shall devolve on the Vice President, and the Congress may by Law provide for the Case of Removal, Death, Resignation or Inability, both of the President and Vice President, declaring what Officer shall then act as President, and such Officer shall act accordingly, until the Disability be removed, or a President shall be elected.][8]

The President shall, at stated Times, receive for his Services, a Compensation, which shall neither be increased nor diminished during the Period for which he shall have been elected, and he shall not receive within that Period any other Emolument from the United States, or any of them.

Before he enter on the Execution of his Office, he shall take the following Oath or Affirmation:—"I do solemnly swear (or affirm) that I will faithfully execute the Office of President of the United States, and will to the best of my Ability, preserve, protect and defend the Constitution of the United States."

Section 2. The President shall be Commander in Chief of the Army and Navy of the United States, and of the Militia of the several States, when called into the actual Service of the United States; he may require the Opinion, in writing, of the principal Officer in each of the executive Departments, upon any Subject relating to the Duties of their respective Offices, and he shall have Power to grant Reprieves and Pardons for Offenses against the United States, except in Cases of Impeachment.

He shall have Power, by and with the Advice and Consent of the Senate, to make Treaties, provided two thirds of the Senators present concur; and he shall nominate, and by and with the Advice and Consent of the Senate, shall appoint Ambassadors, other public Ministers and Consuls, Judges of the supreme Court, and all other Officers of the United States, whose Appointments are not herein otherwise provided for, and which shall be established by Law: but the Congress may by law vest the Appointment of such inferior Officers, as they think proper, in the President alone, in the Courts of Law, or in the Heads of Departments.

The President shall have Power to fill up all Vacancies that may happen during the Recess of the Senate, by granting Commissions which shall expire at the End of their next Session.

Section 3. He shall from time to time give to the Congress Information of the State of the Union, and recommend to their Consideration such Measures as he shall judge necessary and expedient; he may, on extraordinary Occasions, convene both Houses, or either of them, and in Case of Disagreement between them, with Respect to the Time of Adjournment, he may adjourn them to such Time as he shall think proper; he shall receive Ambassadors and other public Ministers; he shall take Care that the Laws be faithfully executed, and shall Commission all the Officers of the United States.

Section 4. The President, Vice President and all civil Officers of the United States, shall be removed from Office on Impeachment for, and Conviction of, Treason, Bribery, or other high Crimes and Misdemeanors.

ARTICLE III
Section 1. The judicial Power of the United States shall be vested in one supreme Court, and in such inferior Courts as the Congress may from time to time ordain and establish. The Judges, both of the supreme and inferior Courts, shall hold their Offices during good Behaviour, and shall, at stated Times, receive for their Services a Compensation, which shall not be diminished during their Continuance in Office.

Commanding the armed forces: The president is commander-in-chief of the armed forces of the United States.
Granting pardons: The president can grant pardons for federal crimes, except in cases of impeachment.

Checks and balances: Treaties and appointments. The president can sign treaties with other countries. But the Senate must approve treaties by a two-thirds vote. The president can name certain officials and federal judges, but the Senate must approve the president's choices.

Powers of leadership: The president can propose ideas for new laws and reports to Congress on the State of the Union. In emergencies, the president can call Congress into special session.

Checks and balances: Impeachment. Presidents and federal officials can be removed from office if they misuse their powers.

Article III: The Judicial Branch
The judicial branch consists of the Supreme Court and other federal courts. Congress has set the number of Supreme Court justices at nine. The margin notes that follow point out some of the specific powers of the judicial branch.

8. Changed by the Twenty-Fifth Amendment

Article IV: Relations between the States

Section 2. The judicial Power shall extend to all Cases, in Law and Equity, arising under this Constitution, the Laws of the United States, and Treaties made, or which shall be made, under their Authority; —to all Cases affecting Ambassadors, other public Ministers and Consuls; —to all Cases of admiralty and maritime Jurisdiction; —to Controversies to which the United States shall be a Party; —to Controversies between two or more States, —[between a State and Citizens of another State;][9] —between Citizens of different States, —between Citizens of the same State claiming Lands under Grants of different States, [and between a State, or the Citizens thereof, and foreign States, Citizens or Subjects.][10]

In all Cases affecting Ambassadors, other public Ministers and Consuls, and those in which a State shall be Party, the supreme Court shall have original Jurisdiction. In all the other Cases before mentioned, the supreme Court shall have appellate Jurisdiction, both as to Law and Fact, with such Exceptions, and under such Regulations as the Congress shall make.

The Trial of all Crimes, except in Cases of Impeachment; shall be by Jury; and such Trial shall be held in the State where the said Crimes shall have been committed; but when not committed within any State, the Trial shall be at such Place or Places as the Congress may by Law have directed.

Section 3. Treason against the United States, shall consist only in levying War against them, or in adhering to their Enemies, giving them Aid and Comfort. No Person shall be convicted of Treason unless on the Testimony of two Witnesses to the same overt Act, or on Confession in open Court.

The Congress shall have Power to declare the Punishment of Treason, but no Attainder of Treason shall work Corruption of Blood, or Forfeiture except during the Life of the Person attainted.

ARTICLE IV
Section 1. Full Faith and Credit shall be given in each State to the public Acts, Records, and judicial Proceedings of every other State; And the Congress may by general Laws prescribe the Manner in which such Acts, Records and Proceedings shall be proved, and the Effect thereof.

Section 2. The Citizens of each State shall be entitled to all Privileges and Immunities of Citizens in the several States.

A Person charged in any State with Treason, Felony, or other Crime, who shall flee from Justice, and be found in another State, shall on Demand of the executive Authority of the State from which he fled, be delivered up, to be removed to the State having Jurisdiction of the Crime.

[No Person held to Service or Labour in one State, under the Laws thereof, escaping into another, shall, in Consequence of any Law or Regulation therein, be discharged from such Service or Labour, but shall be delivered up on Claim of the Party to whom such Service or Labour may be due.][11]

Section 3. New States may be admitted by the Congress into this Union; but no new State shall be formed or erected within the Jurisdiction of any other State; nor any State be formed by the Junction of two or more States, or Parts of States, without the Consent of the Legislatures of the States concerned as well as of the Congress.

9. Changed by the Eleventh Amendment
10. Changed by the Eleventh Amendment
11. Changed by the Thirteenth Amendment

The Congress shall have Power to dispose of and make all needful Rules and Regulations respecting the Territory or other Property belonging to the United States; and nothing in this Constitution shall be construed as to Prejudice any Claims of the United States, or of any particular State.

Section 4. The United States shall guarantee to every State in this Union a Republican Form of Government, and shall protect each of them against Invasion; and on Application of the Legislature, or of the Executive (when the Legislature cannot be convened), against domestic Violence.

ARTICLE V

The Congress, whenever two thirds of both Houses shall deem it necessary, shall propose Amendments to this Constitution, or, on the Application of the Legislatures of two thirds of the several States, shall call a Convention for proposing Amendments, which, in either Case, shall be valid to all Intents and Purposes, as Part of this Constitution, when ratified by the Legislatures of three fourths of the several States, or by Conventions in three fourths thereof, as the one or the other Mode of Ratification may be proposed by the Congress; Provided that no Amendment which may be made prior to the Year One thousand eight hundred and eight shall in any Manner affect the first and fourth Clauses in the Ninth Section of the first Article; and that no State, without its Consent, shall be deprived of its equal Suffrage in the Senate.

ARTICLE VI

All Debts contracted and Engagements entered into, before the Adoption of this Constitution, shall be as valid against the United States under this Constitution, as under the Confederation.

This Constitution, and the Laws of the United States which shall be made in Pursuance thereof; and all Treaties made, or which shall be made, under the Authority of the United States, shall be the supreme Law of the Land; and the Judges in every State shall be bound thereby, any Thing in the Constitution or Laws of any State to the Contrary notwithstanding.

The Senators and Representatives before mentioned, and the Members of the several State Legislatures, and all executive and judicial Officers, both of the United States and of the several States, shall be bound by Oath or Affirmation, to support this Constitution; but no religious Test shall ever be required as a Qualification to any Office or public Trust under the United States.

ARTICLE VII

The Ratification of the Conventions of nine States, shall be sufficient for the Establishment of this Constitution between the States so ratifying the Same.

Done in Convention by the Unanimous Consent of the States present the Seventeenth Day of September in the Year of our Lord one thousand seven hundred and Eighty seven and of the Independence of the United States of America the Twelfth In Witness whereof We have hereunto subscribed our Names.

Article V: Amending the Constitution
This article describes how the Constitution can be amended, or changed. Amendments must be ratified (approved) by three fourths of the states.

Article VI: The Constitution as the Supreme Law of the Land
This article makes the Constitution the supreme (highest) law of the nation. No federal or state law can contradict the Constitution.

Article VII: Ratifying the Constitution
This article says that the Constitution must be ratified (approved) by 9 of the original 13 states.

The Bill of Rights and Later Amendments

Congress cannot make laws that violate Americans' basic freedoms, including freedom of speech, religion, and the press. Citizens have the right to gather peacefully and to ask the government to correct wrongs.

Citizens have the right to own and carry weapons for use in state militias.

In peacetime, the government cannot force citizens to let soldiers stay in their homes.

Government officials cannot search citizens or their property, or seize their belongings, without good reason. Normally, searches and seizures require a warrant approved by a judge.

Citizens who are accused of crimes have certain basic rights. They cannot be tried twice for the same crime, or be forced to testify against themselves. They cannot be jailed or lose their property except through proper legal actions.

Citizens who are accused of crimes have the right to a trial by jury that is fair and public. They have the right to question witnesses, and they have the right to a lawyer.

Citizens have the right to demand a jury trial to settle disputes over things of value.

Original Ten Amendments: The Bill of Rights
Passed by Congress September 25, 1789. Ratified December 15, 1791.

AMENDMENT 1
BASIC FREEDOMS

Congress shall make no law respecting an establishment of religion, or prohibiting the free exercise thereof; or abridging the freedom of speech, or of the press, or the right of the people peaceably to assemble, and to petition the Government for a redress of grievances.

AMENDMENT 2
RIGHT TO BEAR ARMS

A well regulated Militia, being necessary to the security of a free State, the right of the people to keep and bear Arms, shall not be infringed.

AMENDMENT 3
QUARTERING OF SOLDIERS

No Soldier shall, in time of peace be quartered in any house, without the consent of the Owner, nor in time of war, but in a manner to be prescribed by law.

AMENDMENT 4
SEARCH AND ARREST

The right of the people to be secure in their persons, houses, papers, and effects, against unreasonable searches and seizures, shall not be violated, and no Warrants shall issue, but upon probable cause, supported by Oath or affirmation, and particularly describing the place to be searched, and the persons or things to be seized.

AMENDMENT 5
RIGHTS IN CRIMINAL CASES

No person shall be held to answer for a capital, or otherwise infamous crime, unless on a presentment or indictment of a Grand Jury, except in cases arising in the land or naval forces, or in the Militia, when in actual service in time of War or public danger; nor shall any person be subject for the same offence to be twice put in jeopardy of life or limb, nor shall be compelled in any criminal case to be a witness against himself, nor be deprived of life, liberty, or property, without due process of law; nor shall private property be taken for public use, without just compensation.

AMENDMENT 6
RIGHT TO A FAIR TRIAL

In all criminal prosecutions, the accused shall enjoy the right to a speedy and public trial, by an impartial jury of the State and district wherein the crime shall have been committed; which district shall have been previously ascertained by law, and to be informed of the nature and cause of the accusation; to be confronted with the witnesses against him; to have compulsory process for obtaining witnesses in his favor, and to have the Assistance of Counsel for his defence.

AMENDMENT 7
RIGHTS IN CIVIL CASES

In Suits at common law, where the value in controversy shall exceed twenty dollars, the right of trial by jury shall be preserved, and no fact tried by a jury shall be otherwise re-examined in any Court of the United States, than according to the rules of the common law.

AMENDMENT 8
BAIL, FINES, PUNISHMENT
Excessive bail shall not be required, nor excessive fines imposed, nor cruel and unusual punishments inflicted.

Bail and fines that are set by a court must be reasonable. Punishments for crimes cannot be cruel or unusual.

AMENDMENT 9
RIGHTS RETAINED BY THE PEOPLE
The enumeration in the Constitution, of certain rights, shall not be construed to deny or disparage others retained by the people.

The government must respect all the rights of Americans, including rights that are not listed in the Constitution.

AMENDMENT 10
STATES' RIGHTS
The powers not delegated to the United States by the Constitution, nor prohibited by it to the States, are reserved to the States respectively, or to the people.

The states and the people keep any powers that the Constitution does not specifically give to the federal government.

Later Amendments

AMENDMENT 11
LAWSUITS AGAINST STATES
The Judicial power of the United States shall not be construed to extend to any suit in law or equity, commenced or prosecuted against one of the United States by Citizens of another State, or by Citizens or Subjects of any Foreign State.

Ratified February 7, 1795.

People cannot sue a state in federal court if they are citizens of a different state, or of a foreign country.

AMENDMENT 12
PRESIDENTIAL ELECTIONS
The Electors shall meet in their respective states, and vote by ballot for President and Vice-President, one of whom, at least, shall not be an inhabitant of the same state with themselves; they shall name in their ballots the person voted for as President, and in distinct ballots the person voted for as Vice-President, and they shall make distinct lists of all persons voted for as President, and of all persons voted for as Vice-President, and of the number of votes for each, which lists they shall sign and certify, and transmit sealed to the seat of the government of the United States, directed to the President of the Senate;—The President of the Senate shall, in the presence of the Senate and House of Representatives, open all the certificates and the votes shall then be counted;—The person having the greatest number of votes for President, shall be the President, if such number be a majority of the whole number of Electors appointed; and if no person have such majority, then from the persons having the highest numbers not exceeding three on the list of those voted for as President, the House of Representatives shall choose immediately, by ballot, the President. But in choosing the President, the votes shall be taken by states, the representation from each state having one vote; a quorum for this purpose shall consist of a member or members from two-thirds of the states, and a majority of all the states shall be necessary to a choice. [And if the House of Representatives shall not choose a President whenever the right of choice shall devolve upon them, before the fourth day of March next following, then the Vice-President shall act as President, as in the case of the death or other constitutional disability of the President.][12] The person having the greatest number of votes as Vice-President, shall be the Vice-President, if such number be a majority of the whole number of Electors appointed, and if no person have a majority, then from the two highest numbers on the list, the Senate shall choose the Vice-President; a quorum for the purpose shall consist of two-thirds of the whole number of Senators, and a majority of the whole number shall be necessary to a choice. But no person constitutionally ineligible to the office of President shall be eligible to that of Vice-President of the United States.

Ratified June 15, 1804.

The vice president will be elected separately from the president. In the original Constitution, the candidate who finished second in the voting for president automatically became vice president. Under that system, the president and vice president were likely to be political enemies. The Twelfth Amendment allows the same political party to win the elections for both president and vice president.

[12]Superseded by Section 3 of the Twentieth Amendment

No person in the United States can be kept as a slave. No person can be forced to work for someone else, except as a legal punishment for a crime.

All Americans, including former slaves, have the right to be treated as citizens. For example, states must respect the constitutional rights of all citizens. States must give all their citizens equal protection in their laws. In addition, they cannot deny the right of eligible men to vote in federal elections. If they do, they will lose some of their representatives in Congress.

The Fourteenth Amendment also deals with other questions that arose because of the Civil War. For instance, it prevents people who have rebelled against the United States from being elected to office. It also says that the federal government is not responsible for Confederate debts.

States cannot deny anyone the right to vote because of the person's race or color, or because the person used to be a slave.

AMENDMENT 13
END OF SLAVERY

Section 1. Neither slavery nor involuntary servitude, except as a punishment for crime whereof the party shall have been duly convicted, shall exist within the United States, or any place subject to their jurisdiction.

Section 2. Congress shall have power to enforce these article by appropriate legislation.

Ratified December 6, 1865.

AMENDMENT 14
CIVIL RIGHTS

Section 1. All persons born or naturalized in the United States, and subject to the jurisdiction thereof, are citizens of the United States and of the State wherein they reside. No State shall make or enforce any law which shall abridge the privileges or immunities of citizens of the United States; nor shall any State deprive any person of life, liberty, or property, without due process of law; nor deny to any person within its jurisdiction the equal protection of the laws.

Section 2. Representatives shall be apportioned among the several States according to their respective numbers, counting the whole number of persons in each State, excluding Indians not taxed. But when the right to vote at any election for the choice of electors for President and Vice-President of the United States, Representatives in Congress, the Executive and Judicial officers of a State, or the members of the Legislature thereof, is denied to any of the male inhabitants of such State, being twenty-one years of age, and citizens of the United States, or in any way abridged, except for participation in rebellion, or other crime, the basis of representation therein shall be reduced in the proportion which the number of such male citizens shall bear to the whole number of male citizens twenty-one years of age in such State.

Section 3. No person shall be a Senator or Representative in Congress, or elector of President and Vice-President, or hold any office, civil or military, under the United States, or under any State, who, having previously taken an oath, as a member of Congress, or as an officer of the United States, or as a member of any State legislature, or as an executive or judicial officer of any State, to support the Constitution of the United States, shall have engaged in insurrection or rebellion against the same, or given aid or comfort to the enemies thereof. But Congress may by a vote of two-thirds of each House, remove such disability.

Section 4. The validity of the public debt of the United States, authorized by law, including debts incurred for payment of pensions and bounties for services in suppressing insurrection or rebellion, shall not be questioned. But neither the United States nor any State shall assume or pay any debt or obligation incurred in aid of insurrection or rebellion against the United States, or any claim for the loss or emancipation of any slave; but all such debts, obligations and claims shall be held illegal and void.

Section 5. The Congress shall have the power to enforce, by appropriate legislation, the provisions of this article.

Ratified July 9, 1868

AMENDMENT 15
VOTING RIGHTS

Section 1. The right of citizens of the United States to vote shall not be denied or abridged by the United States or by any State on account of race, color, or previous condition of servitude.

Section 2. The Congress shall have the power to enforce this article by appropriate legislation.

Ratified February 3, 1870.

AMENDMENT 16
INCOME TAXES
The Congress shall have power to lay and collect taxes on incomes, from whatever source derived, without apportionment among the several States, and without regard to any census or enumeration.

Ratified February 3, 1913.

Congress has the power to collect taxes from individual citizens based on their income (wealth).

AMENDMENT 17
SENATORIAL ELECTIONS
The Senate of the United States shall be composed of two Senators from each State, elected by the people thereof, for six years; and each Senator shall have one vote. The electors in each State shall have the qualifications requisite for electors of the most numerous branch of the State legislature.

When vacancies happen in the representation of any State in the Senate, the executive authority of such State shall issue writs of election to fill such vacancies: *Provided,* That the legislature of any State may empower the executive thereof to make temporary appointments until the people fill the vacancies by election as the legislature may direct.

This amendment shall not be so construed as to affect the election or term of any Senator chosen before it becomes valid as part of the Constitution.

Ratified April 8, 1913.

Members of the Senate will be elected directly by voters. Previously, senators were elected by state legislatures.

AMENDMENT 18
PROHIBITION OF LIQUOR
Section 1. After one year from the ratification of this article, the manufacture, sale, or transportation of intoxicating liquors within, the importation thereof into, or the exportation thereof from the United States and all territory subject to the jurisdiction thereof for beverage purposes is hereby prohibited.

Section 2. The Congress and the several States shall have concurrent power to enforce this article by appropriate legislation.

Section 3. This article shall be inoperative unless it shall have been ratified as an amendment to the Constitution by the legislatures of the several States, as provided in the Constitution, within seven years from the date of the submission hereof to the States by the Congress.

Ratified January 16, 1919. Repealed by the Twenty-First, December 5, 1933.

This amendment outlawed the making and selling of liquor (alcohol) in the United States. The 21st Amendment removed this amendment from the Constitution.

AMENDMENT 19
WOMEN'S SUFFRAGE
The right of citizens of the United States to vote shall not be denied or abridged by the United States or by any States on account of sex.

Congress shall have power to enforce this article by appropriate legislation.

Ratified August 18, 1920.

Neither the federal government nor the states can deny people the right to vote because of their sex. This amendment guaranteed the right of women to vote.

This amendment changes the dates when elected federal officials began serving their terms. It also deals with special situations, such as the death of a president-elect before the start of the president's term in office.

AMENDMENT 20
TERMS OF OFFICE

Section 1. The terms of the President and Vice President shall end at noon on the 20th day of January, and the terms of Senators and Representatives at noon on the 3d day of January, of the years in which such terms would have ended if this article had not been ratified; and the terms of their successors shall then begin.

Section 2. The Congress shall assemble at least once in every year, and such meeting shall begin at noon on the 3d day of January, unless they shall by law appoint a different day.

Section 3. If, at the time fixed for the beginning of the term of the President, the President elect shall have died, the Vice President elect shall become President. If a President shall not have been chosen before the time fixed for the beginning of his term, or if the President elect shall have failed to qualify, then the Vice President elect shall act as President until a President shall have qualified; and the Congress may by law provide for the case wherein neither a President elect nor a Vice President shall have qualified, declaring who shall then act as President, or the manner in which one who is to act shall be selected, and such person shall act accordingly until a President or Vice President shall have qualified.

Section 4. The Congress may by law provide for the case of the death of any of the persons from whom the House of Representatives may choose a President whenever the right of choice shall have devolved upon them, and for the case of the death of any of the persons from whom the Senate may choose a Vice President whenever the right of choice shall have devolved upon them.

Section 5. Sections 1 and 2 shall take effect on the 15th day of October following the ratification of this article.

Section 6. This article shall be inoperative unless it shall have been ratified as an amendment to the Constitution by the legislatures of three-fourths of the several States within seven years from the date of its submission.

Ratified January 23, 1933.

AMENDMENT 21
REPEAL OF PROHIBITION

The Eighteenth Amendment is repealed (removed from the Constitution).

Section 1. The eighteenth article of amendment to the Constitution of the United States is hereby repealed.

Section 2. The transportation or importation into any State, Territory, or Possession of the United States for delivery or use therein of intoxicating liquors, in violation of the laws thereof, is hereby prohibited.

Section 3. This article shall be inoperative unless it shall have been ratified as an amendment to the Constitution by conventions in the several States, as provided in the Constitution, within seven years from the date of the submission hereof to the States by the Congress.

Ratified December 5, 1933.

AMENDMENT 22
TERM LIMITS FOR THE PRESIDENCY

Presidents cannot serve more than two full terms in office.

Section 1. No person shall be elected to the office of the President more than twice, and no person who has held the office of President, or acted as President, for more than two years of a term to which some other person was elected President shall be elected to the office of the President more than once. But this Article shall not apply to any person holding the office of President when this Article was proposed by Congress, and shall not prevent any person who may be holding the office of President, or acting as President, during the term within which this Article becomes operative from holding the office of President or acting as President during the remainder of such term.

Section 2. This article shall be inoperative unless it shall have been ratified as an amendment to the Constitution by the legislatures of three-fourths of the several States within seven years from the date of its submission to the States by the Congress.

Ratified February 27, 1951.

AMENDMENT 23
WASHINGTON, D.C., SUFFRAGE
Section 1. The District constituting the seat of government of the United States shall appoint in such manner as the Congress may direct:

A number of electors of President and Vice President equal to the whole number of Senators and Representatives in Congress to which the District would be entitled if it were a state, but in no event more than the least populous State; they shall be in addition to those appointed by the States, but they shall be considered, for the purposes of the election of President and Vice President, to be electors appointed by a State; and they shall meet in the District and perform such duties as provided by the twelfth article of amendment.

Section 2. The Congress shall have power to enforce this article by appropriate legislation.

Ratified March 29, 1961.

This amendment gives the District of Columbia the right to participate in electing the president and vice-president. The District of Columbia is the nation's capital and is not part of any state.

AMENDMENT 24
ABOLITION OF POLL TAXES
Section 1. The right of citizens of the United States to vote in any primary or other election for President or Vice President, for electors for President or Vice President, or for Senator or Representative in Congress, shall not be denied or abridged by the United States or any State by reason of failure to pay poll tax or other tax.

Section 2. The Congress shall have power to enforce this article by appropriate legislation.

Ratified January 23, 1964.

No state can deny someone the right to vote because the person failed to pay a special voting tax. Before this amendment, some states used a tax to prevent African Americans from voting.

AMENDMENT 25
PRESIDENTIAL SUCCESSION
Section 1. In case of the removal of the President from office or of his death or resignation, the Vice President shall become President.

Section 2. Whenever there is a vacancy in the office of the Vice President, the President shall nominate a Vice President who shall take office upon confirmation by a majority vote of both Houses of Congress.

Section 3. Whenever the President transmits to the President pro tempore of the Senate and the Speaker of the House of Representatives his written declaration that he is unable to discharge the powers and duties of his office, and until he transmits to them a written declaration to the contrary, such powers and duties shall be discharged by the Vice President as Acting President.

This amendment deals with situations in which the president dies or is unable to carry out his or her duties. It spells out when the vice president should act for the president or take over as president. It also says how a new vice president should be elected if the vice president dies or leaves office between elections.

Section 4. Whenever the Vice President and a majority of either the principal officers of the executive departments or of such other body as Congress may by law provide, transmit to the President pro tempore of the Senate and the Speaker of the House of Representatives their written declaration that the President is unable to discharge the powers and duties of his office, the Vice President shall immediately assume the powers and duties of the office as Acting President.

Thereafter, when the President transmits to the President pro tempore of the Senate and the Speaker of the House of Representatives his written declaration that no inability exists, he shall resume the powers and duties of his office unless the Vice President and a majority of either the principal officers of the executive department or of such other body as Congress may by law provide, transmit within four days to the President pro tempore of the Senate and the Speaker of the House of Representatives their written declaration that the President is unable to discharge the powers and duties of his office. Thereupon Congress shall decide the issue, assembling within forty-eight hours for that purpose if not in session. If the Congress, within twenty-one days after receipt of the latter written declaration, or, if Congress is not in session, within twenty-one days after Congress is required to assemble, determines by two-thirds vote of both Houses that the President is unable to discharge the powers and duties of his office, the Vice President shall continue to discharge the same as Acting President; otherwise, the President shall resume the powers and duties of his office.

Ratified February 10, 1967.

AMENDMENT 26
18-YEAR-OLD SUFFRAGE
Section 1. The right of citizens of the United States, who are eighteen years of age or older, to vote shall not be denied or abridged by the United States or by any State on account of age.

Section 2. The Congress shall have power to enforce this article by appropriate legislation.

Ratified July 1, 1971.

AMENDMENT 27
CONGRESSIONAL PAY RAISES
No law, varying the compensation for the services of the Senators and Representatives, shall take effect, until an election of Representatives shall have intervened.

Ratified May 7, 1992.

The federal government and the states cannot deny citizens who are 18 years and older the right to vote.

Congress cannot change the pay of senators and representatives who are serving in that session of Congress. Changes in pay will take effect only after the next election for the House of Representatives.

Presidents of the United States

1. George Washington — 1789-1797 — (no party)
2. John Adams — 1797-1801 — (Federalist)
3. Thomas Jefferson — 1801-1809 — (Democratic-Republican)
4. James Madison — 1809-1817 — (Democratic-Republican)
5. James Monroe — 1817-1825 — (Democratic-Republican)
6. John Quincy Adams — 1825-1829 — (Democratic-Republican)
7. Andrew Jackson — 1829-1837 — (Democrat)
8. Martin Van Buren — 1837-1841 — (Democrat)
9. William Henry Harrison — 1841 — (Whig)
10. John Tyler — 1841-1845 — (Whig)
11. James Knox Polk — 1845-1849 — (Democrat)
12. Zachary Taylor — 1849-1850 — (Whig)
13. Millard Fillmore — 1850-1853 — (Whig)
14. Franklin Pierce — 1853-1857 — (Democrat)
15. James Buchanan — 1857-1861 — (Democrat)
16. Abraham Lincoln — 1861-1865 — (Republican)
17. Andrew Johnson — 1865-1869 — (Democrat/National Union)
18. Ulysses Simpson Grant — 1869-1877 — (Republican)
19. Rutherford Birchard Hayes — 1877-1881 — (Republican)
20. James Abram Garfield — 1881 — (Republican)
21. Chester Alan Arthur — 1881-1885 — (Republican)
22. Grover Cleveland — 1885-1889 — (Democrat)
23. Benjamin Harrison — 1889-1893 — (Republican)
24. Grover Cleveland — 1893-1897 — (Democrat)
25. William McKinley — 1897-1901 — (Republican)
26. Theodore Roosevelt — 1901-1909 — (Republican)
27. William Howard Taft — 1909-1913 — (Republican)
28. Woodrow Wilson — 1913-1921 — (Democrat)
29. Warren Gamaliel Harding — 1921-1923 — (Republican)
30. Calvin Coolidge — 1923-1929 — (Republican)
31. Herbert Clark Hoover — 1929-1933 — (Republican)
32. Franklin Delano Roosevelt — 1933-1945 — (Democrat)
33. Harry S Truman — 1945-1953 — (Democrat)
34. Dwight David Eisenhower — 1953-1961 — (Republican)
35. John Fitzgerald Kennedy — 1961-1963 — (Democrat)
36. Lyndon Baines Johnson — 1963-1969 — (Democrat)
37. Richard Milhous Nixon — 1969-1974 — (Republican)
38. Gerald Rudolph Ford, Jr. — 1974-1977 — (Republican)
39. James Earl Carter — 1977-1981 — (Democrat)
40. Ronald Wilson Reagan — 1981-1989 — (Republican)
41. George Herbert Walker Bush — 1989-1993 — (Republican)
42. William Jefferson Clinton — 1993-2001 — (Democrat)
43. George Walker Bush — 2001- — (Republican)

The Pledge of Allegiance

I pledge allegiance to the Flag
of the United States of America,
and to the Republic
for which it stands,
one Nation under God, indivisible,
with liberty and justice for all.

The Star-Spangled Banner

September 20, 1814
By Francis Scott Key

Oh, say can you see, by the dawn's early light,
What so proudly we hailed at the twilight's last gleaming?
Whose broad stripes and bright stars, through the perilous fight,
O'er the ramparts we watched, were so gallantly streaming?
And the rockets' red glare, the bombs bursting in air,
Gave proof through the night that our flag was still there.
O say, does that star-spangled banner yet wave
O'er the land of the free and the home of the brave?

On the shore, dimly seen through the mists of the deep,
Where the foe's haughty host in dread silence reposes,
What is that which the breeze, o'er the towering steep,
As it fitfully blows, now conceals, now discloses?
Now it catches the gleam of the morning's first beam,
In full glory reflected now shines on the stream:
'Tis the star-spangled banner! O long may it wave
O'er the land of the free and the home of the brave.

And where is that band who so vauntingly swore
That the havoc of war and the battle's confusion
A home and a country should leave us no more?
Their blood has wiped out their foul footstep's pollution.
No refuge could save the hireling and slave
From the terror of flight, or the gloom of the grave:
And the star-spangled banner in triumph doth wave
O'er the land of the free and the home of the brave.

Oh! thus be it ever, when freemen shall stand
Between their loved homes and the war's desolation!
Blest with victory and peace, may the heaven-rescued land
Praise the Power that hath made and preserved us a nation.
Then conquer we must, for our cause it is just,
And this be our motto: "In God is our trust."
And the star-spangled banner forever shall wave
O'er the land of the free and the home of the brave!

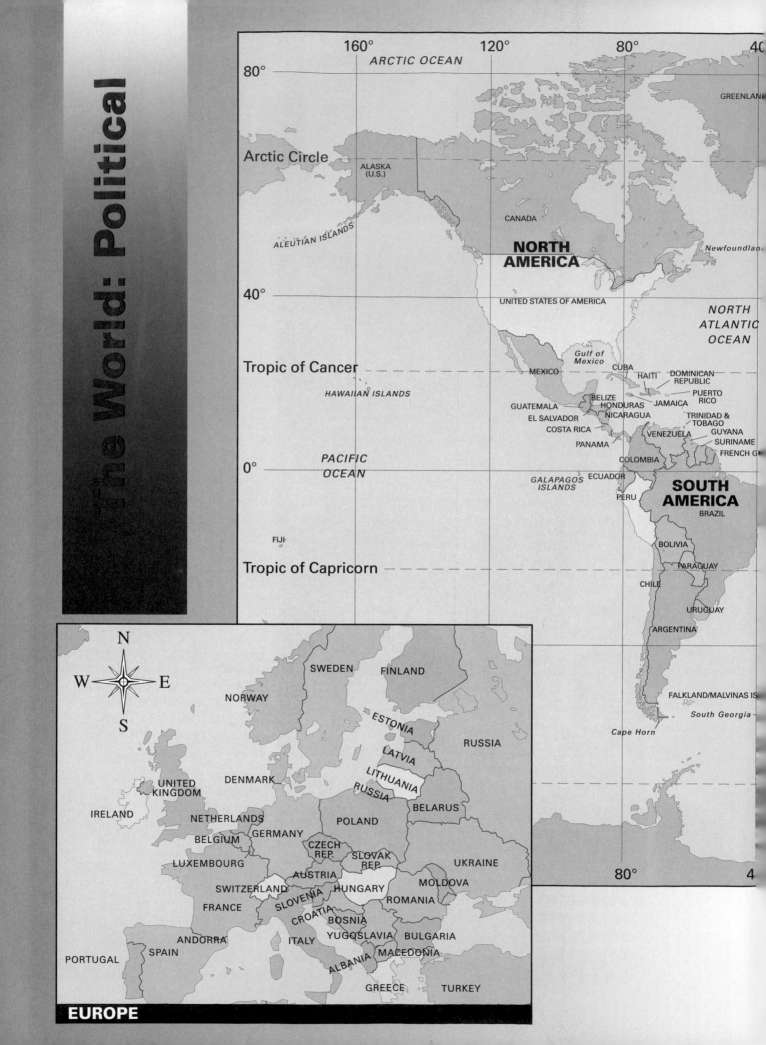

The World: Political

80°   160°   120°   80°   40

ARCTIC OCEAN

Arctic Circle

ALASKA
(U.S.)

GREENLAN

ALEUTIAN ISLANDS

CANADA

**NORTH
AMERICA**

Newfoundlan

40°

UNITED STATES OF AMERICA

*NORTH
ATLANTIC
OCEAN*

Tropic of Cancer

*Gulf of
Mexico*

MEXICO   CUBA   HAITI   DOMINICAN
REPUBLIC

HAWAIIAN ISLANDS

BELIZE   PUERTO
RICO

GUATEMALA   HONDURAS   JAMAICA

EL SALVADOR   NICARAGUA   TRINIDAD &
TOBAGO

COSTA RICA   VENEZUELA   GUYANA

PANAMA   SURINAME

FRENCH G

COLOMBIA

0°   *PACIFIC
OCEAN*

*GALAPAGOS
ISLANDS*   ECUADOR

**SOUTH
AMERICA**

PERU

BRAZIL

FIJI

BOLIVIA

PARAGUAY

Tropic of Capricorn

CHILE

URUGUAY

ARGENTINA

FALKLAND/MALVINAS IS

South Georgia

Cape Horn

80°   4

EUROPE

N
W   E
S

SWEDEN   FINLAND

NORWAY

ESTONIA

RUSSIA

LATVIA

DENMARK   LITHUANIA

UNITED
KINGDOM   RUSSIA

BELARUS

IRELAND

NETHERLANDS

POLAND

BELGIUM   GERMANY

UKRAINE

LUXEMBOURG   CZECH
REP.   SLOVAK
REP.

AUSTRIA   MOLDOVA

SWITZERLAND   HUNGARY

SLOVENIA   ROMANIA

FRANCE

CROATIA   BOSNIA

ANDORRA   ITALY   YUGOSLAVIA   BULGARIA

PORTUGAL   SPAIN   MACEDONIA

ALBANIA

GREECE   TURKEY

0°   40°   80°   120°   160°

SVALBARD   ARCTIC OCEAN   SEVERNAYA ZEMLYA   ARCTIC OCEAN   80°
ZEMLYA FRANTSA IOSIFA
Novaya Zemlya

Arctic Circle

Area of Inset

RUSSIA

EUROPE   ASIA   ALEUTIAN ISLANDS

KAZAKHSTAN   MONGOLIA

40°
GEORGIA   UZBEKISTAN   KYRGYZSTAN   NORTH
ARMENIA   AZERBAIJAN   TAJIKISTAN   CHINA   KOREA
CYPRUS   TURKMENISTAN   SOUTH   JAPAN
TUNISIA   SYRIA   IRAQ   KOREA
MOROCCO   LEBANON   IRAN   AFGHANISTAN
ISRAEL
ALGERIA   LIBYA   JORDAN   PAKISTAN   NEPAL   BHUTAN   Tropic of Cancer
WESTERN   EGYPT   SAUDI   QATAR   TAIWAN
SAHARA   ARABIA   U.A.E.   INDIA   BANGLADESH   PACIFIC
RITANIA   AFRICA   ERITREA   OMAN   BURMA   OCEAN
MALI   NIGER   CHAD   YEMEN   LAOS
GUINEA   BURKINA   SUDAN   DJIBOUTI   THAILAND   VIETNAM
FASO   NIGERIA   CAMBODIA   PHILIPPINES
ERRA   IVORY   CENTRAL   ETHIOPIA   SRI
EONE   COAST   AFRICAN REPUBLIC   LANKA   BRUNEI
LIBERIA   CAMEROON   SOMALIA   MALAYSIA
BIA   GHANA   UGANDA   KENYA   MELANESIA
NEA-BISSAU   TOGO   CONGO   RWANDA   EAST INDIES   0°
GABON   BURUNDI   SINGAPORE   INDONESIA   PAPUA   SOLOMON
BENIN   REPUBLIC   TANZANIA   NEW   ISLANDS
EQUATORIAL   OF CONGO   GUINEA
GUINEA   ANGOLA   INDIAN   Coral Sea   VANUATU   FIJI
MALAWI   OCEAN
SOUTH   ZAMBIA   MOZAMBIQUE
TLANTIC   NAMIBIA   ZIMBABWE   MADAGASCAR   MAURITIUS   AUSTRALIA   Tropic of Capricorn
OCEAN   BOTSWANA   RÉUNION   AUSTRALIA
SWAZILAND   North I.   40°
SOUTH   LESOTHO   NEW
AFRICA   ZEALAND
South I.

N
W   E
S

0   2000   4000 miles (at equator)

0   2000   4000   6000 kilometres (at equator)

Gall Projection

Antarctic Circle

ANTARCTICA

0°   40°   80°   120°   160°

Maps   **493**

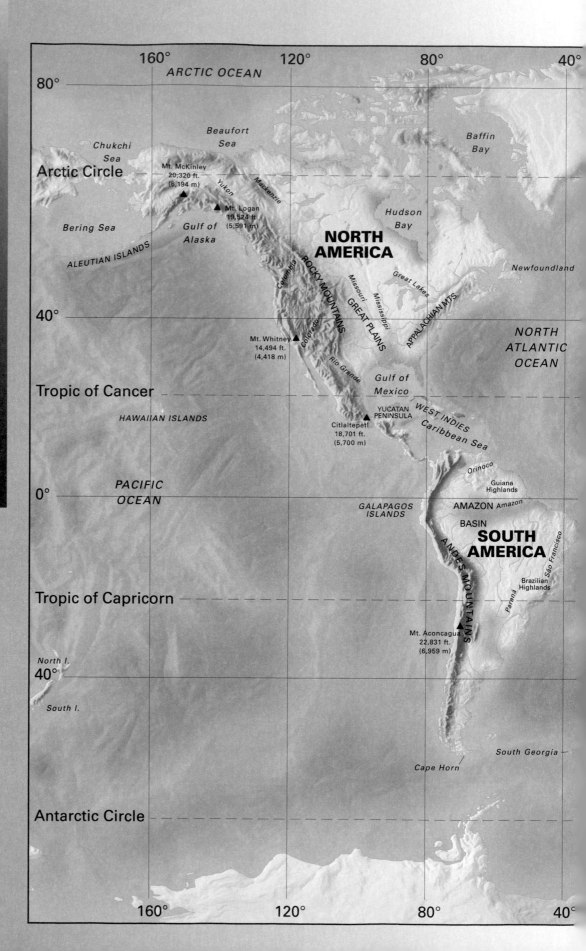

The World: Physical

ARCTIC OCEAN

80°

Chukchi Sea

Beaufort Sea

Baffin Bay

Arctic Circle

Mt. McKinley
20,320 ft.
(6,194 m)

Yukon

Mackenzie

Hudson Bay

Mt. Logan
19,524 ft.
(5,591 m)

Bering Sea

Gulf of Alaska

NORTH AMERICA

Newfoundland

ALEUTIAN ISLANDS

Columbia

ROCKY MOUNTAINS

Missouri

Great Lakes

APPALACHIAN MTS.

40°

GREAT PLAINS

Mississippi

Mt. Whitney
14,494 ft.
(4,418 m)

Colorado

NORTH ATLANTIC OCEAN

Rio Grande

Gulf of Mexico

Tropic of Cancer

HAWAIIAN ISLANDS

YUCATAN PENINSULA

Citlaltepetl
18,701 ft.
(5,700 m)

WEST INDIES

Caribbean Sea

Orinoco

0°

PACIFIC OCEAN

GALAPAGOS ISLANDS

AMAZON *Amazon*

Guiana Highlands

BASIN

SOUTH AMERICA

ANDES MOUNTAINS

São Francisco

Brazilian Highlands

Paraná

Tropic of Capricorn

Mt. Aconcagua
22,831 ft.
(6,959 m)

North I.

40°

South I.

South Georgia

Cape Horn

Antarctic Circle

160° 120° 80° 40°

0°   40°   80°   120°   160°

ARCTIC OCEAN
SVALBARD
ZEMLYA FRANTSA IOSIFA
SEVERNAYA ZEMLYA
ARCTIC OCEAN   80°

Norwegian Sea
Novaya Zemlya
Laptev Sea
East Siberian Sea
Chukchi Sea

Arctic Circle

Barents Sea
Kara Sea
Dvina
Indigirka
Kolyma

North Sea
Baltic Sea
Ob-
Nizhnyaya Tunguska
Lena
Bering Sea

NORTH EUROPEAN PLAIN
Ob-
Yenisey
Angara
Lena
Aldan
Sea of Okhotsk
ALEUTIAN ISLANDS

EUROPE
Volga
Tobol Ishim
LAKE BAIKAL
ASIA

ALPS
Don
Ural
Irtysh
Sea of Japan   40°

Black Sea
Caspian Sea
Aral Sea
K2 28,250 ft. (8,611 m)
GOBI (DESERT)

Mediterranean Sea
Huang He
Yellow Sea

ATLAS MTS.
Indus
HIMALAYAS
Chang Jiang
East China Sea

SAHARA
THAR DESERT
Ganges
Mt. Everest 29,028 ft. (8,848 m)
Tropic of Cancer

Nile
Red Sea
ARABIAN PENINSULA
DECCAN PLATEAU
South China Sea
PACIFIC OCEAN

SAHEL
Niger
AFRICA
Bay of Bengal
Philippine Sea

Uele
White Nile
Mt. Kenya 17,058 ft. (5,199 m)
Celebes Sea
0°

CONGO BASIN
Congo
EAST INDIES
MELANESIA

Mt. Kilimanjaro 19,340 ft. (5,985 m)
INDIAN OCEAN

SOUTH ATLANTIC OCEAN
Coral Sea

KALAHARI DESERT
AUSTRALIA
Tropic of Capricorn

Orange
GREAT VICTORIA DESERT

Tasman Sea
North I.   40°

South I.

N
W   E
S

0   2000   4000 miles (at equator)

0   2000   4000   6000 kilometres (at equator)

Gall Projection

Antarctic Circle

ANTARCTICA

0°   40°   80°   120°   160°

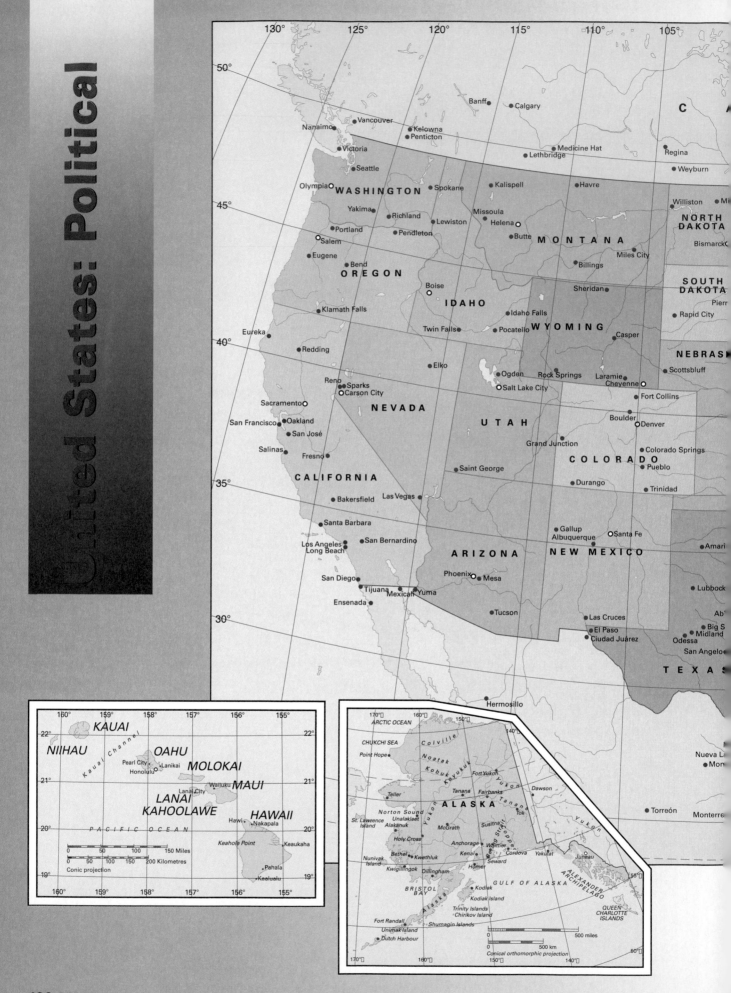

130° 125° 120° 115° 110° 105°

50°

C

Banff • Calgary •

Vancouver •
Nanaimo •
Kelowna •
• Penticton
Victoria •
Medicine Hat • Regina •
Lethbridge • Weyburn •
• Seattle

Olympia○ WASHINGTON • Spokane • Kalispell • Havre Williston • Mi
45° Yakima • Richland Lewiston Missoula NORTH
Portland • Helena○ DAKOTA
Pendleton • Butte MONTANA Bismarck •
Salem○
Eugene • Miles City •
Bend • OREGON Billings •
SOUTH
Klamath Falls • Boise○ IDAHO Sheridan • DAKOTA
Pierr
40° Idaho Falls • Rapid City •
Eureka • Twin Falls WYOMING
Redding • Pocatello • Casper •
NEBRAS
Elko • Ogden • Rock Springs Laramie • Scottsbluff •
Reno Cheyenne○
Sparks • Salt Lake City○ Fort Collins •
Sacramento○ Carson City○
NEVADA UTAH Boulder •
San Francisco • Oakland • Denver○
San José • Grand Junction • Colorado Springs •
Salinas • COLORADO
Fresno • Pueblo •
35° CALIFORNIA Saint George • Durango •
Bakersfield • Las Vegas • Trinidad •
Santa Barbara • Gallup •
Los Angeles • San Bernardino • Albuquerque • Santa Fe○
Long Beach • ARIZONA NEW MEXICO
Amari •
San Diego • Phoenix○ Mesa •
Tijuana • Yuma Lubbock •
Mexicali
Ensenada • Tucson • Las Cruces • Ab°
30° El Paso • Big S
Odessa • Midland •
Ciudad Juárez San Angelo •

TEXAS

Hermosillo •

160° 159° 158° 157° 156° 155° 170° 160° 150°
22° KAUAI 22° ARCTIC OCEAN 140°
NIIHAU OAHU CHUKCHI SEA Colville
Pearl City MOLOKAI Point Hope • Noatak Fort Yukon • Nueva L
Honolulu • Lanikai Kobuk Keyukuk Yukon • Mon
21° Lanai City MAUI 21° Teller • Tanana Fairbanks Dawson •
LANAI Wailuku ALASKA Tanana
KAHOOLAWE St. Lawrence Norton Sound Tok •
HAWAII Island Unalakleet
20° PACIFIC OCEAN Hawi Nakapala 20° Alakanuk McGrath Susitna
Keahole Point Keaukaha Nunivak Holy Cross Anchorage • Cordova
0 50 100 150 Miles Island Bethel • Kwethluk Kenal • Whittier Yakutat
0 50 100 150 200 Kilometres Kwigillingok Dillingham • Homer Seward Juneau •
Conic projection Pahala • BRISTOL Kodiak GULF OF ALASKA ALEXANDER 55°
19° Kaalualu 19° BAY Alaska Kodiak Island ARCHIPELAGO
160° 159° 158° 157° 156° 155° Fort Randall Trinity Islands Chirikov Island QUEEN
Unimak Island Shumagin Islands CHARLOTTE Torreón •
• Dutch Harbour ISLANDS Monterr •
0 500 km
0 500 miles
Conical orthomorphic projection 50°
170° 160° 150° 140°

United States: Physical

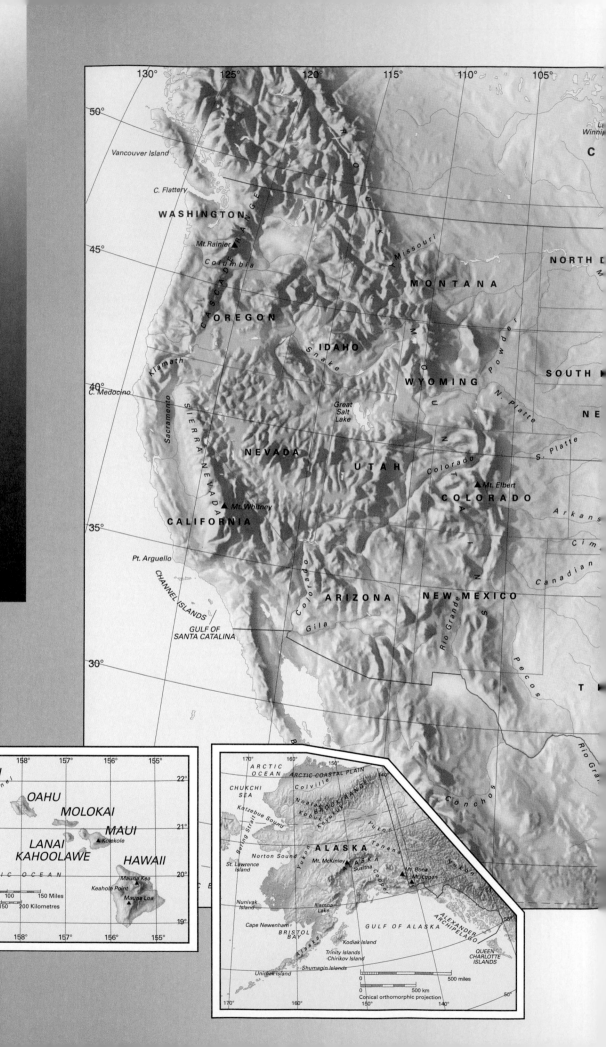

498 Maps

A

abolitionists people who favored abolition, the ending of slavery

adapt to change in order to survive in a new or different environment or situation

agrarian a person who favors an agricultural way of life and government policies that support agricultural interests

AIDS: Acquired Immune Deficiency Syndrome, a disease that weakens the body's ability to fight off infection and illness

aliens people who have come from other countries and are not yet citizens

ally a nation that joins another nation in some common effort, such as winning a war

amendment a change to the constitution

annex To add a territory to a country. Such an addition is called an *annexation.*

arsenal a place where weapons and ammunition are stored

Articles of Confederation The first written plan of government for the United States. A "confederation" is an association of states who cooperate for a common purpose.

assembly an elected group of lawmakers

assimilation the process by which immigrants or other newcomers acquire the attitudes, behaviors, and cultural patterns of the society around them

B

bicameral Having two lawmaking parts. *Bicameral* comes from Latin words meaning "two rooms."

bill a proposed law

Bill of Rights a formal listing of the basic rights of citizen

blockade a closing off of an area to keep people or supplies from going in or out

boycott To refuse to buy one or more goods from a certain source. An organized refusal by many people is also called a boycott.

C

capitalism an economic system based on the private ownership of farms and businesses

carpetbaggers northerners who went to the South after the Civil War to gain money and political power

cash crops crops, such as tobacco, sugar, and cotton, raised in large quantities in order to be sold for profit

checks and balances the system that allows each branch of government to limit the powers of the other branches

civil rights the rights that are guaranteed by the Constitution to all people as citizens, especially equal treatment under the law

civil servants employees of the government

civil war a war fought between the people of a single country

class A part of society defined by such qualities as wealth, occupation, and inherited titles or honors. A society may have an upper class, a middle class, and a lower class.

collective bargaining a method for negotiating labor issues in which union representatives bargain with employers on behalf of the union's members

colony a new settlement or territory established and governed by a country in another land

compromise an agreement in which both sides in a dispute agree to give up something they want in order to achieve a settlement

Confederacy the independent country declared by 11 southern states, who called themselves the Confederate States of America

conquistadors Spanish soldier-explorers, especially those who conquered the native peoples of Mexico and Peru

conservation the effort to protect something valuable from being destroyed or used up

constitution a written plan that provides the basic framework of a government

converts people who accept a new religion

corporation a business that is owned by many investors

cotton gin a hand-operated machine that cleans seeds and other unwanted material from cotton

cultural region an area in which a group of people share a similar culture and language

culture a people's way of life, including beliefs, customs, food, dwellings, and clothing

D

Declaration of Sentiments A formal statement of injustices suffered by women, written by the organizers of the Seneca Falls Convention. *Sentiments* means "beliefs" or "convictions."

defendants people who are required to defend themselves in a legal action; an example is an accused person who is put on trial for a crime

deforestation the clearing away of forests

democratic Ruled by the people. In a democracy, citizens elect representatives to make and carry out laws.

diplomacy The art of conducting negotiations with other countries. People who engage in diplomacy are called *diplomats.*

discrimination unequal treatment based on a person's race, gender, religion, place of birth, or other arbitrary characteristic

doctrine a statement of official government policy, especially in foreign affairs

draft a system for requiring citizens to join their country's armed forces

E

economy the way a society organizes the manufacture and exchange of things of value, such as money, food, products, and services

Electoral College The group established by the Constitution to elect the president and vice president. Voters in each state choose their electors.

emancipation the act of freeing people from slavery

embargo a government order that stops merchant ships from leaving or entering a country's ports

Enlightenment the "Age of Reason" in 17th and 18th century Europe. Enlightenment thinkers emphasized using rational thought to discover truths about nature and society

entrepreneur someone who starts a business and is good at making money

environment all of the physical surroundings in a place, including land, water, animals, plants, and climate

executive branch the part of government that "executes" (carries out) the laws

expansionists Americans who favored extending the United States' power by taking control of new territories

F

federalism the constitutional system that shares power between the national and state governments

feminist a person who is actively concerned with achieving social, political, and economic equality for women

First Great Awakening a revival of religious feeling and belief in the American colonies that began in the 1730s

folk art art made by ordinary people (as opposed to trained artists) using traditional methods

foreign policy guidelines for how a country handles political and economic interactions with other countries

forty-niners the people (almost all young men) who joined the rush for gold in California in 1849

freedmen African Americans who had been set free from slavery

fugitive a person who flees or tries to escape (for example, from slavery)

G

Great Depression a drastic decline in the economy that led to widespread unemployment and poverty in the 1930s

guerrillas soldiers who operate on their own and are not part of a regular army

H

habeas corpus a written order from a court that gives a person the right to a trial before being jailed

heritage the traditional beliefs, values, and customs of a family or country

homestead a plot of land where pioneers could build a home, farm, or ranch

homesteader a farmer who is given a plot of public land (called a *homestead*) in return for cultivating it

I

immigrant A person who moves from one country to another. Such a movement is called *immigration*.

impeach to formally accuse an official of a crime related to official duties

imperialism the policy of extending a nation's power by gaining political and economic control over other countries

inauguration a formal ceremony to mark the beginning of something, such as a president's term of office

indentured servant A person who signed an indenture, or an agreement to work for a master for a period of years. Indentured servants were not free until they completed their term of service.

independence freedom from control by another government or country

Industrial Revolution The dramatic change in economies brought about by the use of machines to do work formerly done by hand. The Industrial Revolution began in England in the late 1700s and spread to America and the rest of Europe.

industrialist a person whose wealth comes from the ownership of industrial businesses and who favors government policies that support industry

industrialization the birth and growth of businesses that make and distribute products through the use of machinery

interest group an organization that actively promotes the views of some part of the public on specific issues

Internet a network that allows computers in locations around the world to share information

interstate commerce trade and other business dealings that cross state lines

irrigation a system for bringing water to farmland by artificial means, such as using a dam to trap water and ditches to channel it to fields

isolationism a policy of avoiding political or military agreements with other countries; first established by George Washington

J

Jim Crow laws Laws enforcing segregation of blacks and whites in the South after the Civil War. "Jim Crow" was a black character in an entertainer's act in the mid-1800s.

judicial branch the part of government, consisting of the Supreme Court and lower federal courts, that interprets the laws

L

laissez-faire The theory that economies work best when governments do not interfere with them. (*Laissez-faire* is French for "leave alone.")

legislative branch The lawmaking part of government, called the *legislature*. To *legislate* is to make a law.

Loyalists American colonists who were loyal to the British government

M

Manifest Destiny the belief that it was America's right and duty to spread across the North American continent

mass production the use of interchangeable parts and assembly lines to make large quantities of identical goods

mercenaries professional soldiers who fight for anyone who will pay them

migrate To move from one place and establish a home in a new place. A move of a large number of people is called a *migration,* and the people are called *migrants*. Some animals also migrate, usually with the seasons.

militarism a policy of glorifying military power and military ideas and values

militia a small army made up of ordinary citizens who are available to fight in an emergency

mission A place established by missionaries for their work. A typical California mission included such things as a church, a residence, workshops, and large areas of land for raising crops.

missionaries people who travel to a territory or community in order to make converts to their religion

monopoly a company that controls all production and sales of a particular product or service

Mormons Members of the Church of Jesus Christ of Latter-Day Saints. *Latter-Day* means "modern," while *saints* are people who dedicate their lives to following God's teachings.

N

nationalism devotion to a national or ethnic identity, including the desire for independence from rule by foreign countries

nativism an attitude of superiority and resentment toward the foreign-born

natural resources useful materials found in nature, including water, vegetation, animals, and minerals

neutrality a policy of not choosing sides in a war or dispute between other countries

New World The European name for the Americas. These continents were a "new" world for the Europeans, but not for the native peoples who lived there.

nullify To refuse to recognize a federal law. This action by a state is called *nullification*.

O

oppression the feeling of being weighed down or held back by severe and unfair force

Oregon Trail an overland route that stretched about 2,000 miles from Independence, Missouri, to the Columbia River in Oregon

P

Parliament the lawmaking body of England, consisting of representatives from throughout the kingdom

party an organized political group

passport a document issued by a citizen's home government that identifies a person and permits him or her to travel to other countries

Patriots American colonists who believed that the colonies had the right to govern themselves

petition (noun) a formal, written request

petition (verb) to make a formal demand or request

plantation a large area of privately owned land where crops were grown through the labor of workers, usually slaves, who lived on the land

platform a statement of the policies favored by a political party

pogroms Organized and often violent persecutions of minority groups. The word *pogrom* comes from Russian words meaning "like thunder."

popular sovereignty the idea that the authority of government comes from the people

populist devoted to the needs and interests of common people

Progressive movement a political reform effort of the early 1900s that focused on improving American life by fighting for such causes as equal rights, better working conditions, and protection of wilderness areas

public schools schools that are paid for by taxes and managed by local government for the benefit of the general public

Puritans People who wanted to "purify" the English Church. Puritans wanted to simplify the Church's ceremonies and its ranks of authority.

Q

quota a limit based on numbers or proportions—for example, the proportion of a country's population allowed to immigrate to the United States

R

racism prejudice based on race

rancho A grant of land made by the Mexican government. Most ranchos were used for raising cattle and crops.

ratify To formally approve a plan or an agreement. The process of approval is called *ratification*.

Reconstruction the period after the Civil War when the federal government ruled the southern states in order to rebuild them and allow them back into the Union

reformers people who work to correct failings or injustices

refugees people who flee their homes or countries because of war, persecution, or other causes

regulation the enforcement of laws that control conduct or practices; government regulations control the way goods, food, and drugs are produced and sold to the public

reparations debts imposed on a defeated nation to pay for the harm done during a war

repeal to take back, or to cancel, a law

republic a country governed by elected representatives

reservation An area of land set aside ("reserved") by the government for Native Americans. Reservations generally were on poor land that settlers didn't want.

Revolutionary War The struggle of the former British colonies in America to gain their independence from Britain. Also called the War for Independence, or the American Revolution.

rights powers or privileges that belong to people as citizens and that cannot or should not be taken away by the government

S

scalawags white southerners who supported the federal government after the Civil War

secede to withdraw from an organization or alliance; in this case, to withdraw from the United States

secession the act of withdrawing from an organization or alliance, such as the withdrawal of the southern states from the Union

Second Great Awakening A revival of religious feeling and belief in the 1820s and 1830s. The First Great Awakening swept through the American colonies in the 1700s.

secretary of state The head of the State Department, who oversees matters relating to foreign countries. The secretary of state is an important member of the president's cabinet.

sedition the crime of encouraging rebellion against the government

segregation the social separation of groups of people, especially by race

self-incrimination the act of giving testimony that can be used against oneself

self-made achieving wealth or influence through one's own effort rather than being born to a privileged family

slavery The treatment of people as property for the purpose of forcing them to do labor. People who are denied freedom in this way are called *slaves* and are said to be *enslaved*.

slave trade the business of capturing, transporting, and selling people as slaves

Social Darwinism the idea that people and societies compete for survival, with the fit becoming wealthy and successful while the weak struggle to survive

spiritual a religious folk song of African American origin

spoils system the practice of rewarding political supporters with government jobs

states' rights All rights kept by the states under the Constitution. Supporters of states' rights sometimes argued that states were not obliged to honor federal laws that they believed violated the Constitution.

strategy An overall plan (for example, for winning a war). Specific ways of carrying out a strategy are called *tactics*.

subsidy money or other things of value (such as land) that a government contributes to an enterprise

suffrage the right to vote

T

tariff a tax imposed by the government on goods imported from another country

tenement buildings crowded and usually run-down buildings with many small, cheap apartments

territory A region designated by Congress and organized under a governor. A territory may apply to become a state when it has a large enough population.

trade unions early labor organizations that brought together workers in the same trade, or job, to fight for better wages and working conditions

tradition a belief, custom, or way of doing something that has existed for a long time

traitor a person guilty of the crime of treason, or disloyalty to the government

transcendentalism a philosophy which taught that people should "transcend" (go beyond) logical thinking to reach true understanding with the help of emotion and intuition

transcontinental railroad a railroad that crosses a continent (*trans* means "across")

trappers adventurers who capture and kill animals, such as beavers, for their fur

treaty a formal agreement between nations

trust a group of corporations that unite in order to reduce competition and control prices in a business or industry

tyranny The unjust use of government power. A ruler who uses power in this way is called a *tyrant*.

U

undocumented immigrants people living in the United States without official permission from the government

the Union The United States as one country, united under a single government. During the Civil War, "the Union" came to mean the government and armies of the North.

urbanization the growth of cities

V

veto To reject a proposed law or a bill. Only the president can veto bills.

visas government documents that allow people from other nations to enter the country for a limited period of time

W

warrant an order from a judge that authorizes police or other officials to take a certain action, such as searching someone's property

well-born born to an upper-class (wealthy, respected) family

Y

yellow journalism the practice of publishing sensational and often exaggerated news stories in order to attract readers

A

Abenaki people, 1
abolitionists, 246–247, 249, 294
   and Congress, 289, 328–329
   voices against slavery, 450–452
Act Concerning Religion, 44
Adams, Abigail, 156, 434
Adams, John
   in Continental Congress, 80, 84, 434
   as Patriot, 70, 73
   as president, 155–156, 164–165, 166
   presidential campaign (1800), 157, 436
   as vice president, 134, 146
Adams, John Quincy, 172, 185
   anti-slavery proposal, 289
   election to president (1824), 179, 188
   Fourth of July Address (1821), 437
Adams, Samuel, 68–69, 70, 73, 106
adobe, 11, 236
Africa
   Barbary States, 166–167
   migration from South to, 334
   slave trade, 40, 45, 55, 84, 112
African Americans
   in the American Revolution, 90, 431
   and black codes, 325
   civil rights of, 326, 418, 421
   in colonial society, 55
   culture of, 279–282
   education for, 246, 325, 332, 460
   Fifteenth Amendment and, 328, 332
   Fourteenth Amendment and, 326, 333, 421
   free blacks in the North/South, 264, 265, 270–271
   freedmen, 324–325, 326, 327, 328, 332
   and Jim Crow laws, 181, 333, 394, 457–458
   in the military, 90, 317, 403, 431
   National Association for the Advancement of
      Colored People (NAACP), 394
   in public office, 329
   support for the Republican Party, 328
   in U.S. population, 111, 263, 269
   voting rights, 325, 328, 328–329, 332, 421
   See also slavery, slaves
African Methodist Episcopal Church (AME), 271
agrarians, 256, 259, 386–387
agriculture
   effect of Industrial Revolution on, 259

Native American, 3, 13, 14
   in the Southern economy, 256, 460–461
   See also farming, homesteads
Aguinaldo, General Emilio, 404
AIDS, epidemic, 422
Alamo, Battle of the, 202–203
Alaska, purchased from Russia, 400
Algonquian languages, 13
Alien Act, 155
Allen, Ethan, 81
Allen, Richard, 271
ally/allies, 63, 94
amendments
   to prevent ties in presidential election, 158
   process, 127
   protecting individual rights, 127, 421
   See also individual amendments
American Anti-Slavery Society, 328
American Expeditionary Force (AEF), 412
American Federation of Labor (AFL), 366
American Notes (Dickens), 448
American Red Cross, 309
American Revolution, 80
   African Americans in, 90, 431
   American strengths/weaknesses during, 88
   battles of, 90–97, 98–99
   British strengths/weaknesses during, 89
   First Great Awakening and, 429
   foreign aid during, 88, 94, 96
   impact on rest of world, 100
   Minutemen in, 75–76, 431
   surrender of British in, 97
   Treaty of Paris ending, 100
American Slavery As It Is (Weld), 451
American System, Clay's, 178
Amnesty Act of 1872, 331
Anaconda Plan, 308
Angel Island, 378
Anglican Church, 39, 43, 44
annexation, of Texas, 203
Anthony, Susan B., 240, 250, 445–446
Antietam, Battle of, 310–311
Anti-Federalists, opposition to the Constitution, 116
Antislavery movement. *See* abolitionists
Appeal to the Colored Citizens of the World (Walker),
   451–452
appellate courts, 124–125
Appomattox, 319, 320

architecture, southwest Spanish-style, 236
arms, right to bear, 138
Arnold, Benjamin, 81
arsenal, 105
art, early American, 180
    See also literature; music
Articles of Confederation, 103, 104, 116
    revising, 105, 108, 109, 110
Asia
    American expansion into, 400–401
    land bridge from, 2
assembly, elected, in the colonies, 38, 42
assembly, right to peaceful, 137
Audubon, John James, 180
Austin, Moses, 201
Austin, Stephen, 201
Aztecs, 20

B

Baltimore, Lord, 44
Bank of the United States, 142, 153, 178
    established by Congress, 151
    Jackson's battle against, 191
Barbary States, piracy, 166–167
Barton, Clara, 309
Bear Flag Republic, 207
Bedford, Gunning, 110
Bell, Alexander Graham, 357
Beringia, land bridge, 2
Berkeley, Lord John, 42
Bessemer, Henry, 356
bicameral legislature, 121
Biddle, Nicholas, 191
Bidwell, Annie, 221–222
bill, 122
Bill of Rights, 127, 133–134
    English, 52
    U.S., text of, 482–483
Bingham, George Caleb, 183
Black Americans. *See* African Americans
black codes, 325
    See also Jim Crow laws
Black Hawk, 192–193
Blackwell, Elizabeth, 249
Blaine, James G., 329
blue laws, 53
Bolívar, Simón, 171
Booth, John Wilkes, 323
Boston (Massachusetts) 51, 63
    British retreat from, 81
Boston Massacre, 69–70
Boston Tea Party, 70–72
boycott, of British goods, 69

Braddock, Edward, 65
Bradford, William, 39
Brandeis, Justice Louis, 139
Breed's Hill, 80
British East India Company, 71
Brook Farm, 243
Brooks, Preston, 295, 296
Brown, John, 294–295, 298–299
Brown v. Board of Education, 421
Bryan, William Jennings, 387, 400
buffalo, 12, 221, 342, 345
Buffalo Soldiers, 334
Bull Run, Battle of, 308–309
Bunker Hill, Battle of, 80
Burgoyne, General John, 93, 94
Burr, Aaron, 157
business, growth of big, 354–355, 359–360, 388–389
Butler, Andrew P., 295

C

cabinet, president's, 146
Cabot, John, 27
Calhoun, John C., 169
    debate with Daniel Webster, 453–454
    nullification crisis and, 190
California
    America's claim of, 206–207
    building of Central Pacific railroad in, 342–343
    Californios' legacy in, 217
    Chinese immigration to, 225–226
    gold rush, 224–225
    mid-19th century travel to, 441–442
    Native American cultural region, 3, 4–5, 8
    Spanish missions, 216
    statehood and slavery issue, 290
Californios, 216–217
Calvert, Cecil, Leonard, and Sir George, 44
Canada
    British control of, 163, 169
    British troops' capture of, 65
    early explorers in, 25, 26, 27
    Loyalists settling in, 100
    Nez Percé flight to, 339
    and Oregon country, 205
    runaway slaves and, 292
canals, building of, 260
Canyons of the Colorado (Powell), 444–445
Cape Horn, sailing around, 441
capital, location of nation's, 150–151, 156
capitalism, 178
Caribbean
    early explorers, 18, 19, 22
    slave trade in, 20, 84

Carnegie, Andrew, 356, 367, 388–389
carpetbaggers, 328
Carteret, Sir George, 42
Cartier, Jacques, 25
Carver, George Washington, 460–461
cash crops, 38, 55, 201, 255, 272
Cather, Willa, 459
Catlin, George, 180
cattle ranching, 216, 231
Cayuse people, 219–220
Champlain, Samuel de, 25, 26
Charles II, king of England, 32, 41, 43
Chávez, César, 422
checks and balances system, 126
Cherokee people, 192, 193, 439–440
Cheyenne people, 350
Chickasaw people, 192
Chief Abraham (Seminole), 200
Chief Joseph (Nez Percé), 219, 338–339
child labor, 392, 448–449
China, 17
    American trade with, 400–401
Chinese
    at Angel Island, 378
    in California gold rush, 225–226
    as immigrants, 378–379
    as railroad workers, 342–343
Choctaw people, 192
church
    for free blacks, 271
    for slaves, 281
    position on slavery, 264
    separation from state, 135, 435
Church of England, 39, 43, 44
Church of Jesus Christ of Latter-Day Saints, 222–223
cities
    in the colonies, 51
    growth of, 265, 361–362
citizens, protection from government abuse, 138–139
Civil Rights Act of 1866, 326
Civil Rights Act of 1964, 421
civil rights movement, 418
Civil War
    African American soldiers in, 317
    costs of, 320
    death toll of, 311, 320, 454
    draft during, 312, 313–314
    generals of, 454–455
    letters from soldiers, 456–457
    medical care during, 309, 311
    secession leading to, 300
    strengths/weaknesses, North vs. South, 304–305
    surrender of Lee, 319–320
    Union blockade during, 310
    weaponry of, 311
    women in, 308, 309
    See also individual battles
Clark, William, 204, 212–215, 338
Clay, Henry
    American System, 178
    Bank of the United States, 191
    Compromise of 1850, 291
    and the Missouri Compromise, 288
    presidential campaign (1824), 179, 188
    on Texas annexation, 203
    as War Hawk, 169
Clemenceau, Georges, 413
Cleveland, Grover, 401
Clinton, Hillary Rodham, 251
Clinton, Sir Henry, 95, 96
Cochrane, Josephine, 461
Cole, Thomas, 180
collective bargaining, 366
college
    for African Americans, 334, 394, 460
    for veterans, 419
    for women, 246
colonies
    African Americans in, 54, 55
    city life in, 51
    class differences in, 54
    crime/punishment in, 53
    farming in, 37–46, 50
    formation of militias, 73
    government in, 38, 39–46, 52
    rights of colonists in, 52
    See also individual colonies
Columbian Exchange, 19
Columbus, Christopher, 17, 18–19, 22, 27, 427
Command of the Army Act, 326
commerce clause, of Constitution, 128
Common Sense, (Paine), 82, 430
community property law, 237
Compromise of 1850, 291–292
Compromise of 1877, 331
computers, 417, 420
Concord (Massachusetts), 63, 75–76, 90
Confederacy, 303, 304, 305, 306, 308
    See also Civil War
Confederate States of America, 303
Congress, U.S., 121
    deadlock over the Tallmadge Amendment, 287
    division and violence over slavery, 295
    impeachment by, 124
    and national bank, 151
    passage of Force Bill, 190
    passage of laws by, 122
    powers of, 122

and Reconstruction, 324–327
    refusal to ratify the Treaty of Versailles, 414
    structure of, 121
    Supreme Court and, 125
Connecticut, 37, 41
    ratification of Constitution, 133
conquistadors, 20, 22–23
conservation movement, 393
Constitution
    amending, 127
    elastic clause of, 122, 151
    Father of, 107
    federal judges and, 125
    Federalists' support for, 116
    as living document, 119, 421
    preamble to, 120, 474
    ratification of, 115
    text of, 474–481
Constitutional Convention, 106–115
    delegates to, 106–108, 473
    issue of presidential selection, 113–114
    issue of slave representation, 111–112
    issue of state representation in the government, 109–110
    system of checks and balances, 126
    and three-fifths compromise, 112
    views and beliefs of delegates, 107–108
constitutions, state, 108, 329, 433
Continental Army, 80, 87
    defeat in New York, 91
    end of the Revolutionary War and, 100
    soldiers' life in, 432
    strengths/weaknesses, 88
    victory in Trenton, 92
Continental Congress, 73, 80, 84
Cooper, James Fenimore, 438
copper mining, 230
Cornwallis, Lord Charles, 96, 97, 100
Coronado, Francisco Vásquez de, 22, 23, 24
corporations, set up of, 359
Cortés, Hernán, 20
cotton,
    and slavery, 272–273
    effect on soil, 256, 460–461
    in Southern economy, 253, 256, 261, 262
    and tariffs, 190
    in Texas, 201
cotton gin, 256
coureurs de bois, 25
court system, federal, 124–125, 126
    See also Supreme Court
Covey, Edward, 276, 277
cowboys, 231, 232, 238, 345–346, 444
Crandall, Prudence, 246, 248

Crawford, William, 188
Creek people, 192, 193
"Crime Against Kansas" (Sumner speech), 295
Crisis, The (Paine), 92
Crocker, Charles, 341, 342
Crockett, Davy, 182, 202
Crook, General George, 349
Crow people, 218
cruel and unusual punishment, 141
"Cry of Dolores" (Hidalgo speech), 171
Cuba, 402–403, 465
Custer, George, 350

D

D'Angelo, Pascal, 374, 375
Darwin, Charles, 389
Davis, Captain Isaac, 76
Davis, Jefferson, 304–306
Dawes, William, 75
de la Salle, Robert, 26
de Niza, Marcos, 23
death penalty, 141
Decatur, Stephen, 167
Declaration of Independence
    drafting and adoption of, 83–84
    text of, 470–472
    and debate over slavery, 84
Declaration of Sentiments, 249
defendants, rights of, 139–140
deforestation, 254, 393
Delaware, 37
    ratification of Constitution, 133
Delaware people, 43
democracy, 38, 153
Democracy in America (Tocqueville), 175, 177
Democratic Party
    northern/southern split, 299
    origins of, 188
    and the Populists, 387
    and Reconstruction, 328–333
    vs. Republican Party, 188, 299, 328, 414
departments, executive, 124, 146
Dewey, Admiral George, 404
Dickens, Charles, 448
Dickinson, Charles, 187–188
Diné (Navajo) people, 426
discrimination
    African Americans, 270–271, 317, 394, 418
    Chinese, 226
    immigrants, 266, 372, 382
    Jews, 377, 463
    Mexicanos, 229
    religious minorities, 418

district courts, 124–125
District of Columbia, 151, 156
Dix, Dorothea, 244, 309
Dodge, Grenville, 341–342
Douglas, Stephen A., 293–295, 298, 299, 303
  Lincoln's debates with, 298
Douglass, Frederick, 247, 270, 271, 279
  abolition movement and, 247
  publisher of *North Star,* 247
  and treatment of slaves, 275, 276, 277–278, 282
  and voting rights, 250
  "What the Black Man Wants," 452
draft, 312, 313–314
Dred Scott decision, 296–297
DuBois, W. E. B., 269, 394
due process, 140
Dutch, in New World, 30–33

E

Eastern European immigrants, 372, 376–377, 382, 463
Eastern Woodlands, Native American cultural region, 3, 4–5, 13
economy, 50
  affected by Constitution, 128
  building of national, 178
  changes in the 20th century, 467–469
  Hamilton's and Federalist party's view of, 150
  Jefferson's and Republican party's view of, 153
  See also Capitalism
Edison, Thomas, 357
education
  in the colonies, 57
  for freedmen in the South, 325, 332
  Horace Mann's reform of, 245–246
  improvement of opportunities through, 419
  Jewish immigrants and, 377
  in the West, 221–222
  for women, 57, 246, 249
Edwards, Jonathan, 429
18-year-old vote, 127, 421, 488
Eighth Amendment, 141, 483
elastic clause of Constitution, 122, 151
election, presidential, 114
  of 1796, 155
  of 1800, 157–158, 436
  of 1824, 179, 188
  of 1828, 185, 188
  of 1860, 299
  of 1876, 331
  of 1960, 418
  of 2000, 114
Electoral College, 114, 155, 157, 158
electric power, 357

Ellis Island, 374, 376, 377
Emancipation Proclamation, 312
Embargo Act (1807), 167
Emerson, Ralph Waldo, 243, 292
Enforcement Acts, 330
England
  Hamilton and, 151
  Jefferson and, 153
  War of 1812, 169–170
  See also Great Britain
English Bill of Rights, 52
English colonies
  Middle Colonies, 37, 42–43
  New England Colonies, 37, 39–41
  Southern Colonies, 38, 44–46
Enlightenment philosophy, 108
environment
  Native Americans and, 3, 6, 15, 426
  protection of, 393
equality
  civil rights and, 326, 418, 421
  Fourteenth Amendment, 326, 329, 333, 421
  Nineteenth Amendment, 127, 396, 421
  Thirteenth Amendment, 127
  Twenty-sixth Amendment, 127, 421
  See also women's rights
Erie Canal, 260
Europe, outbreak of World War I, 408
European exploration
  Dutch, 30–32
  English, 27–29
  French, 25–26
  Spanish, 18–24
Exclusion Act, Chinese, 378
executive branch of government, 109, 123–124, 126, 146
  departments of, 124, 146
  powers of, 124
expansionism, 399–400
  Louisiana Purchase and, 198–199
  manifest destiny and, 197
exploration
  European, 18–32
  Frémont, John C., 213
  Lewis and Clark expedition, 212–215
  Pike, Zebulon 213

F

factories, 257–259, 353
  mass production in, 357
  working conditions in, 364, 448–449
  See also Triangle Shirtwaist Factory
famine, in Ireland, 266

Farmers' Alliances, 387
farmers/farming
    in the colonies, 37, 38, 45, 50
    irrigation and, 234
    Mexican, 234, 381
    Native American 6, 11, 13, 14
    protest against big business, 386–387
Farragut, Admiral David, 310, 315
Federal system, and state government, 128–129
Federalist Papers, 116
Federalist Party
    Alexander Hamilton and, 149–151
    division during 1800 presidential campaign, 157, 165
    opposition to the War of 1812, 168, 170
    preferred form of government, 150
    Republican party vs., 147–148, 154
    support for Constitution, 116, 133
    view of French Revolution, 148, 153–154
Feminine Mystique, The (Friedan), 422
feminism, 419, 422
fiestas, 216, 238
Fifteenth Amendment, 328, 329, 332, 484–485
Fifth Amendment, 139–140, 297, 482
54th Massachusetts Infantry, 317
Finney, Charles G., 242
First Amendment, 135–137, 482
First Continental Congress, 73, 74
First Great Awakening, 56, 242, 429
Five Civilized Tribes, 192
Florida
    Spanish control of, 22, 23, 163, 200
    U.S. invasion and acquisition of, 200
folk art, 180
Force Bill, 190
Ford, Henry, 420, 461–462
foreign policy
    of Adams (John), 164–165
    of Adams (John Quincy), 437
    in Asia and the Pacific, 400–401, 404–405
    Congress and, 128
    of Jefferson, 166–167
    in Latin America (late 1800s), 402–403, 405–406
    of Madison, 168–170
    of Monroe, (Monroe Doctrine), 171–172
    of Washington, 161, 163
    in World War I, 408, 410, 411
Fort Duquesne, 64
Fort McHenry, 169, 175
Fort Sumter, 300, 303
Fort Ticonderoga, 81
Fort Wagner, 317
forty-niners, 224–225
Foster, Stephen, 181

Fourteen Points, 413, 414
Fourteenth Amendment, 326, 329, 333, 421, 484
Fourth Amendment, 139, 482
Fox people, 192
France
    Adams and U.S. relations with, 164–165
    ally of the Continental Army, 94
    and American ships, 167
    Canada, claim to, 25–26
    in Florida, 23
    influence of the Revolution on, 100
    Louisiana, claim to, 26, 198
    Ohio Valley conflict and, 164, 165
    role in American Revolution, 88, 94, 96
    role in World War I, 408, 409, 412
    See also French Revolution
Franklin, Benjamin, 49, 55, 84, 88, 107
    antislavery views, 111
    at Constitutional Convention, 107, 113, 115
Franz Ferdinand, Archduke, 408
free blacks, 264, 269, 270–271
freedmen, 324–325, 326, 327, 328, 332
Freedmen's Bureau, 324–325
    and public schools, 325, 332
freedom of assembly, 135, 137
freedom to petition, 135, 137
freedom of the press, 136–137
freedom of religion, 135–136, 435
freedom of speech, 135, 136–137
free-soilers, 294
free states, 286
Frémont, John C., 206, 213
French and Indian War, 63, 65
French Revolution
    Americans' view of, 163
    Hamilton and, 151
    impact of American Revolution on, 100
    Jefferson and, 147–148, 153–154
Frick, Henry Clay, 367
Friedan, Betty, 422
fugitive slave clause, of Constitution, 112
Fugitive Slave Law, 290, 291, 292, 300
Fuller, Margaret, 447
Fulton, Robert, 260
Fundamental Orders, 41
fur trade, 25, 26, 31, 217–218

G

Gadsden Purchase, 208
gag rule, 289, 290
Gage, General Thomas, 69, 74, 75
Garrison, William Lloyd, 247, 451
Genet, Edmond, 154, 155

George, David Lloyd, 413
George II, king of England, 46
George III, king of England, 66, 69, 72, 74
   American Revolutionary War and, 89, 100
   answer to the First Continental Congress, 74
   crimes of, in Declaration of Independence, 83,
     470–472
Georgia, 38, 46
   opposition to ending slavery, 112
   ratification of Constitution, 133
   Sherman's march through, 319
   slave owners' issues with Florida, 200
Germain, Lord George, 89–90
Germany, 89, 266, 408–414
Gerry, Elbridge, 111, 115
Gettysburg, Battle of, 312–314
Gettysburg Address, 314
Giants in the Earth (Rolvaag), 459
Gibbons v. Ogden, 179
Gideon v. Wainwright, 421
Gilded Age, 355
Glorious Revolution, 52
gold mining, 19, 224–225, 230, 338, 343–344, 443
gold rush, California, 224–225
Gompers, Samuel, 366
Gooding, James Henry, 317
government
   Articles of Confederation, 103, 105
   branches of, 121–125
   developed at Constitutional Convention, 109–110
   popular participation in, 130, 391
   separation of powers, 128–129, 142
grand jury hearing, right to, 139
Granges, organization of, 386–387
Grant, General Ulysses S.
   in Civil War, 310, 316, 318, 319, 320, 455
   presidential campaign (1868), 328, 455
Great American Desert, 213, 346
Great Awakening
   First, 56, 429
   Second, 242
Great Basin, Native American cultural region, 3, 4–5, 9
Great Britain
   U.S. relations with, 151, 153, 163, 164
   impressment of American sailors, 166, 168
   In World War I, 408–410
Great Compromise, 110
Great Depression, 419
Great Law of 1682, 43
Great Plains, Native American cultural region, 3, 4–5,
   12
Great Seal, of the United States, 160–161
Greeley, Horace, 211, 294
Greene, General Nathaniel, 96

Greenhow, Rose, 308, 309
Gregg v. Georgia, 141
Gregory v. Chicago, 137
Grenville, George, 67
Grimke, Angelina and Sarah, 247, 248
Guadalupe Hidalgo, Treaty of, 208, 229
guerillas, 96

H

habeas corpus, 313
Hamilton, Alexander, 116, 145, 149
   Federalist Party and, 149–151
   presidential campaign (1800), 157
   supporting Jefferson, 158
   view of human nature, 149
   Whiskey Rebellion and, 147
Hancock, John, 106, 133, 134
Harlan, Justice John Marshall, 333
Harrison, William Henry, 169, 170
Hartford (Connecticut), 41
Hawaii, annexation of, 401
Hay, John, 403
Hayes, Rutherford B., 331
Haynes, Lemuel, 271
Henry, Patrick, 73, 79, 106
Hidalgo, Miguel, 171
Hispanics. *See* Mexican Americans
Hitler, Adolf, 414
Homestead Act, 340
Homestead (Pennsylvania) strike, 367
homesteads, 220, 346–347, 444
Hooker, Thomas, 41
House of Burgesses, 45
House of Representatives, 109, 110, 121, 124
   powers described in Constitution, 474–476
   powers of impeachment, 124, 327
housing
   economics of, in the 20th century, 468
   in the Gilded Age, 354, 355
   Native American, 5, 7, 8, 10
   on the prairie, 347
   for slaves, 275
   in tenements, 361, 375, 377, 464–465
Houston, Sam, 203
How the Other Half Lives (Riis), 464–465
Howe, Elias, 258
Howe, General William, 80, 81, 90, 92, 95
   occupation of Philadelphia, 93, 94
Hudson, Henry, 30
Hudson River School of painting, 180, 182
Huron people, 26, 31
Hutchinson, Anne, 40

I

Ice Age, migration and, 2
"I Have a Dream" (King speech), 418
immigrants
    assimilation of, 372, 382
    Chinese, 225–226, 378–379
    discrimination against, 226, 229, 266, 372, 377, 382, 463
    Eastern European Jews, 371, 376–377, 463
    Irish and German (1845–1860), 266
    Italian, 374–375
    as labor for industry, 353, 371, 372, 388
    as labor for agriculture, 381
    living conditions of, 361, 375, 377, 464–465
    Mexican, 380–381
    as refuges, 266, 372, 376, 380
    religious diversity of, 372
    Russian, 347, 463
    undocumented, 420
    in the West, 459
immigration
    between 1820 and 1990, 373
    restriction of, and quota system, 382
impeachment, of president, 124
    of Andrew Johnson, 327
imperialism, 400
impressment, of American sailors, 166, 168
"Inaugural Address, First" (Jefferson), 436
inauguration
    Jackson's, 186
    Washington's, 146
Incas, 21
indentured servants, 35, 45, 54, 58
Independence Hall, 106, 120
Indians. *See* Native Americans
Indian Removal Act, 192, 349
Indian wars, 334, 339, 349–350, 439
Industrial Revolution, 257–259
industrialists, 257, 259, 388–389
industry, 263, 363
    growth in 1800s, 258–259, 356–357, 388
    See also factories
information economy, 420
initiative, 391
interest groups, 130
International Ladies' Garment Workers' Union (ILGWU), 367
Internet, 420
interstate commerce, national regulation over, 128
Intolerable Acts, 72–73, 79
Inuit people, 3
inventions
    airplane, 462–463
    automobile, 461–462
    blue jeans, 462
    cotton gin, 256
    dishwasher, 461
    electrical devices, 357
    for farming, 259, 460–461
    for industry, 258
    moving assembly line, 420
    reaper, 259, 461
    sewing machine, 258
    steamboats, 260
    steam locomotives, 260
    steel plow, 461
    telephone, 357
Iroquois people, 13, 26, 31
    Dutch settlers and, 31
    French settlers and, 26
irrigation, 11, 234, 444
Irving, Washington, 182, 217, 438
isolationism, 163, 164, 168, 172, 437
    Madison's abandonment of, 169
Italian immigrants, 374–375

J

Jackson, Andrew, 179, 187–188
    Battle of New Orleans, 170
    inauguration of, 186
    Indian policy of, 192–193
    "kitchen cabinet," 189
    as president, 189–191
    presidential campaign (1824), 179, 188
    presidential campaign (1828), 185, 188
Jackson, Rachel, 185, 187
Jackson, General Thomas (Stonewall), 309
Jacksonian Democracy, 188
James, Duke of York, 32, 42, 52
James I, king of England, 28, 44
James II, king of England, 41, 52
Jamestown, 28–29, 45
Japan, trade treaties with, 401
Jay, John, 116, 150, 164
Jay Treaty, 164
Jefferson, Thomas, 83, 106, 107, 134, 145, 152, 172
    Alien and Sedition acts, 156
    election of, 157–158
    "First Inaugural Address" (1801), 436
    foreign policy of, 166–167
    interest in Florida, 200
    loss of election to Adams (1796), 155
    Louisiana purchase by, 198–199
    Republican party and, 152–154, 155
    as vice president, 155
    view of human nature, 152
Jewish immigrants, 362, 376–377
    and religious freedom, 31, 44

Jim Crow laws, 181, 333, 394, 457–458
John, king of England, 52
John Brown's Raid, 298–299
Johnson, Andrew, 324, 325, 326
    impeachment of, 327
    president after Lincoln's assassination, 323
Joliet, Louis, 26
Jones, Mary Harris (Mother Jones), 392
judicial branch of government, 109, 124–125, 126
judicial review, 125, 126
Jungle, The (Sinclair), 395, 397
jury
    right to hearing by a grand, 139
    right to trial by, 140
Justice Department, 124

K

Kansas-Nebraska Act, 293–294
Kearny, General Stephen, 206
Kelley, Oliver, 386
Kemble, Fanny, 450
Kendall, Amos, 189
Kennedy, John F., 418
Kentucky, adoption of Alien and Sedition acts, 156
Key, Francis Scott, 169, 175
King, Martin Luther, Jr., 418
King, Rufus, 110
Kitty Hawk (North Carolina), 462
Knights of Labor, 366
knowledge workers, 420
Knox, Henry, 81, 145, 146
Ku Klux Klan, 330

L

La Follette, Robert, 391
labor. *See* factories, unions
labor laws, child, 392
labor unions, 366–367
Lafayette, Marquis de, 94, 95
laissez-faire doctrine, 354
Land Ordinance of 1785, 104
Last of the Mohicans (Cooper), 438–439
Latin America, foreign policy and, 171–172, 405–406, 437
Latinos. *See* Mexican Americans
Lazarus, Emma, 371
League of Nations, 413, 414
Lee, General Robert E., 305, 454–455
    battle of Antietam, 310–311
    defeat and surrender, 318–319, 320
    waging a defensive war, 313
legal system
    in the colonies, 53

influence of Mexican, 237
    rights and protections of the people, 139–141
Legend of Sleepy Hollow (Irving), 438
legislative branch of government, 109, 121–122, 126, 127
Leisler, Jacob, 42
Lemon v. Kurtzman, 135
Lewis, Meriwether, 204, 212–215, 338
Lewis and Clark expedition
    claim of Oregon and, 204
    map and images of, 214–215
    Nez Percé and, 338
Lexington (Massachusetts), 75, 90
Liberator, 247
Lieberman, Joseph, 418
Liliuokalani, queen of Hawaii, 401
Lincoln, Abraham, 285, 304, 306
    assassination of, 323
    Emancipation Proclamation, 312
    Gettysburg address, 314
    Jefferson Davis vs., 305–306
    northern opposton to war, 313
    planning of Union's war strategy, 308
    position on slavery, 300
    as president, 285, 300
    presidential campaign (1860), 299
    reelection of, 318
    run for Senate, 298
Lincoln-Douglas debates, 298
literature
    early American, 182, 438–439
    See also individual titles
Little Big Horn, Battle of, 350
Little Rock Nine, 422
Livermore, Arthur, 287
Locke, John, 108
Lodge, Henry Cabot, 400, 405
Lone Star Republic, 203
long drive, 345–346
Longfellow, Henry Wadsworth, 182, 295
Los Niños Héroes, 208
Louisiana
    French claim on, 26
    purchase of, 198–199
    Spanish control of, 163
Louisiana Purchase, 198–199
Louis XIV, king of France, 26
L'Ouverture, Toussaint, 199
Lowell, Francis Cabot, 258
Lowell (Massachusetts) textile mills, 258, 448–449
Loyalists, 63, 70, 81, 83
    and the Boston Tea Party, 73
    resettlement in Canada, 100
    in the Revolutionary War, 92, 96
Lusitania, sinking of, 410

M

Madison, James
  and Constitutional Convention, 103, 105, 107, 108, 109, 112, 113
  drafting Bill of Rights, 134–135
  Father of the Constitution, 107, 134
  and *Federalist Papers,* 116
  on Latin America, 171–172
  as president, 168–169
  and War of 1812, 169–170
Magna Carta, 52
Maine, as a free state, 288
Maine, U.S.S. sinking of, 402, 465–466
malaria, 28, 58, 406
Manhattan, settlement of, 30–31
Manifest Destiny, 197, 203, 208, 399
Mann, Horace, 245, 246
maps
  Agricultural Regions, 1900, 363
  Agriculture, 1860, 262
  America in 1820, 176
  Barbary Coast, 166
  Battle of Yorktown, 99
  Civil War, 1861–1865, 307
  Colonial America in 1770, 36
  Comparing the Worlds of North and South, 262–263
  Compromise of 1850, 291
  Dred Scott Decision, 297
  European Settlements in North and South America, 1682, 32
  Exploration of the Americas, 21
  Free and Slave Population, 1860, 263
  Immigration to the United States, 1820–1990, 373
  Indian Removals, 194
  Industry and Raw Material, 1860, 263
  Iron and Steel Production, 1900, 363
  Kansas-Nebraska Act, 294
  Key Battles of the American Revolution, 98
  Land Losses of Native Americans, 348
  Lewis and Clark Expedition, 214
  Mexican Cession, 208
  Migrating Routes of the First Americans, 2
  Military Reconstruction and the Readmission of the South, 326
  Missouri Compromise, 288
  Native American Clothing, 4
  Native American Cultural Regions, 4
  Native American Food, 5
  Native American Housing, 5
  North America in 1763, 66
  North American Territorial Claims in 1796, 162
  Oregon Country, 205
  Railroads, 1860, 262
  Slave System, 1801–1860, 273
  Triangular Trade and the Enslavement of Africans, 84
  U.S. Expansion Around the World, 1867–1903, 407
March on Washington, 418
marriage
  in the colonies, 58
  of slaves, 279
  state laws for, 129
Marion, Francis, 96
Marquette, Father, 26
Marshall, Chief Justice John, 178–179
Marshall, James, 224
Marshall, Justice Thurgood, 141
Martí, José, 402
Martin, Joseph, 87, 88, 89, 91, 94, 95, 97, 432
Maryland (colony), 38, 44
Mason, Biddy, 221
Mason, George, 115
mass production, techniques of, 357
Massachusetts (colony), 37, 38, 39
  Boston Massacre, 69–70
  Boston Tea Party, 70–72
  farmers' rebellion, 105
  Intolerable Acts against, 72
  ratification of Constitution, 133
  Salem witch trials, 53,
  schools and education in, 57
  start of American Revolution in, 75–76, 430
Massachusetts 54th Regiment, 317
Mather, Cotton, 40
Mayflower, 39
Mayflower Compact, 39, 428
Mayhew, Jonathan, 429
McClellan, General George, 310–311, 318
McClure, Sam, 385, 390
McCormick, Cyrus, 259
McCoy, Joseph, 345
McCulloch v. Maryland, 142, 179
McKinley, William, 399
  annexation of Hawaii, 401
  position on the Philippines, 405
  presidential campaign (1892), 387
  support for Cuba, 402
Meade, General George C., 312
measles, 24, 220
Meat Inspection Act, 395
meatpacking industry, 395
medical care, Civil War, 311
Menéndez de Avilés, Pedro, 23
Mennonites, 347
mentally ill, treatment of, 244
mercenaries, 89

Merrimac, 315
mesa people, 11
Mexican Americans/Mexicanos, 229
    architectural style, 236
    attitudes toward slavery, 237
    cattle ranching and, 231, 232
    food and cooking style, 235
    as immigrants, 380–381, 382
    irrigation system for farming, 234
    legal principles, 237
    mining techniques, 230
    sheep raising system, 233
    Western entertainments, 238
Mexican-American War, 206–208
Mexican Cession, 208, 233, 290
Mexican Revolution, 380
Mexico
    and California, 206–207, 216
    independence from Spain, 171
    Spanish conquest of, 20
    Texas, conflict over, 201–203
    U.S. war with, 206–208
Middle colonies, 37–38, 42–43
    See also colonies by name
Midway Island, 401, 407
migration
    of African Americans from the South, 334
    of the first Americans, 2
militarism, 408
Military Reconstruction Act, 326
militias
    in the colonies, 64, 73
    in the states, 138, 163
    mills, 258, 448–449
miners, 224–226, 230, 343–344, 393
mining law, 237
Minuit, Peter, 30
Minutemen, 73, 74, 75–76, 431
Miranda warning, 139
missionaries, 24, 25, 205, 216, 219–220
Mississippi River
    as boundary of frontier, 176, 198, 211, 213
    as boundary of free vs. slave states, 286
    control of, in Civil War, 305, 310, 315, 316
    French exploration of, 26
    Native Americans and, 169, 192, 195, 439
    as transportation for farmers, 198, 199, 261
Missouri, slavery issue in, 286
Missouri Compromise, 288–289, 290, 293–294, 296–297
Missouri River, exploration of, 212–213, 217
Mittelberger, Gottlieb, 35
Monitor, 315
Monmouth, Battle of, 95
monopoly, 71, 359–360, 390

Monroe, James, 198–199
    Latin America foreign policy, 171–172
    Louisiana Purchase and, 198–199
    as president, 178–179
    road building and, 259
Monroe Doctrine, 172, 402
Morgan, J. P., 359
Mormons, 222–223
Morris, Gouverneur, 111, 113
Mother Jones, 392
Mott, Lucretia, 248, 249, 250, 446–447
mountain men, 217–218
muckrakers, 385, 395
mudslinging, 185
Muir, John, 393
music and dance
    early American, 181
    Mexicano, 238
    of slaves, 181, 280, 281, 282
My Ántonia (Cather), 459

N

Napoleon Bonaparte, 165, 168
National Association for the Advancement of Colored People (NAACP), 394
national bank. *See* Bank of the United States
National Board of United Cloth Hat and Cap Makers, 367
National Council of Colored People, 271
national forest, 393
National Organization for Women (NOW), 422
national parks, 393
National Road, 259
National Woman's Party, 396
nationalism, 408
Native Americans, 3–14
    in American art, 180
    beliefs of, 1, 6, 426
    and the buffalo, 12, 342, 345
    and the colonists, 39, 40, 45, 60
    Five Civilized Tribes, 192
    clothing of, 3, 7, 8, 9, 10 11, 12, 13, 14
    crafts of, 7, 8
    cultural regions, 3, 4, 6–15
    and European diseases, 19, 20, 24, 26, 45, 216, 220, 225
    food of, 2, 3, 5, 7, 8, 9, 10, 11, 12, 13, 14
    housing of, 2, 3, 5, 7, 8, 9, 10, 11, 12, 13, 14
    Jackson's policy on, 192–194
    land losses of, 348
    migration routes, 2
    missions and, 216, 220
    railroads and, 342
    relations with early explorers, 19–20, 24–25, 26, 30–31

reservation life, 337, 338, 339, 349
resistance to white settlers, 169, 170
Trail of Tears, 193–194, 439–440
treaties, 192, 338, 439–440
wars, 169, 192–193, 338–339, 349–350
See also individual tribes
nativism, 382
Nebraska, 293–294
neutrality, U.S.,163, 164–167, 408
Nevada, 342
New Amsterdam, 31–32
New England colonies, 37, 39–41
See also colonies by name
New England Primer, 57
New France, 25–26
New Hampshire (colony), 37
New Haven (Connecticut), 41
New Jersey (colony), 37, 42, 68, 133
plan for state representation in the government, 109
New Mexico, 24, 208, 291
New Netherland, 30–32
New Orleans, 198, 280
Battle of, 170, 185, 188
Napoleon's plans for, 198
as river port, 198, 261
New Spain, 20
New York (colony), 32, 37, 42, 68
Washington's defeat in, 91
newspapers
abolitionist, 247, 289, 451
in the colonies, 49, 67, 120
freedom of the press, 136–137
on secession, 300, 301
on sinking of the *Maine,* 465–466
on settling the West, 197, 211
Nez Percé people, 213, 219, 338–339
Niagara Movement, 394
Nineteenth Amendment, 127, 396, 421, 485
Ninth Amendment, 142, 483
North
advantages/disadvantages in the Civil War, 304–305
African Americans free in, 265–266, 271
comparison of South and, 262–263
economy of, 257–259
geography of, 254
opposition to Civil War, 313
society of, 265–266
tensions between South and, 190
transportation in, 259–260
North, Lord, 69, 71, 72, 100
North Carolina (colony), 38
Northern Securities Company, Antitrust Act and, 390

Northwest Coast, Native American cultural region, 3, 4–5, 6–7
Northwest Ordinance of 1787, 104, 286
Northwest Passage, 25, 26, 30, 212
Northwest Territory, 104
nullification crisis, 190

O

Oberlin College (Ohio), 246, 249
Oglethorpe, James Edward, 46
Ohio Valley conflict, 64, 164
oil business, 359, 389, 390
Olive Branch Petition, 82
Oñate, Juan de, 24
Oregon Country, 204–205, 214
Oregon Trail, 219–221, 442
Orlando, Vittorio, 413
Osceola people, 193
Ostend Manifesto, 293
O'Sullivan, John, 197
Our Lady of Guadalupe, 238

P

Pacific, American expansion in, 400–401
Pacific Railroad Act, 340–341
Paine, Thomas
Common Sense, 82, 430
The Crisis, 92
Panama Canal, 405–406
Paredes, Mariano, 206
Parker, Captain John, 75
Parks, Rosa, 418
Parliament
founding of English, 52
repeal of Stamp Act, 67
repeal of Townshend Acts, 69
parties. *See* political parties
Patriots, 63, 64
"America's Forgotten," 431
Boston, 68, 69–70, 71–72, 73
forming militias, 73
Patrick Henry, 79
Thomas Paine, 82
in the Revolution, 88, 89, 91, 92, 100
Patterson, William, 108, 109
Paul, Alice, 396
Pearl Harbor, 401
Penn, William, 43
Pennsylvania (colony), 37, 38, 43
ratification of Constitution, 133
Pennsylvania Gazette, 49
People's Party, 387

Perry, Oliver Hazard, 169
Pershing, General John J., 412
personal computers, 420
Peru, conquest of, 21, 22
petition, right to, 137
Philadelphia, 37, 43, 51, 106, 120, 416
    occupation of, 93, 94
Philippines, 404–405
Pickett, George, 313
Pike, Zebulon, 213
Pilgrims, 39, 45, 428
Pinckney, Charles, 113, 157
piracy, 53, 166–167
Pizarro, Francisco, 21
Plains Indians, 12, 342, 344, 345
plantations, 38, 256–257, 274, 279, 320
Plateau, Native American cultural region, 1, 3, 4–5, 10
Pledge of Allegiance, text of, 490
Plessy v. Ferguson, 333
Plymouth Rock, 39, 45
Pocahontas, 29
pogroms, 376
political parties, 114, 130, 149, 153
    reform of, 375
    See also specific parties by name
Polk, James K.
    manifest destiny and, 203
    Oregon issue and, 205
    War in Mexico, 206, 290
poll taxes, 332, 421
Polo, Marco, 17, 18
Ponce de León, Juan, 22
Poor Richard's Almanac, 49
popular sovereignty, 120
population
    free/slave, 111, 263, 269
    Native American, 3, 192
    in New Amsterdam, 31
    in the New World colonies, 51, 64
    United States in 1790, 109, 111
    United States in 1850, 269
    United States in 20th century, 417
Populists, 386, 387
Populist Party. *See* People's Party
Portsmouth (Rhode Island), 40
poverty rate, in 2002, 420
Powell, John Wesley, 444–445
Powhatan, 28, 29
Preamble, to the Constitution, 120, 433
president
    debate over the title of, 146
    election of, 113–114, 123
    powers of, 124, 126
    removing from office, 124

term of office, 123
veto power, 122
    See also presidents by name
press, freedom of, 136–137, 156
Preston, Captain Thomas, 70
privacy, right to, 138, 142
Proclamation of 1763, 66
Progressive Movement, 385
Promised Land, The (Antin), 463
Promontory Point, Utah, 343
property
    community, 237
    protection of private, 140
Providence (Rhode Island), 40
public schools, 245–246
    See also education
Pueblo people, 24, 234
Puerto Rico, 22, 403
Pure Food and Drug Act, 395
Puritans, 39, 40, 41, 53, 56, 57
Putman, Israel, 80

Q

Quakers, 38, 43, 49
    on slavery, 246, 247, 248, 249, 445
Quartering Act, 68
quartering troops, 68, 138
Quebec, 26
Quetzalcoatl, 20
quota, immigration, 382

R

racism, 181, 269, 333, 394
    See also discrimination
railroads, 260, 261, 262, 380, 388
    Central Pacific, 342–343
    ranchers' transportation, 345–346
    steel industry and, 356
    transcontinental, 340–343, 378
    Union Pacific, 341–342
Raleigh, Sir Walter, 27, 45
ranchos, 216–217, 231
Randolph, Edmund, 113, 115
Rankin, Jeanette, 396
reaper, 259, 461
recall, 391
Reconstruction
    congressional, 326–327
    end of, 330–331
    presidential, 324–325
    reversal of, 332–333
    southern, 328–329

redcoats, 70
referendum, 391
reform movements
    in education, 245–246
    in Progressive era, 385–396
    women and, 244, 247–250
refugees, 372
    See also immigrants
religion
    in the colonies, 38, 39, 40, 43, 44, 56
    freedom of, 135–136, 435
    for slaves, 281
    See also missionaries
religious freedom, 38, 39, 40, 44, 347, 376
    guaranteed by Constitution, 135–136
Renaissance, 18
reparations, paid by Germany, 413
Republican Party
    views of, 152–154
    vs. Democratic Party, 188, 299, 328, 414
    vs. Federalist party, 147–148, 152–154, 155, 436
    and Reconstruction, 330–331
    reform of, 391
reservations, for Native Americans, 337, 338, 339, 349
Revere, Paul, 63, 69, 70, 75
Revolutionary War. *See* American Revolution
Rhode Island (colony), 37, 40
Rice, Thomas Dartmouth, 181
right to bear arms, 138
right to petition, 52, 137
right to privacy, 138
right to speedy, public trial, 140
right to vote
    election of 1828 and, 186
    freedmen, 328
    Nineteenth Amendment and women's, 130, 328, 396
    Twenty-fourth Amendment and poll taxes, 421
    Twenty-sixth Amendment and 18-year-olds, 421
rights, natural, 83
rights of accused persons, 139–141
Ripley, George, 243
roads, building, 178, 179, 259
Roanoke Island, 27
Rockefeller, John D., 388, 389
    Antitrust Act and, 390
    Standard Oil Company trust, 359, 385
rodeos, 231, 238
Rolfe, John, 29
Rolvaag, Ole E., 459–460
Roman Catholics, 24, 25, 44, 375, 381, 418
Roosevelt, Theodore
    ally of expansionists, 399
    investigation of meatpacking industry, 395
    national forests, expansion of, 393
    and Rough Riders, 403
    as trust-buster, 390
    and Panama Canal, 405–406
Ross, Nellie Tayloe, 443
runaway slaves, 200, 237, 278, 292
Russia, 376, 400, 408, 412

S

Sac people, 192
Sacagawea, 212–213
Salem (Massachusetts), witch trials, 53
Salt Lake City, settlement of, 223
San Martín, José de, 171
San Salvador, 18
Santa Anna, General Antonio López de, 202–203, 207
Savannah (Georgia), 96
Sawyer, Philetus, 391
scalawags, 328
Schneiderman, Rose, 366, 367
schools. *See* education
Schurz, Carl, 400, 405
Schuyler, Elizabeth, 149
Scott, General Winfield
    invasion of Mexico, 207–208
    planning of Union's war strategy, 308
search and seizure, unreasonable, 139
secession, 288, 300, 453, 454
Second Amendment, 138, 482
Second Great Awakening, 242–243, 289
Secotan people, 15
secretary of state, 172
Sedition Act, 155–156
segregation, 271, 333, 334, 394, 417, 457–458
    Supreme Court and, 421, 422
self-incrimination, 139
Seminole people, 192, 193, 200
Senate, 109, 110, 121–122, 124, 126
    powers described in constitution, 474–478
    power to try impeachments, 124
Seneca Falls Convention, 249–250
separation of church and state, 135, 433, 435
Separatists, 39
Sequoyah, 192
Serbs, 408
Serra, Junipero, 216
servant, indentured, 35, 45, 54, 58
Servicemen's Readjustment Act, 419
Seven Cities of Cibola, 22–23
Seventh Amendment, 140–141, 482
Seward, William, 400
Seymour, Horatio, 328
sharecropping, 327
Shays's Rebellion, 105
Sheridan, General Philip, 318

Sherman, General William Tecumseh, 318, 319
Sherman, Roger, 110, 113
Sherman Antitrust Act, 390
Shoshone people, 212, 213
Siberia, 2
silver mining, 230, 343–344
Sinclair, Upton, 395
Sitting Bull, 349
Sixth Amendment, 140, 421, 482
slave quilts, 268, 280, 281
slave rebellions, 278
slave trade, 20, 40, 45, 55, 112
slavery
    and the abolitionists, 246–247, 450–452
    addressed in state constitutions, 433
    debated at Constitutional Convention, 111
    debated during drafting of Declaration of
        Independence, 84
    economics of, 256–257, 272–273
    opposition to, 450–452
    resistance to, 277–278
    Thirteenth Amendment ending, 127, 324
    in Virginia, 45
slaves
    buying and selling, 270, 279
    control by owners, 270, 276
    fugitive, 278, 290, 292
    in Mexicano communities, 237
    introduction to America, 19–20
    in the Revolutionary War, 90
    rural vs. urban, 270
    in the South, 274–282
smallpox, 19, 20, 21, 24
Smith, Captain John, 28–29
Smith, Jedediah, 204–205
Smith, Joseph, 222
Smith, Samuel Francis, 181
Social Darwinism, 389
Song of Hiawatha (Longfellow), 182
Sons of Liberty, 67, 71–72, 73
South
    advantages/disadvantages in Civil War, 305
    African Americans free in, 270
    comparison of North and, 262–263
    economy of, 111, 256–257, 272
    geography of, 255
    reconstruction and, 324–329
    society of, 264
    tensions between North and, 190
    transportation in, 261
    See also Civil War; Confederacy
South Carolina (colony), 38
    opposition to ending slavery, 112
Southeast, Native American cultural region, 3, 4–5, 14
Southern colonies, 38, 44–46

See also colonies by name
Southern Democrats, 299, 328
Southwest
    as America's fruit basket, 234
    Native American cultural region, 3, 4–5, 11, 426
    Spanish-style architecture of, 236
    water in, 11, 234, 444–445
    See also Mexican Americans
sovereignty, popular, 120
Spain
    ally of Continental Army, 94
    and battleship Maine, 465–466
    claim to Oregon, 204
    Florida's purchase from, 200
    Latin American revolutions and, 171
    New World conquests, 18–19, 20–23
    in the Philippines, 404
    role in slavery, 19–20, 24
Spalding, Henry and Eliza, 219
Spanish-American war, 402–403
Spanish borderlands, 22, 23–24
speech, freedom of, 136–137
spoils system, 189
St. Augustine (Florida), 23
St. Mary's City (Maryland), 44
Stamp Act, 67
Standard Oil, 359, 385, 389, 390
Stanford, Leland, 341
Stanton, Elizabeth Cady, 248, 249, 250, 446
"Star-Spangled Banner," 169, 175, 181
    text of, 491
Starving Time, 29
state constitutions, 108, 329, 433
State Department, 124
state government, powers of, 128–129
states' rights, 142, 156
    in McCulloch v. Maryland, 179
    in nullification crisis, 190
Statute for Religious Freedom (Jefferson), 435
steam engines, 260
steel, 356
Stephens, Uriah, 366
Steuben, Baron Friedrich von, 95
Stone, Lucy, 249
Story, Justice Joseph, 138
Stowe, Harriet Beecher, 292–293, 450
Strauss, Levi, 462
Stuart, Gilbert, 180
Stuyvesant, Peter, 31, 32
suffrage, 396
    for 18-year-olds, 127, 421, 488
    for African Americans, 325, 328–329, 332, 421,
    447
    for women, 222, 248–250, 396, 434, 445–447
Sumner, Charles, 295–296

Supreme Court, 125
First Amendment and, 135
judicial nationalism and, 178–179
justices, 124, 125
school segregation and, 333, 422
on the slavery issue, 296–297
See also individual case names

T

Taino people, 18
Tallmadge Amendment, 286–287
Taney, Chief Justice Roger, 296, 297
Tarbell, Ida, 385, 390
tariffs, 178, 190, 401
Taylor, Zachary, 207
Tea Act, 70, 71
technology
industry and improvement of, 356–357
transformation of American economy, 419, 420
Tecumseh, 169, 170
Tejanos, 201, 202, 231
telephone, 357
tenement housing, 361, 375, 464–465
Tenochtitlán, 20
Tenth Amendment, 142, 483
Tenure of Office Act, 326, 327
Texas, 201–203, 206
Thanksgiving, first, 39
theocracy, in Massachusetts, 38
Third Amendment, 138, 482
Thirteenth Amendment, 127, 484
Thoreau, Henry David, 243
three-fifths compromise, 112
Ticonderoga, Fort, 81
Tilden, Samuel J., 331
Tillman, Ben, 331
Tippecanoe Creek, Battle of, 169
tobacco, 29, 38, 45, 55, 253, 255, 256
Tories, 63
See also Loyalists
Tocqueville, Alexis de, 175, 177, 182
on slavery, 183
Townshend Acts, 68–69, 70
trade
Latin America and, 171
in New World colonies, 37, 40, 42, 43, 46
trade unions, 366–367, 422
Trail of Tears, 193, 194, 439–440
transcendentalism, 243
transcontinental railroad, 340, 341–343
transportation
American System and, 178
in the North and South 259–261, 262

to the West, 220, 340–341, 441–442
trappers, 25, 217–218
Travis, William, 201, 202–203
Treasury Department, 146
Treaty of Ghent, 170
Treaty of Greenville, 439
Treaty of Guadalupe Hidalgo, 208, 229
Treaty of Paris, 100, 104
Treaty with the Six Nations, 439
Treaty of Versailles, 413–414
Trenton (New Jersey), 92
trials, 139, 140, 141
Triangle Shirtwaist Factory, 358, 360
fire, 353, 368
ILGWU strike and, 367
location and code violation, 362
and state investigations, 392
working conditions at, 365
Tripoli, 166–167
Trumbull, John, 97
trust, 359–360
Truth, Sojourner, 241, 246, 247
Tubman, Harriet, 278
Turner, Nat, 277, 278, 289, 290
Turner's Rebellion, 278
Tuskegee Institute, 394, 460
Twain, Mark, 355
Twelfth Amendment, 158, 159, 483
Twenty-fourth Amendment, 421, 487
Twenty-sixth Amendment, 127, 421, 488
tyranny, 66

U

Uncle Sam, symbol of national unity, 177
Uncle Tom's Cabin (Stowe), 292–293, 450
Underground Railroad, 278
Union, the, 286
See also Civil War
Union Pacific Railroad, 341–342
unions, 366–367, 422
United Farm Workers Union, 422
urbanization, 265, 361–362, 417
Utah, 222, 223, 444

V

Vallejo, General Mariano Guadalupe, 207
Valley Forge, 94–95, 432
Van Buren, Martin, 193
Vanderbilt, Cornelius, 354
Vanderbilt, Mrs. William Kissam, 354
vaqueros, 231, 232
Venezuela, 171

Vesey, Denmark, rebellion of, 278
veto, 122
Vicksburg, Battle of, 316
Virginia (colony), 38, 45
    adoption of Alien and Sedition acts, 156
    House of Burgesses, 108
    plan for state representation in the government,
        109
    ratification of Constitution, 134
Virginia Plan, 109
Virginia Resolutions, 156
visa, required for immigration, 382
voting rights. *See* suffrage

W

War Hawks, 169
War of 1812, 169–170, 197
Washington, Booker T., 394
Washington, D.C., 151, 156, 177, 180, 291
Washington, George, 64, 65, 73, 145
    in American Revolution, 80, 81, 88, 91–95, 96
    at Constitutional Convention, 106, 107, 113, 115
    foreign policy under, 154, 163
    as president, 134, 146–148, 161, 163, 166
water, conflicts over, 237, 444
Weaver, James B., 387
Webster, Daniel, 178, 185, 186, 291, 292
    debate with John Calhoun, 453–454
Weld, Theodore, 247, 451
West
    conservation in, 393
    expansion into, 198–199, 203, 204–208
    exploration of, 212–214
    farming and ranching in, 216, 231–234, 387
    immigrants in, 347, 459
    Kansas-Nebraska Act and slavery in, 293–296
    in literature, 182, 438–439, 459
    mining in, 224–226, 230, 343–344
    pioneers in, 219, 220–222, 442–443
    trappers in, 217–218
    water in, 11, 234, 237, 444–445
    See also railroads; Native Americans
"What the Black Man Wants" (Douglass), 452
Whigs, 63
    See also Patriots
Whiskey Rebellion, 147
White, John, 15, 27
White, Ryan, 422
Whitman, Marcus and Narcissa, 219–220
Whitney, Eli, 256, 258, 357
Wilder, Laura Ingalls, 443
William of Orange, 52
Williams, Roger, 40

Wilmot Proviso, 290
Wilson, James, 108, 110, 113
Wilson, Woodrow
    engagement during World War I, 411–412
    neutrality during World War I, 408
    Treaty of Versailles and, 413–414
Winthrop, John, 39
Woman in the Nineteenth Century (Fuller), 447
women
    in abolition movement, 246–247, 248
    as Civil War supporters, 309
    earnings in 2003, 418
    education for, 57, 246, 249, 434
    equal rights for, 248–250, 445–447
    pioneers, 220–222, 442–443
    property rights, 237, 248, 250
    role in Iroquois society, 13
    unions and, 367
    voting and, 130, 222, 248–250, 396, 434, 445–447
women's rights, 241, 248–250, 396, 434, 445–447
Woodward, Charlotte, 250
workers' rights, 392
    See also unions
working conditions
    in industry, 364, 392, 448–449
    for slaves, 264, 274, 276
World Anti-Slavery Convention, 248, 446, 447
World War I, 408–410
    America enters, 411–412
    armistice, 412
    at sea, 410
    trench warfare, 409
World Wide Web, 420
worship, freedom of, 135–136
Wright, Wilbur and Orville, 462–463

X

XYZ Affair, 164

Y

yellow fever, 406
yellow journalism, 402
Yorktown, Battle of, 96–97, 99
Yosemite National Park, 393
Young, Brigham, 222–223

Z

Zenger, John Peter, 136

Correlation of History Alive! Materials to State History–Social Science Standards

Below is a correlation of *History Alive! The United States Through Industrialism* to California Content Standards. For correlations to other state standards, go to **http://www.historyalive.com**.

California History–Social Science Standards, Eighth Grade	Where Standards Are Addressed
8.1 Students understand the major events preceding the founding of the nation and relate their significance to the development of American constitutional democracy.	
1. Describe the relationship between the moral and political ideas of the Great Awakening and the development of revolutionary fervor.	pp. 56, 429
2. Analyze the philosophy of government expressed in the Declaration of Independence, with an emphasis on government as a means of securing individual rights (e.g., key phrases such as "all men are created equal, that they are endowed by their Creator with certain unalienable Rights").	pp. 83, 470–472
3. Analyze how the American Revolution affected other nations, especially France.	p. 100
4. Describe the nation's blend of civic republicanism, classical liberal principles, and English parliamentary traditions.	pp. 52, 106–108 Online Resources: Ch. 8 Enrichment Essay 5
8.2 Students analyze the political principles underlying the U.S. Constitution and compare the enumerated and implied powers of the federal government.	
1. Discuss the significance of the Magna Carta, the English Bill of Rights, and the Mayflower Compact.	pp. 39, 52, 428
2. Analyze the Articles of Confederation and the Constitution and the success of each in implementing the ideals of the Declaration of Independence.	pp. 103, 106–108, 117
3. Evaluate the major debates that occurred during the development of the Constitution and their ultimate resolutions in such areas as shared power among institutions, divided state-federal power, slavery, the rights of individuals and states (later addressed by the addition of the Bill of Rights), and the status of American Indian nations under the commerce clause.	pp. 106–116, 119–130, 133–143
4. Describe the political philosophy underpinning the Constitution as specified in the Federalist Papers (authored by James Madison, Alexander Hamilton, and John Jay) and the role of such leaders as Madison, George Washington, Roger Sherman, Gouverneur Morris, and James Wilson in the writing and ratification of the Constitution.	pp. 106–116
5. Understand the significance of Jefferson's Statute for Religious Freedom as a forerunner of the First Amendment and the origins, purpose, and differing views of the founding fathers on the issue of the separation of church and state.	pp. 135–136, 435–436
6. Enumerate the powers of government set forth in the Constitution and the fundamental liberties ensured by the Bill of Rights.	pp. 120–125, 128–129, 134–143
7. Describe the principles of federalism, dual sovereignty, separation of powers, checks and balances, the nature and purpose of majority rule, and the ways in which the American idea of constitutionalism preserves individual rights.	pp. 120–130, 134–142

California History–Social Science Standards, Eighth Grade	Where Standards Are Addressed
8.3 Students understand the foundation of the American political system and the ways in which citizens participate in it.	
1. Analyze the principles and concepts codified in state constitutions between 1777 and 1781 that created the context out of which American political institutions and ideas developed.	pp. 106–108, 433 Online Resources: Ch. 8 Enrichment Essay 6
2. Explain how the ordinances of 1785 and 1787 privatized national resources and transferred federally owned lands into private holdings, townships, and states.	p. 104
3. Enumerate the advantages of a common market among the states as foreseen in and protected by the Constitution's clauses on interstate commerce, common coinage, and full-faith and credit.	pp. 128–129
4. Understand how the conflicts between Thomas Jefferson and Alexander Hamilton resulted in the emergence of two political parties (e.g., view of foreign policy, Alien and Sedition Acts, economic policy, National Bank, funding and assumption of the revolutionary debt).	pp. 149–158, 436
5. Know the significance of domestic resistance movements and ways in which the central government responded to such movements (e.g., Shays' Rebellion, the Whiskey Rebellion).	pp. 105, 147
6. Describe the basic law-making process and how the Constitution provides numerous opportunities for citizens to participate in the political process and to monitor and influence government (e.g., function of elections, political parties, interest groups).	pp. 121–122, 130
7. Understand the functions and responsibilities of a free press.	pp. 136–137
8.4 Students analyze the aspirations and ideals of the people of the new nation.	
1. Describe the country's physical landscapes, political divisions, and territorial expansion during the terms of the first four presidents.	pp. 145–158, 163–170 (political divisions), 198–200 (expansion), 176–177, 254–255 (landscapes)
2. Explain the policy significance of famous speeches (e.g., Washington's Farewell Address, Jefferson's 1801 Inaugural Address, John Q. Adams's Fourth of July 1821 Address).	pp. 148 (Washington), 436 (Jefferson), 437 (Adams)
3. Analyze the rise of capitalism and the economic problems and conflicts that accompanied it (e.g., Jackson's opposition to the National Bank; early decisions of the U.S. Supreme Court that reinforced the sanctity of contracts and a capitalist economic system of law).	pp. 191 (Jackson and National Bank), 178–179 (Supreme Court decisions) Online Resources: Ch. 7 Enrichment Essay 4
4. Discuss daily life, including traditions in art, music, and literature, of early national America (e.g., through writings by Washington Irving, James Fenimore Cooper).	pp. 180–182, 438–439 Online Resources: Ch. 11 Enrichment Essay 7
8.5 Students analyze U.S. foreign policy in the early Republic.	
1. Understand the political and economic causes and consequences of the War of 1812 and know the major battles, leaders, and events that led to a final peace.	pp. 168–170

California History–Social Science Standards, Eighth Grade	Where Standards Are Addressed
2. Know the changing boundaries of the United States and describe the relationships the country had with its neighbors (current Mexico and Canada) and Europe, including the influence of the Monroe Doctrine, and how those relationships influenced westward expansion and the Mexican-American War.	pp. 171–172, 197–208, 216–218
3. Outline the major treaties with American Indian nations during the administrations of the first four presidents and the varying outcomes of those treaties.	pp. 192–194, 439–441
8.6 Students analyze the divergent paths of the American people from 1800 to the mid-1800s and the challenges they faced, with emphasis on the Northeast.	
1. Discuss the influence of industrialization and technological developments on the region, including human modification of the landscape and how physical geography shaped human actions (e.g., growth of cities, deforestation, farming, mineral extraction).	pp. 254, 257–260, 262–263, 265–266, 448–449
2. Outline the physical obstacles to and the economic and political factors involved in building a network of roads, canals, and railroads (e.g., Henry Clay's American System).	pp. 176–179, 259–261
3. List the reasons for the wave of immigration from Northern Europe to the United States and describe the growth in the number, size, and spatial arrangements of cities (e.g., Irish immigrants and the Great Irish Famine).	pp. 265–266
4. Study the lives of black Americans who gained freedom in the North and founded schools and churches to advance their rights and communities.	pp. 265–266, 270–271
5. Trace the development of the American education system from its earliest roots, including the roles of religious and private schools and Horace Mann's campaign for free public education and its assimilating role in American culture.	pp. 57, 245–246 Online Resources: Ch. 18 Enrichment Essays 9, 10
6. Examine the women's suffrage movement (e.g., biographies, writings, and speeches of Elizabeth Cady Stanton, Margaret Fuller, Lucretia Mott, Susan B. Anthony).	pp. 248–250, 396, 445–447
7. Identify common themes in American art as well as transcendentalism and individualism (e.g., writings about and by Ralph Waldo Emerson, Henry David Thoreau, Herman Melville, Louisa May Alcott, Nathaniel Hawthorne, Henry Wadsworth Longfellow).	pp. 180, 182, 243 Online Resources: Enrichment Essay 8
8.7 Students analyze the divergent paths of the American people in the South from 1800 to the mid-1800s and the challenges they faced.	
1. Describe the development of the agrarian economy in the South, identify the locations of the cotton-producing states, and discuss the significance of cotton and the cotton gin.	pp. 253, 256–257, 261, 264
2. Trace the origins and development of slavery; its effects on black Americans and on the region's political, social, religious, economic, and cultural development; and identify the strategies that were tried to both overturn and preserve it (e.g., through the writings and historical documents on Nat Turner, Denmark Vesey).	pp. 43, 55, 111–112, 245–247, 256–257, 264, 269–283 Online Resources: Ch. 19 Enrichment Essays 11; Ch. 20 Enrichment Essays 12, 13

California History–Social Science Standards, Eighth Grade	Where Standards Are Addressed
3. Examine the characteristics of white Southern society and how the physical environment influenced events and conditions prior to the Civil War.	pp. 255–257, 261, 264
4. Compare the lives of and opportunities for free blacks in the North with those of free blacks in the South.	pp. 270–271
8.8 Students analyze the divergent paths of the American people in the West from 1800 to the mid-1800s and the challenges they faced.	
1. Discuss the election of Andrew Jackson as president in 1828, the importance of Jacksonian democracy, and his actions as president (e.g., the spoils system, veto of the National Bank, policy of Indian removal, opposition to the Supreme Court).	pp. 185–195
2. Describe the purpose, challenges, and economic incentives associated with westward expansion, including the concept of Manifest Destiny (e.g., the Lewis and Clark expedition, accounts of the removal of Indians, the Cherokees' "Trail of Tears," settlement of the Great Plains) and the territorial acquisitions that spanned numerous decades.	pp. 192–194, 197–209, 211–227, 337–351, 439–440, 441–443
3. Describe the role of pioneer women and the new status that western women achieved (e.g., Laura Ingalls Wilder, Annie Bidwell; slave women gaining freedom in the West; Wyoming granting suffrage to women in 1869).	pp. 220–222, 442–444
4. Examine the importance of the great rivers and the struggle over water rights.	pp. 237, 444–445
5. Discuss Mexican settlements and their locations, cultural traditions, attitudes toward slavery, land-grant system, and economies.	pp. 201–203, 216–217, 229–239
6. Describe the Texas War for Independence and the Mexican-American War, including territorial settlements, the aftermath of the wars, and the effects the wars had on the lives of Americans, including Mexican Americans today.	pp. 201–203, 206–208, 229
8.9 Students analyze the early and steady attempts to abolish slavery and to realize the ideals of the Declaration of Independence.	
1. Describe the leaders of the movement (e.g., John Quincy Adams and his proposed constitutional amendment, John Brown and the armed resistance, Harriet Tubman and the Underground Railroad, Benjamin Franklin, Theodore Weld, William Lloyd Garrison, Frederick Douglass).	pp. 111, 246–247, 276–278, 289–290, 298–299, 451–452
2. Discuss the abolition of slavery in early state constitutions.	p. 433 Online Resources: Ch. 8 Enrichment Essay 6
3. Describe the significance of the Northwest Ordinance in education and in the banning of slavery in new states north of the Ohio River.	pp. 286–287 Online Resources: Ch. 18 Enrichment Essay 9
4. Discuss the importance of the slavery issue as raised by the annexation of Texas and California's admission to the union as a free state under the Compromise of 1850.	pp. 203, 290–291

California History–Social Science Standards, Eighth Grade	Where Standards Are Addressed
5. Analyze the significance of the States' Rights Doctrine, the Missouri Compromise (1820), the Wilmot Proviso (1846), the Compromise of 1850, Henry Clay's role in the Missouri Compromise and the Compromise of 1850, the Kansas-Nebraska Act (1854), the Dred Scott v. Sandford decision (1857), and the Lincoln-Douglas debates (1858).	pp. 156, 190, 285–299
6. Describe the lives of free blacks and the laws that limited their freedom and economic opportunities.	pp. 270–271
8.10 Students analyze the multiple causes, key events, and complex consequences of the Civil War.	
1. Compare the conflicting interpretations of state and federal authority as emphasized in the speeches and writings of statesmen such as Daniel Webster and John C. Calhoun.	pp. 190, 453–454
2. Trace the boundaries constituting the North and the South, the geographical differences between the two regions, and the differences between agrarians and industrialists.	pp. 253–267
3. Identify the constitutional issues posed by the doctrine of nullification and secession and the earliest origins of that doctrine.	pp. 156, 190, 286–288
4. Discuss Abraham Lincoln's presidency and his significant writings and speeches and their relationship to the Declaration of Independence, such as his "House Divided" speech (1858), Gettysburg Address (1863), Emancipation Proclamation (1863), and inaugural addresses (1861 and 1865).	pp. 298–300, 303–320, 323 Online Resources: Ch. 22 Enrichment Essay 14
5. Study the views and lives of leaders (e.g., Ulysses S. Grant, Jefferson Davis, Robert E. Lee) and soldiers on both sides of the war, including those of black soldiers and regiments.	pp. 304–320, 454–457
6. Describe critical developments and events in the war, including the major battles, geographical advantages and obstacles, technological advances, and General Lee's surrender at Appomattox.	pp. 300, 303–321
7. Explain how the war affected combatants, civilians, the physical environment, and future warfare.	pp. 303–321
8.11 Students analyze the character and lasting consequences of Reconstruction.	
1. List the original aims of Reconstruction and describe its effects on the political and social structures of different regions.	pp. 324–334
2. Identify the push-pull factors in the movement of former slaves to the cities in the North and to the West and their differing experiences in those regions (e.g., the experiences of Buffalo Soldiers).	p. 334
3. Understand the effects of the Freedmen's Bureau and the restrictions placed on the rights and opportunities of freedmen, including racial segregation and "Jim Crow" laws.	pp. 324–325, 332–334, 457–458
4. Trace the rise of the Ku Klux Klan and describe the Klan's effects.	pp. 330–331
5. Understand the Thirteenth, Fourteenth, and Fifteenth Amendments to the Constitution and analyze their connection to Reconstruction.	pp. 324–329

California History–Social Science Standards, Eighth Grade	Where Standards Are Addressed
8.12 Students analyze the transformation of the American economy and the changing social and political conditions in the United States in response to the Industrial Revolution.	
1. Trace patterns of agricultural and industrial development as they relate to climate, use of natural resources, markets, and trade and locate such development on a map.	pp. 343–344, 346–347, 354–355, 359–362
2. Identify the reasons for the development of federal Indian policy and the wars with American Indians and their relationship to agricultural development and industrialization.	pp. 192–194, 338–350
3. Explain how states and the federal government encouraged business expansion through tariffs, banking, land grants, and subsidies.	pp. 340–341, 346–347, 354–355 Online Resources: Ch. 24 Enrichment Essays 15
4. Discuss entrepreneurs, industrialists, and bankers in politics, commerce, and industry (e.g., Andrew Carnegie, John D. Rockefeller, Leland Stanford).	pp. 341, 354–357, 388–389
5. Examine the location and effects of urbanization, renewed immigration, and industrialization (e.g., the effects on social fabric of cities, wealth and economic opportunity, the conservation movement).	pp. 353–368, 371–382, 393, 464–465
6. Discuss child labor, working conditions, and laissez-faire policies toward big business and examine the labor movement, including its leaders (e.g., Samuel Gompers), its demand for collective bargaining, and its strikes and protests over labor conditions.	pp. 353–368, 392
7. Identify the new sources of large-scale immigration and the contributions of immigrants to the building of cities and the economy; explain the ways in which new social and economic patterns encouraged assimilation of newcomers into the mainstream amidst growing cultural diversity; and discuss the new wave of nativism.	pp. 371–382, 463–464 Online Resources: Ch. 26 Enrichment Essays 17, 18
8. Identify the characteristics and impact of Grangerism and Populism.	pp. 386–387
9. Name the significant inventors and their inventions and identify how they improved the quality of life (e.g., Thomas Edison, Alexander Graham Bell, Orville and Wilbur Wright).	pp. 356–357, 460–463 Online Resources: Ch. 25 Enrichment Essay 16

Historical and Social Science Analysis Skills

In addition to the content standards, students demonstrate the following intellectual reasoning, reflection, and research skills, which are reinforced throughout the program.

Chronological and Spatial Thinking

1. Students explain how major events are related to one another in time.

2. Students construct various time lines of key events, people, and periods of the historical era they are studying.

3. Students use a variety of maps and documents to identify physical and cultural features of neighborhoods, cities, states, and countries and to explain the historical migration of people, expansion and disintegration of empires, and the growth of economic systems.

Historical Research, Evidence, and Point of View

1. Students frame questions that can be answered by historical study and research.

2. Students distinguish fact from opinion in historical narratives and stories.

3. Students distinguish relevant from irrelevant information, essential from incidental information, and verifiable from unverifiable information in historical narratives and stories.

4. Students assess the credibility of primary and secondary sources and draw sound conclusions from them.

5. Students detect the different historical points of view on historical events and determine the context in which the historical statements were made (the questions asked, sources used, author's perspectives).

Historical Interpretation

1. Students explain the central issues and problems from the past, placing people and events in a matrix of time and place.

2. Students understand and distinguish cause, effect, sequence, and correlation in historical events, including the long- and short-term causal relations.

3. Students explain the sources of historical continuity and how the combination of ideas and events explains the emergence of new patterns.

4. Students recognize the role of chance, oversight, and error in history.

5. Students recognize that interpretations of history are subject to change as new information is uncovered.

6. Students interpret basic indicators of economic performance and conduct cost-benefit analyses of economic and political issues.

Credits

New York. **p. 154:** The Granger Collection, New York. **p. 155:** The Granger Collection, New York. **p. 156:** The Granger Collection, New York. **p. 157, upper:** The Granger Collection, New York. **p. 157, lower:** The Granger Collection, New York. **p. 158:** The Granger Collection, New York. **p. 159, left:** Library of Congress. **p. 159, right:** The Granger Collection, New York.

Chapter 12
p. 160: Library of Congress. **p. 161:** Len Ebert. **p. 163:** © Laurie Platt Winfrey Inc./Woodfin Camp and Associates. **p. 164:** The Granger Collection, New York. **p. 165:** The Granger Collection, New York. **p. 167:** The New-York Historical Society. **p. 168:** The Granger Collection, New York. **p. 169:** Library of Congress. **p. 170:** The Granger Collection, New York. **p. 171:** O'Gorman, Juan (1905–1982). *Panel of the Independence*, detail of center with Farther Hidalgo. Mural. 1960/61. Museo de Nacional de Historia, Castillo de Chapultepec, Mexico City, D.F., Mexico. Schalkwijk/Art Resource, New York. **p. 172:** The Granger Collection, New York. **p. 173:** Courtesy, Winterthur Museum.

Chapter 13
p. 174, upper: Composite photograph of the 190-year-old Star-Spangled Banner, the flag that inspired the national anthem. National Museum of American History, Smithsonian Institution © 2002. **p. 174, lower:** Selma to Montgomery march, 1965. © Matt Herron/Take Stock. **p. 175:** Len Ebert. **p. 177:** Charles Burton (active c. 1819–1892), *View of the Capitol*, 1824. Watercolor, gum Arabic, and graphite on off-white wove paper. 16 x 24 3/4 in. The Metropolitan Museum of Art, Purchase, Joseph Pulitzer Bequest, 1942. (42.128) Photograph © The Metropolitan Museum of Art. **p. 178:** *Portrait of James Monroe* by Samuel F. B. Morse, c. 1819, oil on canvas. White House Historical Association. **p. 179:** *Fairview Inn or Three Mile House on Old Frederick Road*, 1814, by Thomas Cole Ruckle. Watercolor on paper. The Maryland Historical Society, Baltimore, Maryland. **p. 180:** Thomas Cole, *The Subsiding of the Waters of the Deluge*, 1829. Oil on canvas, 35 3/4 x 47 3/4 in. (90.8 x 121.4 cm). Smithsonian American Art Museum, Gift of Mrs. Katie Dean in memory of Minnibel S. and James Wallace Dean and museum purchase through the Smithsonian Institution (1983.40). **p. 181:** *Dance in a Country Tavern*, by George Lehman, n.d. (BB61K89). The Historical Society of Pennsylvania (HSP), Philadelphia. **p. 182:** The Granger Collection, New York. **p. 183:** *The Verdict of the People* by George Caleb Bingham, 1854–1855. The Saint Louis Art Museum. Gift of Bank of America.

Chapter 14
p. 184, upper and details: The Granger Collection, New York. **p. 185:** Len Ebert. **p. 186:** Library of Congress. **p. 187:** © George Lepp/Corbis. **p. 188, upper:** Library of Congress. **p. 188, lower:** The New-York Historical Society. **p. 189:** The Granger Collection, New York. **p. 190:** source unknown. **p. 191:** Library of Congress. **p. 192:** Library of Congress. **p. 193:** The Granger Collection, New York. **p. 195:** Library of Congress.

Chapter 15
p. 196, upper and details: *American Progress* by John Gast, 1872. Library of Congress. **p. 197:** Len Ebert. **p. 198:** Library of Congress. **p. 199:** The Granger Collection, New York. **p. 200:** © Corbis. **p. 201:** Texas State Library. **p. 202:** *Fall of the Alamo* by Robert Jenkins Onderdonk, courtesy of the Friends of the Governor's Mansion, Austin. **p. 203:** Oldest Known Lone Star Flag, Republic Period. Collection of the Star of the Republic Museum. Gift of Cletus Brown Jr. **p. 204:** *Approaching Chimney Rock* by William Henry Jackson, Scotts Bluff National Monument. **p. 206:** E. Punderson, *Exeter, N.H. [Exeter, New Hampshire, volunteers leaving for the Mexican War]*, c. 1846. Daguerrotype, 1/4 plate. P1979.33. Amon Carter Museum, Fort Worth, Texas. **p. 207:** The Granger Collection, New York. **p. 209:** *Emigrants Crossing the Plains* by Albert Bierstadt, 1867. National Cowboy & Western Heritage Museum.

Chapter 16
p. 210: Leutze, Emanuel Gottlieb (1816–1868). *Westward the Course of Empire Takes Its Way*, (mural study, U. S. Capitol), 1861. Oil on canvas, 33 1/4 x 43 3/8 in. (84.5 x 110.1 cm). Smithsonian American Art Museum, Washington, DC/Art Resource, NY. **p. 211:** Len Ebert. **p. 212:** *Lewis and Clark at Three Forks* by E. S. Paxson, Oil on canvas, 1912. Photo by Don Beatty. Courtesy of the Montana Historical Society. **p. 213:** The Granger Collection, New York. **p. 215, upper left:** Library of Congress. **p. 215, upper right:** Library of Congress. **p. 215, center left:** Library of Congress. **p. 215, center right:** *Lewis and Clark Expedition* by C. M. Russell, from the collection of Gilcrease Museum, Tulsa, Oklahoma. **p. 215, lower left:** The Granger Collection, New York. **p. 215, lower right:** The Granger Collection, New York. **p. 216:** *Hacendado y Su Mayordomo* by Carlos Nebel, Museum Collection Number 980, History Collections, Los Angeles County Museum of Natural History. **p. 217:** The Granger Collection, New York. **p. 218:** *Trappers at Fault – Looking for the Trail* by Arthur Fitzwilliam Tait, The Anschutz Collection. **p. 219:** © Corbis. **p. 220, upper:** Oregon Historical Society. **p. 220, lower:** Oregon Historical Society. **p. 221:** The Granger Collection, New York. **p. 222:** The Granger Collection, New York. **p. 223:** *Handcart Pioneers, 1900* by C. C. A. Christensen/Museum of Church History and Art. **p. 224:** Nahl, Charles Christian (1818–1878) and Frederick August Wenderoth (1819–1884), *Miners in the Sierras*, 1851–1852. Oil on canvas, 54 1/4 x 67 in (137.7 x 198.8 cm) Smithsonian American Art Museum, Washington, DC/Art Resource, NY. **p. 225:** California State Library. **p. 226:** © Corbis. **p. 227:** Library of Congress.

Chapter 17
p. 228: Courtesy of the Arizona Historical Society, Tuscon, AHS#19431. **p. 229:** Len Ebert. **p. 230:** Courtesy of the Arizona Historical Society, AHS#14546. **p. 231:** Bancroft Library, University of California, Berkeley. **p. 232:** *California Vaqueros* by James Walker/The Anschutz Collection. **p. 233:** *Mission San Gabriel Arcangel* by Oriana Day/Fine Arts Museums of San Francisco/Gift of Eleanor Martin, DY37556. **p. 234:** Courtesy of the Arizona Historical Society, AHS#3767. **p. 235:** *Mariana Coronel Grinding Corn* by A. Harmer, Museum Collection Number 1000. History Collections, Los Angeles County Museum of Natural History. **p. 236:** © David Muench. **p. 237:** "Ramona Martinez Cruz and Carlos Cruz," Museum Collection Number 3875. History Collections, Los Angeles County Museum of Natural History. **p. 238:** The Granger Collection, New York. **p. 239:** Getty Images.

Chapter 18
p. 240: Library of Congress. **p. 241:** Len Ebert. **p. 242:** The Granger Collection, New York. **p. 243:** The Granger Collection, New York. **p. 244:** © Corbis. **p. 245:** The Granger Collection, New York. **p. 246:** State Archives of Michigan. **p. 247, upper:** Library of Congress. **p. 247, lower:** The Granger Collection, New York. **p. 248:** *Pic Nick Camden Maine* by Jerome B. Thompson/ Museum of Fine Arts, Boston. Gift of Maxim Karolik for the M. and M. Karolik Collection of American Paintings, 1815-1865. **p. 249:** © Bettmann/Corbis. **p. 250, upper:** © Corbis. **p. 250, lower:** The Schlesinger Library/Radcliffe Institute. **p. 251:** © AP/Wide World Photos. **p. 251, inset:** © AP/Wide World Photos.

Chapter 19
p. 252, upper: The Granger Collection, New York. **p. 252, lower:** Library of Congress. **p. 253:** Len Ebert. **p. 254:** © Stephen J. Krasemann/DRK Photo. **p. 255:** © Stephen G. Maka/DRK Photo. **p. 256:** The Granger Collection, New York. **p. 257:** © Corbis. **pp. 258-259:** © Corbis. **p. 260:** Decker, Herman. *Lonsdale Wharf, Providence, RI*, 1878. Guache, 24 x 38 in. Museum of Art, Rhode Island School of Design/Mary B. Jackson Fund. **p. 261:** Library of Congress. **p. 264:** The Granger Collection, New York. **p. 265:** The Granger Collection, New York. **p. 266:** The Granger Collection, New York. **p. 267:** The Granger Collection, New York.

Chapter 20
p. 268, upper: Harriet Powers, American, 1837–1911. *Pictorial Quilt*, 1895–98. Pieced, appliqued, and printed cotton embroidered with plain and metallic yarns. 175 x 266.7 cm. Museum of Fine Arts, Boston, Gift of Maxim Karolik for the M. and M. Karolik Collection of American Paintings, 1815–1865; 46.852. **p. 268, lower:** © Corbis. **p. 269:** Len Ebert. **p. 270:** The Granger Collection, New York. **p. 271:** The Granger Collection, New York. **p. 272:** © Bettmann/Corbis. **p. 274:** © Bettmann/Corbis. **p. 275:** Library of Congress. **p. 276:** Library of Congress. **p. 277:** The Granger Collection, New York. **p. 278:** Library of Congress. **p. 279:** Library of Congress. **p. 280:** *Kitchen Ball at White Sulphur Springs, Virginia*, 1838 by Christian Mayr, North Carolina Museum of Art, Raleigh. Purchased with funds from the State of North Carolina. **p. 281:** Harriet Powers, *Bible Quilt*. National Museum of American History, Smithsonian Institution. **p. 282:** The Granger Collection, New York. **p. 283:** Library of Congress.

Chapter 21
p. 284, upper: © Bettmann/Corbis. **p. 284, lower:** Library of Congress. **p. 285:** Len Ebert. **p. 287:** The Granger Collection, New York. **p. 289:** © Bettmann/Corbis. **p. 290,** © Corbis. **p. 292:** The Granger Collection, New York. **p. 293:** Library of